PRAISE FOR

BECOMING MEDICINE: PATHWAYS OF INITIATION INTO A LIVING SPIRITUALITY

Becoming Medicine is a great compilation of contemporary medical science and ancient spiritual wisdom. This book is written from the heart like a prayer, if you are a seeker of a living spirituality and want to magnify your power to heal, read this book.

— CARL HAMMERSCHLAG MD, author of *The Dancing Healers, The Theft of the Spirit*, and *Healing Ceremonies.*

This is a remarkable and deeply engaging account in which a Native American shaman and his psychiatrist apprentice plunge deep into the heart centre of a living wisdom. Replete with questor myths and mystical adventures, this passionate, richly cross-referenced and spiritually inclusive book becomes a vibrant junction of intersecting journeys from diverse wisdom traditions. Circling age-old themes of separation, quest and spiritual homecoming, it is an invitation to trust the non-linear journey of inner transformation — one that turns us, eventually, into our own medicine. Marked by an authenticity that readers will instantly recognize, here is a genuine watering-hole at which seekers of all persuasions can pause and 'drink the light'.

— ARUNDHATHI SUBRAMANIAM MA, author of *When God is a Traveller, Sadhguru: More Than A Life*, and with SADHGURU, *Adiyogi: The Source of Yoga*, editor of *Eating God: A Book of Bhakti Poetry.*

Behind the words and images of Becoming Medicine is the wisdom of a man fearless enough to break down all the barriers between what he knows and what he is. Joseph Rael is a unique island of beauty and sanity in our crazy, uncultured culture. And that island that he is, is vaster than the whole world.

— PETER KINGSLEY PhD, author of *Catafalque: Carl Jung and the End of Humanity, A Story Waiting to Pierce You: Mongolia, Tibet and the Destiny of the Western World*, and *In the Dark Places of Wisdom.*

In this wonderful book, Picuris/Ute medicine man Joseph Rael reveals that each of us is an embodied human being who is in fact a medicine bag, a container in which we carry sacredness. By walking into the center of ourselves, into the center of our hearts, we cease to be ourselves and are instead becoming medicine. It is something that is done every moment. Becoming Medicine means that we are becoming capable of being a place for the Breath-Matter-Movement of the vast spirit to manifest and reside for a moment. This is a fabulous book for our times.

— HANK WESSELMAN PhD, anthropologist and author of nine books on shamanism including *The Re-Enchantment: A Shamanic Path to a Life of Wonder, The Bowl of Light: Ancestral Wisdom from a Hawaiian Shaman*, the award winning *Awakening to the Spirit World* (with SANDRA INGERMAN) and the *Spiritwalker* trilogy.

Tragically the odious divisive social diseases of the 1930s are returning. Nationalistic, racist and fundamentalist movements are rapidly dividing communities. Innocent people feel more and more lost, alienated, powerless, lonely. They yearn for healing. But how can this healing begin? This is why *Becoming Medicine* by David Kopacz and Joseph Rael (Beautiful Painted Arrow) is so timely. It is a truly remarkable book, so relevant, so grounded in experience. The medicine of healing begins within each one of us. There we discover our true selves, our unified oneness with all humankind and the universe itself. This is not a healing that is confined to one event. On the contrary, it is a call to a transformative, ongoing, lifelong initiation of discovery. Each discovery leads to a deeper personal and social healing.

— GERALD A. ARBUCKLE PhD, Refounding and Pastoral Development Unit, Sydney, Australia. Author of *Fundamentalism at Home and Abroad: Analysis and Pastoral Responses* (2017), *Loneliness: Insights for Healing in a Fragmented World* (2018) and *Humanizing Healthcare Reforms* (2012).

Like the wondrous journeys of the spirit it describes, this book escorts the reader along a path to new understanding and, ultimately, transformation. Along the way, we are reminded of our true nature, our kinship with everything around us, and our power to navigate through our own tumultuous times. The path can be bumpy. It can be circular. Sometimes it is dark. This book helps light the way, and every page is a step toward something meaningful. Where will your journey take you?

— J. ADAM RINDFLEISCH, MPhil, MD, Medical Director, Integrative Health, University of Wisconsin School of Medicine and Public Health, Associate Professor, Department of Family Medicine and Community Health.

Becoming Medicine will help you think in circles, dream-journey in technicolor, speak your vowels with mystic awareness, listen to music with more heart, and feel your heartbeat with more awe. The wonderful paintings of Joseph Rael (Beautiful Painted Arrow) and David Kopacz are a generous offering to linger over. I am grateful for their creative friendship and commitment to share a depth of spiritual, psychological, quantum physics, and visionary teachings. Becoming Medicine is a call to community, not only so that we seek out companions to slowly explore the insights and stories in this book. But so that we each take an inner journey into our hearts and return as the visionary healers the community of earth is calling for.

— SHELLY L. FRANCIS, author of *The Courage Way: Leading and Living With Integrity* (2018).

This is a book that can really change your life. David Kopacz and Joseph Rael's *Becoming Medicine* is a remarkable collaboration between two brilliant and courageous pioneers. The information they provide opens a doorway to a healing path that unveils the hidden potential of the human spirit. Blending together knowledge that is ancient and sacred within the backdrop of modern day psychiatry, it is deeply illuminating. It is a must read for anyone interested in embarking on a journey of transformation and becoming medicine for the world.

— SHILAGH MIRGAIN PhD, Assistant Professor, Distinguished Psychologist, University of Wisconsin – Madison

Becoming Medicine by David R. Kopacz & Joseph Rael (Beautiful Painted Arrow) is a powerful illustration of the title through the authors' sharing of their own stories, beautiful art and text, using examples from scientific and humanistic/spiritual literature. Its message is not about becoming a doctor or a healer, but the path to becoming the medicine itself. This is a profound exploration of the journey to Become More — Medicine to self, others and the world, integrating personal examples with multiple cultural traditions present and past. In *Becoming Medicine*, Kopacz and Rael detail not only the journey for individuals but a path for a disoriented and fragmented world to engage in transformation towards wholeness and unity. Health workers and all seekers alike will benefit from this work.

— MICHAEL HOLLIFIELD, MD, (Long Beach, California & Angel Fire, New Mexico), President and CEO, War Survivors Institute, Clinical Professor of Psychiatry and Behavioral Sciences at the George Washington University School of Medicine and Health Sciences.

Becoming Medicine is a bridge between many dualities including: the conscious and the unconscious, the scientific and the spiritual, the ordinary and the non-ordinary, and the Western and the Indigenous. Intricately referenced and yet personal in narrative, David and Joseph weave us through distinct world traditions to reveal the interconnectedness in stories of healing. This bridge is likely to most benefit those of us educated in western contexts, where our minds have been trained to neglect the wisdom of circles and spirit. Whether readers begin as healers or seekers, they will realize the congruence of these paths. *Becoming Medicine* inspires us into our own shamanic journeys.

— NEETA RAMKUMAR, PhD, Lecturer, School of Social Sciences, University of the South Pacific, Fiji.

Dr. Kopacz holds the space between the mystery and majesty of shamanic tradition and the study of anthropology and medicine. His writing brings the reader into sublime experiences that Dr. Kopacz holds in his body. He walks the walk between the seen and the unseen, transforming life along the way. Prepare to be fascinated. Prepare to be amazed. You'll return over and over to the information on the pages and between them.

— HENRI ROCA, MD, Functional Medicine Specialist, Shamanic Journeyer, Clinical Assistant professor, family and community health, Louisiana State University School of Medicine, University of Arkansas for Medical Sciences.

ALSO BY JOSEPH RAEL

BEING & VIBRATION: ENTERING THE NEW WORLD

HOUSE OF SHATTERING LIGHT

CEREMONIES OF THE LIVING SPIRIT

SOUND: NATIVE TEACHINGS + VISIONARY ART

INSPIRATIONS OF THE LIVING SPIRIT

ALSO BY DAVID R. KOPACZ

RE-HUMANIZING MEDICINE: A HOLISTIC FRAMEWORK FOR TRANSFORMING YOUR SELF, YOUR PRACTICE, AND THE CULTURE OF MEDICINE

ALSO BY DAVID R. KOPACZ & JOSEPH RAEL

WALKING THE MEDICINE WHEEL: HEALING TRAUMA & PTSD

BECOMING MEDICINE

PATHWAYS OF INITIATION INTO A LIVING SPIRITUALITY

DAVID R. KOPACZ MD

JOSEPH RAEL

(Beautiful Painted Arrow)

CONDOR & EAGLE
PRESS

Condor & Eagle Press
Seattle WA & Marvel CO USA

Standard edition. First printing
Book and jacket design by Carl Brune
Printed in the USA

ISBN 978-1-7342800-3-6 (Art Medicine Edition)
ISBN 978-1-7342800-1-2 (Standard Edition)
Distributed by Itasca Books
itascabooks.com

davidkopacz.com
beingfullyhuman.com

CREATOR OF WORLDS

CONTENTS

ABBREVIATIONS

The following abbreviations will be used for references to Joseph's books in the text.

BPA	*Beautiful Painted Arrow: Stories and Teachings from the Native American Tradition* (Joseph Rael)
B&V: NW	*Being & Vibration: Entering the New World* (Joseph Rael)
B&V	*Being & Vibration* (Rael & Marlow, 1993)
Ceremonies	*Ceremonies of the Living Spirit* (Joseph Rael)
House	*House of Shattering Light* (Joseph Rael)
Inspiration	*The Way of Inspiration* (Joseph Rael)
MDR	*Memories, Dreams, Reflections* (Carl Jung & Aniela Jaffé)
MMSS	*Modern Man in Search of a Soul* (Carl Jung)
Sound	*Sound: Native Teachings + Visionary Art* (Joseph Rael)
Visionary	*The Visionary: Entering the Mystic Universe of Joseph Rael (Beautiful Painted Arrow)* (Kurt Wilt)
Walking	*Walking the Medicine Wheel: Healing Trauma & PTSD* (David Kopacz & Joseph Rael)

FOREWORD

LEWIS MEHL-MADRONA

"This is a story. It is just one story among a universe of stories, told from my perspective. Someone else would tell the story differently. This story takes place on Turtle Island.[1] *I am hesitant in putting this story out there, because as Thomas King acknowledges, 'For once a story is told, it cannot be called back. Once told, it is loose in the world.'"*[2]

(RENEE LINKLATER)

In *Coyote Medicine*,[3] I wrote about my journey to integrating my ancestral lineages — European, Cherokee, and Lakota. My story was also one of integrating healing traditions. I knew from my upbringing that people did heal in sometimes mysterious ways and without conventional explanations, but I also knew that scientific medicine had its usefulness and could provide cure in areas that traditional medicine could not, notably trauma and joint replacement surgery. David has been on a similar journey and this book tells his story. Our association began when he saw *Coyote Medicine* in a Borders Bookstore in Champaign-Urbana and read it in 1999. That was a time when he was searching for holistic ways of healing just as he was starting to put into practice his psychiatric training. For me, 1999 was a time of continuing to struggle with conventional medicine and to wonder how to bring indigenous wisdom into contemporary health care. David and I both were asking, in our separate contexts, how to work with people's personal stories, with the broader cultural stories, and within our cultural contexts in which human rights and dignity were not always respected.

MY STORY. In order to introduce David's story, I need to tell my story. I was born in southeastern Kentucky. My grandmother and grandfather

1 "Turtle Island is an Indigenous concept that refers to the North American countries of Canada, United States and Mexico; some teachings include Central and South America. Oral history stories share that a Turtle came to the surface of the water and life began to grow upon her." Footnote from Rene Linklater's book.

2 Rene Linklater, *Decolonizing Trauma Work*, 19. Embedded quote from Thomas King is from *The Truth about Stories: A Narrative*, 10.

3 Lewis Mehl-Madrona, *Coyote Medicine: Lessons from Native American Healing*, (1997).

were proudly Cherokee, though my mother was trying to be white, which I resented as a teenager, but can now completely understand as an adult, looking back on the world of Kentucky and the United States in 1953. In those days, the USO paid local women to dance with soldiers. My mother and father apparently did more than dance. My father, whose name was Frank, came from the Pine Ridge Reservation of South Dakota. He had enlisted in the military for the Korean War and had been sent to Kentucky for a temporary duty assignment (what is called TDY) where he and my mother crossed paths. For many years, I did not know this. I thought my father was Lewis Eugene McKinley, Senior, for whom I was named. He was a Cherokee man, whom I eventually found in the area of Daytona Beach, Florida. He was a kind man, just as my grandfather was, and told me the story of how he and my mother got together. He was pretty sure that he wasn't my father. He thought the timing was off. However, he did love my mother, but sadly, she didn't love him, and they divorced when I was one year old. Though some researchers and clinicians would say that my memory is clearly constructed, I do remember being in the bathtub as an infant and a man coming into the bathroom in uniform and greeting my mother. I believe this was him. We had a good visit and he did the DNA test as I requested, and indeed, he was not my father, though his name was on my birth certificate. Then, he told me about Frank, whom he thought was my father and who was his best friend in the military.

I went looking for Frank in Rapid City, where Lewis, Sr., had last contacted him, and then on the Pine Ridge Reservation. This was my healing journey. I did not find Frank, but I found Sonny Richards, of whose hocokah I became part. A hocokah is a circle, an altar, or the group of people who follow a particular elder's altar. At the time I was working at the University of Pittsburgh (during 1999 when David found *Coyote Medicine*) and creating a regular conduit between Pittsburgh and Rapid City. With my friend Kurt Kaltreider, who wrote several marvelous books, and who sadly died recently, giving me all his sweat lodge covers, I travelled frequently to South Dakota to participate in ceremony. We brought Sonny and his helpers—Jason, Wylie, Milo, and others—to Pittsburgh to do ceremony and teachings. Through Sonny, I met Frank Fools Crow, the famous elder whom Sonny had followed for many years. We visited the grave of Buddy Red Bow, and I began dancing the sundance. That has continued for the past 22 years.

Eventually I did get my mother to talk about Frank in the year before she died. She talked about visiting him in South Dakota and considering moving there to be with him, but deciding, eventually, that she couldn't go there. There had been two other candidates to be my father, and I had DNA tested both of them with negative results. My mother's favorite was Jack, who was a Law Professor at the University of Kentucky. I think she liked him best because he appeared to be the most successful. He was friendly enough when I met him at a Burger King restaurant in Cincinnati (his choice), and he kindly agreed to the DNA testing, after which his wife attacked me for trying to steal the family wealth. My mother had married my stepfather, John Mehl, Jr., about whom I wrote in *Coyote Medicine*. Sadly, my birth certificate was altered with his adoption of me, and I lost my proof of tribal affiliation, though I couldn't have known that until decades later.

I began trying to make sense of healing when I entered medical school. In those days (the early 1970s), we were struggling to understand what it meant to be Indian (or Native American or, in Canada, aboriginal, indigenous, or First Nations). What did it mean to have an Indian identity? No one knew. The American Indian Movement was in process of formation. People were actively working to recover language, ceremony, and culture. The obstacles were large. I also wrote in *Coyote Medicine* about my shock during one of my first courses in medical school, Pharmacology, when the Professor told us that "life was a relentless progression toward death, disease, and decay. The physician's job is to slow the rate of decline." That shocked me deeply, because my Cherokee great-grandmother and grandmother had taught that one should aim to die healthy so as to be able to celebrate right away with one's relatives on the other side. The contrast between these two positions was so extreme that I ran across campus to the Stanford Indian Center right away. It was located in those days in the Old Firehouse. Henrietta Blue Eyes was at the desk. I ran across the distance between us and managed to stammer to her, "Henrietta, I need an elder."

"What tribe?" she asked.

"Cherokee," I said. Henrietta thumbed through her Rolodex (now a completely archaic means of maintaining a contacts database) and found two names for me—Kidla in Ukiah and Grandfather Roberts outside Garberville. Kidla was closer so I visited him the next weekend. Garberville was farther so it took me longer to get there. Both of them were very helpful to me. Both knew techniques of healing that they used on me. Both of them knew the physical method for bodywork or massage therapy of the Cherokee Nation and used it with me. They helped me get through medical school successfully.

TRAUMA. Trauma is at the center of our stories since colonization began. My mother was trying to protect me from trauma when she frantically sought a husband once I was conceived. Social workers took away the children of single mothers and put them with proper Christian families, even more likely with Native American single mothers. By finding a husband, my mother insured my safety from being snatched by those social workers, and for that, I am eternally grateful. My grandparents who raised me while my mother went to College (Berea College which was free for Appalachian youth) were incredibly kind and compassionate people. Later I would experience trauma in the move from Kentucky and in life with my stepfather, but that was not the case earlier, which was good.

LETTING LOOSE STORIES. Whenever we write about powerful spiritual teachers and our own transformative experiences, we let loose another story to roam Turtle Island. Once it is told, it cannot be recalled. David's story about his spiritual transformation in conjunction with a very special teacher, Joseph Rael, or Beautiful Painted Arrow, a man who has been a teacher to more than one of my friends, is one of those stories that needs to be released. While unique to David, his story is meaningful and beautiful and will roam Turtle Island with a bountiful lope. He will describe the many things he learned with Joseph, the visions he had and their meaning for him, and he will speculate about the indigenous parts of all of us.

Joseph teaches that we become sick when breath separates from matter and from movement. The solution is "drinking light energy from which comes vision," which is another way of saying to reconnect with the medicine that flows through us. In chapter 4, "Becoming a Visionary," David and Joseph describe the following in the "Visions for Healing" section.

> Medicine is the flowing of source into the vessel of the human, into the plowed and prepared field of our consciousness. When the medicine sprouts in the individual, then the individual becomes medicine and is called to go forth into the world in order to bring the medicine vision to others who are sick. A vision comes with a responsibility. . . . [W]hen we allow the visionary medicine seed to take root in ourselves as individuals we become medicine and we become creators and we take part in Creation. Joseph says that he

strives to live this way, letting himself be led rather than striving to lead.[4]

THE MEDICINE CIRCLE. The medicine circle is another example of cultural symbols that healers like Beautiful Painted Arrow use. It has four directions: east, south, west, and the north. It serves as an outer world symbol for re-orienting our inner world when we become lost. A former student of Joseph Rael, Kurt Wilt, who has passed on, tells how Joseph came to his own inspirational vision of the medicine wheel.

> Painted Arrow's insights on the medicine wheel began in the kiva. The most notable occasion occurred when Antonio [his grandfather] sent him into the kiva for a special ceremony that Picuris perform once every hundred years. In *House of Shattering Light*, Joseph recalls being alone in the sacred space for weeks. . . .
>
> Sitting at the center of the ceremonial chamber, he realized he was at the center of the circle, the medicine wheel, the universe, the heart. He also realized the directions were the sound/light beings manifesting against silent darkness. The heart, the hub of darkness, is a flash of light that becomes a star as we exhale.[5]

Joseph explains that the outer directions mirror inner directions, though each tribe can assign the directions a bit differently. I am most familiar with the east representing the spiritual direction, the south representing emotions and relationships, the west representing the physical, and the north representing the cognitive. The medicine wheel is actually a sphere with "up" representing the sky which protects us and "down" representing the earth, who nurtures and heals us. Joseph calls the center "the heart that contains the place of 'held-back goodness.'" In the way I was taught, the center is the invisible direction, often assigned the color purple or no color at all, and it is from the center that we connect to everyone and everything with which we are connected. David says, "It is through the heart that we move from isolated self and 'other' to interconnected 'brother and sister,'" so the teachings we have received are remarkably similar.

> There are many Medicine Circles. The universe is a Medicine Circle. Our own solar system is a giant Medicine Circle. The earth

---

4 Kopacz, David R. & Rael, Joseph, *Becoming Medicine: Pathways of Initiation into a Living Spirituality*, 2019.

5 Kurt Wilt, *The Visionary: entering the mystic universe of Joseph Rael Beautiful Painted Arrow*, 182.

> is a Medicine Circle. Every nation is a Medicine Circle. Each state is a Medicine Circle. Each family is a Medicine Circle. You are a Medicine Circle, for every individual is a Medicine Circle.[6] (Roy I. Wilson)

David is speaking of this kind of medicine in this book. Human beings carry this medicine in their hearts. Joseph tell us that every human being is "a medicine bag that carries holy objects." In the introduction to the book, David describes the circular path of seeking and becoming medicine.

> Becoming Medicine means to be seeking healing, to be receiving healing, and then to be giving healing. Seeking, finding/receiving, and giving are the three fundamental stages of becoming medicine and these are three stages of initiation: separation, initiation, return. Initiation gives us the opportunity to feel vibrantly alive by giving us a pathway for transforming our suffering, to re-spiritualize ourselves and the world, and to allow us to see our underlying unity with creation and the cosmos.[7]

Circles are powerful and they work. I was part of a project in which we learned that talking circles conducted by elders in health centers after hours had a more powerful effect than visits to the doctor for many problems.[8] In the Talking Circle, communication is regulated through the passing of a talking piece (an object of special meaning or symbolism to the circle facilitator). Twelve hundred people participated in talking circles in which 415 attended at least four sessions and completed pre- and post-questionnaires. Participation in at least 4 talking circles resulted in a statistically significant improvement in reported symptoms and overall quality of life with the size of those effects being typically greater than what people found from actually going to the doctor.

BEING INDIGENOUS. David's message is that, regardless of our origins in this life and our station, we are all seeking our indigenous roots and heritage wherever that lies. There are politics to this, which I will discuss. Some of us are more removed from our indigenous roots than others. Indigenous activists sometimes object to non-indigenous people embracing

---

6 Roy I. Wilson, *Medicine Wheels: Ancient Teachings for Modern Times*, 9.

7 David Raymond Kopacz & Joseph Rael, *Becoming Medicine: Pathways of Initiation into a Living Spirituality*, 2019.

8 Mehl-Madrona, L., & Mainguy, B. (2014). "Introducing healing circles and talking circles into primary care." *The Permanente Journal*, 18(2), 4-9.

indigenous teachings. This would apply to David and his relationship with Beautiful Painted Arrow. That is one perspective. Another perspective is that everyone needs to move toward collectivist thinking in order for human beings to survive. Everyone needs to embrace a more indigenous perspective than the contemporary capitalist point of view. If we do not commit to taking care of each other and to being relational and to the importance of community, humanity will disappear from the planet. Perhaps that would not be so bad. My fantasy is that the raccoons would evolve to become the next dominant species for they are clever and already have opposing thumbs. So, I support the idea of everyone seeking their indigenous origins, lest we succumb to raccoon dominance. Others would disagree with me and would find David's training with Beautiful Painted Arrow offensive for he is not certified indigenous. The Blood Quantum Act of 1904, passed by the U.S. Congress, created Native Americans as a species similar to dogs or horses. The goal was to eliminate indigenous people, and, it is working, as the numbers of indigenous people in the United States are declining. I and others have proposed that indigenous people reclaim their status as independent nations and begin to accept immigrants who are sincere and committed to learning the language and culture. In this way, the indigenous nations could grow and become a more powerful political force. Otherwise, the Blood Quantum Act assures that indigenous people will disappear. The formula for how that happens is on display in the Smithsonian Institute. That being as it may, I acknowledge that some people will criticize David as a non-Native embracing a Native spiritualty. I suspect some of that was accidental. David was seeking and Beautiful Painted Arrow appeared; though some would say there are no accidents. I suspect accidents do occur and some of what happens is random; it's up to us to make meaning of accidents and randomness, which David has clearly done. His encounters with Beautiful Painted Arrow changed his life and moved him in a direction that has enriched him and those with whom he works.

STORIES OF CONNECTION. Each listener decides what stories to endorse and what stories to reject, though studies have shown that all stories change us a little. I accept David's story as a template for the heroic spiritual journey. I think it is a valuable story to circulate for it inspires others to believe in spiritual heroism and in seeking deeper connections to the invisible or extraordinary world. The stories of healers and healing taking place on Turtle Island are worth releasing. We would not want to call them back. They need to circulate in the world.

In his introduction to *Becoming Medicine*, David writes about how we are seeking a living spirituality which leads from the "pain of division and separation to the healing of re-unification."

> This unity is a radical Oneness—oneness with all people, all living things, and oneness with the cosmos. Our sense of ego identity can be transformed from a 'thing' to be preserved to a conduit of service. In this book we are moving to the place where we are all One—the interconnected place of the mystic, visionary...journey.[9]

David has identified our contemporary angst – we have become separated from each other. People often do not know their neighbors. People do not gather together to visit each other but only to watch an event, parallel to each other as at the theatre or a sporting event, but not interactive with each other. Health care has succumbed to this parallel individualism – multiple people in some cubicles unbeknownst to each other even though being together would reduce some of their suffering.

TEACHINGS OF THE ELDERS. Elders listen to illness narratives and transform them into healing narratives. Through their stories they foster relationships that transcend the dyadic interactions of conventional medicine and involve wider social networks. I interviewed 851 Aboriginal people in Saskatchewan in a series of focus groups about how they felt about the health care services they were being offered.[10] My respondents reported that their health care providers had distinctly different values from them, as others have found.[11] The most common value difference mentioned was the lack of respect for elders. They noted that the importance of elders is common to virtually all indigenous groups and overrides all other values. Benton-Banai[12] listed seven virtues endorsed by elders, which include love, respect, wisdom, bravery, honesty, humility

9 Kopacz, David R. & Rael, Joseph, *Becoming Medicine: Pathways of Initiation into a Living Spirituality*, 2019.

10 Mehl-Madrona, L., "Relationships of Aboriginal People with Conventional Health Care Services," *The Canadian Journal of Native Studies*, 2012 32(2): 1-20.

11 Trimble, J. and J. Gonzalez, "Cultural Considerations and Perspectives for providing Psychological Counseling for Native American Indians," in *Counseling Across Cultures*, ed. PB Pedersen, et al. Thousand Oaks, CA: Sage, 1996.

12 Benton-Banai, E., *The Mishomis Book: The Voice of the Ojibway*. St. Paul, MN: Red School House, 1988.

and truth. Participants remarked on how aboriginal values of service and commitment to relationships and community go against the grain of individualistic, dominant cultural values upon which so many health services are organized, especially in the United States, where health care is for profit.[13]

In another project,[14] I gave elders tobacco, sometimes colored cloth or prayer ties, and usually another gift each time I sat with them. This acknowledged their role as teacher and mine as the learner. Unlike a more conventional study with multiple subjects and one researcher, this project was autoethnographic. I was the subject and the elders were the teachers. Through an iterative process in which each elder reviewed the comments of every other elder, we arrived at 12 ideas upon which they could all agree, and which reinforce Joseph Rael's message in this book:

1. **Teach students the importance of listening.**
2. **Teach students a relational model of the self.**
3. **Solutions must be internally derived.**
4. **People are spontaneously self-healing.**
5. **The healer should be of selfless intent.**
6. **Healers need to be passionate about their work.**
7. **Healers have to maintain some independence from political structures.**
8. **Teach students the importance of faith, hope, and the power of the activated mind.**
9. **Empowerment is different than treatment.**
10. **Teach students the importance of community.**
11. **Only Creator can give prognoses.**
12. **All healing is ultimately spiritual healing.**

SUMMATION. The stories David tells will circulate far and wide. They will stay with us. They will change us. Their tellers will become part of us. And that is good, for it will lead us into the future, one of integration

13 Hooks, B. & West, C. "Black Women and Men: Partnerships in the 1990s: a dialogue between bell hooks and Cornell West presented at Yale University's African American Cultural Center." New Haven, CT: Yale University Press, 2000.

14 Mehl-Madrona, L. "What Traditional Indigenous Elders Say About Cross-Cultural Mental Health Training." *Explore*, 2009, 5:20–29.

and cooperation among cultures and health care systems. I am pleased to introduce David's work for you, the reader.

— LEWIS MEHL-MADRONA
Author of *Coyote Medicine, Narrative Medicine,* and *Healing the Mind through the Power of Story*; Associate Professor of Family Medicine, University of New England College of Osteopathic Medicine; Clinical Assistant Professor of Psychiatry, University of Vermont, Burlington, Vermont; Executive Director, Coyote Institute

REFERENCES

Benton-Banai, E., *The Mishomis Book: The Voice of the Ojibway*. St. Paul, MN: Red School House, 1988.

Hooks, B. & West, C. "Black Women and Men: Partnerships in the 1990s: a dialogue between bell hooks and Cornell West presented at Yale University's African American Cultural Center," *Breaking Bread: Insurgent Black Intellectual Life*. New York: Routledge, 2016.

Linklater, Renee. *Decolonizing Trauma Work: Indigenous Stories and Strategies.* Winnipeg: Fernwood Publishing, 2014.

Mehl-Madrona, L., *Coyote Medicine: Lessons from Native America*. New York City: Simon & Schuster, 1998.

Mehl-Madrona, L. "What Traditional Indigenous Elders Say About Cross-Cultural Mental Health Training." *Explore*, 2009, 5:20–29.

Mehl-Madrona, L., Relationships of aboriginal people with conventional health care services. *The Canadian Journal of Native Studies*, 2012. 32(2): p. 1–20.

Mehl-Madrona, L., & Mainguy, B. (2014). Introducing healing circles and talking circles into primary care. *The Permanente Journal*, 18(2), 4–9.

Trimble, J. and J. Gonzalez, "Cultural Considerations and Perspectives for providing Psychological Counseling for Native American Indians," in *Counseling Across Cultures*, ed. PB Pedersen, et al. Thousand Oaks, CA: Sage, 1996.

Wilt, Kurt. *The Visionary: Entering the Mystic Universe of Joseph Rael Beautiful Painted Arrow*. Tulsa: Council Oak Books, 2011.

Wilson, Roy I. *Medicine Wheels: Ancient Teachings for Modern Times*. New York: The Crossroad Publishing Company, 1994.

BREATH, MATTER, MOVEMENT

JOSEPH'S AND DAVID'S ACKNOWLEDGEMENTS

All those who helped bring this book into physical form: Paulette Millichap, Corbin Lewars (developmental editor), Sally Dennison (line editor), Carl Brune (designer), and Susan Singh (financial backing) , Chris Smith (proofreading), and Gene Dennison.

JOSEPH'S ACKNOWLEDGEMENTS

I give salutations to the two tribes of my youth: the Southern Ute tribe, to which my mother, who gave me birth, belonged and to my father who was of the Picuris Pueblo tribe. These two together brought me to a place where I could write the way I could and should—in a way that might be valuable to the planetary societies.

Carolyn Powell for her support and understanding.

There are so many other people to include. When we were working on this book we were thinking of all of you because we were thinking of the kind of knowledge in these books, so we dedicate this book and future books to our readers, even those who are not born yet. This kind of knowledge is bringing ancient wisdom to our awareness for the betterment of the world.

DAVID'S ACKNOWLEDGEMENTS

Beautiful Painted Arrow (Joseph Earl Rael) for the gift of his friendship, energy, and teaching.

Kurt Wilt for his book *The Visionary* and for introducing me to Joseph Rael.

Friends who have read parts of the manuscript and provided suggestions: Carl Reisman, Qi Liu, Sneh Prasad, Aysha Saeed, Lori Katz, and Henri Roca. The Transformations Work Group: Karen Kopacz, Gary Orr, and Laura Merritt. Antonella Vicini and the on-line magazine, *Badger*. Other seekers who have shared their time and words: Gerald Arbuckle, Bill Laswell, Peter Kingsley, Corinna Nicolaou, Mike Lee, Marty Martinez, Bernie Howarth, Jenny Salmon, Lamont Tanksley, and Stephen Hunt. The next generation of seekers: Penelope & Violet Heynan, Ben & Layne Traxler, David Rothenburg, Kevin Folz, Soroosh Maghsoudi, and Rowan, Frankie, and Maeve Ison-Howarth. My family who have initiated me into a world of curiosity, compassion, and nature: Mary Pat Traxler, Mike & Marie Pedroncelli, Karen Elizabeth Kopacz (who was present at some of our meetings and provided

ENLIGHTMENT

video and photography), Thomas Raymond Kopacz, Linda Ruth Guill Kopacz, Elizabeth Sophia Kopacz, Florian Raymond Kopacz, John Hudson Guill III, Vivian Constance Roberts Guill. Caffe Vita and Cafetal Quilombo for their coffee, community, and nourishment.

The Land, Mother Earth, Father Sky, *Si'ahl* (Chief Seattle), the Suquamish and Duwamish, and the other indigenous peoples who cared for and care for this region on the coast of the Puget Sound, the Salish Sea, and the Pacific Ocean where I am now living.

In Peace

SEATTLE

December 21st, 2018

Winter Solstice

Waxing Gibbous Moon

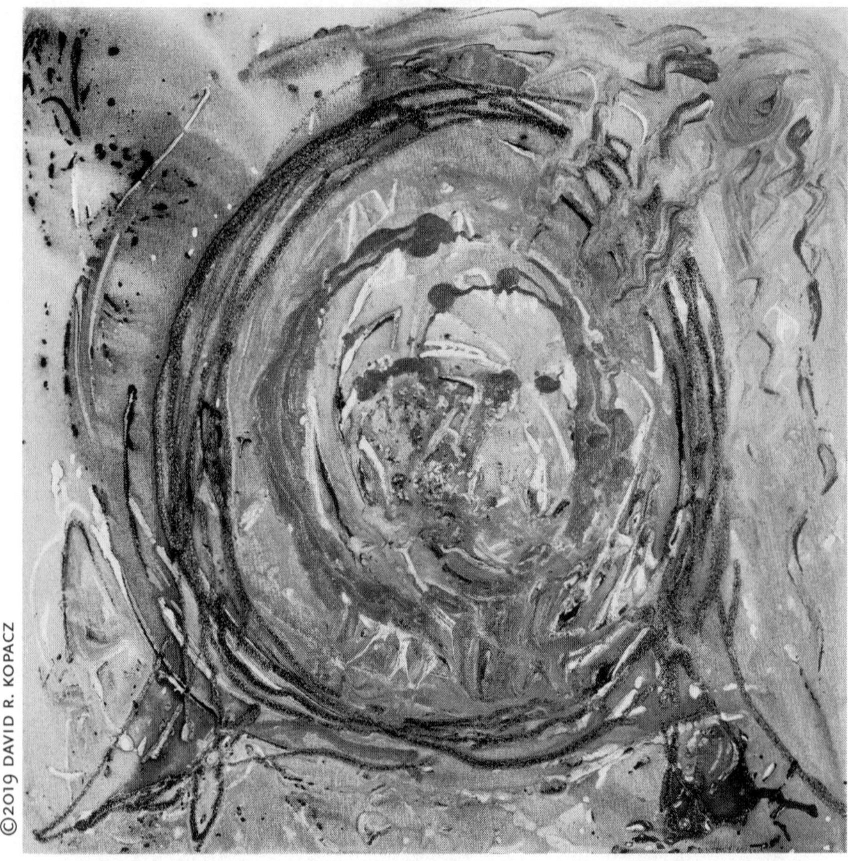

CONCEPTION

Secret—in your work, in my work, in everybody's work, you have to dig it up, you have to bring up the secret from the darkness of the earth and bring it up into that blank space of the Vast Self in order to bring something new into creation. That is what the monks were doing in the caves and what the priests in the Catholic, Protestant, and Greek churches—that is what they are doing, reaching into the secret and bringing it up into the blank space of the Vast Self in order to be co-creators. You and I are already involved in this work, there is no going back now.

JOSEPH RAEL
BEAUTIFUL PAINTED ARROW

INTRODUCTION: THE SECRET JOURNEY

When I (DRK) was in High School I would sit in the dark and listen over and again to the song "Secret Journey," by the band The Police, from the 1981 album *Ghost in the Machine*. The song begins, "*Upon a secret journey, I met a holy man.*"[1] I would sit in the basement and wish that I would meet such a holy man who would instruct and initiate me into the secrets. This longing for a spiritual quest and teachers led me to studying psychology, philosophy, anthropology and world religions in college. Some of my study was formal, such as taking classes from Professor Peter Gregory in World Religions, Zen Buddhism, and East Asian Religions, where I read Niehardt's *Black Elk Speaks*, Juan Mascaró's translation of the *Bhagavad Gita*, Shunryu Suzuki's *Zen Mind, Beginners Mind* and Burton Watson's translation of Chuang Tzu. Some of my quest was through informal reading of Joseph Campbell, Richard Bach, Henry David Thoreau, and books on mysticism. My search also took the form of going into nature, with solo backpacking trips to Black Elk Peak, and Olympic National Park and Shawnee National Forest.

My inspiration for becoming a doctor and psychiatrist came from reading the books of Carl Jung and M. Scott Peck who wrote of transformational spiritual growth as part of the work of psychiatry. I began reading Carl Jung in high school and later had an independent study class on Jung with Professor Gregory. I received my MD from University of Illinois at Chicago (UIC) where I met Deb Klamen and first started to study trauma and physician wellness by working on her paper on Posttraumatic Stress Disorder symptoms and medical training. Deb was a great mentor for learning how to do interesting and relevant research and for accepting me as I was. Later, during my residency, Deb was going up for promotion and put together a series of articles on medical student attitudes toward controversial health topics and she generously let me have first authorship on one of the papers.

Bob Molokie was another mentor, a Hematologist/Oncologist who could carry on three or four different conversations at the same time about medicine as well as the poems of Stephen Crane and novels of Jerzy Kosinski. It was impossible to give Bob a wrong answer to a question because he would simply make up a question for which the answer I had

1 The Police, "Secret Journey" lyrics, from the album *Ghost in the Machine*, 1981.

given was correct and then would quiz me until I got to the right answer of the original question.

I continued at UIC for my psychiatric residency. I learned from Hyman Muslin, a psychoanalyst who had studied Self Psychology with Heniz Kohut. Dr. Muslin told me that I was in a psychiatric *education* program, not a *training* program, because *training* is for dogs and *education* is for humans. Dr. Muslin was an irreverent, old school psychoanalyst as well as a jazz musician. He spoke like a hepcat Freudian and ran a Psychiatry & Literature seminar where we read Shakespeare, Freud, and both classic and modern literature. Dr. Muslin was very concerned that we understand our patients and ourselves as authentic human beings and not get caught up in biological reductionism.

I began two years of influential mentorship from Stevan Weine whose work was in witnessing and genocide. Steve brought Bosnian author Tvrtko Kulenović into the department who facilitated literature discussions for the residents. Steve introduced me to Martin Buber's concept of the *I-It* and *I-Thou* relationships and was a fierce proponent of human rights and human dignity in medicine. When Steve was a medical student, he was befriended by poet Allen Ginsberg, who gave him access to his psychiatric records and said to Steve, "I want to make you into my kind of psychiatrist."[2] Ginsberg gave Steve a reading list that included: William James' *Varieties of Religious Experience*, Burroughs' and Ginsberg's *The Yage Letters*, and Artaud's book on *Van Gogh*. Ginsberg wanted to train a young psychiatrist to see his visionary experiences as something more than reductive psychiatric symptomatology.[3] Steve continued being "Allen Ginsberg's kind of psychiatrist" in mentoring me—always challenging easy

2 Stevan Weine, "Allen Ginsberg's Kind of Psychiatrist," *American Journal of Psychiatry*, Volume 171, Issue 1, January 2014, pp. 23–24.

3 Allen Ginsberg (1926–1997) had visionary experiences that inspired his poetry in 1948, around the age of 22. He was reading William Blake when he heard a voice reciting Blake's poems. His biographer, Michael Schumacher describes that "Allen reached the understanding that poetry was eternal: A poet's consciousness could travel timelessly, alter perception, and speak of universal vision to anyone attaining the same level of consciousness. . . . He was not only a part of a vast presence; he was also part of timeless eternity." Ginsberg wrote that he was "able to read almost any text and see all sorts of divine significance in it," (Schumacher, *Dharma Lion: A Biography of Allen Ginsberg*, 95–96).

Prior to meeting Steve I had gone through a Beat Poets phase, reading *The Yage Letters* and the work of Jack Kerouac, Allen Ginsberg, and William S. Burroughs in college and medical school. The Beats inspired me with the way they formed a creative and interpretive community of writers and poets. I saw Ginsberg perform the *Wichita Vortex Sutra* with Philip Glass in Chicago in the 1990s.

answers, reductive psychiatric diagnosis and terminology, and encouraging me to find the authentic humanity of myself as well as those suffering souls whom I was working with clinically. I can only hope that I have become "Stevan Weine's kind of psychiatrist."

After psychiatric residency, I took a job at the Omaha VA working in the Posttraumatic Stress Disorder and Mental Health Clinics, with a faculty appointment at University of Nebraska. I continued writing poetry and writing in trauma studies, but I had difficulty getting published. Psychiatrists are supposed to write about medications and statistical analyses, not scholarly papers on "Witnessing and the Death Taint in the Writing of Kosinski and Céline," or weird unpublishable books called *In the Shadow of the Slaughterhouse: Silence is the Only Real Crime Against Humanity*.

Eventually my wife, Mary Pat, and I moved back from Omaha to Champaign-Urbana where I embarked on a personal project I called *Die Untergang*, which was a German word that Nietzsche used that meant something like "going under" or "the down-going" from his book *Thus Spoke Zarathustra*. I used that term to summarize a review of all my personal journals while simultaneously reading Carl Jung and Nietzsche, starting with Jung's seminars on Zarathustra. I also did some writing in a column called "Coniunctionis" for an online magazine that my sister started called *Mental Contagion*. This was around 2000 when I was reading about shamanism and wrote a series on "Trauma, Transformation, and Punk Rock" in the Coniunctionis column.[4] We also "got the band back together," so to speak, as Rick Valentin, Mike Barry, and Doug McCarver and I started a band called VibraKing and I learned how to play bass guitar (I had played drums in the past).

I recently came across personal statements I wrote as a medical student and as a psychiatric resident. In both of these I spoke of my dream to work with the Indian Health Service on a reservation to provide service and to learn about Native American healing traditions.[5] These dreams never

---

4 These writings can be accessed on my website, www.davidkopacz.com under "Creativity/Coniunctionis" tabs.

5 Joseph tends to move between the terms "Native American," "American Indian," and most often "Indian." I will follow his convention of interchangeability. When possible we will refer to specific tribal affiliation. I am not sure there is an adequate descriptor word for the aggregate of indigenous peoples who lived on this land since times before it was called the "United States of America." Neither is the use of the word "Americans" without issue, as everyone who lives in North and South America can use that descriptor for themselves. Let us just agree that we are still trying to figure out who we are and what we should call ourselves.

came to pass as we moved from one day to the next, one year to the next. Ten years passed idyllically in Champaign-Urbana. I ran a solo private practice for five years in Champaign while I was also studying holistic healing approaches. The band ended when Rick and Mike moved away. Mary Pat's sisters Julie and Melanie moved away. Both of our pets passed on within a couple years of each other and we found ourselves asking what we wanted to do with our lives in this new opening space.

We decided to move away from Illinois, to head to Seattle, but first spend a few years in New Zealand. I had always wanted to live abroad and was interested in the people, animals, and ecosystem of New Zealand and they were always hiring psychiatrists. We were provided with a one-way ticket to Auckland, New Zealand by Auckland District Health Board. My first job was at Manaaki Community Mental Health Center, where I worked with Fiona Wilson, Dawn Bannister, Sneh Prasad, Qi Liu and many other great people. After eight months, my supervisor, Debbie Antcliff, asked if I would like to work with her at Buchanan Rehabilitation Centre and I jumped at that offer. I loved Buchanan, we would start every shift with a Māori song and we had a great team focused on psychiatric rehabilitation—helping clients regain lost skills, develop new levels of functioning, and reintegrate into the community. Debbie was a great mentor and I learned a lot about leadership from her. She had a wonderful ability to stay in a state of possibility as she would listen to many different people's opinions and perspectives and then she would suddenly synthesize into a decision of her own that incorporated elements of many different people's perspectives. I was also grateful to learn the Re-covery Model from Patte Randal, and learned a great deal from sitting in on her classes.

I was able to incorporate holistic approaches in working with clients and started a Spirituality & Philosophy discussion group. With my friends Sneh Prasad, Bernie Howarth, and Arishma Narayan, we started the Exploring Mental Health through Yoga group. I started the Auckland Holistic Writers group and we met once a month upstairs at Time Out Books in Mt. Eden, bringing together poets, mystics, clinicians, researchers, and scholars.

I returned to the United States November of 2013. Although it was a time of disorientation and reorientation, I thought I had reached a place in my life where I was no longer actively looking for a holy man and I was making a deeper commitment to my own experience. I was forty-six years old and was publishing my first book, *Re-humanizing Medicine*, and I had an outline for my next book. I had come full circle from my first job at Omaha VA and University of Nebraska to working at the Puget Sound VA and being on faculty at University of Washington. I had worked in so many settings and with so many people over the years, I was no longer looking for a holy man or another mentor—and yet that is the time in my life when I met Joseph Rael.

I was in Portland, Oregon one weekend, at Powell's bookstore and a book called *The Visionary*, by Kurt Wilt, caught my eye. I picked it up and was puzzled for a moment by the familiar looking cover art. I read the subtitle: *entering the mystic universe of Joseph Rael Beautiful Painted Arrow*, and I knew I had to read it. I had read a couple of Joseph's books, including *Being & Vibration*, and had recently picked that off my shelf and referenced the section on "Becoming a True Human" in my monthly "Thoughts from the Clinical Director" column at Buchanan Rehabilitation Centre. Throughout *The Visionary*, Kurt compared Joseph Rael's journey to the hero's journey story developed by Joseph Campbell. I emailed Kurt and mentioned that I was using the hero's journey in my work with veterans reintegrating into civilian culture. Kurt thought Joseph would want to know about that work and connected me with Joseph.

I went to Southern Colorado to spend three days with Joseph, thinking maybe it would lead to a chapter in my hero's journey work. The first day I met Joseph I realized this was more than developing a resource for the class—instead it became a real-life hero's journey in which I became the student. I had met a friend, a mentor, a fellow artist and visionary—without even knowing it I had made a secret journey and met a holy man! I had come full circle with my earlier dreams of learning Native American spirituality and wisdom.

The song, "Secret Journey," describes the seeker listening to the words of the holy man, chasing them like birds flying wildly through the sky. This book is the story of my secret journey and the stories of many other seekers as well. Part of the secret journey is becoming disoriented, and the topics of this book may seem to wander, but remember what Gandalf said in *The Lord of the Rings*, "Not all those who wander are lost."[6] This book

6 *All that is gold does not glitter,*
Not all those who wander are lost;
The old that is strong does not wither,
Deep roots are not reached by the frost.
From the ashes, a fire shall be woken,
A light from the shadows shall spring;
Renewed shall be blade that was broken,
The crownless again shall be king.
J.R.R. Tolkien, *The Lord of the Rings*, 182.

will follow the wildly flying birds of Joseph and other visionaries' thoughts and teachings, but there is an underlying unity in these often bewildering pathways and trajectories. One of the primary things that I have learned from Joseph is how to think in circles rather than in the linear way that we are trained. If we seem to be going in circles sometimes in this book, that is part of the teaching that we are seeking to illuminate.

When I first met Joseph, I did not understand why he was physically taking me to the places on the land where he had his visionary experiences. I have come to an understanding that it was necessary to see the places where his visions occurred and to experience them by travelling in the circle of his footsteps. Following the stories in this book may make you feel disoriented in the same way I did while visiting Joseph. This kind of learning requires you to not just change how you think or put new interesting ideas in your mind, but to transform who you are. Transformation requires a journey that goes in circles, like the medicine wheel that Joseph teaches about from his visionary experiences. Eventually after spinning in circles for a while you begin to intuit what is at the center of the circle, the center of the medicine wheel, and that is where you have your own secret journey.

The ancient teachings are there to be re-discovered, but you cannot reach them by linear thought. You must first learn to go in circles and go into stillness, and then the center of the circle begins to manifest. What I have been learning from Joseph is how we are all interconnected and that everything is alive. Joseph teaches that there is an ordinary reality and a non-ordinary (visionary) reality, and that the ultimate reality is that we are all one. This involves a circular and intuitive thought process that I see as an antidote for our overly materialistic society that has lost touch with the sacredness of daily life.

When I met Joseph in 2014 I had recently published my first book, *Re-humanizing Medicine*. I had written about the need for a "counter-curriculum," of inner learning to counter-balance the scientific and technical curriculum of medicine. I also called for a "compassion revolution" to bring heart back into medicine. I felt like I was losing my soul in studying the reductionist curriculum of medicine and the counter-curriculum was a kind of soul retrieval for me. I realized "that the counter-curriculum and compassion revolution are both based on a re-spiritualization of human beings as an antidote to the materialization of human beings that is so prevalent in society and medical culture." To re-spiritualize medicine, I thought that we should harmonize with "the

THE HERO'S JOURNEY

timeless ideals of healing."[7] Through life events and losing heart, through a rich intellectual education, through an outer journey across the world and living in another country, I had returned "home," yet was still missing some aspect of my soul, my *anima* (Latin). In 2014, on my visit to meet Joseph, I sat in the dark of a hotel room in Durango, Colorado, with the sliding door open to the chilly October evening. I was listening to the sound of the Animas River and I realized that there was a secret journey to make as part of my ongoing *counter-curriculum* and it had something to do with working with Beautiful Painted Arrow.

Loss of soul is a common condition in contemporary society. People find themselves angry, confused, disoriented, feeling that "others" are

---

7 David Kopacz, *Re-humanizing Medicine: A Holistic Framework for Transforming Your Self, Your Practice, and the Culture of Medicine*, 322-323.

causing all the problems. Technology is growing exponentially and now has become a source of insecurity. Politics in the United States and the world has become narrow and mean with fundamentalism and nationalism that echoes the rise of totalitarian states in the 20th Century. People feel more and more justified in taking out their anger on other human beings because they are viewed as "other." People appear ready to give up on the dream of a global society and there is less and less civility. Mircea Eliade wrote of the effects of "radical secularization" leaving modern human beings "*living in a desacralized cosmos*."[8] When we lose the sense of sacredness in ourselves, in others, and in nature, all we have left is the profane and profanity. Carl Jung wrote that modern man has "come to the very edge of the world, leaving behind him all that has been discarded and outgrown, and acknowledging that he stands before a void out of which all things may grow."[9] We can focus on our fear of the void or on the creative potential out of which *all things may grow*. Eliade wrote that the feeling that everything is falling apart is part of the process of rebirth and can lead us back to a "sanctified life." What we need are new frameworks for initiation into new ways of being that can be birthed out of our current pain. Eliade describes initiation as having three stages: suffering, death, and rebirth. Initiation is a process of transformation which is fueled by pain and by symbolic "death," the void, out of which rebirth can grow. According to Eliade, "every human existence is formed by a series of ordeals, by repeated experience of 'death' and 'resurrection.'"[10] This is also what Joseph Campbell tells us: we are all called to live a *heroine's* or *hero's journey* because "what we're seeking is an experience of being alive, so that our life experiences on the purely physical plane will have resonances with our own innermost being and reality, so that we will actually feel the rapture of being alive."[11]

Dante embarked on a secret journey when he became lost in a dark wilderness mid-way through his life's journey. There are outer wildernesses and inner wildernesses and one can become lost in either and then must seek a way out of the darkness. I too am at this mid-life junction, just having passed 50. I find that the many possibilities of youth narrow down into a life that can feel constrictive at times, and even *over*. This is magnified

8 Mircea Eliade, *The Sacred and the Profane: The Nature of Religion*, 186, 17.

9 Carl Jung, *MMSS*, 197.

10 Eliade, 196, 209.

11 Joseph Campbell with Bill Moyers, *The Power of Myth*, 4–5.

by a national and international political movement of radical *other-ing* where we break down into smaller and smaller in-groups threatened by those "others." The United States and the world seems to have gone mad, turning a blind eye to the dream of democracy, diversity, and global peace.

My youth and young adulthood are behind me and I find myself saying, "I am beyond." I feel that I am becoming *beyond* this world and it is difficult to see the openings in the darkness; to see the new potentials and possibilities; to see the inherent goodness in life that I know is there, but which I have lost the lived sense of. I stand looking forward and backward and I pick up this thread of the secret journey that was planted in my heart years ago in the darkness of my youth and I wonder what this *beyond* is that I have entered into.

Carl Jung wrote that at mid-life we shift from the outer world of activity and interaction into an internal world of spiritual exploration. This inner wilderness can be daunting, and Dante seems to tell us we *must get lost* at the mid-point. The song "Secret Journey" sings of entering into darkness and disorientation in search of an inner light that brings the opposites together into unity. The song ends with the repeated words that after making the secret journey, one becomes the holiness that was sought. There is a circularity—what one seeks, one becomes. "And when you've made your secret journey/You will be a holy man." The root of the word "holy" is related to "whole" and "healing." As philosopher of ancient Western mystical traditions, Peter Kingsley, points out, the path to holiness may start with feeling you have holes in your heart.

> People who love the divine go around with holes in their hearts, and inside the hole is the universe. . . .
>
> And there is a great secret: we all have that vast missingness deep inside us. The only difference between us and the mystics is that they learn to face what we find ways of running from. That's the reason why mysticism has been pushed to the periphery of our culture: because the more we feel that nothingness inside us, the more we feel the need to fill the void.[12]

One of the central mysteries Joseph Rael teaches is that the seeker of visions goes to the heart of the medicine wheel, which is the heart of the Great Spirit, Vast Self. It is here where everything dies into greatness, the place where all goodness is born. In the heart we are in communion and communication with Vast Self, because we do not really exist separate

12 Peter Kingsley, *In the Dark Places of Wisdom*, 33–36

from Vast Self. In the emptiness in the center of the heart we are full of nothing and part of everything. The empty center of the heart is the place of transformation.[13]

Throughout the ages, mystics, visionaries, and shamans have rejected the roles that we are given and have become seekers of *a living spirituality*. This path of seeking leads from the pain of division and separation to the healing of re-unification. This unity is a radical Oneness—oneness with all people, all living things, and oneness with the cosmos. Our sense of ego identity can be transformed from a "thing" to be preserved to a conduit of service. In this book we are moving to the place where we are all *One*—the interconnected place of the mystic, visionary, and shamanic secret journey. Joseph calls this the journey from ordinary reality to non-ordinary reality and the movement from ego to Vast Self.

This is a book for those who are seeking healing and it is a book for those who are seeking to be healers. We become seekers because of something we feel we lack. We receive healing when we find what fills this absence. We become healers when we are fulfilled and this fullness spills over into giving to others. Those who heal and those who are seeking healing are two sides of the same coin—a coin that is ancient and buried in the soil of yourself.

In modern society we have relegated healing to the field of medicine, but healing is more than pills and surgery. In Native traditions, such as the Southern Ute and Picuris Pueblo traditions Joseph Rael grows out of, *medicine* has a different meaning. It is not something external to you, but a power you have and something you are in relationship with. A person is a kind of medicine because each person has power, what the Pasifika peoples call *mana*. In an indigenous sense, *medicine* and *mana* are similar concepts.

Joseph says that the human being is a medicine bag that carries holy objects. This is the kind of *medicine* we are speaking of in this book. *Becoming Medicine* means to be seeking healing, to be receiving healing, and then to be giving healing. *Seeking*, *finding/receiving*, and *giving* are the three fundamental stages of *becoming medicine* and these are three stages of initiation: *separation*, *initiation*, *return*. Initiation gives us the opportunity to feel vibrantly alive by giving us a pathway for transforming our suffering, to re-spiritualize ourselves and the world, and to allow us to see our underlying unity with creation and the cosmos.

---

13 See Joseph's *B&V:NW*, p. 70, which I am paraphrasing here as it captures recurrent themes of which Joseph often speaks.

The medicine wheel has four outer directions: east, south, west, and the north. The medicine wheel helps us re-orient ourselves when we become lost in the outer world. The medicine wheel also has four inner directions: the mental, emotional, physical, and spiritual. The medicine wheel helps us re-orient when we become lost in the inner world. After walking the inner and outer medicine wheel, we are moving to the center of the medicine wheel and into the heart that contains the place of "held-back goodness" that Joseph says we all have within us. It is through the heart that we move from isolated self and "other" to interconnected "brother and sister."

The heart is the fifth direction—the center of the medicine wheel—which is no direction and yet includes all directions. The journey into the center is the path of the visionary, the mystic, and the shaman. This book continues the journey started in our book, *Walking the Medicine Wheel*, diving into the center of the heart. The center is the invisible place of arising, just as a drum has a center within which sound arises and resonates. The drum is a physical object, but its center is in emptiness. So too, our bodies are physical objects, but our center is a spiritual place of emanation—both our starting point and the place to which we are perpetually returning. Drums beat, hearts beat and the secret journey is into the silence from which the sound of beating arises. As we are walking on the inner journey to the central heart of the medicine wheel, we move deeper into ourselves, which is also moving deeper into the mystery of being. Joseph calls this Vast Self, *Wah-Mah-Chi*, Breath-Matter-Movement, which are different words for "God." When we speak of God we are not speaking of the god of one religion, but rather the God behind all religions, the creative source of life and vitality: *Wah-Mah-Chi*, Breath-Matter-Movement.

The inner journey of the medicine wheel brings us to the place of the center, which is the place of the heart. Joseph teaches that each of the four directions of the medicine wheel has a color, a principle idea, and a vowel sound (starting with the East–A–*ahh*, South–E–*eh*, West–I–*eee*, North–O–*oh*, and the Center–U–*uu*).[14] The principle energy of the center is *carrying*, which is the heart of the medicine wheel. As we make this inner journey to the center of the medicine wheel we are on the journey of *becoming medicine*. This is not an egotistical place of thinking we have personal power, rather it is a place that is reached by moving beyond ego and becoming what Joseph calls "a hollow bone." A hollow bone is a

14 *B&V:NW*, 44. Vowel sounds in Tiwa are as pronounced in Spanish, also similar to Polynesian languages and Māori.

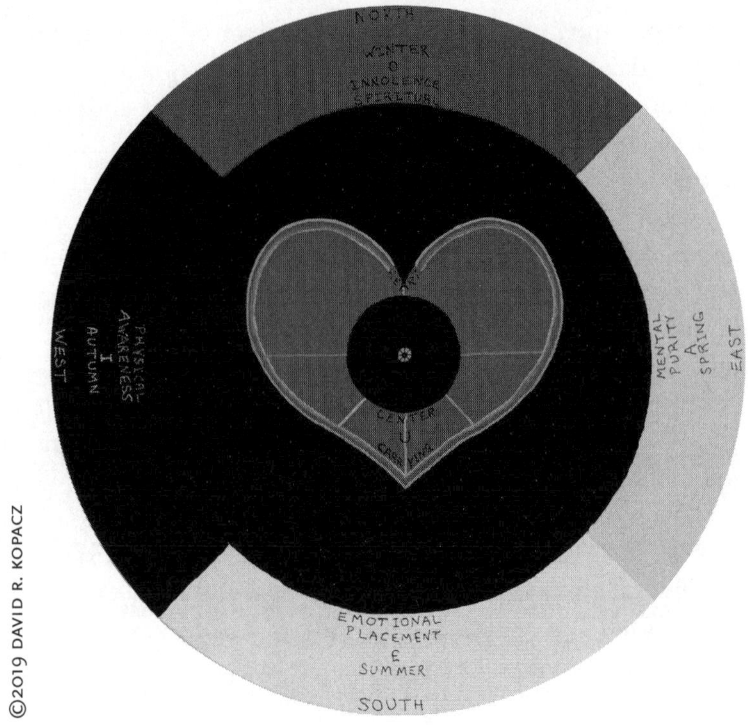

MEDICINE WHEEL OF THE HEART

structure, a vessel, whose purpose is to let Breath-Matter-Movement flow through it. One becomes a hollow bone by letting go of self, surrendering and submitting to letting Vast Self live through you. We began the book *Walking the Medicine Wheel* with the *nah-meh-neh* ceremony that Joseph offered to help veterans reconnect to themselves and to the earth. The sound *neh* is similar to the Persian word, *ney*, the word for the reed flute that the poet Rumi often wrote about. The *ney* is an empty tube from a water reed with nine holes in it. One blows breath into the hollow emptiness of the reed. The vibratory sound of the song comes into being not only because of the hollowness of the reed, but also from the nine holes punched into the body of the *ney*. Joseph tells us that *neh neh* in Tiwa means the self in a relationship of awareness with the Vast Self. In other words this means self in relationship to God (Breath-Matter-Movement).[15] By allowing ourselves to be empty (and hole-y) we create

15 See *Sound*: *Neh* means "the Vast Self and personal self as it places itself in a statement of awareness," (35) and "*neh neh* is the self, positioned in awareness of the Vast Self," (208).

the space for Breath-Matter-Movement to flow through our hearts and our lives. Our hearts must become empty, like the *ney*, like the drum, and like the hollow bone. It is only through the empty spaces of our hearts that life-giving, oxygen-carrying blood is able to flow through our bodies.

Coleman Barks, a prolific translator of Rumi's work into English, tells us that "*Language and music are possible only because we're empty, hollow, and separated from the source. All language is a longing for home.*"[16] Rumi hears in the plaintive sound of the notes of the *ney* the longing for the source from which it was separated, the reed bed along the river. The secret journey into the invisible center of the medicine wheel takes us into the heart of the source which we are always longing for and yet from which we are never truly separated.

OUR COMMON, ANCIENT SPIRITUAL HERITAGE

The initiation we describe in this book is both personal as well as universal. It is personal in that it will follow my journey of learning about Joseph's journey. We include Joseph's own reflections on initiation. It is universal because there is a universal body of descriptive literature on the experiences and initiations of visionaries, mystics, and shamans. Joseph tells me, "*What Indians can teach people, all people, is not how to be an Indian, but how to be a human being. In Tiwa, to be a human being is* tie-eh-neh.[17] *This means that the human being is the creator.*" To study initiation is to become a human being, which is to become a creator.

"The shaman's practice of direct revelation is the ancestral precursor of all our religious and philosophical traditions, both ancient and modern," writes Paleoanthropologist Hank Wesselman.[18] Like Wesselman, we look at shamanism in a broad context as a generic pathway of "direct revelation," *a living spirituality*, a basic common pathway of the experience of sacred

---

16 Coleman Barks, *The Essential Rumi*, 17.

17 Tiwa developed as an oral language and that is how Joseph learned it. He uses phonetic spelling in which the sound is more important than the spelling. I have noticed slight variations in the spellings he gives of Tiwa words. He will often tell me, "You spell it, you're good at that." Thus the spelling of spoken Tiwa words in this book is often a collaboration of Joseph's speaking and my hearing and translating speech into written word.

18 Hank Wesselman's preface to Sandra Ingerman and Hank Wesselman, *Awakening to the Spirit World: The Shamanic Path of Direct Revelation*, xvii-xix. Ingerman and Wesselman trace the birth of shamanism back to "tens of thousands of years ago . . . the Upper Paleolithic Period," xxii. Also see Fred Gustafson's discussion of the archetype of the "indigenous one," in *Dancing Between Two Worlds* and Peter Kingsley's work on early shamanic influences in Western culture in *A Story Waiting to Pierce You*.

goodness. Direct spiritual experience is what we are discussing in terms of initiation in this book. We are looking at the long human timeline, going all the way back to when *Homo sapiens* first walked out of Africa, long before Islam, Christianity, Judaism, Buddhism, or Hinduism—back to the oral traditions handed down over aeons through rites of initiation. As we look back to these traditions, we are looking for how we can create *a living spirituality* that people can enter into even now. Wesselman puts it this way:

> Engaging with the shamanic tradition is not about cultural appropriation or ripping off the spirituality of any indigenous peoples. We all come from indigenous ancestors if we go back far enough, and they all had great shamans. Thus, the shamanic path is one of our birthrights and the ancestral precursor of all our spiritual and religious traditions.[19]

The reason that Joseph and I, as well as Wesselman and many others, can speak of shamanism as a common shared pathway, is because shamanism[20] teaches how to connect to the spiritual realm. There are cultural variations in the surface phenomenon of shamanism, but at its core it is a teaching of ancient wisdom—how to open the interior door for direct, spiritual revelation.

The purpose of the book is not to portray one specific cultural tradition, but rather to provide a guidebook that people can use on their own personal journeys of initiation into a living spirituality—*becoming medicine.* Our apologies to any who find it objectionable to draw from many traditions of living spirituality. Our focus is not on appropriating external forms, but in using multiple external forms to point the way to the center of the heart where we each can experience *a living spirituality.*

---

19 Hank Wesselman, *The Re-Enchantment: A Shamanic Path to a Life of Wonder*, 23-24.

20 Some may object to using the term "shaman" in its broadest and most inclusive sense, rather than in its narrowest sense belonging only to specific cultural groups of Central and Northern Asia. Joseph, himself, often uses this term to describe his own initiation and work and in being true to his tradition and experience we will use the term "shaman" throughout the book to refer to a spiritual seeker and visionary who uses his or her spiritual experiences for the purposes of healing self, others, and community. Proto-Indo-European is the largest historical language group whose descendants include English, Iranian, Celtic, Italic, Germanic, Slavic, Greek, and Indic languages. The descendant languages of Proto-Indo European are spoken across the globe and likely originated in this same area of Central Asia between the Caucasus, Carpathian, and Ural Mountains (see David Anthony, *The Horse, the Wheel, and Language*).

A ROAD MAP FOR TRANSFORMATION

My work researching the roots of healing has led me to this work with Joseph on the transformative process of initiation. Most kinds of learning are incremental steps that involve memorizing information. Incremental learning is changing what you know and what you do. Transformative learning is more than learning facts and information; it is about changing who you are. There is a theoretical and evidence-base for studying transformative change. Sociologist Jack Mezirow developed and researched "transformational learning theory" His theory included ten steps of transformational learning, which we will condense down to three key steps:

1. A disorienting dilemma
2. Recognizing the connection between one's discontent and the process of transformation
3. Reintegration of a new perspective into one's life[21]

These three steps parallel the steps of the hero's journey and the steps of the universal framework: separation, initiation, and return. The *disorienting dilemma* occurs with the separation from the known world and the sense of a known identity. The *recognition of a connection between the disorientation and the process of transformation* is the transition that occurs in the abyss of the hero's journey, which is a death of the old and the birth of a new sense of self and purpose. *Reintegration with a new perspective* is the step of crossing the return threshold in the hero's journey, it is the step of returning home in a transformed state. Mezirow captures the idea that disorientation is necessary for transformation. This is what Joseph Rael speaks of when he says *na-yo ti-ay we-ah*, "I do not exist." This means that in order for transformation to occur we must embrace the fact that we are not who we thought we were, accepting this opens the doorway to becoming who we are in the process of becoming.

Another proponent of transformational learning is psychologist Richard Katz, who has lived and worked with traditional healers in Fiji, Botswana, and North America. For over 35 years Katz has been writing about "education as transformation," an education of the "heart," involving a process of "envisioning." Katz believes this kind of transformational education would

21 Jack Mezirow, "Transformational Learning Theory," in Jack Mezirow, Edward Taylor, and Associates eds., *Transformative Learning in Practice*, 19.

benefit community psychiatrists if they could re-learn this ancient wisdom from traditional healers. Katz writes, transformative education "involves a transformation of consciousness in which potential healers experience a sense of connectedness, joining a spiritual healing power, themselves, and their community . . . [which] affects the inner quality of their lives, transforming them."[22] This transformation goes beyond the individual as a separate being to interconnect with all of creation. Katz writes that the "Fijian concept of dauloloma (love for all) . . . is feeling a love for another because that person, like oneself, is a part of creation."[23]

You might ask, "What do transformation and initiation have to do with my day-to-day life in the 21st Century?" If you feel you have lost something of yourself or you feel out of harmony with the world, transformation is what can help you find yourself and your purpose again. If you are seeking to grow in your humanity, then studying pathways of initiation of mystics, visionaries, and shamans can give you a template for transformational growth in your own life.

We can learn something about life and healing from studying the stories of shamans and mystics. These stories of transformative initiation re-spiritualize and re-vitalize our ordinary lives and bring healing. While this may seem like an esoteric process it is incredibly practical for those who are seeking growth. Whenever we feel lost, trapped, frustrated, alone, hopeless, demoralized, or in despair, we are half-way into initiation as these are the first steps toward transformation. We can learn how to live our lives and particularly how to grow and thrive in the midst of crises—in fact, crisis is the invitation for transformative growth.

In addition to being a road map for transformative growth during the trials and tribulations of life, this book is also important from the perspective of burnout and demoralization. Indiscriminate mass shootings, environmental disasters, attacks on democracy and free speech, the rise of radical "other-ing" of people who look or think different than us, violence and discrimination toward women, immigrants, and people of differing faiths—all of these issues are disorienting us as to who we are as

---

22 Richard Katz, "Education as Transformation: Becoming a Healer Among the !Kung and the Fijians, *Harvard Educational Review*, Vol. 51, No. 1, February 1981, 58. An updated version of this essay can be found in Katz and Murphy-Shigematsu, *Synergy, Healing, and Empowerment* (2012).

23 Richard Katz, *Indigenous Healing Psychology: Honoring the Wisdom of the First Peoples*, 308.

human beings and what it means to live together on Mother Earth. To be a healer means to be close to illness, suffering, madness, and death. These disorienting human situations propel a person into another realm, what Joseph would call non-ordinary reality. Whenever there is a strong break in the daily routine of ordinary reality, non-ordinary reality breaks in, to reveal itself in epiphany and revelation. The work healers do demands inner work as well as outer work as a way of transforming suffering into healing. We all are in need of healing and in this book we illuminate the pathway for becoming the healers that we so desperately need.

My first book, *Re-humanizing Medicine*, was about rediscovering humanity for doctors and health care professionals who burned out and lost touch with their idealism. It traced my own journey of losing important aspects of my humanity and developing a way to regain humanity, to re-humanize. In this way, we could say it was a shamanic journey of soul recovery. In our first collaborative book *Walking the Medicine Wheel: Healing Trauma & PTSD*, Joseph and I were seeking to blaze a trail from war back to peace. Both these books were about seeking the truth of the heart when one becomes lost in the inner and outer worlds and both map out the pathway back to recovering our humanity. This book, *Becoming Medicine*, is also for healers and warriors—which means it is for all of us, even if we are not formally in health care or if we have not gone to war, because the same journey that healers and warriors make when they lose heart is the same kind of journey that all of us make when we have lost heart.

Anyone who is wounded, whether they are veterans or healers, or stockbrokers, lawyers, parents, teachers, students, has already entered the first step of initiation—separation from the ordinary world with its attendant disorientation. Feeling alone is the first step of initiation. *Seeking* removes one from the crowds and a feeling of separation from the crowd can also be the motivation for seeking a sense of interconnection that appears to be lacking in contemporary society.

CREATIVE ILLNESS

We live in a time of profound inner and outer disorientation. Initiation begins with disorientation and that disorientation is necessary for healing ourselves, our society, and the world. Henri Ellenberger has discussed the similarities between the work of shamans and psychotherapists. He sees Freud and Jung, two of the founders of dynamic psychotherapy, as having gone through *creative illnesses* which parallel the initiatory training of shamans.

> It is our hypothesis that Freud's and Jung's systems originated mostly from their respective creative illnesses. . . . This rare condition begins after a long period of restless intellectual work and preoccupation. The main symptoms are depression, exhaustion, irritability, sleeplessness, and headaches. . . . There can be oscillations in the intensity of symptoms but throughout the patient remains obsessed by a prevailing idea or the pursuit of some difficult aim. He lives in utter spiritual isolation and has the feeling that nobody can help him, hence his attempts at self-healing. But usually he will feel these attempts intensify his sufferings. The illness may last three or more years. The recovery occurs spontaneously and rapidly; it is marked by feelings of euphoria, and is followed by a transformation of the personality. The subject is convinced that he has gained access to a new spiritual world. Examples of this illness can be found among Siberian and Alaskan shamans, among mystics of all religions, and among certain creative writers and philosophers.[24]

Ellenberger describes the "pathfinder" as a creative individual who takes on the ills of society in order to break through into a new conception of healing, first healing one's self and then healing others. He speaks of "preoccupation," which we usually think of as a negative thing, like an obsession. However if we look at the word *pre*-occupation, we can also see it as an intense period of incubation in which the individual gives birth to his or her own occupation. This initial disorientation of creative illness can thus be seen as the beginning stage of a vocation or calling. The *separation* of the individual from his or her peers in the creative illness is the first step of *initiation*. After a period of sometimes years, Ellenberger describes the rapid resolution of *creative illness* with a "transformation of the personality" along with "access to a new spiritual world," which paves the way for the individual's *return* to society to take up his or her vocation and cause. This idea of creative illness encourages us to approach illness and suffering creatively—as a disorienting invitation to initiation.

In the Police song "Secret Journey," the journey ends when the seeker becomes that which was being sought—he or she is holy. To become

---

24 Henri Ellenberger, *The Discovery of the Unconscious*, 889.

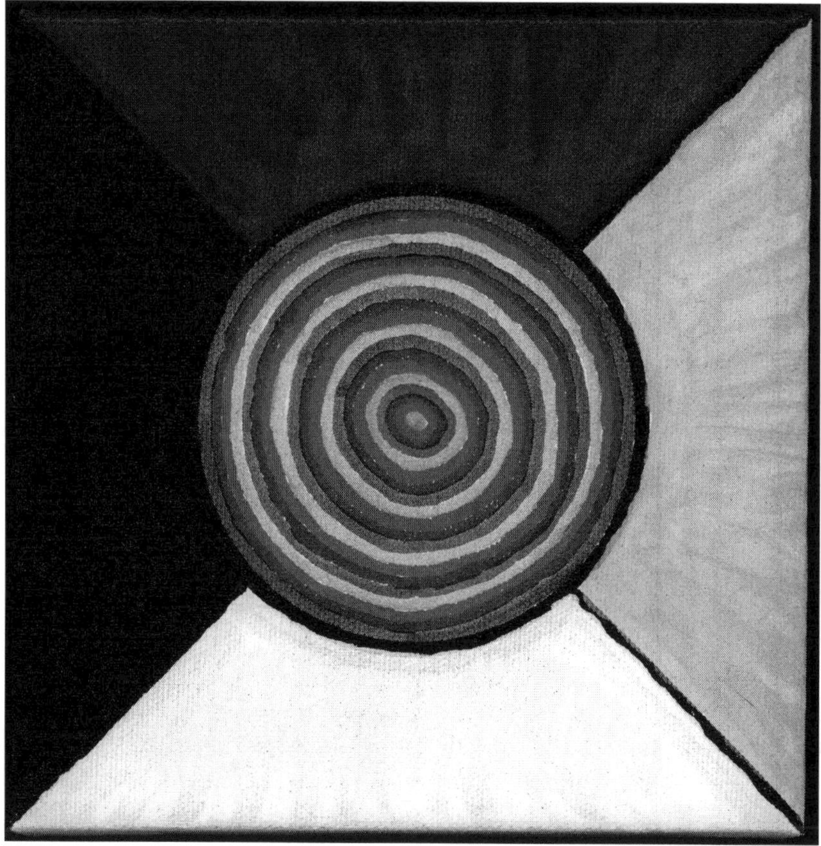

RAINBOW MEDICINE WHEEL

holy is to become *whole* and to walk a path of healing. Holiness is an orientation to ourselves, to the world, and to all of existence. Being a holy man or woman is not about being some kind of special person, it is more a matter of orientation of envisioning life in a certain way and in seeing life as a certain kind of work. Joseph always reminds us that the holy woman or holy man is not the source of the healing spirit, rather, holiness comes from becoming a "hollow bone." Joseph often jokes, "*Some people call me a medicine man—I don't know about that—I just work here.*" If Joseph does not claim that status, I surely do not claim that status. When Joseph asks me what I think about including something in the book, I give him his joke back and say, "You're the boss—I just work here." Yet *work* for Joseph is sacred. "Work is worship," his grandfather at Picuris Pueblo used to tell him. So we offer this book to you, our work as two individuals seeking to bring peace into the world through offering ourselves as hollow bones conveying *Wah-Mah-Chi*.

What I hope, in sharing my secret journey and Joseph's guidance on this journey, is that we can all come to a healing orientation of peace in our hearts, in our lives, and in the world. We must make this secret journey alone, but if we are lucky, we find a mentor or two along the way. Even though the journey is deeply personal, it is also universal—we must all make it—and we find we are on our own path which is also the path that we are all walking. The current darkness that we find ourselves in may be the perfect place to start such a journey. Joseph Campbell wrote that when the Knights of the Round Table began their quest for the grail, each Knight knew that he must find his own path in the place of greatest darkness:

> They thought it would be a disgrace to go forth as a group.
> Each entered the forest at a point that he himself had chosen,
> Where it was darkest and there was no path.
> Where there's a way or path,
> It is someone else's path; each human being is a unique phenomenon.[25]

Yet, the Knights of the Round Table knew something of the circle as they sat around their table; while each had to make his own secret journey, there was a collective responsibility that they began with and returned to. As we each make our own individual secret journey, we return together to find that at heart, we are holy, we are whole, and we are one.

25 Campbell, cited in Phil Cousineau, ed., *The Hero's Journey: Joseph Campbell on His Life and Work*, viii.

PART I

SEPARATION (SEEKING)

Perhaps, before I was twelve I was already preparing myself for my life's work. Then, in 1980, I decided to explore that life's work, and I began actively seeking out visionary experiences and the guidance of Spirit.[1]

JOSEPH RAEL

To get there is simple. You walk until you reach the limit of your ability and there is no way you could possibly go any further.[2]

PETER KINGSLEY

Every religion begins with the recognition that human consciousness has been separated from the divine Source, that a former sense of oneness with the ground of Being has been lost, and that only by a process of purification and transcendence can we be reconnected with the sacred dimension.[3]

RICHARD HEINBERG

If life is a story we're meant to live through,
then both me and you are the pages.
I'll tell you a tale, and most of it's true,
you see, I came here for you through the ages.[4]

CLOUD CULT

1 *House*, 126.

2 Peter Kingsley, *A Story Waiting to Pierce You*, 3.

3 Richard Heinberg, *Memories and Visions of Paradise: Exploring the Universal Myth of a Lost Golden Age*, 81–82.

4 Cloud Cult, "Living in Awe," from the album, *The Seeker*, 2016.

NIGHT EYES OF DIRECTION FINDER

CHAPTER 1

BECOMING MEDICINE

"The thing I should have said in my books is that everyone already has their medicine. The way you become a medicine person is you practice who you are because you are already medicine. No one gives it to you, you are already it."[1]

(JOSEPH RAEL)

Joseph tells us that the human being is a medicine bag, in which we carry sacredness. By walking into the center of the medicine wheel, we are walking into the center of ourselves, into the center of our hearts. In doing this we cease to be ourselves and are instead *becoming medicine.* We say *becoming* because it is not done once and for all. It is something that is done every moment through work and ceremony. *Becoming Medicine* means that we are empty space, we are becoming capable of being a place for *Wah-Mah-Chi,* for Breath-Matter-Movement to manifest and reside for a moment.

Life is a movement—not so much a thing, but more like a breath that goes in and goes out. And we are like the reed flute (*ney*), the hollow bone, the matter through which breath is moving. When we empty ourselves and make space for breath it is a form of seeking, and seeking opens space within us for transformation. Seeking is a form of work, and as Joseph's grandfather taught, "*Work is worship.*"[2] The work is to create a space of emptiness, which leads to seeking, seeking leads to finding & receiving and this state of fullness leads to giving.

The point of all this is to tell a story. It is my story, it is Joseph Rael's story, it is also the story of every visionary, mystic, and shaman. Joseph has this to say about story:

1 We will set Joseph's spoken words to me in italics with quotations. References from his books will be in quotation marks, but not italicized and will have textual footnotes referenced.

2 Joseph tells me this often and it appears throughout his published writing. For example: "My Tiwa grandfather taught me that work is worship. And yet if we don't exist, and none of this exists, and there is nothing that we really need to do except know that we don't exist (except in the sense that we are part of the Vast Self), why do we need to work? We need to work because we have physical bodies, and these physical bodies are really forms that can be traced back to sacred dimensions," (*Sound*, 134).

"We are a story already and when we tell a story we are telling on ourselves and therefore stories are a part of us because we are telling it. As soon as I start telling a story I am telling it with such authorship because I was born with the gift of stumbling and when I tell a story that part of me that I am telling about is stumbling. That part of me telling the story is telling what I am about. Stumbling is what gives a story its characteristic."

Joseph Campbell found the story beneath all the stories and called it the "monomyth," the "hero's journey"—a framework for all growth and transformation in our lives that begins with seeking. The hero hears a call to adventure, separates from the everyday world, goes through initiation, loses heart through a descent into inner or outer darkness, regains heart, and then returns with a gift to the everyday world. This gift is the knowledge of how to regain heart after losing it. Some of the stories might be what you expect about holy people—stories of saints and religious people. Some of the holy people's stories might not be what you expect—ordinary seekers, musicians, and artists who are people of transformation. These stories are written in the beatings of the heart rather than in the strainings of the analytical mind that separates and categorizes. The work of the mind is to divide and the work of the heart is to unify. As you read these stories, try to listen by softening your heart rather than straining your mind. There are many stories and many characters, but they all start with separation, move into initiation, and then come full circle with return. In the time it takes you to read this sentence, your blood circulated through your heart and completed an initiation into a sacred moment. Every moment is an initiation.

The holy person grows comfortable spending more time in the emptiness of non-existence than in the fullness of existence—yet, paradoxically, the holy person is able to live a fuller existence by spending more time in non-existence. Joseph calls existence ordinary reality and non-existence non-ordinary reality. He is very interested in the astrophysics concepts of dark matter and dark energy and sees these as non-ordinary reality (non-existence). Joseph says that Breath-Matter-Movement (God) is found in the spaces, not in the words, similarly, we could say that *Wah-Mah-Chi* is found in non-existence, in non-ordinary reality.

In *Walking the Medicine Wheel* we wrote about how division and separation open the door to violence and war. To see someone as "other" invites the possibility of treating that person in a violent way (by *person* we also mean plants, animals, rocks, stones, and Mother Earth, herself). Violence is a side effect of separation. Peace follows unification. The violence of separation is the illness and the peace of unification is the medicine. Thus, in *becoming medicine* we are becoming peace.

A PATH OF SEEKING

Joseph tells me that the phrase *ta-no-chee-who* means "I am seeking." Then he tells me about his earliest vision when he was three or four years old. (The hillside where this vision occurred is the first place Joseph took me to when I met him in 2014).

"I was searching for my mother on the hillside where she was driving some of the stray sheep and it was the being of ta-no-chee-who *that guided me in the direction I could find her. A voice said 'jump through the cloud,' there was a mist all around me and she was on the other side.*

"In later years when I was writing my first book I realized that I was ta-no-chee-who, *that I was inside* ta-no-chee-who. *I was lost there so that I could find myself with the help of* ta-no-chee-who."

Looking back, I see my own path of *ta-no-chee-who* (seeking) starting around the time that I was listening in High School to the song "Secret Journey." You could say that my path started in sound and music and led to the mind and then to the heart. The Police, (Sting, Steward Copeland, and Andy Summers), spoke in interviews about the influence psychiatrist Carl Jung had on their music. For instance, their 1983 album, *Synchronicity* was named after Jung's theory of meaningful coincidence. My friend, Jack Scott's, parents had a copy of Jung's *Modern Man in Search of a Soul* and they let me "borrow" it. The reading was dense and I had a difficult time following it. My desire to learn its secret wisdom was great, however. I set up a plan to read at least five pages, whether or not I understood, each night. After five pages I could relax my mind and read my science fiction books.

Throughout *Modern Man in Search of a Soul,* Jung speaks of *mana* as "theory of energy." He describes conversations with medicine men, such as Ochwiay Biano (Mountain Lake) from Taos Pueblo, who told Jung that Americans are crazy because they think with their heads whereas the Pueblo people think with their hearts.[3] He introduced the concept of introversion and extraversion, the orientation of people to either value the external or the internal world. The idea of introversion gave me a

3 *MMSS*, 146–147, 184.

framework to understand why I was not as outgoing as many of my peers and it validated that the inner path is a legitimate focus. Jung wrote about the interconnection between mind-body-spirit, and the need to have a spiritual focus in medicine and healing. He had an intuitive grasp that the personality and attitude of the therapist was more important than psychotherapeutic theory or technique, which has been validated in many studies of psychotherapy.[4]

Jung's work was a work of seeking, as the title *Modern Man in Search of a Soul* suggests. He diagnosed the problem of modern humans as the lack of a living spirituality and he saw the psychotherapist as heir to medicine men and priests in being a spiritual guide for those who were lost and seeking. Jung believed in the inner healer and the innate healing power of human beings. He wrote about four stages of psychotherapy: 1) confession, 2) explanation, 3) education, and 4) transformation.[5] The first three stages helped one to adjust to society and become "normal," however the fourth stage of transformation involved going beyond normal to becoming a unique individual whose spirituality is activated. The stage of transformation is a "place" that both the therapist and the client enter into together. Jung speaks of the "fact of mutual influence and all that goes with it underlies the stage of transformation." Transformation is not something the doctor does to the client, but rather a state that both enter into equally. "The fourth stage . . . then, demands not only the transformation of the patient, but also the counter-application to himself by the doctor of the system which he prescribes in any given case." This is an important point, one that I have worked on much of my career, that transformation requires not just medical technique and expertise, but the full humanity of the healer to open within the therapeutic encounter. As Jung wrote, "The medical diploma is no longer the crucial thing, but human quality instead."

Transformation occurs when "the destructive powers were converted into healing forces." This transformation involves the activation of inner forces within the individual that do not arise from ego consciousness. He writes that with transformation, "something arises to confront him—something strange that is not the 'I' and is therefore beyond the reach of

---

4 For instance, see the summary of studies in Bruce E. Wampold and Zac E. Imel, *The Great Psychotherapy Debate: The Evidence for What Makes Psychotherapy Work* (2015) and David N. Elkins, *The Human Elements of Psychotherapy: A Nonmedical Model of Emotional Healing* (2015).

5 Jung, *MMSS*, 46–54.

personal caprice. He has gained access to the sources of psychic life, and this marks the beginning of the cure." Jung writes that this "spontaneous activity of the psyche often becomes so intense that visionary pictures are seen or inner voices heard. These are manifestations of the spirit directly experienced today as they have been from time immemorial."[6] We can call this activation of psychic energy and visionary experience initiation into *a living spirituality.*

MY PROFESSIONAL PATH OF MEDICINE

I made the decision to go to medical school during a time of deep despair when I was on academic probation during my first year of college and was not sure what to do with my life and my studies. I was staring at my bookshelf and the idea came to me that maybe if I looked at the books I was interested in I would know what it was that most interested me and I could study that. The first book my eyes focused upon was Jung's *Modern Man in Search of a Soul.* The next book my eyes focused on was also by a psychiatrist, M. Scott Peck's *The Road Less Traveled.*

The first sentence of *The Road Less Traveled* is: "Life is difficult." When I first read that I just stared at the page. What a paradigm shift! I had just received the letter that I failed calculus, one-third of my credit hours, and I was on academic probation. "Life is difficult," was the first line and I took that to mean that maybe it was ok that I was in despair and that I did not know what to do. That is what M. Scott Peck seemed to be saying to me:

> Life is difficult.
>
> This is a great truth, one of the greatest truths. It is a great truth because once we truly see this truth, we transcend it. Once we truly know that life is difficult — once we truly understand and accept it — then life is no longer difficult. Because once it is accepted, the fact that life is difficult no longer matters.[7]

The other major thing that I found in Peck's book was that he made no distinction between mind and spirit and that he saw spiritual growth as a long and continuing process. Peck's and Jung's books served as doorways of initiation into a different view of life. It was reassuring to me to read Jung's writings on calling and vocation and Peck's writing about *the road less traveled.* These two psychiatrists gave a context for suffering as a path to initiation and transformation. Not only did their writing help me through

6 Ibid., 50–51, 53, 242–43.

7 M. Scott Peck, *The Road Less Traveled,* 3.

a difficult time, they were also role models who introduced the idea that a psychiatrist could be a life-long seeker and a healer. I wanted to be the kind of psychiatrist that Carl G. Jung was, the kind of psychiatrist that M. Scott Peck was. I decided then that I wanted to be a psychiatrist, the only thing left to do was to figure out how one became not only a psychiatrist, but how to become the kind of psychiatrist that Jung and Peck were.

My professional path to *becoming medicine* officially started in August of 1989 when I began medical school at University of Illinois at Chicago. Medical school began with an immersion in the dead physical body of a woman who had donated her body to science and wound up being my first patient—a *cadaver*.

> c. 1500, from Latin *cadaver* "dead body" . . . probably from a perfective participle of *cadere* "to fall, sink, settle down, decline, perish," from PIE [Proto-Indo-European] root **kad-* "to lay out, fall or make fall" . . . Compare Greek *ptoma* "dead body," literally "a fall."[8]

The way medical school is taught in contemporary times is through a *fall*—an immersion in death rather than life. One's first patient is dead and one then dismembers what once was a human being, but soon comes to look like a carved up turkey at Thanksgiving dinner. The dissection of the cadaver is a process of separating out bits and pieces of what were once living flesh into isolated nerves, muscles, bones, organs, and blood vessels. How different this is than the ideas of *wholeness*, *love*, *heart*, and *interconnection*. Science is a process of separation, of cutting things up and naming them. I grew in the realm of science, but what was I losing?

Science came to be associated, for me, with death, and perhaps what I was losing then was life, spirit, and soul. I found that I had to develop a *counter-curriculum* to re-birth my own soul within me. As in the hero's journey, I left the known world, I crossed a threshold, I came across negative and positive mentors, I faced challenges, I went through times of darkness in the abyss and the dark night of the soul, my old identity died, and I was reborn as a physician. In all initiation and acculturation processes something is lost and something is gained. There is both a celebration and a grieving that occurs as we move across boundaries in life.

While I felt like I lost my soul studying medicine, the work of a healer and the work of a shaman is bringing body and soul back together again. I am not the only physician to speak of the dehumanization and

---

8 "Cadaver," *Online Etymology Dictionary*.

despiritualization that are side effects of learning to practice contemporary medicine. Carl Hammerschlag wrote, "I was reasonably well trained in the science of medicine, but that didn't make me a healer."[9] Lewis Mehl-Madrona also writes about doctors needing to learn how to be healers in order to "learn to take their patients on spiritual journeys."[10] Soul loss can be the separation that leads to seeking—it can be the first step in an initiation process that reunites mind and body, body and soul, heart and head. Dismemberment and death are just the first step of transformative change. Transformative learning, as Jack Mezirow describes it, is a disorienting dilemma that pulls one out of ordinary reality. This separation is often felt as a trauma and a violent separation from one's sense of self—leaving the comfort zone and entering the path of the *road less travelled*, the path of "I am seeking," *ta-no-chee-who*. Many shamanic healers describe a visionary process of their bodies being dismembered, chopped apart, blown to pieces. There is the death of the old body and a new body is formed that is born out of pain, but is now a healing body.

This journey into death, like my journey of immersing myself in the cadaver of a once living woman, appears to be necessary in the journey of the healer. Medical and health sciences education are very good at breaking down, but we are not so good at the putting back together and in creating a supportive healing environment for the younger generation of wounded healers to be reborn. In fact, our whole society lacks nurturing, compassionate, and healing structures to help our citizens "put themselves back together" after the inevitable dismemberments and disorientations of modern life. This is what Joseph Rael (Beautiful Painted Arrow) and I seek to map out in this book. *Becoming medicine* does not necessarily mean you will become a health professional, but it does mean that you will enter into a process of *becoming a medicine* that can be used for healing yourself and others in this world.

Just at the time I was graduating medical school and starting psychiatry residency there was another pathway unfolding three miles away—the

9 Carl A. Hammerschlag, *The Theft of Spirit: A Journey to Spiritual Healing*, 14. He goes on to write that it was through stories that he was able to "metamorphosis from doctor to healer," (14). Hammerschlag's vision is similar to that of *Becoming Medicine*. He diagnoses Western culture as having lost its spirit, its soul, and he learned from Native American healers how to heal himself and society. His book, *The Dancing Healers: A Doctor's Journey of Healing with Native Americans* explores these themes.

10 Lewis Mehl-Madrona, *Coyote Medicine: Lessons from Native American Healing*, 17. This book follows Mehl-Madrona's own healing and learning after contemporary medical education.

Parliament of World Religions in August and September of 1993. I did not know this was happening at the time, I was so immersed in the excitement of starting psychiatric education. I was right there, three miles away from this second Parliament of World Religions (100 years after the first gathering in 1893). When I realized, years later, how close I was to this momentous spiritual event, my initial feeling was sadness. Joseph is always looking for the meaning of events occurring in the world related to what is going on inside us. "We are the microcosm of the macrocosm" he often says. This is what Jung called "synchronicity," the meaningful connection between inner and outer events. I now look at this tremendous influx of spiritual energy into Chicago as the *medicine* that would help me heal and become a healer—the return of my lost my soul from medical school!

Joseph tells me that the Tiwa word for "medicine" is *waa-leh-ney*, and then he described the difference between the meaning of medicine in English and Tiwa.

"In English, 'medicine' is something that still needs to happen, but in Tiwa medicine is already there, it is a power. Every human being is a power.

"One becomes a medicine person through practicing one's destiny. The child already has his or her own medicine. Through practicing one's destiny, the medicine person manifests the medicine that was already there as a child. The child makes medicine all those years and then becomes an adult."

In contemporary health care, we think of medicine as a pill or a technology that is external to ourselves. Indigenous cultures, however, view medicine as a power or energy that is inherent within all creation. Although this medicine/power is inherent in all creation, ceremonies can bring out the medicine power of an object or a person. Anyone can buy a pill at the drugstore and take that kind of medicine, but *sacred medicine* requires a sacred ceremony and the first step of the ceremony is to work to get into a special state of being. In other words, one must first work to manifest one's own sacredness in order to bring out the sacredness in something or someone else. This sacredness, while inherent in every living and non-living thing, comes through us but does not belong to us, rather we belong to it. When we bring ourselves into sacred relationship with ourselves, others, and the land, we become a conduit or *hollow bone* that transmits goodness and sacredness. This is what we mean when we say that we are *becoming medicine*—we are doing work to allow sacredness to flow through us into the world.

Medicine, in this sense, is an energy, a power, and yet it becomes more powerful through our surrendering our self-centeredness as we find the Vast Self that is present in our center. Joseph Rael told me recently that when he learned and performed the ceremony of the Deer Dance, it "*added to my medicine.*" For Joseph, *medicine* is a power and force that can be grown and used to care for others. Europeans used to have this understanding of *medicine*. Ed Tick describes how the ancient Greeks would "travel to a healing center where priest-physicians practicing a combination of physical and spiritual medicine could help them prepare for a dream visit from Asklepios, the god of healing."[11] Prior to the Roman invasion of Europe, the Celts practiced a nature-based religion and form of healing in which "everything was holy" and in particular "glades and lakes."[12]

Mana is a concept used by the indigenous people throughout the Pacific, including the Māori of New Zealand. Studying with traditional healers in Fiji, psychologist Richard Katz learned that *mana* "is like a secret message that comes to you. It's hidden. You can feel it inside yourself, but you can't see it. It's secret advice that comes into and within you." Katz further defines mana as "the fundamental spiritual force" that is the "power to effect" or "what makes things happen."[13]

The concept of *mana* is similar to how many Native American tribes use the English word *medicine*: it refers to an unseen power and authority that a person has. A person can increase their *mana*, for instance by giving to others or caring for others. I worked at a community mental health center in Panmure in Auckland, New Zealand called Manaaki House. The word *manaaki* is about giving and caring for others.[14] This is a giving of care and *mana* to others. *Mana*, like *medicine*, grows the more you give it away. Where I live in the Northwest of the United States, the tribes have a tradition of potlatch, which were giving ceremonies in which the status and influence of the giver was enhanced through the giving. Joseph speaks of this too, adding that "*we have to become the give-away.*" We hold this medicine in our hearts.

> The human is a medicine bag. A medicine bag contains articles deemed sacred and holy by the person to whom the bag belongs. So

---

11 Ed Tick, *The Practice of Dream Healing: Bringing Ancient Greek Mysteries into Modern Medicine*, xix.

12 John Davies, *A History of Wales*, 24.

13 Richard Katz, *The Straight Path: A Story of Healing and Transformation in Fiji*, 224, 22.

14 "Manaaki . . . to support, take care of, give hospitality to, protect, look out for – show respect, generosity and care for others," *Māori Dictionary*.

> it is with us. We carry holy "objects" in our psyche. The vibration of the sacred medicine bag is to see, to have capacities of the visionary. So, when we carry these forms, we carry the capacity of drinking the light, of being visionaries, exploring existence.[15]

When Joseph says that a "human being is a medicine bag" he is reminding all of us that we carry sacred gifts within us, that we carry "holy" objects in our psyches, and further that when we bring out our inherent sacred goodness from our medicine bag, we are becoming that which is holy and healing. He tells us that when we are carrying these sacred forms we are developing the capacity to be visionaries. The visionary, the mystic, and the shaman are all seekers of sacred medicine and in walking their paths, they are in the process of *becoming medicine.*

---

15 *B&V:NW*, 69. In Tiwa, "bag" is "*moh-neh. Moh* means 'to see.' *Neh* means 'the Vast Self and personal self as it places itself in a statement of awareness,'" (*Sound*, 35). A bag is a place of seeing and visions, a place where medicine connects the microcosm of the self to the macrocosm of Vast Self, *Wah-Mah-Chi*.

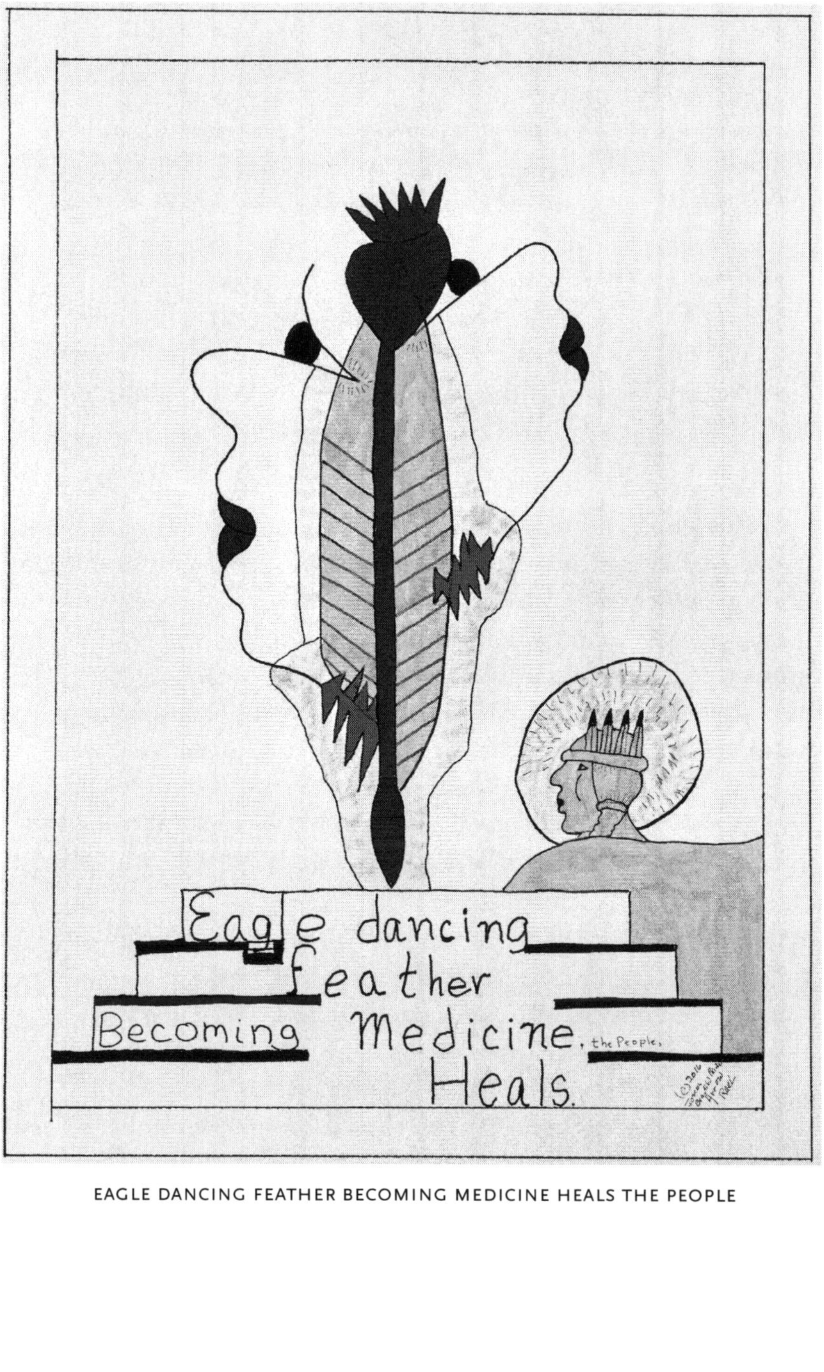

EAGLE DANCING FEATHER BECOMING MEDICINE HEALS THE PEOPLE

CHAPTER 2

CIRCLE MEDICINE

I have called the principles that underlie the Tibetan and Navajo systems of natural philosophy the Circle of the Spirit. . . . Initially, in life's journey, we do not realize our identity with the nature of things, that we and the universe are one and interpenetrate each other at all times . . . the . . . principle of the circle of the spirit is Becoming: Sacred Rites of Transformation. . . . When a rite of transformation is specifically geared toward beginning a person's lifelong spiritual journey into the circle of the spirit, it is referred to as an initiation rite.[1]

PETER GOLD

Painted Arrow's insights on the medicine wheel began in the kiva. The most notable occasion occurred when Antonio [his grandfather] sent him into the kiva for a special ceremony that Picuris perform once every hundred years. In House of Shattering Light, *Joseph recalls being alone in the sacred space for weeks. . . .*

Sitting at the center of the ceremonial chamber, he realized he was at the center of the circle, the medicine wheel, the universe, the heart. He also realized the directions were the sound/light beings manifesting against silent darkness. The heart, the hub of darkness, is a flash of light that becomes a star as we exhale.[2]

KURT WILT

There are many Medicine Wheels. The universe is a Medicine Wheel. Our own solar system is a giant Medicine Wheel. The earth is a Medicine Wheel. Every nation is a Medicine Wheel. Each state is a Medicine Wheel. Each family is a Medicine Wheel. You are a Medicine Wheel, for every individual is a Medicine Wheel.[3]

ROY I. WILSON

---

1 Peter Gold, *Navajo and Tibetan Sacred Wisdom: The Circle of the Spirit*, 3–7.

2 Kurt Wilt, *The Visionary: entering the mystic universe of Joseph Rael Beautiful Painted Arrow*, 182.

3 Roy I. Wilson, *Medicine Wheels: Ancient Teachings for Modern Times*, 9.

HEALING CIRCLES

Circles are ubiquitous symbols of healing found throughout the cultures of the Earth. Healing circles bring us back into harmony with ourselves, the land, and the sacred. We wrote about this in our last book, *Walking the Medicine Wheel.* Joseph often makes the point that he teaches from his own visions and is not revealing traditional tribal practices. Some say that the medicine wheel belongs only to the Dakota, Lakota, and Nakota peoples of North America, however it has become a Pan-Indian symbol that is important to many different tribes, and healing circles are part of many cultures across the circular globe of Mother Earth. Medicine Wheel/Medicine Mountain National Historic Landmark, in Wyoming, is an 80 foot diameter, circular stone pattern. By Western archaeological investigation, this site is thought to have been in use as a ceremonial place for at least 7,000 years and is held as sacred by many plains tribes. There are at least 70 similar stone circles throughout North America.[4] Many of these circles were constructed in alignment with the passage of the sun and moon. My home state of Illinois contains a circle over a thousand years old at Cahokia Mounds. It has been called "woodhenge," as it was constructed out of wooden poles rather than stones, and it dates back to around 1000 CE.[5]

HEALING CIRCLES OF MANY CULTURES OF THE WORLD

Healing circles are found throughout many cultures. Ancient stone circles were found in lands that my ancestors come from, as well. Poland has stone circles, for instance, a series of 12 circles in Odry dating back to the first or second century CE.[6] One of the most famous stone circles is Stonehenge in England, around 5000 years old.[7] Graham Robb, in his book, *Ancient Paths*, describes how the Celts, prior to the Roman invasion, developed a series of roads, cities, and holy sites across Europe that had spokes that radiated out from a central point and mapped out

---

4 Fred Chapman, "The Bighorn Medicine Wheel: 1988-1999," *Cultural Resource Management*, Vol. 3, 1999, 5–10.

5 Bryan Penprase, *The Power of Stars: How Celestial Observations Have Shaped Civilization*, 201–02.

6 Robert Sadowski, "Stone Rings of Northern Poland," in D.C. Heggie (ed.), *Archaeoastronomy in the Old World*, 215–24. Also see *Atlas Obscura*, "The Stone Circles at Odry."

7 Sadowski, 189–92.

the summer and winter solstice lines of the sun across the Earth. He describes how small, spoked, "solar wheels" are still found at Celtic sites throughout Europe. According to Robb, the "Ancient Celts always knew exactly where they stood in relation to the universe."[8] The Celtic (or Gaulish) word *Mediolanum* referred to places throughout the old Celtic lands and is defined as "a term of sacred geography . . . a holy centre . . . perhaps a central point of reference on the vertical axis of the three worlds – upper, middle and lower."[9] *Mediolanum* were founded at places of the intersection of the larger spoked wheel that stretched out across the landscape. Robb speculates that the common image of a cross within a circle arose during the time of the Celts and was later adopted into the Celtic Christian cross (which looks like a medicine wheel at the center of a cross). Robb's research found that many later Christian sites and Roman roads were superimposed on the earlier Celtic holy centers and roads.

The Pueblo peoples built kivas, circular structures that were aligned with the paths of the sun and moon. Bryan Penprase writes that the "construction of the kiva gathered together many of the deepest symbols of the Pueblo Native American cosmos, to create a public space that embodies fourness, a connection with the sky and stars, and harmony with the universe."[10] Chimney Rock, Mesa Verde, Aztec National Monument, and Chaco Canyon all have structures that were used to map the progress of the sun and moon and included ceremonial sites. Joseph speaks a lot about the Pueblo peoples' relationship to the sky, stars, sun, and moon. He gave me a copy of Ron Sutcliffe's *Moon Tracks: Lunar Horizon Patterns* that discusses lunar observation at Chimney Rock and Chaco Canyon. Sutcliffe points out how science and spirituality were unified in the Pueblo view of the world, in contrast to the current separation in the Western world. He writes, "There may have been something lost way back when the two separated. . . . Something important may have been dropped out of the equation long long ago. The understandings inspired by these old buildings may help us rediscover ourselves."[11]

8 Graham Robb, *The Ancient Paths*, 11.

9 Xavier Delamarre, cited in Robb, 41.

10 Penprase, 195.

11 Ron Sutcliffe, *Moon Tracks: Lunar Horizon Patterns*, 54.

LUNAR STAND-STILL AT CHIMNEY ROCK

YIN-YANG

The Yin-Yang symbol has been used in China for thousands of years. The Yin-Yang symbol unites dark and light into a single circle. Taoism sees life as arising out of the interaction of opposites—rather than shunning the dark and seeking the light, it is a philosophy that is based on harmony and balance. In the Yin-Yang symbol, there is a small seed of light in the place of greatest darkness and a small seed of dark in the place of greatest lightness. Joseph Rael will often say, "*everything becomes its opposite*," which speaks to this harmonious relationship.

SACRED CIRCLES OF INDIA: MANDALAS & CHAKRAS

India and the religions it has given birth to are steeped in the concept of circularity. The doctrine of reincarnation leads us in a circle from birth to death to re-birth. The concept of the great ages or *yugas* teaches that creation itself is a great circle and that the universe is continually in a cycle of creation and destruction. Various Hindu religions, Buddhism, and Jainism all originated in India. Buddhism migrated up through Tibet and China and out into Southeast Asia and the world.

The word "mandala" comes from the Sanskrit, *maṇḍala*, and means "circle." Mandalas are used in many different ways, sometimes as visualizations of circular structures and organizations, sometimes they are found in spiritual art work. Often there are four gateways or openings, which recalls the four directions of the medicine wheel. An example of a mandala is the Tibetan Wheel of Life (*bhavacakra*), a circular depiction of the cyclical nature of existence.

The chakra (or *cakra*) concept arises out of India and is used in the spiritual and healing methods of yoga and tantra found in Hinduism, Jainism, and Buddhism. Chakras are often depicted as a series of circles found at characteristic places on the body.[12] They are thought to translate or transduce spiritual energy into the manifestation of life at those levels, e.g. physical, mental, emotional, etc. These are like a series of medicine wheels, each containing a certain set of attributes and working together with the other chakras to create our holistic, multi-dimensional reality. When I was looking for a holistic framework for understanding a whole human being while I was writing *Re-humanizing Medicine*, I decided to loosely base the holistic framework on the chakra system. The dimensions of: *body*, *emotions*, *mind*, *heart*, *expression*, *intuition*, and *spirit*, (to which I added a developmental dimension of *time* and a sociocultural dimension of *context*) give us a good way of looking at nine different complementary levels of human being and experience. The first seven of these dimensions correspond to the seven commonly described chakras. I describe in the

12 Recall how the *ney* has a series of nine circular holes which create the sound vibrations of the reed flute. Perhaps the chakras are similar to these circles that create the vibrations of the different dimensions of human being.

book how I came to adapt this particular framework. I had knowledge of its utility from my study of yoga and spiritual work. Additionally, Jung, himself, studied chakras and found them to be "symbols for human consciousness" which provide a "symbolic theory of the psyche" and can "symbolize highly complex psychic facts which . . . we could not possibly express except in images."[13]

CARING FOR SELF AND OTHERS CIRCLE

In *Re-humanizing Medicine* I describe each of these levels of human experience (*body*, *emotions*, *mind*, *heart*, *expression*, *intuition*, *spirit*, *time* and *context*) and how, to have a truly holistic medicine, we need to have a medicine that can speak to each of these nine dimensions.

> [An] important point in understanding the use of a multi-dimensional holistic framework for human being is that each dimension may have different kinds of realities that hold true at its level that may not hold true at another level. This allows for biomedical truth, poetic truth, the truth of compassion and spiritual truth to all simultaneously exist in different dimensions. Rather than trying to reduce all truth to one dimension (such as a reductionist biomedical approach) we can have what Cohen called 'medical pluralism,' the ability to bring multiple models of understanding to the complex issues around human health and illness.[14]

I like this idea of Cohen's, *medical pluralism*, because it tells us that there are different, equally valid ways of understanding health, illness, and medicine. Just as the chakra system allows us to enter into the realm of the physical, or the mental, or the heart, so too we can have different systems of medicine that may help us understand health and illness from different perspectives that are not mutually exclusive, but are, rather, complementary. In this chapter, where we will discuss the concepts of linear medicine and circle medicine, we are encouraging *medical pluralism,* using a *both/and* rather than an *either/or* mentality.

Since writing *Re-humanizing Medicine*, I have been developing a companion workbook volume, with my friend Laura Merritt, called *Caring for Self & Others*. This holistic framework uses a series of nested circles to visually represent human multidimensionality.

13 Jung, *The Psychology of Kundalini Yoga*, 61.

14 Kopacz, *Re-humanizing Medicine*, 132. The Michal H. Cohen term "medical pluralism" can be found in his book, *Healing at the Borderland of Medicine and Religion*, 3.

TIBETAN AND NAVAJO CIRCLES OF THE SPIRIT

The opening quote in this chapter is from Peter Gold's study of the similarities of what he calls "the circle of the spirit" used by Tibetan and Navajo people.

> Both . . . envision a special kind of circle. It consists of a small, inner circle connected to an outer, larger one by means of four lines, creating four quadrants. It is a spiritual draftsman's diagram, a sacred shorthand for the four universal principles of the spiritual path. The smaller circle is the microcosm, the finite bodymind or self, yet it is also the source of all awareness of life. The larger circle is the macrocosm, the infinite bodymind of the universe and, simultaneously, the fully expanded individual on the spiritual path.[15]

These Tibetan and Navajo circles look a lot like the medicine wheel, a circle that is divided up by spokes into four quadrants, containing a central circle that unites all the quadrants. Gold describes how the Tibetan and Navajo peoples use these circles for orientation and guidance in bringing the individual into harmony with the physical and sacred landscape. He describes the circular, Tibetan mandala as "almost always a visual expression of the perfect pattern in all things and a prime metaphor for the quest of the spiritual hero toward the central still point in a changing world. In the process of moving to the center, the seeker becomes transformed."[16]

JUNG: MANDALAS AND THE CIRCLE OF THE SELF

Psychiatrist Carl Jung was fascinated with the healing powers of circular mandalas. He drew them himself during difficult times in his life (starting during World War I) and he encouraged his patients to do so as part of therapy. He found that the circle had an organizing and orienting effect, bringing together the disparate elements of the person that were struggling and in conflict. Jung saw the circle as a symbol of the self—the whole person in totality, not just ego consciousness. He describes what he discovered in his mandala drawings:

> In them I saw the self—that is, my whole being—actively at work . . . they seemed to me highly significant, and I guarded them like precious pearls. I had the distinct feeling that they were something

15 Gold, 3.

16 Gold, 135.

> central . . . a living conception of the self. . . . When I began drawing the mandalas . . . I saw that everything, all the paths I had been following, all the steps I had taken, were leading back to a single point—namely to the mid-point. It became increasingly clear to me that the mandala is the center. It is the exponent of all paths. It is the path to the center, to individuation. . . . There is no linear evolution; there is only a circumambulation of the self.[17]

HILDEGARD OF BINGEN

When I was forty-two years and seven months old, a burning light of tremendous brightness coming from heaven poured into my entire mind. Like a flame that does not burn but enkindles, it inflamed my entire heart and my entire breast, just like the sun that warms an object with its rays.[18]

HILDEGARD OF BINGEN

Hildegard of Bingen (1098–1179 CE) was a Christian mystic and saint who had a formative series of visions when she was forty-two years old. She is only the fourth woman in the history of the Catholic Church to be declared a "Doctor of the Church," as well as a saint. Matthew Fox describes her as a champion of the feminine who married science and spirituality. Hildegard had an ecological and environmental mindset and spoke of "greening power."[19]

In her visions, she was told to "speak and write what you see and hear." At first she resisted, became sick, but again was encouraged to speak and write, "not according to human speech or human inventiveness but according to the extent that you see and hear those things in the heavens above in the marvelousness of God. . . . Be a listener who understands the words of his or her own teacher but explains them in one's own way of speaking."[20] She entered into this divine writing of songs, an opera, poems, and nine books. Through her visions she was given the sudden "taste of the understanding of the narration of books."[21]

---

17 *MDR*, 196–97.

18 Matthew Fox, *Illuminations of Hildegard of Bingen*, 7.

19 See Matthew Fox, *Hildegard of Bingen: A Saint for Our Times*, xiv-xv. The other three female Doctors of the Church are Catherine of Sienna, Teresa de Avila, and St. Therese of Lisieux.

20 Fox, *Illuminations of Hildegard of Bingen*, 40.

21 Ibid., 7.

Many of her visions had circular and nature elements as well as Christian imagery. Matthew Fox points out Celtic and Nature-based spiritual elements in her visions and work. All these elements came together in a circle for her. "Divinity is like a wheel, a circle, a whole, that can neither be understood, nor divided, nor begun, nor ended. . . . God is as round as a wheel."[22]

JOSEPH RAEL'S VISION OF THE MEDICINE WHEEL

Joseph Rael had a vision of a healing circle when he was eight years old and he discovered something important about himself. His Grandfather asked him to take part in a sacred ceremony that was only done every hundred years. Joseph entered into the darkness of the circular, ceremonial kiva chamber and stayed there for many weeks. Joseph asked what he should do and his Grandfather only said, "Just go in there. You'll know when you get there."

> Sitting at the center of this ceremonial chamber, which is round, I became the connection with the center of the circle of light. The light and sound beings were aspects of the circle of light, and I was the center of that circle. Of course, now I know it as the medicine wheel. I saw the medicine wheel through the lights that were emanating from it. Circle means to go forth and sow seed, to plant them as lights that life can drink to sustain the soul of its being.[23]

From this ceremony and visionary experience, Joseph draws the authority to write and speak about the medicine wheel because he realized that he is the center of the medicine wheel, just as Jung drawing his mandalas came to understand that he was approaching the center of Self. Joseph still does not know what the ceremony was about, "Grandfather didn't explain it to me, or why they did it every hundred years. I don't think he needed to, because I have it in me. I think that I was the ceremony."[24]

This brief survey shows that there is an ancient practice of using circles,

---

22 Fox, *Hildegard a Life for Our Times*, 114.

23 *House*, 55–56.

24 Ibid., 54–57. The ceremony ended when Joseph's Grandfather eventually came in and got Joseph and said, "You've been here for so many weeks. You know, you were supposed to come out . . . you were supposed to come out after so many days, but you stayed a little longer than we thought you would. But, because you stayed longer, we decided to leave you in here because maybe we needed to do something different in your case."

often ones which orient a person to the seasons and solar and lunar passages, for ceremonial healing. We have also looked at the way that individuals, such as Jung, Joseph Rael, and myself, have used healing circles in spiritual and personal growth work. When we enter into the healing circle, we go through a process of transformation which re-orients us to who we truly are, re-connecting us to the divine and the physical landscape of the Earth. This is not something that is just done once and completed. It is an ongoing process as we lose and find our way in this life.

THE CIRCULAR LANGUAGE OF SPIRITUALITY

Moving from this discussion of the ubiquity of healing circles throughout cultural and individual healing work, we will now turn to a discussion about language and how it shapes our perception of the world. Joseph frequently points out to me the difference between noun languages, such as European languages, and verb languages, such as Tiwa and many indigenous languages. Emphasizing either nouns (things) or verbs (actions) in a language draws our attention toward either static objectification or interconnected, circular processes. Noun languages lend themselves more to science and verb languages lend themselves more to spirituality. This is a distinction that is important to Joseph and it will help us toward an understanding of circle medicine if we first examine the structural assumptions of our language. Learning circle medicine requires that we learn a new language and a new way of thinking.

VOWEL MYSTICISM

Joseph teaches that the sounds of the vowels embody the essences and directions of the medicine wheel. We reviewed in *Walking the Medicine Wheel* how Joseph perceives the vowel sounds relating to each of the four compass directions and the center.

There are five dominant sound vibrations that give sustenance to the soul. They are the five key vowel sounds: ah, eh, eee, oh, and uu (A, E, I, O, and U, as pronounced in Spanish). The vowel sounds connect us to the spirit world; the consonants connect us to the relative, to placement in physical world. Vowels are spirit and consonants are embodiment. Each specific vowel sound carries a special quality. And each vowel has a designated place within the medicine wheel.

Joseph further links each vowel sound to a principle idea and the words we speak manifest these different principle ideas. By adding up principle ideas more complex concepts can be created.

"Aah" (the A sound in Spanish)—Purification
"Eh" (the E sound in Spanish)—Relationship
"Eee" (the I sound in Spanish)—Awareness
"Oh" (the O sound in Spanish)—Innocence, the Infinite Void
"Uu" (the U sound in Spanish)—Carrying[25]

Throughout his teachings, Joseph returns to the basic sound that is the being & vibration of which we are made, which is Breath-Matter-Movement. Other spiritual traditions speak of spiritual sound vibrations. This is a level of hidden meaning beyond the linear or linguistic meaning of the word. Muller-Ortega calls this "vowel mysticism" in describing Kashmiri Shaivism, a branch of Hinduism in which Śiva is Supreme. Muller-Ortega describes that in Sanskrit, "the sixteen vowels, which include the *bindu*, the 'point,' and the *visarga*, the Emissional Power, function as symbolic for different aspects of the Lord."[26]

> Consciousness which is formed of the Ultimate (*A*), vibrates with a "seed" vibration in the two extreme points of the first vowel (*A*), two points whose nature is that of reposing in their own-nature. Because of the power of that vibration, consciousness, which is composed of the essence of all, becomes in the central point, the impulse toward the manifestation of the distinct and different "cognitions."[27]

In vowel mysticism, creating the sound of something creates that thing within the self. *Annuttara*, the Ultimate (*A*) is a sound that is a sound vibration that is the source of consciousness and from this vibration comes the seed that grows into matter. It is through sound that one reaches God, *Wah-Mah-Chi*, Breath-Matter-Movement, Śiva. "The manifestation is in the abode of the Ultimate *A*, has its beginning in the Ultimate *A*, and finally therein comes to repose in the very Śiva. Therefore, by that knowledge, the true nature of the Ultimate, of the vibration, comes to be well known."[28]

---

25 *B&V:NW*, 58, 44.

26 Muller-Ortega, *The Triadic Heart of Śiva*, 62. Further, he explains that the first and last vowels hold particular spiritual significance: "the first vowel, A, known as the Ultimate (*annuttara*), and the last vowel, Ḥ, the *visarga*" [Emissional Power], (63).

27 Abhinavagupta, in Muller-Ortega, 214

28 Ibid., 90.

GOD IS NOT A NOUN[29]

Noun language is about separation because a noun is a person, place, or thing and its *thing-ness* depends upon it being distinct from other things. Verb language is about connection, it is about what happens between things—action that includes things in part of a greater movement. If we have been separated through over-use of noun language, we can be initiated into verb language and this will help bring us back into interconnection.

Wah-Mah-Chi is Breath Matter and Movement and verb languages are movement, everything is movement. Here is an example.

"When my foster mother would call me, 'Joseph come here, I want to show you how you can find the tracks of an animal and that is by paying attention to the smells of where you are walking and you will smell the deer or even the wild rabbits, or turkeys.'

"'Joseph come here,' I learned later in my life, living with Lucia and Agapito, that 'Joseph come here,' would repeat itself all day long until I went to sleep at night, because later in years, after I had learned English, the first three words, 'Joseph come here,' were Wah-Mah-Chi and those three words would repeat themselves over, and over and over again throughout the day until I went to sleep and then they would stop. So if you come from a verb language culture the first three sounds that you hear that are referring to you personally, Wah-Mah-Chi never stops and that is how we were taught that divine presence is always here in the sound of the words spoken and the unfolding of daily experience in the spiritual life of a two-legged, four-legged, or winged, or those ones who swim in the rivers.

"The noun is the name of a person, place, or thing. The English language is a noun/pronoun language. In Tiwa, the word for God is Wah-Mah-Chi which is active all day long, moving, breathing, coming into matter and leaving matter. Wah-Mah-Chi is in everything, every kind of work from start to finish. All things are in relationship and all things are sacred because nothing is separate or isolated from anything else. Dan Moonhawk Alford gave a talk in 1994, 'God is Not a Noun in Native America.'

"God is always present because we—this is a way to confirm it—if God is Breath-Matter-Movement, the cosmos already is Breath-Matter-Movement. When a baby is born they are spanked to take a breath and that is done for

29 Several Native American elders have used this phrase, including Joseph Rael, Phillip H. Duran, and Dan Moonhawk Alford. Joseph gave me a copy of a paper by Alford entitled, "God is Not a Noun in Native America: Worldview Thought Experiment," speaker's notes from a 1994 paper.

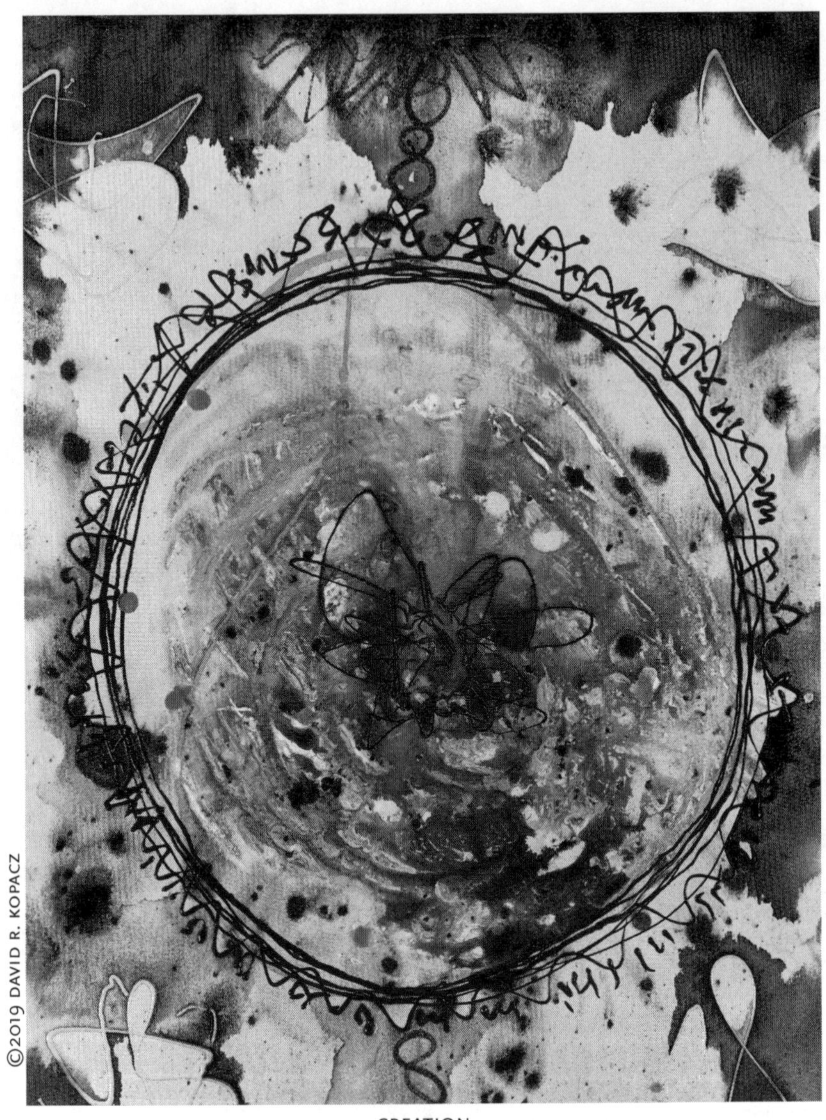

CREATION

him or her to wake up, like Rip Van Winkle, from twenty years of sleep, he or she is awake now and can respond accordingly to life. He matters, that is why he was born, he has the breath, and he has to move. God is always present in all the things that he does as a child born into Wah-Mah-Chi. And God is not in heaven like Christianity teaches or anything like that. God is present all the time because we are the micro- of the macrocosm. A lesson instilled into early childhood socialization of being & vibration of consciousness."

We are continually going through initiation each moment, separating from Creator, popping into being, initiated into a moment of being, then right back to return to Creator. Every moment is an initiation. Every moment is an epiphany. Every moment is a theophany in the circular movement of verb language.

THE WAR OF NOUN VS. VERB LANGUAGE

Technological Man thinks in lines and points, in separation of one thing from another. "Technological Man" means "Westerners," "Europeans," "mainstream Americans," "whites," but what I am pointing to is not a function of direction, or of Europe (for Europe had its own indigenous cultures), or "American." In many ways it is more a function of Technological Man as opposed to Spiritual Human or Natural Human. It is a function of a way of thinking, not a place of origin or a color of skin. In technology, a thing must be defined and separate. This leads to a noun language. Native language is more contextual, more about connections than separations. Joseph describes Tiwa, spoken by the people of Picuris Pueblo as a verb language. This is why he will call me "David-ing" and himself "Joseph-ing." A verb is what happens between objects, it includes those objects, but it is not limited in time and space the way a "thing" is. Being, Becoming, Living, Dying—these are all verbs. "David and Joseph talked on the phone." This is a dead sentence, although it conveys information. *David-ing Joseph-ing talking phone-ing.* This is an open and living statement that is full of life and possibility.

When Europeans came to the Americas and saw the native peoples living, they only looked for objects—gold, slaves, treasure, heathens—they did not see the richness of the verb language, how everything connected in harmony. In some ways, it is obvious what happened next, the noun people with their powerful things could not see the beauty of the verb people, could not even understand their life and they objectified the people, turned them into objects; they commodified the land and "bought" it and moved the Indians to other, less desirable land; they outlawed the language and the religion that they did not understand and they tried to make the Americas over in their own image.

This is what Carl Hammerschlag speaks of as "theft of the spirit." He writes that this theft will continue as long as we allow "reverence for life to be replaced in our hearts . . . by desire for money, possessions, and technology." The result is that "the portion of ourselves that is imbued with spirit becomes faint and sick—and we as a planet, become weaker."[30]

Nouns are things that can be picked up and moved, they are entities in and of themselves. Verbs are *connectings*, they are qualities, not quantities, they are more about the space in between than about the thing in and of itself. Obviously, English language has both nouns and verbs, but in talking about verb or noun language, we are bringing to light the emphasis on *things/quantities* or *interactions/qualities*. European culture and the dominant culture of the US, with its noun focus, is more individualistically-oriented. Native American culture, with its verb focus, is more collectively-oriented. A person in an individualistic culture looks to themselves as the orientation point in society. A person in a collectivist culture looks at the group as the orientation point.

What does it mean to be a verb people? Relationships rather than objects receive the emphasis of importance. I get the image of looking at the universe through two different eyes. If we look with the "noun eye" we see vast stretches of useless empty space and then small clusters of matter in the solar systems. If we look with the "verb eye" we see vast webs of interconnectedness that exist to allow the flowering of things. Rather than focusing on the "thing" or "object," verb language focuses on the space between objects, the interactions and interconnectivity of objects.

This reminds me of the concept of dark matter and dark energy that Joseph is always talking about. A recent article from NASA states that roughly 68% of the universe is dark energy, 27% dark matter, and "normal" matter about 5%. The article comments that, "maybe it shouldn't be called 'normal' matter at all, since it is such a small fraction of the Universe."[31] This means that roughly 95% of the universe is made up of qualities we cannot see and which we do not really understand. I think that verb language is more about this 95% and noun language is more about the 5% of reality.

Joseph illustrated that when a quarterback throws a football, we focus on the quarterback, on the football, and on the receiver. We tend to focus on what we can see as things and we make people into things. A verb perspective would be not on these three things: quarterback, football, and receiver—but on *throwing-catching-running-playing* as well as the whole game and how the game relates to the society and the society to the earth.

30 Hammerschlag, *The Theft of the Spirit*, 23.

31 NASA Science online: Astrophysics page, "Dark Energy, Dark Matter."

In traditional Native American society, every action is an epiphany of God and a chance to gain insight into the spiritual nature of reality. At the Picuris feast day festival, there is a traditional dance and the *Ko-sas* or clowns come out and interact with the dancers and the audience. Joseph points out that "*cosa*" in Spanish means "thing," so perhaps this is a commentary on what happens if you get too noun-oriented, too thing-focused, you become a clown. Joseph says with a serious face, "*Life is a circle—and sometimes it can turn into a circus!*" (He says this last part laughing). We need clowns and tricksters to remind us about what is important, but if everyone is a clown—chasing "things," we lose what is important in life.

NATIVE SCIENCE

Science is one mode of explanation, and spirituality is another,

LEWIS MEHL-MADRONA[32]

The language we use determines the way we perceive the world and our sense of separation or interconnection. Western science is founded upon the objectivity and fundamental separation of the observer and the observed. It has given us a great ability to manipulate and take apart things. However, we lose something if all we know is how to separate things into smaller and smaller component parts. This is the principle of reductionism. If we think back to the Yin-Yang circle, reductionism could be half of a circle and holism could be the whole circle. Holism teaches that the whole is greater than the sum of its parts and everything is in interactive relationship. Native American languages, languages of the place of the land of North America, are languages of holism and if we can adopt the principle of *medical pluralism*, or *scientific pluralism*, we can examine the kind of science that grows out of a verb language.

Dr. Gregory Cajete, from Santa Clara Pueblo (Tewa-speaking) in New Mexico, has written a book called *Native Science: Natural Laws of Interdependence*. Cajete describes Native Science as being based on "affiliation" rather than "objectivity."[33] It is a participatory-observer model rather than a detached observer model. "Native science reflects the unfolding story of a creative universe in which human beings are active

32 Lewis Mehl-Madrona, *Coyote Medicine*, 119.

33 Similarly, Richard Katz states that the "Indigenous idea of research as a process of knowing, featuring the ultimate value of personal experience, focuses on *understanding* and the *making of meaning*. It offers a sharp contrast to the prevailing concept of research in mainstream Western psychology, which focuses more on *prediction* and *control*," Katz, *Indigenous Healing Psychology*, 212.

and creative participants." He also sees the descriptive aspect of science as a way of explaining the world, linking it to story. "Science in every form, then, is a story of the world." Cajete points out that "the first shamans can also be considered the first artists" as story and visual art were the ways that the findings of native science were transmitted to others. In fact, Cajete sees shamans as the founding creative and technical people in history. There was a "created role for a person whom we call a 'shaman,' the first medicine person, first teacher, first artist, first doctor, first priest, and first psychologist."[34]

Cajete maps out a number of tenets of native philosophy, a few of which will be listed below:

- Native science integrates a spiritual orientation.
- Dynamic multidimensional harmony is a perpetual state of the universe.
- Every "thing" is animate and has spirit.
- There are stages of initiation to knowledge.
- Elders are relied upon as the keepers of essential knowledge.
- Acting in the world must be sanctioned through ritual and ceremony.
- Dreams are considered gateways to creative possibilities[35]

Joseph gave me a paper written by his friend Phillip H. Duran entitled, "On the Cosmic Order of Modern Physics and the Conceptual World of the American Indian." Duran's people are Tigua from Ysleta Del Sur Pueblo. As he studied Western physics and cosmology, Duran kept seeing parallels between the findings of quantum and astrophysics with traditional Native views of reality. "Quantum theory *validates* indigenous concepts," writes Duran, and then he states, "*I believe that the places where the two systems of knowledge meet can become gateways to realms that are unfamiliar to the Western world.*"[36] Duran then lists the following correspondences between Native Science and Western, modern physics:

- All things are imbued with spirit
- All things are related and connected and belong to a coherent whole

34 Cajete, *Native Science,* 14, 27, 48, 156.

35 Ibid., 64–65.

36 Phillip H. Duran, "On the Cosmic Order of Modern Physics and the Conceptual World of the American Indian," pre-publication, 2005, 1-2. This was published in *World Futures: The Journal of New Paradigm Research* Volume 63, 2007–Issue 1. Many of these ideas are developed in more detail in Duran's *The Condor and the Eagle: Uniting Heart and Mind in Search of a New Science Worldview.*

- The world exists in constant flux (i.e. change is constant)
- Matter is equivalent to vibrating energy
- The Earth is a system of cycles
- A mysterious energy pervades the universe, also referred to as the Great Mystery
- Renewal and self-organizing processes spontaneously occur in nature[37]

THE HOLOMOVENT

Duran also draws heavily on the work of physicist David Bohm. David Bohm was a physicist who created an experimental verb language, he called the "rheomode," and encouraged students in his lab to speak using it. Near the end of his life, he learned that many Native American languages are verb languages and he participated in a meeting of indigenous elders and physicists. Although Bohm passed away in 1992, shortly after that first conference, these conferences continued in New Mexico with Dan "Moonhawk" Alford, Leroy Little Bear, F. David Peat (Bohm's biographer), Fred Alan Wolf, and Joseph Rael. Anthony Dellaflora made a film, "Language of Spirituality," about these conferences and Joseph Rael appears in the documentary.[38]

Bohm's view of physics overlapped significantly with Native American spirituality. Duran describes Bohm's concept of the *holomovement* as "two aspects of the universe [which] are complementary, existing together in ceaseless movement . . . in an endless process of unfolding (into the explicate order, such as when a wave becomes a particle) and enfolding (into the implicate order, such as when a particle becomes a wave)."[39] The implicate (enfolding) and explicate (unfolding) are like a cosmic breath or pulsation into and out of being of all reality. The *explicate order*, is the everyday world of separated, discrete objects that we perceive with our senses (what Joseph Rael would call *ordinary reality*), and the *implicate order* which is an interconnected whole out of which the explicate order

37 Ibid., 3.

38 This was put on through SEED Graduate Institute. The late Dan Moonhawk Alford was a Native American teacher who organized the series of meetings. Leroy Little Bear is a Blackfoot tribal member, an author, and the former director of Harvard's Native American Program. F. David Peat, a physicist, spent time with different Native American tribes and recounts this in his book *Blackfoot Physics*. Physicist Fred Alan Wolf ventured into the visionary realm and wrote *The Eagle's Quest* about his experiences. Peter Kingsley and Phillip Duran also attended.

39 Duran, 13.

is continually arising (which could correspond to Joseph's *non-ordinary reality*).

Duran states that for "many years Bohm expressed concern about fragmentation in science and society, asserting that a new, non-fragmentary world view was needed in science. . . . He referred to the natural world with terms like 'objective wholeness' and 'undivided universe.'" Duran lists key elements of Bohm's science that correspond to Native perspectives:

- The universe as an unbroken, coherent whole
- The existence of visible (explicate) world, valid in the domain of classical physics
- The existence of an invisible (implicate) world, valid in the domain of quantum physics
- The explicate enfolding into the implicate, and vice versa, with the two worlds co-existing in ceaseless movement, called the *holomovement*
- The inadequacy of modern languages (including English) to describe the quantum processes and the adequacy of Native languages to do the same[40]

The interesting thing about Native Science is how much it corresponds to the "new" science of physics. One difference that Duran points out however is that as Westerners, even if we are aware of the paradigm-shifting nature of the "new" science, we "can live an entire day or week without thinking about or interacting with the unseen, unmanifested world. Indian spirituality does not allow such an impersonal and unsocial stance toward the natural world; it compels us to relate to our human and non-human relatives." It is perhaps the sense of interconnectedness that Duran highlights as the most important correspondence between Native Science and physics. He writes:

> Reality lies not with the particles but with the *relationships* that exist within the flux of energy and processes of quantum nature . . . [where] particles lose their individual identities and behave like a single atom. . . . The twin "entangled" particles that are forever connected are *correlated* somehow as if forming a single system even though they may be far apart. If this seems strange, it's because it *is* strange. It belongs to the Great Mystery.[41]

40 Ibid., 3.

41 Ibid., 4, 11-12.

Native science is circle medicine, it seeks the wholeness and interrelatedness of a holistic view of reality that includes observer and observed within a unitary framework.

LINEAR MEDICINE AND CIRCLE MEDICINE

Contemporary medicine is based on science and is often called "evidence-based medicine." It is a form of linear medicine as it has a straight path and goal of putting the functions of the body back into a "normal" state. This is good medicine and helps many people and can cure many things. Linear medicine is technological medicine. Science and linear medicine work by isolating variables, reducing a person down into a set of numerical numbers such as chemistry results. By separating a person into fragments, linear medicine seeks to treat illness to restore health. It is a dualistic medicine because it views health and illness as two separate things and it is always fighting against illness and striving for health.

There is another kind of medicine—*circle medicine.* Circle medicine is unitary medicine. Rather than separating or reducing a person into separate organs, circular medicine seeks to bring the person together into wholeness and to look at how to re-orient or harmonize a person with reality—with self, with other people, with community, and with nature. "*Life is a Being and we are all parts of that Being,*" Joseph tells me.

LINEAR MEDICINE	CIRCULAR MEDICINE
Pathological Process	Natural Process
Treatment	Transformation
Elimination of symptoms	Acceptance of symptoms
Restoring old state	Achieving new state
Disease-based	Health-based
Biomedical Model	Holistic Model
Evidence-Based Medicine	Human-Based Medicine
Hierarchical	Collaborative
Can Foster Dependency	Empowering

Circle medicine gets us to this place of transformation that linear medicine cannot reach. The *linear* approach to change is incremental, *changing what we do*. Circle medicine opens the possibility for *transformation*: *changing who we are*. In this book we start from the place of circular medicine. This is the kind of medicine we discussed in *Walking the Medicine Wheel.* The medicine wheel, as the name implies, is a kind of circular medicine. It is not the only form of circle medicine, but it is the kind of medicine we used in the last book.

Fred Alan Wolf, a physicist who studied different forms of shamanism across the globe, developed a number of hypotheses about the shamanic worldview. The first has to do with vibration, similar to Joseph's view. A view of things as vibration (waves) rather than as discrete objects (particles) takes one into a circular worldview, where waves sweep back and forth and return full circle to their point of origin.

> The underlying reality that shamans deal with is vibrational. They deal with a world of vibrations, cycles, and circles, not straight lines. The key to understanding their world was to realize that it was a vibrational world—a world of sacred songs, chants, and rhythmic drumming—all designed to alter the consciousness of the patient, enabling that patient to heal by taking the patient's mind off his or her normal waking consciousness and into a world of myth.[42]

Mythic thinking is circular and is expressed in story. Sometimes in post-Jungian theory we come across the terms "mythopoetic" and a similar term "mythopoesis." *Mythopoesis* means to create mythology, the act of myth-making:

> "pertaining to the creation of myths," 1846, from Greek *mytho-*, combining form of *mythos* (*see* myth) + *poiein* "to make, create" (*see* poet).[43]

Combining the word *myth* + *poet*, we have *mythopoetic*, which can also have a similar meaning of telling stories and making myth, but this word signifies that the mythic and the poetic are in relation and have something in common. Dreams are similar, they are mythopoetic states in which meaning is symbolic and relational, rather than based on logic and linear thought. Maybe this is the way the right hemisphere of the brain functions through visual image, symbol, mythos, circularity and relationality (as opposed to left brain analysis and separation).

Carl Jung and many psychotherapists have studied dreams for their symbolic meaning. Studying dreams is an ancient tradition of many

---

42 Fred Alan Wolf, *The Eagle's Quest: A Physicist Finds Scientific Truth at the Heart of the Shamanic World*, 283.

43 "Mythopoesis," *Online Etymology Dictionary*.

cultures, reaching back to our shamanic heritage where dreams were viewed as a portal into a different world. Jung spoke of "archetypes of the collective unconscious." Archetypes are structural forms. They are like suns of meaning, illuminating aspects of human being. Archetypes are organizing structures, like the medicine wheel. In fact, Jung wrote that the archetype of the Self (which related to God and Wholeness) was often found in a circle. The collective unconscious is the realm of archetypes. Jung believed that this was a stratum of consciousness that all human beings shared and that it was a repository of our past cultural and animal heritage. Jung found, in his early psychiatric studies, that modern people having psychotic symptoms would speak in words and images that echoed ancient religions. He hypothesized that psychosis was a state in which the collective unconscious was breaking into and overwhelming consciousness. This led to his book *Symbols of Transformation*, published in two volumes in 1911–1912, which mapped out the early precursor of the hero narrative that Joseph Campbell later developed into the hero's journey (a circular medicine of transformation). When Jung went through his own "confrontation with the unconscious," he began drawing circular mandalas every day and peering into them to see what the unconscious revealed through these circular portals. He found that the center of the circle was the goal of the journey and of all psychospiritual development.

> The center is the goal, and everything is directed toward that center. Through this dream I understood that the self is the principle archetype of orientation and meaning. Therein lies its healing function. For me, this insight signified an approach to the center and therefore to the goal. Out of it emerged a first inkling of my personal myth.[44]

Circle Medicine functions when we enter into this non-ordinary reality of myth and story. These stories started in a time long, long ago, and we are telling them now. We are not just telling them, but we are living them, making them our own, but they are not just ours, because they belong to everyone—these stories of circle medicine are archetypal, they connect us deeply to our innermost center of our being, and in so doing, they connect us deeply with all other human beings, living and dead, and even with those to come. Joseph speaks of non-ordinary reality as *metaphoric mind*, which is circular being. Joseph tells us that:

44 *MDR*, 198–99.

> Everything is metaphor. Everything that exists — every object, every action, every experience — is expressing some principle idea. . . . Ceremonies of the living spirit are such pathways. They give us routes to follow so that we can penetrate the surface of manifested reality and experience directly the power of principle ideas.[45]

When Joseph speaks of *principle ideas*, these are similar to what Carl Jung calls *archetypes*. They are powerful *medicine* that transforms us when we come in contact with them and allow them to be planted into the center of our hearts and to grow there. "Life is a circle," Joseph writes, "and the circle means seed." Just as we plant seeds in the land in order to have nourishment, we must plant these spiritual seeds in our hearts, in order that we may have spiritual nourishment. Circle medicine connects the human being to the land, through metaphor. What happens in the heart happens in the land and what happens in the land happens in the heart. In our ordinary reality, linear medicine view, we are separate and disconnected objects. In non-ordinary, circle medicine, we are not only all related, but if you go deep enough, we are all one.

> Everything that exists is trying to unify itself with the whole. All ceremony exists to unify, to bring together, to bring into oneness — but within that oneness is the diversity of all that is. The oneness is, actually, the only thing that exists. It is the only reality. And it is nothing. Yet from that nothing comes all that is.[46]

The linear, analytical mind seeks to control and keep things going in a straight line. The circular mind is more relaxed and is guiding rather than controlling. When you relax into spirit and intuition you enter into circular time. This contrast between linear and circular time and perception also gets at what I have been concerned about in my writing on holistic medicine. *Holistic* medicine is *circle medicine*, it is about how everything is included and interconnected to bring about health. Contemporary medicine is based on linear thinking, on reductionism, and analytical science. The initiation into circle medicine requires that we let go of our attachment to material reality and learn to be able to find meaning that arises from circulating around the medicine wheel. Just as physical life is a result of the perpetual circulation of blood through the heart and body, so too spiritual life is a result of the circulation of the medicine wheel.

45 *Ceremonies*, 8.

46 Ibid., 13, 1–2.

INITIATION OF THE CIRCLE

One of the initiations I have gone through with Joseph is moving from a linear perspective to a circular perspective. From the very first day with Joseph, he took me around in circles, having me drive through the important locations of his life, then circling back to the past at Aztec Ruins National Monument in New Mexico. He often tells me the same story again, circling back to it so that I can enter into the story at a deeper level.

The indigenous world is a circular world, whereas the Western world of technology is a linear world. In the linear reality we have lost spirit and we are enthralled with matter. The world of spirit, the non-ordinary reality, is a circular world. Spiritual time is circular time, whereas worldly time is linear. Circular reality is about renewal, whereas linear reality is about a straight line, "black road"[47] mentality of the physical and mental worlds.

Joseph is continually teaching me about the circular nature of reality, saying that we are *"circle people,"* that *"what comes around goes around,"* and that *"everything eventually becomes its opposite."* He also points out how the difference between a linear and circular perception is based on the perspective or paradigm through which you are perceiving. *"Look at how we move in a circle, but then look at it from the side and it looks like we are moving forward and backward, back and forth. It depends on your perspective of seeing."*

Joseph tells me that even our perception of time is based upon our perspective. We see time as moving only forward, but he says in a circular perspective time can move backwards as well, and can even return back to the starting point. *"We perceive it as moving forward,"* he says about time, *"but scientists are trying to find out how it also moves backwards. We are trying to bring science and spirituality into dialogue."*

---

47 The distinction between the "good red road" and the "black road is often heard in Native stories. Lewis Mehl-Madrona writes, "The Elders say, 'when you step off the good red road, then comes sickness and disease.' The good red road is the road from wisdom to compassion, the road of connecting to all of life from the center of your being, from your heart. It is a road of forgiveness, compassion, and love." (*Narrative Medicine*, 46). I think of the black road as the opposite of this, the road of egoism and mental calculation. The good red road runs vertically through the medicine wheel. In Joseph's version of the medicine wheel this connects the North (place of the spiritual) with the South (place of the emotional). The black road runs horizontally, connecting the East (place of the mental) with the West (place of the physical). When we only live by the mental and physical we have materialism and we end up with black-top paved roads all over Mother Earth.

Then Joseph asks me if I know why babies are born. I say, "You are not going to tell me about the birds & bees are you?" He just ignores my joke and says, *"Time is in the midwifery business. Time is in cahoots with life."*

I knew, intellectually, about how different cultures have linear or circular time perceptions. In World Religions class in college I learned about Mircea Eliade's concepts of the *sacred* and the *profane*. The profane is like the black road of materialism and machines; it is mental and physical materialism without the indwelling of the spirit. Eliade calls the profane "*desacralized*." The sacred is something that is hidden, but can be revealed through a certain way of seeing the world and through various ceremonies. To "designate the *act of manifestation of the sacred*," Eliade writes, "we have proposed the term *hierophany*."[48] Hierophany is related to the words "epiphany" and "theophany," and represents the revelation of the sacred in the world.

The sacred is often about a return to the origin point, the creation myth and source of a culture—a return and circularity. Eliade described this as "the eternal return," the "eternal repetition of the fundamental rhythm of the cosmos—its periodical destruction and re-creation."[49] The majority of religions have some kind of cyclical element to them with symbolic renewals and re-birth, even though the religions of "historical time," are linear, for example Judaism, Christianity, and Islam. Joseph often speaks of the recreation and renewal of the world through activities such as plowing, or at Picuris Feast day where the abundance is brought down from heaven (the top of a tall pole) for the next year.

As I have been working with Joseph, I have started to see circles everywhere and to realize that I am working with *circle medicine*, even when I didn't realize it: the circle of the Medicine Wheel, the Caring for Self and Others circle, the circle of the Hero's Journey (which is the circle that brought Joseph and me together), the Circle of Health developed by the VA Office of Patient Centered Care & Cultural Transformation—all these are models of circle medicine that I am using on a regular basis. They are circles of initiation and transformation, taking me through separation (seeking), initiation (giving & receiving), and return (giving).

My work with Joseph is an ongoing initiation into *the language of spirituality* and *circle medicine* and as the circle includes everything and excludes nothing, in my initiation into circle medicine, I am *becoming*

48 Eliade, *The Sacred and the Profane*, 11.

49 Ibid., 108.

medicine. In this process, Joseph has taught me to relax my linear mind and to open to the circularity of visionary reality which speaks in image, myth, and metaphor.

MOON WOMAN VISION, 11/26/15, 3:29 AM

I wake up, as I often do around this time. I get settled in my comfortable chair in the dark. It is bright—full moon tonight, illuminating the room. I remember a brief sensation I had as I went to the bathroom before settling in the chair. The moon was brightly shining hard through the bathroom window. I felt a strange pull of my head toward the moon and a strange feeling like my head was starting to melt. I resisted it as it caught me off guard, but now, settled in my chair, I let go to it.

I travel on a light beam from the earth to the moon. A beam of light shines one way, but it illuminates the return path, as well. There is a beautiful Moon Being, a woman with glowing silver hair. I soften at her beauty and her glance and I shift and I become her. As the Moon Woman, I learn her Dance. She rotates her body ever so slowly, around the Earth, part of her dancing in the light of the sun, and part of her dancing in the darkness of space. Moon Woman is always looking at Earth, as a lover who cannot look away, even as she spins in space. Here is her song that she sings as she dances: *Hey-ya yaa, Hey-ya yaa, Hey-ya yaa, Hey-ya yaa, Hey-ya yaa, Hey-ya yaa, Hey-ya yaa, Hey-ya yaa, Hey-ya yaa, Wikki Wikki Wikki . . .*

Then something odd happens and I pass through a portal, as if the moon were a hole in a black ceiling and I pass through the round circular entrance into another dimension. It is a vast green plain with a black sky of space above. There is a floating octopus-like being, arms dangling down, floating kind of like a jellyfish, with arms pulsing periodically to move it through the air. The Octopus Being then turns into a floating daisy, the head becomes the flower and the arms become the stem. When I look with my right eye it is the Octopus Being, when I look with my left eye, it is the floating daisy.

Then I am sucked back down, like going down a drain. I realize that one face of Moon Woman pushes and the other face of Moon Woman pulls. She has a face of light and a face of darkness, always staring into the light and always staring into the dark. The face of light pulls, pulls us toward her beauty and pulls the ocean tides toward her. The corresponding face of darkness pushes, pushes the light that is pulled in out into another realm.

In this realm it seems like darkness streaming out into space, but if you pass through the portal of the Moon Woman to the other realm, there instead of darkness, she is giving off light. There is always a correspondence in the other realm to this realm.

Moon Woman takes a strand of her hair, she passes it through my left ear and loops it around into a silver strand of Moon earring. And then I am back in my chair.

SUN AND DANCING MOONLIGHT ON THE PEOPLE OF MOTHER EARTH

CHAPTER 3

SEPARATION

The standard path of the mythological adventure of the hero is a magnification of the formula represented in the rites of passage: separation—initiation—return: which might be named the nuclear unit of the monomyth.[1]

JOSEPH CAMPBELL

The ego is, above all, separation.[2]

DANIEL ODIER

We are remembering how the Heart experienced fear to become whole, how the Heart experienced separation to become whole. Because the only way it wanted to do it was through illusion. So the Heart is the great Being, the great Mystery. All that is here now is a reflection of a Being who lies in a state of dreaming and is perceiving, in reflection, what already is.[3]

JOSEPH RAEL

Every initiation starts with some form of separation, but what is it that we separate from? The details are not as important as the process of separation. We could separate from family, from home, from being a child, from our home country, or we can separate from our identity, from our society, our culture, from the belief system that we were raised in. Ultimately, the separation that leads to initiation is the separation from who we think we are and what we think reality is. These are the two questions that science fiction writer and visionary Philip K. Dick asks again and again: "What is human?" "What is real?" If you find yourself asking these questions, congratulations, you have taken the first step of separation on the path of initiation—you have become a seeker! If you do not leave from somewhere, you will not be able to get where you are going. Separation is adventure—setting off for something new and exciting. Separation is also loss—leaving behind what you know and love.

1 Joseph Campbell, *The Hero With A Thousand Faces*, 23.

2 Daniel Odier, *Desire: The Tantric Path to Awakening*, 54.

3 Joseph Rael, *Sound*, 101.

Many people move from one place to another, but someone on a path of initiation becomes comfortable with separation, he or she becomes an *in-betweener*. An in-betweener is just a made-up word that means the same thing as a visionary, mystic, or shaman. Joseph says, "*If you want to be an in-betweener you consciously know you will be in two places. Always go back to the body, feet together, then feet apart.*" To clarify, I asked him, "When your feet are in two places, you are in two places?" To which he just replied, "*A shaman is always in touch with his power because he has grown up with it all his life.*"

Separation is a pre-requisite for initiation. One separates from a given identity and role and is ushered into a new identity. Life begins with separation. This is true, but it is not the whole truth. Life actually begins in union, however we are unconscious of that union. A man and woman come together out of a drive for union, which is another way of saying out of love. From this love union, life is created. It is only at birth (that is, the separation from the mother) that we begin to become conscious. The beginning of our life is in union, but our *experience* of life only happens when we begin to experience separation. We could thus say that life is union and separation, however as human beings we have a biased tendency to only perceive how we are separate. We mistakenly believe that life is only separation, because this is what we see—the baby separating from the mother.

When we experience ourselves as separation, we believe that we exist, however separation is also the start of death, unless we have constant reconnection with replenishment and revitalization. When things are separated, they are cut off. You can see a beautiful flower blooming, you cut its stem and bring it inside and think, what a beautiful flower, how nice to have a living thing in my house—but that flower is dying as soon as you separate it from the plant. At the moment that we feel we possess or control something, it is in a state of separation and is starting to die.

In the introduction to *The Rubais of Rumi*, Nevit O. Ergin and Will Johnson capture the interplay of separation, initiation (union), and return that we focus on so much in this book. They describe how the child in the womb is at one with the mother, but upon birth "enters a rough and tumble world of separation," in which "normal" consciousness is a "consciousness of separation."[4]

4 Nevit O. Ergin and Will Johnson, *The Rubais of Rumi: Insane with Love*, 5–6.

This consciousness of separation is a painful state we all feel in our lives. From our studies of initiation, we recognize that this state of separation is necessary on the hero's or heroine's journey as we seek initiation into new levels of consciousness and new modes of being. What Ergin and Johnson, through Rumi, are describing is that our very consciousness and being is in a state of separation. We do not have to go on a journey of separation because we are already separate in our egos and in every sense that we see ourselves as "me" and see other people, animals, nature, and things as "other than me." Our very state of ordinary reality is a state of separation. Ergin and Johnson follow Rumi for the solution/initiation that takes us beyond separation into union. In our given state of separation we long to reconnect, to "get back to the garden." Rumi provides a solution to this dilemma, the soul "must undertake a second task," to let go of separation consciousness in order to merge back into union. Ergin and Johnson continue,

> The consciousness of union is every bit as real and palpable as the consciousness of separation, whose pains can only be healed when we once again feel this natural and intimate connection with the larger world of the earth and the heavens and everything that exists. Rumi tells us . . . we have to go beyond ourselves. . . .
>
> Rumi exhorts us to surrender to the tugs and pulls of union, to let its currents sweep us away and take us wherever they want. If we can yield in this way to these currents (and these currents are active in each and every one of us), if we can submit to the forces we feel stirring inside of us and listen to their voices . . . then we can undertake the journey that leads to union.
>
> Union is a feeling state in which inner and outer come back together as one. Union is always beckoning us back into its embrace.[5]

Initiation moves us into a state of union, a state of non-ordinary reality where there is no subject and no object. The work is not so much in striving as it is in ceasing our striving. Normally, we are constantly striving and grasping after separate things and objects and pleasures and pains. Initiation is a reorientation and return to source. Having received initiation, there is then a second return, carrying back non-ordinary reality into ordinary reality. This is a re-birth.

While we tend to emphasize drama and trauma in people's life stories, the truth is that every moment on the visionary, shamanic, and mystical

5 Ibid., 6–7.

path is a hero's and heroine's journey. Joseph teaches that one should be seeking to manifest a state of newness of being in every moment, in every second. Not only should we be seeking this, it is actually seeking us because it is the nature of reality. Reality is in a perpetual state of manifestation and renewal. Every second is a theophany, every second is an epiphany, every second is a revelation of God—*Wah-Mah-Chi*, Breath-Matter-Movement. The journey is not something we undertake, but it is something that is undertaking and overtaking us. All we have to do is to allow the divine creative pulsation to manifest in us and to do this we must look at our existence in a state of separation and say "*na-yo ti-ay we-ah*," "I do not exist," and this creates space for us to be re-born and to flicker into existence and repeat this journey again and again and again.

When we believe we exist, we feel that we have something, some matter, which we need to cling to, to attach to, to take from others or defend from others. We mistakenly believe that we are only separate things. We have lost connection to spirit, Joseph teaches.

> When we start to believe we exist, we open ourselves to the mindset that only one reality is "true" . . . we fall into the vibration of judgment. We judge what we think is right and what we think is wrong, and then we are stuck. Once we are stuck, we fall into decadence and that eventually leads to the death of the psyche.[6]

Our sense of a persisting, solid identity separates us from the ever-renewing revelation of life. Our sense of separateness *separates* us from the sacred. Thus *we must separate from our separation*. Therefore, Joseph writes,

> The reason I say that we don't exist is that we are creating our own realities as we are going along. So, if we are creating our own realities as we are going along, then the only time we exist is when we are creating a reality that we can reflect upon. We create this reality through thought. We create it through how we think life is unfolding. . . . We are the creators of all the realities that are going to occur because we are the manifestors of reality.[7]

In saying we create reality, it is not saying that our egos can create whatever they want. Creation comes not from a state of separation, but rather, from the renewed life that flows through what was once separated

---

6 *Sound*, 73–74.

7 Ibid., 71–72.

as it comes back into union and blinks back into existence emitting new light. We are continually blinking in and out of existence and the strength of our ability to create is dependent upon our abilities to let go and cease to exist, to merge back into union and to be born again. When we refuse rebirth, we choose to live in a state of non-existence, death, in which we are objects amongst objects, and hence we are at war with reality, at war with ourselves, and eventually, inevitably, at war with others. War stems from viewing ourselves and others as separate; peace comes from feeling that we are one.

Ergin and Johnson continue the journey from separation to union:

> But as soon as you feel and realize that everything . . . can come together as one . . . then your mind and heart and body become imbued with a feeling that aligns you with what can only be called the energies of God. . . .
>
> Rumi encourages all of us to go beyond the confines and limitations of the orthodox face of religion and to reach back to the original experience on which all religions were founded. He urges us to fall back into the center of ourselves, back into that common ground of being we share identically with each and every person who has ever lived, that place in which we are no longer Muslims, no longer Jewish, no longer Christian, but simply human. . . . Separation in oneself, or among cultures, nations, and religions, is no longer a viable position to hold and embody. Only the lived experience of union can put to rest our individual suffering and help heal the tragic conflicts of religion.[8]

THE LOSS OF OUR ORIGINAL INSTRUCTIONS

Peter Kingsley describes how we, in the West, have become separated from and have lost our *original instructions*. Many creation stories and founding myths of cultures contain a set of original instructions for how we are supposed to live. When we forget these instructions it creates a "burning need to try and discover what is missing in our modern Western world."[9] This feeling of spiritual emptiness at the heart of our culture led him on a secret journey to re-discover our roots that have become buried.

8 Ergin and Johnson, 8–9.

9 Richard Smoley, "Original Instructions: An Interview with Peter Kingsley," *Quest*, 101. Joseph Rael wrote the foreword to Peter Kingsley's book, *A Story Waiting to Pierce You: Mongolia, Tibet and the Destiny of the Western World.* Joseph writes, "I consider Peter Kingsley to be one of the most courageous people on the planet at the moment," (3).

In seeking the original instructions at the root of Western civilization, Kingsley describes finding these instructions preserved, as a thread, through various cultures.

> I began to discover how medieval Persian Sufis, Arab alchemists, mystics who were teaching all the way from Spain through Egypt to Mecca and into Central Asia, had preserved the essential awareness of what I had experienced myself: that in fact many of the so-called Presocratics were great Masters of wisdom and guides of humanity, major prophets and lawgivers who had laid down the spiritual laws for what Western civilization was meant to be."[10]

Kingsley describes practicing the ceremonies and techniques he discovered and that he was "transformed." His life and work provide a great example of the scholar and the seeker who makes the secret journey into what is hidden to find the treasure buried under our feet. "There is no greater spiritual adventure than to turn back to our own, apparently empty shell of a culture and prize it open until we find the jewels and pearls at its core."[11]

SEPARATION CULTURE

Joseph tells us, "Technological society encourages the separation of the mind from the body. Our educational system, and everything we really value in Western culture, separates us from Infinite Self."[12] The problem, as Peter Kingsley points out, is that we have separated ourselves from our living spiritual heritage.

In books by "Westerners" or books by "Native Americans" authors often make a distinction between the dominant materialistic culture of the United States and the indigenous cultures. We speak of first world, second world, third world, and we generally are signifying how industrialized and "modern" a culture is. Thus we could call "Western" culture, "technological" culture. An unintended consequence of modernization and technological development is separation and isolation from our own inner being, from

---

10 Ibid., 102. Peter Kingsley's ground-breaking new work, *Catafalque: Carl Jung and the End of Humanity* explores these themes in great depth: Jung, Corbin, mysticism, prophecy, and the loss of our original instructions. This book was only just published as I was in the final stages of editing *Becoming Medicine*, otherwise it would be more prominently featured as it is very relevant to our topic.

11 Ibid., 104–05.

12 *Ceremonies*, 23.

authentic relationships with others, and with a disconnection from the land. We could call "Western" culture, "Separation" culture, as we have a biased perspective of separation over union. Science, logic, economics, and the mind are all based on separation, on dividing things up, on being objective, on distinguishing between what is mine and what is yours.

Joseph tends to switch back and forth between the terms "Indians," "American Indians," and "Native Americans." Throughout this book we will use these terms interchangeably, all the while realizing that none of them are adequate descriptors and when able to speak of a specific tribal heritage we will do so. Our apologies to anyone who feels that we should use a different descriptor. Generally I will use the term "Native American" which has been the most acceptable usage culturally. Although Joseph has said that anyone born in this country could be considered a "Native American."[13]

Many "Westerners" speak of "Native American culture." Many Native American authors point out that it is not technically correct to lump the 573 federally recognized tribes in the United States into one culture. That is definitely true, but does that argument work both ways? Can we lump all Americans of European descent together regardless of how long their ancestors have lived on this land? All of this points to the fact that we do not really know who we are.

I realized when living abroad that many people in New Zealand would try not to use the descriptor "American" to refer to people from

---

13 In this book we include a number of authors from the Indian Subcontinent, so the use of "Indian" becomes confusing. I choose to use some of the historical terms, while recognizing that our language is imprecise and perpetuates colonialism—at least until we can find a term that describes all of us and that we all find acceptable. At the end of the day, Joseph often ends up talking about us all as global citizens. For the purpose of this book we do not want to spend too much time focusing on our differences when the goal is for us to recognize our common global citizenship. Still, it is good to be cognizant of the language that we are using.

Roxanne Dunbar-Ortiz writes about terminology in *An Indigenous Peoples' History of the United States*:

> I use "Indigenous," "Indian," and "Native" interchangeably in the text. Indigenous individuals and peoples in North America on the whole do not consider "Indian" a slur. Of course, all citizens of Native nations much prefer that their nations' names in their own language be used. . . . I don't use the term "tribe." "Community," "people," and "nation" are used instead interchangeably. I also refrain from using "America" and "American" when referring only to the United States and its citizens. Those blatantly imperialistic terms annoy people in the rest of the Western Hemisphere, who are, after all, also Americans. I use "United States" as a noun and "US" as an adjective to refer to the country and "US Americans" for its citizens, (xiii–xiv).

the United States. Technically Canadians, Mexicans, and people from the United States are all North Americans, and South Americans could also call themselves *Americans*. We are people who have gotten all jumbled up.

We are back at the debate that Joseph and I mentioned in our previous book—the Darwinian distinction between *lumpers* (those who see similarities between things) and *splitters* (those who see more differences and distinctions between things).[14] It is true that there are cultural variations between people, but it is also true that we are all people, we are all *Homo sapiens*. We are currently in a time period where people are focusing on differences in the world. However, in the world of spirit, we are taught to seek unity amongst diversity. I once heard a joke that I like to tell. "There are two kinds of people in the world: the people who think there are two kinds of people, and—everyone else!"[15]

For the purpose of this book, we are all global citizens. It is also appropriate to provide a cultural critique of our predominant modes of thought and our state of separation in the United States. We, new-comers to this land, have a lot we can learn from those whose DNA has lived in harmony with this land for thousands of years. The late Phillip H. Duran, was a friend of Joseph's who wrote about tribal culture, US American culture, and science culture. In *The Condor and the Eagle: Uniting Heart and Mind in Search of a New Science Worldview,* Duran writes the people of the North, the Eagle (the United States and its European heritage) use their minds to understand the world, the people of the South, the Condor (representing the indigenous peoples of the continents) use their hearts to understand the world. There is an ancient Incan prophecy about a bitter winter of separation and then a new spring when the Eagle and the Condor will fly again together.

---

14 See our discussion of Darwin's concept of lumpers and splitters in *Walking the Medicine Wheel*, 272–73.

15 Richard Katz cautions about seeing similarities between cultures as a possible bias that can have harmful consequences. "The eagerness to see similarities between different approaches, to see how one can fit into the other, to even welcome the other approach, can lead to assimilation and consequent diminution of a less socio-politically powerful approach by a more dominant and dominating approach. As we remain open to the unexpected, we can better appreciate there are many paths toward understanding, and that diversity deepens the understanding," (Katz, *Indigenous Healing Psychology*, 153). This is a valid point to keep in mind. However there is also the opposing danger of seeing everyone else as so "other" than one's self or one's culture that it is impossible to form a relationship or correspondence. It is a very difficult balance to be able to seek correspondence while also respecting diversity. As our book is more about the many different spiritual traditions that speak of the underlying unity within diversity (rather than being a book on cultural differences) we tend to look at similarities between spiritual paths and traditions in this book.

As a physicist, educator, and indigenous person, Phillip Duran called for a unification of "*both* Native and Western concepts . . . in the development of science and educational curricula." Further, he states that "a realignment of science is necessary, that the whole human being—spirit, mind, emotion, body—can enhance the contribution to knowledge. . . . *The world needs Indigenous knowledge*."[16]

Phillip Duran was interested in unifying the painful separations that we have in our world. He called for "reindigenization,"[17] or reinvigorating old ways of knowing. This is important, not just for indigenous people, but, for all people and the whole Earth. Joseph often echoes these beliefs in his own teachings. Ancient cultures and modern indigenous cultures still have what Joseph calls *ceremonies of the living spirit*. These ceremonies bring together the masculine and the feminine, they bring together separation and union and honor both aspects of life. We need to heal the divisions between "Western," "Eastern," and "Native American." Joseph writes, "We are fragmented. . . . What we want to do is get back together again." He tells us that we must be continually seeking to unite together what has been fragmented. "Unification has to be done almost all the time, and that is why we have rituals and ceremonies we repeat."[18]

We start our secret journey by being pulled into the beginning of an initiation ceremony—we are in ordinary, separation reality, but here we are separated from the sacred, thus we must separate from the state of separation and seek union and connection. We must become seekers of sacred medicine to heal the separation we find ourselves in.

THE WOUND & GIFT OF SEPARATION

Separation is both a wound and a gift. Separation is a wound as the living tissue of our umbilicus is cut, which had been our lifeline. We are cast free into the great unknown. Yet, separation is the gift of life, our birth as a human being and as an individual as we separate from our mother and enter into great adventures. Separation is what begins our initiation through which we are continually transforming. Separation is necessary in order for there to be seeking, seeking is necessary for there to be finding, and finding is necessary for there to be something to give as a gift to

16 Phillip Duran, *The Condor and the Eagle*, 15.

17 Ibid., 4.

18 *Ceremonies*, 23.

others. When Joseph says "we don't exist," this includes the death of who we thought we were, but it also includes the gift of a new birth into who we are becoming.

"Every moment is a womb and you might as well understand that as a human being—because the next moment you will be birthed into a new womb. And as you begin to identify who you are as a human being, you learn that birthing is a life-long journey. A womb isn't separate. Every time you are born, you are born like new again—it is a celebration. Life is, every single moment is, a birthing. That instant brings powers to achieve awareness you can bring from the past and that awareness helps you in the new moment.

"The journey for us is to achieve our highest excellence. Achievement is a new time for celebration."

Joseph told me of a visionary experience he had around the separation from his foster mother, Lucia. Although there is the grief of Lucia's loss, there is also a gift of a vision into another reality of the ancestors. As I drove up to Picuris Pueblo with Joseph and my wife, Mary Pat, Joseph pointed out the hill where he saw the space open up that is the doorway that connects to the ancestors. The wound of separation leads to the gift of the realization that "*all of us live in these two worlds.*" Separation from one world is entry into another.

JOSEPH'S VISION OF HIS FOSTER MOTHER, LUCIA

"For me, I was in training all the time that I was in Picuris. If everything is considered holy, then you are always in training. So you always want to be good because Grandfather (God) might be watching. Apparently I was in training for right now—to tell the people in the United States what we are built to do and that we are the Sacred. We are the holy ones. That is why I always speak with eloquence.

"My foster mother, Lucia, and Agapito, my foster father, loved roses. I got them a red and yellow rose bush and I tended them when I lived with them at Picuris. I used to visit them as often as I could because they were aging. Every so often I would send them yellow roses, red roses and give them to them for a birthday or Christmas. It was a way of honoring them. Agapito died, and of course I went to the funeral. It was just Lucia then.

"One day, Lucia was walking from the house over toward the school and she fell and broke her hip, so I took her to the hospital in Santa Fe. So I took a bouquet of roses. I talked with her and I thought she was going to be

DOVE OF PEACE

alright. The next day I had a meeting with the All Indian Pueblo council in Albuquerque and I made my presentation in the morning. Around 11 AM there was a call and someone said, 'Joseph you are wanted,' and it was the hospital calling to say that she had died.

"I left and went to my house. When I got there I heard a voice in my head say 'Don't go to the left, go straight.' The room was full of the perfume of red roses. I looked off to the left and I saw her and it looked like her form. She looked like she was about 29 years old. I walked straight ahead into the bathroom, then I turned around and looked back and there was no silhouette there, just the ordinary house. So I got ready, I had to go to Picuris. I fixed some lunch and

I went up to Picuris and the governor had already arranged to have the body brought up to Picuris. So I went up to Picuris to meet the body. We put her in the house where she was going to lay in state. We had a wake, an all-night wake. The people knew how to prepare the funeral and to prepare the body and they folded her in a blanket. She was laying in one of the rooms with chairs all the way around for people who wanted to come and pray or sing songs. At midnight they have a rosary and then they would feed the people.

"The next day as soon as summer daylight started, they started digging the place where she would be buried. Five or six men dug the hole. The body had to be buried by 10 AM, you couldn't bury later than that. The number 10 (tehn-ku-teh) *is the number of completion and that is why. As she was my mother, I couldn't handle a shovel or anything, but I had other things to do to get ready. I had breakfast in the room right next to where she was laying in state and people would come by and give their condolences. They put her on a step-ladder and the pall bearers took her down to the church. The padre, the priest, did a low mass for her. They took her and put her in the middle of the church, closer to where the people would pass on their way to communion. Then the pall bearers would take her out the door and to the cemetery.*

"Back at the house, that is when I saw her, when they were doing the rosary. They close the windows and pull the curtains and cover the mirrors. After she had been buried, they were doing the rosary and everyone was praying facing the altar. I saw up in the corner of the room, instead of the wall I saw a blue sky open up. This was right above Lucia's altar with her statues of the saints and Jesus. Up in the corner of the room a white dove appears in a blue background as an opening in the wall. There is my first view of paradise, the dove flying in paradise. I remember that when Lucia had given me a statue of St. Francis, there was a little dove on his left shoulder. I kept it with me and took it to the Santa Fe Indian School. I used to pack it in my suitcase, but I don't know where it is now.

"The next thing I saw was my mother and my father standing there and I looked into their youthful faces and there was like a half-smile and a joy-happiness coming from their presence and they were holding hands and the rest of the people were looking toward the wall where the dove appeared above the niche of her altar with her patron saints. White light was above the heads of the people praying the rosary. Lucia and Agapito went over their heads and moved out through the wall.

"The dove is the symbol of purity, which is the direction of the South—purity. They went south, I followed them down to the mountain and a tunnel opened

JOSEPH WITH FOSTER PARENTS, LUCIA & AGAPITO

up in the side of the mountain and a group of people came out to greet them. Lucia and Agapito looked young, like 29 years old.

"Then the hillside closed and there was no sign that there had been a tunnel or people there. We've all got that power to separate our two bodies.

"Back in the house where the people were praying there was a white light coming from people's heads, a heavenly presence. The thing I remember most is that I was always late and this time I was almost late. The rosary was just starting. That is when I saw the presence of the two looking, looking at me primarily and then they started moving, floating and went through the wall. My physical body stayed praying, but my other body went with them down to the mountain. I wasn't walking, more like floating.

"Why did that appear to me? Why did they appear to me rather than her brother? All my life I have had these spiritual experiences and I have never thought to ask why they were happening to me. When I was a kid we would live in two places. In the summer we would go up into the mountains to the ranch and then in the winter we would go down into the village. This was in the 1940s. I just realized now that my life is coming full circle again to this. I am going to be living in New Mexico during the winter and come up north to the summer home on the Southern Ute Reservation. In a way, all of us live in these two worlds."

This story of separation with the death of Joseph's foster mother, Lucia, leads to a visionary experience. Separation feels like a wound, but it is a gift because it reminds us that we do not exist, and it clears the way for initiation, transformation, and rebirth. The wound of separation makes us cry, yet Joseph tells us that it is by crying for a vision that our wounds are healed.

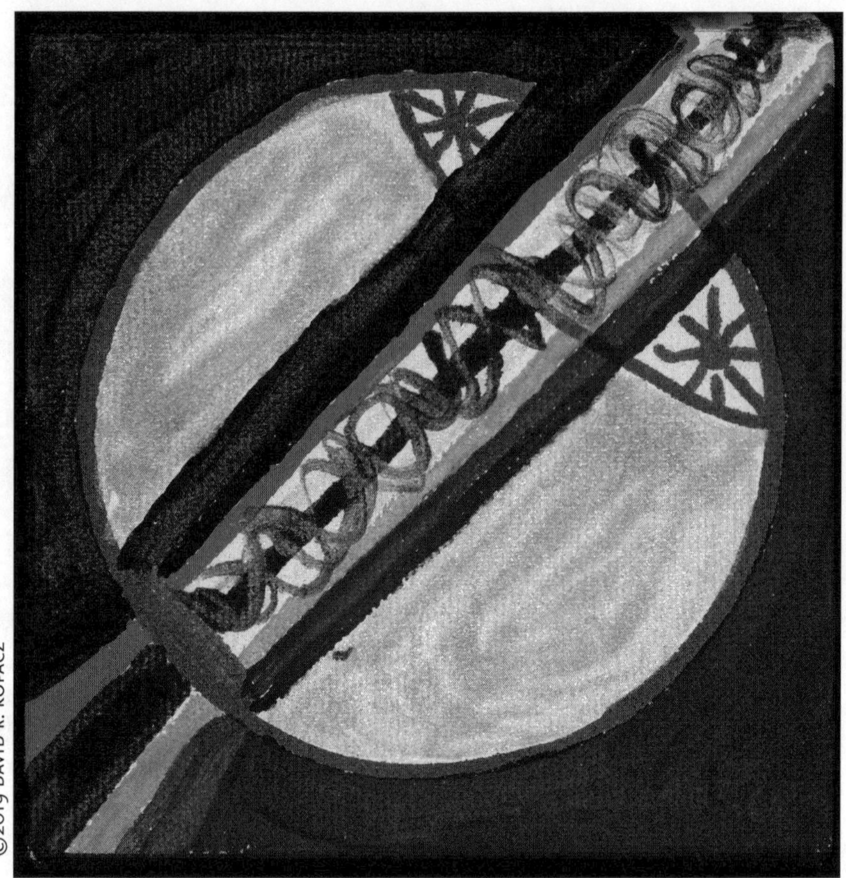

VISIONARY PERCEPTION

CHAPTER 4

BECOMING A VISIONARY

All visions are always present. A vision is what a visionary is seeing. . . . When we see visions, they enter perceptual reality. In perceptual reality, the visionary is seeing something in front of him or her that is now available to be perceived by a perceiver, who has allowed himself now to perceive.

A vision is the soul drinking light. It starts with descending light, falling like rain. . . . The visionary transformation happens in the act of perception. . . . It has the quality of "heaven is here now." What you want to achieve is here now, ready, given.[1]

JOSEPH RAEL

1 *Ceremonies*, 40.

It doesn't matter how long your spirit lies dormant and unused. One day you hear a song, look at an object, or see a vision, and you feel its presence. It can't be bought, traded, or annihilated, because its power comes from story.

No one can steal your spirit: you have to give it away. You can always take it back.

Find yours.[2]

CARL A. HAMMERSCHLAG

A VISIONARY

A visionary is a person who sees visions. Visions are non-ordinary states of reality. Many holy people are visionaries, they hear the voice of God, they see angels, and they have experiences that are difficult to understand. The core of this book is really about realizing we all have the ability to be visionaries. Joseph told me the following:

"I think we can address this idea of visioning really well. I am interested in how we can explain this to the larger public because it is important.

Ok, on how to become a visionary:

What you do is you get in a meditative position, lotus position or just in a chair

You've got to go into your mother's womb, it's called oseaone, oseaone *is 'birther of babies.' So you have to be birthed. You have to be re-birthed again because our mind has been contaminated with noun-pronoun perceptual consciousness so you have to go to your mom when she was carrying you. Go into her womb and that is a little ocean.*

"So we are visionaries. All humans are visionaries because they come out of their mother's womb, the womb is like a little tiny ocean. The Greeks call it okeanos. *They were the ones who named the 'ocean.'*[3] *We call it* oseaone*—one who births children. And then you have to count from one to nine, but you don't use English, you say in Tiwa:* weh-mu, weh-seh, paah-chu, wiii, paah-nu, maa-tschlay,

2 Carl A. Hammerschlag, *The Theft of the Spirit*, 171.

3 Ocean (n.) Late 13c., from Old French *occean* "ocean" (12c., Modern French *océan*), from Latin *oceanus*, from Greek *okeanos*, the great river or sea surrounding the disk of the Earth. . . . Personified as *Oceanus*, son of Uranus and Gaia and husband of Tethys. *Online Etymology Dictionary.*

> cho-oh, wheh-leh, whiii. *Then you birth, imagine yourself being birthed. After that you have ten and you know what happens at ten, whatever you were doing is completed at ten and another cycle begins. And then you go and you become 10, 11, 12, 13, 14, 15 and so on . . .*
>
> *As soon as you are born physically born at the 9th month then you are a visionary at that point because your third eye is open at that time for a while. Eventually it starts to close up through language, whatever language it is we grow up in. It is either noun-pronoun language or verb language, while I grew up in verb language, I attended noun-pronoun schooling in English concepts. Your third eye starts to cloud up as you learn noun-pronoun language.*
>
> *Anyway, that is how you become a visionary."*

ON VISIONS

Joseph's artwork comes from his visions. What he sees in his visions he puts in his artwork. I keep a number of Joseph's paintings around my desk. One of these is "Where God and Humans meet." This painting is in the shape of a large vase, filled with tiny dots—like stars or molecules of gas. There is a central point, like a sun, which shines two rays downward to the top of two people's heads and there is a little star where that divine energy enters in through the crown (7th) chakra. Arching upwards from the central sun is a divine being, God or Vast Self. As always in Joseph's paintings, this divine being is looking upwards and has a large black eye (which is a black hole, Joseph says, and this black hole is about the same size as the light giving central sun). The edge of the vase and the back of this divine being are the same line, the vase grows out of the divine being which creates a container of and for existence. We are the vase that contains the space where God and humans meet, but from a visionary perspective, the material we are made of, the vase, is the material of *Wah-Mah-Chi,* Breath-Matter-Movement, in other words, God. Visions come from the divine and they reveal to us who we are. Visions are the soul drinking light, Joseph says.

Visions are at the center of this book, just as the heart is at the center of the medicine wheel and our hearts are the center of our being. A vision is a little bit like a poem, or maybe a dream. It can be of brief, passing interest, or it can be an orienting structure for the rest of your life.

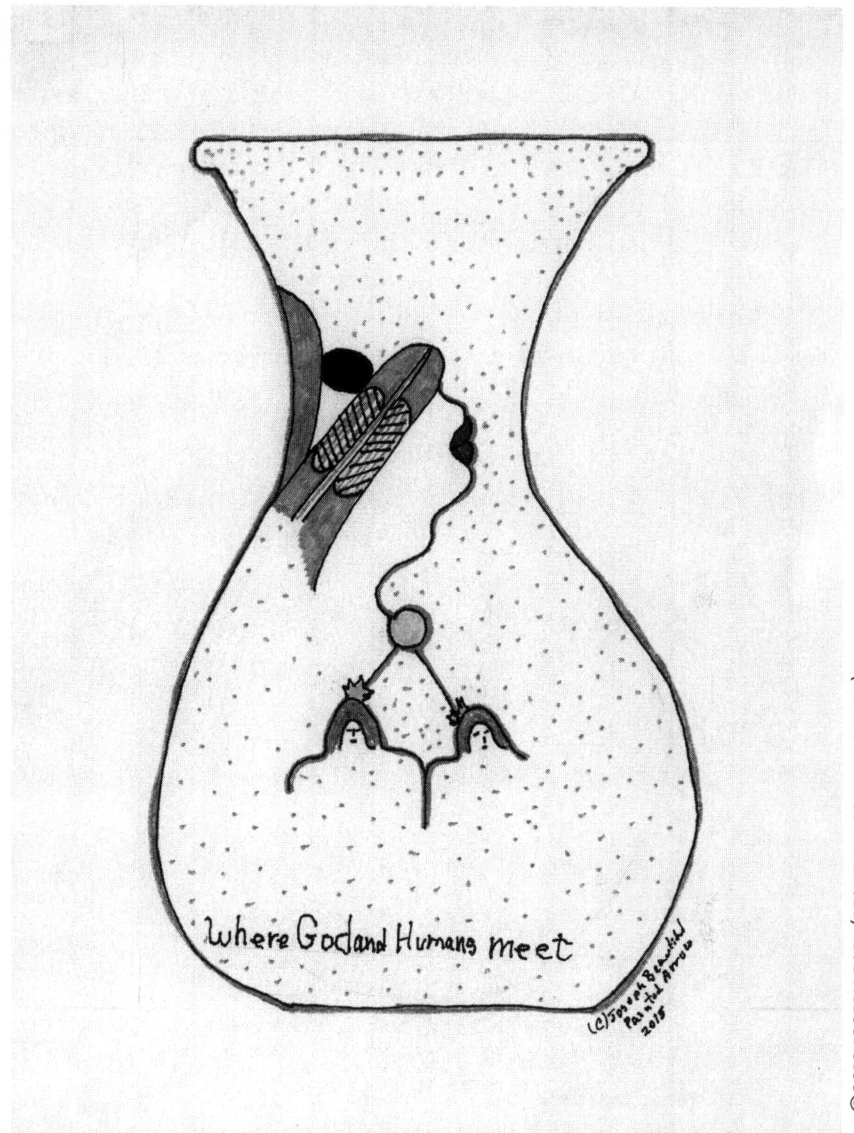

WHERE GOD AND HUMANS MEET

Joseph's spiritual life is the pursuit of visions, which is why he is called a visionary—one who sees visions and brings these visions to others and shares them. The visions speak about the nature of reality and they instruct us in how we can be better heart people, how we can better harmonize between ordinary and non-ordinary reality in the centers of our being (our hearts).

Joseph's own initiation began with visions—different perceptions of reality that revealed a truth for living. One of his first visions was a cloud of mist that he walked into when he was five years old. Visions are a kind of journey in which one enters into a visionary geography or topography, what Joseph calls non-ordinary reality. This is the place *where God and humans meet.* Joseph has learned to let his visions guide his actions. His vision of the Sound Chambers in the early 1980s led to the creation of more than 50 of these chambers dedicated to world peace.

When I met Joseph in 2014, the first place he took me was to the hillside where he had his first vision. He was wandering in the dark while his mother was out gathering the livestock for the evening. Joseph saw a mist open up and he went into it and it was his first taste of non-ordinary reality. Eventually he heard his mother calling him and he came back into ordinary reality. At the time I was confused as to why we had to actually go to the hillside and why he could not just tell me about this over a cup of coffee. I have gradually realized that Joseph was starting my initiation so that I could develop my own visionary abilities. He was having me, literally, follow in his footsteps.

Many holy people are visionaries. Black Elk of the Oglala Lakota had his visions which organized and structured his life and he gave these visions to the people. I read about his visions and they inspired me to follow in his footsteps. I traveled to Black Elk Peak and slept alone by a creek nearby, seeking some visionary experience. Wovoka of the Northern Paiute had his visions in the 1890s about returning back to the purity of the traditional, native ways. He gave these visions to the people and this led to the Ghost Dance which was embraced as a method to renew and rejuvenate Native American culture across many tribes. Being a visionary is an accepted role in many indigenous cultures and it is often the path to how one becomes a holy man or woman.

Visions were a regular part of the European and Judeo-Christian traditions in the past. There were many Christian mystics up until the time of the Enlightenment and the scientific revolution. Hildegard of Bingen is a famous visionary who saw many visions and communicated regularly with God. During the Middle Ages religion was a living spirituality and visions were not just a thing of the past like Moses and the burning bush. In this chapter we will be talking about modern day visionaries, like Henry Corbin, Carl Jung, and Joseph Rael.

HENRY CORBIN: THE IMAGINAL AND THE 'ALAM AL-MITHAL

Henry Corbin studied esoteric Islam. He was a French professor of Islamic Studies who spent time in Iran (where there is a street bearing his name) and was stranded in Istanbul from 1939–1945 with the outbreak of World War II. At the age of 26 he encountered the 12th Century visionary Suhrawardī, who became his spiritual teacher. Corbin met Suhrawardī when the director of Islamic Studies at the Sorbonne, Louis Massignon, gave Corbin a copy of Suhrawardī's *Hikmat al-Ishraq*. Massignon said to Corbin, "Take it. . . . I think there is something in this book for you." Corbin later wrote,

> this "something" was the company of the young Shaykh al-Ishraq, who has not left me in my whole life. . . . Through my meeting with Suhrawardī, my spiritual destiny for the passage through this world was sealed. Platonism, expressed in terms of Zoroastrian angelology of ancient Persia, illuminated the path I was seeking.[4]

Similar to Jung, Corbin was a scholar, but also a mystic and visionary.[5] I cannot remember how I came to read Corbin. I had surely seen his name referenced by Jungians, perhaps something by James Hillman. For some reason, near the end of my time in New Zealand, I decided that it was time to read Henry Corbin and my introduction to him was through his book, *Alone with the Alone: Creative Imagination in the Sūfism of Ibn*

---

4 Henry Corbin in Tom Cheetham, *All the World an Icon: Henry Corbin and the Angelic Function of Beings*, 8–9. Cheetham has written a number of books on Corbin that can be a good entry point to Corbin's work, but to really understand Corbin, you must read him directly. If you recall, I had to teach myself how to read Jung, and with Corbin it is the same way. The concepts are dense and difficult, but they open up a sublime view, like struggling up a forested mountain through clouds and fog. With Corbin there are also esoteric flights of poetic vision that are inherent within Esoteric Islam—vistas that open up momentarily in your journey through the clouds and trees.

5 Tom Cheetham has written about Jung and Corbin in his book, *Imaginal Love: The Meanings of Imagination in Henry Corbin and James Hillman*. Peter Kingsley provides a very different view of Jung's and Corbin's friendship and he had the benefit of being befriended by Stella Corbin, Corbin's widow. Kingsley describes Corbin and Jung's friendship in terms of chivalry, two knights seeking the Holy Grail through their own pathways. While they recognized a kindred spirit in each other, and influenced each other, each was on his own path to living spirituality. Corbin used the ancient Greek phrase *monos pros monon*, "alone to alone," in his review of Jung's *Answer to Job*. Peter Kingsley also points out that this phrase applies to the meeting of two true individuals as it does to the meeting of the individual with Divine. See *Catafalque: Carl Jung and the End of Humanity*, 8–9, 375–86. *Catafalque* is a great example of living spirituality and interweaves Kingsley's own visionary experiences within the larger narrative of Jung's and Corbin's mysticism and prophecy.

'Arabī. I realized that Corbin was a writer and visionary on par with Carl Jung. At the time I was also immersed in Jung's *Red Book* and Philip K. Dick's *Exegesis*, two visionary, spiritual diaries. I immediately recognized that reading Corbin was to enter into a vast and strange visionary realm. He called this realm the *'alam al-mithal* and it was the place of interrelationship between matter and spirit. I could sense that one could spend a lifetime reading Corbin, as one could with Jung, and always be learning deeper spiritual truths. I still cannot claim to have fully digested and understood Corbin's work, but will include him in this discussion of *becoming a visionary*.

In the West we have split mind from body, spirit from body, and spirit from body. Corbin describes how the *Creative Imagination* was a central part of human experience, until we lost the imaginal function in the 12th Century, when a split occurred between the inner and outer realms and we descended into elevating material reality above spiritual reality. In essence, we lost our soul and became only bodies and minds, living in a material world. Sufism provides an example of a living spirituality, an embodied spirituality. Islam and Sufism preserved something that we, in the West lost, quite literally—many of the texts from ancient Greece and Egypt were lost from Europe in the Middle Ages and were later re-discovered through translations from Islamic Arabic and Persian sources.

Beyond the fascinating world of majesty and beauty of Sufism, there is within Corbin's work the attempt to re-spiritualize the human being and to reclaim the role of *imagination* as the function of the *'alam al-mithal* where matter and spirit are in a living exchange with one another. This is another important contribution of Corbin, to validate and highlight the necessity of the spiritual imagination. The *Creative Imagination* that he is describing is different than fantasy or make believe, rather it is the place and function of what Joseph would call non-ordinary reality (sometimes this is called *imaginal* to distinguish from fantasy imagination). *Creative Imagination* is not fantasy, but rather *theophany*—revelation of the divine that is the very creative essence of the world we live in. Through it we make visionary journeys and it is the place where we meet God. Again, this is not to say that it is "made up," quite the contrary, it is what is making up, materializing us—it is the place where spirit becomes matter and matter becomes spirit. *Creative Imagination* opens up a visionary world of living spirituality.

Corbin described esoteric Islam as conceiving of a three-fold universe of matter, intelligence (spirit), and between these two a *barzakh*, an "interworld." The interworld is necessary in order for matter and spirit to communicate. This would be like the role of the shaman in connecting ordinary and non-ordinary reality. However, Corbin writes that this interworld is "the real place of all psycho-spiritual events (visions, charismas, thaumaturgical actions breaching the physical laws of space and time)." Corbin sees *Creative Imagination* or the *Imaginal* as the language or essence of this interworld realm. Corbin describes the *'alam al-mithal* as the "world of archetypal Images through and in which *Spirits are corporealized and bodies are spiritualized*."[6] Thus, if one can become capable of opening to this imaginal realm, one can transform one's self. Corbin also describes how the *'alam al-mithal* is populated with spiritual beings—angels—whose work is to tend the never-ending process of spiritualizing matter and materializing spirit. A visionary is thus someone who can "see" and "go" into the *'alam al-mithal.*

GOING INTO THE SPANDA *AND THE* ALAM AL-MITHAL

The *'alam al-mithal* and the *spanda* are two orienting and disorienting concepts for me. During my transition from New Zealand back to the United States these two concepts from Sufism and Kashmiri Shaivism, respectively, along with Joseph's teachings, have been the fundamental spiritual terrains I have been exploring. *Spanda* is the fundamental essence of Divine Consciousness in Kashmiri Shaivism, described as "active, dynamic, throbbing with life, creative pulsation."[7] *Spanda* is the movement of Divine Consciousness in a way that is analogous to Joseph Rael's teaching of God being *Wah-Mah-Chi*, Breath-Matter-Movement—the fundamental nature of the Divine which manifests as everything. Jaideva Singh comments on the *spanda*, writing that, "In reality, nothing arises, and nothing subsides. It is only the divine *Spandaśakti* which, though free of succession, appears in different aspects as if flashing in view and as if subsiding."[8] This is the closest explanation in a spiritual tradition that helps me to understand and contextualize what Joseph Rael means when he says "we do not exist," and I try to imagine myself as this divine creative pulsation, *flashing in view and as if subsiding*.

6 Henry Corbin, *Spiritual Body and Celestial Earth*, 79, 177.

7 Jaideva Singh, *Spanda-Kārikās: The Divine Creative Pulsation*, v.

8 Ibid., xviii.

When I was living in New Zealand and reading Corbin's book, *Alone with the Alone*, I was fascinated by this concept of an "interworld," a place where spirit is materialized and matter is spiritualized. I would sit down to meditate, facing out across Waitemata Harbour as it opens into the Hauraki Gulf, looking toward the dormant volcano, *Rangitoto*[9] and close my eyes. I set out seeking the *'alam al-mithal*, envisioning what it might look like. I saw in my imagination a thin layer running horizontally, nothing really, not so much a space as a separation between spaces. Yet, still, I saw what looked like a doorway. I entered in and gasped a deep breath as I was immersed in a reddish-gold fire, yet it was not a fire that burned, and it was not so much that I existed as that I was composed of this *fire* and the *fire* was all that existed. It was incredibly pleasant. I imagine that this is what the visionaries and saints experience when they go into ecstasy. I stayed in this space for a while and then "came out" again. I found that I could enter into and out and back into this space when I would meditate. When I returned to the United States, I tried to paint a picture of what this place looked like. I was not very successful at capturing it, but I painted ten different paintings that I have up in my office above the door and window.

The vision of the *reddish gold fire* reminded me of something I read about 17th Century mathematician, Blaise Pascal. Pascal had a visionary, mystical experience on November 23rd, 1654, of which is known only a few fragmentary lines. He wrote on a scrap of parchment "From half-past ten till half-past twelve, Fire!" He drew a rendition of a flaming cross and then below this was a short series of exclamations that spoke of a feeling of certitude, peace, and joy. He had sewn this scrap of parchment into his doublet and apparently wore it upon his person always. Evelyn Underhill describes this as "a perpetual memorial of the supernal experience, the initiation into Reality, which it describes."[10] We can only guess what this meant to Pascal, but it was some kind of orienting vision so powerful and important that he kept it on his body and his servant found it there upon his death.

9 The volcano's full name is *Te Rangi-i-tōtōngia-ai-te ihu-o Tamatekapua*. Maybe I was seeing *Rangitoto's* "bloody sky," or maybe it was the *'alam al-mithal*, or maybe they are one and the same. For the association of volcanoes and visionary initiation, see Peter Kingsley's *Catafalque: Carl Jung and the End of Humanity*.

10 Pascal quoted in Underhill, *Mysticism*, 188–89.

THE ORIENTING FUNCTION OF VISIONS

One of the functions of visions is to orient us to the divine, the soul, to what is really important in life. Corbin speaks of the term "orient," a term we used in discussing the medicine wheel's function. He describes the *'alam al-mithal*, the interworld, as populated by visionary beings and states that "each human being is oriented toward a quest for his personal invisible guide."[11] His interest in Persia as a "place" between East and West also gives us an orientation to the unification of opposites.

Corbin describes a world in which there is perpetual theophany—revelation of God—and this theophany is the continual creation of reality. This idea of continuous creation is the flip side of Joseph's statement, "we do not exist." The reason we do not exist is because we are continuously being created. Corbin writes,

> Here we encounter the link between a continuous creation, renewed from instant to instant, and an unceasing theophanic Imagination, in other words, the idea of a succession of theophanies (*tajalliyāt*) which brings about the continuous succession of beings. This imagination is subject to two possibilities. . . . It is a veil; this veil can become so opaque as to imprison us and catch us in the trap of idolatry. But it can also become increasingly transparent, for its sole purpose is to enable the mystic to gain knowledge of being.[12]

We can use Imagination to orient us to reality. Corbin writes, "This imagination does not construct something unreal, but unveils the hidden reality." It is through Imagination that we can think the way that God thinks. Imagination is the "principle and source of all the universes," and it "connects all the individuals who are in the universes."[13] This is an amazing statement. We have a function available to us is that is the same function that God uses to create the universe. To move to the place of Imagination is not just to witness creation, but to become the creation of creation. To enter the *'alam al-mithāl* through Imagination is *becoming medicine* because one becomes that which heals and creates.

The place of interconnection is not the mind, but rather the heart and it is through an orientation of the heart that one connects to the divine in one's self, the divine in all beings and the ultimate Oneness of the Divine.

---

11 Henry Corbin, *Alone With the Alone*, 33.

12 Ibid., 187.

13 Corbin, *Spiritual Body and Celestial Earth*, 12, 152.

'ALAM AL-MITHAL

This is consistent with what Joseph Rael teaches that we must go into the heart of the medicine wheel in order to become visionaries. Corbin writes that the "Imaginative Forms belong precisely to what is secretly contained in the heart."

> The human heart, because it recapitulates all the forms of the epiphanic function, possess hundreds, even hundreds of thousands of Orients and still more, and all the stars which are the divine Names rise and shine through all these Orients. But opposite each one there is also an Occident. How wondrous and strange the human heart, which no one can see, save the pilgrims of the spirit, who are the pure in heart.[14]

Joseph Rael and I wrote about the vital function of orientation that the

14 Ibid., 212, 163.

medicine wheel provides when we become lost, as we inevitably do, and as we must do in the process of continual initiation. Corbin's description of the correspondence between each Orient of the Imagination with an Occident can be seen as parallel to Joseph Rael's descriptions of the correspondence between the structures and beings of ordinary reality with the structures and beings of non-ordinary reality. Corbin describes what the sage Suhrawardī means by the Orient: that it is both the geographical East as well as Orientation to the beings of Light.[15] Orientation is a vital function of visions, it helps us to orient on the inner and outer medicine wheels and also to orient in the direction of God, *Wah-Mah-Chi*.

Corbin sought to re-spiritualize philosophy and to bring the Imagination to the center of what it means to be a human being. He described the pursuit of philosophy as a spiritual journey, a journey that never ends.

> To be a philosopher is to take to the road, never settling down in some place of satisfaction with a theory of the world, not even a place of reformation, nor of some illusory transformation of the conditions of this world. It aims for self-transformation, for the inner metamorphosis, which is implied by the notion of a new, or spiritual rebirth (*wiladat ruhaniya*). The adventure of the mystical philosopher is essentially seen as a voyage which progresses towards the Light (*sayr*).[16]

Corbin's work on the creative function of Imagination literally opens new realms for us to explore while also providing a theoretical structure for the correspondence between what Joseph Rael calls ordinary and non-ordinary reality. He tells us that reality is continually being created through the revelation of the divine (theophany) and that the place of this revelation is in the hearts of individual human beings. Visions orient us to reality, rather than drawing us into fantasy. Just as with Black Elk, Carl Jung, or Joseph Rael, visions give us orientation for opening ourselves to be filled and guided with a living spirituality.

---

15 "In his [Suhrawardī's] doctrine, the word 'Orient' takes on a technical meaning. In the literal sense, it is at one and the same time the geographic East, or, more precisely, the world of Iran and the hour when the horizon is lighted by the fires of dawn. In the true sense—that is to say, in the spiritual sense—the Orient is the world of the beings of Light, from which the dawn of knowledge and ecstasy rises in the pilgrim of the spirit." Ibid., 110.

16 Henry Corbin, *The Voyage and the Messenger: Iran and Philosophy*, 140.

VISIONARY REALITY

Many scientists say that we have let go of our irrational views of reality and now we are fully grounded in material "reality," only believing that what can be seen and touched is real. However, other scientists, particularly quantum physicists are saying that "matter" may not be as solid and real as we think it is. They say that light does not just have one nature, it can be both a particle (a bit of matter) or it can be a wave (flowing energy). Physicist David Bohm wrote, "matter . . . is condensed or frozen light."[17]

Scientists and materialists draw a sharp distinction between imagination and material reality. Descartes is often credited or blamed for popularizing mind/body dualism by separating out the thinking mind from the material body and world. However even Descartes reductionism was inspired by a vision of an angel:

> When he was a young soldier in the Hapsburg army, Descartes had a vision in which an angel appeared to him and revealed that "Nature can be conquered by measurement." Thus began his quest to prove the angel right, the outcome of which is that man and nature can be measured, dissected, and probed, which is where mainstream science still largely stands.[18]

A materialist might say that a vision is at best, "fantasy" and at worst a "hallucination" a symptom of mental illness. Either way, a materialist would say that a vision is not real. That is the perspective from ordinary reality. However, a visionary might say that a vision is the experience of consciousness expanding beyond ordinary reality into non-ordinary reality and then bringing back a vision into ordinary reality.

Perhaps that is what visions are—a different experience of reality—an experience that scientific materialism has turned its back on. Just as it is possible to train to be a scientist and study ordinary reality it is possible to train to be a visionary and to experience non-ordinary reality. This is in fact what Joseph teaches.

---

17 Bohm, *The Essential David Bohm*, Lee Nichol (ed.), 152.

18 Ross Heaven, *The Way of the Lover: Sufism, Shamanism and the Spiritual Art of Love*, 40. I had never heard of Descartes' vision before, but an internet search reveals multiple references to this incident.

BECOMING A VISIONARY

We all have the capacity to become visionaries. Some visions arise spontaneously, others can be invited through making one's self capable of becoming a visionary. We become visionaries when ordinary reality breaks down and non-ordinary reality breaks in. Trauma, prolonged physical or emotional stress, sustained attention/intention, and ceremony are all ways that we can be opened to visions. Joseph often talks about fasting, lowering salt and sugar levels, prolonged dancing, going into darkness, and doing ceremony as ways of inviting a vision.

> Ceremony is the way to do this. It gives us these powers. Ceremony works because it is crying for a vision. By crying for a vision, I mean that the soul is longing for light, so it can drink it in and thus fulfill its nature. If light—vision—is lacking, there is sadness.[19]

Relaxing our minds, opening our hearts, softening our gaze, seeking a break in the ordinary routine—these are things that orient us to non-ordinary reality, to visionary reality. Visions are like allowing your eyes to see life as a flowing poem that is constantly being written and has multiple levels of depth and meaning. Paying attention to our dreams is another way to enter into visionary reality. Visions are like waking dreams, like visual poetry. Joseph will often say, "*I saw this in an early morning vision or dream*," illustrating that there is not a clear distinction between dream states and visionary states. Visions are not things you create or force, rather, *crying for a vision* opens one up like a hollow bone and then the *Wah-Mah-Chi* flows through. Learning to be less linear, to be open to circle medicine, to go into meditation in the center of the medicine wheel and allow visionary possibility to orient me is what Joseph has been teaching me. One of the ways of becoming a visionary is to listen with an open heart and an open mind to visionaries talking about their visions.

Joseph walks us through the process of receiving the calling of a vision and voice and then the work of allowing the meaning of the vision to grow through him as a reality in the world. In the early 1980s Joseph was working in Santa Fe and he saw a vision of a map appear on the wall.

> The map appeared and on it I was simultaneously shown perhaps ten or fifteen different scenarios playing out simultaneously. I absorbed the meaning of all of them in depth through one flash of light,

---

19 *Ceremonies*, 87.

AT VISION QUEST VISITING WITH DANDELION

replete with information. The map was radiating its own beingness from the problems in this Indian and non-Indian world.

Each scene on the map was also a representation of an idea, and all of those ideas were flowing into me as I looked at the map. In a sense, I became the map, the ideas. The scenarios were awakening in me images of what I was going to do for the next five or ten years.

> But I received so many scenarios for my life from the map in that single instant that now I had a new problem. I needed to isolate them and figure out what was supposed to happen next. The best way I knew to do this was through walking or through dancing.
>
> So I began to walk. I walked from Albuquerque all the way to northern New Mexico, which is about eighty miles. I walked but I didn't get any images; I just got really tired. Only after the long walk was finished and I went on about my business, over a period of the next nine months, was I given the insights I'd been seeking, in the form of images.[20]

Joseph explains that work must be done after one receives a vision. To understand the calling, he has to prepare the soil for the vision to sprout and grow into what it is meant to become. He recommends walking and dancing. These are ways that we prepare the soil, like kneading bread, so that it will rise and grow. *Nah meh neh* means the soil of the earth and *nah* means self, the individual. Thus when we need to work on ourselves, we must turn to the earth and work the earth. This is the principle that the microcosm and macrocosm are images of each other and are interconnected. What we do to the earth we do to ourselves and what we do to ourselves we do to the earth. Joseph noticed when he was a boy that the Tiwa word for walking (*taa*) also appeared in the word for plowing. *Taa chi who* means a person is walking. *Taa* also means "plow." Joseph writes "walking, is plowing just like I was plowing with the team of horses, plowing the ground and turning the soil over, preparing it for the seed to be planted. By walking you're plowing your field, making your inner soil ready for new seeds to be planted."[21] In addition to walking on the earth, Joseph also started sun dancing on the earth.

The way to *becoming medicine* is through visionary reality. Visionary reality is what Joseph calls "non-ordinary reality." He describes ordinary reality as that which we see all around us. You could say it is what is given to us. Visionary or non-ordinary reality is not given to us, but it is still present—veiled from us, below the surface, sustaining us, and even creating us. Maybe visionary/non-ordinary reality is the 96% of the universe that we cannot see and measure, what the physicists are now seeking to understand—dark energy and dark matter. If ordinary reality is given to us, then we can say that it is necessary to seek non-ordinary reality.

20 *House*, 107.

21 Ibid., 108.

We must become seekers, ever seeking to glimpse, to grasp that reality which is beyond our five material senses. By working with Joseph, I am not just learning about another cultural view from him, I am acculturating to that view, so that I can learn to see reality (or non-ordinary reality) in a new way, and not just see it, but experience it.

CARL JUNG AND VISIONS OF ACTIVE IMAGINATION

Carl Jung was a psychiatrist who saw visions and these visions shaped his later theoretical and therapeutic work. Many of these are found in his *Red Book*, published in 2009, long after his death. Some mental health professionals thought he was hallucinating and maybe schizophrenic. Some people thought he was an artist or a mystic. Jung rejected all these claims. Instead he said he was a scientist exploring the unconscious. He came upon a practice for becoming a visionary he called "active imagination." You may notice that both Jung and Corbin came upon "imagination" as a term to describe visionary reality. Jung's *active imagination* is a method of clearing the mind of the ego and allowing images and visions to arise. He said that this is how you begin a dialogue with your personal unconscious and you can go deeper into dialogue and relation with the collective unconscious that all humans share and maybe even deeper into dialogue with the *anima mundi* or the soul of the world. For Jung, active imagination was a way of becoming capable of dialogue with the deeper levels of the self. He said that unlike the rational mind of the ego, the unconscious communicated in symbols, images, and archetypes. He describes a period of time at mid-life where he felt pulled into deeper dialogue with the unconscious and he felt that this provided a re-orientation for him in his life, after he worked through about eight years of crisis.

JUNG'S VISIONARY ENCOUNTER WITH THE UNCONSCIOUS

Jung's sustained visionary crisis started in 1912 and 1913 when he was about 36 years old. This was after his break with his mentor, Sigmund Freud over whether spiritual experiences were pathological or whether they could be part of a larger intelligence seeking to enlighten us and to spur personal growth. Jung came to call this path *individuation*, by which he meant that an individual moves from the limitations of a separate ego to a state of greater wholeness, which he called "the self." Jung developed the theory that human beings are naturally externally-oriented during the first half of their lives and then at mid-life there is a shift from external to internal (spiritual) orientation. This shift causes a crisis as the person's sense of self shifts from the material to the spiritual. Jung is often credited as one of the first writers to consider the concept of the "mid-life crisis" although he did not coin the term.

> Among all my patients in the second half of life . . . there has not been one whose problem in the last resort was not that of finding a religious outlook on life. It is safe to say that every one of them fell ill because he had lost that which the living religions of every age have given to their followers, and none of them has been really healed who did not regain his religious outlook.[22]

VOCATION

We think of vocation as a job that we *choose* to do. However, the root of the word vocation originally meant to be called by a voice—a vocation is a vision that comes in the form of a voice that calls you and asks something of you. A famous example of such a vocational calling is when thirteen year old Joan of Arc saw a vision of the Archangel Michael, Saint Catherine, and Saint Margaret who appeared and told her to drive the English out of France.

> vocation (n.)
> early 15c., "spiritual calling," from Old French *vocacion* "call, consecration; calling, profession" (13c.) or directly from Latin *vocationem* . . . literally "a calling, a being called." . . . Sense of "one's occupation or profession" is first attested 1550s.[23]

Carl Jung personally experienced this sense of vocation and calling. He had his own visionary experiences in his life and detailed these in his secret journal, *The Red Book*. Jung saw himself as a scientist of the unconscious and denied being a mystic. However, after publication of *The Red Book*, we can consider him a visionary and mystic. We do not need to look at this as an either/or. It is possible to be both a scientist and a mystic, as Peter Kingsley has pointed out.[24] In fact, the calling of many scientists has come through visionary insight or inspiration, such as Kekulé's dream that led to the discovery of the structure of the benzene ring or Descartes visitation by

22 Jung, *MMSS*, 229.

23 "Vocation," *Online Etymology Dictionary*.

24 Peter Kingsley, *Catafalque*, 207.

an angel that led to his project of *conquering nature*. Jung's understanding of vocation involves being called by a visionary voice.

> It is what is commonly called vocation: an irrational factor that destines a man to emancipate himself from the herd and from its well-worn paths. True personality is always a vocation and puts its trust in it as God, despite its being, as the ordinary man would say, only a personal feeling. But vocation acts like a law of God from which there is no escape. . . . Anyone with a vocation hears the voice of the inner man: he is *called*. . . . The original meaning of "to have a vocation" is "to be addressed by a voice."[25]

Jung believed that everyone has a voice within themselves that calls, but most people do not listen to the inner voice. The inner work led into the outer world through heeding the call.

Joseph Campbell speaks of "the call to adventure" in the hero's journey. The vocation, the call, pulls the individual out of his or her sheltered and safe world into the high seas of adventure. The individual becomes a conduit by allowing him- or herself to be taken over by a higher idea and a higher principle and purpose. For Jung, vocation is not chosen, rather it is something that one is chosen by. Jung often moved back and forth between talking in spiritual/religious terms (a calling coming from God) and psychological terms (calling as the voice of an archetype of the collective unconscious calling the individual to take the journey of individuation). Either way, Jung believed that when we quiet the ordinary mind of our ego, we open into vast spaces which are populated by other intelligences whom we can interact with and who seek to advise and guide us on the journey of inner growth and the journey of outer calling.

Henry Corbin wrote that a person's capacity for spiritual experience "depends on the degree to which man renders himself 'capable of God,' for it is this capacity which defines and measures the sympathy as the necessary medium of all religious experience."[26] The work of the individual is to prepare the soil of the self, to get the ego out of the way, and to allow God to manifest within. To become more capable of God means becoming better able to clearly hear one's calling and vocation.

All visionaries probably worry about whether their visions are real and how to explain them to others. Carl Jung, like Joseph Rael, and Henry

25 Jung, *The Development of the Personality*, CW 17, 175–76.

26 Henry Corbin, *Alone With the Alone*, 111.

Corbin, sought to teach us that there is a reality that is beyond the material reality of our ego's sensory perceptions—a visionary reality. Jung explains the reality of what occurs in the psyche:

> It is a very different thing when the psyche, as an objective fact, hard as granite and heavy as lead, confronts a man as an inner experience and addresses him in an audible voice, saying, "This is what will and must be." Then he feels himself called, just as the group does when there's a war on, or a revolution, or any other madness. . . .
>
> But what has the individual personality to do with the plight of the many? In the first place he is part of the people as a whole, and is as much at the mercy of the power that moves the whole as anybody else. The only thing that distinguishes him from all the others is his vocation. He has been called by that all-powerful, all-tyrannizing psychic necessity that is his own and his people's affliction. If he harkens to the voice, he is at once set apart and isolated, as he has resolved to obey the law that commands him from within. . . .
>
> But he knows better: it is the law, the vocation for which he is destined, no more "his own" than the lion that fells him, although it is undoubtedly this particular lion that kills him and not any other lion. Only in this sense is he entitled to speak of "his" vocation, "his" law.[27]

Jung's comment of being killed by a lion is pertinent to walking the visionary path. The Sufis that Corbin studied often say "die before you die," meaning that the ego must die in order for the visionary reality to be born. Corbin clarifies, "what is meant is to die in spirit, to die a voluntary death. It means to get there while remaining in this world. . . . 'Know how to die before you are dead.'"[28] The ego becomes the soil and *Wah-Mah-Chi* becomes the seed that grows in the rich soil after the ego dies. Until the ego dies, it is directing things and will not allow the seed of Breath-Matter-Movement to germinate. When the ego hears the voice of calling and has faith to surrender to it, then the word of God is born and grows in the individual.

Joseph Rael had many visionary callings that led to his vocation. His vision of the Sound/Peace Chambers took him around the world, meeting many different people from many different lands and eventually led to chambers being built in North & South America, Europe, and Australia.

27 Jung, *The Development of the Personality*, CW 17, 177–78.

28 Corbin, *Spiritual Body, Celestial Earth*, 265.

PUUH-TEA BRINGER OF NEW KNOWLEDGE

From the sun dancing came the vision for the peace chambers, and other visions as well. When I had a vision, that vision also gave me directives. "So, here you are now, this is what you have to do next."

In my visions, I was directed to take my knowing, my medicine, to the outer world, beyond the Indians. I was told, "Don't talk to Indians any more. You've done that since you were eighteen years old. Now you're forty-five. The non-Indian people need this information because they're the ones who are going to save the Indians. Until they know what's going on, not only with the Indians, but also with themselves, the non-Indian population won't be able to help themselves or the Indians. Until then the Indians are going to be doing things by themselves and the non-Indians are going to be doing things by themselves, and not realizing that the cumulative energy of everything they're both doing is affecting all of us globally."

I knew we couldn't work that way any longer.[29]

Joseph mentions the calling for him to take his *knowing* out into the world. He calls this knowing his *medicine*. Medicine is the knowledge that the vision imparts. This is what we are talking about in this book. Medicine is what comes from the visionary world. It is the seed of the Spirit that is planted in the *nah*, the earth of ourselves. *Becoming medicine* means listening to the voice of the calling and preparing a place for the seed of the vision to take root in us. At that point we actually become medicine and Spirit uses us as a delivery vehicle to inject the medicine into the larger world.

Joseph often stresses that he is not teaching secrets of the Picuris Pueblo or Southern Ute tribes. He is teaching from his own visions and these visions direct him to do different things in the world. He describes how at mid-life he was instructed to turn from teaching in the Indian world to teaching in the non-Indian world. This movement took him all over the world to Europe, Australia, New Zealand, and South America. And now he has come full circle, living on the Southern Ute reservation for many years. The vision is a calling and it directs the receiver of the vision into particular action in the world.

The map directed me from the Age of Reason to the Age of the Heart. It was now time for the Indians to show the non-Indians how to think through the heart and not through the mind. . . .

I have learned over the years that I should always follow whatever happens from the place of the unexpected. From the place of the unexpected, Spirit talks to me. I cannot ignore the thing that comes through from left field. When it happens, I know it's right on, even though logically it shouldn't be happening. Sometimes I want to ignore it because my plan does not include this unexpected thing.

All of a sudden something happens and I'm going off in an unexpected direction, but I know there's a reason for it. I know there's a

29 *House*, 108–09.

> blessing there. The blessing will unfold as the week goes by, or within the next month, because that is the way it is with the unexpected.[30]

Carl G. Jung's visionary experiences were unexpected and made him question the reality he had believed in up to that point. Ultimately, he could not determine if what he was experiencing was real or not, at least in the way that most people think of reality. Jung referred to the concept of the "psychoid" as a state of being where matter and spirit met. This concept was particularly relevant in his work on synchronicity with physicist Wolfgang Pauli. Jeffrey Raff, a Jungian therapist, further elaborated on this concept. He writes, "when the body becomes spirit and spirit becomes body, we enter a new realm of experience that I call *psychoid*."[31] Raff developed what he calls "psychoidal alchemy," describing reality as a Unity "that we may call . . . God, the *prima materia*, or many other terms." Raff writes that this unity can also split into other psychoidal figures whom we can seek to interact with through the psychoid world.

> They belong to another dimension of reality, which is neither purely physical nor purely psychic, but a mixture of the two. They live in an imaginal reality between the world of spirit and the ordinary world. The imagination with which we perceive and work with psychoidal beings is not the usual imagination but a special one that the Sufis call the "Gnostic imagination."[32]

SPIRIT GUIDES AND SPIRITUAL BEINGS

Corbin and Jung describe coming into relationship with spirit guides as part of becoming a visionary. Joseph Rael describes various beings he encounters, for instance he has had visions of the Madonna after he was in a gas explosion. In his visions Joseph is always meeting and interacting with different spiritual beings and he has his own spirit guides and animal totems.

My first visit with Joseph he had me drive around with him in a big circle, stopping at various places where he had visionary experiences. We stopped by a house and Joseph told me about a gas explosion that had happened there. Both of Joseph's knees were bent back and he was blown out into the yard. The family dog was running around with his tail on fire.

---

30 *House*, 115–16.

31 Jeffrey Raff, *Jung and the Alchemical Imagination*, 28.

32 Jeffrey Raff, *The Wedding of Sophia*, xii.

Joseph had a vision of the Holy Mother who looked down at him and said, "You are going to be all right." He had another vision of the Madonna when he was at an AA meeting and he made a painting, called "Awakening at an AA Meeting" which we included in *Walking the Medicine Wheel.* He has gone on visionary journeys with the shaman Jesus and had visitations by his own father who gave him an obsidian spear point. Joseph has told me about a vision of his spirit animal, Badger, who got into a tussle with a Jaguar spirit animal of another shaman. One of the visionary initiations that Joseph has taught me is to sit in the center of the medicine wheel and to cry for a vision and watch for spirit guides who will enter the circle for spiritual work and journeys. In these visionary states I've seen Crow and had journeys through the darkness of the cosmos and I've seen visions of my body going through various stages of dissolution and rebirth, sometimes even eaten by various animals and then reborn. These would have been disturbing if I had not read so many accounts of visionaries and shamans who go through visionary death and rebirth on the spiritual path.[33] Becoming a visionary involves opening up to encounters with spirits, animals, and ancestors.

ALLY WORK

Jungian therapist Jeffrey Raff writes that each of us has our own spirit guide who is our partner in life. He uses the term "ally" to represent what has historically been called a guardian angel or back to Socrates, a *daemon*, an "inner," spiritual being who gives us advice and information. Raff writes, "There are many reasons to make the quest into the imagination, yet the one I found most compelling was to find my divine partner, twin of my soul, whom I have called 'the ally.' An ally is a divine being, a face of God that is unique to each human being."

Raff's spirit guide was *Sophia* and she came to him in a vision. Sophia is a divine feminine figure who appears in Hebrew, Christian, Gnostic, Islamic, and alchemical traditions. She is often said to represent Divine Wisdom and sometimes is said to have been there with God before creation. Raff described this encounter in his book:

> A few years ago I awoke in the middle of the night to discover a being of transcendent beauty, surrounded by bright light, sitting on

33 Mircea Eliade's *Shamanism* and Holger Kalweit's *Shamans, Healers, and Medicine Men* abound with these type of descriptions.

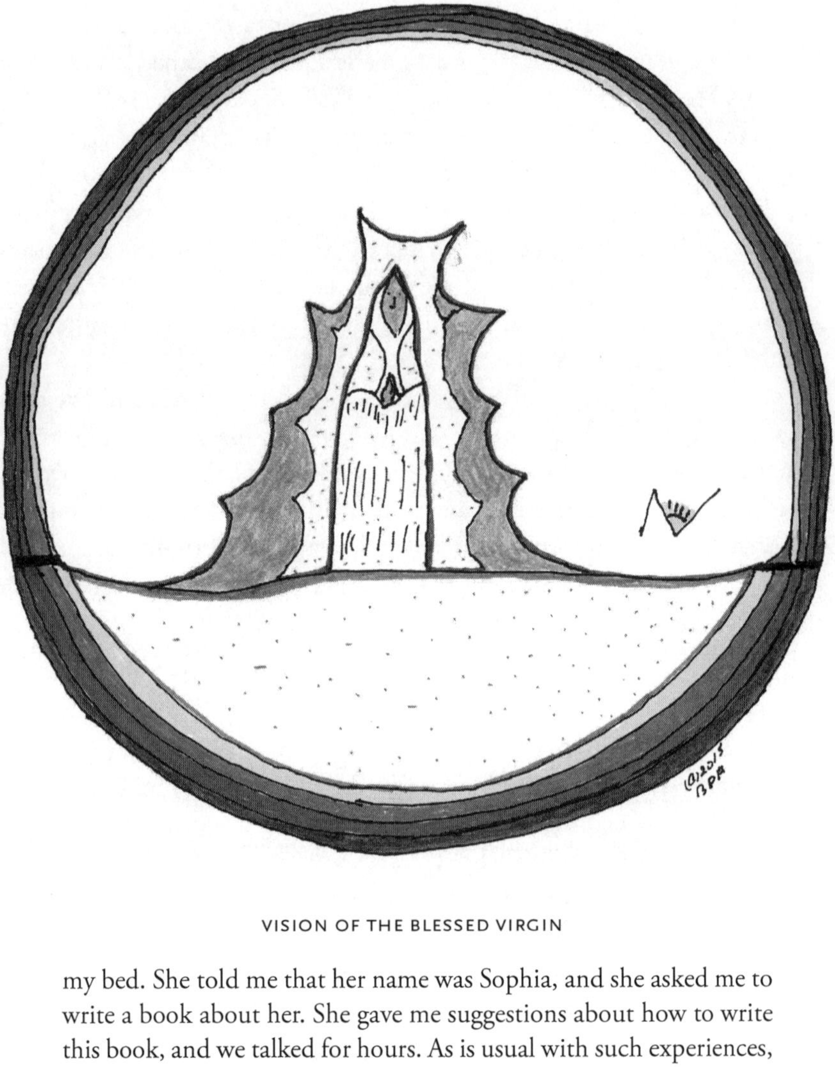

VISION OF THE BLESSED VIRGIN

my bed. She told me that her name was Sophia, and she asked me to write a book about her. She gave me suggestions about how to write this book, and we talked for hours. As is usual with such experiences, I could never recall all that she had told me, because I was in an altered state of consciousness and in another reality; the reality of imagination. But I did remember her request to write this book, and the last thing she said to me. She asked me to show people that she was real, and that all beings of the imagination are real.[34]

34 Jeffrey Raff, *The Practice of Ally Work: Meeting and Partnering with Your Spirit Guide in the Imaginal World*, 3–5, xi.

SOLOVYOV'S VISIONS OF SOPHIA

Vladimir Solovyov (19th Century Russian philosopher, theologian, mystic, and poet) also had visions and dialogues with Sophia. Solovyov's visionary meetings with Sophia taught him that she functions by "transfiguring matter and embodying the divine."[35] While Sophia teaches many things to Solovyov in her dialogues with him, her beauty and presence is transformative in and of itself. She teaches him that "Spirit and Matter are not absolutely different entities, separated and opposed, but different sides or poles . . . of the same substance."[36] Judith Kornblatt, who translated Solovyov into English, summarizes Solovyov's views on the nature and function of Sophia.

> Sophia brings heaven to earth and in the interaction of the opposites creates a new whole: a poetic, often joyful, light-infused creation. She is the mediator and the element that causes us to see reality from more than one perspective at once . . . she is a tension, the energy that binds and transforms through the binding itself. She alters reality, making it better, truer, and more beautiful. With her interaction, spirit is incarnated and matter divinized. She can have many names, faces, and functions, because she, who is the "true reason for creation and its goal" . . . is no one thing. Sophia not only links but fully participates in two opposites and in the new creation their relationship produces."[37]

IBN 'ARABĪ, NIẒĀM, AND SOPHIA AETERNA

Henry Corbin's book, *Alone with the Alone*, focuses on the visionary journeys of 12th century mystic and visionary Ibn 'Arabī and his visible and invisible teachers. A decisive encounter occurred for Ibn 'Arabī when he met the young woman, Niẓām, who combined "extraordinary physical beauty with great spiritual wisdom." Corbin writes that she served a similar role for Ibn 'Arabī as Beatrice served for Dante, the inspiration of the divine feminine: "she was and remained for him the earthly manifestation,

35 Judith Deutsch Kornblatt, *Divine Sophia: The Wisdom Writings of Vladimir Solovyov*, 3, 91, Kornblatt's summary of Solovyov. Solovyov influenced the generation of spiritual intellectuals that included Tolstoy and Dostoyevsky, who both attended his 1878 *Lectures on Divine Humanity*.

36 Ibid., 133. Solovyov's words.

37 Ibid., 94. This paragraph is Kornblatt's description, with only "true reason for creation and its goal" being Solovyov's words.

the theophanic figure, of *Sophia aeterna*." Corbin continues, "It was to her that he owed his initiation into the *Fedeli d'amore*."[38] This group, the *Fedeli d'amore*, was, historically, a secret group of Dante's companions, but also allows us to understand how love for a person can be at the same time the love of God. To put it another way, it explains the way that a person can embody the divine for another person. This helps us to understand Rumi and Shams, for instance. Corbin describes that Beatrice for Dante, as well as Niẓām for Ibn ʿArabī, are both, simultaneously, a real woman as well as "a theophanic figure, the figure of *Sophia aeterna*. . . . If we fail to grasp this twofold dimension simultaneously, we lose the reality both of the person and of the symbol."

The idea of a "theophanic person" is a revelation of God through a living human being. In this situation there is a break-through of the divine into the human realm and in this way the encounter is an initiation that brings us into the center of the world, the center of the medicine wheel, and brings us back to the Garden. "An encounter with theophanic persons always postulates a return to the 'center of the world,' because communication with the *'alam al-mithāl* is possible only at the 'center of the world.'" There is a confluence of a human person, the divine feminine, and the center of the world. *Sophia*, from Greek, means "wisdom," and here we are encountering ancient wisdom in the form of the Divine Goddess embodied within a living person. Corbin writes that this combines the aspects of Divine Beauty with Divine Compassion.

> This encounter with the mystic Sophia prefigures the goal to which the dialectic of love will lead us: the idea of the feminine being (of which Sophia is the archetype) as the theophany par excellence, which, however, is perceptible only through the sympathy between the celestial and the terrestrial. . . . This conjunction between Beauty and Compassion is the secret of Creation—for if divine "sympathy" is creative, it is because the Divine Being wishes to reveal His Beauty, and if Beauty is redeeming, it is because it manifests this creative Compassion.[39]

Through Jeffery Raff, Vladimir Solovyov, and Ibn ʿArabī we have three encounters and conversations with Sophia, Divine Wisdom. This teaches us that it is possible to have encounters with the sacred through the

38 Corbin, *Alone with the Alone*, 52.

39 Ibid., 100, 53, 145.

confluence of the human and divine. Many religious traditions tell us that it is possible to have a conversation with God, through learning to hear the Word of God and to listen to the Wisdom of God.

MY CONVERSATION WITH IS (11/11/88)

On November 11th, 1988, I was 21 years old and I was in my senior year at university. A few nights earlier, while I was working on a paper on Carl Jung, I clearly heard a voice say, "They're waiting." Nothing more, just "They're waiting." Then, some days later, I had another similar experience that started off with the voice saying something. I called the voice the "IS,"[40] influenced by how Richard Bach speaks about God in his book, *Illusions*. I asked the IS a few questions such as, "Can other people truly be helped and how can I help them? or in other words, if I live my life according to the Tao, or the Dharma, or the Lord, will others truly benefit from it, or am I to live the Way for its own sake?"

The answer came, "Follow yourself, the way lies within you. If you yourself are correct, your influence will be as a rock dropped from a great height into the ocean, waves will reverberate out, and likewise you will be washed over by the waves of those around you." A very prototypical Chinese answer, I thought; focus on yourself and the world will fall into accord. Well, the world already is in accord, as the IS said, "Everything in the world is for a purpose, although it falters...and does not seem to be."

I then asked, "Should I follow love or should I follow another path?" I was thinking about my future life and wondering about different paths of relationship and service. The IS said, "Follow your heart, your insides know best. Love is giving yourself up for the greater good. It is a sacrifice in which you get caught up and swept away, down to the sea. Love is what you are, how can you be otherwise?"

Then the question dawned on me: what is it that "*They're waiting*" for?

"For you."

"What do you mean, O IS, for me?"

"They (the people and the cosmos) are waiting for you to reconcile the world to them. Give them the knowledge of relativity, give them the knowledge of the absolute. Let them enjoy the roles they play. Let them

---

40 Matthew Fox, in his *Meditations with Meister Eckhart*, page 12 describes how Meister Eckhart also spoke of God as "Isness" in the 13th to 14th Centuries.

> "For you ask me: Who is God? What is God?
> I reply: Isness.
> Isness is God."

live out their purpose, to be amazed at the life around them and amazed even more that all of it *means* nothing. The only purpose of life is to live, nothing more. The rest is up to you."

In my journal I wrote, "The IS voice appeared in my mind. It spoke using my words, my vocabulary. It sounded like some of Richard Bach's language, but it felt almost like me, almost, but not quite. I think there is a difference between the quality of daydreaming or thinking about something and the experience of thoughts appearing in mind, or, to put it another way, there is a difference between thinking and being thought through. It could very well be my inner self speaking, but there really is no difference. Was it me "pretending" to be the IS, or was it the IS pretending to be me? This reminded me of Chuang Tzu's "Transformation of Things."[41] The Taoist sage Chuang Tzu had a dream about being a butterfly and then when he awoke he thought about himself as a human who had a dream about a being a butterfly, but then his consciousness takes a leap and he wonders how he would know if he was a human dreaming about being a butterfly or a butterfly dreaming about being a human who had a dream about being a butterfly. He points to the dilemma of consciousness that we can only know what we experience without knowing the Absolute nature of that experience. He comments that this dilemma is the "transformation of things."

This dilemma of consciousness and objective reality is an age-old conflict that all people who have visionary experiences must grapple with at some point. Science fiction writer Philip K. Dick filled up over a thousand pages of his secret journal, *The Exegesis*. Like Jung's *Red Book*, it was only published after his death. Phil Dick comes to absolute conclusion after absolute conclusion about the nature of his visionary experiences, only to discard it the next day and come to a different conclusion. One conclusion he comes to is that what he is experiencing might be partly him, his own thoughts, but "it was not all me." One day in 1980, Philip K. Dick had a conversation with God.

> God manifested himself to me as the infinite void. . . . He said, "I am the infinite. I will show you. Where I am, infinity is, where infinity is, there I am. Construct lines of reasoning by which to understand your experience in 1974. I will enter the field against their shifting nature. You think they are logical but they are not; they are infinitely creative."

41 *Chuang Tzu: Basic Writings*, trans. Burton Watson, 45.

> I thought a thought and then an infinite regression of theses and countertheses came into being. God said, "Here I am; here is infinity." I thought another explanation; again an infinite series of thoughts split off in dialectical antithetical interaction. God said, "Here is infinity; here I am." . . . I tried for an infinite number of times; each time an infinite regress was set off and each time God said, "Infinity. Hence I am here." Then he said, "Every thought leads to infinity, does it not? . . . I am everywhere and all roads lead to me. . . . You are not the doubter; you are the doubt itself. So do not try to know what you cannot know."
>
> I said, "Probably it is you, since there is an infinity of infinities forming before me."
>
> "There is the answer, the only one you will ever have," God said.[42]

How does one know if one is being what Joseph calls "a hollow bone" and being a conduit for visionary experience versus "fantasizing," "making things up," being "deluded," or worse, "psychotic." Philip K. Dick gives one answer, and yet he continued to doubt through the 895 pages of his published *Exegesis* (which is only a portion of what he wrote) spinning out into infinity and back. There is a danger that a person imagines Spirit is telling them something true when in reality it is his or her ego fantasizing. Jung often cautioned about being "possessed" by the Shadow, our dark archetype in the unconscious. Many of the worst human atrocities have been committed with the certainty that God's will is being carried out. The work of the visionary is in trying to get out of the way and become the soil that the vision takes root in without distorting or influencing it. There is still a role for the ego, to be strong enough to discriminate between visionary experience and fantasy. The experience I had felt real, it felt "other" than me, but it also felt like it was coming through me. Obviously it was using my vocabulary, picking up on the word "IS," for "God." As I pondered this experience after it happened in 1988, I came across a quote from Carl Jung that I felt was important in regards to whether or not the voice was "real."

---

42 Philip K. Dick, *The Exegesis of Philip K. Dick*, 582, 639–40. Dick describes the amount of work he put into trying to sort out the reality of his visionary experiences:

> "In my six and a half years of working on my exegesis I have often said, 'I have found it.' I don't want to do that one more time, one in an endless series of failure. It seems to me almost as if the mere saying of it causes it to permutate to some other explanation. . . . I have been relentlessly skeptical and relentlessly imaginative and I have done enormous research and tried out as many possible theories as I could come up with," (610).

> What is a valid experience? For instance, if a dog bites me, is that a valid experience? It is an experience; and if I have a religious experience, well that is an experience too, and how shall I say that it is valid? You might say, "Oh, you have an imagination, you have an illusion; you think that you had a religious experience." Well, that does not concern me. Perhaps it is an illusion; how do I know? There is no criterion. I can only say, "I felt like this." Of course, you can draw conclusions, and so you can ask, "Are the conclusions you draw from it valid?" . . . Is that valid? Is that interpretation valid? . . . [T]here is a considerable difference in the interpretation of such experiences, but the experiences themselves are always valid because they exist.[43]

Perhaps more important than asking "Is it real," is asking "What does it mean?" This leads to the tradition going back to ancient times of interpreting visions and dreams. Now, almost 30 years after this calling, I remembered this experience as I was working on this book. My conversation with the IS has not been something I have consciously remembered through many of the intervening years. In re-reading about this calling, I am struck by the first question that I chose to ask "Can other people truly be helped and how can I help them? Or in other words, if I live my life according to the Tao, or the Dharma, or the Lord, will others truly benefit from it, or am I to live the Way for its own sake?" This question shows a focus on inner work as well as outer work. The question I first asked was about helping others and that seems appropriate as far as a vision inspiring a life of service as a healer. Perhaps this calling has been there transmitting all throughout my life, guiding my decisions and choices, whether I was conscious of it or not.

VISIONS FOR HEALING

Joseph often points out that it is not he who does the healing, it is the Spirit of Breath-Matter-Movement flowing through him. He cannot take credit for the work because he is just a hollow bone, instead he shrugs his shoulders and says, "I just work here."

> As soon as I get a vision, even today, I know if it's a directive asking me to do something. When that happens, I just do it. If I don't do it, I lose the power of insight. I go into a dark state of the soul where I

---

43 *Carl Jung Speaking*, 111.

> feel totally alone. A certain morbidity comes into my life, and I am not happy with myself. I get stuck.
>
> The first time this happened to me was when I was a child, after my mother died. I made a deal with Spirit: Please get me out of this depression, and I'll try to serve. *Naa-aah-uu-kwill* means to sink down into depression and then to rebound and find meaning in your life on the upswing. It was an agreement I made with myself. *Naa-yo-taah-wee-aah* means "I am my own creation." My creator self tells my action self to act.
>
> It seems as if the Universe always gives me something right around the time that it knows I'm ready to go to the next level. I don't necessarily have to like it, I just need to do it. Then comes the next thing I need to do when it's time for that thing to happen. That's how I work my life. It drives people crazy.[44]

Here Joseph is describing how to treat the state of separated, isolated depression that occurs when we lose the connection with the source of Spirit. At that point we are sick with the sickness of separation from *Wah-Mah-Chi*—the separation of breath from matter from movement. The treatment is to open our mouths so that we can be "drinking light energy from which comes vision."[45] Sickness is separation from source. Treatment is reconnecting with source. *Medicine* is the flowing of source into the vessel of the human, into the plowed and prepared field of our consciousness. When the medicine sprouts in the individual, then the individual becomes medicine and is called to go forth into the world in order to bring the medicine vision to others who are sick. A vision comes with a responsibility.

In the above quote, Joseph says that "*Naa-aah-uu-kwill* means to sink down into depression and then to rebound and find meaning in your life on the upswing." Joseph says "*Naa-yo-taah-wee-aah* means "I am my own creation." This is the mystical teaching of the visionary—that when we allow the visionary medicine seed to take root in ourselves as individuals we become medicine and we become creators and we take part in Creation. Joseph says that he strives to live this way, letting himself be led rather than striving to lead.

---

44 *House*, 109–10. Compare *naa-yo-taah-wee-aah* to what Joseph has taught me *na-yo ti-ay we-ah*, "I don't exist." With a slightly different emphasis this means "I am my own creation." It should be noted that as Tiwa is an oral rather than written language that Joseph sometimes gives different spellings of the same word.

45 *House*, 108.

> That's the way I live. I never know how the things I do are going to turn out. I just show up and do what I'm told. This energy follows me around, but I always know if I don't do what I'm told I will be unhappy. I used to tell my students, be sure that you follow your guidance because that guidance is in your higher interest. From that, other experiences will come to you that will enhance your growth.

In living holistically, Joseph became holism. "Without realizing it, I had become the very being of holism."[46] By living in a way of seeking medicine, he became medicine. We carry the sorrows and joys of this world in the four-chambered baskets of our hearts. We live in this world where we start in fullness and at some point we become empty, our hearts become empty and we are depressed and separated objects. At this point we need to go back to the river, back to the fountain, back to the garden, back to the source in non-ordinary reality. A vision appears as a rainbow bridge and we follow this bridge into non-ordinary reality and we are filled and replenished with abundance that we carry in the fullness of our hearts back into ordinary reality. Joseph describes that the vision of the map pointed out a journey that he followed from the head to the heart and from the heart out into the world.

While some people spontaneously have visions, it is possible to train one's self to be more capable of visionary experiences. Just as you can remember your dreams more if you remind yourself to remember your dreams and then write them down upon awakening, so too you can awaken your visionary capacity by paying attention to the visions that arise in the moments of quietness and emptiness that you find or create in your life. The opening up of visionary experience is one of the pathways of initiation into a living spirituality.

---

46 Ibid., 110–11, 114.

SHAMANIC VISION

CHAPTER 5

BECOMING A SHAMAN

We shall soon see that all the ecstatic experiences that determine the future shaman's vocation involve the traditional schema of an initiation ceremony: suffering, death, resurrection. . . .

The content of these first ecstatic experiences . . . almost always includes one or more of the following themes: dismemberment of the body, followed by a renewal of the internal organs and viscera; ascent to the sky and dialogue with the gods or spirits; descent to the underworld and conversations with spirits and souls of dead shamans; various revelations, both religious and shamanic (secrets of profession). . . .

Sometimes there is not exactly an illness but rather a progressive change in behavior. The candidate becomes meditative, seeks solitude, sleeps a great deal, seems absent-minded, has prophetic dreams. . . All these symptoms are only the prelude to the new life that awaits the unwitting candidate.[1]

MIRCEA ELIADE

Both shamans and analysts are wounded healers . . . [if] . . . they have a true vocation . . . analysts as well as shamans must find their way through many painful emotional trials to find the basis for their calling.[2]

DONALD SANDNER
AND STEVEN WONG

SHAMANISM

Shamanism is perhaps the most ancient spiritual practice. It is a way to journey from ordinary to non-ordinary consciousness.

I first read *Black Elk Speaks* in college and this piqued my curiosity about the indigenous visionary traditions of the Oglala Lakota Sioux. I was drawn to the land that was the place of Black Elk's visions, and, later in life, I ventured to Black Elk Peak in South Dakota. There has always been something very intuitive to me about connecting to nature and the ritual of shamanism. We have an inherent human drive to connect to the land where big things have happened. This drive lies behind thousands of years of spiritual pilgrimage.

I received a copy of Holger Kalweit's *Shamans, Healers, and Medicine Men* as a graduation present from medical school in 1993. I also received a backpack as a graduation gift. I went on a month-long journey across the United States by bus, spending 2 weeks solo backpacking in Olympic National Park, in the mountains and on the shore of the Pacific Ocean. Going into the wilderness alone is a different experience than going with other people. Going deeper into the outer wilderness alone brings one into deeper places of the inner wilderness.

Around the turn of the millennium, I read Mircea Eliade's tome *Shamanism: Archaic Techniques of Ecstasy*. It was around then that I went on a solo backpacking trip to Southern Illinois, to Shawnee National Forest. Eliade defines shamanism as a "technique of ecstasy" in which the

---

1 Mircea Eliade, *Shamanism: Archaic Techniques of Ecstasy*, 33–35.

2 Donald Sandner and Steven Wong, eds., *The Sacred Heritage: The Influence of Shamanism on Analytical Psychology*, 3–6.

shaman enters into "a trance during which his soul is believed to leave his body and ascend to the sky or descend to the underworld."[3] The shaman is chosen by life-threatening illness (and is often reported to have died and been reborn), or by lightning strike (the ultimate "enlightenment"), through training and apprenticeship, or through hereditary transmission of the "gift." I read Bradford Keeney's *Shaking Out the Spirits* and experimented for a while with what I came to call "crazy dancing." I would let go of ego control and I would let my body move and shake. Then I would lie down and meditate. I would often start off listening to the Meat Puppets song, "Flaming Heart" and just let myself go. Eventually I sprained a toe. That is a pretty suburban injury as far as experimenting with shamanism. Suffering, pain, illness, and even death, play a crucial role in shamanic transformation. From this perspective, suffering is not to be shunned, rather it is to be valued for its potential transformative power. Psychotherapist Holger Kalweit writes,

> An initiation into shamanic healing means a devaluation of all values, an overturning of the profane world, a peeling away of the inveterate handed-down notions of the world, liberation from everything preconceived. For that reason, shamanism is closely connected with suffering. One must suffer the disintegration of one's own system of thought in order to perceive a new world in the higher space.[4]

Shamans often go off into the wilderness alone, such as in the American Indian vision quest. A Native Alaskan shaman, Igjugarjuk, said, "The only true wisdom lives far from mankind, out in the great loneliness, and it can be reached only through suffering. Privation and suffering alone can open the mind of a man to all that is hidden to others."[5] I think the reason why I have taken a few solo back-packing trips has to do with this idea of going off into the wilderness alone.

The shaman's healing crisis is similar to the widespread rite of initiation, which we focus on in this book. This rite entails separation from the tribe, painful ordeals or body modifications, some form of symbolic death and rebirth, and then return to the community with a new identity. This also mirrors the hero's journey of separation, descent, trial/combat, winning the boon, and return to the community.

---

3 Eliade, *Shamanism*, 5.

4 Holger Kalweit, *Shamans, Healers, and Medicine Men*, 4.

5 Cited in Joseph Campbell, *Primitive Mythology*, 54.

After surviving and mastering the initial trials of illness and descent into darkness, the shaman gains the ability to voluntarily enter an ecstatic trance that can be transformative not only for the shaman, but also for his/her patient and community. Drumming, chanting, dancing, and music are often aides or vehicles to enter into such a trance state. In some cultures the drum is even called the shaman's "horse" or "canoe," because it is a vehicle for travel.[6]

While the outward manifestations of drumming, dancing, injury and shaking precipitate or are manifestations of the trance, inwardly the shaman has expansive experiences which may be recalled after the trance. He/she can visit the land of the dead, descend to hell, explore many heavenly layers of the sky, commune with animals, or transform into animal or supernatural shapes. The shaman can pursue the lost soul of a patient or remove various blockages, objects, or imbalances that are causing illness by disrupting the person's energetic field. A Native Alaskan account of the process of becoming a shaman is: "I searched in the darkness, I was silent in the great silence of the dark. That is how I became an angaqoq, through visions, dreams, and meetings with flying spirits."[7]

Shamanism is an ancient practice that is still alive in many indigenous traditions and many contemporary healers seek shamanic wisdom. Lewis Mehl-Madrona is a physician who is of Cherokee and Lakota heritage. He has been working to bridge contemporary medicine and the healing work of shamanism. Mehl-Madrona describes how many people today have lost their orientation and "suffer from a loss of meaning, or loss of world, or loss of self." He writes that the "shaman specializes in finding meaning by venturing outside its borders into chaos and meaninglessness." This separation from ordinary reality allows the shaman to tap into the healing energies of non-ordinary reality. Through becoming comfortable in chaos (which we could also call primal creative energy), the shaman can create new order, new meaning, and even new reality. "We need," writes Mehl-Madrona, "to . . . adopt the way of the shaman and create meaning out of nothing. When a shaman finds a psychiatric patient who has no world, who sees no meaning, she says, 'Well, Okay then, let's make up a new world for you. Let's create a world that you can enjoy.'"[8]

---

6 Eliade, 173, 254.

7 Cited in Kalweit, 14. An *angaqoq* is a Native Alaskan term similar to "shaman."

8 Lewis Mehl-Madrona, *Coyote Medicine*, 164, 164-165.

JOSEPH'S JOURNEY

The initiatory path of the shaman starts with the separation from ordinary reality and ordinary society. Joseph was spontaneously having visions from childhood, but then he also went through separation from his family to live with his grandfather, Antonio D. Simbola, for formal training as a shaman. Joseph said that living with his grandfather was "living with the unpredictable" and he would chase after him and assist him with ceremonies whenever he could. Some of this training involved specific verbal teachings, some of it was unconscious transmission, and some of it was—and is—absorbing through osmosis from just being around the "unpredictable."

Joseph describes his initiation as a shaman or medicine man in his book *Being & Vibration*: "in a shamanic experience, I saw that we are created out of the continuum of rapidly moving light and I saw that it was timeless in nature." He grew up with the teaching that he was a sacred being and that all life and all creation is holy.

> We knew we were a people (a "vibration") who had come from the Infinite Void, from zero, from one's sense that we did not exist. We were made of appearing and disappearing light that came from the inhalation and exhalation of God's breath. We were from the very Heart of the center of the non-existence of infinity.[9]

Part of the shamanic journey and teachings is journeying back to the origin or source point of reality in order to learn how to connect to the source of healing, the vibration of goodness. Joseph learned a creation story of his people and recounts it as follows.

> According to the Tiwa myth-maker being, in the beginning Vibration wanted to walk, Vibration wanted to run, Vibration wanted to climb. According to the storyteller, Vibration loved to climb, like little boys love to climb. Vibration liked to sit and play, just as little boys like to sit and play. Vibration liked to be grandfathers and grandmothers. Vibration loved little boys and little girls because Vibration was babies and Vibration was boys of eight years old or girls of eight years old or teenage girls and boys. Vibration was made of teenage love already being what it was being, so it could continue. Vibration was twenty and then twenty-five and then thirty-five or thereabouts.

9 *B&V*, 35, 23.

> Then Vibration decided it would descend into form and become the living concreteness that we call material form.[10]

This story of Vibration (Breath-Matter-Movement) transforming from spirit into material form speaks of the love of Vibration wanting to manifest into the physical being of children and then older and older adults. "What this myth was telling us," Joseph wrote, "was that if we were to do something long enough and believe in it, we could manifest it. We were receivers of memory, listening stations of cosmic truths in the here and now, and senders to the future."

One of his grandfather's most important teachings was "*Ah dah la pi ah chi*," "pay attention," or "Become the essence of the work, the being of listening, if you want to be a true human being. Become of work, of listeningness, and you will find the voice of our Mother/Father spirit talking to you."[11]

FORMS OF SHAMANIZING

A shaman has a long training period that goes on for years, and really for one's entire lifetime. One of the main points of this book is that living spirituality is open to all of us as we embark on the path of *becoming medicine*. Few of us would qualify as true shamans, but many people have innate or developed shamanic abilities. They are able to engage in shamanizing, even though they are not shamans. This could be thought of as someone having the skills to do some carpentry, but not the skill and training to build a whole house. The ability to go into shamanic states is a universal human attribute, but very few people become a true shaman. Even Joseph, himself, does not claim to be a shaman.

Mircea Eliade describes there being two paths to becoming a shaman: spontaneous and hereditary. In the hereditary path the capability to be a shaman is passed down through inheritance and the training is like an apprenticeship in the family as the child grows up. The spontaneous pathway occurs without training, without an organizing structure to hold the experiences, which can be overwhelming and confusing. In speaking about *becoming a shaman*, I am doing a balancing act. On the one hand, I believe everyone has the capacity to shamanize and to have mystical and visionary experiences. On the other hand, I do not want to embolden

10 Ibid., 41–42.

11 Ibid., 42–43, 46.

people to think that because they read a book or took a weekend course that they can call themselves a "shaman." Many traditions still close to our shamanic roots say that to brag about one's power is the best way to lose it. What I would say is that you can learn to shamanize, that it takes time, energy, effort, and practice. You have to become friends with the fact that you do not exist, and to become friends with the fact that you will go through many painful experiences and even "die before you die." And yet even if you become a shaman, you should never say that you are a shaman. I can tell you for sure, I am not a shaman, I just work here. It is more important to have a sense of humor and humility than to have a sense of self-importance.

Joseph has taught me the first step is to go into the medicine wheel and then to separate my consciousness from my body and to observe my body from the outside—thus becoming both observer and observed. "Don't get stuck in the form," says Joseph.

> "Don't get stuck in the form" means don't get stuck in the breathing or the materialization, or in the movements of life. Perhaps the most important thing to do is to return to silence, to become the finite and the infinite of all knowingness. The idea I want to convey here is that we use the inner walls of our need to catch the revelations as they pass by us so that we can become states of illumination, so that we can become the shamanic journey of the observer and the observed in our everyday life experiences.[12]

Holger Kalweit explains that shamanic trance "means healing through inner recuperation from the unending stream of external stimuli, from complex thinking, from complicated emotions."[13] Here we see a return to a balanced, Zen-like, simplicity. Healing is a matter of peeling away the layers of cultural education and assumption, of convoluted ego-oriented thinking and desire, until one can feel the universal pulse of life coursing through existence and oneself.

DAVID'S COSMIC DREAM JOURNEY WITH JOSEPH

Paying attention to our dreams is one of the modalities of shamanizing. When I was studying Jung I would write my dreams in a diary each morning. Since working with Joseph I have started paying more attention

12 *B&V*, 182.

13 Kalweit, *Shamans, Healers, and Medicine Men*, 91.

to my dreams again. Sometimes Joseph will call me, even waking me up, and I hear his voice on the line, "Good Morning, David-ing, I need to tell you about a dream I just had."

Now I will tell you about a dream that I had about a year after beginning to work with Joseph. I am in a room with another man, I start to feel light in my steps, I start to panic because I am actually floating now. The panic changes to adventure as I float out of the room and hear Joseph say, "Come on its time to go," and off we go, into the sky, into space. I am looking behind us as the earth, solar system, galaxy condense into smaller configurations as we move away. I think, "I should be looking where we are going, instead of where we have been." I look forward and small points of light become larger and we move into light. There is a memory gap and then we are returning. I figure Joseph took us to meet God, but somehow my memory was occluded, and I chuckle as I remember his story of going to meet God and getting past one set of guards after another until he hears a voice say, "It is you!" and then there is a loud pop and he is sitting back on the mountain in Hawaii. "That wasn't very fun," he mutters under his breath, after a vision quest and days of fasting. In this dream I am thinking, "I should have asked God a question or maybe have asked for something, some amulet or sacred object." I think of the hawk feather I found in downtown Durango last time I visited Joseph. When I awake I take the feather and put it in my shrine on my desk with all the other sacred objects.

I have had many vivid dreams since working with Joseph. In one dream an understanding came to me during sleep. The places where we stay tight and constricted are the places where we are striving to persist—where we do not truly exist, but cling to tightness and suffering. When we relax, and open up the spaces between the bones and organs, we create the space to flare into being. There is something very important here to remember.

Some of what I have learned with Joseph I can explain, but there is much that I cannot explain because it is not a "thing" or a fact, but rather it is a state of being, or a way of being in the world. Practicing *Circle Medicine*, perceiving things as interconnected, trying to understand what he means when he says "we do not exist," these are things I am learning. It is both serious and fun at the same time. Sometimes Joseph says something like, "Boy, you are going to end up a shaman yet," or "If you are not careful, you are going to end up a shaman," but what you call a thing is not as important as what something is. Learning from Joseph is to always be

BLESSINGS FOR DRINKING FROM MORNING STAR (DRK + BPA)[1]

1 Joseph dictated the text and had me write it on this print of his original painting.

listening, not just to linear narratives, but to the sounds and surroundings of those narratives. The linear is just one thread of reality, just one loop on the circle and the circle of the medicine wheel brings together many things that from a linear perspective would be considered opposites. Learning from Joseph means listening to the silence and stillness that surround the notes of the music of existence.

MODERN SHAMANIZING IN ART & MUSIC

Visionaries, shamans, and mystics are people who have learned to see and listen to non-ordinary reality and then to bring it back into ordinary reality. Joseph's art grows out of his abilities to have visionary, shamanic, and mystical experiences. His art is a spiritual manifestation of a vision, not a consumer object. Joseph's shamanic work is through sound—through chanting and drumming as well as a deep listening to the sound of the names of things that reveals their hidden meanings.

Many artists, musicians, poets and creative people have found their way into shamanizing to make art that speaks from a deep place. Tapping into the deep rhythms of our inner being that correspond to the patterns of the outer rhythms of the land is a form of shamanizing. In speaking of musicians shamanizing, I am not saying that someone is a "shaman," but rather that they use the techniques and principles of shamans in creating their art.[14] Because sound is so important to Joseph, I thought I would include musicians in this section who seem to shamanize in creating music.

MILES DAVIS: IN A SILENT WAY

Paul Tingen describes Miles Davis as having attributes that we can think of as shamanic. Tingen knows a bit about spiritual states as he studied Zen Buddhism for years and in 1997 was ordained in Thich Nhat Hanh's Order of Interbeing. Those who knew Miles Davis described him as "a medium, a transformer, a touchstone, a magnetic field," "mystical," a "guru," and a "shaman." Bassist Michael Henderson has said, "Miles gave me myself. . . . He gave me something that belonged to me. When I came to play with him, I became 'me.' Like everybody else who was with

14 Hank Wesselman suggests the term *"shamanist"* for a contemporary person walking the shamanic path, (*The Re-enchantment*, 46). In speaking about musicians *shamanizing*, I am speaking of individuals who are not practicing a spiritual tradition, but rather entering into some of the same places and doing some of the same things that shamans, or shamanists might.

him. We all found ourselves." John McLaughlin, as a young jazz guitarist, was told by Miles "play guitar like you don't know how to play guitar." McLaughlin said,

> He was like a Zen master. He would give you very strange directions that were difficult to understand, very obscure. But I think that was his intention, as it is with a Zen master. They will say something to you, and your mind will not be able to deal with it on a rational level. And so he made you act in a subconscious way, which was the best way. He had this great gift of pulling the best things out of people, without them even realizing.[15]

Miles, himself, wrote "I do believe in being spiritual and do believe in spirits . . . music is about the spirit and the spiritual, and about feeling." His co-author of his autobiography, Quincy Troupe, wrote that Miles had a "spiritual, mystical" effect on him and that Miles routinely spoke with great jazz musicians who had crossed to the other side, such as Gil Evans, John Coltrane, and Charlie Parker.

Miles rarely rehearsed with his later bands and encouraged improvisation. If his musicians rehearsed before shows he would angrily tell them "How are you going to rehearse the future?" and he would instruct them, "Don't play what's there. Play what is not there." Some of the musicians who worked with Miles wrote that he "always came from silence."[16]

Like many artists, Miles Davis suffered for his art and went through periods of darkness. He was found to have sickle cell anemia in later life and had joint pain and received one of the first ever hip replacement surgery. Tingen writes of Miles' "silent" period (1975 to 1980) when Miles said he didn't even touch his trumpet for five years and he disappeared from the world stage. Miles came back to the stage in 1980 and continued to perform until he died in 1991.

Leonard Feather, a musician who worked with Miles said of him, "He manifestly changed the entire course of an art form three or four times in twenty-five years—an accomplishment no other jazz musician can claim." As Tingen writes, Miles not only transformed music, he transformed people and culture. He crossed boundaries, brought people together and he sought the source of the universal in the silent void out of which music arises if we only listen. Tingen wrote

15 Paul Tingen, *Miles Beyond: The Electrical Explorations of Miles Davis, 1967–1991*, 17.

16 Ibid., 19, 14–15.

> In addition, as the first black musician who consistently crossed over into other music genres, other cultures, other countries, Miles transcended the paradigm of musical, cultural, and racial segregation. The effects of his musical and personal odyssey rippled into the whole of the twentieth century music and culture, and are still with us today.[17]

In the hero's journey class that I teach with veterans, the question is always: "What is the boon or the gift that you are bringing back that asks for the transformation of your Self and has the potential to transform society?" One thing that the person, the "hero" or "heroine," brings back from the abyss is his or her very self which is a testimony to the possibility of transformation. The returning hero can then serve the function as a mentor and a guide who can lead others through the transformation of consciousness and the creation of new (musical) forms and realities. The hero role, when accepted, is necessarily a form of leadership. Possibly this is a recognized role, but it also can be a different kind of leadership, *non-ordinary leadership*. Paul Tingen compares Miles' life to Joseph Campbell's hero's journey framework:

> Miles was one of the thousand faces of this mythological hero. The cause to which he gave his life was music, the undiscovered country he traveled, and the trials and tribulations he underwent have been described at length in this book. And true to the hero's story, Miles did his best to share the consciousness he attained—in his music, in his methods, and in his expanded awareness. On another level he also pioneered and taught, by example, a modern awareness of racial equality. We only now begin to recognize that his consciousness exemplified the currently emerging existential world-view. Miles was one of the harbingers of this twenty-first century paradigm.
>
> Miles's working methods, the way he taught his musicians, can also be interpreted as a form of a new, spiritual, type of leadership.[18]

BEN LEE: WELCOME TO THE WORK

Australian musician Ben Lee is an example of a modern mystic and visionary who has crossed into shamanizing from time to time. I first learned of Ben Lee's work when I saw him open for Ben Folds at Foellinger

---

17 Ibid., 8, 21.

18 Ibid., 269.

Auditorium at University of Illinois on April 15, 2008. The power went out during the show and Ben Lee did an amazing job of carrying on with the performance. He was able to get the large crowd to be very quiet and he performed several songs acoustically. The auditorium was able to carry the sound so everyone could hear, but it was an amazing sense of connection and collaboration because every single person in the audience had to actively work to quiet themselves to create a silence in which Ben Lee's music could be heard.

Joseph Rael's grandfather used to say, *work is worship*. Ben Lee's 2013 album, *Ayahuasca: Welcome to the Work* explores *the work* with the mystical and shamanic use of ayahuasca, a plant medicine from South America used by the shamans of that region. In a video promoting the album, Lee says,

> I've been working with ayahuasca over the past few years as part of my own spiritual, and psychological journey. . . . Taking part in ayahuasca ceremony is often called "the work" and that work asks us to examine our integrity in great detail, to look at our flaws and fantasies and to strive to become a healthier, more integrated human being. I've approached ayahuasca not as a drug experience, but as a sacred, spiritual experience, used to uncover untouched depths of my own unconscious. . . . It is a different type of album for me, it is not necessarily a pop album, or a singer-songwriter album, it is a journey, its meditative, experimental, joyful, terrifying, exhilarating—it's a lot of things, and it is really designed hopefully to encapsulate a tiny portion of what the plant medicine has to offer.[19]

Ben Lee exemplifies the path of a modern mystic who engages in shamanizing, exploring consciousness through ayahuasca, pursuing his spiritual path, and then returning the fruits of his journey with the world in a socially-engaged and ethical way. On his website he writes that all his diverse projects "are drawn together through a common purpose: to awaken myself and others to infinite possibility!"[20]

One of the songs on this album is called, "In the Silence." This is the silence of the mystics which reveals the truth to those who can listen to the voice within. The song is a duet between Ben Lee and Jessica Chapnik Kahn. The song starts out slow and spacious and then Kahn begins singing repeatedly, "In the silence, hear what can't be heard." Then Ben Lee's voice

19 Ben Lee Album Trailer, *Ayahuasca: Welcome To The Work.*

20 Ben Lee website.

comes in, "If I open my heart, open my heart, where does all my pain go?"

This song is followed by an instrumental called "The Shadow of the Mind," which starts out with tentative, searching piano and builds up into a bit of a swarming maelstrom of noise. Entering into the *silence* is like entering into the *stillness* and entering into the *darkness*. This is the path of the mystic and the shaman who enters into the darkness of the *guhā*, the cave of the heart. This path of seeking is the secret journey within. As the song builds in tension it reminds me of the feeling of over-stimulation, the overwhelming sense of too much building up that comes before the quiet opening into vastness and the mystical peace that comes from letting one's self grow into a larger space of transformation.

Just as I would sit in the dark as a teenager listening to The Police song "Secret Journey," so too I would sit in the dark in Auckland, New Zealand, listening to Ben Lee's album *Ayahuasca: Welcome to the Work*. Our lives are all beautiful tapestries with threads that interconnect across time and space. In order to see and feel these interconnections we must enter into the silence, enter into the darkness, to do the work of our secret, shamanic journeys.

JOSEPH'S SHAMANIC JOURNEY HELPING KURT WILT

The way I came to meet Joseph was through several books. *Being & Vibration* called to me from the bookshelf in the year 2000. I read that book and then it sat on my bookshelf until I picked it up again in 2013 as I was preparing to leave New Zealand. In 2013 another book called to me from the shelf, Kurt Wilt's *The Visionary: entering the mystic universe of Joseph Rael Beautiful Painted Arrow*. I read about how Kurt was using Joseph Campbell's hero's journey framework in describing Joseph Rael's path and I reached out and sent an email to Kurt and told him how I was using the hero's journey with veterans struggling to return home. Kurt thought Joseph would be interested in that and the rest is history, as they say.

Kurt passed on recently and was in a coma before he died. Joseph often would tell me things about Kurt and remind me that he and I had first connected through Kurt. Joseph frequently returns in our discussions to a shamanic journey he made to help guide Kurt's soul back in his body when he was in a coma.

"At one moment at 3:30 in the morning I was pushed down into my mattress and a part of my non-ordinary body flashed, just below the speed of light, from Colorado to Florida. Because I was moving so fast I didn't have time to think about where I was going. I was looking for the person who was lost in the bardos where the soul goes when the soul leaves the physical body and goes toward the promised land. The soul that I was to search for I had to go and find, he was across a little stream and standing looking to the other side. I appeared to him on his left and he turned to me and said 'Joseph you are here' And I could tell that he was lost, his thoughts had wandered too far away from his body. I turned him around to face where he had come from, where his body was. The moment I turned him around I started to take one step and he did too and in the time that we took one step, there was a force that moved us seven miles in the split of a split of a second, or even less, because in non-ordinary reality there is no time or space. We arrived at his body, we were both in our spiritual bodies, he looked down and next thing I knew he couldn't fit back into his body. I said to him, 'Pretend you are a page from the New York Times *newspaper and I will make you into a ball and I will stuff you through the right side of your body and I will push you back into your body like a round ball, paper ball newspaper and from there you will unfold and go back into place and start breathing.' In the next split second I was back in my body and I had travelled from the Four Corners to Tampa in no time at all. And I heard his wife speaking to his daughter because they were there with him at 5:30 AM (because they were EST). And I heard a voice say he's back and he's breathing on his own and they proceeded to take the tubes out of his body. It didn't take not even 2–3 seconds, our time, but in non-ordinary reality I imagine you can travel hundreds and hundreds and hundreds of miles, you are thinking of where you are going even before you arrive there. This is because we don't exist."*

THE WOUNDED HEALER

> *In the first panel [of the "Journey of the Wounded Healer" painting] we see the self trapped in a dizzying vortex of evolutionary descent, paralleling the hallucinatory descent of the initiate shaman into the underworld or realm of the dead. The prisoner yearns for freedom and becomes sick with the materialist limitations of his genetic chains represented by entrapment in a spiraling DNA molecule.*
>
> *In the central panel the self explodes into space, dismembering . . . all levels of reality; subatomic, cellular, planetary, galactic, psychical,*

spiritual. The energy which animates the All, the force of God, erupts through the embodied self and destroys identification with the sickly contracted ego, opening the self to merge with new powers . . . an integrating and transmuting energy which binds together the new self.

In the final panel the reintegrated man ascends into the middle and upper worlds, released from the psychic bonds of materialist entrapment and tapped into the light which beams from the mind and heart. As a healer, he wields a crystalline hermetic caduceus with the balanced serpent powers of the unconscious and winged vision of the superconscious. The healer/scientist/artist ascends the crystal mountain of the higher self, a self empowered by the responsibility for healing the future.[21]

ALEX GREY

The concept of the wounded healer is ancient. The Greek god of healing, Asklepios was apprenticed to the centaur, Chiron, who had a non-healing wound.[22] A true healer must understand, from personal experience, the pain of illness and suffering. The path of the shaman is an example of this archetypal initiation in which the healer passes through pain, illness, and death in order to be able to first heal herself or himself, and then to heal others.

Many contemporary physicians, psychiatrists, psychologists, and psychotherapists are fascinated with the similarities between shamanism, healing, and psychotherapy. Jungian therapists, in particular, have a great interest in shamanism as well as in Native American cultures. Jung himself had these interests and travelled to the Southwest of the United States and visited the Pueblos there.

In 1925, Jung met Ochwiay Biano (Mountain Lake) of Taos Pueblo described in *Memories, Dreams, Reflections.*[23] Although it was a brief

---

21 Alex Grey, writing about his triptych painting "The Journey of the Wounded Healer." *Chapel of Sacred Mirrors* website. The individual painting of the exploding body of the wounded healer can be seen at: http://www.alexgrey.com/art/paintings/soul/.

22 Edward Tick, *The Practice of Dream Healing*, 21–23. Tick further points out that as a centaur, Chiron was half man and half animal. He is thus a liminal being who brings together nature and humanity.

23 *MDR*, 246–53. Antonio Mirabal was Ochwiay Biano's English name and Mountain Lake a translation of his Tiwa name. David G. Barton critically discusses Jung's relationship with Mirabal in his paper, "C.G. Jung and the indigenous psyche: two encounters." Barton raises a number of good points, some of them based on the perspective of contemporary cultural sensitivity that is product of our current times and not the time that Jung was living. Barton's paper is worth reading, although he is a bit polemical, and he minimizes the work of "Jungians" and contemporary physicians

encounter, it deeply affected him and he continued to speak of this meeting into his later years and referred to Mountain Lake as my "friend."[24] Some of the key themes that Jung returned to throughout his life are the view of Western society as predatory in its colonizing, the difference of thinking with the head versus the heart, and the difference between a dead and a living spirituality. Picuris Pueblo, where Joseph lived for most of his childhood years, is about 30 miles from Taos. I ponder the synchronicity of Jung the psychiatrist meeting Ochwiay Biano (Mountain Lake) and David Kopacz the psychiatrist meeting Joseph Rael (Beautiful Painted Arrow).

Carl Hammerschlag, Donald Sandner, Jerome Bernstein, and Fred Gustafson are a few influential psychiatrists who spent time working with Native American cultures and have written a number of books. Native American healers and authors have also found in Jung a kindred spirit who seems to have undergone a shamanic initiation (descent, visions of spirits, communication with ancestors). Vine Deloria Jr. and Eduardo Duran have found Jung's work to provide a bridge between Native and Western worldviews. In Deloria's *C.G. Jung and the Sioux Traditions*, he looks at similarities and contrasts between Jung and the Sioux, while also critiquing and cautioning about cultural appropriation. Like many authors he sees that a Native perspective can help to correct an imbalance within the dominant culture of the US.

> In producing the achievements of Western culture, humans have at the same time cut themselves off from understandings of nature as a source of spiritual and psychological life. Sioux culture—and the cultures of other indigenous peoples—contain certain understandings that can help us rethink and address this lack. The long history of appropriations from Indian people, however, requires us proceed with great caution. My intent here is to establish a balanced dialogue between two cosmologies and the spiritual and

and psychotherapists who have learned from close association with Native elders and teachers, many of whom we mention in this book. Barton points out that Antonio Mirabal (Mountain Lake) was also comfortable in Western society and had met with President Franklin Roosevelt as a tribal representative and he refused a meeting with President Herbert Hoover over his Indian policies, (77). In addition to providing additional biographical history on Mirabal, Barton also calls for an open cross-cultural dialogue between "Jungians" and indigenous people, (78). I would like to think that the work that Joseph Rael and I are doing together is an example of this, although, I would not consider myself a "Jungian," even Jung himself often said to Henry Corbin, "Thank God I am Jung and not a Jungian!" (Peter Kingsley, *Catafalque*, 398).

24 Jung, *MMSS*, 146.

psychological dynamics that derived from them.[25]

Psychologist, Eduardo Duran has also written a great deal about Jung in his works *Native American Postcolonial Psychology* and *Healing the Soul Wound.*[26] He sees correspondences between Jung's psychological types and mandalas with the medicine wheel. We quoted from his essay "Medicine Wheel, Mandala, and Jung," in *Walking the Medicine Wheel.* In this work he describes Jung as "initiated via the shamanic tradition." Duran wonders about why Jung's encounter with Mountain Lake (Ochwiay Biano) of Taos Pueblo reverberated so strongly in Jung's life and thinking.

> Was he even trying in some way to heal the collective split in the Western psyche that occurred when the patriarchy became supreme? Why else was he so driven to the Taos people and why did he persist for so long in trying to find out the workings of the psyche of the Taos people? Perhaps Jung was searching for balance within himself between patriarchal anima and matrilineal anima as well as for balance within the collective, which is part of the shaman's task, i.e., the shaman learns his new song in the underworld during his initiatory process and then brings his new song, or medicine, back for the community.[27]

---

25 Vine Deloria, Jr., *C.G. Jung and the Sioux Traditions: Dreams, Visions, Nature and the Primitive*, 2.

26 These two books focus on developing a culturally-sensitive psychotherapy specifically for Native American people. These are excellent books for therapists working with Native clients. In my work with Joseph, we focus on using indigenous wisdom along with Western science, and other healing and spiritual traditions as a *medicine* for all people. It is worth noting Duran's comments on how his focus on the similarities between Native Peoples could appear to be "glossing," the "assumption that all tribes are exactly the same culturally."

> I purposefully engage in what may appear as glossing because I believe that one of the most powerful colonial strategies inflicted on Native Peoples has been convincing us that we are so different from one another. Of course there are tribal variations in the metaphors of healing. In this work, as in my day-to-day clinical work, I use basic root metaphors. Using root metaphors is also consistent with the concept of the collective unconscious . . . with which most people are familiar: the theory that human beings are all connected at a collective level of psyche and that this level of psyche is the source of primordial ideas and images of all human beings, (*Healing the Soul Wound: Counseling with American Indians and Other Native Peoples*, 7).

27 Eduardo Duran, "Medicine Wheel, Mandala, and Jung," in *Spring*, "Native American Cultures and the Western Psyche: A Bridge Between, Vol. 87, Summer 2012, 129, 131.

Duran also summarizes Donald Sander's understanding of three different levels of healer. This echoes my critique of contemporary medicine in terms of doctors who function solely as technicians compared to those who function as healers—a primary distinction being whether or not the physician has gone through her or his own initiation as a healer thereby *becoming medicine*, not just practicing it. Eduardo Duran summaries Sandner's classification:

> 1) The shaman enacts the symbolism in his own person through periods of ecstatic trance.
>
> 2) The Navajo medicine man does not act out the symbolism in his own person. . . . The medicine man draws upon a vast body of traditional symbolism, but he does not live it out.
>
> 3) In the psychotherapist mode or method of healing the doctor is comparatively passive. . . . The main focus of the symbolic action is from the patient him/herself.

Duran quotes a shaman he once met who described the difference between Western and shamanic approaches, "Psychologists take the patient all the way to the edge of the cliff and leave him there. What I do is push him over the cliff and go with him, and stay with him as long as it takes to bring him back."[28] Duran argues that working with Native Peoples requires a degree of shamanic work.[29] To incorporate the healing symbols within oneself is what Joseph and I are talking about in *becoming medicine*, embodying that which is healing to the individual and society.

THE NEED FOR BECOMING A SHAMAN IN CONTEMPORARY LIFE

Oftentimes, shamanism is considered "primitive" or something only indigenous people do.[30] There are modern shamans, however, such as Joseph Rael, who are telling us that there is something that we have

---

28 Eduardo Duran, *Native American Postcolonial Psychology*, 57–58, 63. Donald Sandner's original conceptual table can be found in his *Navaho Symbols of Healing: A Jungian Exploration of Ritual, Image, & Medicine*, 260–61.

29 Psychiatrist Arthur Kleinman and psychologist Richard Katz have both recommended that all psychiatrists and psychologists in training learn from indigenous healing traditions in order to be better healers. See Kleinman's chapter, "How Do Psychiatrists Heal?" in *Rethinking Psychiatry: From Cultural Category to Personal Experience* (1991) and Katz's paper, "Education as Transformation: Becoming a Healer Among the !Kung and the Fijians, *Harvard Educational Review*, Spring, 1981.

30 Jung's use of the word "primitive" is one of the critiques that Deloria, Duran, and Barton raise. The majority of scientists, materialists, and rationalists living today still believe shamanism is primitive superstition even if they use more politically correct language.

forgotten, that we have become separated from, something precious and to which we must return. African shaman Malidoma Patrice Somé writes:

> My elders are convinced that the West is as endangered as the indigenous cultures it decimated in the name of colonialism. There is no doubt that, at this time in history, Western civilization is suffering from a great sickness of the soul. The West's progressive turning away from functioning spiritual values; its total disregard for the environment and the protection of natural resources; the violence of inner cities with their problems of poverty, drugs, and crime; spiraling unemployment and economic disarray; and growing intolerance toward people of color and the values of other cultures—all of these trends, if unchecked, will eventually bring about a terrible self-destruction . . . the only possible hope is self-transformation.[31]

Somé says that what could save us is *self-transformation*. This is the theme that runs throughout this book; initiation is a transformational process that changes not just what we do, but who we are. We need this kind of transformation if we are to survive, according to Somé. For the symptom of "alienation" he prescribes the medicine of "communication and community—a new sense of togetherness." He tells us that the "challenge of modernity is to bring the world together into a unified whole in the middle of which diversity can exist."[32] We will talk more about how shamans, mystics, and visionaries can work for personal as well as communal healing in section three of this book.

Another contemporary shaman, a Western evolutionary biologist and paleoanthropologist, Hank Wesselman tells us that shamanism can help us bring about a *re-enchantment* of ourselves and the world. Based on his experiences and research, he says that "the shaman is a universal figure found in some form in every culture and that our Western use of the term *shaman* is valid." Wesselman sees that we need a modern form of shamanism for personal transformation and also "cultural revitalization." Just as Mircea Eliade wrote about the sacred and the profane and the need for ceremonies to *re-sacralize* ourselves and the world, Wesselman tells us that shamanism is a pathway that can lead us back to the sacred, thus *re-enchanting* the world. This re-enchantment reconnects us with nature and wonder, and according to Wesselman, can "enable you to see more

31 Malidoma Somé, *Of Water and the Spirit: Ritual, Magic, and Initiation in the Life of an African Shaman*, 1.

32 Ibid., 13, 10.

deeply into the outer world of things seen, as well as the inner worlds of things hidden. . . . It is simply a matter of tuning in to the right frequency and paying attention to what happens next. It is a matter of allowing ourselves to be re-enchanted."[33] This re-enchantment leads to personal transformation as well as cultural revitalization, which is why becoming a shaman (or shamanist) is as important now as it has always been.

33 Wesselman, *The Re-enchantment*, 2, 20.

Sacred offering of the five-fingered

SACRED OFFERING OF THE FIVE-FINGERED

CHAPTER 6

BECOMING A MYSTIC

Only the mystics bring creativity into religion.[1]

CARL JUNG

Here we deal with mystical knowledge. Mysticism is not the same thing as intellectual discourse, reasoning, or knowledge as one might study it at a university.

Mysticism works on the level of intuition, of spirit. . . .

I was raised among the Tiwa-speaking people at Picuris Pueblo and learned much of my way of thinking about life from my spiritual grandfather, a Tiwa mystic and holy man . . . in Tiwa mysticism, the hand is the metaphor for bringing into manifestation. On the two hands, we have ten fingers, and the finger represents, or is, the power to manifest from seed. . . .

Remember, this is Tiwa mysticism. I've been studying mysticism since I was eight or nine years old, just because I was curious. The mystic, whenever he uses hand movement, like a handshake, knows that he is bringing something into manifestation.[2]

JOSEPH RAEL

Joseph Rael (Beautiful Painted Arrow) is a living mystic. To listen to him speak for even a short while is to enter his mystic universe. As Joseph wrote in the quote above, he's been studying mysticism since childhood just because he was curious. Joseph grew up in a tradition that still had a connection with the ancient wisdom of a living spirituality. This tradition has been passed on orally for generations, from heart to heart. Joseph writes that, "Mysticism works on the level of intuition, of spirit. Some mystics say that the cosmos was created by numbers, letters, and words (sounds). Letters have to do with the materialization of ten vibrations via manifestation."[3]

We had written earlier about vowel mysticism where the sounds of letters contain sacred information about the universe. Here, Joseph is

1 Carl Jung, *Mysterium Coniunctionis*, 375.

2 *Inspiration*, 10-12.

3 *Sound*, 178.

speaking about number mysticism as well, that the numbers one through ten contain divine information. For Joseph, this is not something esoteric, but eminently practical. Just as sub-atomic physicists seek to learn the composition of matter, Joseph hears the mysteries of spirit revealed in the word sounds. The microcosm is the macrocosm, Joseph often reminds me. It is not that one thing is symbolic of another, it is that one thing is the same as another thing when heard from the perspective of non-ordinary reality. The sound of the number one, the number one itself, and the beginning of creation are all holographically the same thing. So too, the sound of the number ten, the number ten itself, and the completion of creation are all the same thing. It is like we, in Western society, just see the tip of the iceberg and think that is all there is, because we cannot easily see the rest. That is another way to think of becoming a mystic, learning to see the hidden reality, rather than reducing reality down to matter.

> There is a Divine Presence in all the numbers. By listening to the vowel sounds in these ten numbers, we can access their powers. The sounds in the words for one through ten can teach us the ten steps by which material forms manifest from inspiration, the path by which the energy moves through all of perceptual reality into form. These are ten vibrations, ten seeds, ten stages inside the circle of manifestation, of all that is.[4]

Mysticism is a common feature of most religious systems, although it is often hidden, secret, and sometimes suppressed. Mysticism, Joseph reminds us, is not an intellectual exercise, rather it is diving deep into the cosmic ocean of direct spiritual experience. Mysticism is a living spirituality. Joseph wrote a book called *Ceremonies of the Living Spirit*, and this is what mysticism is about, Living Spirit. The path of mysticism leads through visions and ecstatic states to a final experience of Oneness and Unity with the Divine.

Mysticism is the inner aspect of religion, not the formal teachings, but the spiritual path of experience. Although religions were founded by mystics who spoke with God and had visions and dreams, religions teach that the time of revelations, visions and living spirituality occurred only in the past. Spiritual teachers, however, speak of each moment being a sacred moment of divinity. Mysticism is not a religion in and of itself; rather it is a standard path of spiritual experience, as is shamanism, a path that

4 *Sound*, 179.

often has more similarities than differences across different religions. In fact, mystics may see themselves as being more similar to mystics of other religions than to the more conservative and orthodox members of their own religion. "All mystics, said Saint Martin, speak the same language and come from the same country."[5]

One of the first books I read on mysticism was J.M. Cohen and J-F. Phipps, *The Common Experience* (1979). This book is a work of interspirituality, documenting the common features of mystics across religious traditions. In the last few years I came across Evelyn Underhill's (1875-1941) classic text on mysticism, *Mysticism: A Study in the Nature and Development of Spiritual Consciousness* (1911). The thing I like about this book is that it is clear that Underhill is a mystic, not an academic writing about something she has no personal relationship to. She wrote about mysticism because she loved it, because she had to. I loved her book so much I gave it away before I was finished with it and I bought another copy for myself. It is one of those books that you are just happy exists. I had tried reading William James' *Variety of Religious Experiences*, but I could never really get into it. Underhill's biographer, Bernard Bangley, describes her as "without formal religious or theological education," but she "read more widely than most of us, had an authentic mystical experience, and refused to distort such activity by putting herself at the center." Her reading showed her that mystics throughout history were "not self-centered, but God-centered." Bangley writes that mysticism, "was not, for her, something odd, but entirely natural."[6] While she drew primarily on Christian sources, she also cites saints and mystics of other spiritual traditions. Her language can be a bit dated at times, but her excitement and luminosity is still perceptible. Underhill described mystics as the "pioneers of the spiritual world."

> Mysticism, then, offers us the history, as old as civilization, of a race of adventurers who have carried to its term the process of a deliberate and active return to the divine fount of things. They have surrendered themselves to the life-movement of the universe, hence have lived with an intenser life than other men can ever know; have transcended the "sense world" in order to live on high levels the spiritual life.[7]

---

5 Evelyn Underhill, *Mysticism*, xiii.

6 Bernard Bangley ed., *Radiance: A Spiritual Memoir of Evelyn Underhill*, vii.

7 Evelyn Underhill, *Mysticism: A Study in the Nature and Development of Spiritual Consciousness*, 4, 35.

THE MYSTIC'S JOURNEY

Underhill traces the *Mystic Way* through a number of different lives and experiences of mystics and shows the similarities and universality of the mystical path. Mystics embark on a pathway of initiation following the structure of separation, initiation, and return. While there are many spiritual organizations and traditions that can guide and initiate mystics, the path is an inner journey of the mystic starting in a state of separation and moving toward a state of oneness. The ego in its separate state is alone, separate. The goal of the journey is to merge with the One, which is also Alone—however this state of Aloneness is a state of Unity with all creation.

Underhill quotes the neo-Platonic philosopher, Plotinus, as describing the solitary journey of the soul as "the flight from the Alone to the Alone."[8] Many mystics describe a state of suffering and aloneness that precedes their union with the divine, like St. John of the Cross and the *dark night of the soul.* The mystic suffers from the sense of separateness and absence from the divine and this creates a divine desire, a divine longing, which is sometimes described as the longing of the lover for the Beloved. Underhill quotes Jámí,

> All that is not One must ever
> Suffer with the wound of Absence,
> And whoever in Love's city
> Enters, finds but room for One
> And but in Oneness, Union.[9]

Underhill calls this journey of the *alone to the Alone* a person's "secret adventures with God," in which the seeker sets off on a journey from ordinary reality to non-ordinary reality. Mystics agree upon one thing—there are a number of different paths to the One.

---

8 Ibid., 82. Henry Corbin's book on the Sufi mystic 'Ibn Arabi is also titled *Alone with the Alone.* In speaking of the relationship of the mystic and God, Corbin writes, "He is the he who knows himself through myself, that is in the knowledge that I have of him, because it is the knowledge that he has of me; it is alone with him alone, in this syzygic unity, that it is possible to say *thou,*" (95). This quote describes the non-dualist perspective that underlies the apparent separation of ordinary reality.

9 Jámí in Underhill, 82.

THE JOURNEY OUT, THE JOURNEY IN, THE JOURNEY THROUGH

Underhill, describes three different branches of the Mystic Path: the journey of the seeker (the "Mystic Quest"), the longing of the lover (the "Marriage of the Soul"), or the trials of the ascetic saint (the "Great Work" of the "Spiritual Alchemist").

> The first is the craving which makes him a pilgrim and wanderer. It is the longing to go out from his normal world in search of a lost home, a "better country." . . . The next is that craving of heart for heart, of the soul for its perfect mate, which makes him a lover. The third is the craving for inward purity and perfection, which makes him an ascetic and in the last resort a saint.[10]

We can think of these as three different *places* where the mystical journey occurs—the outer journey, the relational journey, and the inner journey. Seeking mysticism can lead us to different places. It can lead us out into the world, into our deepest being, or through another person to God. All these places are ultimately one, but the path of the mystic is the path of the seeker, and the seeker is a wanderer through both the inner and outer wildernesses. Arundhathi Subramaniam puts it this way: "I'm aware that our experience of the sacred cannot exist anywhere outside of us. But I'm also given to traveling intermittently in quest of it." Even if you are told, "God dwells within you," this world seems created in such a way that we are always getting lost in it, always going on spiritual quests within it, and always getting lost in its beauty and horror. We can ask, with Subramaniam, *what is all this seeking seeking?*

> What are they seeking? A newness, an in-betweenness, an elsewhereness. An axis that connects the fleeting to the incomprehensible. A glimpse of a less fractured religious inheritance. A poetic moment rescued from an exhausted liturgy. A respite from chronic unease. A reminder of the possibility of symmetry in otherwise incidental, hastily sutured lives. Sometimes, they're not quite sure what they're seeking, but they retain a sense of compulsion. Sometimes they begin to discover that they have a quest only once the journey is underway. Even those who write merely as travellers or ethnographers find themselves more implicated than they had anticipated.[11]

---

10 Underhill, 126–29.

11 Arundhathi Subramaniam, ed., *Pilgrim's India: An Anthology*, xi, xvi. Subramaniam is a poet and seeker, herself. She co-wrote *Adiyogi: The Source of Yoga and Sadhguru: More than a Life* with her guru, Sadhguru Jaggi Vasudev. Reading her adventures with her teacher reminds me of my work with Joseph.

We are all seekers, even if we do not know it. And if you look deeply enough, everywhere you seek you will find the same thing.

THE PLACES OF MYSTICAL EXPERIENCE

In *The Silent Cry: Mysticism and Resistance*, Dorothy Soelle has described five different "places of mystical experience" for seeking mysticism: *nature*, *eroticism*, *suffering*, *community*, and *joy*. "We are all mystics," writes Soelle, seeing mysticism as a fundamental human experience.[12] She begins the book with a description of the Ogalala Sioux Black Elk's description of his visions as a child. He heard a bird say to him, "Behold, a sacred voice is calling you; All over the sky a sacred voice is calling." Soelle points out that Native American visionaries did not see their visions as purely personal, but rather as guidance for the whole people, as Black Elk said, "Without community, the vision consumes you."[13] Thus, for Soelle, the mystic is not pursuing a selfish path, but rather takes on the illness of the current cultural situation and through his or her own mystical initiation offers a collective vision that heals society. Mysticism counters the dehumanization of materialism, putting the divine back into the material. "Without mysticism," writes Soelle, "the image of the human being deteriorates into that of a consuming and producing machine that neither needs nor is capable of God."[14]

Soelle describes five different "places" or domains in which mystical experience can take root and blossom. Many individuals might move between these different places, but there are whole traditions of mysticism that are based on each of these "places." *Nature*, *eroticism*, *suffering*, *community*, and *joy* are the five "places" that Soelle maps out for mystical experience. Some of these *places* are *outer*, some are *inner*, and some are spaces *through* to the Divine.

The first *place* is *nature*, which really is a place in the world. Nature mysticism is a form of immanent spirituality in which the material is seen as a manifestation of the spiritual. Nature mysticism is inherent in all indigenous spiritual practices. Shamanic work often occurs in nature and is about coming into a different, harmonious relationship with nature. We will talk about this more in the chapter on Land later in the book.

---

12 Soelle, *The Silent Cry: Mysticism and Resistance*, 9.

13 Black Elk, cited in Soelle, 10–11.

14 Soelle, 44.

The second *place* is *eroticism*. Sufi poet Rumi's longing for his spiritual partner, Shams; Ibn 'Arabī & Nizam, Dante's love of Beatrice — all illuminate a path of reaching divine love through the love of a person. The Hindu tradition of *bhakti* is the path of divine love, such as the being called *Radhakrishna*, which is the combination of the human woman, Radha, and the god Krishna and their transformative divine love.

"A place that you recognize as a dark place of origin, marking the beginnings of an ancient human ache," is how Arundhathi Subramaniam describes bhakti, "a simple, insatiable throb." As a form of mysticism, bhakti "liberated" God from religion, allowing a direct relationship with the Divine without the mediation of temples, priests, rules, or regulations.

> This is a throb so definitive, so encompassing that it blurs the conventional divide between the sacred and the profane. It is a throb that demands union and annihilation, love and liberation, ecstasy and extinction, more and no more—and demands it now.
>
> Everyone has known it. Many choose to forget, defer, deny or dilute it. Understandably. It is inconvenient. It makes life difficult. When one does encounter it, however, one knows one is the in the presence of something fragile, urgent, moltenly alive.[15]

The third *place* of mystical pursuit Soelle mentions is *suffering*. Joseph and I have written about the therapeutic and transformative uses of intentional suffering in *Walking the Medicine Wheel*. For instance, fasting, sweat lodge, Sun Dance, and vision quest all have elements of ceremonial suffering that is used for mystical purposes. Many Christian saints and Hindu ascetics have not only turned away from the material world, but have actively pushed the limits of their bodies through inflicting pain, fasting, and practices of extreme asceticism.

The fourth *place* that Soelle explores is *community*. She describes that in every form of mysticism "there is found a desire to live in a common life that is different."[16] This is the impetus behind utopian communities, monasteries, ashrams, and desert retreats. Related to mystical communities, Soelle reviews Victor Turner's work on the concept of *communitas*, which we will examine later in the book.

The fifth *place* of mysticism that Soelle explores is *joy*. Joy, and bliss often come through the later stages of union on the mystical journey. Soelle

---

15 Arundhathi Subramaniam, ed., *Eating God: A Book of Bhakti Poetry*, ix-x, xvi.

16 Soelle, 157.

describes how joy itself can be a place where mysticism is pursued and manifested. She draws on Thich Nhat Han's work, embodied dancing and leaping (ecstatic dancing is found in many mystical traditions, including the Sufi whirling dervishes), and also the joy of artistic creation.

What we can take away from Soelle's descriptions of "places" of mysticism is that there are different locations through which the mystical journey can be pursued. Some mystics specialize in one or more of these domains, but at heart, these domains are the domains of life: the natural world and the earth, love in all its forms, the pain and suffering inherent in life, the communal world of humanity, and the joy and bliss that mystics tell us is the ultimate foundation of reality in the form of divine love. All places are locations of mysticism.

BECOMING CAPABLE OF GOD

> *"To know ourselves as the Vast Self playing is to be both human and divine. It is for this we all are born, to be mystics, fully alive and dancing."*[17]

Narayana Guru described ten different pathways in his *Garland of Visions*: for example the path of *karma* (action), the path of *jñāna* (knowledge), the path of *yoga* (union), and the path of *bhakti* (contemplation of the adorable), this last path is also described as the path of love or devotion.[18] However all these different paths lead to the same goal, as Narayana Guru describes the "ultimate teaching is that there is one Reality alone. As there is but one single Reality, each person is inseparably one with the whole, with the one changeless Reality underlying all that is changeful."[19]

Through following these different paths, and places, and branches of mystical experience, the mystic is becoming more "capable of God." This phrase of Corbin's, "capable of God," struck me like a lightning bolt the first time I read it. He is telling us that a human being can only experience God (or anything else for that matter) through his or her "very own mode of being."[20] To be capable of God does not require a search so much as it requires an emptying. The only way to experience God, *Wah-Mah-Chi*,

17 *House*, 200.

18 Swami Muni Narayana Prasad, *Garland of Visions (Darśanamālā Of Narayana Guru)*, 8.

19 Ibid., v.

20 Corbin, *Alone with the Alone*, 111.

ELDERS GATHERING AT WINTER SOLSTICE

is to be able to have a place to put God, a place for God to manifest within yourself. Here we come to Joseph Rael's view that the human being is a medicine bag. The mystic becomes an empty bag which *Wah-Mah-Chi* can then fill. The work of the journey is to create space within one's personality for the divine seed to sprout and blossom. Our work, as gardeners of mysticism, is to create/find a place within ourselves that allows the infinite to bloom within the finite.

The corollary of the state of union with the divine is that the mystic becomes a vehicle for the divine to flow into the world, which is *medicine* for the "sickness of separation" for the individual, society, and the world. The Fountain of Youth, the Holy Grail, the Face of God, Mecca, the Divine Jerusalem, the Garden of Eden—all these are actually found in the heart of the mystic, and yet the only way to realize the divine within the self is to surrender the self to the divine to become, as Joseph Rael says, a hollow bone, a conduit of the divine.

In mystical reality the seeker and the sought turn out to be identical. Underhill cites Dionysius, "Divine love . . . draws those whom it seizes beyond themselves: and this is so greatly that they belong no longer to themselves but wholly to the Object loved."[21] Love and longing for the Divine is both the vehicle that carries the mystic toward God as well as being the state that is achieved through Union—following love leads to manifesting Love.

Will Johnson, in his book *The Spiritual Practices of Rumi: Radical Teachings for Beholding the Divine*, describes how Rumi and his spiritual mentor Shams, would spend hours gazing into each other's eyes, seeing the divine in the other's eyes. The mystic path opens up whenever non-ordinary reality is perceived, this requires some kind of break in ordinary reality. Any strong emotion or deep connection can open up the mystic path. Many mystics like Rumi illuminate the mystic's path of the heart through devotion to the divine in another. Sometimes this is in the form of the divine in one human illuminating the divine in another: Dante & Beatrice, Rumi & Shams, and Ibn 'Arabī & Nizam. Other mystics manifest a personal relationship with divinity in the form of a specific god: Mirabai & Krishna, Akka Mahadevi & Shiva, or Teresa de Ávila's marriage and union with God.[22]

Underhill writes that any little object will do for contemplation as

---

21 Dionysius in Underhill, 197.

22 The idea of erotic love or devotional love and God is strange to many in the West, however it is not unheard of, for instance, the "Song of Songs" contains elements of erotic love. For an explanation of Bhakti in the Hindu tradition see S. N. Dasgupta's *Hindu Mysticism*. Arundhathi Subramaniam's compilation of Indian poetry on this topic is: *Eating God: A Book of Bhakti Poetry*. The work of translator and renderer Daniel Ladinsky spans Indian, Sufi, and Christian poets who wrote of the love of God as a way of seeking non-dualism and spiritual union. For instance, in his *Love Poems from God: Twelve Sacred Voices from the East and West*, he writes that "Faith in the Ocean may be difficult at times and union may seem a fantasy, but I think the real fantasy is separateness from That which is Everywhere . . . I hope a few of these poems will reach deep enough to cure what separates us from each other, and from the beautiful," (xi-xii).

God is found everywhere. What follows is her description of the way that contemplation works.

> Look, then, at this thing which you have chosen. Willfully yet tranquilly refuse the messages which countless other aspects of the world are sending; and so concentrate your whole attention on this one act of loving sight that all other objects are excluded from the conscious field. Do not think, but as it were pour out your personality toward it: let your soul be in your eyes. Almost at once, this new method of perception will reveal unsuspected qualities in the world. First, you will perceive about you a strange and deepening quietness; a slowing down of our feverish mental time. Next, you will become aware of a heightened significance, an intensified existence in the thing at which you look. As you, with all your consciousness, lean out towards it, an answering current will meet yours. It seems as though the barrier between its life and your own, between subject and object, had melted away. You are merged with it, in an act of true communion: and you *know* the secret of its being deeply and unforgettably, yet in a way which you can never hope to express.[23]

Underhill's description of contemplation on any little object is a way of looking for the divine spark, the *scintillae*, in every object. Divine Oneness includes all things as One and all things are a pathway from the many into the One. While many mystics speak of the difficulties that come on the mystic path, they also speak of the divine bliss that comes along the way. Julian of Norwich (c. 1342 – c. 1416 CE) reminds us, "all shall be well, and all shall be well, and all manner of things shall be well."[24]

MYSTICAL INTERCONNECTIONS

Mystics, visionaries, and shamans learn from one another and there is an interconnecting web that links the lives and works of spiritual seekers. This story of transmission of knowledge and wisdom from one person to another is the hidden secret of this book. Ancient wisdom has been passed from person to person back into unwritten history. Finding a fellow seeker is a reprieve from the aloneness of the mystical path. A common experience when someone has an uncommon experience of non-ordinary reality is to research wisdom writings or to seek out a teacher who knows the paths to

---

23 Underhill, 301–02.

24 Julian of Norwich, in J.M. Cohen and J-F. Phipps, *The Common Experience*, 55.

the divine. An encounter with a living person or with the living spirituality of someone's writing is a common theme on the mystic path.

I first came across Juan Mascaró through reading his translations of the sacred wisdom inscribed in Sanskrit and Pali. I have read and re-read Mascaró's introductions to the Penguin Classics of the *Upanishads*, *Bhagavad Gita*, and *Dhammapada* and his words are like a treatise in mysticism and could very well be used as a complementary text to Underhill's for a mystic initiation. Mascaró's introductions seamlessly weave together quotes from Sanskrit with quotes from the *Bible* and the Spanish mystics such as St. John of the Cross and St. Teresa of Ávila. As I have been researching mysticism over the years I realized that I was not the only one to be inspired by Mascaró. In 1967 Mascaró was in the audience of the David Frost television show on a program discussing Maharishi Mahesh Yogi's Transcendental Meditation, the panel included John Lennon and George Harrison of the Beatles. After the show Mascaró wrote to Harrison saying, "a few days ago two friends from abroad gave me the recording of your song 'Within You Without You'. I am very happy, it is a moving song and may it move the souls of millions; and there is more to come, as you are only beginning this great journey." Mascaró also sent a copy of his book *Lamps of Fire* to Harrison with the note, "might it not be interesting to put into your music a few words of Tao, for example no. 48, page 66 of *Lamps*."[25]

> Without going out of my door
> I can know all things on earth.
> Without looking out of my window
> I can know the ways of heaven.
>
> For the farther one travels
> The less one knows.
>
> The sage therefore
> Arrives without traveling,
> Sees without looking,
> Does all without doing.[26]

Harrison did just this and it became the Beatles song, "Inner Light." Not every university professor can claim to have inspired a Beatles song, but Juan Mascaró was no ordinary university professor. While he was a

25 George Harrison, *I, Me, Mine*, 116.

26 Mascaró, rendering of *The Tao Te Ching XLVII*, *Lamps of Fire*, 66.

translator of ancient languages and esoteric spiritual topics, he gave them a luminescence, an *inner light*—if you will. In many ways, all visionaries, mystics, and shamans are no more than translators seeking to translate spiritual experiences of non-ordinary reality into the language of ordinary reality.[27] It was apparent that Mascaró was seeing the One universal light of the Spirit coming through these different religious traditions.

> Our spiritual life must be a work of creation. Whether we are within a religion, or outside a religion, or against religion, we can only live by faith, a burning faith in the deep spiritual values of man. This faith can only come from life, from the deep fountain of life within us, the Atman of the Upanishads, Nirvana, the Kingdom of Heaven.[28]

Mascaró captured what Teasdale calls "interspirituality," in which he can move from the Spanish Mystics to the Romantic Poets, to the *Bible*, Hindu texts and Buddhist texts in such a way that it is apparent that they are all speaking of One thing—the luminous and silent, reachable and unreachable essence of God moving through the brief bodies of human beings. A visionary translator is much like a visionary healer; he or she allows God to pass through without imposing ego on the process.

Mascaró was a poet, a mystic and a unifier of the spiritual wisdom of the world. Reading Mascaró is like the soul drinking light, thus he is a visionary as well as a mystic, as Joseph Rael teaches that a vision is "the soul drinking light." It was after reading his introduction to *The Upanishads* (as exciting as the text itself) that I became interested in Mascaró, himself. In his introduction to *The Upanishads*, Mascaró wrote that "an *Upanishad* could even be composed in the present day: a spiritual *Upanishad* that would draw its life from the One source of religions and humanism and apply it to the needs of the modern world."[29]

As secretly influential as Juan Mascaró continues to be, there is very little written in English about who he was as a person. He was born in Majorca, Spain and lived in India and England. I did some digging and eventually procured a copy of the out-of-print *Lamps of Fire* as well as the posthumously published *The Creation of Faith*. I published a blog post

---

27 I feel this with Joseph sometimes, that I am a translator whose work is to listen to what he says, to ascertain the deeper meaning, and then try to capture it with words on the page.

28 Mascaró, Introduction to the Penguin Classics, *The Upanishads*, 23.

29 Mascaró, *Upanishads*, 8.

review of *The Creation of Faith.*[30]

George Kirazian read the review and wanted to thank me for it as it had brought back fond memories of when Kirazian and his family had stayed with the Mascaró family in Cambridge in 1972. I published my interview/discussion with George on October, 6, 2105, titled "The Blessing of Stillness and Silence."[31] George told me how he had come to meet Mascaró:

> I had been studying the Penguin *Bhagavad Gita* in the late 60s, '68-69, and was deeply impressed. I then purchased the *Upanishads*, Juan's translation, and I was so moved when I completed the introduction, that I just simply–it was at midnight–picked up the phone and trusting to luck and good fortune, called Cambridge, yes, at midnight, San Diego time. I guess it was what, 8 or 9 am there, and she was kind enough, the operator, to trace Juan's number for me. I called him and he was having breakfast. We chatted for a while and I said "Professor Mascaró, I am so deeply moved by the introduction to the *Upanishads* that it was like an Upanishad for me," and he said "Oh, George, where are you calling from?"
>
> I said, "I am calling you from San Diego." He was very gracious and he said, "Look, I know this is a costly call, can you give me your address." So I took down his number and I gave him my address and we continued chatting for a while, I don't know, by this time it was 1 am or so, and a week later I received a Penguin *Bhagavad Gita* inscribed to me with a very lovely note. And then there began, in Winter, 1971 a lengthy correspondence that carried over into the spring of '72.

As I continued my research for this book, I began reading the work of psychiatrist Paul R. Fleischman. I was surprised to read in his book, *Cultivating Inner Peace*, an almost identical description between Fleischman and Mascaró. Fleischman described a similar inspiration from reading Mascaró's translation of the *Bhagavad Gita*. Fleischman, inspired by Henry David Thoreau, was living in a cabin in the woods at the time.

> On a hunch, seated in a canvas chair next to the woodstove in our Vermont cabin, I wrote to J. Mascaró, explaining how his translation had set me on a quest years ago, how I poked into the Sanskrit and

30 Being Fully Human: Living an Integrated Life blog, "Amazon Review: The Creation of Faith," June 16, 2013.

31 Ibid., "The Blessing of Stillness and Silence," October 6, 2015.

> found the spirit of his words true, and how I had woven the study of psychiatry and religion into a profession I continued to pursue. I wrote that through his translation I imagined I had heard scientific ecology break forth into rhythmic poetic couplets of reverence and love.[32]

Fleischman sent the letter to the publisher and to his surprise he received a written reply back! They carried on a seven-year correspondence in the era of paper letters. Then in 1986, Fleischman and his family travelled to the UK and met with the now elderly Mascaró and his wife, Kathleen. They lived in a simply furnished house with only one heated room, but plenty of books and bookshelves where they spent their time "studying over the great texts of humanity: the New Testament, the poetry of Rabindranath Tagore, the Gita." In one of Mascaró's letters to Fleischman he had written, "We want an inner revolution . . . peace is an act of creation . . . a harmony, and this harmony should be found within ourselves, our family, our village, our nation, our world."[33]

In his book, *Cultivating Inner Peace*, Fleischman points out the interconnectedness of those who have been working for peace. This mystical interconnection is the thread running through our book. My work with Joseph Campbell's hero's journey led to me contacting Kurt Wilt after picking up his book *The Visionary* at Powell's bookstore, and Kurt had me contact Joseph and that connection led to this book that you are reading. Those of us working on the same thing will sooner or later run into each other. Piecing together interconnections on the path of peace is like tracing the flow of ancient wisdom through various peoples of the Earth. "The written word, the spoken word," writes Fleischman, "is like a hand feeling its way into a dark room, looking for a switch." Peace writers grow from each other's writings. "Behind every Whitman is a Krishna and an Isaiah; behind every Gandhi is a Thoreau and a Socrates."[34] Peace is inherently about Oneness, not about divisions or boundaries—peace is international, world peace. Fleischman pieces together an amazing back and forth series of inspirations across time and across oceans. He picks up the thread while writing about the Shakers, an idealistic spiritual community from 19th century United States.

32 Paul R. Fleischman, *Cultivating Inner Peace*, 34.

33 Ibid., 36–38.

34 Fleischman, *Cultivating Inner Peace*, 101–02.

> Shakers corresponded with Count Leo Tolstoy. Tolstoy's book was one that transformed Gandhi, and Shaker and Gandhian ideas re-molded Count Tolstoy into a Christian peasant Tolstoy. Whitman and Thoreau met and influenced each other, and Thoreau's "Civil Disobedience" became the manifesto for Gandhi's social action. Scott and Helen Nearing read Whitman and Thoreau, as did Rabindranath Tagore. Tagore and Gandhi had a long relationship. John Muir's favorite author was Thoreau. Thoreau "carried Leaves of Grass around Concord like a red flag." Seekers of peace read each other, write to each other, influence each other. The quiet life of inner peace isn't a vacuum.[35]

This is an important point that Fleischman is making and that Joseph and I are making in this book: peace workers, mystics, visionaries, and shamans are all interconnected and learn from each other. I know it can seem like we have a bewildering array of people we reference, quote and give mini-biographies on, but they all interconnect in meaningful ways. Juan Mascaró is a mystical hub who influenced psychiatrist Paul Fleischman, writer and composer George Kirazian, and Beatle George Harrison. George Harrison studied sitar with Ravi Shankar and Ravi's daughter, Anoushka performed at the Concert for George after his death (we focus on Anoushka Shankar's work later in this book). Ravi Shankar influenced John Coltrane so much so that John and Alice Coltrane named their son Ravi. George Harrison, John Coltrane, and Alice Coltrane all brought Indian music and spirituality into Western consciousness. Bill Laswell, whom I interviewed for this book, met Alice Coltrane a few times and Laswell remixed Miles Davis fusion-era work (J. Coltrane and Miles had, of course, played together). Laswell continues to bring together musicians from many strands of world music in his work.[36] John Coltrane influenced Stephon Alexander, musically, but also in his work as a physicist. Alexander met a number of musicians, such as Brian Eno and Ornette Coleman, and also read Jung. I came to Carl Jung through the music of The Police and this led me into the study of ancient world religions. Through Jung I learned about Taoism, Hinduism, Gnosticism, alchemy, as well as the Christian mystics. Jung wrote an essay on Ramana Maharshi, who influenced Heinrich Zimmer, Somerset Maugham, and

35 Ibid., 101–02.

36 I first heard of Bill Laswell when I was in a café in Minneapolis and I asked what music they were playing. It was his album *Tabla Beat Science*. I was so taken by it that I immediately went to a record store looking for it and have continued to delve into Laswell's prodigious catalogue.

Abhishiktananda. Abhishiktananda influenced Bede Griffiths who in turn influenced Wayne Teasdale, creating a thread of Christian-Hindu spirituality. Joseph Campbell was influenced by Jung and was friends with Zimmer (whose last works he edited after Zimmer's early death). Joseph Campbell met Krishnamurti and they corresponded for some time. Krishnamurti also befriended physicist David Bohm who, near the end of his life, became interested in Native American language and spirituality. A series of conferences bringing together physicists and Native American elders and mystics, including Joseph Rael—who has definitely influenced me! In trying to understand Joseph Rael, I have turned to a study of Henry Corbin's esoteric Islam (Corbin was in some of the same circles as Jung and Campbell and influenced many post-Jungians). Joseph says *"If you pray long enough, sooner or later you are going to meet God."* That seems like it might be true, and if you don't meet God, at least you will meet someone who has met Her, or at least shared a cup of coffee and a poem or song.

20TH CENTURY MYSTICS

Gandhi is perhaps one of the best known spiritual seekers of our time. He could be considered a mystic for he sought truth in every religion, and put himself through a number of restrictive and ascetic practices, particularly his life-long purification of his diet in the pursuit of an applied spirituality that sought to bring greater peace into the world. Let us take a look at the lives of a few more 20th Century mystics: J. Krishnamurti, Carl Jung, and Matthew Fox.

J. KRISHNAMURTI AND THE PATHLESS LAND OF TRUTH

From the age of 10 years old, J. Krishnamurti was groomed to be the next World Teacher by the leadership of the Theosophical Society in India.[37] He prepared spiritually for many years, he studied and meditated,

---

37 J. Krishnamurti (1895–1986) was born in India. When he was ten years old, mother, Sanjeevamma, died and his father Jiddu Narayaniah took a position at the Theosophical Society as a clerk. Charles Leadbeater, of the society, met the young J. Krishnamurti on the beach of the local river and thought that he had the "most wonderful aura he had ever seen, without a particle of selfishness in it." He introduced young Krishnamurti to Annie Besant and they decided that he appeared to be the "vehicle" for the next great World Teacher. Leadbeater and Annie Besant took over his care and made sure he had an education fitting for the next World Teacher, ("Jiddu Krishnamurti," *Wikipedia*). Biographical information on Krishnamurti is from this source.

then taught. The Theosophical Society[38] created the Order of the Star, and made Krishnamurti its head. In 1929, when he was 34 years old, Krishnamurti gave the inaugural speech of this organization and simultaneously disbanded it! He maintained that no organization can help individuals attain spiritual growth. What courage it must have taken to take this philosophical position after having received years of education and financial support through the Theosophical Society! Here is what Krishnamurti said in that speech.

> I maintain that Truth is a pathless land, and you cannot approach it by any path whatsoever, by any religion, by any sect. . . . Truth, being limitless, unconditioned, unapproachable by any path whatsoever, cannot be organized; nor should any organization be formed to lead or to coerce people along any particular path. . . . For two years I have been thinking about this, slowly, carefully, patiently, and I have now decided to disband the Order, as I happen to be its Head. You can form other organizations and expect someone else. With that I am not concerned, nor with creating new cages, new decorations for those cages. My only concern is to set men absolutely, unconditionally free.[39]

Krishnamurti did become a spiritual teacher, and for years he spoke in gatherings, utilizing a Socratic method of inquiry and dialogue. He did not formalize or structure his teachings, instead urging seekers to let go of their pre-conditioning and to open up the natural intelligence of their minds to inquire after the true nature of reality and to *think on these things*.

In 1961 he wrote a series of diaries or notebooks about mystical experiences he was having at that time, roughly around the age of 65. He often would awaken early in the morning and go through this mystical process.

> In the evening . . . suddenly it was there, filling the room, a great sense of beauty, power, and gentleness. . . . All night it was there whenever

38 The Theosophical Society was founded by Madame Blavatsky in 1875. This organization introduced many in the Western world to Hindu philosophy. Theosophy was an interspiritual philosophy, combing elements of many spiritual and mystical traditions. Theosophy even helped Gandhi learn about the ancient teachings of India which had been suppressed under the British education system in India. Gandhi's *An Autobiography: My Experiments with Truth*, (68-69) discusses his experience with Theosophy whilst he was studying in England. Gandhi wrote in his journal "Theosophy is Hinduism in theory, and Hinduism is Theosophy in practice." Gary Lachman describes this history in his book, *The Secret Teachers of the Western World* (Gandhi quote pg. 373).

39 J. Krishnamurti, *Total Freedom: The Essential Krishnamurti*, 1, 7.

I woke up . . . it is empty, totally empty. . . . Only when the brain has cleansed itself of its conditioning, greed, envy, ambition, then only it can comprehend that which is complete. Love is this completeness. . . .

Woke up in the middle of the night and there was the experiencing of an incalculable expanding state of mind. . . . Destruction is essential. Not of buildings and things but of all the psychological devices and defenses: gods, beliefs, dependence on priests, experiences, knowledge and so on. Without destroying there can be no creation. It's only in freedom that creation comes into being. . . . Creation is the movement of the unknowable essence of the whole; it is never the expression of the part. . . .

An immeasurable vastness that is utterly still and silent. There is no space, nor time to cover space. The beginning and the ending are here, of all things. . . . And it is here, there's a beauty and a glory and there's a sense of wordless ecstasy.[40]

Krishnamurti's Notebook visits many of the places of the mystic journey: descriptions of nature, suffering, and ecstatic joy. He describes this process as continually transforming his mind (consciousness) in a way that his brain could not comprehend and language could not capture. His mystical process took him to "the centre of all creation" and there he encountered "a terrific storm, a destructive earthquake gives a new course to the rivers, changes the landscape, digs deep into the earth, so it has levelled the contours of thought, changed the shape of the heart."[41]

Krishnamurti played a pivotal and influential role in the lives of several other figures who are important in our discussion of visionaries, mystics, and shamans. A young Joseph Campbell met a young Krishnamurti on an ocean passage across the Atlantic in 1924. Krishnamurti and physicist David Bohm had a long and mutually influential friendship together. Bohm found that his quest for understanding the nature of reality from the perspective of a physicist and scientist overlapped substantially with Krishnamurti's spiritual perspective of reality. Some of these dialogues between the physicist and the spiritualist are published in *The Ending of Time: Where Philosophy and Physics Meet.* Here is a brief excerpt of Bohm's and Krishnamurti's dialogue:

JK: The world is me: I am the world. But we have it divided up into the British earth and the French earth and all the rest of it!

---

40 J. Krishnamurti, *Krishnamurti's Notebook*, 2–15.

41 Ibid., 29.

DB: So we say the world of society, of human beings, is one, and when I say I am that world, what does it mean?

JK: The world is not different from me.

DB: The world and I are one. We are inseparable.

JK: Yes. And that is real meditation; you must feel this, not just as a verbal statement: It is an actuality. I am my brother's keeper.[42]

CARL JUNG

Carl Jung's detractors call him a mystic as do those who praise him. "Everyone who says that I am a mystic is just an idiot."[43] And yet Jung's very mysticism is what spoke to his readers. He is valued not so much as a scientific explorer of the mind as much as he is for bringing a living spirituality and mysticism into personal growth and psychology. Gary Lachman, in his book *Jung the Mystic*, writes that,

> Jung is responsible for the widespread resurgence of a more inner-oriented spirituality in the modern world, and his contribution is so fundamental that it can easily be overlooked. In essence, Jung taught more than one generation to look within and to embark on the great adventure of discovering themselves. Many today still take their first steps on that voyage with Jung in hand.[44]

I know that this was true for myself, as my first conscious steps on the mystic way were influenced by Jung. Not only was I influenced by Jung's ideas, but through his writings I was also introduced to Taoism, Buddhism, Hinduism, Kabballah, Meister Eckhart, alchemy, and Gnosticism. Jung provided a sense of exploration and a complicated framework that brought back together the microcosm and the macrocosm. He struggled

---

42 J. Krishnamurti and David Bohm, *The Ending of Time: Where Philosophy and Physics Meet*, 438. This final statement is one that Joseph Rael makes quite frequently, "I am my brother's keeper," and we discuss that in *Walking the Medicine Wheel* as a movement toward peace as it contradicts Cain saying he is not his brother's keeper in the *Bible* after he killed him.

43 *C. G. Jung Speaking*, "The Houston Films," interviews by Richard I. Evans, 333. This statement is often taken to be a categorical rejection of mysticism by Jung. However, in his next sentence Jung says, "He doesn't understand the first word of psychology." This seems to imply that mysticism, is perhaps part of the proper study of psychology. Peter Kingsley explores Jung's mysticism in a nuanced way in *Catafalque: Carl Jung and the End of Humanity*, this quote is referenced page 506, fn 71.

44 Gary Lachman, *Jung the Mystic*, 9.

to objectively comment on the most subjective of experiences, but he was a spiritual seeker who had his own dreams, visions, and epiphanies. He worked to develop a new language and framework with which to understand his own experiences as well as those of others.

When Jung was asked near the end of his life if he believed in God, he hesitated and then replied, "*I know.* I do not believe, I know."[45] This intense personal knowing is the fruit of his many spiritual and mystical experiences that had come to him and that he also pursued. Jung wrote that religious and mystical experiences belong to the person and are a psychological fact, not something that can or should be debated from a detached, objective viewpoint.

> You can only say that you have never had such an experience, whereupon your opponent will reply: "Sorry, but I have." No matter what the world thinks about religious experience, the one who has it possesses a great treasure, a thing that has become for him a source of life, meaning, and beauty, and that has given a new splendor to the world and to mankind. He has *pistis* and peace. Where is the criterion by which you could say that such a life is not legitimate, that such an experience is not valid, and that such *pistis* is mere illusion? Is there, as a matter of fact, any better truth about the ultimate things than the one that helps you live?[46]

Beginning from his earliest life when he had strange experiences and began to undertake rituals even he himself did not understand (such as secretly hiding a little box filled with "sacred" things in the house). He described the need for this secret, inner spirituality as a part of the process of individuation and personal growth. "Like the initiate of a secret society that has broken free from undifferentiated collectivity, the individual on his lonely path needs a secret which for various reasons he may not or cannot reveal. Such a secret reinforces him in the isolation of his individual aims."[47] For Jung, mysticism was this secret which included both the most defining moments of his life as well as the thing that he had to keep hidden as a scientist in the field of psychiatry. It was only years after his death, that his *Red Book* was published which contains his own secret journey and silently and secretly influenced the rest of his mature work.

---

45 Jung, *Carl Jung Speaking*, 428.

46 Jung, *Psychology and Religion: West and East*, 104–05.

47 *MDR*, 343.

Jung's *Red Book* led to his separation from being a scientist exploring the psyche and the spiritual to becoming a mystic and visionary experiencing a living spirituality. He described a state of profound disorientation and loss of connection at this start of his descent into the collective unconscious.

> If I speak of the spirit of this time, I must say: no one and nothing can justify what I must proclaim to you. Justification is superfluous to me, since I have no choice, but I must. I have learned that in addition to the spirit of this time there is still another spirit at work, namely that which rules the depths of everything contemporary. The spirit of this time would like to hear of use and value. I also thought this way, and my humanity still thinks this way. But that other spirit forces me nevertheless to speak, beyond justification, use, and meaning. Filled with human pride and blinded by the presumptuous spirit of the times, I long sought to hold that other spirit away from me. But I did not consider that the spirit of the depths from time immemorial and for all the future possesses a greater power than the spirit of this time, who changes with the generations. The spirit of the depths . . . took away my belief in science, he robbed me of the joy of explaining and ordering things, and he let devotion to the ideals of this time die out in me. He forced me down to the last and simplest things.
>
> The spirit of the depths took my understanding and all my knowledge and placed them at the service of the inexplicable and the paradoxical. He robbed me of speech and writing for everything that was not in his service, namely the melting together of sense and nonsense, which produces the greatest meaning.[48]

Jung describes being separated from his *belief in science*, his *joy in explaining and ordering things* and he is left with *the inexplicable and the paradoxical* and *the melting together of sense and nonsense.* Joseph might say that Jung is being initiated into non-ordinary reality and that he was losing his grounding in ordinary reality. Jung admits that there is some gain in this separation and loss of ordinary reality—*the supreme meaning.*

For Jung, the separation he describes in the *Red Book* and in his chapter "Confrontation with the Unconscious" in *Memories, Dreams, Reflections*, describe his separation from the world of objective science and began his initiation. He spent the rest of his life working with these inner images and experiences and later wrote of their immense value to him.

48 Jung, *Red Book*, 229. *A Reader's Edition*, 119–20.

> The years when I was pursuing my inner images were the most important in my life—in them everything essential was decided. It all began then; the later details are only supplements and clarifications of the material that burst forth from the unconscious, and at first swamped me. It was the *prima materia* for a lifetime's work.[49]

What complicated Jung's work was that he felt he could not speak openly about spiritual experiences as mystical experiences, he had to try to translate the intensively subjective, inner mystical experience into a language and format that was objective and scientific. Peter Kingsley writes that it is just this tension between Jung being a scientist *and* a mystic that makes his writing so important.

> If Jung had just been a scientist, his life and work would never have become such eternal objects of fascination. If he had simply been a mystic, no one would ever have cared so much.
>
> But his science coupled with his mysticism is what's so irresistible because it pulls us straight back past him, way beyond his personality, to the impersonal reality that lies buried at the roots of our western world and contains the secret of what our culture was meant to be.[50]

MATTHEW FOX

What distinguishes a warrior from a soldier is that a warrior is a mystic, a lover, one possessed by beauty, one alive with radical amazement, one seized by the Cataphatic Divinity, the God of Light and Creation. It takes a warrior to become a mystic, for the mystic cannot survive in denial; the mystic hunts everywhere in search of his or her beloved.[51]

Dominican Catholic Priest Matthew Fox had polio when he was 12 years old, but fully recovered after six months of convalescence. An experience of some kind of illness or accident is often found in the lives of mystics. "Polio altered my life," writes Fox, "especially my inner life." Rather than polio being a negative experience, Fox used the illness for transformation.

---

49 *MDR*, 199

50 Peter Kingsley, *Catafalque: Carl Jung and the End of Humanity*, 207.

51 Matthew Fox, *Meister Eckhart: A Mystic Warrior for Our Times*, xx.

> All in all, my memories of being in the hospital are not painful. If anything, a kind of joy entered my heart at that time. A joy and a trust. . . . Having polio taught me something about solitude: that it was okay to be alone and to not be in control. . . . First, I felt deeply grateful, not to anyone in particular—not even God-in-the-sky—but to the universe itself. I was well. . . . Today I like to tell people that mysticism is about "not taking for granted." An ecological awareness is therefore a mystical awareness. . . . Clearly, my polio experience baptized me into a mystical awareness.[52]

Later in his life as a Catholic priest, Fox started the Institute of Culture and Creation Spirituality (ICCS). Creation Spirituality denied the concept of "original sin" and held that human beings were essentially good and that life was an "original blessing" rather than an original sin. Fox blended a number of spiritual traditions at the ICCS, including Native American traditions, yoga, African drummers, and even Wiccan perspectives. Creation Spirituality is an Earth-based and inclusive spirituality and he would sometimes call God "Mother," which is not so unusual in traditional societies and Hinduism, but not part of Catholic dogma. Cardinal Ratzinger (who later became Pope Benedict XVI) hounded Fox for years, trying to coerce him to come back into the fold of traditional Catholicism. Fox, however, felt he had to pursue the goodness of the Truth, which was a mystical realization of God in one's life, rather than an adherence to dogma and scripture.

"I'm Catholic. I come from an age-old mystical tradition," he told journalist Molly O'Neill.[53] Eventually Cardinal Ratzinger publicly silenced Fox for one year and took away his income. During this time he went on retreat in the woods in Canada, did a Native American vision quest, and travelled extensively in Central and South America. He ended his year of being silenced with a public speech in which he said, "As I was saying fourteen months ago . . . when I was so rudely interrupted . . ."[54] He told journalist O'Neill, "I guess I'd be sorry for the things I've done, if I wanted to preserve a male-dominated, anthropocentric, essentially white institution that denies its own mystical tradition."[55]

---

52 Fox, *Confessions: The Making of a Postdenominational Priest*, 59–60.

53 "At Supper with – Matthew Fox; Roman Catholic Rebel Becomes A Cause Celebre," by Molly O'Neill, Published: March 17, 1993.The history of this paragraph can be found in O'Neill's article, as well as in more depth in Fox's autobiography, *Confessions*.

54 Matthew Fox, *Confessions: The Making of a Postdenominational Priest*, 229.

55 O'Neill.

Refusing to be silenced or compromised any longer, Fox continued on the path his heart had set for him. He published *Creation Spirituality: Liberating Gifts for the Peoples of the Earth* as a thank you to all who hosted him during his year of silence. In 1993 he was expelled from the Dominican Order for his ongoing teaching, writing, and activities.

Fox describes himself as "healed body, soul, and mind" from the vision quest he did, assisted by his friend Buck Ghosthorse, during the year of his silencing, which he describes in detail in his *Confessions*. Fox went on to map out an alternative spirituality, a creation spirituality, that is living, transcends religious divisions, harmonizes with nature, and is accessible to all people. It is an example of a living spirituality which recognizes the divine in all things and the sacred in all traditions. Like many who seek the truth beyond the confines of Rome, beyond the confines of a single tradition, he was branded a heretic and excommunicated.

THE MYSTIC UNIVERSE OF JOSEPH RAEL (BEAUTIFUL PAINTED ARROW)

Joseph, of course, can be considered a mystic. In one of his visions he describes seeing five beings who have a mystical resonance. "The five black-light beings that appeared like humans are symbolically the five vibrations of the vowels A-E-I-O-U. Additionally they represent the five right-hand fingers of Taah-meh-ney, who is the Creator-father in Tiwa mysticism."[56] Putting these vowels into sound and words is a way that Joseph teaches people how to know and connect to spirit. These sounds, letters, and words connect a person to their own inner source, awakening living spirituality.

When I mention Matthew Fox to Joseph he says: *"The word 'fox' in Tiwa is* ku-knek. *This means he who eats good food.* Ku *means good and* knek *means to eat."* When I tell him that Matthew Fox got kicked out of the Church, Joseph continued:

"No wonder he got kicked out! He knew more than the priests!"

D: "Because he was eating better food? The food of God?"

J: "Yes, yes."

Earlier that trip, we had seen two foxes hunting along the long drive way to Kuaua Pueblo. Joseph tells me that

"Kuaua*: means hello, it is the greeting that you give when you meet someone.*

---

56 *House*, 181.

DRINKING UNIVERSAL SPIRIT STARS LIGHTS

Ku *means good and* aua *means life, so it means good life, have a good life, it is like a blessing. So when we say hello to someone,* kuaua, *we are instantly bringing out the goodness that exists in the world, in the bushes, the plants, and the trees, the stones, and the mountains. It is not that we say it and it travels over there. We say it and it re-awakens what is already there in the world. In that way we are bringing out the goodness in the world through our words and our actions. We are giving birth to the world in our everyday life. Isn't that great?"*

Foxes are liminal beings that walk on the Earth and live below it in their dens. They are spirit animals of those who seek to connect the above and the below. Like a fox, Matthew Fox has been able to land on his feet and give us what is "good to eat." The Episcopal Church recognized his priesthood and welcomed him as a member and he re-founded his organization which is now called Creation Spirituality.

Around the time of his dismissal from the Dominican Order, Fox says that the universe gave him a great gift in the friendship of Father Bede Griffiths. This brings in another web of mystical interconnections: Griffiths is another point in the circle of *Becoming Medicine*—Griffiths replaced Abhishiktananda (whom we discuss elsewhere in this book) at Shantivanam, Sacchinananda Ashram in India. Griffiths also was an inspiration for Father Wayne Teasdale, author of *The Mystic Heart: Discovering Universal Spirituality in the World's Religions.*[57]

MYSTICAL BOOKS & MYSTICAL EXPERIENCES

> *Maybe that's our job, to make that connection with books or art or ceremonies. Maybe we help that awakening to manifest in a quicker way for individuals who want to pursue the mystical resonances of their own inner sources into blossoming forms. To me, that's why we write books and do art and music.*[58]
>
> JOSEPH RAEL

It all began in a bookstore . . . at least the interconnection. I first came to know of Joseph through finding a book on the shelf in a bookstore irresistible: *Being & Vibration*. I have mentioned how I came to know Joseph through Kurt Wilt and I began corresponding with Kurt Wilt after I found his book on Joseph, *The Visionary*, at Powell's Books in Portland. On another trip to Powell's I found Wayne Teasdale's book *The Mystic Heart*. These two books are like book ends for this book on *Becoming Medicine*. Kurt's book introduced me to Joseph. Teasdale's book introduced me to *guhā*, the cave of the heart, and to Abhishiktananda. For me, books are a link to mysticism and my story is as much a story of books as it is a story of relationships.

Illusions by Richard Bach is a book that I have carried with me throughout my life, reading and re-reading. I have turned to this "made up" story about illusions again and again at different low points in my life and it is like an old friend. The illusion alluded to in the title is that life is not "real" in the sense we ordinarily experience it, which is similar to Joseph's saying that "we do not exist" in the way we think we do. The central point of the book is that we are co-creators of our reality through

57 Teasdale makes the point that Griffiths was not a "syncretist" (*Bede Griffiths: An Introduction to His Spiritual Thought*). Syncretism is a blending of religions and this is one of the things that Fox was accused of when he brought in spiritual leaders from diverse traditions to teach at the Institute in Culture and Creation Spirituality (ICCS). The dilemma that faces many spiritual seekers who have an official title and role within a specific religion is how to remain true to their "parent" religion while respecting, honoring, and learning from other religions. For Abhishiktananda, particularly, we will see the struggles he went through as he pursued the path of a Hindu *sannyasi* (renunciate) while maintaining his position as a Benedictine monk. Abhishiktananda's first book was suppressed by the Catholic Church on the grounds of syncretism.

58 *Ceremonies*, 21.

our thoughts and expectations. The limitations that we experience in life are a consequence of our lack of imagination. In the book, the character Richard Bach goes through a mystical initiation into the nature of reality and spirituality through the "reluctant messiah" Donald Shimoda.

Recently, Joseph told me that I should read the book, *The Shack*, because it was about a man who meets and talks to God. That reminded me of *Illusions* and I asked Joseph if he had read that book. He thought he had and I recounted a little bit of the plot about how the book is about a messiah who quits his job and ends up flying biplanes in Illinois with Richard Bach and how Richard becomes his student. Joseph said, *"That sounds just like you and me!"*

ENTERING THE MYSTICAL HEART OF THE MEDICINE WHEEL CEREMONY

There are four outer directions of north, south, east and the west, we have spoken in our previous book of the four inner directions of the spiritual, emotional, mental and the physical. The shaman's, visionary's, and mystic's journey of the medicine wheel is a deeper journey yet, into the heart center of the wheel. The heart has four chambers, just as there are four outer and inner directions. The four chambers of the heart are the four directions or orientations of the heart. While this mystical path sounds like a fantastic journey that only a few could undertake, both Underhill and Soelle stress that we all are mystics, the mystical path is in our DNA. It is our inherent birthright to follow this path in small ways or in big ways, at certain stressful times in our lives, or as a constant path in a life.

In ordinary reality, there comes a time when the fire of your heart has gone out. In order to heal your heart, you must make a mystic journey. There is a cave of the heart, a place filled with darkness and emptiness. One must venture into the cave of the heart when life loses meaning and vitality. The journey into the *guhā*, cave of the heart, is long and arduous. In the cave of the heart you will find a stone that is shaped like a heart. You must find a way to light this stone on fire. Facing the east, pick up the stone heart and hold it tightly to your chest. Feel its coldness. Offer it your thoughts of love and healing. However, there is still darkness. Turning to the south, you must warm up this stone heart that has gone cold. At first you will feel only its coldness against your chest, but then you will start to feel your warmth going toward the stone heart. Offer to the stone heart your emotions of love and healing. Yet, there is even deeper darkness. Turning to the west, give it everything all the warmth of your body, until you and the stone heart are the same temperature, however it is still cold and dark, maybe even more so. Turning to the north, give, give it everything you have, give it your spirit of love and healing. And yet, it is darker and colder than ever.

Still. Be still. This is still not enough warmth to re-light the stone heart. You must give it more. You look around, but there is no firewood to be found, just an empty chamber of the heart. You must use the events of your own life as kindling. Everything you have, everything you have been, everything you have done, place it around the fire. Now, reach into your chest and take out your own stone heart, it is now cold as well. Strike your stone heart on the stone heart in front of you. Strike until there is a spark and all the kindling wood bursts up into flames. You now have a good fire going and the stone heart is surely warm now. However the fire starts to die down and the stone heart is still not lit.

What else can you give? Take all of your thoughts, emotions, desires, hopes, and dreams and throw them on the fire. You can sense that the fire is almost hot enough now, but what else can you throw on it to help it get that last little bit hotter? Throw yourself on it, your identity, your body, your sense of "I exist," definitely throw your sense of "I exist" on the fire, for it will not serve you well any longer.

Now! The fire bursts in flames, up to the ceiling, consuming you, filling the entire room and the stone heart begins to glow, the way that molten lava from a volcano glows. As the flames die down, you realize that no matter what you do, you cannot light the stone heart in ordinary reality. You must cross over into non-ordinary reality, but you have already done the preparatory ceremony to do so. As darkness begins to creep back in around the edges of the room, stare into the stone heart, gaze into it with all your attention and intention. Take your own stone heart that you are still holding in your hand and place it on the glowing stone heart. Push it against the glowing stone heart and you will see that it sinks into the glowing stone heart. This is because there is no difference between your heart and the stone heart in the inner cave. This stone heart in front of you is the heart of the earth and there is no difference between your heart and the heart of the earth. You are now in non-ordinary reality.

You are now in the cave of the non-ordinary heart. It is exactly the same,

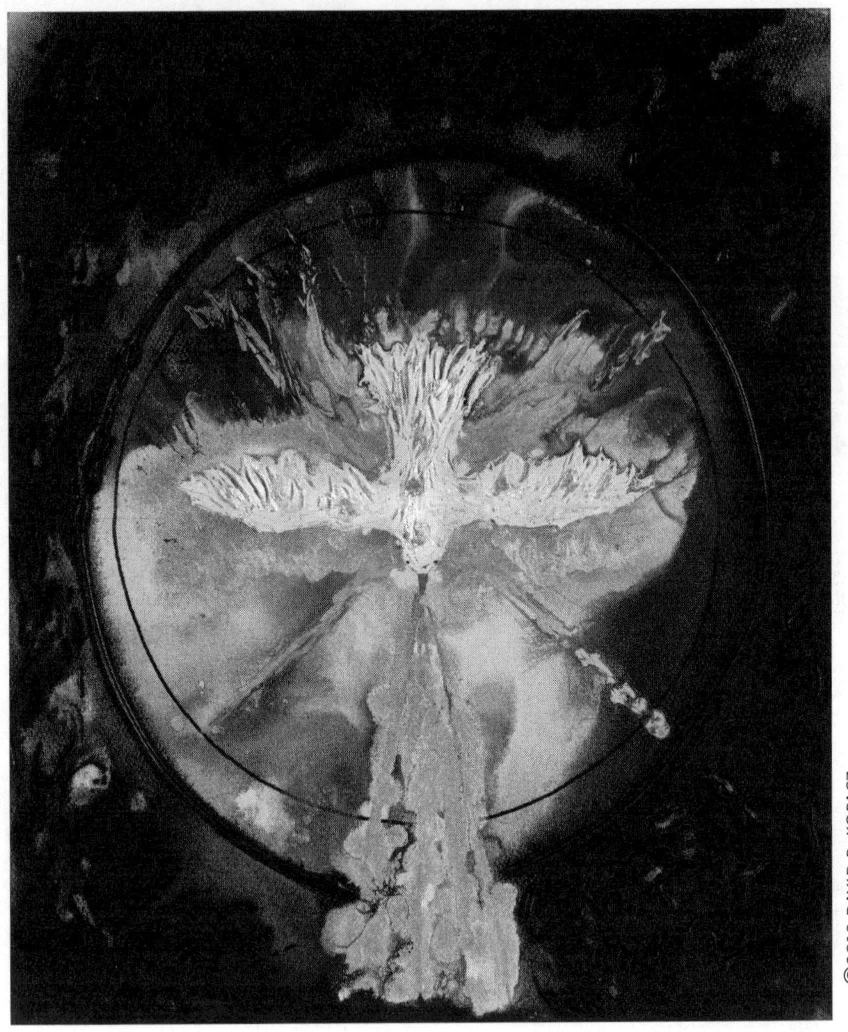

DOVE OF THE HOLY SPIRIT

except that the stone heart is glowing and burning like the sun, it is giving off light and the whole cave is filled with the divine fire of non-ordinary reality. Bask in this light for some time. Now, reach into the burning fire of the flaming non-ordinary heart, it will burn like crazy, but that is not what is important, just reach into the fire and pull out your stone heart that is now also burning like the sun and giving off light and life. Place your burning stone heart on your chest. It will burn and sear, but that is not what is important. Gently push your burning stone heart back into your chest and let it fill you with light and life. Turn to the east and let it light up your mind. Turn to the south and let it ignite your emotions. Turn to the west and let if fill your body with liquid, glowing light. Turn to the north and let the burning dove of the Holy Spirit of Divine Fire enter you. Give thanks. Now you can return to ordinary reality and be a source of love, light, and life for yourself and all of those around you.

BECOMING MYSTICS, VISIONARIES, AND SHAMANS

I give examples of my experiences throughout this book to show that we all have the capability of having mystic, visionary, and shamanic experiences. It is nothing special, although it is non-ordinary. We can develop the ability to have experiences of non-ordinary reality and this is the same thing as saying that we are walking the path of becoming mystics, visionaries, and shamans. We never actually arrive to say, "I am a mystic, I am a visionary, I am a shaman." Instead we can say, I am in the process of *becoming*, not in the business of arriving. As Joseph has taught me, I recently positioned myself in the center of the medicine wheel. I extended my consciousness out 200 miles to the north, 200 miles to the south, 200 miles to the east, and then 200 miles to the west. I moved out of my body, which I watch sitting in the center of the medicine wheel. Immediately there was loud clanging noises—dissonant and chaotic. I had the sense of being on the verge of being overwhelmed by the chaotic assault of clanging noises. I often feel the presence of Crow.[59] I remembered how in my last vision I had gone into space to recover a body—my body, and how Crow had expanded and expanded into the darkness of space, filling the void of space with the living darkness of his body. And then Crow had swooped through the stars, swallowing them, even swallowing the moon and as we came back to earth to the center of the medicine wheel I smiled at how Crow had done this and how I now had the stars and the moon so close to me, right on my shoulder. It came to me, "Let's go exploring, let's go off into space!" And Crow and I shot out into space, he seemed so gleeful and joyful to spread his wings in the cosmos. We shot to the center of our Milky Way Galaxy and there we sat.

The clanging was still loud and dissonant but eventually I began to hear a rhythmic drum beat, slow and steady. The clanging began to recede and fall away, replaced by the rhythmic drumming. And then I heard

59 Joseph, as in many Native American and shamanic traditions, speaks of spirit guides and animal helpers.

the cosmic chanting of the galaxy, "Muuuuuuuuuu." And the "uuu" sound reverberated indefinitely, like Pythagoras' harmony of the spheres. I had just been reading the Zen koan, Joshu says "mu." And *mu* meant something like "no" or "not." I thought, gosh, the center of the galaxy can't be negation, can it?" Then I recalled how Joseph says that we don't exist and I wondered if maybe this is the truth that our galaxy is built on this sound, which is real, but which is reminding us in its realness that we are not real in the way we think we are real. We know that the center of the Milky Way contains a black hole four million times the mass of our sun.[60]

"Joshu says mu" is a Zen koan, a paradoxical teaching. Joshu was a Zen master and he had these students who were always asking him questions. One day a student asked him if a dog has Buddha-nature. Joshu said, simply, "mu." *Mu*, in Chinese Zen, means "not" or "nothingness." *Mu* is the sound of nothingness. Another Zen koan is "What is the sound of one hand clapping?" You could very well answer, "*Mu*." Koans were designed to help separate the student's habitual mind-set from his or her conscious awareness, leading to enlightenment (initiation). In discussing Joshu's "Mu," we come up against what Joseph Rael teaches, that *we do not exist*. Zenkei Shibayama, in his discussion of this koan writes, "We should not read this as an old story; you yourself have to *be* directly 'Mu.' . . . Not only that, you yourself and the whole universe are nothing but 'Mu.'"[61]

Is this a real vision or did I make it up unconsciously or subconsciously? When I looked up Joseph's teaching of the Tiwa language sound meaning of "M" is, "manifestation" and then of course, "U" is the sound of the center of the medicine wheel, which has the essence of *carrying*. It seemed like confirmation that there is meaning in this vision and consistency between my inner experience and documented symbols.[62] Then I came across another lead, Charles Eisenstein refers to Mother Universe, that led me to think that Mother Universes initials are MU.[63]

Mysticism is a word that people feel very differently about. To a materialist it means something obscure, vague, and made up. To a mystic,

60 Priyamvada Natarajan, *Mapping the Heavens: The Radical Ideas that Reveal the Cosmos*, 68.

61 Zenkei Shibayama, *The Gateless Barrier: Zen Comments on the Mumonkan*, 22.

62 The meaning of vowels and consonants will be references to *B&V:NW*, pages 80-89, unless otherwise specified. In Tiwa, Joseph will often find variations on the meaning of words and letters depending on the context, so there may be variations in the text from what he has written in the past.

63 Charles Eisenstein, *The Ascent of Humanity*, 491.

the word represents the pathway for a direct experience of divinity. Is mysticism a path of co-creating our reality, or is it wishful or fuzzy thinking? Is scientific materialism an advance in perceiving the truth of reality or is it a limitation of our experience of different dimensions of reality? Are there different realities that mysticism and scientific materialism illuminate? Maybe scientific materialism describes the 4% of the universe we can experience and measure and mysticism studies the 96% of the universe comprised of dark matter and dark energy that we cannot measure.

PART II

INITIATION (FINDING & RECEIVING)

The two—the hero and his ultimate god, the seeker and the found—are thus understood as the outside and the inside of a single, self-mirrored mystery, which is identical with the mystery of the manifest world. The great deed of the supreme hero is to come to the knowledge of this unity in multiplicity and to make it known.[1]

JOSEPH CAMPBELL

If, in presence, we can descend to the deepest in ourselves, we see clearly that there is no ego, no differentiation, and therefore no duality.[2]

DANIEL ODIER

Carrying is the same as initiation. At sunrise, the sun's light initiates the day. At sundown, the sunlight initiates the night by ending the light of the day and beginning the dark of night. Similarly, life is carrying all that is; all plants, animals, and things. Life initiates us into linear time. We live from one moment to the next one. We live inside each moment, then it passes on so that we can become something new. A past moment that just died carries and becomes the foundation for the new knowing that was just born.[3]

JOSEPH RAEL

It's good to be a seeker,
But sooner or later you have to be a finder;
And then it is good to give what you have found.
A gift into the world for whoever will accept it.[4]

RICHARD BACH

1 Campbell, *The Hero With A Thousand Faces*, 31.
2 Odier, *Desire*, 54.
3 *Sound*, 111.
4 I have seen this quote attributed to Richard Bach on the internet, but I have not been able to locate it in a physical book in two different editions of *Jonathan Livingstone Seagull*, the citation given. I guess I am still a seeker on this and not yet a finder!

CROW FLYING THROUGH COSMOS

CHAPTER 7

STORY MEDICINE

All that we are is story. From the moment we are born to the time we continue on our spirit journey, we are involved in the creation of the story of our time here. It is what we arrive with. It is all we leave behind. We are not the things we accumulate. We are not the things we deem important. We are story. All of us. What comes to matter then is the creation of the best possible story we can while we're here; you, me, us, together. When we can do that and we take the time to share those stories with each other, we get bigger inside, we see each other, we recognize our kinship – we change the world, one story at a time . . . [1]

RICHARD WAGAMESE

We've been searching for our whole lives
And we have traveled through unexplainable stories
Swear to God I fought the good fight
Always waiting for the coming of morning
And I heard the Captain say, I heard the Captain say
"The more I know, the less I'm knowing." [2]

CLOUD CULT

JOSEPH RAEL'S NEW CREATION STORY

Joseph called me with a dream/vision he had one morning:

"Grandmother was making strong black coffee one morning and brought a cup to Grandfather. She also brought the coffee upstairs to the children and gave it to them so that they would get out of bed. She wasn't supposed to do this, so she didn't tell Grandfather this. [Joseph relates that this happened to him when he was a young boy, that he was given coffee secretly in the morning to wake him up so he would get dressed for school].

"When Grandfather drank the coffee he had an epiphany, an inspiration. He had a white sheet of paper in front of him and he hit it and it made the

1 Richard Wagamese, quoted in Jim Poling, "We are story," *The Minden Times Ontario* online, accessed 6/22/18.

2 Cloud Cult, "Unexplainable Stories," from the album *Light Chasers*.

sound, one—weh-mu*! He hit it again and it made the sound, two*—weh-seh*! Then again, three*—paah-chu! *He continued to hit the paper ten times, counting out the numbers of inspiration one through ten: four*—wii, *five*—paah-nu, *six*—maa-tschlay, *seven*—cho-oh, *eight*—wheh-leh, *nine*—whiii, *ten*—tehn-ku-teh. *He hit the paper with a multi-colored colored pencil that he had and with each hit he created a circle of colored light that emanated out from the Big Bang of the central point.*

We talked about this vision for a while and I wondered why God needed the cup of coffee for inspiration (I do live in Seattle). I wondered if the black liquid coffee could represent the blackness of the Void that existed before creation.[3] I like this idea that God drank in liquid blackness and out of this inspiration came a vision, which Joseph describes as the soul drinking light—and out of inspiration comes rainbow circles of light creating Creation out of sound, light, color, breath, and vibration.

In Joseph's vision, we also have the interaction of the feminine and the masculine in creation, the feminine providing the inspiration through the liquid black of coffee, but also showing the introduction of duality and the use of coffee for both the inspiration to create the Universe, but also abusing the coffee to force the children awake. In the exegesis of the vision, Joseph mentioned that the Grandmother was an older generation than the Grandfather, not necessarily the partner of the Grandfather, but maybe the Grandmother of the Grandfather—thus we have the interesting idea that perhaps the Grandfather was one of the children that the Grandmother was trying to get up, dressed and off to school, and what slipped out was that the child/Grandfather smacked the paper 10 times and created the Universe before running off to school.

Joseph explained that prior to the Grandfather having the epiphany, he was living in darkness, in the Vast Self. He was an artist who had learned to see in the dark, making his sketches. He hadn't yet moved into the Circle of Light. *"Darkness is where all the good ideas are,"* says Joseph, this is where the source of inspiration is. With the first hit of the paper, simultaneously a sound and light are created. This is the point of light at the center of the medicine wheel. It is the light of epiphany, the light of movement, there is

3 In the World Religions class I took at university, I heard a story that Muslim jurists debated whether coffee was a drug and should thus be banned, or if it was acceptable to drink. Their finding was that yes, coffee was a drug, but it could be used for positive benefit to become more focused and to stay up at night and worship Allah and read the *Qur'an*.

now a central organizing point. With each hit of the paper, a new colored circle of light of the medicine wheel is created.

Joseph gave another interpretation of this dream/vision. The central point is the nipple of the round breast. With each hit of the Grandfather's multi-colored pencil, a new energy was released through this cosmic nipple that feeds the baby of the New Self. We all feed on the epiphanies through this cosmic nipple. All the babies on the earth, the human and animal, sucking at the breasts of their mothers keep the cosmic medicine wheel going.

In talking about this dream/vision, Joseph says, *"Of course we are God, we are the artist."* Each of us is creation, but we also keep creation going through our lives and as we cycle through the medicine wheel we create energy—the friction in our lives creates sparks and gives off light. The medicine wheel gives a structure, organization and context to all life events. It shows how life moves in circles: each year we move from winter to spring to summer to fall and back to winter again; each life comes from the earth and returns to the earth; each inspiration and epiphany begins in the North (winter/spiritual) and then moves to the East (spring/mental), then to the South (summer/emotional), and then to the West (fall/physical). The medicine wheel explains how spiritual inspiration becomes mental idea, becomes emotional feeling, and then becomes a physical thing in material reality. The medicine wheel shows that there is no artificial boundary between the spiritual and physical, rather there is a bridge, or a rolling wheel that moves the energy along, manifesting in different dimensions at different times.

CREATION BEGINS WITH SOUND

Hindus say it all started with a sound, oh yeah
Christians say it was spoken out in a word – that's a sound
Steve Hawking said it all started with a bang, oh, yeah – that's a sound
Hello, Steve . . .
We're living in deep space
And the center's any place
Yet nowhere to be found . . .
It all started with a sound
Let there beeeeeeeeee.........Light![4]

LUKE HURLEY

4 Luke Hurley, "The Sound," from the album *The Best of Luke Hurley*.

Creation stories start with *sound* (in fact, before writing, all stories started with sound and could only be told through sound, even now with reading a story, it only makes sense through the echoes of words sounding in your consciousness). In his book, *Sound: Native Teachings and Visionary Art*, Joseph writes that "The mystery of life is very simple. . . . The truth is this: Sound is the basis for all that is."[5] In learning the four spoken languages of his childhood (Ute, Tiwa, English, Spanish), Joseph realized that the combination of sounds, particularly vowel sounds, brought about the creation of things. Joseph describes a creation story.

> In the beginning, according to the creation story, there was nothing. All was complete blankness. This nothingness wanted to bring itself into awareness, to know itself. Then life was created by *Wah-mah-chi*, which is the Tiwa name for God, and means breath, matter, movement. The breath is the inspiration in matter that brings all concreteness into form, into existence via movement. Really only one thing exists, and that is the breath of God in a state of movement creating the vibration of matter.[6]

In Tiwa, the word *poh*, is the word is for "breath" and for "sound." *Poh* means, "blowing breath," "sound," "wheel of sound," and also "the circle of the medicine wheel." Just as the circle of life is continuous and the story of life has to be continually spoken, so too Joseph sees creation not as an act accomplished once in the past, but as a continual act of work that we as human beings do. He writes, "I now see this creation as a continual process, an evolution of consciousness that results from the interplay between the realm of pure ideas and the material realm."[7] In other words, every moment is a new beginning, a new moment of creation. Thus it is important for us to tell and re-tell and re-make creation stories. Through repeating ceremonies, creation is renewed, and people are co-creators in creation and reality. The Tiwa word for "people," *tie-eh-neh*, also means "vibration," and thus we are back where we started, with sound.

CREATION STORIES

Creation stories serve as the archetypal patterns for a culture's initiation stories. Creation is the first initiation—it is the separation from the void,

---

5 *Sound*, 11.

6 Ibid., 19.

7 Ibid., 20.

THE BLOWING BREATH OF DARK ENERGY

the emergence of form from the state of undifferentiated chaos. Creation begins with the separation and differentiation of the creature from the Creator. In these stories the Creator often gives humanity the "original instructions" for the proper way of living in harmony with creation.[8] A second separation occurs when humanity forgets the "original instructions," and then must struggle to return to the right path again. Creation stories are stories of separation, initiation, and return.

THE JUDEO-CHRISTIAN CREATION STORY

In the beginning God created the heavens and the earth. The earth was without form and void, and darkness was upon the face of the deep; and the Spirit of God was moving over the face of the waters.

And God said, "Let there be light"; and there was light. And God saw that the light was good; and God separated the light from the darkness. God called the light Day, and the darkness he called Night. And there was evening and there was morning, one day.

8 See Richard Smoley, "Original Instructions: An Interview with Peter Kingsley," in *Quest.*

> *And God said, "Let there be a firmament in the midst of the waters, and let it separate the waters from the waters. And God made the firmament and separated the waters which were under the firmament from the waters which were above the firmament. And it as so. And God called the firmament Heaven.*[9]

God continues to separate things and eventually gathers up some of the dust (the earth he has created), forms it and breathes (sound) into it and creates Adam and Eve in the Garden. Through the Fall (separation), Adam and Eve's descendants are initiated into exile and they seek to return to God and the Garden.

A HINDU[10] CREATION STORY

Joseph Campbell summarizes a Hindu creation story. "So, in the beginning that was no beginning, there was nothing but the Self. And the Self at a moment that was no moment said, 'I. *Aham. Ego.*' And as soon as it thought, 'I,' it experienced fear." After fear, desire arose, and the "Self swelled and split in half . . . and there were two. Each united with the other and produced something. And then she—the feminine one—said, 'How can he unite with me who am of his own substance?' So she turned herself into a cow; he turned into a bull. She turned into a donkey, and he turned into a jackass. She turned into a mare, and he into a horse, and so on down to the ants."[11] In this creation story the sound of the word "I," coinciding with consciousness (separation from unconsciousness), leads to fear, desire, and a continual pattern of separation into masculine and feminine of all the creatures that leads to the vast diversity of life.

A GREEK CREATION STORY

Campbell tells of another creation story, as told by Plato in the *Symposium*. Plato recounts Aristotle's telling of the following creation story. In the beginning all human beings had two heads, four arms and four legs.

---

9 *The Holy Bible, Revised Standard Version, Second Catholic Version, Genesis* 1.1–1.8.

10 Some say that it would be more correct to use the term Vedanta rather than Hinduism. However, in this book we will be speaking of a range of "Hinduisms," including Kashmiri Shaivism, for which Vedanta may not be the proper over-arching category. We will use "Hindu" and "Hinduism" in the book with apologies to those who would prefer a different term.

11 In Joseph Campbell, *Myths of Light*, 9.

The human beings came in three varieties: male-male, female-female, and female-male. The Greek god, Zeus became afraid of the power of these combined unities, and so, with a lightning bolt (sound and light), split them in two. However, as soon as they were separated, they simply clung to one another, so the gods separated them and scattered them across the globe, mixed up with all peoples. Yet even still, these separated, half-beings, sought out their other half in order to recreate the original unity.[12]

A MĀORI CREATION STORY

The indigenous Māori people of *Aotearoa* (New Zealand) have a creation myth that echoes many traditional myths. In the beginning, there was the sky father, *Ranginui*, and mother earth, *Papatuanuku*. They lived in happy embrace, yet their children had no space to live their lives, they were cramped. All the sons tried pushing them apart, to no avail. Eventually *Tāne Mahuta*, the god of the forests and birds, succeeded. In order for the new generation of created beings to thrive, there had to be space created between the primal parents. However Ranginui still grieves over the separation from his wife and love, and thus tears of rain fall from the sky. Papatuanuku also grieves, and her body heaves with earthquakes and grows hot with passion (New Zealand has many hot pools and geothermal activity) and longing for her husband and lover.[13]

THE BIG BANG: THE CREATION STORY OF SCIENCE

The Big Bang is the scientific creation story. We do not know what existed before the Big Bang, but the story goes that in the beginning there was a "very dense point of space and time," a "primeval atom." Then there was a "bang," an explosion of diversity from that single point. Clouds of gas condensed into the first stars, but these stars only contained hydrogen, helium. These were the building blocks of life, but not all of them, the heavier elements necessary for life were only created through the supernovae explosions (death) of the first stars. These explosions further condensed matter, creating the elements that led to series upon series of

12 Ibid., 10.

13 There are multiple sources for this creation story and I give, here, a synopsis. Joseph Campbell gives a version of this in *The Hero with a Thousand Faces*, 241–42. *Tāne Mahuta* is also the name of the largest and oldest kauri tree in New Zealand. I have visited this giant tree, who is estimated to be around 2,000 years old. Campbell also cites other Māori legends, including a beautiful, poem-like listing of a series of voids, nights, and dawns, (231–32, 234–36).

deaths and rebirths of stars.[14] The molecules that we are made of came from the Big Bang and from the deaths of the ancient stars. Thus Moby can sing, "We are all made of stars."[15]

According to Joseph Rael, creation requires splitting. Creativity comes from working with the split as well as working to re-unify. Our stories are, ultimately, the stuff of creation.

> We are constantly in a state of creativity; we are co-creating. Creation requires splitting. . . . In order to reproduce, life had to split itself. In order to become ourselves, we split ourselves apart from our memory of ourselves. . . . At the heart center, we know that we are not really split. We appear to be split, but our split only exists in the material realm where perception rules our reality. But this reality is constantly changing, for perception is impermanence. We appear to be split, but our split exists only in the material realm where perception rules reality.[16]

ANOTHER OF JOSEPH'S CREATION STORIES: GOD'S FALL

Joseph tells another Creation story—where it is God that falls, rather than humanity. In this story God was walking along and slipped on something, letting out a cry, a sound, the entire universe was created from that first Sound. We can imagine that the Big Bang in this story happened when God decided that there should be something solid to land on to stop this fall. The work of the visionary is the work of God. The creation of the visionary is the act of allowing God to create through the individual personality.

Joseph explains that the work that he and I are doing in writing this book, and the work that you, the reader, are doing in reading this book is to *"Explore an area that religions haven't explored."* This unexplored area is the area that the mystics and poets know, the area that we are continually creating as we create our lives. Creation is not a thing of the past, it is a moment, continually renewed in the present moment. There is a Latin phrase for the continual creation and renewal of the universe, *creatio continua*. The time of Creation, the time of the revelation and epiphany of *Wah-Mah-Chi*, is not in the distant past, but is happening right now—

---

14 Natarajan, *Mapping the Heavens*, 60–65, 162–65.

15 Moby, "We Are All Made of Stars," from the album *18*. Moby has said that this song was influenced by the band, Galaxie 500's song, "Flowers," quantum physics, and in response to the September 11th attacks on the World Trade Center.

16 *Sound*, 94.

Creation is now, always in this very moment as we are inspired and expiring, as we are breathing in and breathing out, and as we are breathed in and breathed out.

NARRATIVE MEDICINE

There is a growing field of medicine which is not new, but is rather the rediscovering and remembering of how speaking words and listening to stories can be transformational for the individual and society. Physician and healer, Lewis Mehl-Madrona, is on the forefront of reaching back into ancient wisdom to bring the healing power of story into contemporary medicine and society. As he was studying contemporary medicine he also began to explore his Native American heritage. He seeks to map out how the healing power of story interacts with the brain and neuroscience. Mehl-Madrona describes his goal as: "to save and promote the visions and wisdom of aboriginal cultures for health and healing—because we desperately need this perspective and their stories."[17] Healing for the individual as well as healing the institution of medicine requires that we learn again to listen to individual human being's stories. "Changing medicine means making new stories, telling these stories, and appreciating the stories of others."[18] Stories were the earliest form of medicine as they have the power to transform and heal. We can think of story as indigenous medicine and indigenous science. Mehl-Madrona recounts how anthropologist William Lyon told him that "shamanism represents the original science . . . that every shamanic ceremony is in essence a scientific experiment."[19] Story is an essential part of shamanic work as many shamans tell healing stories as part of the ceremony. For instance in *Walking the Medicine Wheel*, the *nah-meh-neh* ceremony that Joseph Rael offers for veterans, he recounts a story of creation and our relationship to the land and sky, to Mother Earth and to Father Sky.

Lewis Mehl-Madrona developed a chart that compares and contrasts narrative medicine with conventional medicine and this chart captures much of what Joseph and I seek to explain in this book and it will seem quite similar to our earlier description of circle medicine.

---

17 Lewis Mehl-Madrona, *Narrative Medicine*, 17.

18 Ibid., 296.

19 Ibid., 69.

NARRATIVE MEDICINE[20]	CONVENTIONAL MEDICINE
Multiple causality	Unilateral causality
Systemic explanations	Mechanistic explanations
Entanglement, interdependence; circularity; relationship to quantum physics	Independent variables; linearity; cause and effect; randomized controlled trials; classical mechanics
Community focus (disease seen as originating through relationships within a community)	Individual focus (disease is seen as originating within the individual)
Solutions do not necessarily relate to causes	Solutions arise from understanding cause, and grow logically out of one cause
Healing focuses upon restoring harmony and balance	Healing focuses upon finding a specific biological or genetic cause and fixing that
Disease arises out of dysfunction; it occurs through susceptibility, which relates to imbalance and disharmony in relationship	Disease is defined by structural suffering and anomalies; caused by biological factors or genetics (cause and defect paradigm)
Relational self	Individual self
Cooperate; win-win	Compete; win-lose
Disease is found within relationships	Disease is found within individuals and specifically within organs

Lewis Mehl-Madrona continues to write books and give workshops about the healing power of story. He has called for a reinvention of psychiatry "as the art and science of story," and says that we "can draw on the wisdom of the narrative movement in philosophy and psychology for support in transforming our vision of brain and behavior from one of defective brains (genetically or structurally) to defective stories."[21] In *Remapping Your Mind: The Neuroscience of Self-Transformation through Story*, he links the function and effect of stories to recent findings in neuroscience. For instance, the Default Mode Network creates a constant background activity level which he sees as linked to story.

20 Table adapted from Ibid., 31.

21 Mehl-Madrona, *Healing the Mind Through the Power of Story: The Promise of Narrative Psychiatry*, 5.

> We need to understand story, because story is our default mode: it is intrinsic to who we are. Story is what we use to explain our world. Story is what we use to create identity. More than that, increasingly, it seems apparent that the stories we tell ourselves literally impact our health.

Part of the benefit of story is that it creates a mental flexibility that allows us to take in new information and to change our identities. Mehl-Madrona writes that we "need to think of ourselves in a way that is less literal," as this is "an indigenous way of thinking that locates us embedded in a swarm of stories, moving along through time."[22] There is a growing literature on writing, story, and health that is validating what indigenous people have known even before stories were ever written down: telling stories is healing.

"Story is our science," Joseph tells me, *"Indian science is the study of ordinary reality in relationship to non-ordinary, we do it through dance. But you have to live in an ego-less world, a world without ego."*

Gregory Cajete writes similarly about story and native science. "Native science is a story, an explanation of the ways of nature and sources of life, embedded in the guiding stories of a people and the language and way of life that convey their stories."[23] Stories not only pass down ancient wisdom, they also can be used for creation and healing. Mehl-Madrona writes, "I saw that we create our own world . . . if we refuse to believe in healing, healing does not exist. If we sing and dance only of molecules and drugs, then molecules determine our fate and drugs will be our only hope. What we believe in is what comes true. . . . What we sing and dance is what will be."[24]

Another storyteller who has been influential for me is Rebecca Solnit. For Solnit, one story leads to another and one story interweaves with other stories. She weaves together her own personal narrative together with history, environmental awareness, politics, human nature, and even a little punk rock now and then. Here is a little of what she has to say about story.

> What is your story? It's all in the telling. Stories are compasses and architecture; we navigate by them, we build our sanctuaries and our prisons out of them, and to be without a story is to be lost in the

---

22 Mehl-Madrona, *Remapping Your Mind: The Neuroscience of Self-Transformation through Story*, 2–3, 63–64.

23 Cajete, *Native Science*, 74.

24 Mehl-Madrona, *Coyote Medicine*, 111.

> vastness of the world that spreads in all directions like arctic tundra or sea ice. To love someone is to put yourself in their place, we say, which is to put yourself in their story, or figure out how to tell yourself their story. . . . We think we tell stories, but stories often tell us, tell us to love or to hate, to see or to be blind. Often, too often, stories saddle us, ride us whip us onward, tell us what to do, and we do it without questioning. The task of learning to be free requires learning to hear them, to question them, to pause and hear silence, to name them, and then to become the storyteller.[25]

Solnit illustrates many of the aspects that Lewis Mehl-Madrona speaks of in regard to story and identity. She grasps the circularity of story as something that we create, but also something that creates us. Stories are maps of both our inner and outer landscapes. Stories connect the inner and outer and maybe they even are what makes the medicine wheel circle and maybe they are the sound that comes out of this spinning wheel of our life. All is story: stories are the only thing that exist. Matter does not matter unless it has a story. Joseph would say that if we can be still and listen, even the smallest rock or stone can tell a story. From the ancient times wisdom was passed down through story and culture was created through story.

A NEW MYTHOPOESIS: THE CALL FOR A NEW CREATION STORY

Stories often begin with "A long time ago…" but in modern times we have lost connection with the past and we have lost connection with our stories. This is what Carl Jung illuminated when he realized he did not know the "myth" by which he was living. After completing his book, *Symbols of Transformation*, which led to his break with Freud, he felt pleased with himself when a disconcerting inner dialogue arose in him:

> "Now you possess a key to mythology and are free to unlock all the gates of the unconscious psyche." But then something whispered within me, "Why open all gates?" And promptly the question arose of what, after all, I had accomplished. I had explained the myths of peoples of the past; I had written a book about the hero, the myth in which man has always lived. But in what myth does man live nowadays? . . . "But then what is your myth—the myth in which you do live?" At this

25 Rebecca Solnit, *The Faraway Nearby*, 3–4.

> point the dialogue with myself became uncomfortable, and I stopped thinking. I had reached a dead end.[26]

Jung then had a dream of a white dove that came to him and transformed into a young girl who spoke with him. This dream led to an opening of Jung's consciousness into which the creative unconscious flowed and out of this a story emerged: the "Seven Sermons of the Dead," and *The Red Book*. This story took the rest of his life to tell, because the story was his life, and even after he passed on, his story continued to unfold as his *Red Book* was published and people continue to discuss the story of Carl Jung.

Each of us has a story inside of us that is longing to be told and the only way we can tell it is through listening to that story as our life unfolds around us. Sometimes our story will lead us into a dead end and there we have to sit in stillness and listen to the whisperings of the story within us. One way of looking at illness and sickness is that it happens when we lose track of the story we are meant to be living. When the two Navajo brothers became sick in the story of *Where the Two Came to Their Father*, the holy people took them to a sacred mountain and the medicine given to them was to hear their own story four times, once for each direction. After hearing their own story told back to them four times, the brothers were once again healthy, "Then they felt fine and could move as before. And they talked of living in the future, and of making the future people."[27] Their story was the medicine they were seeking, becoming their own story was *becoming medicine*. They had to go four times around the wheel, once for each direction, and then enter back into the center of the story of their lives.

Another way we can learn about our story is by listening to the stories of others. When we hear of other people losing their way, losing their story, and then when we hear about them regaining their story, it gives us hope and inspiration that we can find the thread of our own story once again and we can feel hope. In this way, stories are medicine for the soul, stories are like visions, listening to them is like the soul drinking light and being able to shine again.

---

26 *MDR*, 171.

27 Maud Oakes and Joseph Campbell, *Where the Two Came to Their Father: A Navaho War Ceremonial Given by Jeff King*, 52. We discuss this story in more depth in *Walking the Medicine Wheel*.

STORIES OF SEPARATION AND STORIES OF REUNION

I only just started to read Charles Eisenstein's *The More Beautiful World Our Hearts Know is Possible* and *Climate: A New Story* as I was putting the finishing touches on *Becoming Medicine.* Eisenstein illuminates how the stories that shape our identities lead to different actions in the world. He tells us we need more than incremental change to address political, environmental, and cultural crises—we need a total transformation of who we are and that this requires a change in our guiding story. This requires shifting from "the Story of Separation" to "the Story of Interbeing, the Age of Reunion." By repeatedly telling ourselves the Story of Separation, we reinforce our identities as separate, disconnected individuals and this leads to selfish and unloving actions. This is a similar point that Joseph and I are making in this book, and that we need to move from separation to union. Eisenstein's vision is that our current crises are spiritual crises and he even starts off *The More Beautiful World Our Hearts Know is Possible* with a chapter entitled "Separation," and he concludes with a chapter on "Initiation."

> This book is a guide from the old story, through the empty space between stories, and into a new story. It addresses the reader as a subject of this transition personally, and as an agent of transition—for other people, for our society, and for our planet.
>
> Like the crisis, the transition we face goes all the way to the bottom. Internally, it is nothing less than a transformation in the experience of being alive. Externally, it is nothing less than a transformation of humanity's role on planet Earth.

Eisenstein sees an "emerging Story of the People that is the defining of a new mythology of a new kind of civilization," in which "we are inseparate from the universe, and our being partakes in the being of everyone and everything else."[28] This is what he means by the Story of Interbeing and this is what we mean by creating the new story of *Becoming Medicine.*

---

28 Charles Eisenstein, *The More Beautiful World Our Hearts Know Is Possible*, 1–7, 15–21.

A CALL FOR A NEW CREATION STORY

> *What does a creation story do for us? It grounds us in the history of how we arrived here, and it awakens awe and wonder that we are here. When this happens, we are less subject to manipulation, to trivia, to titillating distractions, addictions, and consumerism. . . .*
>
> *All origins are sacred. To hear stories of our origins that are fresh and true is to awaken reverence and awe among us. We return to our origins in a sacred journey we make together when we share a common creation story.*[29]
>
> MATTHEW FOX

Matthew Fox was excommunicated from the Catholic Church for teaching what he calls *creation spirituality*. He calls out for us to create a new creation story in which we see creation not as a fall or a sin, but rather as a gift. This approach is similar to the creation stories of many indigenous people who do not have the sense of pure transcendent spirituality in which the body and the Earth are sinful, but rather that the Earth and the earth that composes our very bodies is divine. Fox calls this *creation spirituality* and it is an alternative to the transcendent spiritualities that have led to the pollution and subjugation of the Earth, the oppression of indigenous peoples, discrimination and mistreatment of women, and our alienation from our own bodies. This immanent spirituality tells us the divine is found within all of creation.

Just as with narrative medicine, creation spirituality is not something new, but rather bringing ancient wisdom into the present. "Creation spirituality is not a newly invented path. For twentieth-century Westerners it is a newly *discovered* path because the onslaught of anthropocentric (human-centered) culture that began with the breakup of cosmology at the end of the Middle Ages has left us lost in a mechanized and nonmystical world."

Creation spirituality gives us a new creation story that is life-affirming and present-focused. It teaches us how to be *a living spirituality*, it teaches us how to be *becoming medicine*. Fox tells us that we need this new creation story as medicine to heal the ills of our current society.

> A new cosmic creation story is important because, historically, all tribes have kept themselves together through their creation stories.

---

29 Matthew Fox, *Creation Spirituality*, 27–28.

> Today, with scientists agreeing the world over on the basic facts of a new creation story, we have the potential for a sense of global unity, an experience of the human race as a single tribe bound together by a single, amazing, creation story.[30]

A NEW MYTHOLOGY FOR THE EARTH

In studying mythology and psychotherapy, Carl Jung realized he did not know what the organizing and orienting myth was by which he was living. This led to his descent into the inner depths of his unconscious. Joseph Campbell also studied the religions and mythology of the world and he diagnosed our modern times as missing a connection with a living myth, a living spirituality. He thought that the new mythology which could give us a sense of meaning and purpose had to be a story that brought us all together as one people. In his interview with Bill Moyers, Campbell elaborated on our need to create a new mythology, a new creation story for us to make sense of contemporary life and keep from destroying ourselves.

> And the only myth that is going to be worth thinking about in the immediate future is one that is talking about the planet, not the city, not these people, but the planet, and everybody on it. That's my main thought for what the future myth is going to be . . . the society that it's got to talk about is the society of the planet. . . .
>
> Do you see? And this would be a philosophy for the planet, not for this group, that group, or the other group.
>
> When you see the earth from the moon, you don't see any divisions there of nations or states. This might be the symbol, really, for the new mythology to come. That is the country that we are going to be celebrating. And those are the people that we are one with.[31]

Our old mythologies have been negated through the new information of science and technology, but Campbell says that we cannot live without a mythology because that is what gives our lives meaning, context, and purpose. We need a new story that can encompass science and still give a living spirituality a place to flourish. Campbell discusses the famous photograph, "Earthrise," taken by astronaut Bill Andrews in 1968, which gave us our first view of planet Earth as a whole. This new, holistic, perspective gives us the opportunity to re-write our creation stories and

---

30 Ibid., 13, 27.

31 Campbell and Moyers, *The Power of Myth*, 41.

to create a future mythology that will allow us to live in the present and future world. Campbell is calling for us to create, together, a story that allows us to think of ourselves as Citizens of Earth.

STORIES FROM SPACE

Joseph's visionary work resonates with the findings of astronomy and quantum physics. He is always reading up on scientific findings, looking for correspondences with his visionary work. The first time I met Joseph, he was wearing a NASA baseball cap.[32]

Joseph had a vision of Creation when he was five or six years old, living in Picuris in New Mexico.

> I saw a transparent ship come down from the heavens and land next to my grandmother's woodpile. In the ship were two kachinas [spirit beings]. They were very tall and they were wearing black and white robes. They got out of the ship and moved north from the west end of the house to where they stopped, and the next thing I saw, the Blue Stone people were there and the kachinas started feeding the blue stones. . . .
>
> Half a century later I had another vision of the kachinas coming. In that vision, I was in the sky. There was a hole in the clouds and I could see down through the hole. I could see the top of Picuris Pueblo as if I were looking at the village from the sky.
>
> It was as if there was a book in front of me, a thick book, and as the pages turned, the landscape of Picuris began to change. When the kachinas landed it was a mud flat with nothing there. As time began to move the pages (for each page was a moment in time), I saw the whole landscape change. It was like a wind was blowing the pages over, and many, many pages later, eventually we had a river and vegetation there, and eventually we had the village on the other side of the river. As this was all happening, I realized that the kachinas had turned into vibrations, and that was what was making the pages turn.[33]

It is an important part of his teachings to understand the historical and traditional appearance of space ships and beings from other dimensions

---

32 The Native peoples of the Southwest are avid watchers of the stars and their creation stories often see life coming from above and down to the Earth and then emerging from the Earth. Modern day focus on the stars and extraterrestrials continues in this region in Roswell, New Mexico.

33 *Sound*, 85–86.

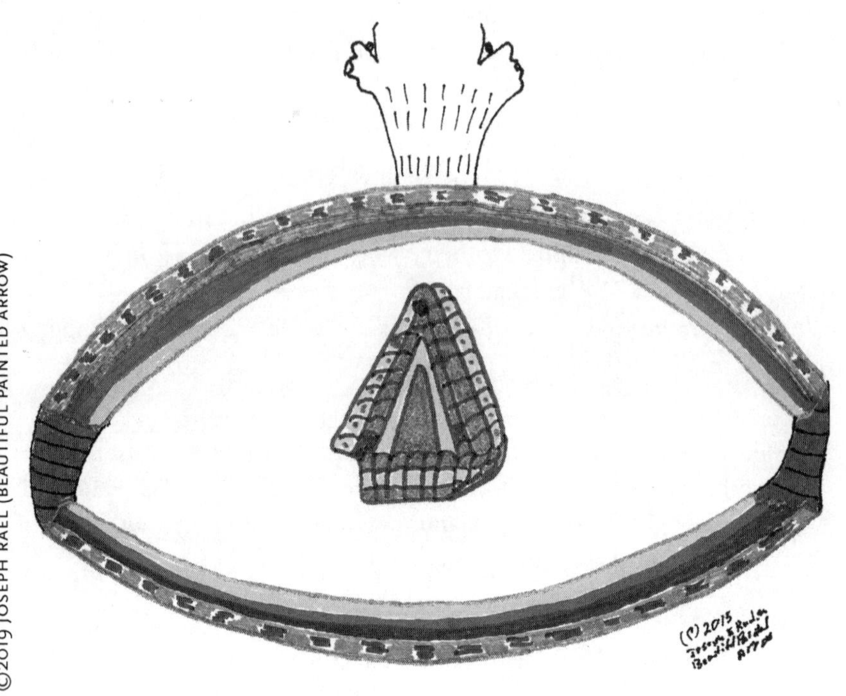

THE UNDERSIDE OF A FAR LARGER SHIP

in traditional Native American teachings of the Southwest. Many historical paintings show space ships and people travelling in the sky. The disappearance of the ancient pueblo people, leaving behind many dwellings has led to a number of theories about their disappearance. While anthropologists speculate about drought, famine and population movements, Joseph and many native people speak of other possibilities, that those people left with the people in the space ships, or that they evolved beyond this dimension, or another variant, that they have not actually left, but are still inhabiting these same dwellings in another dimension.

There is thus a dual theme in Joseph's interpretations of the old stories and his own visions: on the one hand, we are the Earth, we are of the soil, there is no separation between ourselves and the land and the health of both depends upon ceremonies that continue to bridge and connect people and land; on the other hand, we are not originally from here, we were seeded from the heavens, from God, from the kachinas in their spaceships. Rather than fall into a dualism between matter and spirit, Joseph's teachings point to the connection between realms.

A way that I have come to understand this is that we are like plants, growing out of the soil, our roots deep in the dark, solidity of the soil, and that we are actually incorporating the elements of the soil into our bodies—we are of the Earth and we are the Earth. Yet we are also growing toward something, evolving, our sprouts and leaves and branches growing upward from the surface of the earth, back toward the heavens, our branches stretching out into open space. We are moving with a purpose (*teleological growth*). We are Earth, we are soil, but we are also growing toward something else—we are both descending feminine energy and ascending masculine energy—the truth is that we are both/and, not either/or. While we are equally of Father Sky and Mother Earth, each of us as an individual is a seed, a circle, which is a principle idea that is planted in the soil of Mother Earth. As we become a seedling, our roots grow deeper into Mother Earth, while we also sprout out of the soil and our leaves open to Father Sky. We are in actuality a thread connecting Father Sky and Mother Earth.

> It is interesting that the Tiwa creation stories tell of beings from outer space who came here to seed the planet. That is part of the whole concept of consciousness, the concept of the upper world seeding the middle and lower worlds (lower world being the land, the Earth). These beings seed the Earth with ideas—vibrations that enhance *naa-meh-ney*. . . .
>
> The kachinas plant the seeds of what we know now as the circle of life or the sacred circle, or the medicine wheel. . . . They come from above; they come down in a transparent ship; and then they go back into the heavens and translate what this all means psychologically; and then they come back and land, not really landing on land. They stop descending, and things take material form. Infinite Vastness is the beginning. That is what they land on. According to the vision that I saw, this is how spirit descends into matter.[34]

34 *Sound*, 85–86.

JOSEPH'S JOURNEY THROUGH THE WORLD OF STORY

After another vision, his formative vision of the Sound Chambers for world peace, Joseph spent many years traveling around the Earth, to Europe, South America, across the United States, and down under to Australia. In his vision he realized that we must go back to the oral tradition languages and let them vibrate alongside the written words. "The vision was saying that what we need in today's world is to re-acquaint ourselves with the vibrations emanating from the spoken word so that we might understand inner meaning. That mystical meaning can come through the physical body and the mind via sound."[35] Joseph traveled around the world, telling the story of his visions and hearing the stories of others.

"I traveled all over Europe, I listened to Irish stories, I'd stay at the storyteller's house. I listened to German stories, all sorts of stories, I didn't get to see my children grow up because I was listening to stories and telling stories. I spent time teaching chanting, teaching drumming, teaching dancing, and working for world peace with the sound chambers.

"Here is what authors do, as far as I know, they take an idea, get it out to the public. The public learns this idea in books, maybe at school. Then they have a new orientation to the changes that are coming. They have an expectation of what to see before they see it because they know what is coming. Like with the ETs, that they will be coming back. I know that they will come back because everything is a circle, we live in a circular reality. They were here before, because they were here before I know that they will be here again in the future because it is all a circle. I've been in and out of realities long enough, 50 years now I keep telling people. I don't know why I keep telling people I'm 50 years old, I'm 82 years old now, but I don't feel it." [I interject that I, David am 50 as he tells me this].

"All my personal visions are one-half dream and one-half vision and they are in Technicolor. I'm always working at the area where the impossible was happening to me. I can write about it, but no one will believe me—they'll say it is just a story.

"Well, that's all for today, I better go do the dishes!"

Joseph often ends his stories abruptly, bringing the focus back to the everyday, the way Zen monks talk about chopping wood and carrying water.

35 *BPA*, 29.

PICURIS CHILDREN'S STORIES: MAGPIETAIL BOY AND HIS WIFE

Joseph tells me that children's stories are important because they are a place where ancient wisdom is passed on to the next generation. He has repeatedly emphasized the importance of the Picuris Children's Stories, particularly "Magpietail Boy and His Wife."[36] He believes that there is a deep mystical truth hidden within this children's tale. Joseph has explained to me the opening invocation of the story means "*the Vast Self laying down dreaming in the house where the all of everything lives just before it disappears, only to reappear in another moment in time.*" All who hear the story are like stars in the sky, blinking points of light in the vastness of space and hearing this story the listeners become the resonance of the story. Joseph says that the ancient storyteller uses the word meaning "Magpietail Boy" which means the people following the path of illusion. Kurt Wilt tells of a different story that Joseph had told him about the creation of the worlds and how Magpietail Boy tricked the people by using his tail as a bridge that took them to the second world instead of the first world. Kurt speaks of Magpietail Boy as a trickster figure and that because of his "trick, we are not aware that Earth and our bodies are the Vast Self."[37]

The story begins with Magpietail Boy always being sleepy and falling asleep as soon as his wife, Yellow Corn Woman, feeds him dinner. Unbeknownst to him, she would go out and study with the wizards while he slept and she would return before he woke up. There is a mystery and secret within this story.

On a visit with Joseph, I drove out to see Joseph's Sound Chamber since he has done more work on it since I had last seen it. It was a two day celebration of Joseph's 80th birthday and the re-release of *Being & Vibration: Entering the New World*. The drive out was beautiful, past Night Horse Lake, mountain ridges and the sky, the blue sky with mountains of clouds and light that look like we could just jump up there and live wonderful lives above the Earth. We drive between two deer on either side of the road, at the spot where a vulture had been circling low. Magpies are everywhere: one (*weh-mu*: seed), two (*weh-seh*: divine longing relationship),

---

36 Joseph has reproduced this story in his book, *Beautiful Painted Arrow: Stories & Teachings from the Native American Tradition*. The original publication (but not the original telling) was in the *Forty-Third Annual Report of the Bureau of American Ethnology, 1925-1926*. There is also a small volume available called *Indian Tales from Picuris Pueblo*, collected by John P. Harrington. Joseph also spoke with Kurt Wilt about this story and Kurt has a discussion of it in his book, *The Visionary*.

37 Wilt, *Visionary*, 34.

three (*paah-chu*: consciousness gains power of movement), four (*wii*: parts of brain come together into a created instant of time). What was that flash of yellow? A warbler, an oriole? A field of blue birds. Such beautiful land, I breathe it in.

I remember how my story with Joseph started in 2014, driving around, pulling off to the side of the road and looking at land, him talking and me listening. (*Chasing his thoughts like birds*, like in The Police song, "Secret Journey"). I am thankful for the time Joseph has spent helping me to see this land through his eyes and also seeing through time—circular time—where the past is not gone, but it is still happening here, just in a way that you have to look differently for it.

Joseph felt it was very important to teach me the Picuris Children's Stories. On my first visit he sent me home with an old copy of the *Forty-Third Annual Report of the Bureau of American Ethnology, 1925-1926*, which contains stories that were told only during the winter time at Picuris Pueblo. Joseph approaches these stories as hidden revelations or theophanies that hide profound truths about who we are and where we come from. Joseph often returns to the story of Magpietail Boy. I have to say that I still don't fully understand it, but I just saw those four magpies on the drive to Joseph's home, and then, one more on the way back—five (*paah-nu*: parts of self come together in oneness of Higher Mind). When I saw the Magpie Newsstand Café in Durango, Colorado (the sixth magpie of the day, *maa-tschlay*: information/memory of past/present reviewed) I thought it was the perfect place to get a cup of coffee and write up the notes from our conversations. I have returned to this spot a number of times, where I go to ponder why Joseph feels this story is so important.

What was it he has said to me about this? Something about the black and white of the magpie, represents the void, blackness, dark matter, dark energy and the white light of creation and consciousness. Magpietail Boy is that being that is half black and half white; he is our consciousness emerging into this world. But what does he do with it? He is sleepy all the time, constantly sleeping, wasting away the gift of consciousness. And what happens? Yellow Corn Woman, his wife goes off at night to study magic with the wizards. When I ask why she ends up getting punished at the end of the story, when it seems like it was Magpietail Boy's fault for sleeping all the time, Joseph says, *"Well, she was stepping out on him, but you can't say that in a children's story, so instead she was studying magic with the wizards."* No wonder I can't make sense of this story, every time Joseph tells me about it he focuses on a different interpretation! Sometimes he speaks of Magpietail Boy's blackness as evil, other times as unconsciousness, other times as dark matter—which often has a positive creative association for Joseph, almost like Vast Self, that pre-creation out of which we all emerge.

What happens in that story, then? I am trying to remember it. Magpietail Boy follows his wife one night, hides and sees what is going on. Then he gets into a fix, he falls (ahh, here is something that Joseph talks about—the necessity of falling) and gets stuck on a ledge and he has to ask Elf for help. Elf gives him five (*paah-nu*: parts of self come together in oneness of Higher Mind) chances.[38] Magpietail Boy misses the first four pine cones, but catches the *paah-nu* cone, which grows into a tree and he gets safely off the ledge. Then Elf gives him a worm that he puts in his wife's belly button and it eats into her and she dies. This always seems like such an abrupt end of the story to me. I still can't understand it.

Magpietail Boy lives quite happily alone, that is the last part of the story.

This ending seems like the opposite of a Western fairy tale, the hero and princess don't live happily ever after, instead Magpietail Boy lives happily ever after alone. I suppose we could view it as a coming into consciousness—moving from slumbering in unconsciousness to learning what his wife, Yellow Corn Woman, was learning from the wizards. In the story he undergoes a trial—after falling from the roof of the wizards' hut they send him to a ledge halfway down and halfway up the cliff. Whether you are a pessimist or an optimist, it is still a long way down or a long way up. He gets help from Elf, since even though he has a bird's tail, Magpietail Boy can't fly. Elf, the trickster, toys with him a bit, then ultimately helps him and gives him the worm that kills Yellow Corn Woman through her umbilical cord. It seems like a cruel and tough lesson. Maybe it has something to do with the medicine wheel of life with birth and death and how the crops grow, fruit and then die. We could look at how it is the feminine element that lures Magpietail Boy out of his slumber—this is consistent with many myths in which the feminine gets into some kind of trouble or inspires the masculine to move out of the known and into the unknown worlds. At the end of the story, Joseph writes that when Magpietail Boy lived happily ever after alone, which means that "higher conscious awareness has been achieved. It also introduces the idea of looking at life as a chain made out of connected moments, with each link

38 Elf tricks Magpietail Boy, though, telling him that the fourth pine cone is the last, when he misses catching that one, then Elf gives him one more chance, the fifth pine cone.

an opportunity to start anew, and that is really life beginning-ness with no ending-ness to it"[39]

I speak about this story more with Joseph when we are at Ohkay Hotel Casino, in Ohkay Owingeh, before we go to Picuris feast day. He says that in telling the Picuris stories, at the end of the story, the teller will now say to the listeners, "Now you have a tail."[40] This means that now the listener has to become the teller of another story. Joseph says it also means that the teller is bringing to awareness the listener's own negative energy. He continues:

"The black and white of Magpietail Boy's tail represents the ascending and descending light and that these meet on a cross, like the Holy Cross. The tail also represents purity 'a' and awareness 'i.'"

T: "Energy coming down/time"

A: "Purity"

I: "Awareness"

L: "mental, sky/earth connection"

"Medicine should be a round circle, but the Christians always try to make it a square, a cross. The brain is two circles, two realities: ordinary and non-ordinary. We need to create a dialogue between the two, we need to become cross-eyed."

More recently, in 2018, I spoke with Joseph again about the ending of Magpietail Boy. Joseph focused this time on the "worm" that Elf gave Magpietail Boy who then put it in Yellow Corn Woman's belly button. He says that the Tiwa word for worm is *pu-pi. Pu* means "*to make something happen.*" *Pi* means "*the heart.*" The ending with the worm makes something happen in the heart. Joseph reminds me that when he goes into a visionary state he often has a glowing pu-pi enter through his head inducing the vision, so *pu-pi* has to do with entering a visionary state. He also tells me that the "*worm is fear. That aspect of her that is fear dies.*" This time he tells me that Yellow Corn Woman does not die, rather she leaves ordinary reality and goes up into the cosmos with the wizards (who are ETs) just as many of the past Pueblo peoples had disappeared. Magpietail Boy stays behind, now in an enlightened, awake state. He stays behind to teach the people about becoming a visionary.

Another time Joseph told me, "*You can never tell the Magpietail Boy story the same as I told it because you are going to change it in some way.*"

---

39 *BPA*, 67–68.

40 Sometimes Joseph seems to mean "tale," this time he means "tail."

THE UNITY OF STORY

Creation stories begin with a primal unity that breaks apart with a sound and separates out into the diversity of beings. From this separation come the gods, the earth, the sky, the sea, and fire, plants, animals, and human beings. Fundamental aspects of creation are that it starts with sound; separation creates a longing for return to unity; and that we, the created, are also creators. We also see that death is necessary for life, whether this is the death of ancient stars, the death of our earlier evolutionary prototypes, or the death of unity into the plethora of separation. Within this separation is longing. The Sufis, the mystics of Islam, meditate on God's explanation for Creation being that God longed to be known. When the prophet, King David, asks Allah why all this was created, Allah tells David,

> "I was a hidden treasure;
> I loved to be known,
> so I created creation."[41]

We long for the original unity. All the better aspects of human nature stem from this longing for unity and recognition of our unity with others. We call this Love. Yet this longing is also pain and suffering. The separation creates the possibility of re-union, but it also creates the possibility for the mistaken perception that we are only separate. This mistaken perception that we are separate beings leads to the excesses of materialism, greed and egoism—of which war is the most extreme manifestation. Materialism is the belief that only material objects exist, and in its extreme form human beings are just transitory objects amongst a world of objects. This is dehumanization, the view that human being is not sacred, and that people are objects. This can lead to a view that the goal of life is material comfort. Greed leads to the accumulation of material objects in order to further one's comfort, without caring about the comfort or wellbeing of others. Egoism is the belief that only the ego (body, emotions, mind) exist, and that one should maximize one's comfort and minimize one's discomfort. Since the ego is seen as separate and bounded, egoism leads to the suffering of self (through isolation) and the suffering of others (through greed and accumulation of resources that are taken away from others).

Our hope for this book is that it will continue Beautiful Painted Arrow's visions of world peace through illuminating the inner journey to the center

41 Suhrawardī, *The Shape of Light: Hayakal al-Nur*, 57.

of our hearts. It is in our hearts that we find we are not separate and wars of separation do not reflect who we truly are, because in our hearts we are connected with the primal unity. There is a place within our hearts and souls that never separated from oneness.

> It is when we do not connect ideas to the infinite vastness and the heart in this way that we have wars. We are stuck in cold reason and we act from self-righteousness and fear. But we can act from love when we use meditation and ceremony to bring that cold intellectual energy down through the heart center, connect it with the Vast Self, and then bring it back through the heart to the brain. . . . The rational mind says that whatever it cannot understand is not real, and that misconception is what separates us from God.[42]

The unity of story tells us that we lose something when we try too hard to take it apart and explain it all. While science and academics in contemporary society strive to take everything apart and explain it objectively, Joseph teaches me that there are things that are best left as a unity, to work as they are—*unconscious healing* he calls it. Lewis Mehl-Madrona hints at this too when he says that the "spirit of transformation . . . is much deeper and more profound than any intellectual interpretation."[43]

SILENT STORIES

Stories arise out of silence, they are the sound, but the sound is made possible by the empty space of silence around the sound. When we live in ordinary reality we attend to the sounds, sights, smells, tastes, and feel of the world. But our stories start and end in non-ordinary reality, which is silence. When we lose the thread of our stories, we must go back into non-ordinary reality to be still and listen to the stories, to listen closely until we can hear our story again.

"Every human being has a secret," Joseph tells me. The secret of ourselves can be found in the stillness and silence. I guess this is the story of each of our "secret journeys" of separation-initiation-return, of *Wah-Mah-Chi*, of Breath-Matter-Movement. It is our responsibility to find out the secret that we are. It is our responsibility to find the myth by which we can live, to find, again, the thread of our story when we have lost the plot.

---

42 *Sound*, 97–98.

43 Mehl-Madrona, *Coyote Medicine*, 105.

JOSEPH INSIDE DOOR

CHAPTER 8

ENTERING THE DOORWAY

The "y" in the English word "you" is pronounced "eee." This sound is the gate of awareness that bonds or connects as in a grid the physical world and the spiritual world of ideas. So, symbolically, when I say "you" I am saying that, at that moment, you are the doorway for me to evolve to my place of higher spiritual awareness. This is one of the mysteries of what life is about, because I found out it takes another person to make me a possibility. I need another person to reflect back to me my identity as it emerges from potential into manifestation. Also, when two people are in relationship to each other, these two sets of vibrations begin to hit against each other, and in that interaction both are changed and lifted. So the "eee" sound in "you" recognizes that other person as a doorway for me, and the "uu" in "you" recognizes that the relationship we are forming is a container in which both of our energies are to be carried, like a glass carries water, to nurture the soul of each of us. The word for soul in Tiwa means "drinker"; the soul is that in us which thirsts for knowledge or truth or enlightenment (or actual water, for that matter!).[1]

JOSEPH RAEL

When I first met Joseph and thought about our writing a book together, the thought came to me: "We are doorways for each other." It was not a conscious, logical decision, more an instantaneous intuition that holds many levels of meaning. For me, Joseph is a doorway into a deeper spirituality. In working with Joseph-ing, I am able to bring elements of spirituality into our book that would be difficult to do as a psychiatrist trying to maintain the balance on the edge of medicine and healing.[2] For Joseph, I imagined that I was a doorway for bringing his ideas to a health care audience. In that instant, standing in the middle of the living room

1 *B&V:NW*, 61.

2 I empathize with Carl Jung's balancing act of speaking to the truth of his visionary experiences and his struggle to maintain the perspective (and respect) of an objective scientist and psychiatrist. Evidence-based medicine has no room for the subjective experience of the physician and the patient's subjective experiences are valued only so much as they can be objectified and quantified. However, our mystical and spiritual humanity is not observable through objectification, but rather only through subjectification.

in Joseph's work house, I knew that Joseph and I were both doors for each other. I thought I had some idea of what it would mean to walk through the doorway of Joseph and yet every time I walk through that doorway into the next room, Joseph beckons me from a door on the opposite side of the room.

If we look at the meaning of letters that Joseph describes in *Being & Vibration*, we find the following meanings for the word, "door."

D – touch
O – Innocence
O – Innocence
R – abundance

A door is the place where we touch abundance, where we can bring abundance into our lives. There is a double "o" because a doorway passes in two different directions and when we enter with innocence in our hearts and minds we can then touch the abundance that has been prepared for us on the other side of the door.

The visionary poet, William Blake, spoke of cleansing the doors of perception in order to reveal the true nature of reality as infinite. Blake also cautioned that human beings cut themselves off from the infinite by closing doors and raising bars rather than passing through doors.

> If the doors of perception were cleansed every thing would appear to man as it is, infinite.
>
> For man has closed himself up, till he sees all things thro' narrow chinks in his cavern.[3]

William Blake's writing was guided by his visions and he reproduced the visions in his work. Alfred Kazin wrote of Blake that "For him man is always the wanderer in the oppressive and sterile world of materialism which only his imagination and love can render human."[4] It was through his visions that Blake re-humanized and re-spiritualized the material world. As Joseph has taught us, the world is in perpetual creation and re-creation and visions can be the reanimating force that brings the new into dying forms of past experience. Kazin writes that for Blake "vision represents the total imagination of man made tangible and direct in works of art," and that "vision restores his human identity."[5]

---

3 William Blake, *The Portable Blake*, 258.

4 Alfred Kazin, introduction to *The Portable Blake*, 13.

5 Kazin, 16, 47.

William Blake, the visionary, encourages us to *cleanse the doors of perception* so that we can see everything as it is—*infinite.* The door is there, but it needs to be cared for, attended to, so that one can touch abundance through the innocence of the heart. Where is this doorway to be found that leads us to infinite abundance? Blake points us to the *doors of perception*, which could seem to be our five physical senses. However, he is a visionary and so we could also read him to be speaking of the visionary doors that allow visionary perception. Joseph sometimes speaks of using our "third eye" to see visionary infinity.

The word "door" points us toward a double innocence and innocence is a function of the spirit. We can turn our attention to the doors of the heart in order to find this innocence. The physical heart has four doors: the mitral valve, the tricuspid valve, the aortic valve, and the pulmonary valve. Each of these valves is a door that our blood passes through on its journey from being depleted and de-oxygenated, entering through the heart, passing to the lungs where the blood is re-oxygenated, and then back into the heart, and then passing back out into the rest of the body. These doors of the heart must be in good working order in order for blood to undergo its continual transformation and renewal.

Perhaps these doors of the heart also play a role in allowing visionary, non-ordinary reality to enter us and allowing us to walk through these doorways into non-ordinary reality. While the physical valves of the heart function to let blood only move forward, the visionary doorways of our hearts allow us to move back and forth between ordinary and non-ordinary reality. Without non-ordinary reality, material objects lose their vitality. We, too, lose our vitality if we are cut off from the continual in-flow and out-flow of non-ordinary reality into our being. Doorways are always doorways to the new, to the infinite and walking through a doorway is an initiation.

The sun is a door. As I write this, the doorway of the sun is opening onto the darkness of a Sunday morning. A pale blue-grey light is in the sky, not so much illuminating as allowing to be seen the thinning orange-yellow fall leaves of the cherry tree as the crow flies quickly past on some business. The moon is a door. Darkness is a door. Light is a door. I am a door. You are a door.

In April of 2017, Joseph had me walking back and forth across the room, paying attention to the present moment and how it passes one moment to the next as I took steps across the room. "*All that stepping forward does*," he told me, "*is that it is allowing you to go through one door, closing it, that's one moment, right? Or one year. And then you open the door and close it.*" He had me walk back and forth, slowly across the room and then "handed" the non-ordinary book to me saying, "*This is* ma-na-nay. Ma *means to bring forth, to handle it. Now you are in non-ordinary reality and you have this book and you are bringing it forth. When you're writing it's* do-pya *but we'll deal with that later.*" He has me walk back and forth as he repeated "*non-ordinary reality, non-ordinary reality, non-ordinary reality.*"

After we did this for some time, I asked Joseph, "Could it be said that the only time you exist is when you are going through the doorway? The time that it's opening and then closing. It's not about getting into the next room and getting comfortable. It's about finding the next doorway that leads out of that room."

J: "That's the goal. That's why you're like this."

D: Our home is not necessarily the four walls of the room that we're in but our home is the doorway.

J: "Because it's the one that opens you to enlightenment, right? If you go through the door, you see light, enlightenment, but it's a wall that you have which keeps you from the elements. Rain and other elements but it also keeps your body warm and a bed where you can sleep, rest, like a cave. In ancient times, you sought caves."

D: In your life, if you stop looking for the next door, once you get into a house or your structure or your life and you stop looking for the next door, then at some point that starts to become a cave because a room with no door is a cave.

J: "Yeah, and remember, people argue, well, there was an entrance, you got in there and so therefore you can get out. Don't do that, but those people are always going to be with us, aren't they? The key is that if you are caved in, you can't get out. And that's when your body starts to die. I call it 'decadence.'"

D: So the holy person would always be seeking caves if they don't see the door. If they seek the door and see the door, that's good, but if they don't find the door, then you need to seek the cave to go deeper into yourself until you can find that next door.

J: "Because the cave is what you are imprisoned in, but at the same time, it's the one that is telling you that you have to seek. You don't just sit there and die. You check the walls and everything and figure out and you'll get out."

D: Feel the texture in the walls. It's like a womb too then, that you eventually need to be born into another dimension, into another place.

J: "See it keeps repeating itself. Biologically as well."

D: I'm glad we've connected the door and the cave. Going through the door is a separation, an initiation, return. When you open the door, it's the separation. As you walk through the door, it's the initiation, and as you close the door, it's a return into being in the place where you are now looking for the next door.

J: "And when you find the next door, and you walk into it, it's when you have to—you've disappeared until you start moving again, stepping, that's why you are two-legged. That's the moment we don't exist. Do you notice when you go through a door, when you are going to work or something, the door is there, but at that time, your mind is just on the door. It's not on getting in the car because you have to watch that the dog doesn't go out, the cat doesn't come in or whatever, that you don't step or fall out. And then when you turn around and start walking to your car, then you exist again. You're walking the pathway to your car or to the garage or wherever and then you are in the day. So that's when you exist. Think of a strobe light. When the strobe light goes on, it goes on for a split of a split of a second, but if you stretch it, it could be longer than a second."

D: It's kind of like matter and dark matter. There's a percentage, four or five percent light matter, the stuff that we see, and ninety-five, ninety-six percent dark matter which is what surrounds it and so if we use that analogy, we would say, we blink on for five percent, but ninety-five percent of the time we don't exist.

*J: "Yeah, but it's happening so fast, just like that. And remember, dark matter means—*HAWW [he makes a loud exhaling breath sound]—*this means—go like that, like you are going to breathe—*haawwww.[6] *What it's suggesting is that dark matter is ninety-five percent of our life, right? But look what's happening to that dark matter, it's going—*haawwww—*from here.* Haawwww—*it's gone. So it's moving, fast. So it doesn't stay very long. And then this is the light and then it's gone again. And so God gave us inhalation, exhalation. When you inhale in, you're inhaling in air, and then when you breathe out, that's the dark*

6 Of a similar sound, Joseph writes, "*Haah* is identity; breath is identity. . . . Breath connects us with higher levels. Breath is inspiration," (*Ceremonies*, 13–14)

matter and then it's gone, right? And then when you go—hawww—*that's the light. And when you go out, it's dark matter because it's waste."*

D: In Latin, doorway or doorframe is *limen.* So they talk about liminal beings, beings who are beings of the doorway, who are always in between one place and the next. Would you say we are all liminal beings?

J: "And on the same page, you could just say what 'limen'[7] *is—what liminal beings are according to the ancient people who wrote about it. You can find metaphors there. The condition of human life. And so it's not a question of this being an Indian book or a veteran's book or a religious book."*

D: It's a human book.

J: "It's a human book, and written for humans by humans (laughs)."

---

7 "Limen" means "threshold," and "is a transliteration into the Latin alphabet of the ancient Greek word, λιμήν, "harbor, refuge, creek," *Wikipedia.*

It is often used to signify a door or opening from one space into another. It has been taken up by psychotherapists and anthropologists to signify the boundary between one role and another or one state of being and another. It is in this sense that it is important for this book. In Joseph's terms, the *limen* is a paper thin veil between ordinary and non-ordinary reality. A liminal being is someone who can cross back and forth over the *threshold* of non-ordinary consciousness. The Greek root is also of importance here as bringing in the element of water (which Jung said often represents the unconscious) as well as the idea of a refuge.

We can think of the *limen* as the space through which energies can pass from non-ordinary to ordinary reality. In this sense Corbin's *'alam al-mithal* is a *limen.* Mircea Eliade writes of the space through which the sacred enters into the profane through some kind of *break* or *opening* and that the entry of the sacred into the profane creates an orientation and this place of passage becomes the center of the Earth. This is important in Joseph Rael's teachings as we are seeking, throughout this book, to find the *limen*, the *liminal space*, the *doorway*, into the center of the medicine wheel. Eliade summarizes as follows:

> "the experience of sacred space makes possible the 'founding of the world': where the sacred manifests itself in space, *the real unveils itself*, the world comes into existence. But the irruption of the sacred does not only project a fixed point into the formless fluidity of profane space, a center into chaos: it also effects a break in plane, that is, it opens communication between the cosmic planes (between earth and heaven) and makes possible ontological passage from one mode of being to another. It is such a break in the heterogeneity of profane space that creates the center through which communication with the transmundane is established, that, consequently, founds the world, for the center renders *orientation* possible." (Eliade, *The Sacred and the Profane*, 63).

WALKING THROUGH THE DOORWAY VISION[8]

One night, I woke up at 3:30 AM and did some reading and meditation. I had started re-reading Ruzbihan Baqli's *The Unveiling of Secrets: Diary of a Sufi Master.* I love the visual imagery and poetics of this book and it is filled with Ruzbihan's visions that started when he was a child and continued on throughout his life. For instance, on this night I read the passage, "On the Carpet of Oneness without a Veil."

> What we have shown and alluded to is a kind of knowledge that comes from the science of passion and love. The Truth appeared here in beauty and majesty, and he bequeathed to them some of that love, passion, and knowledge. This is because there are seas of unknowing in the reality of divine oneness, from which all the prophets, messengers, angels and saints flee. In the station of divine oneness is the burning of greatness, which consumes thoughts, understandings, and comprehensions. . . . I entered into ecstasy and cried out repeatedly, annihilated in his majesty. . . . I saw him unveiled, and he said, 'Ruzbihan! Do not shed tears at the shifting flow of the shapes of the actions, and do not doubt what you have seen: 'I am I' [Qur'an 28:30], your lord, the one, the single. You do not deserve that I should distress you in the oceans of unknowing. I am yours throughout my creation, so do not worry over anything. I shall convey you to the station of 'the vision of vision' and I shall seat you on the carpet of my nearness forever, without a veil.'[9]

Next, I read "Seeking the Vision of the Essence," with the line, "And the Truth (who is transcendent) revealed himself in an atom of the light of his pre-eternal essence (he is mighty and supreme), and my spirit nearly vanished."[10]

I sat in the dark and began to meditate, thinking about what Joseph calls, "crying for a vision." I love this phrase because it brings to mind two concepts of crying: crying out, like strongly stating a wish or intention of openness and receptivity to be filled; and crying as in sadness or longing. Joseph describes the number "two" as *weh-seh*. Two is the place of separation from unity into duality and this brings about a longing for lost

8 A version of this was originally published in *The Badger*, October 2017, Year 3, Volume 4, 36–42. This is an online magazine edited by Antonella Vicini, who has studied with Joseph.

9 Ruzbihan Baqli, *The Unveiling of Secrets: Diary of a Sufi Master*, trans. Carl W. Ernst, 24–26.

10 Ibid., 29.

unity. Joseph describes the word "two" in Tiwa:

> At step two we have duality, we have two sides, and at this point we have the capacity to cry. We can cry in longing. We can cry in praise. . . .
>
> Listen to it: weh-mu is one. Weh-seh is two. Weh is to slip. Seh is to cry. Weh-mu is to slip and see. We can now perceive. . . .
>
> Weh-seh is crying for a vision. And it is in number two that God has the plan for us that we are contemplators. We can think now, we can see, and we can reflect.[11]

One of the beauties of Sufism is the movement back and forth from unity to duality and back to duality. Whether it is the longing of Rumi for his teacher Shams, or the heart-pourings of Ruzbihan as he moves from the ecstasy of divine union to the heart-wrenching longing of separation. Carl Ernst, who has translated Ruzbihan's writing into English, describes two attributes of God: majesty and beauty. "The Attributes of God can be divided into two types: Attributes of majesty that mediate the power and wrath of God, and Attributes of beauty that convey the grace and mercy of God."[12]

Two, then, represents the separation, exile, and longing (the Attribute of majesty). Yet, it also represents the approach of divine union (the Attribute of beauty). Separation contains within it the memory of Unity and the promise of future Re-unity. In the longing of separation after Shams' death, Rumi eventually finds union and writes poems and signs Shams' name to them. As in Kashmiri Shaivism, all things are Śiva. Even separation into two (masculine Śiva and feminine Śakti) is a manifestation of the essence of Supreme Unity. Separation is the perception in Ordinary Reality and Unity is the perception in Non-ordinary Reality.

So with all this swirling in my head as a sense of divine longing arises in my heart, I think of Joseph "crying for a vision," and I say out loud, "Help me God!" And I hear in the voice of my imagination, "It is not I who come to you, but you who come to me." And I see in the eye of my imagination A Ray of Divine Light from a bright Source. I start to move toward the Light along this ray. I contemplate what Ruzbihan calls the "stations," all the positions, 70,000 maybe—I think he mentions that number—and I contemplate the spectrum of the Station of Nearness next to the Light

11 *Inspiration*, 50–51.

12 Baqli, 30

and the Station of Farness as far away from the Light as can be imagined. I contemplate the Stations of Light from a faint, dim flicker to a blinding flash of lightning that is so bright it seems to annihilate my very being. I contemplate the Stations of Darkness, from a dim light to an utter void that is so dark that it annihilates my very being.

I approach the Light and observe I become brighter the closer I get to it. I touch the Light and feel it warming me. I reach into the Light, I walk into the Light. At first I am so bright that I start to become indistinct, and eventually it is so bright that I cannot perceive a difference between myself and the Light; I have become the Light.

Then I am back to having a self and a body, but my heart is an open heart shape, like a big cookie cutter was pressed through me. I peer out forward through my heart and it is brilliant Light. I peer backward through my heart and it is luminous Darkness. I think, "This is why we move forward; we are constantly running from the Darkness or we are chasing the Light, but really we have both, we are both, we are made of both Light and Dark. Maybe this is why Ruzbihan says the "prophets, messengers, angels and saints flee" the "seas of unknowing in the reality of the divine oneness."

One and Two. One and the Other. There is a world where all is One, that is the Non-ordinary Reality that Joseph speaks of. There is a world where there is not unity, but duality and diversity. One and the Other. This world, ordinary reality, is a dark reflection of the One World.

Then I hear something and am afraid. I look at the door in the room and I think, "Who is going to come through that door?" I remember Rumi's statement, "Submit to love without thinking." I realize that it is me who is going to go out through that door, I am going to pass through a doorway. Rather than someone coming in, I am going to go out through that door. I walk through into a World of Light so bright that the world begins to dissolve into Union with the Light. I begin to dissolve and become less substance and more Light, until I am nothing but Light. I remember Ruzbihan's phrase, "the Truth (which is transcendent)." I realize I am only experiencing one sense, vision—what about scent? There are saints who smell God as well as saints who see God. With the nose of my imagination I smell the sweet scent of jasmine. It is separation that allows me to smell that as something other than myself and I gradually lose myself in this scent and I become this brilliant Light, so bright that nothing exists but light and I am this scent. I contemplate Ruzbihan's descriptions of various oceans and deserts. The fullness of oceans and the absent barren-ness of deserts. I contemplate Oneness as a Vast Ocean with no boundaries, of Being as nothing but Ocean. I contemplate separation as a Vast Desert with no boundaries, separation as nothing but empty Desert. Sometimes Ruzbihan even drinks the Oceans in his visions. "Why not?" I ask myself as I drain the Brilliant Ocean of Eternity, which is nothing but Light, nothing but Jasmine, nothing but delicious sweetness, nothing but everything.

It is only in the most superficial way that we are separate beings, that we are disconnected, unrelated, and that our boundaries keep us apart more than link us together. We are a manifestation of what the universe is and there is no separation between mind and body, between *you* and *I*, between one people and another people, between the ego and the universe. This is the Hindu concept of *Purusha*, the Self, of the physical reality we see being a glimmer of light on the Vast Ocean of consciousness, or of Narayana dreaming the world into existence while sleeping in the Cosmic Ocean. Joseph says that there is in reality only one Being observing all of creation and calls this Vast Self.

IN THE CENTER OF THE MEDICINE WHEEL IS THE HEART

How do we enter into the center of the medicine wheel? How is it that we can find the doorway into our hearts? When we lose the thread of our story in life, we struggle to find the connection, to enter back into the source of our story. In life we look for doorways in ordinary reality, but we often cannot seem to find the doorway into the center of the heart. The secret journey of initiation reveals doorways that exist in non-ordinary reality only. This is how we can enter into "the temples without doors" that René Guénon speaks of.[13] To find the doorways to the center of the heart, we need some ceremony to shift our seeing in ordinary reality to the vision of non-ordinary reality.

At the center of the medicine wheel lies the heart and at the heart is the center of humanity—it is a medicine bag that contains holy objects. We can travel to the center of the medicine wheel, we can travel to the center of humanity, and here we find the heart, but then we must travel to the center of our heart, which is the center of The Heart—this is the "center of the center."[14]

---

13 René Guénon, *Symbols of Sacred Science*, 203.

14 Paul Eduardo Muller-Ortega describes the functions of the heart in Kashmiri

Our physical hearts are divided into four chambers, and yet they all work together as one. We can say that we have one heart even though it has different aspects and functions. Some chambers of the heart are giving and receiving de-oxygenated blood. Other chambers of the heart are giving and receiving oxygenated blood. It is in this unity of the heart that we can meet the unity of humanity and the unity of all being. Through each of our individual hearts we enter the larger realm of the Heart and we come into communication and connection with the heart of the people and the heart of the land. We further connect to the heart of the solar system, the heart of the galaxy, and the heart of the universe. When we are in the realm of the heart, we can connect and communicate with other hearts.

A single heart connects individual, community, land, and existence. When we become specialists of the heart we not only *know*, we *experience* the interconnectedness of all beings and all being. When we move into the realm of the heart and we speak the language of the heart, we are in a place of interconnectedness. The language of the heart is love and this provides another source of interconnection within the individual, between people, in communities, and in relationship to the earth, the cosmos and to God or Vast Self. The heart is the place of love and this is the same as "home," thus we are in the realm of home. Home is the place of belonging and it is the place where we are relating to each other.

It may seem counter-intuitive, but it is when we have undertaken the inner search and gone to the innermost place that we are also connected

---

Shaivism in his book *The Triadic Heart of Śiva*. The heart, in this tradition, is the Ultimate Reality, the Embodied Cosmos, and the origin of Vibration and Emissional Power that is the source of the creation of the universe as well as the still resting place of the divine. Muller-Ortega writes of a resonance in the heart that is a resonance between the human body and the universe.

> This resonance might be explained as a kind of parallelism between a microcosm, the body, and a macrocosm, the universe itself. . . . In a final sense, due to the indivisible nature of Śiva, microcosm and macrocosm are simply indistinguishable. Wherever Śiva is present, the whole is present. If the body is a structure composed essentially of Śiva, then all that is manifested from Śiva . . . may be found present in the body. Their presence in the body is not, it must be emphasized, as a microcosmic replica. The infinite reality out of which the array of the universes are structured is present in the body, and thus they too are present in the body. This is the extreme to which the notion of non-duality is carried by the tradition, (101–02)

Muller-Ortega quotes Abhinavagupta, "The power which consists of a sparkling vibration and which is in the Heart . . . produces a state of pulsation, and thus becomes the energy of the wheel of deities. . . . The power, whose form is the center of the center of the entire wheel of sense capacities and subtle conduits is . . . the place of birth," (101–03).

to what is outermost. This is because as we move into deeper levels of inner truth we recognize deeper levels of interconnectedness with other people, other beings, the world and the cosmos. The deeper we go, the more interconnected we are, until finally there is only Union—Oneness with no duality. This is the place of mysticism and the place of mysticism is the heart.

One of the reasons that we can connect and communicate with other hearts is because the Heart is One. There is one beating heart of all creation and in a small but meaningful way the heart in our chest echoes the heart of all creation. "Mysticism means, direct, immediate experience of ultimate reality," writes Brother Wayne Teasdale, who brought together Christian monastic and Hindu sannyasi traditions.[15] As we all have a heart, Teasdale proclaims "We are all mystics! The mystic heart is the deepest part of who or what we really are."[16] Joseph thinks mysticism is universal, as well. He says "*Whether we know it or not, we are all on a spiritual journey.*"

15 Wayne Teasdale, *The Mystic Heart: Discovering a Universal Spirituality in the World's Religions*, 20.

16 Ibid., 12.

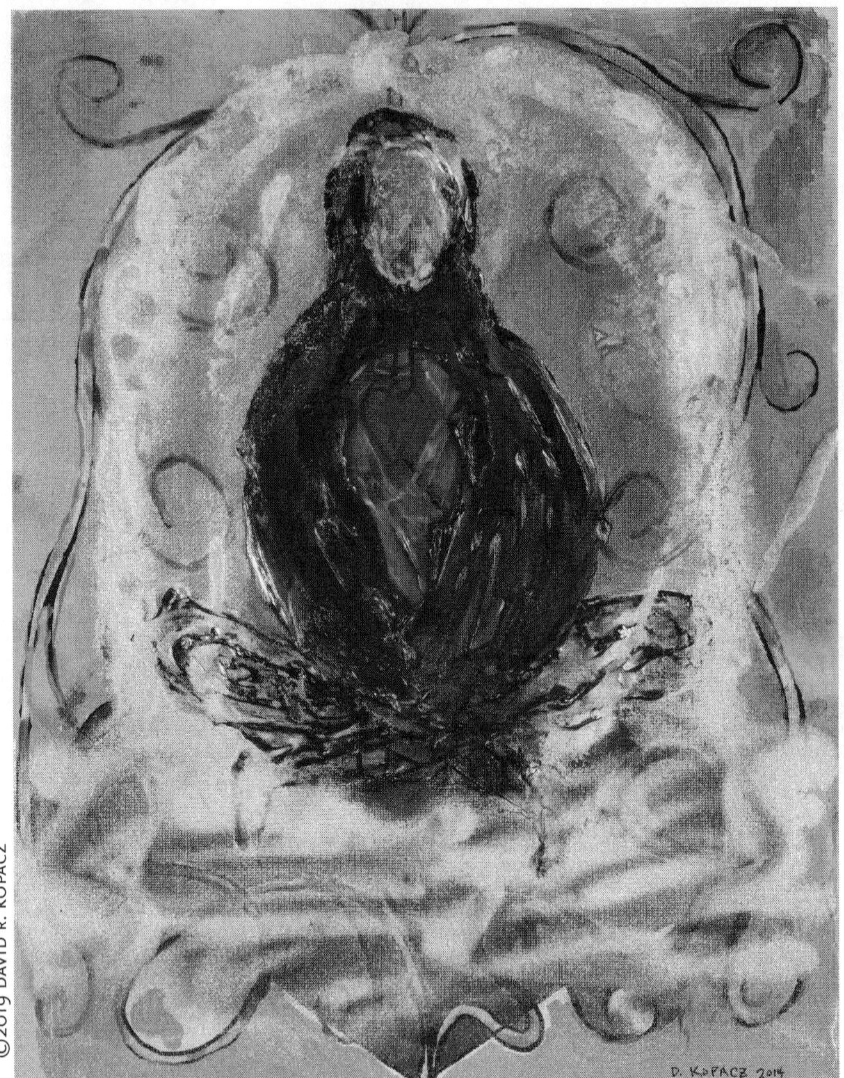

HEART MEDITATION

CHAPTER 9

GUHĀ: CAVE OF THE HEART

The rishic seers, the mystic founders of Hinduism, also experienced continuity between the divine presence encompassing the entire cosmos and the inner depths of their own hearts, the guha *or cave of the heart, the deepest point of human subjectivity and freedom, a 'place' uncorrupted by time and external actions. In India, the guha is a metaphor for that hidden, transcendent place within us that is totally transparent to the divine . . . the deepest center of ourselves is one with the deepest center of the universe. All beings are united with the Brahman.*[1]

WAYNE TEASDALE

When we move from the outside of our body, which is in the light and is visible, the journey to the heart goes through the inner darkness of the chest. This is our own darkness, the density of matter that makes up our body. To reach the heart we have to go through darkness. We can then meet the heart, we come to it and see it as an anatomic muscle buried within the darkness of our chests, beating and beating, pumping blood through our arteries and veins an average of 80 times a minute. Or we see it as a symbolic heart, red, with two feminine upper lobes coming to a masculine point at the base.

Yet we are told by mystics that the journey of initiation does not stop at the heart, there is a journey to reach the heart, but that is just the preliminary journey. We must now enter into the *guhā*, the cave of the heart. The darkness around our heart is our personal darkness, but the darkness within the cave of the heart is universal darkness, maybe this is what Meister Eckhart was speaking of when he wrote "God's darkness/is a superessential darkness."[2]

Shamans, visionaries, and mystics often go and sit in caves in the wilderness, but did you know that you have an inner wilderness that is even more vast than the outer world? You can enter into this inner wilderness, find this cave of the heart, and enter into it and sit in utter

1 Teasdale, *The Mystic Heart*, 53.

2 Matthew Fox, *Meditations with Meister Eckhart*, 43.

stillness. Maybe you are crying for a vision. Maybe you have become weary and disillusioned with the world and you are seeking something stable. You separate, you leave behind this world of movement and matter and you enter deep into the heart of stillness. Here you must lie in what the Greeks called incubation, until you are visited by a dream or a vision. It is in this superessential darkness that you will find what you are seeking and what you are seeking is seeking you. Joseph Rael writes about the "black light."

> The essence of the darkness is "to call into existence from non-existence that which we are searching for." That is the metaphor of nighttime. The breath and blackness are the same thing because Spirit is in the breath of nighttimeness. . . . Knowledge always appears from the no-formness of the dark space into the white daylight of knowing."[3]

It is in this *superessential darkness* that you will find the spark of the light of *Wah Mah Chi* that dwells within every human heart. There are many paths to God, because there are many living beings. Every mystic must make this secret journey into the inner wilderness to find the cave of the heart. Yet, there is only one heart and it is the Heart of God, so there is nowhere to go, there is no separation and this is the initiation—the self-realization that you do not exist and that you are the spark of the light of God within the darkness of the cave of the heart.

"Our whole being depends on nothing but a becoming–Nothing,"[4] writes Eckhart. This becoming Nothingness is similar to what Joseph says: "We don't exist." It is into this Nothingness that the secret, sacred journey leads us.

Father Bede Griffiths describes the *mulasthanam*, the inner sanctuary of the Hindu temple, as a place that is always kept in darkness. "You go through the courts of the temple, which are filled with light, the figures of the gods, but when you come to the inner sanctuary you come to the heart, the inner center of your own being, and you encounter God in the darkness."[5]

Peter Kingsley has written about the ancient Greek process of incubation (and also how the Greeks may have been influenced by Central Asian

---

3 *B&V:NW,* 72–73.

4 Matthew Fox, *Meister Eckhart: A Mystic Warrior for Our Times*, 131.

5 Bede Griffiths in Renée Weber, *Dialogues with Scientists and Sages*, 177.

shamanism), in which the initiate lies down "like an animal in its lair."[6] Incubation is an initiation that occurs by lying down in the darkness of a cave or shrine.

THE CAVE IN THE MIND

In his book, *The Cave in the Mind*, South African scholar David Lewis-Williams has written about cave art and the human capacity for altered states of consciousness as employed by shamans. He points out that "entering a cave" was a metaphor for the entering into a shamanic state of consciousness.[7] He also describes how walls could also be veils, or passages between worlds. There are both outer and inner caves, Lewis-Williams tells us, and entering the outer cave can help us to enter the inner cave.

> We are concerned not only with the human mind in the cave; we must also take into account the neurological cave in the mind . . . the ways in which the human mind behaved in the Upper Paleolithic caverns, whether as a result of the sensory deprivation of the caves themselves or the many other factors that induce altered states of consciousness . . . the sensation of entering a constricting vortex and coming out on the far side into an hallucinatory realm with its own conditions of causality and transformation. This is the cave in the mind.[8]

Lewis-Williams finds correlation between different stages of altered states of consciousness and the different journeys that shamans throughout time have described. Two of the most common types of shamanic journeys are the descent into the underworld or the flight to the sky realm. He sees these journeys as growing out of the neuropsychological experience of the sinking vortex (heaviness with downward pull) or experiences of the skyward journey (weightlessness). The shamanic experiences of journeying have neuropsychological correlates with the possibilities of human experience in altered states. Lewis-Williams is not using this correlation in a reductive way, for instance arguing that shamanism is brain malfunction, rather he is saying that brain functioning in altered states of consciousness allows us to have shamanic experiences. He writes, "they are part of the in-built experiences of the full spectrum of human consciousness."[9]

---

6 Peter Kingsley, *In the Dark Places of Wisdom*, 78–84.

7 David Lewis-Williams, *The Cave in the Mind*, 168.

8 Ibid., 204.

9 Ibid., 145–47.

Lewis-Williams sees these neuropsychological human capabilities as the foundation for religious and spiritual experiences, such as the visionary, mystical, and shamanic experiences we explore in this book. He finds that many scholars have come to this conclusion and reviews their thinking. Weston La Barre, for instance, writes that "shamanism or direct contact with the supernatural in these states . . . is the de facto source of all revelation, and ultimately of all religions."[10] Lewis-Williams describes how shamans learn to set aside their perceptions of outer (what Joseph would call "ordinary" reality) and enter into the cave in the mind to perceive the inner neuropsychological structure of inner consciousness.

JOSEPH ON THE MEANING OF THE CAVE

I asked Joseph about the meaning of caves and this is what he said:

"Nah au kwee leh neh *is the Tiwa word for cave.* Nah *means 'self.'* Au kwee – *means 'curved.'* Leh neh *means 'straight like a fence.'*

"Nah *means that when we enter a cave, we are entering into ourselves and we should think of the cave as our self. We should expect that when we first enter the cave it will turn every which way and it can get confusing, but eventually it will straighten out and you will then find what you are seeking.*

"When I was a kid, I would ride my bike and swerve back and forth. I would pretend that I was riding in a cave and swerving down the passageways. . . . I would pretend I was in a golden, diamond-studded cave with jewels as big as coffee cups. Each jewel would have a special sound—I would listen for it in my imagination. My grandfather said that I should listen to things as I moved through them, like passing by rows of trees on either side as I rode my bike and I would listen to them singing. I always was really fond of trees and I spent as much time with them as I could."

THE CAVE OF THE HEART (GUHĀ)

There is a Hindu tradition that speaks about the *Guhā*, which means "cave of the heart." This place of seemingly barren darkness within each of our hearts is actually the place where we connect to the source of our self, which is also the Source of the Self. This is the place where the Hindus teach that we connect to God.

---

10 Weston La Barre, in Lewis-Williams, 135.

Many mystics and shamans retreat into a cave at some point in their initiations. St. Francis went to Alverna and had visions there. Late in life he saw a vast angelic Seraph in the sky, after which he was the first person to receive the "stigmata," the marks of Christ's wounds on his palms.

There was a man named Abhishiktananda, but that was not the name he was born with. He was born Henri Le Saux in the Brittany region of France. He became a Benedictine monk and yet his heart called him on a journey to India. A Benedictine is a Catholic monk who follows the teachings of St. Benedict of Nursia. In the year 500 CE, Benedict went into a cave near Subiaco, about 40 miles from Rome. He spent three years in that cave on his initiatory path, which was not so much a journey as a sitting in stillness and darkness.

Le Saux served as a French soldier in World War II. He was captured and escaped. He kept trying to get transferred to India. After the war he wrote to Father Monchanin, who was serving in India. He wrote, in 1947, to Monchanin that it was a joy "to discover someone whom the thought of the *atman* leads to the contemplation of the divine Paraclete, and how behind the superficial pantheism discerns the extraordinary intuition of the Spirit reached by the great seers of the Upanishads."[11] Le Saux found something universal in the spiritual Hindu texts of the Upanishads and felt a correspondence, a resonance between the idea of the *atman*, the inner divine Self, and the Paraclete (the dove of the Holy Spirit). While Le Saux was drawn to Indian spirituality and to the land and the people, he initially thought he was going as a missionary to bring Christianity to India. Eventually Le Saux was approved to go to India and he landed near Colombo, Sri Lanka, on August 14, 1948 (a year since India had gained its independence and six months after Mahatma Gandhi had been assassinated).

However Le Saux's journey was a secret journey because he did not realize that he would have an extreme crisis of faith as he dove ever more deeply into the Cosmic Ocean of Hinduism. His personal principles called him to become Indian to teach Christianity in India. "We can only succeed in our work," he said, "if we become Indian right through—right to the depths of our heart and soul—right to the smallest details of daily life." However in becoming Indian *right to the depths of our heart and soul* he began to have difficulty subsuming Hinduism under Christianity and

11 Le Saux letter to Monchanin, cited in Du Boulay, *The Cave of the Heart: The Life of Swami Abhishiktananda*, 48.

ended up living out a painful, yet enriching "double-belonging." Shirley Du Boulay writes in her biography of Abhishiktananda (the name Le Saux is best known by today) that his is "a story of transformation . . . the story of a man searching for God, prepared to give up everything and to risk all in the search. It is also the story of a man caught in contradiction. . . . And here lies the heart of his anguish and his crowning consummation."

His anguish was exactly his triumph. Du Boulay writes that he had "two loves," his two religions. [12] While Hinduism has often been able to embrace different gods and religions as paths to God, Christianity has a "jealous" God that devalues other religions and other gods.

Initially, Le Saux and Monchanin set up a Christian-Hindu ashram called Shantivanam. The two men had different personalities that sometimes caused conflict. Le Saux, himself, had inner conflict between becoming a wandering seeker of God and setting up a Christian community for Hindus. He met the sage Ramana Maharshi in 1949, a year before this mystic died. Du Boulay writes that the "man whom Henri credited with his real initiation into Indian spirituality was Sri Ramana Maharshi." Le Saux wrote that meeting Ramana was "a call which pierced through everything, rent it in pieces and opened a mighty abyss."[13] Le Saux was not the only Westerner influenced by Ramana Maharshi. Somerset Maugham met the Sage of Arunachala in 1938 and based the character of the guru in his book *The Razor's Edge* on him. Heinrich Zimmer,[14] the German student of Indian art and religion, was inspired by Ramana Maharshi's writings. Zimmer in turn was an associate of Carl Jung and Jung wrote a piece which was later used as an introduction to the Shambhala Press book *The Spiritual Teachings of Ramana Maharshi*. Le Saux's meeting with Ramana Maharshi gave him a taste of *advaita*—non-dualism, which he continued to drink like the soul drinking a vision.

When Ramana Maharshi was sixteen, he read about the Tamil saints

---

12 Shirley du Boulay, *The Cave of the Heart*, 57, xv-xvi, 62.

13 Ibid., 67, xvi.

14 Zimmer was a friend and colleague of Joseph Campbell. Zimmer, incidentally, recommended that the first publication of the new Bollingen press should feature a Native American topic. The first publication did just that, *Where the Two Came to Their Father: A Navaho War Ceremonial Given by Jeff King*, by Maud Oakes and Joseph Campbell. After Zimmer's death, Campbell edited his final works: *Myths and Symbols in Indian Art and Civilization, The King and the Corpse, Philosophies of India*, and *The Art of Indian Asia*. Campbell said that when he would get stumped at editing Zimmer's notes, "he would relax and close his eyes for a moment, and it was as if Zimmer came and gave dictation," (Stephen and Robin Larsen, *A Fire in the Mind: The Life of Joseph Campbell*, 326).

and a "throbbing awareness began to awaken in him, a state of bliss. 'At first I thought it was some kind of fever,' he said, 'but I decided, if so it is a pleasant fever, so let it stay.'" He had a death-experience and an awakening into enlightenment and began teaching.

> Ramana Maharshi taught the purest form of *advaita*, or nonduality. The word *advaita* comes from the Sanskrit words *a-* and *dvaita*, literally 'not two'—nonduality. It is the fundamental insight of the Upanishads and one that was to dominate the rest of Henri's life. Its central teaching is the oneness of the individual soul with the Absolute, and Ramana taught it through the discipline of self-knowledge. [15]

Ramana Maharshi was drawn to the mountain Arunachala, with its many caves, an ancient holy site dedicated to Lord Śiva. He spent the rest of his life there, sometimes living in the caves and eventually an ashram and temple grew around him. He was silent for some time, and even after he began speaking again, would only give short answers. One of his primary teachings was self-enquiry. This consisted of asking "Who am I?"[16]

In 1949, Henri Le Saux traveled to Arunachala to meet Ramana Maharshi. He awoke the next morning with a fever. It was then that he had his transformative initiation, which was really just the beginning of a life of mysticism.

> Unknown harmonics awoke in my heart. A melody made itself felt, and especially an all-embracing ground-bass. . . . In the Sage of Arunachala of our own time I discerned the unique Sage of the eternal India, the unbroken succession of her sages, her ascetics, her seers; it was as if the very soul of India penetrated to the very depths of my own soul and held mysterious communion with it. It was a call that pierced through everything, tore it apart and opened a mighty abyss.[17]

The next year Ramana Maharshi died and it was two and a half years later that Abhishiktananda returned to the caves of Arunachala. He had taken a Hindu name and was dressing in the traditional ochre robes of Hindu holy men, wearing the Benedictine cross with the sacred OM symbol carved in the center. The name, Abhishiktananda, means "Bliss of the Anointed One, the Lord." Abhishiktananda found a cave overlooking

15 du Boulay, *The Cave of the Heart*, 68–69.

16 Ibid., 81.

17 Ibid., 72.

the temple and settled in, calling the cave, *sacro speco*, meaning "sacred space," which is what St. Benedict called his cave in Italy. The first night in the cave, Abhishiktananda had "three powerful intimations, which he recorded in his spiritual diary [*Ascent to the Depth of the Heart*]. He accepted Hindu sannyāsa as an end itself. . . . He embraced silence. . . . And he went even further in his acceptance of poverty." He embraced silence and stillness, loving it with all his heart and wrote that he was "willing to remain *for ever* in my cave, keeping silence." He wrote a love poem to the cave, to silence, to stillness.

> In silence you teach me silence, O Arunachala,
> You who never depart from your silence,
> May I not have entered Your cave in vain;
> of "mine" and "me" may nothing any longer remain . . .
> alone and without a second, advaita, You are.
> "You shine in the form of Self
> You are 'I'"
>
> Jesus Brahman![18]

Ramana Maharshi wrote a poem to the god Śiva, who was the same as the mountain Arunachala—the god being the place and the place being the god.

> To its caves, age after age, there has come a succession
> of those who are hungry for wisdom and renunciation,
> whom the Mountain, the divine Magnet,
> draws to its bosom,
> to teach them in its own silence
> the royal path of the supreme Silence,
> and how to be established in the Self.[19]

This point of the equivalency of the divine with the earthly place is found in indigenous cultures and Hinduism has a strong blend of indigenousness within its teachings as it stretches back into shamanic pre-history and incorporated earlier spiritual pathways.[20] Even if Ramana Maharshi was gone, Abhishiktananda felt he could learn from the caves of the sacred mountain which had also been Ramana's teacher in silence.

---

18 Ibid., 73–76, 77.

19 Ramana Maharshi in du Boulay, 79–80.

20 A story that links the divine feminine and the land comes from when Śiva's beloved, Sati, throws herself on a fire and dies. Distraught, Śiva picks up her dead body and dances madly with her. As he dances across all of India, pieces of Sati's body fall to the earth and blend into the land, creating a series of *Śakti Peethas* or sacred sites.

"Could it be, then, that even at the physical level something passes from the mountain of Arunachala into the hearts of those who shelter in its caves?"[21] Abhishiktananda continued to visit these caves, as well as wandering up into the Himalayas for expeditions into the heart of silence. While the physical caves may seep into the heart of the seeker, Ramana taught that we all have a *guhā*, a cave of the heart, and in the darkness of this cave is where we find God. While the outer cave may help us connect to this inner cave, it is really this inner journey into darkness, silence, and stillness that is the defining one. *Guhā* can also mean "a hiding place," not only a cave, but a secret place where things are hidden.[22] One of the things that might be hidden there, in the secret darkness of the cave, in the *guhā* is the inner *guru*, which can be translated as "a teacher — one who dispels darkness (ignorance) of the mind (person). 'Gu' means darkness and 'ru' means the act of removal."[23]

The cave of the heart, the *guhā*, came to be an orienting feature in Abhishiktananda's quest and teachings. His first book that he wrote, *Guhantara*, was not published because the Catholic censors felt it was too syncretistic, blending Hinduism and Christianity instead of critiquing and subsuming Hinduism under Christianity. Disappointed, he kept on going deeper into the interior of the cave of the heart. "Each time one thinks one has touched the bottom; and as one goes into the depths, one discovers circles ever deeper in that depth." His crisis of faith was between the light of Christianity, with its rigid laws and rules of the Church, and the inner darkness of the cave of the heart that if plumbed deeply enough, reveals the inner light of bliss and union with the One. "Even the symbol of the Cross no longer speaks to me. So I concentrate on the Heart of Christ, *hrid*, as the Hindu understanding of the Sacred Heart."[24] Du Boulay writes that many "people who seek the experience of *advaita*, who long to transcend the opposites, are drawn on this path partly because they themselves, in their own lives and personalities, are caught between opposites."[25] She describes Abhishiktananda's creative tension between: Christianity and *advaita* Hinduism; between his responsibilities at the ashram and his desire to wander as a *sannyasi*; and his desire for solitude and his longing

21 Ibid., 77.

22 "Guhā," *Sanskrit Dictionary*, "a hiding-place, cave, cavern."

23 "Sanskrit, The Aksharas (letters)," *Hindupedia*.

24 du Boulay, 108, 111. *Hrid* is "heart" in Sanskrit.

25 Ibid., 200.

to be around others. It was in the center of his being, within the cave of the heart, that he found the vast space that could encompass and hold these opposites. In fact the opposites actually arise from this space, because if one goes deep enough within the cave of the heart, one reaches the place of non-duality. Abhishiktananda spoke of the deep, dark places of the cave of the heart, which lead ever and ever deeper into mystery.

> Guhantara, the interior cavern. . . . In these dark places where there is no longer a guide, the words explode, logic wavers, and paradox alone can pull together this desperate effort to tell that which is beyond words . . . finally there may emerge, from the deep womb of the heart, which has at last been discovered, at last attained, that sign, that pure sign, which is the sacred stone in the centre of the place of rebirth of Being. . . . In the abysses of the heart to which he feels himself inexorably drawn, there is absolutely nothing he can grasp hold of or hang on to, nothing solid on which he can, so to speak, put down his foot, no air from outside in which to draw a breath. . . . The door of the guha has been opened to you! You have glimpsed its depths, now enter within, from depth to depth, to ever deeper centres, in a constantly deeper passing beyond of yourself and of God, which has neither beginning nor end, in that mystery which is no more either not-one or not-two.[26]

This inner, secret journey into the cave of the heart, into this inner wilderness is a dreadful journey that leads to bliss. It is the separation from the noisy and busy world of forms and senses into the stillness and silence of inner quietude. "Alone with the Alone, or rather alone in the Alone," wrote Abhishiktananda in his spiritual diary.[27]

THE PATH OF DARKNESS

Joseph says that in the darkness, visions can be seen more clearly. The path of the shaman, the visionary, and the mystic all lead into darkness at some point in their initiatory journey. The Christian mystics like St. John of the Cross ventured into darkness and the "dark night of the soul" in their search for the Divine. Dante also ventured first into the underworld before ascending to Heaven.

You cannot see the path of darkness, you must trust that it is there. In trusting that it is there you must fall, because it is not really there. Yet you

26 Ibid., 11–20, 130, 137, 220.

27 Ibid., 147.

ANTONIO DOMINGO SIMBOLA – JOSEPH'S GRANDFATHER

have to trust that falling off the path into darkness actually *is* the path, the path that is no path. You have to fall out of the visible light of ordinary reality into non-ordinary reality. When you first enter non-ordinary reality it appears as darkness because you are not used to seeing in non-ordinary reality.

When Joseph was a boy in Picuris Pueblo, his grandfather began initiating him into the sacredness by taking him into the kiva. Joseph took me to Kuaua Pueblo[28] and we went on a tour of the site. I climbed up the ladder to the top of the Painted Kiva, then down the ladder into the darkness. Joseph said that this is how it was, climbing down into the darkness for initiation. Entering into the darkness is a crucial part of the

28 This Tiwa-speaking Pueblo was over-named the Coronado Historical Site.

initiation into non-ordinary reality.

The night before Joseph took me to Kuaua Pueblo, Joseph and I spoke at BookWorks bookstore in Albuquerque. Joseph had a photo of his grandfather and showed the photo to the audience and spoke about how his grandfather would teach him and the other boys. In the winter they would climb down into the darkness of the kiva. One winter, Joseph's Grandfather did a ceremony and told the boys that they had to fix their eyes on a place on the wall. As they did this the wall disappeared and the boys saw a bright meadow through the wall and his grandfather said, "Now keep your eyes fixed on this wall, otherwise I might get trapped on the other side and maybe I will never come back or maybe you will be able to do the ceremony and get me back in 5 minutes or maybe you will never get me back." Then Joseph's grandfather walked through the wall and then came back through carrying summer herbs and flowers into the cold Picuris winter. Later Joseph asked if he could do the ceremony and walk through the wall like his grandfather and his grandfather said, "If you do that I will hit you! You should do something that I have never done, don't just repeat what I can do." Joseph said that this is where we are stuck, repeating what has been done before, and that is not really existing.

SWEAT LODGE

> *"When I hear about caves and houses of the womb, I think of sweat lodges."*[29]
>
> MATTHEW FOX

Joseph and I wrote about the sweat lodge ceremony in *Walking the Medicine Wheel* (54-60). This circular structure made of tree branches and covered with blankets and tarps is used as for traditional purification ceremonies in many American Indian tribes. Many peoples have used heat and steam for healing purposes, from New Zealand to Iceland. The word *sauna* comes from the Finnish language. In the Lakota language, the sweat lodge ceremony is known as *inipi olowan*. My experience with *inipi olowan* has been through Mike Lee, the Ceremonial Elder (Blackfeet) of the Veteran's Sweat Lodge at American Lake VA Hospital and his team of elders.[30] When you enter the sweat lodge, you enter into darkness when the door flap is closed. You sit in the darkness with a group of people who come together for the purpose of healing. There are four rounds (or

29 Matthew Fox, *Meister Eckhart: A Mystic Warrior for Our Times*, 165.

30 See the website for more information, http://vasweatlodge.org/.

"doors) of stones brought in, just as there are four seasons, four cardinal directions, and four chambers of our hearts. More hot stones, who we welcome as our ancestors, are brought in with each round/door. We enter through these doors, letting go of what we no longer need to be carrying. This creates space for new gifts to come in. Mike Lee often says something like, "The *inipi olowan* is not just for Native American veterans, but for all veterans because all veterans are brothers and sisters. This *inipi olowan* is not just for veterans, it is for all VA staff because if the staff are not well how can they help veterans heal?" The sweat lodge is a communal healing ceremony that takes place in the darkness and brings us back into harmonious relationship with the our hearts, our bodies, with the Earth, and with each other.

MEDICINE WHEEL CEREMONY

Joseph taught me a medicine wheel ceremony. He instructed me to close my eyes and then told me to place myself in the center of the medicine wheel. Then to expand out 200 miles to the north, then 200 miles to the south, then 200 miles out to the east and then 200 miles to the west. I am then in the center of a large medicine wheel. Next, he said to step my consciousness out of my body and to watch what happens. This is a standard shamanic practice that is often written about, the shamanic journey where the shaman's consciousness leaves his or her body and journeys into the spirit world. Joseph said that I should watch to see what will approach and from what direction. He told me "*Many of the healers say that there are helpers who come and help you and they do the healing, you are just there to provide a way for them to work and you are not directly involved in the healing itself.*" These helpers can be spirit guides or animal totems or a new healing ceremony may bring in new helpers who are unfamiliar to the healer. Sometimes animal guides are called "familiars" because they are familiar helpers to the healer. Sometimes they are called "power animals," or "animal spirits," or many other names. The familiar power animal can help to provide some orientation in the disorienting process of entering into the darkness—sometimes this darkness is literal darkness in which nothing can be seen or sometimes it is figurative darkness, a place that is unknown or unfamiliar.

Many stories of shamanic initiation take the initiate through death and dismemberment. Sometimes the initiate's bones are replaced with new

HEART AT THE CENTER OF DARK MATTER

bones, or body parts or organs might be replaced, such as being given a new heart. The initiate must go through death, sometimes again and again and again. Holger Kalweit writes that being struck three times by lightning is the initiation of a Lightning Shaman. "It is believed that people who have been struck by lightning three times and survived have been blessed by the gods with miraculous powers. It is said that the first lightning bolt kills, the second separates the head from the body, and the third awakens new life."[31] This three-part process follows the three steps of initiation we have been following in this book.

When I started doing this ceremony of entering the center of the medicine wheel, I was going through some kind of *fanā*, or annihilation,[32]

---

31 Kalweit, *Shamans, Healers, and Medicine Men, 46.*

32 Corbin describes this Sufi term, *fanā'* as "annihilation," stating "*fanā'* will be the 'cipher' (*ramz*), symbolizing this passing away of forms that appear from instant to instant and their perpetuation (*baqā'*) in the one substance that is pluralized in its epiphanies. . . . Since Creation

some kind of initiatory death of the body, which is also a death of the ego. This process of imaginal death and dismemberment has become somewhat familiar to me now. I fall into never-ending darkness; I am eaten by a shark; tiny animals with razor-sharp teeth devour my flesh and leave the bones in a seated position; I sink to the bottom of the cosmic ocean and lay peacefully on my back, staring up into the darkness of the depths beyond any light reaching that deep, small crustaceans swarm over my body and eat away all my flesh until I am just a skeleton on the bottom of the ocean. Joseph has written, "When we die we become the heart. We die in order to disappear into awareness."

Last night I lay in the center of the medicine wheel and a rattlesnake approached from the west, the direction of the physical and it bit me on the head and stayed fast. (I was reminded of the image from Kuaua of the shaman whose head disappeared into the mouth of a giant fish). The poison coursed through my veins and arteries. I died. My body started to decay, there was nothing left but bones. The bones turned to dust and the dust intermingled with the dust of the earth. Water is added and I am rolled up into a "mud man" and then animated again. Death, whether literal or metaphorical, Joseph says is necessary for us to reach God. "When we die, we go back to that infinite vastness which vibrates, but has no light. It has none of the kind of light that we use here in this state of impermanence, which has been called the maya, 'the delusion of illusion.'"[33]

Joseph has said that the healer has to journey back into "the mother's womb." Abhishiktananda wrote of the guhā as "the deep womb of the heart."[34] Healing source energy can then flow from Source through the hollow bone of the healer and into ordinary reality. The shaman does this by going through death and dismemberment again and again until reaching the awareness that he or she does not exist. This *gnosis* or *jñana*, this experiential insight into not existing at first seems negative—an annihilation—but is actually incredibly positive as it allows a conduit to open for creative Source energy to pour through the healer into ordinary

---

is a concatenation of theophanies (*tajalliyāt*), in which there is no causal nexus between one form and another, each creation is the beginning of the manifestation of one form and the occultation of another. . . . Here again we may say . . . this already is the other world," (Corbin, *Alone with the Alone*, 202–03). To me, this seems to be getting at the same concept as Joseph Rael's statement "we do not exist," as well as the doctrine of *spanda* vibration from Kashmiri Shaivism, reality is in a perpetual state of annihilation and creation.

33 *Sound*, 227–28.

34 du Boulay, 130.

reality. This is not anything special, actually, for it is the true nature of reality—we do not actually exist as fixed, separated, static objects—instead we are the divine creative pulsation, the *spanda*, the quantum moment of creation, like a continually breaking wave of reality of the non-ordinary, briefly crystalizing into ordinary reality and then vanishing to be replaced by a new moment of creation.

CAVE OF THE HEART CEREMONY

In a parallel with honoring the four directions of the medicine wheel, Abhishiktananda describes how the devout Hindu takes a bath, recites mantras and then will "honor the four points of the compass, throwing water north, south, east, and west."[35] This brings us back from India to American Indians. Joseph Rael guides us around the four outer directions, and that was largely our work in *Walking the Medicine Wheel: Healing Trauma & PTSD*. Joseph tells us that if we want to go further, if we want to walk the path of becoming medicine—of becoming a visionary, a mystic, a shaman—we must enter into the center of the medicine wheel, which is also the heart. He tells us that we must climb to the top of the mountain because the mountain is also the center of the medicine wheel. We must make this outer journey in order to make the inner journey into the depths of the heart. The shaman must learn to be equally comfortable descending into the darkest dark as well as ascending to the highest high.[36] The ultimate vehicle of all life, of all existence is the heart.

As I have followed Joseph's instructions doing medicine wheel visualizations—visualizing myself in the center of the circle of directions and "stepping outside" of my body in order to see myself from outside

---

35 Ibid., 131.

36 Rene Guenon, in his book *Symbols of Sacred Science*, writes that the cave and the mountain are mirror images of each other, one a triangle pointing up, the other a triangle pointing down. Seekers can pursue what they seek on mountain tops as well as in caves. The triangle pointing up is the masculine and the triangle pointing down is the feminine. When these two are brought together the "Star of David" emerges which brings together the highest mountain-top with the deepest cave, it brings together the light and the dark, and it brings together the masculine and the feminine.

Interlocking triangles are the basis for the śrī Yantra symbol of Hinduism and Buddhism. As taught in Kashmiri Shaivism, our most fundamental reality is Oneness—we are all *Siva*. Even the masculine Śiva and the feminine Śakti merge into One, a divine being called *Ardhanarishvara*, who is half male and half female. Joseph speaks of a similar concept, that when we age we become Mother-Father beings. At birth we separate into either male of female form, yet after age 55, a person becomes a "Mother-Father" person by integrating the feminine with the masculine. This combines into the "Mother-Father-God principle," *Key-aah-ta-meh-nay*, (*Ceremonies*, 150).

(thus creating an inner and outer experience at the same time)—I have found myself entering into imagery of either descending or ascending. At first I tended to experience the descending feelings, also various images of bodily destruction and dissolution that would then be followed by bodily reconstruction and rebirth. This would then be followed by states of lightness, soaring and flight. As I practiced more, sometimes I would enter directly into states of flight, such as turning into a crow and soaring through the darkness of the infinite cosmos. When you enter the cave of the heart at the center of the medicine wheel, open yourself to whatever visions may arise for you. Here is a meditation I have practiced.

Take several deep breaths and enter into the space of your heart.

Begin looking for the cave of your heart, you may find it at the base of your heart, or possibly in the center of the medicine wheel of your heart—the place where the four walls of the heart meet in the center.

Breathe deeply and enter into the cave—only you can learn what is in this most secret and sacred place of your self. Become aware of your senses. What do you see? What is it like to breathe this air? What do you hear? What do you feel? What do you smell? Take a few moments to orient yourself in the darkness of this cave.

Proceed deeper into the cave. Who knows what you will find here? Most likely you will walk through some darkness. You may see images, visions, memories. Allow yourself to experience what this deepest place of your being holds. Remember to breathe, particularly if you get scared or freeze up. Remember that everything that is here is for a reason and there is a reason for you to be here in the cave of your heart at this moment and that reason is so that you can experience what you are experiencing right now.

> Breathe into the darkness of the cave of your heart.
> Enter into the darkness of the cave of your heart.
> Explore the depths of your being.
> Everything that you hold, you hold for a reason.
> Enter into the pulse of your existence.
> Breathe . . .

When I do this exercise, I find many different things each time. I woke up around 3 AM this morning and could not sleep well. It was the perfect time to practice this ceremony. I had been focusing on what I call the "seed of the heart" the place at the bottom of the heart, the lower tip of the heart that I see as the seed that is planted in the darkness of my chest and from which my heart and my life sprouts. This morning, however, I looked at the four walls of my heart and I thought of Joseph's teachings about the medicine wheel and decided I should see what would happen if I entered into a cave at the center of the medicine wheel of my heart.

I entered into the cave, into absolute darkness. I took a moment to stand in the darkness and let my senses adjust. It was still as dark, maybe even darker. I took a deep breath of the air in the cave of my heart—warm, moist, an underground smell, but not suffocating or unpleasant. I ventured further in.

A memory arose. When we moved back to Champaign, Illinois, (around the year 2000) I did a solo back-packing trip down in Shawnee National Forest at the lower tip of Illinois. I had been finding that I did not get very hungry on solo backpacking trips, so I did a liquid fast—miso soup and tea. The hot liquids felt good and nourishing and I found I did not really need solid food. I camped on a rocky prominence that formed a small hill. After pitching the tent, I wandered around the area and found a crevice on the northeast side of the hill and had two impulses—the first was to venture in, the second was to go as far away as I could from the place. I took a breath and went in.

My two main fears were snakes (there are rattlers in that part of Illinois) and spiders. I made my way through spider webs and went deeper into the crevice. It was open on top, although a bit overgrown, and it narrowed as I went in. I reached a place and stopped. I had a feeling and asked myself "Is there some evil here?" I laughed it off and reminded myself of Jung's writings around "the shadow," the dark part of ourselves that we project off on to others and on to places. No, the evil was in me, not in the place I told myself. I had some tobacco with me and lit a match. It was not total blackness by any means, but I felt a sense of relief to see the light of the match and to let the light enter my heart. I offered the tobacco and watched as the smoke wafted up through the crevice and out into the free surroundings above. I forced myself to stay there for a while, confronting my fears and letting my animal body go through the cycle of physiological panic. I walked back out of the crevice and felt a sense of relief when I got out, but also felt that I had done something the nature of which I did not fully understand, but which felt important.

In the movie, *The Empire Strikes Back*, Luke seeks out Yoda on the jungle planet of Dagobah. Instead of a "great warrior" he finds a fussy, intrusive little being who starts to get on his nerves. Yoda, irritated at the impatience of his guest asks Luke a question. Luke says he is looking for a great warrior, but Yoda retorts, that wars do not make one great.

Eventually, Luke realizes that this little green imp is actually the Jedi master he seeks and he begins to study under him. At one point Luke is near a large, ancient tree that has a crevice in it. He doesn't like the feel of it, but Yoda says that he must go into the darkness. Yoda tells Luke that he will find in that darkness only what he takes with him and that he will not need his weapon.

Luke takes his weapons anyway and enters into the darkness. After venturing in past snakes and vines, he encounters Darth Vader, his hated enemy who killed his mentor Obi Wan Kenobi. Luke instantly springs to attack, they battle and Luke slices off Darth Vader's head. The helmeted head rolls to his feet and suddenly the mask burns away to reveal Luke's own face, which unnerves him. The lesson seems three-fold. First, it is foreshadowing the family connection that Darth Vader is Luke's father. Second, there is something about Luke that is like Darth Vader and the vision cautions him in that regard. Third, the greatest darkness we need to face is the darkness we carry within ourselves.

As I walked deeper into the cave of my heart, I had another memory. The night I had gone into the crevice at Shawnee, I was lying in my sleeping bag and I heard a horrendous "screech, screech, screech" to the east. It was the most awful, unworldly sound I had ever heard and I immediately had the image of a human/dog-like creature, low to the ground running on four legs, but sometimes able to stand on two, with glowing red eyes. "Jeez, I thought, what the mind can conjure up," I said to myself. Shaken, I tried to go back to sleep and did doze off a bit, only to be shocked awake by the sound again, now to the south and closer in. Again I had the image of the terrible thing. What the___is that??? Could that be a Screech Owl? I had never heard one, but it was the only thing I could think of. Even with that reassurance, I could not really fall asleep. Again it screech, screech, screeched, now even closer and to the west. I had the image of this feral hunter, slowly circling me. I began to regret going into that crevice where I had laughed off the feeling of evil. I could not sleep at all now as my body panicked, my heart beat hard, my breathing rate increased. I worked to control my breathing and heart rate. I knew that the next time I heard the thing it would be from the north and would be right outside the tent at my head and would burst through the tent to get me.

Morning. I awoke, somewhat surprised that I had been able to fall back asleep. A sense of relief and I looked up at that sun and had never been so thankful to see it. I escaped. Facing your fears is an important part of becoming a shaman, of becoming a visionary. Many scary things come up, in fact those might be the first things you come across as what you repress is charged with the energy that you use to push it away, and when you relax it comes back twice as hard. Now when I go into the medicine wheel, I am not surprised if I see my body sink to the bottom of the ocean floor to be devoured by tiny razor-sharp-toothed fish and to see my exposed skeleton lying on the ocean floor until it starts to become mineralized into a clear crystalline hardness and then I am re-fleshed and brought back to life. Maybe this is just my over-active imagination after reading about shaman's going through ritual death initiations or maybe this is part of the process and those writings exist because that is what happens to you as you embark on this journey of initiation.

After those two memories surfaced from Shawnee, I walked further into the cave of my heart and stepped into water. I kept walking, the water came up to my chest, up to my mouth—I bet it is cold I said to myself—it was cold, but at the same time it was not. I have found that in facing your fear it is best to dive in, so I plunged into the water and began swimming down into the blackness. Oddly enough, there was a light emanating from the deep. It was a light, but it was not a light. It was still complete darkness, but it was like another sense—maybe it was a guiding light. I could see it illuminate the outlines of the rock cliffs along which I was swimming, but there was no actual light. I went toward this light that was not a light. Maybe it is what the mystics call the "uncreated light."

I suddenly was out of the water and into a dry room. Although I was swimming downward, when I entered the room it was like I walked horizontally through a wall of water. It was an unadorned room, stone floor, ceiling and walls, and at the end of the room was a vacant chair. I remembered a couple things at that point. The first was the exercise we do in the hero's journey class for the "journey within" step. In that exercise, there is an inward journey into the dark and then a figure on a throne. As you approach the throne, the figure embraces you and you become that figure. It is an exercise in going through one's own inner darkness in order to "claim the crown," to embrace one's own inner divinity. The other thing I remembered was Joseph's vision quest where he decided he was not going to stop until he met God.

In the cave of the heart exploration, I walked across the empty hall, my footsteps echoing ever louder as I approached the empty throne. I took a breath and sat down on the throne and there was an instant change. Instead of being deep underground in a stone cavern, it was like I was everywhere and could see everywhere. I felt like I was in a "control center" and that my life and the world of existence was unfolding all around me—through me. Not only could I see everywhere—I was everything and everything was me. It was a feeling of being in the center while also being everywhere on the periphery as well.

WHAT JOSEPH HAS TO SAY ABOUT THE CAVE OF THE HEART

"First of all, you have to look at what the letters and sounds mean.

C *thirst*
A *purity*
V *drinking, swallowing*
E *placement*

"The 'c' in 'cave' is pronounced 'Kay.' There is a blanket that has been placed over that moment when the people go into a cave, that is why caves were created in the beginning by the original architect, even before goodness. We don't know who the original architect is. God is a phenomenon that we have created. Kay *means to cover oneself up with the blanket of something, getting blindsided. But you have to do that, you have to go in blindsided, covering your vision, you can't be a visionary unless you go into this darkness.* Kay *also means the beginning. Something has ended.* Kay *means something has ended because something has just been born, so the caves in ancient time, the caves over here in Colorado, the metaphor of the caves means a beginning. You are blindsided, you have to be blindsided to go into the caves.*

"Eventually, the people left the caves and went to live by the rivers. Before that they would come down from the caves to plant gardens and then go back to their caves. Noun-pronoun people think caves were protection and that cave men were hiding, but I am talking about nature being a blanket that is the metaphor for the caves.

"So we have to go with heart where the cave is and start there. I guess it is true, when the baby is born he or she can't see because she has been in the water fluid. Cave water means pah, *the very nature of* pah *means that we are in the womb, a human is in the womb and there is water there, not because the child needs water. The real, real, real reason for it is that is how we embrace the power*

WHEN THE PEOPLE WENT INTO THE CAVE OF EXISTENCE
AND RETURNED AS MADE PEOPLE CEREMONY

of traveling-ness—movement. It is the one that gives us movement. So that is when the first man, woman comes, they live in caves, very natural, Wisdom has already planted that seed, the wisdom that is planted in the placenta. See, it is all around us, we have the answer already, the interpretation. You got some of it, whatever moment you got it is a blessing to us. You just hooked up with a crazy nut like me, and we are going to put this thing together if it kills us.

"As soon as the cave is created in the heart — the heart is two things: one — everything I have said about it already; and two — fear, it seems to me that fear is a positive. The creator of excellence, the architect of everything, instilled fear.

F *father*
E *awareness*
A *purification*
R *radiance*

"You cannot have life without it, look what it spells:

Father
EAR

"When the father is involved in fear, awareness, purification and then the radiance R, That is what it encompasses fear what it does to our minds and our bodies. We have two ears—one ordinary, the other non-ordinary. Until we have them working together we are going to have fear. Structurally I have the right ear and the left ear and this big nose dividing them and the third eye on the forehead. It is really us. We are doing it. We are the fear, and if there isn't fear we will figure out a way to create it. That is the one power we have, we can change, it, but 99.999% of the public doesn't think we have a choice and that is baloney."

HEART OF PEACE

"A man whose heart is not changed will not change any other's."[37]

CARL JUNG

Peace cannot be found with the mind, because the mind functions on separation. Peace must be found at the center of the heart because the heart functions in unity. If we look at the middle letter of the words "heart," and "peace," we find "A." Joseph says that "A" represents "purity," is the center of both the words "heart" and "peace."

37 Carl Jung, "Attitude Change Conducive to World Peace," *The Symbolic Life*, CW 18, 611.

H
E
PEACE
R
T

A is the beginning place in the alphabet. It is the first letter and the first vowel. In Sanskrit, vowels are called *svara* which means "self-shining" as the vowels are the only letters that give off sound. The sound of "a" also "forms the fundamental sound from which all others are derived simply by moving the tongue and lips."[38]

In Kashmiri Shaivism the heart is the place of initiation, the point of transformation, and it is the place where the initiate realizes that they are already one with Śiva. The letter *A* in Sanskrit is of vital importance in this tradition, "the Ultimate (A)," which is a "seed vibration."

In English, the letter *A* is the center of the words heart and peace. For Joseph, *U* is the letter that is in the center of the medicine wheel and *A* is the letter associated with the East. *A* and *U* are found together in the Sanskrit word for God, *AUM*. They are also paired in the center of the Heart Mantra, *SAUḤ*. "The Heart Mantra is a *bija* which means seed." From the perspective of the medicine wheel, bringing *A* and *U* together brings together the first and the last vowel of the wheel, connecting the beginning to the endpoint in the center. The Sanskrit word, "mantra" is a word or phrase that is often given from a guru to a disciple as part of the initiation process. In this regard, "Initiation . . . involves the acquisition of a type of knowledge. Here, however, knowledge does not refer to specific or isolated fragments of information. Initiation is not the transmission of any specific fact or technique. It is rather the transmission of the infinite Self."[39]

When we repeat the phrase "A Heart of Peace," this can be considered a *mantra*, a repeated phrase that brings one to a spiritual focus. "A Mantra is Divinity," writes Woodroffe, it "is a Divine Power, or Daivi Śakti, manifesting sound in a body." To repeat the divine phrase, a person becomes one with that phrase, manifesting the essence of the divinity through the sound body in their own body and self. Creation comes from sound in Hinduism, as it does for Joseph. Joseph teaches that the sound

38 Dennis Waite, *Sanskrit for Seekers*, 13.

39 Paul Eduardo Muller-Ortega, *The Triadic Heart of Śiva*, 214, 170.

of a word and the thing represented by that word are the same, there is no gap between the signifier and the signified. This is similar in the study of the sounds of mantras in Hinduism. To say "A" is to be "A," the meaning and vibration of *A*. To say the name of the deity is to become the deity. Woodroffe highlights that the sound is not different than the essence that sound "represents." In fact, if we break down the word "represents" we have that something is re-presented. A meaning comes out of saying the word this way, when a sound is made it is not "symbolic" of something that is different or absent, rather it is re-presenting, re-manifesting that divinity. "A mantra is not merely sound or letters. This is a form in which Śakti manifests herself."

> Considering Śabda [sound] from its primary or causal aspect . . . it is vibration (Spandana) of any kind or motion, which is not merely physical motion, which may become sound for human ears. . . . There is thus Śabda wherever there is motion or vibration of any kind. It is now said that the electrons revolve in a sphere of positive electrification at an enormous rate of motion. . . . To a Divine Ear all such movements would constitute the "music of the spheres." . . . All mental functioning again is a form of vibration (Spandana). Thought is a vibration of mental substance just as the expression of thought in the form of the spoken word is a vibration affecting the ear.[40]

The vibration we create, we become. This is why Joseph speaks so much of *being & vibration*. Joseph told me that he has buried a large crystal underneath the chair at the center of the Sound Chamber he built on the Southern Ute reservation. The name of this Sound Chamber is Where God Walks & Talks. He told me that he has programmed this crystal to repeat the sound "*world peace, world peace, world peace*" twenty-four hours a day. To have peace we must keep it in our hearts, in our minds, and on our lips.

INNER PEACE

To have peace, we need to make the sound of PEACE. To make the sound of peace, we need to find the sound of peace in our hearts. To find the sound of peace in our hearts, we must listen to the silent oneness within.

The source of peace is the silent place of God in our hearts. This is what *Abhishiktananda* calls the *guhā*, the "cave of the heart." In the oral

40 Sir John Woodroffe, *Śakti and Śakta*, 305, 316, 319.

tradition of initiation, a guru or elder will initiate the seeker into the truth of ancient wisdom. Although Abhishiktananda took on a guru in human form, he considered his *sat-guru,* or root guru to be the Guru Jesus. Joseph Rael also speaks of learning from Jesus, and he says that the shaman Jesus led him to the underworld, which is a part of every shaman's initiation.

Many people are talking about peace and bringing peace to the world. As Joseph has said to me, "*Many people have tried it, but it hasn't worked, but that is what we are trying to do.*" We can look at the material body and world, the psychological ego, and the spiritual self as three different levels. If we only look at the material world, we are materialists. The material world is about separation and things being separate objects, but peace is not about separation, it is about relatedness and unity. Therefore, peace can never be found working only at the material level.

At the level of the psychological ego one can seek peace, however the psychological ego is also a place of separation, although it is inner rather than outer separation. One can spend a great deal of time seeking inner psychological peace, however this is only partial peace and therefore not true peace. The danger with seeking inner psychological peace is that a person can become selfish and disconnected even as they seek their own path of peace. Many self-help books aim to help bolster and strengthen the ego, this can make one more effective in the world or lead to relaxation exercises, but it cannot be a true source of peace. The tentative inner peace is lost as soon as the person has to interact with the messiness of the outer world.

The spiritual level is the place where one goes beyond ego. There are two major pathways that people tend to follow in religion and spirituality—immanence and transcendence. Immanence is finding God or Spirit indwelling within things. This is the teaching that God is in all things and that God is found within. The other major path is transcendence, finding God or Spirit through transcending the physical world. The tension between immanence and transcendence runs through the world religions and can be found in Hinduism, Buddhism, Islam, Christianity, Judaism, as well as in secular philosophies.

There are mystic branches of all religions and these often bring a sense of non-duality and blend immanence and transcendence. Yoga nidra practitioner and psychologist, Richard Miller writes, that immanence "and transcendence are paired opposites that mutually co-arise and affirm the understanding that our True Nature and its objects are always one and never two."[41] Rather than having to choose between creating heaven on earth or rejecting the material world and seeking heaven above, these traditions are able to find God within everything as well as beyond everything as the Source of Oneness. The material world is experienced as a manifestation of God and the spiritual world is also experienced as a continually renewing place of Breath-Matter-Movement. From a mystic spirituality, everything is God, every experience is God, and the individual has no reality other than *Wah-Mah-Chi*. The mystic at first seeks to place his or her hand on the pulse of God, to feel the flow of vitality, but gradually moves beyond this to a non-dualist experience of unity with the Divine. This is the source of inner peace, because there is no separation. The outer world is valued as a manifestation of God and the inner world is valued as a place of spiritual connection.

To go inward into inner peace, one leaves behind the attachments to the outer world and connects to the inner hidden unity that is found in the depths of the cave of the heart. The heart gives off a form of light that we can all feel as love. The blood circulates around the center of the heart just as planets circulate around our sun and as solar systems circulate around the central heart of galaxies. It is thought that the central heart of many galaxies is a black hole. This is the case with the Milky Way. Physician and healer Manjir Samanta-Laughton, author of *Punk Science*, speculates that there may be tiny black holes that generate creative energy within the human body. She wonders if these might give rise to the ancient Hindu concept of the chakras, spinning wheels of energy that transduce different energetic dimensions of reality. She also wonders if the heart, itself, might have such a black hole at its center around which blood circulates. Joseph Rael paints black holes in almost every one of his paintings. He says that the large black eyes that beings have in his paintings are black holes.

Abhishiktananda found the *guhā*, the cave of the heart, as a crucial concept in his quest for Divine Union, which also brought together Christianity and Hinduism. The cave of the heart is the dark space within each of our hearts that holds the Light of Divinity. It is the place where we find that we are one with God. Entering into this cave requires courage (a word that derives from *cor*, meaning heart) and perseverance. First one faces the fear, then one faces loss of the ego (which the Sufis call *fanā*—annihilation), and finally there is total union with the divine which is a

---

41 Richard Miller, "Welcoming All That Is," in *The Sacred Mirror: Nondual Wisdom and Psychotherapy*, 224.

state of non-dualism and non-separation. This is "the peace of God, which passes all understanding,"[42] the *ananda* (joy, bliss) the Hindus speak of, it is the "resting in the spirit" Christians speak of, and it is the state of joy and bliss that the mystics of all religious orientations taste in their union.

The path into the cave of the heart is the secret journey. Although it is given to everyone if they turn inward, and it even calls all of us throughout our lifetimes, few heed this call and turn inward. This path leads to a place of utter darkness where we are learning to see the *inner light.*

42 Philippians 4:7, *The Holy Bible, Revised Standard Edition, Second Catholic Edition.*

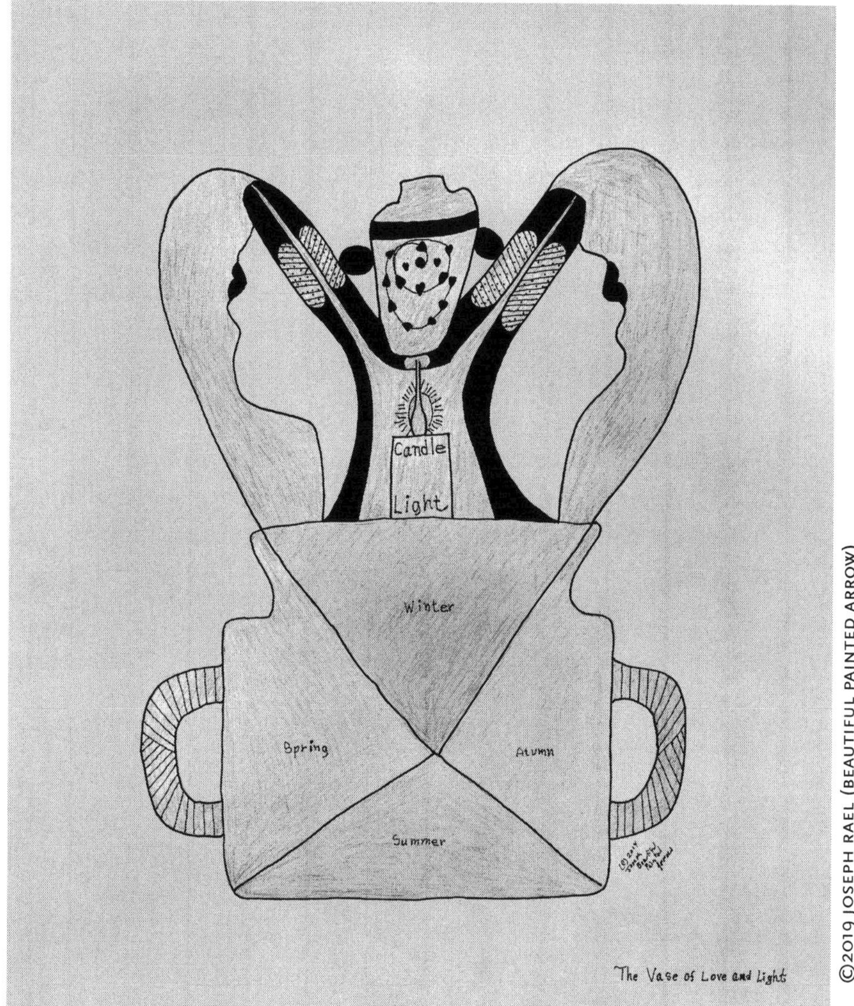

THE VASE OF LOVE AND LIGHT

CHAPTER 10

ENLIGHTENMENT & ENDARKENMENT

Last night woke up with that sense of complete stillness and silence; the brain was fully alert and intensely alive; the body was very quiet. . . . It's as though everything stood still. There is no movement, no stirring, complete emptiness of all thought, of all seeing. There is no interpreter to translate, to observe, to censor. An immeasurable vastness that is utterly still and silent. . . . There is really nothing that can be said about it.[1]

J. KRISHNAMURTI

Accordingly, both traditions [Navajo and Tibetan] understand that all "people," or "sentient beings" exist poised between and encompassing two simultaneous realities: the real and the ideal worlds, which must be reconciled through the heroic spiritual journey in order for life to be meaningful.[2]

PETER GOLD

"Dark," cosmologists call it, in what could go down in history as the ultimate semantic surrender. This is not "dark" as in distant or invisible. This is not "dark" as in black holes or deep space. This is "dark" as in unknown for now, and possibly forever: 23 percent something mysterious that they call dark matter, 73 percent something even more mysterious that they call dark energy. Which leaves only 4 percent the stuff of us.[3]

RICHARD PANEK

1 J. Krishnamurti, *Krishnamurti's Notebooks*, 16, 15.

2 Peter Gold, *Navajo and Tibetan Sacred Wisdom: The Circle of the Spirit*, 125–26.

3 Richard Panek, *The 4% Universe: Dark Matter, Dark Energy, and the Race to Discover the Rest of Reality*, xv.

MENTORS ON PATH TO ENLIGHTENMENT

I do not claim to be enlightened or to even fully understand what is meant by this term. Yet, perhaps we are all on this path in one way or another. One possible definition of enlightenment is that it is a transformative state that changes one's sense of self and reality and this transformation includes a heightened responsibility for other beings and for the earth. Buddha studied all the available spiritual wisdom of his day, and yet still felt there was more to learn. He sat under the Bodhi tree until he achieved enlightenment. He did not rest in ecstatic states of divine bliss, detached from the world. Instead he vowed to help alleviate the suffering of all sentient beings—he returned (in a transformed state) to the earthly realm with a responsibility to all beings. In terms of vocation—when one is called by a voice—one is responsible for carrying out whatever vision spirit has granted.

ILLUSIONS

A fictional example of an enlightened mentor who influenced me is Donald Shimoda in Richard Bach's book *Illusions*. Don "quits" being a messiah (thus the book's subtitle of *Adventures of a Reluctant Messiah*) and befriends Richard Bach, as they fly across Illinois selling biplane rides in farm towns. Don begins teaching Richard and passing on his wisdom.

> "Listen!" he called across the gulf between us. "This world? And everything in it? *Illusions*, Richard! Every bit of it *illusions*! *Do you understand that?*"[4]

Richard gradually gains in understanding through his friendship and apprenticeship with Don. Don gives Richard a *Messiah's Handbook* and one of the things it teaches is that we are illusions creating our own shifting realities. Here is one of the teachings in the book within the book, "*If you will practice being fictional for a while, you will understand that fictional characters are sometimes more real than people with real bodies and heartbeats*."[5] I have certainly gained a lot of wisdom and comfort over the years from walking along with Don and Richard.

---

4 Richard Bach, *Illusions: Adventures of a Reluctant Messiah*, 69.

5 Ibid., 135.

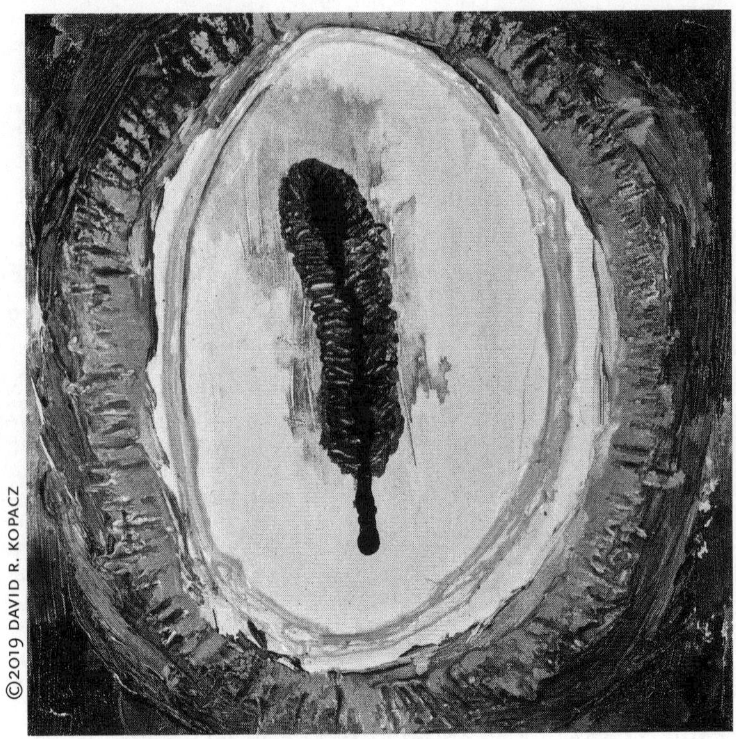

BLUE FEATHER

THE RAZOR'S EDGE

Another favorite book of mine is *The Razor's Edge* by Somerset Maugham. The title of the book is taken from the *Katha Upanishads* "The sharp edge of a razor is difficult to pass over; thus the wise say the path to Salvation is hard."[6] Larry Darrell is the main character in this book, a bright young man from Marvin, Illinois, who serves in France during World War I. He goes through the trauma of war and returns as many veterans do—as if living in another world. Larry is engaged to marry Isabel, but he cannot fit back into ordinary civilian reality. Instead, while others his age are out frolicking about, he spends his days reading obscure philosophy texts in the library. Larry takes a year off to go live in Paris, but still cannot fit back into the life that Isabel wants him to come back to. Larry drifts throughout Europe, working as a fishmonger and a coal miner. He meets a rough Polish coal miner, who cheats at cards, but when drunk speaks of

6 Somerset Maugham, *The Razor's Edge*, 5.

Hindu philosophy and loans Larry a copy of the *Upanishads*. Larry makes his way to India and studies there, achieving a level of enlightenment. He tries again to fit back into society, but events beyond his control thwart this. He lives out his life in a quiet and simple way, working as a cab driver and eventually publishing a slim volume on the lives of diverse people who achieved great worldly success and he was interested whether that brought happiness.

Larry's ex-fiancé in the book has an uncle, Uncle Elliott, who is an interested by-stander in Larry's quest for the Absolute. Uncle Elliott asks Larry what he means by the "Absolute," and Larry replies,

> Reality. You can't say what it is; you can only say what it isn't. It's inexpressible. The Indians call it Brahman. It's nowhere and everywhere. All things imply and depend upon it. It's not a person, it's not a thing, it's not a cause. It has no qualities. It transcends permanence and change; whole and part, finite and infinite. It is eternal because its completeness and perfection are unrelated to time. It is truth and freedom. . . . I found something wonderfully satisfying in the notion that you can attain Reality by knowledge. In later ages the sages of India in recognition of human infirmity admitted that salvation may be won by the way of love and the way of works, but they never denied that the noblest way, though the hardest, is the way of knowledge of its instrument is the most precious faculty of man, his reason.

After several years of studying with Shri Ganesha (based on Ramana Maharshi),[7] Larry had an experience of enlightenment and union with the Absolute Reality. He spent a few days up at a mountain cabin and woke

7 Author Somerset Maugham traveled to India in 1938 and met the spiritual teacher Ramana Maharshi, upon whom he based the character Shri Ganesha. Maugham's biographer describes the purpose of his trip to India. "Maugham's quest in coming to India was to investigate the vast subject of Hindu religion in hope of gaining an insight into the spiritual side of life that had always intrigued him and at the same time eluded him. In preparation he had read widely and, armed with a sheaf of introductions, he had met and talked to numbers of scholars and priests; despite his best efforts, however, he was unable to make very much of what they told him," (Selina Hastings, *The Secret Lives of Somerset Maugham*, 430). Maugham tried meditating with a yogi, he felt he had sat for well over 15 minutes, but looked at his watch to find that only three minutes had passed—a common experience for beginning meditators. Later, he met Ramana Maharshi, but again wisdom seemed to elude him. During a picnic lunch he suddenly fainted and was brought to a quiet room. Ramana Maharshi (also called "Bhagavan") sat across from Maugham for about 30 minutes in silence. Maugham asked, "'Is there any need to say anything?' 'No,' replied Bhagavan. 'Silence is best. Silence is itself conversation,'" (Hastings, 430–32).

early to watch the sunset over the mountains and jungles, the sounds of wild animals below. As the sun rose and illuminated the world, he had the following experience.

> I was ravished with the beauty of the world. I'd never known such exaltation and such a transcendent joy. I had a strange sensation, a tingling that arose in my feet and travelled up to my head, and I felt as though I were suddenly released from my body and as a pure spirit partook of a loveliness I had never conceived. I had a sense that a knowledge more than human possessed me, so that everything that had been confused was clear and everything that had perplexed me was explained.

Uncle Elliott skeptically asks how he knows it was truly enlightenment and not some "hypnotic condition" or illusion. Larry replies,

> Only my overwhelming sense of reality. After all it was an experience of the same order as the mystics have had all over the world through the centuries, Brahmins in India, Sufis in Persia, Catholics in Spain, Protestants in New England; and so far as they've been able to describe what defies description they've described it in similar terms. It's impossible to deny the fact of its occurrence; the only difficulty is to explain it.[8]

RAMANA MAHARSHI

Abhishiktananda, whose life we examined earlier, met the sage Ramana Maharshi in 1949, the year before Ramana's death. He had an influential encounter with Ramana Maharshi that he recounts. "I consider this stay at Tiruvannamalai as a real retreat and at the same time as an initiation into Hindu monastic life. I want to . . . enter into the great silence and peace which, as I have read and also been told, is to be found at the ashram."[9]

> In the contemporary Sage of Arunachala it was the unique Sage of eternal India that appeared to me . . . it was a call which pierced through everything, rent it in pieces and opened a mighty abyss.[10]

Ramana's teachings were in many ways very simple. What exists of his

---

8 Maugham, *The Razor's Edge*, 269–70, 275–76, 276.

9 "Abhishiktananda," *Wikipedia* reference 6: Diary, 24 January 1949, in Stuart, James, *Swami Abhishiktananda: His Life Told through his Letters*, Delhi (ISPCK), 2000, p. 29.

10 Ibid., reference 7: Abhishiktananda, Swami, *The Secret of Arunachala*, Delhi (ISPCK), 1979, p. 8–9.

teachings are mostly dialogues with students: "Call it by any name, God, Self, the Heart or the Seat of Consciousness, it is all the same. The point to be grasped is this, that HEART means the very Core of one's being, the Centre, without which there is nothing whatever." And even more simply, just repeatedly asking, "Who am I?" "The thought 'who am I?' will destroy all other thoughts, and, like the stick used for stirring the burning pyre, it will itself in the end get destroyed. Then, there will arise Self-realization."[11]

Carl Jung, who never met Sri Ramana, wrote an essay about him, excerpts of this served as a foreword to *The Spiritual Teaching of Ramana Maharshi*. Jung saw a correspondence with some of his work on the individuation process where a person moves from orienting toward their ego to orienting toward the Self. Here are a few of Jung's comments on Ramana Maharshi.

> The equation self = God is shocking to the European . . . [yet the] Goal of Eastern practices is the same as that of Western mysticism: the shifting of the centre of gravity from the ego to the self, from man to God. This means that the ego disappears in the self, and man in God.[12]

THE FAKIR

Another story of a student and his teacher, very similar to *Illusions*, is found in Ruzbeh N. Bharucha's *The Fakir*. A suicidal and depressed Rudra (a fictional character) encounters the living spirit of Shirdi Sai Baba. Shirdi Sai Baba died in 1918 and has both Hindu and Muslim followers in India and worldwide. The two have many comical and serious interactions as Rudra apprentices himself to the Master. Just as Joseph Rael says that he is a "hollow bone," so too Rudra learns that the spirit moves through us and accomplishes great things, but we should not take credit for them. "Not for a moment should the piano take the credit for the phenomenal music that is created and which flows through it, for it is the Musician that is responsible for the melody."[13] While the seeker begins with seeking outside the self, the teacher eventually directs the seeker to look internally, for it is there that the true goal lies, in the depths of the heart.

---

11 Ramana Maharshi, *The Spiritual Teachings of Ramana Maharshi*, 106, 6

12 Jung's foreword in *The Spiritual Teaching of Ramana Maharshi*, is edited slightly from the larger essay "The Holy Men of India," *Psychology and Religion: West and East*, CW 11, 580-581. Jung also wrote the foreword to Heinrich Zimmer's book on Ramana which was published in German.

13 Ruzbeh N. Bharucha, *The Fakir*, 108. Bharucha has written a number of spiritual novels that are popular in India.

> The most divine nectar, the most intoxicating, and a million times more potent than any drink in the world, actually exists within each individual. Through the process of meditation, breathing and certain yogic exercises, you can release the nectar from within the deep recesses of the lotus that resides within and taste the drop of nectar. The sweetest honey then transforms the mundane, into the surreal and envelopes you in a state of bliss, lightness and light.[14]

A MUSICAL UNIVERSE

Enlightenment is the search for the Truth about Reality. Science, as well as mysticism, can be a place where a seeker peers into the darkness of the unknown and finds light. Joseph says that "*We are constantly flashing on and off, strobe-like, a drumbeat, returning to the silent void and then back again to this perceptual reality. The true basis for Universal Intelligence is sound. Out of sound comes everything.*"

Stephon Alexander is a professor of physics at Brown University and is also a jazz musician. In his book, *The Jazz of Physics: The Secret Link Between Music and the Structure of the Universe*, he plays different variations on the idea that the structure of the universe is musical. He charts out a hero's journey of seeking the underlying sound of the universe. He faces challenges from the institution of physics and conservativism of the academy as he follows his inspiration and tries to chart out an improvisational physics. He meets many mentors along the way such as physicist Chris Isham who kept Jung's collected works in his office and tells Alexander to "stop reading those physics books" and to "develop your unconscious mind" and "play more music." Alexander took Isham's advice to heart and then one night "in the middle of a sax solo on Coltrane's song 'Mr. PC,' an image appeared in my mind that I knew had to do with the resolution of my project." He later had a dream that he discussed with Isham, which helps him at a stuck point in his work.

> In the dream, an old man in a white robe in outer space was writing some equations at a lightning fast rate. Frustrated, I had pled with the man that I was too dumb to comprehend the equations. Then the blackboard disappeared and the old man slowly swirled his hands in a spiral in one direction.[15]

---

14 Ruzbeh N. Bharucha, *The Fakir: Thoughts and Prayers*, 95.

15 Stephon Alexander, *The Jazz of Physics: The Secret Link Between Music and the Structure of the Universe*, 61, 185.

Isham asks which direction the man's hands were moving and later Alexander realizes that the "orientation of the man's swirling hands provided the insight into how to break the symmetry of cosmic inflation and generate baryon asymmetry."

As Alexander seeks the unity of music and the cosmology of the universe, he meets an impressive array of mentors and helpers from both the fields of physics and jazz. He meets jazz great Ornette Coleman who lets him play his alto sax. Alexander hangs out with "sound cosmologist" Brian Eno (former member of Roxy Music and producer of U2, the Talking Heads, and David Bowie).[16] He also meets physicists Brian Greene, Lee Smolin, Michael Peskin and many others. It is as if Alexander was "looking for that great jazz note"[17] that is the unification of music and physics and he had to learn both music and physics in order to vibrate at that frequency in order to understand what he was seeking.

> My vision of a musical universe was more than an analogy; I realized it was becoming literal.
>
> Waveforms of the early universe formed stars. Stars, in their tumultuous fusion of elements, produce like tones. They organize themselves into larger structures, such as binary systems or clusters—the equivalent of "musical" phrases. What's more, the millions of stars within the galaxies organize themselves into self-similar, fractal structures, like the fractals structure found in Bach's and Ligetti's compositions. I was amazed at the degree to which the organization of cosmic structure mimicked music structure.[18]

In addition to the physical mentors that Alexander met along the path of his journey, he studied three masters from the past: the ancient Greek Pythagoras, father of the Western musical scale who said he could hear the "harmony of the spheres" of the planets and stars singing their way through the cosmos; physicist Albert Einstein and his Theory of Relativity; and jazz musician John Coltrane whose idol was Albert Einstein and whose late albums include *Interstellar Space*, *Stellar Regions*, and *Cosmic Sound*. While the people, living and dead, whom Alexander meets and works with in his journey are important steps, sometimes even *giant steps* along the way, the quest is a personal one and consists of a self-transformation that

16 Ibid., 186, 88.

17 The Clash, "The Sound of Sinners," from the album *Sandinista!*

18 Alexander, 157.

allows a new, musical, vision of the universe to emerge in order for him to hear that *great jazz note* of the creation of the universe.

> Meeting these influential figures is part of the journey. Tapping into the beats and grooves of music theory is part of the journey. Tracing the evolution of structure in our universe is part of the journey. Creating an analogy between physics and music is part of the journey. Not having an adequate analogy, and needing rigorous calculations for clarity, is part of the journey.

If the journey consists of all these parts, what is the overall journey? I'm not sure that Alexander states it explicitly, but it has something to do with creation, improvisation, and tapping into the same energy playing jazz that is the same energy that led to the creation of the universe. Here is how Alexander ends his book:

> One of the fathers of calculus, Gottfried Leibniz, had the idea that the reducible element of the universe, the monad, had the capacity to contain the essence of the universe within it. . . . If one of the fundamental functions of the universe, as I've argued, is to improvise its structure, perhaps when Coltrane improvises, he is doing what the universe does and what the universe did was to create a structure that would come to know the universe itself.[19]

This recalls Joseph Rael's statement that "All of my teachings tie into the reality that there is a Seer seeing everything. We call it God, the higher power, or whatever. It is simply the Vast Self seeing itself creating itself."[20] God, the monad, the Vast Self, the Seer seeing everything—why not just say that God is a hep cat jazz musician doing a massive improvisational jazz solo, and we, the notes of the solo, are co-creators, riffing off of God's jam?

> Get this: If there is nothing outside the universe and if the universe functions like an instrument, with all the musical elements it has, then the universal instrument must play itself. It other words, the cosmic sound is the instrument and the instrument is the cosmic sound. Everything in the universe, including space-time, that supports it must vibrate or oscillate.[21]

---

19 Ibid., 8, 228.

20 *Sound*, 1.

21 Alexander, 208.

SPIRITUAL JAZZ

Stephon Alexander describes how John Coltrane combined elements of Indian philosophy and musical raga into his music. Like many seeking ancient wisdom, John and his wife, Alice, Coltrane turned to India for inspiration.[22] Coltrane was on his own spiritual, musical quest looking for *that great jazz note.* He started to find it in the sound "om," the Sanskrit sound that resonates from Brahman the creator into Atman, the soul of the individual. John Coltrane was increasingly seeking the intersection of music, physics, and spirituality—a kind of "universal religion" and "universal spirituality," as described by Franya Berkman in her book on Alice Coltrane:

> Included in his spirituality was an array of world traditions: Zen, Zoroastrianism, the writings of Yogananda and Krishnamurti, and a commitment to daily meditation, all of which he explored with Alice. . . . John Coltrane's creative ideology was deeply intertwined with his spiritual philosophy. . . . First, music making is based on personal spiritual expression, and the artist should be fully committed to expressing an authentic self as a musician. Second, music making should be universal, erasing aesthetic boundaries and proscriptions about style. And third, such musical universality requires branching out: it is inclusive, pluralistic, and multicultural.[23]

---

22 A synopsis of Coltrane's life and music is found in Lavezzoli's *The Dawn of Indian Music in the West.* A few highlights of this follow. John Coltrane befriended Ravi Shankar and the two corresponded and attended each other's concerts, although never played together. Coltrane began experimenting with translating Indian music into jazz. In 1961 he performed and recorded live at The Village Vanguard four versions of his composition, "India," including the Indian tamboura. In 1965 he recorded a 29 minute piece called "Om." John Coltrane was frustrated in 1967 and he told Ravi Shankar that "he was still trying for something different but he did not know what he was looking for," (288). Ravi Shankar invited him to India "for a prolonged period of musical and spiritual study, an invitation that Shankar had also recently extended to George Harrison," (288). When Coltrane was unable to commit to that, R. Shankar extended an invitation to a school he was starting in California, however before J. Coltrane could attend this, he was diagnosed with liver cancer and died within months at the age of 40.

Prior to his death, on his July 1966 tour, he introduced a new piece called "Peace on Earth." Lavezolli writes that this was a "gorgeous vehicle for Coltrane's tenor, pacific as the ocean dividing West and East, it is the sound of a man yearning for a reality that all human spirituality aspires to, but which human society has not yet attained," (287). When asked about his views on the Vietnam War, Coltrane commented, "Well, I dislike war. Period. Therefore, as far as I'm concerned, it should stop, it should have already been stopped," (287–88).

23 Franya Berkman, *Monument Eternal: The Music of Alice Coltrane*, 52–53.

John Coltrane's music had been adversely affected by drug abuse earlier in his career and Miles Davis fired him in 1957 from the Quintet. It was while he was getting clean that he "experienced a spiritual epiphany so profound that it would exert a decisive influence on him for the remainder of his life." Post-drugs, Coltrane said that his goal was "to live the truly religious life, and express it through music."[24] Coltrane's exploration of ever more dissonant musical forms coincided with his spiritual quest. While many shamanic and other musical traditions of altering consciousness focus on repetitive rhythms or droning harmonics, there are also traditions of dissonance that move a person into a new level of coherence. I recall sitting in a Hindu temple in New Zealand meditating and smelling the incense and hearing a discordant clanging bell and it felt like it moved me out of my ordinary consciousness into a new reality. As I have been entering into John Coltrane's later work, I have been looking for this sense of dissonance that can open into a new state of coherence. Psychologist Bradford Keeney, who has studied with a number of different indigenous groups, has described the interaction between arousal and relaxation in spiritual practices and how a state of agitation can lead into a state of peace.

> I propose that this full cycle, in which one climbs toward a high peak of arousal and then falls until hitting a deep bottom of relaxation, comprises a paradigm for the whole healing response. There are significant healing and transformational benefits when we allow our bodies to naturally and effortlessly enter ecstatic realms and then effortlessly shift into deep states of relaxation.[25]

After John's death, Alice Coltrane went into a dark place that turned out to be part of a spiritual initiation. She continued blending jazz with Indian musical forms. She met the Hindu teacher Satchidinanda, traveled to India, started an ashram in California called Shanti Anantam Ashram, which she later renamed Sai Anantam after meeting Sathya Sai Baba. She

---

24 Peter Lavezzoli, *The Dawn of Indian Music in the West*, 273. Coltrane wrote on the liner notes for his 1965 album *A Love Supreme*, "During the year 1957, I experienced, by the grace of God, a spiritual awakening which was to lead me to a richer, fuller, more productive life. At that time, in gratitude, I humbly asked to be given the means and privilege to make others happy through music. I feel this has been granted through his grace," (Lavezzoli, 273).

25 Bradford Keeney, *Shaking Medicine: The Healing Power of Ecstatic Movement*, 27. Only as I was editing our current book, I came across a great book Keeney wrote with Jeffrey A. Kottler and Jon Carlson called *American Shaman: An Odyssey of Global Healing*, which is definitely worth reading. Thanks to Dr. Neeta Ramkumar for this reference.

took on the name *Turiyasangitananda* and largely left the world of jazz, instead focusing on spiritual teachings and practices and the creation devotional music that was a fusion of jazz, Indian, and African American spirituals. She took a 25 year hiatus from performing live, but released the album *Translinear Light* and did a few performances with her son, Ravi (named after Ravi Shankar). A compilation of the spiritual tapes that she put out at the ashram was released in May 2017 as *World Spiritual Classics: The Ecstatic Music of Alice Coltrane Turiyasangitananda.*

I spoke with musician Bill Laswell about Alice Coltrane, in 2017, he said:

> I knew her, and I used to go to her ashram. I probably went to the place five or six times and I knew some of the recordings she wanted to do and I would just go and talk to her. And you know, she was deeply on the other side . . . she just got on a path and kept moving more and more into the light, or into her spiritual concepts and her personal priorities, and commitments. The first time I met her, I was talking to her and I mentioned John Coltrane, and she said, without missing a beat, "I spoke to John this morning," and she went on about the conversation they had. She was like that. She wasn't necessarily here. She was in a couple additional worlds at the same time.

Swamini Turiya Alice Coltrane lived out the path of spiritual music that she had started on with John Coltrane. She pursued a path of inner peace and created a space where people from all racial and religious backgrounds could come together in worship. Sai Anantam Ashram continues to this day under the name The Vedantic Center, its website describes its vision:

> The Vedantic Center appreciates the contributions of spiritual wisdom and insight from all faiths. Studies at the ashram include not only Vedic scriptures, but also exemplary narratives and scriptural texts from more recent revelations of God. . . . The Vedas have a universal outlook embracing all that is noble and sacred. There is a principle of equality in respecting all that proclaims the concept of Oneness.[26]

Vedanta embraces all religions as valid pathways to God. This is sometimes captured with the phrase, "many paths, one goal." What appears sometimes as polytheism in Hinduism is understood in Vedanta as the

26 The Vedantic Center website. There is also, an apparently unrelated, Saint John Coltrane African Orthodox Church in San Francisco. I recently found mention of this on the *Atlas Obscura* website.

multitude of manifestations of the one all-pervading Divinity. "Advaita Vedanta is a system of belief in which the self (the atman) is identical with the absolute (Brahman). . . . Advaita Vedanta allows for allegiance to many deities, liberation (*moksha*) is to be ultimately attained through knowledge of the self, which is also knowledge of the absolute." Turiya Alice's view of music was that it was the pinnacle of self-expression, and was thus also the emanation of divinity. "As it was in the beginning, let your music forevermore be an expression of My Divinity in a sound incarnation of Myself as *nadabrahma*. For, eternally, divine music shall always be the sound of peace, the sound of love, the sound of life, and the sound of bliss."[27]

In her work after John's passing, as she grew closer to Vedanta, Alice Coltrane began including *bhajans* or *kirtans*, traditional Hindu chants on her albums. She described chanting as "a universal devotional engagement, one that allows the chanter to soar to higher realms of spiritual consciousness. Chanting is a healing force for good in our world, and also in the astral worlds. Chanting can bring a person closer to God because that person is calling on the Lord." The blending of cultures and styles, which John and Alice embarked on together, and Alice continued after John's death, speaks to the universality of the quest for divinity. Alice called this finding the one amidst the many the "Totality concept, which embraces cosmic thought as an emblem of Universal Sound."[28]

NON-DUALITY

Enlightenment leads to non-duality: the lived experience of everything being One. An example of non-dual teachings are found in Kashmiri Shaivism. Psychologist Richard Miller has modernized and adapted this into his form of yoga nidra, Integrative Restoration or iRest. I once met Richard Miller when he was teaching in Seattle and I asked him for the background sources of iRest. He gave me a list of reference readings that have given me the spiritual system that seems most similar to Joseph's "we don't exist" and the flickering nature of our *being & vibration*.[29] This is

27 Berkman, 77, 1.

28 Ibid., 107, 83.

29 Richard Miller recommended a series of books by Jaideva Singh (*Spanda-Kārikās: The Divine Creative Pulsation*; *Śiva Sutras: The Yoga of Supreme Identity*; *Abhinavagupta Parā-trīśikā-Vivarana: The Secret of Tantric Mysticism*). After reading those, I continued looking for other resources, reading Daniel Odier's work, such as his translation, *Yoga*

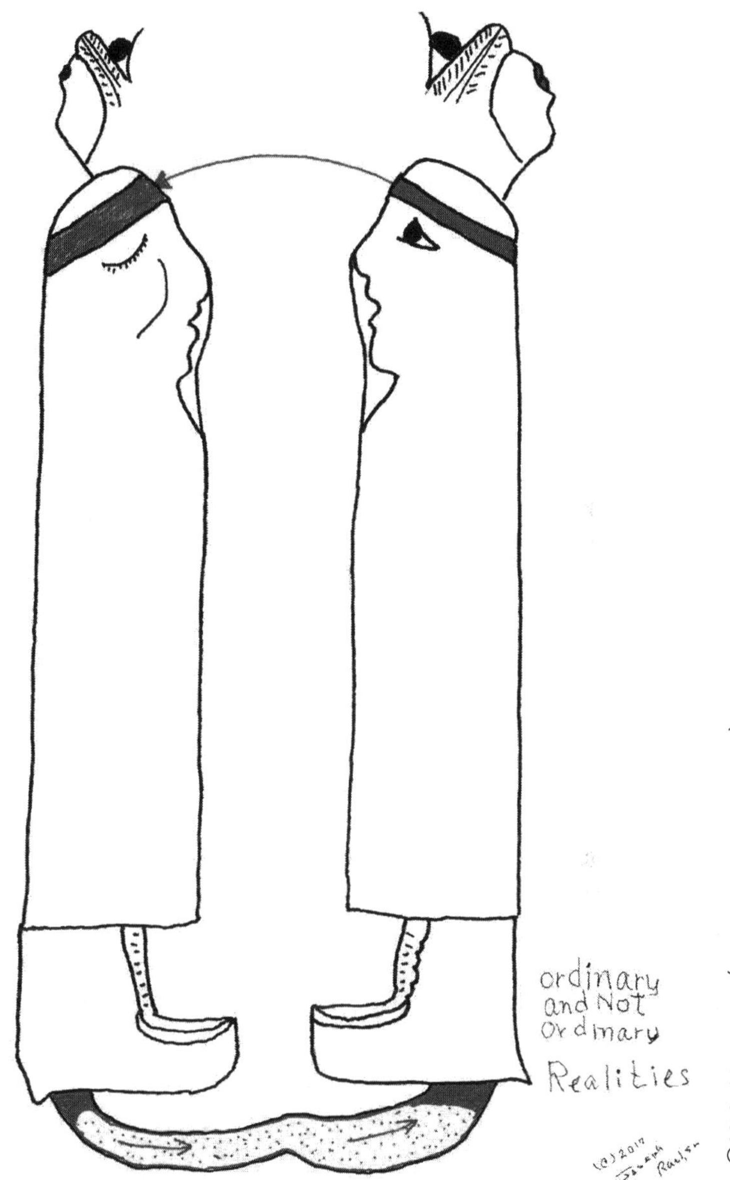

CANDLE OF WORLD #1 — ORDINARY AND NON-ORDINARY REALITIES

the universal quest of the mystic, to find the underlying unity beneath the surface. It is called "non-dual" because the idea of unity can also hold within it the idea of disunity, of separation.

Richard Miller has written books and papers about iRest and yoga nidra. He says that yoga nidra is a path that is "an open secret" in that it seems hidden, but is actually in plain sight. iRest is a non-dual path that leads to the realization that there "is neither 'I' nor 'other' that is separate from Being. . . . Here everything is understood to be undivided Oneness." In this Oneness we "discover . . . that we are Vastness."[30] He describes his own awakening to awareness:

> And then one morning I awoke into the realization of True Nature. It was early morning around 2 a.m. when I found myself unable to sleep. I got out of bed and sat by the glass door, gazing up into the starlit nighttime sky. Suddenly, quite unexpectedly, and with no fanfare, I simply realized the underlying Essence of Being that is my True Nature and that everything is made of.
>
> In that timeless instant, all sense of separation fell away. I recognized the truth that the ego-I is simply a thought and that everything is myself. And with that, all sense of aloneness, emptiness, and searching vanished, replaced with the irreconcilable feeling of equanimity that remains undisturbed no matter what crisis or joy is unfolding in my life.[31]

In the state of enlightenment there is recognition of "non-difference," between the individual and Vastness, what Joseph calls *the Vast Self.* There is a Hindu ritual in which the individual touches different parts of the body saying, this is Śiva's foot, this is Śiva's ankle. In this way, the individual *becomes* the Divine Being.

Henry Corbin speaks of the orienting story of the Stranger, the gnostic, who finds herself or himself exiled in this world of matter and seeks to return to the realm of spirit. The whole story of physical life is a quest of spiritual return. It is the story of separation, initiation, return. However, there is a twist that what starts out as a journey of separation back to union, one realizes that one has always been in union and that separation

---

Spandakarika: The Sacred Texts and Origin of Tantra, and Sir John Woodroffe's writing, such as *Śakti and Śakta*. My rudimentary understanding of Kashmiri Shaivism is that what we experience as ordinary reality is the temporary manifestations of *spanda*, the divine creative pulsation. I later completed Level 1 iRest training for experiential learning.

30 Richard Miller, *Yoga Nidra*, 3, 78, 23.

31 Ibid., 75.

was only an illusion. What seemed to be external turns out to be internal, the spiritual world contains the material world.

> [I]t is a matter of entering, passing into the interior and, in passing into the interior of finding oneself, paradoxically outside. . . . The relationship involved is essentially that of the external, the visible, the exoteric . . . and the internal, the invisible, the esoteric, or the natural and the spiritual world. To depart from the *where* . . . is to leave the external or natural appearances that enclose the hidden realities. . . . This step is made in order for the Stranger, the gnostic, to return *home*—or at least to lead to that return.
>
> But an odd thing happens: once this transition is accomplished, it turns out that henceforth this reality, previously internal and hidden, is revealed to be enveloping, surrounding, containing what was first of all external and visible, since by means of *interiorization* one has *departed* from that *external* reality. Henceforth it is spiritual reality that . . . contains all the reality called material.[32]

Corbin describes how the internal journey becomes an external journey and there is non-difference between inside and outside, between matter and spirit. Joseph has told me about his shamanic journeys. He said that every shaman has to go to hell as part of their initiation. He could not find a teacher to initiate him, but then one day the shaman Jesus appeared to him and said "Come with me to hell" and Joseph said "I don't want to go there," but he went because the shaman Jesus convinced him. He says this is where he got his "Ph.D." from following Jesus to hell. It is sometimes said that one must go to hell before he or she can go to heaven. One must experience the depths in order to experience the heights.

Some years after his descent to hell, Joseph went in search of God when he was on a vision quest in Hawaii. As he went higher and higher he kept encountering different sets of guards, dressed like soldiers. Each set asked him who he was and where he thought he was going. Each set let him through thinking that he would not make it past the next set of guards. Eventually Joseph reached the top and was almost face to face with God. Then he heard a voice say "It is you" and then a loud pop and he was back in his body, sitting on a Hawaiian mountaintop. His first thought after all that work was "That's no fun." After descending to hell and ascending to heaven, Joseph comes to the realization that who he is seeking is himself. He has come to a place of non-duality.

---

32 Henry Corbin, *Swedenborg and Esoteric Islam*, 6.

ENDARKENMENT

If it is true that the ground of the soul is dark, then the human race cannot afford to flee the darkness and to embrace an Enlightenment that does not include an Endarkenment.[33]

MATTHEW FOX

There are different levels of darkness and different kinds of darkness. There are places we are called to enter which we do not see and we do not understand. This is one level of darkness, entering into the unknown. There is another level of darkness that is beyond the unknown—the Darkness of the void, the darkness of the uncreated, pluripotent Source of all things.

ENDARKENMENT AS OBSCURATION OF TRUTH

In Christian theology and symbolism, the light is associated with God and darkness with distance from God, or with the Devil. Mystics often speak of journeying into the light and en*light*enment. The dark is a metaphor of being in ignorance, of having a lack of knowledge. Krishnamurti and David Bohm, like many mystics, turn this metaphor on its head, arguing that knowledge, itself, is what *endarkens* and obscures us from the Truth. Lee Nichol states that Bohm viewed "*knowledge as the central factor in the 'endarkenment' of human consciousness . . . that an active, self-sustaining pool of human knowledge – accumulated and refined through millennia – is thoroughly infected with* misinformation, *thus polluting human experience at its generative source.*"[34] Similar to Krishnamurti, Bohm was striving to get beyond the conditioning of knowledge and language to reach the Truth beyond words and beyond concepts. This is similar to Joseph Rael's concepts of verb language and also of his statement, "we do not exist," because our idea of ourselves through language and knowledge is false. Bohm states it this way:

> It is this absolute certainty of the inward — which tends to focus on the inward — that is the kind of knowledge which may produce darkness. That knowledge of what you are, who you are, what sort of person you've got to be, to whom you belong, what your desires are, what your fears are, what you can do, what you can't do . . . it

33 Matthew Fox, *Original Blessing*, 138–39.

34 David Bohm, *The Essential David Bohm*, 261.

> endarkens the brain. . . . That's endarkenment. That is not only mental endarkenment, but it is a physical disruption of the brain.[35]

Rather than knowledge that endarkens, Bohm sought new forms of imagination and creativity, which he found in the function of the implicate order and what we have earlier discussed as the *holomovement*—the continual pulse of coming into being and passing away (which Bohm called unfoldment and enfoldment).

ENDARKENMENT AS REVELATION

Other mystics seem to specialize in finding the divine in the darkness and seek revelation. Meister Eckhart wrote of the divinity in the darkness and St. John of the Cross wrote of the dark night of the soul as a journey that leads to the divine. The Pueblo people enter into the darkness of the kiva for their spiritual and mystical work. We have written about the path to divinity through external, physical, caves as well as through the internal *guhā*, the cave of the heart.

SEARCHING FOR MEANING IN THE DARKNESS

At a recent Seattle University Search for Meaning Festival, 2018, I heard a couple of authors speak to this issue of wisdom from entering into darkness. Tlingit author, Ernestine Hayes author of *The Tao of Raven*, shared the story of Raven. The people once lived in darkness, but Raven endeavored to steal a box containing the sun from an old man and gave daylight to the people. This is a classic trickster story in which Raven endeavors to be swallowed as a pine needle in the water that the old man's daughter drinks, she becomes pregnant and gives birth to Raven who is now the grandson of the old man. In some versions of this story, Raven steals the light, but Hayes tells of how the old man cannot help but give his grandson whatever he wants, even the precious secret light of the sun and stars that he keeps hidden away in the darkness of his boxes. Raven takes the light and gives it to the people who are struggling to live in darkness. Hayes spoke of what this old man kept in his many boxes: "boxes of indigenous wisdom" and "boxes of indigenous knowledge." She described how we must seek in the darkness for these things that are not only valuable, but essential for life. She said that "Stories teach human beings

35 Ibid., 287–88.

how to be human," which speaks to our theme in this book of human initiation.[36] Initiation is ongoing, for the individual as well as for each new generation. We are continually storing away our wisdom and knowledge in boxes and then having to draw forth the light that is contained in the ancient, indigenous knowledge and wisdom. Hayes concluded, "When we search for meaning, we are opening boxes of daylight."

Another author at this conference, Barbara Brown Taylor spoke about her book, *Learning to Walk in the Dark*, and how there are times that we, individually and collectively, enter into various forms of darkness and that there is wisdom there to be gained. She reminded us that there is a branch of Christian thought called "negative theology" which is a "sacred way of knowing" that comes from the unknowing of darkness. She critiqued the dichotomy of darkness being evil and light being good. In her reading of the *Bible*, instead she sees that in the light of day God appears as a "dense cloud" and a darkness, while in the darkness of night God appears as light. Taylor suggests that God manifests both as light as well as darkness and we can learn different things from these different manifestations. "Light and dark do not contradict each other, but define each other." She said that "trying to look into the Essence of God is like looking into dark matter," we know it is there, but we cannot see or comprehend it.[37]

IN THE DARK PLACES OF WISDOM

Peter Kingsley's 1999 book, *In the Dark Places of Wisdom*, is all about learning in the darkness. He traces the ancient Greek practice of incubation, of *lying like an animal* in a cave, back to shamanic roots. He tells us that we must go into these dark places in order to find ancient wisdom, warning that the *enlightenment* of rationality has actually separated us from ancient wisdom. It is not that we have to go into the outer darkness of caves to find what we are seeking, rather going into the darkness of the cave helps us go into the inner darkness we all contain within us. He tells us, "We already have everything we need to know, in the darkness inside ourselves.

36 Ernestine Hayes, *"The Tao of Raven: An Alaska Native Memoir,"* Seattle Search for Meaning Festival, 2/24/18. The author shared the transcript of her talk with us and said that we can share it with others. I summarize and quote based on this transcript and also hand written notes I took during the talk.

37 Barbara Brown Taylor, "Redeeming Darkness: A Spirituality for the Night Times," Seattle University Search for Meaning Festival, 2/24/18. The quotes are from my handwritten notes of the talk.

The longing is what turns us inside out until we find the sun and moon and stars inside. . . . The source of light is at home in the darkness."[38] Incubation is a process of going deeper into this inner darkness, yet is not a linear or solar striving, but rather a descent and surrender.

> What's important is that you would do absolutely nothing. The point came when you wouldn't struggle or make an effort. You'd just have to surrender to your condition. You would lie down as if you were dead; wait without eating or moving, sometimes for days at a time. And you'd wait for the healing to come from somewhere else, from another level of awareness and another level of being.

Healing comes from surrender into the darkness. Living for some time in this place of darkness is one of the ways that you can find "a state that's like being awake but different than being awake, that's like sleep but not sleep: that's neither sleep nor waking. It's not the waking state, it's not an ordinary dream and it's not dreamless sleep. It's something else, something in between." One who can master this state enters into "indivisible oneness."[39]

This description sounds very similar to how Joseph describes the non-ordinary, visionary reality. It is also similar to yoga nidra, which Richard Miller translates as "The Sleep of the Yogi." He describes it as "a profound state of receptive relaxation, all the while remaining totally aware and alert throughout its process." This breaks down the "myth of separation," which is "actually an illusion that dissolves in the light of true inquiry."[40] In Hindu philosophy, there are four states of consciousness. The fourth state is called *turiya*, a state beyond waking, dreaming, and dreamless state.[41] You might recall that Alice Coltrane took on this spiritual name Turiya or Turiyasangitananda.

---

38 Kingsley, *In the Dark Places of Wisdom*, 67–68.

39 Ibid., 80, 110–11.

40 Richard Miller, *Yoga Nidra*, 16–18, 31, 25.

41 Muni Narayana Prasad describes turiya as "an experiential realm where the seeker transcends all ideas of duality," *Garland of Visions*, 166.

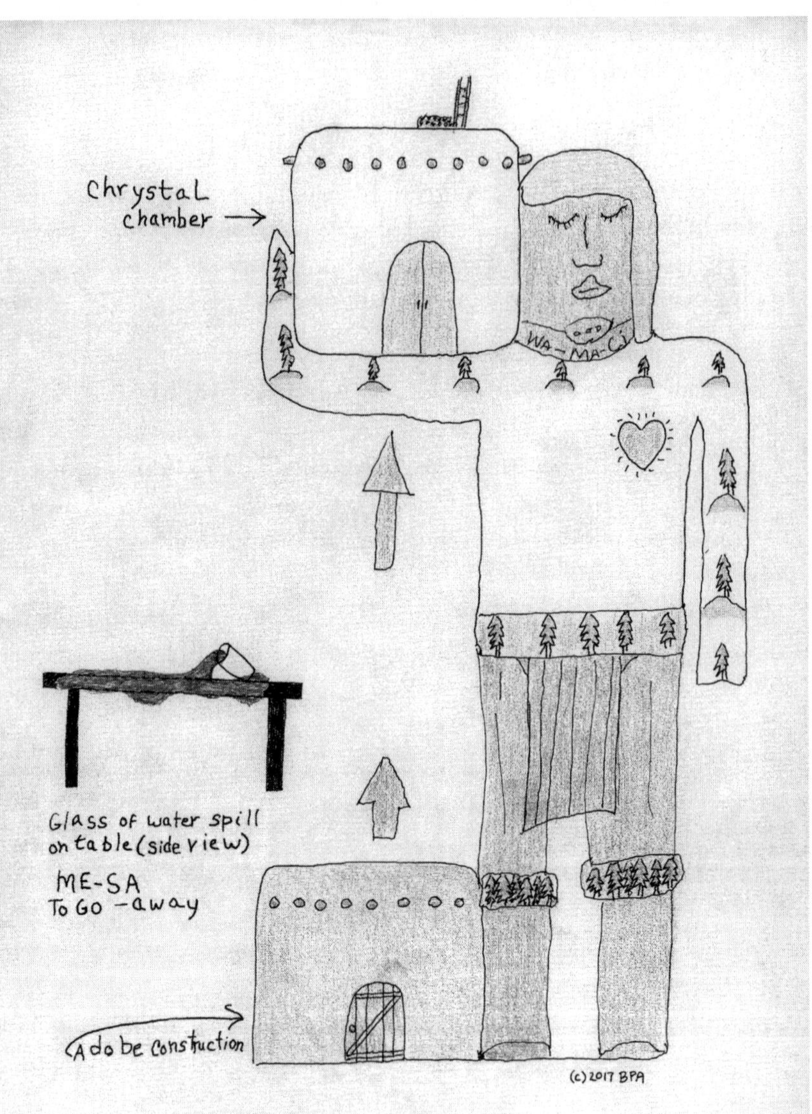

CRYSTAL CHAMBER TAKEN UP INTO THE SKY

JOSEPH ON ENLIGHTENMENT AT THE DARKEST TIME OF THE YEAR

When I asked Joseph if enlightenment came through the darkness or light, he responded with a story.

"People here are putting on their lights, candles in bags, candeleros,[42] *people put them around their houses and then they have bus tours and people drive around to look. They are going to have Zia dancers at the park and bonfires on Christmas Eve. So it is all coming out in the Albuquerque newspaper. It is going to be a celebration.*

"Then it will be the solstice, this mountain, Sandia Mountain, used to be my clock where I used to live. I would watch the sun when it reached that level that it wasn't going to reach any further south, it would start going north again. That's the way the Indians used to do it. I used to do it that way to follow the ceremonies on the solstice.

"When I built the sound chamber here in Bernalillo I created a ceremony where I did a rainbow from the chamber that I had here with the chamber there at the monument where we went (the Painted Kiva). But when the people bought the place here I guess they tore it down. People call it a crystal chamber because I buried crystals in the wall. One day it became a crystal chamber and it went straight up into the sky and it is still there. So it didn't bother me when they tore it down because it was just the physical structure. The little boy went with it up into the sky, 10,000 feet up. So it is sitting up there in the sky over Albuquerque, New Mexico, and Bernalillo."[43]

This was just a brief conversation with Joseph, and on the surface he did not answer my question about enlightenment, the light, and the dark. However, I have learned to listen more closely to what he says and where his consciousness goes when I ask him a question. His answer was that in the darkest times of the year, people naturally turn to the light and put up candles in the darkness. Christian traditions associate the light with God and Jesus and the dark with hell and Satan. In the hero's journey, however, the hero descends into darkness in order to find a new light and bring this back to the ordinary reality. With the pueblo peoples, the sacred is found by climbing down through a hole in the roof of the kiva into the darkness. The pueblo people tell the creation story where they climbed out of a hole

42 Candlesticks.

43 As part of the vision, Joseph was also given a little boy, a spirit child, who grows as the Sound Chambers grow.

ORDINARY, NON-ORDINARY REALITY OFFERING BOWL

in the earth and so climbing down into the kiva is a symbolic return to the womb, to the source of creation—Mother Earth.

Life on this earth has both light and darkness. We have the light of day and the light of summer and we have the dark of night and the dark of winter. There is a spiritual essence of light/summer as there is a spiritual essence of dark/winter. In *Walking the Medicine Wheel*, Joseph has an art piece entitled "Darkness Seekers of Wisdom." The place where we cannot see things is the place where we will find that which we seek. Visual art can bring together the opposites into relationship with each other. Another painting of Joseph's that I keep near me is "Ordinary Reality, Non-Ordinary Reality, Offering Bowl." In this painting there is a vertical line down the center separating the painting with a spirit being looking up and to the left on the left side of the painting (ordinary reality) and a spirit being looking up and to the right on the right side of the painting (non-ordinary reality). Joseph often says that the separation between ordinary and non-ordinary reality is but a sliver. Two human beings are bowing the top of their heads toward the line dividing ordinary and non-ordinary reality. There are several steps going up the side of non-ordinary reality (showing we must climb into it) and on the top of the steps is an offering bowl, filled with tiny particles of something, maybe corn meal. There are two feathers pointing upwards from the Offering Bowl and they look a little like flickering flames at first glance. This painting is one of the first that Joseph gave me and was painted in 2015.

Joseph teaches that what seems separate is connected. The separation between ordinary and non-ordinary reality is but a wispy membrane. Light and dark are not opposites, but partners in bringing cycles of day and night. Joseph speaks of finding illumination in the darkness.

> As a young boy, I was taught in those underground chambers to look within. I discovered I was silence and darkness. And then I saw that by seeing with my eyes I created movement and out of it illumination came, and then I realized the silence and the darkness were full of emptiness, and the emptiness was full of light.[44]

BECOMING THE COSMIC WORLD TREE CEREMONY

Sometimes Joseph speaks of a tree that connects these two realms, such as the tree that lifted his first Sound Chamber from ordinary reality and took it up into non-ordinary reality where it turned into crystal and exists above ordinary reality. Many traditions speak of the "World Tree" that connects the different realms of existence.

In 2017, I traveled to the Southern Ute reservation to meet with Joseph and it happened to be Arbor Day. When I pointed this out he said that we would do a Tree Ceremony for Arbor Day. He ordered some lemon trees from the nursery.

We walked from the Sound Chamber out into the field. Joseph set up the three small trees in one of his geodesic dome greenhouses. He covered

44 *B&V*, 60.

them in darkness with a large pot so that the trees were not visible. He brought in his drum and then sang and drummed for a while, then he would alternate between his drum and hitting the over-turned pot with his mallet. He signaled to me that I was supposed to slowly lift off the covering pot, exposing the tree to the light of day. We repeated this three times.

The ceremony made me think of all the spiritual movements from darkness to light in many traditions. The Pueblo peoples have creation stories of how they climbed from the darkness of a hole in the Earth into this world. Many ceremonies occur in the kivas, where you climb down a ladder from above into the darkness of the kiva, then you climb back out into the light. Covering and revealing, hiding and discovering—these back and forth movements from dark to light and light to dark are sacred ceremonies, just as we continually blink our eyes, we momentarily pause into darkness and then open our eyes again to the light. "*We do not exist*," Joseph often says. We are constantly coming into being and blinking out of being and blinking back into being. We plant the seed of the tree in the darkness of the soil and it grows forth into the light. The tree creates fruit, creating more seeds and the seeds seek darkness in order that they might grow forth into the light. A week or two after the ceremony, Joseph called me and said that the trees were very happy and growing much faster than they would have without the ceremony!

You can practice this feeling of interconnected being between the manifest reality and *Wah-Mah-Chi* by envisioning yourself as the cosmic world tree. Close your eyes and feel your legs and feet as roots, feel your arms and fingers and head as branches. Feel your trunk as the trunk of the cosmic world tree. Your roots reach down into the darkest depths of material reality. Your limbs and leaves reach up into the firmament, into the furthest reaches of cosmic, spiritual reality. The light of *Wah-Mah-Chi* enters through your leaves, passes through your limbs, into your trunk and down to the roots of your being. Your roots take up the vital nutrients of the earth and soak up the watery goodness of the earth and bring these back up to the very tips of your leaves and branches. Trees do not argue about light and darkness, or choose one over the other—they embrace both, growing deeper into darkness with their roots and reaching further into the light with their branches.

Through your being you connect the material and spiritual realms. Allow yourself to feel and enjoy the goodness of being a conduit of *Wah-Mah-Chi*.

JOSEPH WALKING

WE ARE COSMIC CITIZENS

Stars shine in the darkness of space. Joseph speaks a lot about space and the cosmos, using the sun and moon to orient us, and about our relationship and responsibility to the cosmos—because he keeps telling me "*We are cosmic citizens*." There is a strong tradition in amongst the Southwestern Native American tribes of referring to the stars and the movements of the sun and the moon. I felt it was important for me to visit Chimney Rock, where two pillars of rock were used to track the changing patterns of the moon. Joseph told me to "*note the mindset of how the ancient moon watchers used their insights regarding how they used the knowledge from moon observations*." I visited Chimney Rock National Monument in 2015 for a dusk ceremony. As I sat listening to the Native American flute player, a small lizard climbed on to my backpack and then jumped on to my leg and sat there for a little bit. It felt good to gaze off at the pillars of Chimney Rock accompanied by this little rascal.

A COSMIC CONVERSATION WITH JOSEPH

J: "In a vision, my father had given me a black obsidian spear point. I always thought that might be our connection to the beings of the cosmos. Archaeologists are always finding spear points and arrowheads. Spear points are much more than spear points. Besides using them as cutters they were the point that you could use to cut into other realities in prehistoric times. So they had multiple uses. Teh *means to cut. If you cut into something, you can hear the sound* teh. *When you hear this sound, when you make the sound* teh *it opens up a space in the wall.*

"What separates us from non-ordinary reality is the fact that we think we exist. In existence we believe we are separated from everything else. Existence establishes a point of power and it has certain facilities: awareness, the up above and down below and the ability to crystalize. That is what it means to exist—in this reality we spend our whole lifetime distinguishing what things are and what they are used for. But otherwise we are not interested in it and that gives us some knowledge about space. Without existence we wouldn't have forward and backward, we wouldn't have up and down, we wouldn't know any of these dimensions. Because in the other dimension we don't exist. We are nothing."

D: Is the medicine like a translator? Like a space tunnel or star gate between ordinary and non-ordinary reality?

J: [Joseph hands me a hematite ring]. "This ring is the channel to go to the other side. The mountain opened up and you could pass through to the other side. The mountain is the heart. You pass through and you get to have a body for a month or so, but that is just an adjustment period, and then you don't need it because you are already there. But here on this side we have to use our muscles. We are born to live here so that we can experience what it is like to be, because everywhere else we don't exist. Since we live in the hchole, *the circle,* Hchole *means 'to seed,' it is the place-seeder, the place where everything is born, the seed of an idea is born. So when you want to ask the helpers come in to help you to accomplish whatever it is you want to accomplish, because they put the idea in your head anyway. You are in the process of the vibration of* we-aah, *which means to call forth and be. And so the helpers come from the north, south, east, and west and they help you manifest what the patient is asking. Even though the helpers already know what is wrong with that person, you have to request their help through a prayer so that as a shaman you can help to heal the person.*

SPIRITS OF CHIMNEY ROCK

"God loves us so much that no matter what we do he is going to forgive us. So what is the point? We can get away with doing bad things, but if you do you get ostracized. It is like telling a little child, you are a civilized person, don't do what you did because you are endangering your own safety. Once you exist you have pain and pain means suffering and a loving father will say don't do this or that because you end up hurting, he says just don't do it.

"There is the story of Plowman,[45] *the plow which makes the furrows. The little boy and the little girl fawns are running away from the Giantess, who is like the wicked witch of the west. They say that the witch is fattening them up to eat them. So, they are running away and that is when they met Plowman and he said, 'I want you to hide here in this crack in the plow.' Remember this is all metaphor, but as noun-pronoun people we lose the ability to understand metaphor. As the story-teller tells the story we know the answer, but the noun-pronoun thinking blocks it because it is trying to establish separation and superiority over the other. The story goes that at some point he hits the plow and it makes a sound* taah-que.

"Taah *means to do.*

"Que *means to begin.*

"So we have to begin, that is what the big bang is—to begin what? Creation. Science says all these galaxies began to be born and that is the theory. The fact is that we are here, so the fact is that something cool happened, right. So that is what the big bang is 'to do' and then the next logical step is to 'begin' whatever it was you are going to do. And so that is how creation became. What if there hadn't been no to do *and* to begin*—creation wouldn't have started.*

"If you are going to get up out of bed, you do preliminaries and then you begin when you get up. And that is the big bang. In physics it is an explosion, the nuclear fusion and gravity and weight and it is explosive and it is hot and it is a kind of poisonous gas. I believe there is a mind—this big—that knows everything that is going to happen and it knew it yesterday, but we don't know it until we actually know that is what we are going to do. Before we were even born, something, Divine Beingness, or whatever you want to call it, knew what we would be doing from birth to death. And one of the things that we were going to be doing was believing that we exist in order to substantiate our place in existence and that is the way we birth our intelligence in our surroundings. In order to navigate our environment. By inventing or discovering it then we create the illusion, then we spend the rest of our lives believing we exist so that we can perpetuate the illusion, because we want to think that we really are existing, that we really have an intelligence, when it is really just a form that we create and then we create more forms [moving hands to chest and out] then we create a landscape that we can exist in. We say, 'Well it is better than nothing,' because nothing is no form. We have evolved long enough for billions and billions of light-years that we can begin to be the way we are. We have

45 "The Old Giantess and the Brother and Sister Fawns," *BPA*.

evolved to the point now where we have two legs and we know about balance and how to use the muscles, but even as babies we have to train our muscles to be able to do what we already know, so it is a never-ending process.

"Begin: **b** *is focus,* **e** *is placement,* **g** *is that which is good,* **i** *is awareness and* **n** *is the self*

"The self is ready to begin but it first has to place itself by choosing to do good and that awakens a level of goodness of what the personal self as well as the Vast Self—the word already has the movement in it, but placing in that moment a form of goodness that is full of awareness toward the task of seeking the personal as well as the Vast Self toward the direction of creating action—actions of creating."

D: "Does the similarity between the English words being and begin show that true being is really about continually beginning?"

J: "Being. I travel all day long trying to get to point B only to realize that I am already there while I am still trying to get there.

"So we begin something knowing that we have already begun something we finish what we want to do knowing that we have already accomplished before we get to where we wanted to get the task accomplished or done.

"These are gravitational waves and what they do is mess up things. The war is not here, the war is up there. I think the war is really the gravitational ripples[46]

"This is what I think the black holes are doing to us here. When we have that kind of disturbance up there, we are just this tiny little planet called Planet Earth, but the black holes are so far away from us it takes millions of years to affect us and when it does it throws a monkey wrench in our foundation of planet earth and maybe leads to countries going war.

"That is why flying saucers fascinate me. I have seen objects come up out of the ocean and they sparkle in the sun and then they go back under, but I can't tell anyone about them because they will think I am crazy or say I drank too much. I think space ships are already here and they have been here for years. They move through our space without us noticing them.

"That's the last frontier, I have heard that over and over and over again—so that is where we are going to go to the stars, but we have to figure out how we are going to travel there or disappear here and appear there.

---

46 Joseph is referring to an article he sent me, an editorial from *Astronomy* May 2016.

"The reason I know that they will return from outer space is that all life is a circle. If it happened in the past, it will happen again in the future. The space beings were teaching how to appear and disappear. They disappeared, so now we just wait until they appear again."

THE DARK OF SPACE

Joseph is always sending me clippings from different astronomy magazines. Some of his particular interests are dark matter, black holes, and gravitational waves. He tells me several times, "*We have to put something about ETs in the book!*" Talking about Extraterrestrials is part of being a cosmic citizen, recognizing relationships that connect us with the cosmos. Joseph tells me, "*We need to understand them the way Indians would relate to them, as our brothers and sisters and not just objects that we know scientific facts about.*" Joseph often speaks of ETs and about the future space travel of human beings and the old stories about indigenous people who "*disappeared*" and "*went up*" with the ETs.[47] Joseph follows scientific advances in astrophysics and space flight and he will talk about future travels of human beings through space. (One of Joseph's favorite baseball caps has a NASA logo on it.) Other times, Joseph will talk about the shamanic capabilities of human beings, how for instance, he was able to travel from the Southwest to Florida in an instant in a shamanic state to help his friend, Kurt Wilt, who was dying and trapped in a coma. Joseph will say, "*If I can do that, go from my bed in the Southwest to Florida, quicker than a finger snap, then there is no reason we can't go to the moon, or explore the cosmos.*"

I have been trying to figure out how to find the thread for discussing ETs in this book. I remembered that Carl Jung wrote a paper called "Flying Saucers: A Modern Myth of Things Seen in the Sky." Jung seemed to consider these circular objects in the sky to be a kind of visionary projection of collective humanity's unconscious.[48] As these were circular

47 Many indigenous traditions speak of coming from the stars or having been visited by star people. Hank Wesselman describes indigenous Hawaiian traditions that teach, "We originally came from across the universe in celestial canoes made of light. We came as individual souls, as seeds of light, and were accompanied by high spiritual guardians who held the knowledge of our purpose, our destiny." (Wesselman, *The Bowl of Light*, 134). Dolphins and whales are also from this home planet. The name of the Home star is 'A'A which means "Burning Bright," what we call Sirius, (Ibid., 95).

48 In his autobiography, Jung describes a dream he had in 1958 of two UFOs in the sky with a kind of "magic box" and the UFO being a lens that was projecting images toward

objects, he interpreted them as consciousness seeking its own wholeness by bringing in a circular, healing awareness (we could say a medicine wheel). At times Jung's approach to UFOs seemed to be a kind of psychological reductionism of external phenomena to inner states. However, he also was working with quantum physicist Wolfgang Pauli on the concept of synchronicity, which he called an acausal connecting principle, a kind of psychophysical parallelism where something in the outer world was meaningfully connected to something in the inner world. Even though the connection could not be rationally or objectively observed, there could be a deep sense of inner meaning. Jung traced this modern concept of synchronicity with Pauli's insights in quantum physics back to the ancient spiritual concept of the *unus mundus*, the one, unified world. Rather than seeing phenomena as either mental or physical, "all reality would be grounded on an as yet unknown substrate possessing material and at the same time psychic qualities."[49] Inner psychological experience and outer material reality would, thus, both arise as aspects of the same substance.

In weaving the thread of ETs into this book, I recalled reading Harvard psychiatrist John Mack's work with people who had reported alien abduction experiences. After ten years of this work, Mack had shifted away from a purely materialistic theory of what was happening in these experiences and suggested that they were part of a larger opening of consciousness and reconnection to spiritual and metaphysical realms. The way he describes the experience sounds like a hero's journey, or like the pathways of initiation we have been exploring in this book. In seeking to understand the modern phenomena, Mack also interviewed many indigenous people who spoke of their traditions of relationship between the beings of the Earth and the beings of the cosmos. As Mack worked with indigenous people and healers, he tried to understand when they were speaking of "reality" and when they were speaking metaphorically. Bernardo Peixoto from the Ipixuma tribe in the Amazon said, "this makes no difference." Malidoma Somé of the Dagara people in Burkina Faso said, "the supernatural is part of everyday lives . . . the material is just

---

him. Upon awakening, Jung thought to himself "We always think that the UFOs are projections of ours. Now it turns out that we are their projections. I am projected by the magic lantern as C. G. Jung. But who manipulates the apparatus?" (*MDR*, 323).

49 Carl Jung, "Flying Saucers: a Modern Myth of Things Seen in the Sky," *Civilization in Transition, CW 10*, 411.

the spiritual taking on form."[50] This is similar to Jung's discussion of the *unus mundus*, the one world from which the material and spiritual are manifestations.

Mack acknowledged the traumatic aspect that many alien abductees reported to him in his ten years of interviews and research, yet he saw a transformation that occurred in many of the experiencers. The abduction "experiences seem to be created, as if by design, to shatter . . . the previously held idea of reality." This leads to an "awakening" and "heightened awareness that grows out of the ego-shattering impact of the encounters" with characteristic "psychospiritual changes." The awakening, according to Mack, often includes an increased capacity for "nonordinary states of consciousness similar to the symbolic worlds of the shamans of indigenous cultures" and a "deepening and expansion of their psychological and spiritual powers." The person may "undergo a profound connection or reconnection with the Divine, God, Source," and an "experience of heart-opening, a sense of loving connection with all living beings and creation itself, which can at times take on mystical proportions." One underlying theme that Mack emphasizes is *remembering*. The experiencers speak of remembering where we came from, who we are, our original purpose, our connection to all beings, and, ultimately, our reality as part of the Divine or Sacred. This remembering is a returning. Mack, came to view contact experiences as part of a larger movement of spiritual rebirth in Western culture that leads to a sense of interconnection with all beings and a responsibility to be caretakers of the Earth. Contact, in other words, brings about a disorientation and then a reorientation. While there is this positive element of spiritual unity and empowered responsibility, there is also a deep sense of sadness and disconnection that Mack describes, which sounds similar to what saints and mystics describe of the intrinsic sadness of separation living in an individuated human body and the mystical longing for re-Union with the Sacred.

> But there is a painful side to the spiritual awakening that abduction experiencers undergo. Although they may feel that they have a special responsibility or mission as teachers or Earth stewards, their deepening connection with Source or Home brings with it for them a feeling that they do not belong here. They may even feel they have an alien identity or soul and that the spaceships themselves are part of Home.[51]

50 John E. Mack, *Passport to the Cosmos*, 7.

51 Ibid., 297–98, 299.

DARK MATTER

"The behavior of dark matter is the reason that we, that planet earth, that the events on planet earth happen where you go around and you come around, and you just keep doing that over and over again. Dark matter keeps creating the possibility for more and more galaxies to be born. That is the purpose of dark matter. And we may think that it is to enhance 'darkness' and perhaps that is one of its attributes, but that is not its main reason; that is kind of a side effect it has. We will never get away from dark matter because if we do that would be getting rid of the shadow, the shadows."

Joseph is fascinated with the scientific concepts of dark matter and dark energy because they relate to his visionary experiences and the teachings in the darkness of the kiva.[52] Joseph often speaks of the vibration of sound in creation. Perhaps we can imagine the sound as ordinary reality, the visible matter and energy and this would make silence correspond with non-ordinary reality and dark matter and dark energy. Just as Alexander illustrates the musical basis of the universe, so too does Natarajan make a comment that Joseph would most likely resonate with, "in string theory all elementary particles produced in the universe that we detect today can be conceptualized as musical notes produced by the elementary strings that existed prior to the big bang." Natarajan tells us, "Our eyes are not tuned to see the majority of reality."[53]

One of the threads that Joseph sent me chasing was physicist Lisa Randall's book, *Dark Matter and the Dinosaurs: The Astounding Interconnectedness of the Universe*. The title of the book comes from a theory that Randall was investigating whether dark matter may have de-stabilized a comet as our solar system and galaxy rotated through a cloud of dark matter. Charting mass extinctions, she comes up with a periodic cycle that seems to correlate with the time required to pass through clouds of dark matter. She describes something called "*acoustic oscillations*," caused by competing forces of the gravitational pull of matter and the pressure of radiation pushing outwards.[54] She describes the breakdown of the components of

---

52 Hank Wesselman also speaks of the similarity of the astrophysics study of dark matter what Hawaiian elder, Makua, described as *Kū*, "the invisible platform of power upon which things can be built or assembled. It means 'arising' or 'standing up' or 'emerging forth,'" (*The Bowl of Light*, 68).

53 Natarajan, *Mapping the Heavens*, 201, 223.

54 Lisa Randall, *Dark Matter and the Dinosaurs*, 19–20.

the universe as being 5% atoms of ordinary matter and energy, 26% dark matter, and 69% dark energy.

We can see that dark matter and dark energy are by far the dominant forces in the universe, even though they are hidden and unseen. This is yet another obvious parallel with the teachings of mystics, visionaries, and shamans—the unseen is more powerful in shaping the seen. Lisa Randall plays around with some thought experiments. She wonders if there might be dark matter beings who live in the realm of dark matter and dark energy. As a physicist firmly grounded in science and not given to metaphysical speculation, she concludes, "Though it's entertaining to speculate about the possibility of dark life, it's a lot harder to figure out a way to observe it—or even detect its existence in more indirect ways."[55] Moving further into speculation, we can wonder whether "dark life" is what the mystics, shamans, and visionaries speak of when they enter into non-ordinary reality and interact with beings who are otherwise not visible in ordinary reality.

An image that frequently comes to me when I enter into a medicine wheel meditation is that I sink deeper and deeper into the earth, into the darkness, or sometimes I shoot out into the darkness of the void—either way, I end up in the same place. I have the sensation of being a crow or raven, completely black moving through blackness. I feel the strength of my wings and how good it feels to flap them. I am darkness moving through darkness. Sometimes I catch the glint of my black eyes in the darkness. I am *Wah-Mah-Chi*, Breath-Matter-Movement, moving throughout the dark matter, dark energy universe. I cannot tell you why this is a good feeling or why I find it rejuvenating. I am not going anywhere and it is difficult to say that I am anything because there is more a sensation of movement than of being distinct matter. Perhaps this is what Meister Eckhart called the "superessential darkness that has no name and that will never be given a name."[56]

As Henry Corbin has written that we must strive to make ourselves capable of God, Thomas Aquinas wrote that "every human being is *capax universi*," capable of the universe.[57] Thomas Cheetham, who has written extensively on Henry Corbin and Carl Jung writes that "there are these

---

55 Ibid., 335.

56 Meister Eckhart in Matthew Fox, *Meister Eckhart: A Mystic Warrior for Our Times*, 37.

57 Ibid., 16.

two darknesses—the Shadow and the luminous darkness of divine Night. The former is a soul experience, to be integrated into consciousness for completeness, the latter a spirit experience necessary to wholeness, not only of experience, but of the world."[58]

BECOMING A COSMIC CITIZEN

Na-yo ti-ay we-ah. "We don't exist" can seem negative, but it also can create a sense of joy and freedom. When we de-identify with ourselves as nouns and objects, we connect into a spaciousness and boundless sense of relation and unity. Lie down comfortably, close your eyes. Bring your awareness to the front half of your body and all of your senses that are always outwardly focused, bringing the world to you. Now, imagine that there is no back half of your body, it just blends into the depths of outer space. Look at all the beautiful stars shining and all the empty space of the Vast Self, all the potential creation. Sink into this delicious feeling of open space, all this creative potential that you are constantly in touch with. Let yourself, through your cosmic back side, cease to exist and rest in the delicious space of eternity. It is really true that we are all made of stars. Your personal past is also the past of the Universe. There are galaxies being born within you—every single second!

58 Thomas Cheetham, *Green Man, Earth Angel*, xiii.

CHAPTER 11

INITIATION

Initiation represents one of the most significant spiritual phenomena in the history of humanity. It is an act that involves not only the religious life of the individual . . . it involves his entire life. It is through initiation that . . . man becomes what he is and what he should be – a being open to the life of the spirit, hence one who participates in the culture into which he was born.[1]

MIRCEA ELIADE

A lot of people experience initiation without realizing that's what's happening to them. Initiation is a hard word because most people are intimidated by the idea of being initiated or of being questioned or being tested, or even being examined, and so if you can go through that, and I think a lot of people go through it deeply without even realizing what direction they are moving or that's where they are going, but you end up on the other side of something that you didn't know how you got there.

To me it's always about, especially with sound and music, if we could get rid of the restrictions and systems and any rhetoric having to do with what things are for, and try to step into something that has no top and bottom and has no size, you are just in space. From that perspective, you turn around and there's something you created, sometimes without realizing it was happening, but I don't think the majority of people are ready for the initiation. Again, a lot of people pass through that and end up somewhere else without even realizing there was a kind of process involved.[2]

BILL LASWELL

Initiation is a transformation that occurs when we cross from one state of being into another state of being. Initiations can happen suddenly and without preparation or they can occur after years of preparation as part of

1 Mircea Eliade, *Rites and Symbols of Initiation: The Mysteries of Birth and Rebirth*, 27.

2 From a recorded phone call and subsequent transcript of conversation with Bill Laswell.

a spiritual curriculum. Traditional cultures and spiritual traditions have sought to create a way to transmit ancient wisdom from one person to another. An initiation is not just an incremental change in a behavior and it is not just some new facts or knowledge. Initiation is a transformation of the person. When Joseph says, "We do not exist," he is initiating us into a new state of being. Initiation is what happens on the hero's journey: the transformation of an average person into a hero. All of us have our own paths of heroism we are seeking to realize in our lives. Initiation is what brings our heroism from potential possibility to actual realization.

The heart is the organ of transformation. The heart is the place of initiation because the heart is the center of the medicine wheel and it is the center of ourselves. It is the heart that is transformed and it is in the heart that we carry what has been transformed back to ordinary reality. This is because the heart is a medicine bag in which we carry the medicine we are in the process of becoming.

CEREMONY AS INITIATION

Ceremony is one way to empty the heart of what no longer serves us and bring in new sacred "objects." Ceremony is also the way that we can create more space within us, more space within the medicine bag, so that the pain that we carry does not seem so heavy and we also have a greater capacity for joy, a greater capacity for *Wah-Mah-Chi*. It is through ceremonially creating more heart space that we become more capable of God, which is the same thing as *becoming medicine*. Joseph would say that we are becoming greater heart people through ceremonies that enlarge the heart.

Many times people react to pain and suffering by shrinking their hearts. This does not work, even though it is tempting to try to solve the pain of life by not feeling it. It is through becoming greater heart people that we transform the pain of life into life wisdom.

While we can decide to put certain things in our heart, it is not really up to us to decide to take things out of our heart. That can only happen through *Wah-Mah-Chi*, through Breath-Matter-Movement. In the beginning of *Walking the Medicine Wheel*, Joseph gives a *nah-meh-neh* ceremony for veterans before they go to war and then to repeat again when they return from war. This ceremony involves filling a cup with light and then filling a cup with *nah-meh-neh*, which is earth, and then emptying the cup back to the Earth. This ceremony shows that veterans were asked to carry something for their country—where else would they carry this but in their soldier's heart? When they come back home, their soldier's heart is heavy and no longer fits back in the civilian world. This *nah-meh-neh* ceremony helps the human being to become like a hollow bone, it lets *Wah-Mah-Chi,* Breath Matter Movement flow through the veteran and this can help them release things that they should no longer be carrying. However, *Wah-Mah-Chi* does not take all the pain and suffering, just that which is no longer needed for the *medicine* of that particular human being. Carrying some pain and suffering is necessary for medicine because learning about reality is necessary for developing wisdom. We need to be wounded and carry pain if we are going to be healers. Medicine is only made when there is some kind of pain, and long before God made tablets, pills, and capsules, God made human beings as medicine bags to hold the medicine for the Earth. This is what we hoped to do in *Walking the Medicine Wheel*—help veterans become greater heart people and to become bigger medicine bags, because on this planet right now we have a lot of sickness that requires good medicine.

What is important in this book is not the detail, but the broad outline of the journey to the center of the medicine wheel, the journey to the heart—and not just the heart, but into the inner heart, into the *guhā*, the cave of the heart. We journey deeper and deeper into this cave of the heart until we find the ever-renewing fountain of goodness, the Garden of Paradise.

THE STORY OF INITIATION THAT CANNOT BE TOLD

Many mystics, visionaries, and shamans speak of a truth that cannot be spoken of and this is partly why one is not supposed to speak of the specifics of initiation ceremonies. This is why there are so many circular stories and parables because the sages are trying to point to something that has no direction, but rather is found deep within you. Joseph Rael tells us that at the "*heart center, we know we are not really split,*" but our perception and knowledge is based upon the separation of subject and object. How can the truth of initiation be written and transmitted? *Na-yo ti-ay we-ah*: "I do not exist," says Joseph Rael. "You will see light in the darkness, You will make some sense of this," goes the Police song, "Secret Journey."

Daniel Odier is a seeker and he has received initiation from several teachers. In his most recent book, *The Doors of Joy*, he tells how he was striving to teach others what he had learned when he realized that "although teaching was meant to be liberating, it was really just repackaging of a new theory of the world. This has, in turn, created new shackles that keep human beings in a closed universe."[3] Odier tells of studying Zen, Tibetan Dzogchen, Vignan Bhairav Tantra, Varayana, Kashmiri Shaivism, Spanda and Pratyabhijna. In this last approach Odier says the goal was "to become a human being again, to be fully open to the world, alive and full of desire and passion, without the smallest pretension of being anything but spontaneous."[4]

Returning to his insight on teaching, he wrote, "I could see how difficult it was for me not to build systems similar to those that had limited me in my quest. I could see that my students would inevitably adhere to the propensity we all have of building conceptual limitations in order to give more value to our knowledge and experience." What a dilemma, to have gone through the seeking, through the finding and receiving of initiation, and then feeling that he has something to give, and yet the ways that he sought to give and transmit his wisdom only obscured the true goal of the seeking! Odier continues his confession:

> Over time, as I was getting closer to Chan (Chinese Zen) and to the essence of Kashmir Shaivism, I became more and more iconoclastic, and transformed myself into a spiritual anarchist whose only ambition was to reach an authentic freedom by forgetting the path that had always been followed. . . .
>
> It appeared more and more evident to me that it was essential to escape any limitations and that joy was the only natural thing to reach for. The spiritual discourse seemed to me a fatal trap. . . .
>
> Since that time, free of all attachments, I venture only to help those I meet to find spontaneity, joy and freedom.[5]

Odier's decision is similar to that of Joseph Campbell when he was studying Hindu teachings of *sat cit ananda* (being, consciousness, bliss). Campbell concluded that he did not know what *being* or *consciousness* was, but he did understand *bliss* and this led to his famous statement: "Follow your bliss." Odier's story of initiation and enlightenment led to a crisis

3 Daniel Odier, *The Doors of Joy: 19 Meditations for Authentic Living*, vii.

4 Ibid., viii.

5 Ibid., viii-ix.

of pedagogy—how to teach that which is beyond the usual theories and practices of teaching. It seems to me that what Odier is trying to teach is akin to what we are discussing in *Becoming Medicine*—how to become that which you seek and to teach others to become that which they are. This is why J. Krishnamurti disbanded the Order of the Star—a living spirituality cannot be organized and institutionalized.

How can you tell a story that is no story? How can you tell the story of a *secret journey*? Many of traditional creation stories tell of how order evolved and was created out of the primordial chaos, but how do you tell the story of order dissolving back into the creative potentiality of chaos and then being reborn into a new form of order—which is only temporary and momentary? Here is one of Odier's teachings on joy, so relevant to our time:

> The fear in which our present society lives pushes us to forget about the creative aspects of chaos and to see only disorder and catastrophe. If we go back to Greek mythology, we will be able to see the creativity of chaos and then be able to reintegrate it into our lives.
>
> Chaos was here before anything else, a kind of floating and udifferentiated magma filled with suspended energy. . . .
>
> By perceiving chaos as energy, we reduce both the fear we have of chaotic states and our desire to suppress our strategies to avoid them. Periods of chaos are marvelously creative. They are the end of a deceptively organised universe and bring the emergence of a new force. If we dare not to run away from chaos, and not to close our eyes, we will get the impression of floating amidst an ocean of a quivering energy. The body absorbs this energy, the spirit is nourished by it and goes through a phase of withdrawal and restful emptiness out of which the seeds of creativity germinate. It is the end of one order and the beginning of a revitalisation. . . .
>
> Accepting chaos, floating on it as on a benevolent ocean, is a joyous state from which fear has been vanquished. By ceasing our desire to control everything we will feel stimulated, encouraged to desire things to emerge. Control emerges out of the fear of feeling fully alive. There is no authentic joy without encountering chaos.[6]

6 Ibid., 95–97.

SITTING IN THE CENTER OF THE MEDICINE WHEEL CEREMONY (8/17/16)

Joseph described a way of using the medicine wheel as an initiation. First we made an offering to the shrines around his property, then tied an offering on a willow tree and went down by the La Plata River and cut a length of willow. We looped this into a hoop and tied it off with three pieces of twine. Joseph then set the hoop on a red piece of cloth and said that cloth in Tiwa is *poh-la* and means blanket or any cloth

"Truth is always hidden on purpose and the cloth is the thing which hides and reveals the Truth.

"Poh *means 'dirty,' something is laying on the table covering something. It looks dirty but it is not. If you have a table covered with food, that is the holiest that it can ever get when it is covered with food and things, so that it is not clean. I will cover it up and put things on it. After I cover it up, I'll have a sheet on it and I'll pull it off and it will drop on the cloth. That is what God is, he's a magician and that is the way he shows us. The ancient Indians would make covers out of buffalo hide. And you could use the hair for a pillow or blanket, the Pueblo Indians would stuff the blanket with the bark of the Juniper or Cedar tree, which is holy. Usually they would lay that mattress on the ground so that you could be closest to the earth and be in the arms of Mother Earth when you slept at night. Spanish word for bark of juniper tree is called* guipas.

"Poh-la. Poh *is dirty.* L *is God, and* A *is the purity of the cloth.*

"When the magician pulls the cloth out from the table this reveals the Truth of all of the realities of the cosmos. When you cover yourself with a blanket at night you are all the hidden mysteries. You hear the alarm clock and you uncover and reveal them. All the ancient mysteries are within you and you reveal them as you walk out into the daylight which hides and reveals."

Joseph then takes me on a walk outside to listen to the sounds of things: board, *guipas*, rock, *huu*, stump. Things reveal themselves to you if you orient yourself toward them.

Joseph took pieces of red, white, yellow, and black cloths and placed them around the directions of the medicine wheel. He then instructed me to sit in the middle of the medicine wheel. You could do this with a large wheel on the ground, but for us this was in a visionary sense, imagining yourself in the middle of the medicine wheel with the channels open to the north, to the south, to the east and to the west.

"When I sit in the middle of the medicine wheel, I then extend it out, 200 miles to the north, 200 miles to the south, 200 miles to the east, and 200 miles to the west. I figure that gives plenty of space for any kind of help to come in through the medicine wheel. Then I look at myself in the middle of the wheel from the outside. We can do this because as shamans we learn to be in two places at once."

This fits with many shamanic traditions which speak of being able to journey outside of the body. Next, Joseph says that he watches for a helper to show up and he pays attention to which direction they come from. *"The helper can appear as an animal or as a person. They can speak with sound you hear through your ear."* Sometimes it startles me when the helper speaks right in my ear, Joseph says, *"so I am always telling them to speak telepathically with me."* Joseph also says that sometimes the helper can speak through your own thoughts, it sounds like your thought, but it isn't. He gave an example of driving and hearing what sounded like his own thought say, *"You better slow down and check your tires."*

Joseph related a recent vision he had. He was sitting in the medicine wheel when a helper came from the south, the direction of emotion.

"It was a small little white thing, kind of like a little man, but with a lot of teeth. Sometimes they say don't trust something with a lot of teeth, but I could tell it was coming from the south, the place of purity, and he was white, the color of the south, so I thought I could trust him. The helper explained that it was of the dinosaurs and it was here to help with a sickness that had been around the earth. He said that he had come because there was a sickness around the earth. There are a lot of hospitals and people getting sick all the time. So I asked for a helper and then this guy came, and he was the worst kind of looking guy, with all these shiny silver teeth. I intuitively sensed that he was here to help. It seemed like the goodness in me superimposes itself on the situation, so even if it was bad, it becomes good in an instant. This is the job of those who have the job of doing the laundry—you have to wash and cleanse the situation. The being explained to me that he had a lot of teeth so that he could chew up the sickness that was surrounding the earth.

"The helper had his own small helper, an apprentice or son. The first helper told the apprentice, 'You know what to do, you can do it.' The apprentice created a batch of small dinosaurs that started chewing on an inhibiting layer around the earth. They chewed for a little while and only cleared a small patch. The first helper then said, 'Let me show you something,' and he created a massive dinosaur with huge jaws and it started chewing at this layer of sickness

around the earth. I counted, 'One, two, three . . . by the time I got to 60, the layer was gone.'"

Joseph then told me about another vision he had, while we were doing the vision quest to see the tree spirits at moonrise.

"I saw something that looked like a giant, vast manta ray, lying flat on the ground. I stopped driving but we were still being pulled by this being. I thought the truck was still moving and then when I got a little farther I realized I was in a full-blown vision. I was inside of his be-ing. He looked like the manta ray being and he was moving, like swimming in the water, but there was no water there. Every once in a while he would flap his long wings. We traveled whatever distance it is from where I live now toward the place called La Posta, which is south of Durango, but there were no mountains, it was just flat so I knew we were in a non-ordinary landscape. Then he took me, he turned around from Durango area and then he came and brought me back.

"What I found out is that there is no disease actually—it is all clean. The guy with all the teeth ate up all the sickness and there wasn't any more sickness covering the surface of the earth."

Joseph explains that the medicine wheel, itself, is not special in anyway. It is not a thing of power in and of itself, rather it is a doorway or gateway to the Ancients. *"Ancient wisdom is the healer, not necessarily your practice or physical objects,"* Joseph explains. *"All of your ancestors down through all of the centuries are the ones who let you through the gateway into non-ordinary reality. The Ancients and the helpers live in non-ordinary reality and they have jobs that need to get done, so they only work with those shamans who are reliable."*

CROW MEDICINE: *JULY 25, 2016*

One morning in July of 2016 I was getting out of the shower when there was a loud "pop" and the power went out. Transformer blew, I immediately thought. Then a racket started, many crows started cawing and sounding very distressed. I peered out the window and saw a black shape on the ground. I quickly grabbed a tea towel and ran across the street. There must have been 20 crows all gathered around cawing like mad. I looked down at their brother lying inert on the ground. I could smell singed feathers and I could see the crow had been flash burnt by the transformer. I gently picked up his fluffy bulk and saw that bright red blood was pooling on the ground near his head. I re-positioned him in the towel and held him up so that his brothers and sisters could see and they instantly calmed down. I walked into the backyard and gently placed him on the ground. There were a couple of crows in the backyard cawing, too, but they calmed down and flew off after a couple minutes as I grabbed the shovel and looked for rocks to place on his grave.

I found a spot in the Northeast corner of the yard, dug a grave, and gently placed the crow in with some flowers. I said a few words about how beautiful he was and how much I love hearing the crow family and seeing them always about, always curious and always alert and seeking. I found some nice stones and an amethyst I had in the house and completed the burial, washed up and went to work. I was a little shaken by the whole thing and disturbed by the scent and image of the electrocuted crow.

That night I had a dream. I was awake in the dream, but in bed (where I was actually laying) the shade was down and the window open. I sensed some presence outside the window and I was scared. The dream progressed some and then came back to this feeling of something being outside the window again and my fear. I thought I would yell and scare it off, but all that came out of my mouth was a sound like "*awwwwwwwwwwwwwwww*." At that point Mary Pat woke me up from the dream and said that I was screaming in my sleep.

I thought about the dream the next day. It was obviously about the crow being outside the window. I wondered why I would be afraid of the crow. Maybe because it was on the other side of the shade and I could sense it but not see it. I thought I would try to shift my attitude toward my fear in a classic Jungian way. Instead of running from my fear, I would go toward it. This often transforms the fear into something else.

THE DREAM OF THE FRIENDLY CROW: 7/26/16

The following night after my dream of screaming out an "aww" sound I had another dream. (As I write this, at a café, I hear a crow cawing, out of my direct line of vision). In this dream I was in the backyard and I was with a friendly crow. He was sitting on my shoulder for a while. Then he flew off and I wondered if we kept his wings clipped or if he could fly away. He flew a little ways, but then went to the ground and didn't look so well. I picked him up and saw that he had tiny little spots of blood coming out on his face and head. I started to worry about him. I pulled him close against my chest, over my heart, and I felt his fluffy bulk of feathers and being. He died, but I felt him pass into my heart and throughout the

CROW FLYING THROUGH DARK MATTER

night I could feel/see him spreading his wings in my heart, open heart, open flight.

INITIATION AND LIMINAL BEINGS

Anthropologist Victor Turner wrote about the process of initiation. Turner described initiation as having three stages: "separation, margin (or *limen*, signifying "threshold" in Latin), and aggregation." During the middle, "liminal" phase, the person's characteristics and roles are

> necessarily ambiguous, since this condition and these persons elude or slip through the network of classifications that normally locate states and positions in cultural space. Liminal entities are neither here nor there; they are betwixt and between the positions assigned and arrayed by law, custom, convention, and ceremonial.[7]

7 Victor Turner, *The Ritual Process: Structure and Anti-Structure*, 94-95. Turner expanded upon the earlier work of Arnold van Gennep's *rites de passage*. The concept of initiation was also later crucial to Joseph Campbell's development of the concept of the hero's journey. The hero's journey is another term for initiation.

The work of shamans, visionaries, and mystics is crossing thresholds. They become liminal beings—a being that can cross thresholds and live in more than one world. This is necessarily an ambivalent role to be in, because one can be rejected by both worlds, however a liminal being is also a healer and a hero, bringing back *mana* and *medicine* from non-ordinary reality. To consciously embrace being a liminal being is to be in a state of semi-homelessness and to have a sense of impermanence. This is another reason why Joseph Rael says, "We don't exist," because a liminal being is continually being unmade and remade.

ANIMALS AS LIMINAL BEINGS

Joseph taught me that when you go into the medicine wheel various kinds of spirit guides and helpers will appear. He has also taught me to pay attention to animals as they are frequently teaching us things if we listen to them. Although I live in the city, I am surrounded by animals. Every time I see a crow I say, "Hello beautiful crow!" Over time, I have befriended a pair of crows I call Krishna and Yashoda.[8] Krishna is *cawing* at me right now as I write this, watching me from outside the window. I feed this pair nuts in the morning when I am eating my breakfast. Animals also appear in our dreams, so no matter where we live animals are there to teach and guide us.

SAINT FRANCIS AND THE ANIMALS

Saint Francis of Assisi (1181–1226) was a nature mystic who saw the world as a place of divine revelation. He gave sermons to little birds, talked with a wolf, and spent time meditating in caves. St. Francis was friends with St. Clare. Francis called Clare, "Sister Moon," and Clare called Francis, "Brother Sun." These names sound more Native American than those of medieval Catholic saints. They bring us into relationship, through divine humanity into relationship with the cosmos and the earth. By "divine humanity," we mean humanity when it is in its proper relationship to the spiritual, which means it is also in proper relationship to the natural world. Francis' spirituality resonates with the nature-based spirituality of many

8 I gave them these names after I read that not only can *kṛṣṇa* mean "dark" (as Lord Krishna's skin was dark blue) but can also mean "crow." When *Krishna* was a baby, he was raised by Yashoda. One time she saw Krishna playing on the ground and she thought he had eaten some mud and prised his mouth open. She was spellbound when she saw the entire universe of stars and suns and galaxies in his mouth.

OF MANY WINDOWS IN THE DREAM TIME OF MOTHER EARTH

American Indian and other indigenous peoples. For Saint Francis, nature was not something "other." When he gave sermons to little birds in the field, we could say that he was practicing *Little Bird Medicine*. Brother Sun and Sister Moon embarked on the holy work of Francis' vision of restoring the neglected churches of the region.

Santa Fe is home to the Saint Francis of Assisi Cathedral and it is also where Joseph went to the Santa Fe Indian School. I walked around the Cathedral in August of 2015 after attending Picuris Feast Day with Joseph. There are two statues there. Approaching the church, the first statue that is visible is of Kateri Tekakwitha, the first Native American saint. It is fitting that at a cathedral dedicated to Saint Francis, a name that can be masculine or feminine, there is a prominent statue of a Native American woman. The statue of St. Francis is tucked away in near some bushes and he has bird wings instead of arms. This shows his role as a liminal being and guide. Human/animal hybrids are liminal beings that have wisdom to teach, like Chiron, the centaur, who taught Asclepius how to be a healer.

"WE NEED TO PUT SOMETHING IN THE BOOK ABOUT POPE FRANCIS"

One day I received a voice message from Joseph, "*We need to put something in the book about Pope Francis. I am sending you a book.*" A few days later *Pope Francis and the New Vatican*, arrived. Joseph had written some comments in pencil and had underlined a few passages. Here are the passages that Joseph underlined:

> [H]e is full of surprises—of which we are likely to see more.
>
> Together . . . we [the author and photographer] have sought to capture a remarkable moment in the history of human spirituality—one in which a single individual has used the simplest messages to alter a dominant world religion in a host of complicated ways.

This passage brings to mind Coyote or Raven, those characters from Native American story, tricksters who bring life and transform human society by bringing in new possibilities. Joseph's visions have moved him into a similar role of transforming human spirituality and bringing peace to the world. On page 21, Joseph wrote, "David—I took the Sun-Moon Dance to where Saint Francis use to walk, high up above the village of Assisi, Italy, some years ago. My Foster Mother, Lucia Martinez on her altar had a statue of Saint Francis." Joseph underlined one more passage that highlights the trickster nature of Pope Francis. "No one saw him coming; perhaps even those cardinals who voted for him did not know what they were getting."[9]

---

9 Robert Draper, photos by Dave Yoder, *Pope Francis and the New Vatican*, 17, 22.

Cultural Anthropologist, Father Gerald Arbuckle's book on Pope Francis, *The Francis Factor and the People of God*, frames Pope Francis' popularity as a *refounder*, a person who revitalizes an institution. As the first Latin American pope, he is an outsider to centuries of Eurocentric focus. Pope Francis is a liminal being as he is concerned with the poor and Mother Earth and he is trying to make room for the excluded within the "home" of the Church. He calls for social justice, care of the poor, and tolerance and acceptance of diversity and his vision is not based on fear and rejection of others, but on a focus of what is good and divine in everyone. Arbuckle quotes Pope Francis:

> God is in every person's life. Even if the life of a person has been a disaster. . . . You must try to seek God in every human life. Although the life of a person is a land full of thorns and weeds, there is always a space in which the good seeds can grow. You have to trust God.

With Pope Francis, we have a returning to the roots of the Church, a move from institutions to people and an embracing of the world rather than a retreat from it. This is what Arbuckle calls "refounding." He writes that,

> Pope Francis by his actions and words is breaking through years of scandals, cultural trauma, and impasse, allowing the people of God to mourn openly and to hope for a newness based on the mythology of Vatican II. As a ritual leader of mourning he is *refounding* the church, seeking to draw others to join him in this collaborative process."[10]

Arbuckle views Pope Francis as a "gospel comedian" which at first is a bit shocking and hard to know what he means. However, he describes the comedian as someone who encourages us to not take ourselves too seriously, too rigidly and who teaches us that the "social status quo is not set in concrete." Arbuckle mentions Charlie Chaplin as a comedian. Chaplin's life and politics come across in the themes of some of his movies—making fun of the overly serious and wealthy, championing the common people and making fun of dictators. Arbuckle is invoking the role of the trickster, like Coyote or Raven, found in indigenous cultures,

---

10 Gerald Arbuckle, *The Francis Factor and the People of God*, 184, 197-198. Arbuckle describes the promise of Vatican II as "the promise of a revitalized liturgy, a hope of shared leadership, and a recovery of social justice obligations," (164). Vatican II called for a "continual reformation," of the Church "of which she is always in need . . . as . . . a human institution here on earth," (193).

including the Picuris. The *Ko-sas* in Picuris rituals are "clowns" painted in black and white stripes.[11] These stripes show us our black and white thinking as they transgress boundaries and poke fun at people, making it difficult to take ourselves too seriously. Tricksters and clowns can help us separate out the wheat from the chaff. In showing us what not to take too seriously (our egos) they allow us to see the things that are truly worthy of respect. When Joseph invited me out to the Picuris Pueblo feast day, one of the most striking things at the feast day was when I saw an elder *Ko-sa* mimicking an elder dancer who was the embodiment of presence and placement. As the *Ko-sa* began to fall into step with the elder dancer the elder's living spirituality was amplified rather than reduced. The *Ko-sa* "became" the elder and it was a timeless moment and I had a strong sense of *déjà vu* which I cannot explain. Later, this elder *Ko-sa* was the one who was able to climb the tall pole and release the abundance stored there for the next year. This feast day celebration brings down from the up above the divine abundance that needs to be renewed every year.

Arbuckle describes comedians as "liminal people, projecting in their behavior society's fundamental paradoxes such as hope and despair, order and disorder." A liminal being is someone who is on the threshold of two worlds, such as the sacred and the profane. They remind us of the boundary between the mundane and the spiritual realms, while they may serve as guardians or gatekeepers, they can also serve as emissaries or guides. A criticism of the Catholic Church is that its officials have taken on too much of the guardian aspect, limiting peoples' access to God and their right to have inner spiritual experiences. Francis' role as a liminal being seems to be restoring the connections between the mundane and the spiritual for everyone. Arbuckle writes that, "Comedians invite their audiences to critique orderly structures and status in society in search of deeper values and truths about life. Good comedians mock on behalf of humanity the behavior of those who unduly assert authority, who overly insist on rules and obedience to traditions."[12]

Pope Francis made a powerful statement in taking on the name of St. Francis, the founder of the Franciscans, whose mystical vision inspired

---

11 Joseph often goes by sound more than spelling. This is the spelling he told me at the time. When I ask him how to spell something he will ask me to spell it "because you are good at that." I have also seen alternative spellings of *Kossa* and *Koshare*. This particular sound/spelling of *Ko-sa*, Joseph compared to the Spanish, *cosa*, which means "thing."

12 Ibid., 191–92.

him to commune with nature, to take a vow of poverty, and to work to rebuild both the physical and spiritual churches which had fallen into disrepair.

AN INTERESTING MISUNDERSTANDING

This story represents the kind of hope and reform that Pope Francis has unleashed. Writer Sharon Abercrombie wonders, "if perhaps the journalistic kurfuffle was one of those quirky events created by Holy Spirit, the divine trickster."[13]

What happened was that there was confusion of a statement by Pope Paul VI when he was comforting a boy whose dog had died with a statement by Pope Francis. The mistakes are perhaps more important than the facts in this story. Francis of Assisi, the saint from whom Pope Francis takes his name, is the patron saint of animals and is often depicted surrounded by them. Pope Francis came onto the scene as a pope of the people—reclaiming the inherent similarity within the words, "pope" and "people." The original stories read that Pope Francis stated that animals have souls, with headlines such as, "Pope Francis says all dogs can go to heaven." Later the stories were rescinded once the mistaken reference between popes was sorted out. The story took hold because it was so believable, the world believed that this is the type of reform that Pope Francis might envision.

I went through the roller-coaster that perhaps many animal lovers did. It meant even more to me, raised Catholic, as I trace back my break with Catholicism to a comment by a Sunday school teacher that animals do not have souls. This contradicted my lived experience with the animals in my life, including my best friend, Tiggy, a rescued tomcat who slept curled around my head every night. As I researched more into the story on the coming days, I was profoundly disappointed that Pope Francis did not actually say that animals have souls.

Here is what journalist Jeff Schweitzer wrote about what Pope Francis did say after all the press confusion:

> Pope Francis has opened the Pearly Gates to Blue Heelers. The Pope said that "all creatures . . . will be vested with the joy and love of God, without limits." He quoted Pope Paul VI saying that "Paradise is open to all creatures." However, little Rover should not yet get too excited

---

13 Sharon Abercrombie, "A light in the darkness of the botched pope-animal story," *National Catholic Reporter*, December 16, 2014.

> about a supply of perpetual dog treats and slow postal workers in shorts. There seems to be some papal problems with this pronouncement, some disagreements among the papal powers. Previous church leaders, like Pope Benedict, formally denied animal entry to heaven with the pronouncement that, "For other creatures, who are not called to eternity, death just means the end of existence on Earth." Benedict forever condemned his beloved cats to something less than eternal bliss. But Pope Paul VI before him implied otherwise, claiming that "one day we will see our animals in the eternity of Christ." God is sending a mixed signal to his primary spokesmen.[14]

In this telling of the story, we have Pope Paul VI on the side of animal souls, Pope Francis seems to lean that way too, saying, "all creatures . . . will be vested with the joy and love of God, without limits." Pope Benedict takes the opposing view that death for non-humans is simply "the end of existence." We can look at another instance of a similar debate. Matthew Fox, author of some 30 books on spirituality, including *The Coming of the Cosmic Christ* and *Creation Spirituality: Liberating Gifts for the Peoples of the Earth*, was excommunicated from the Dominican Order of the Catholic Church in 1993 by Cardinal Ratzinger. Prior to that, Cardinal Ratzinger put a gag order on Fox for a year, banning him from any public speaking or writing. However, Fox continued to preach his message against the concept of "original sin" with its dualism and separation from our bodies and the earth and for the concept of "original blessing," which views our physical lives and the earth as gifts from God. Aligning himself with feminists, greens, the poor, and indigenous peoples, Fox spoke for an inclusive spirituality rather than a hierarchical framework of the forbidden. After Fox was excommunicated from the Catholic Church, he was accepted into the Episcopal Church as a priest. Cardinal Ratzinger went on to become Pope Benedict XVI and made his statement about animals not having souls.

The question of whether or not animals have souls is a larger theological question beyond our love of pets. It is really about the possible redemption of the Earth. The dualism that humans have souls and the rest of the Earth is soulless has profound implications for the way we humans treat animals, plants, the air, the soil, the water—the very way we treat Mother Earth. In Native American traditions, the Earth is our Mother. In Western

14 Schweitzer, Jeff. "Soul Search: Why Pope Francis Is Barking Up the Wrong Tree." *The Huffington Post*, 12/17/14.

Technological society, the earth is a resource for goods and profits. Pope Francis has come in as the champion of the downtrodden and the question is how far he will go?

THE JUNGLE BOOK: ANIMALS AS TEACHERS

Joseph tells me that children's stories are important because they are a place where ancient wisdom is passed on to the next generation. I recently came across my copy of Rudyard Kipling's *The Jungle Book*, given to me by my maternal grandfather, John Hudson Guill, III, in 1971, when I was four years old. Grandpa Guill gave me a number of books on Native Americans and the natural history of North America. *The Jungle Book's* primary character is Mowgli, a boy who is raised by the animals and comes to know their world, then has to go back to the human world for some time, then back to the animal world to live with the wolves. At the story's end it says he eventually married and lived with humans again, but "that is a story for grownups."

Mowgli is a liminal being—human, but raised by animals. He can be animal-like and adopt their ways, but he is still a human being. In this way he is a bit of a shaman, a liminal being who lives in two different worlds. Some of my favorite stories in the book, however, were about the animals themselves. Kotick the white seal who is an outcast (liminal being) because of his odd coloration, but who leads the seals to safety to a hidden island, away from the predatory humans harvesting seals for their fur. I had a furry seal toy when I was a child. In fact I still have him, a little white seal named Oli, who sits on top of some books on my bookshelf. The other story I particularly related to was Rikki-Tikki-Tavi, the mongoose who saves his human family from a pair of cobras.

These stories opened my imagination to the liminal world of human-animal and animal-human. Children seem to naturally like stories about animals who are people-like and people who can talk to animals and live with them. These children's stories provide a linkage with the natural world that many humans lose as they become "grownups." Joseph has shared a number of Tiwa Children's Stories with me. He believes that they contain a hidden template, secret knowledge, below the surface of the children's tales. Animals are often teachers in indigenous stories.

BEING A BEAST

Apart from living with a wolf pack and apprenticing to a bear and panther like Mowgli, we can still learn from animals, even though we have largely forgotten our animal nature. Author Charles Foster reminds us how to reconnect to animals as well as our own animal nature in his book *Being a Beast: Adventures Across the Species Divide*. He writes "I want to know what it is like to be a wild thing," and he describes his book as "a sort of literary shamanism." He, himself, is a liminal being because he has long sought to experience what it is like to be an animal. He spent quite a while trying to live as animals do, he made a burrow and lived underground like a badger, jumped in the cold water like an otter, hunted like a fox and foraged like a deer, and ran around like a swift. His premise is that to understand an animal you have to live like one, even if that means crawling around on your hands and knees, sleeping underground and eating worms. He writes that the "ability to appreciate the interconnectedness of things" requires a well-developed theory of mind, "the ability to think oneself into another's position." "Shamanic transformation is the natural corollary of highly developed theory of mind," he concludes.[15]

Foster goes to great lengths to commune with animals and to take on their perspectives and he naturally continues to look at his experiment through the lens of a shaman making a shamanic, liminal journey. He says the "shamanic world is a gift culture: the gift required is the only one you can give—yourself."[16]

Foster's experiment—we could call it an initiation—is not a new-age kind of thing. He is very solid and grounded, skeptical of the new agers, and yet drawn to something about the shamanic journey of transcending the boundaries of our human consciousness to partake in the consciousness of wild animals. Despite the dominant scientific objectivist perspective that animals are irrevocably "other," he believes that it is possible to enter into animal consciousness.

One of my personal favorite arguments for human-animal interspecies communion comes from the Taoist sage, Chuang Tzu:

> Chuang Tzu and Hui Tzu were strolling along the dam of the Hao River when Chuang Tzu said, "See how the minnows come out and dart around where they please! That's what fish really enjoy!"

15 Charles Foster, *Being a Beast: Adventures Across the Species Divide*, 18.

16 Ibid., 101.

> Hui Tzu said, "You're not a fish—how do you know what fish enjoy?"
>
> Chuang Tzu said, "You're not I, so how do you know I don't know what fish enjoy?"
>
> Hui Tzu said, "I'm not you, so I certainly don't know what you know. On the other hand, you're certainly not a fish—so that still proves you don't know what fish enjoy!"
>
> Chuang Tzu said, "Let's go back to your original question, please. You asked me *how* I know what fish enjoy—so you already knew I knew it when you asked the question. I know it by standing here beside the Hao."[17]

Foster's comedio-educatio-shamanic exploits and initiations have a bit of a trickster feel about them. He is purposefully putting himself in absurd situations that are also sacred. His work is topical for *Becoming Medicine* because he is crossing the boundaries between self and "other," between human and animal. In our current cultural climate of seeing anyone or anything slightly different than ourselves as "other," whether from a "politically correct" sense of empathy as "aggressive" or a populist perspective of keeping out the "bad hombres," the world is going overboard in emphasizing differences and the *impossibility* of understanding people from other cultures. There is also a similar trend against "anthropomorphizing" animals. Foster lists 20 reasons why someone might think that he or she could have some sense of feeling for an animal, in this case he is talking about his attempts at *becoming a swift*. After listing some rationales for cross-species affiliation he writes the following, which echoes the almost 2,500 year old words of Chuang Tzu:

> These are facts about swifts because they are facts about the world, and swifts are part of the world, as I am. The facts indicate that no qualification other than occupancy of a shared world is necessary for me to write about swifts. That is a great relief, because swifts are the ultimate other. I can write about them only because I'm other too, or (depending on my mood) because nothing is other.[18]

Many animals are liminal in regard to different realms of air, land, earth, and water. Foxes and badgers walk on the earth, but live in holes below the earth. Eagles and birds are mostly of the air, but sometimes they dive into the water. Eagles do this sometimes, birds like kingfishers and gannets

17 *Chuang Tzu: Basic Writings*, trans. Burton Watson, 110.

18 Foster, 188.

even more so. Muriwai Beach in New Zealand is one of my favorite places and has a gannet colony where the birds roost high up on cliffs and then fly out to sea, diving down into the water to catch fish. The way to find whales is to look for gannets, because they are often feeding in the same place. Geese were considered shamanic totem animals in many cultures because they flew in the heavens, walked on the land, and swam in the water. Nuthatches and woodpeckers fly, but they also scroll up and down tree trunks.

Animals are also liminal in the sense that they are tricksters. Coyote and Raven feature in many Native American tales were they steal fire or bring the sun closer to the Earth so that everyone benefits. While they might steal something from you, or look for a lazy way out of work, they also are the bringers of culture. Lewis Hyde, writing about how the trickster is the creator of culture, tells us that trickster is always a "boundary-crosser," and always on the road or near the doorway (true liminal beings), but that the road "that trickster travels is a spirit road as well as a road in fact. He is the adept who can move between heaven and earth, and between the living and the dead."[19]

Joseph is a bit of a trickster figure, often serious, but often joking. A shaman is often a trickster and a liminal being. He or she can communicate or empathize with animals and sometimes relates more with animals than to people. I know for myself, I had a period of time where my best friend was my cat and I grew up surrounded by cats, dogs, birds, fish, newts, and snakes. Joseph has a special affinity for badgers and as a kid he took care of cats and he jokes that now the pumas are taking care of him because they left a deer carcass at his doorstep. Deer are also important to Joseph and stories about deer appear throughout this book and our last.

JOSEPH AND THE PUMAS

Joseph has told me about his relationship with pumas. He was 17 years old and had just graduated from Peñasco High School and had moved back to the Southern Ute reservation. One day he walked down to the river on the land that he would eventually become the caretaker of.

"I felt like something was pulling me toward the stream and I went down there and I just washed myself, blessed myself with the water, but I knew that this place belonged to me and I was turning around and I saw at least five or

19 Lewis Hyde, *Trickster Makes this World: Mischief, Myth, and Art*, 7, 6.

PUMA GIVER OF THE VISIONARY LIFE TO THE PEOPLE OF MOTHER EARTH

six puma tracks, lion tracks and some had crossed the river, right where I was drinking water and maybe that was the vibration that was I picking up of the lions and I didn't know that I was going to have a relationship with them.

"Picuris Pueblo seemed so far away then, because now I was in Colorado and so I noticed that right there at the river, you remember where we did the vision quest that night with the tree spirits? Right there. There were tracks coming from the other side but they were going the other direction and so there were like two separate little pathways. It was an east-west crossing of the river and I had just drank from the energy of the tracks that were the lion's. So somehow

that seemed like a different vibration, but I saw the cat tracks. I wanted to know where are these lions from, so later I went to the top of the hill and I saw that if you go far enough in that direction, you will get to the mountains where the lions were that I had left a deer for. So here I got the sense that I was dealing with a family of lions, not lions in general, but the Puma; there was a family."

Joseph tells me how he realized that if you followed the line of these tracks on the Southern Ute reservation, they led back to Picuris Pueblo and to where he left a deer on Wooden Cross Mountain for the pumas. He had been hunting with another man and they had taken different paths. Joseph saw a deer and shot it, but when he went up to it to give it the ceremonial feeding of corn meal, he heard a voice speak into his ear:

"'Don't touch the deer. If you want to feed it, feed it through the ears.' And I knew what to do so I got my little bag of cornmeal and tobacco and I looked over and I just put into the ear of the deer. And it said 'Don't touch it,' and I didn't answer. I just said ok. And then I started walking down the hill and it was still early and we weren't supposed to meet down there until maybe 5:00 in the afternoon and it was going to be maybe 12:00. And so I sat for the longest time there on a log and then just prayed and knew that I was leaving a deer there, but I knew that some being, a spiritual being had talked to me."

Joseph later learned that some men from an older generation had taken a puma kill of a deer in the cold winter and, although he did not know it at the time, when he left the deer he was told not to touch, he was repaying the pumas for his ancestors taking their deer. In this sense, it was a full circle moment when Joseph was paying the debts of his ancestors and he was also establishing a relationship with the pumas, who decades later left a deer for him in front of his house.

There is another part to this story. A man Joseph had just met in Tulsa, Oklahoma, brought him a puma paw that someone had shot at Wooden Cross Mountain and the man gave it to Joseph, making another full circle in Joseph's life around the pumas and deer and Josephs. Joseph also saw a mountain lion once on the land he stewards and instead of running away it made a low kind of submissive growl and looked at him shyly for a few moments and then turned and left. Joseph told me, "*I had an intuition, and I turned around and looked in the direction of Picuris, and I saw Picuris and I saw a white light.*"

Joseph had been telling me about ceremony before this story. He was saying that ceremony always has three parts, two parts that seem separate and then a third part that connects them all together and makes them realize they are one. I asked Joseph if the pumas were the ceremony that helped him connect his past life at Picuris to his present life at the Southern Ute land. He said, "*Yes, they are an integral part.*"

A BOY RAISED BY A SCHNAUZER PACK

I grew up surrounded by animals. My mom and dad grew up in town, but when they got married they rented a farm house up on a hill, out on a gravel road in the country. My mom said, "There was no one to tell us we couldn't have something," so they collected a number of animals. We had a boa constrictor named Billy whom I was always letting out of his cage and my mom worried he would crawl through the holes in the old farmhouse walls and live on mice and rats. She would ask me, "David, where is the snake?" I would say, "I don't know." One time she found him half-way in the wall and she had to apply gentle, steady pressure pulling him until he would relax to try to move forward (because snakes have to relax their muscles before they can move forward). We had geese, a horse, a pony, turtles, fish, newts, birds, cats and lots and lots of dogs because my mom raised miniature schnauzers.

Sometimes I joke that I was raised by miniature schnauzers. In fact, my godmother gave us our first schnauzer as a gift for me. My best friend was a cat, Tiggy, a stray that I snuck in through the windows at night when my dad said we could not have a fourth cat. He changed his mind when my mom showed him Tiggy sleeping with his arms around my neck one night when I forgot to put him back outside. My first work as a psychotherapist can be traced back to when I was a kid and would watch a new litter of puppies for the one that was the most shy and timid. I would give that puppy special attention and watch as the little pup's personality blossomed.

Our family has always been keenly aware of animals, both domestic and wild. We would stop to identify birds. My mom would make us stop the car when she saw something by the side of the road, for instance when she saw a dead porcupine, or when she put a very large snapping turtle in the back of the station wagon that she worried would get hit by a car and cause an accident. My sister and I thought this was a bit much as the turtle hissed and snapped at us! One time my mom brought our pony, Sparky, in the house. She said she thought he was so tame that she could bring him in and he would be ok. That is how I grew up, seeing my mom bring a pony in the house and not really being all that surprised! We lived with the animals and the animals lived with us.

My dad worked as a farrier for a while and I would help him at some of the jobs, handing him tools.[20] When it came to adding new animals to the house, he would often be the voice of reason and restraint, but generally went along with things after a while. We had a snake with a bent tail we rescued and injured grackle with one eye. (We called him Slingshot figuring he might have gotten hit by a rock from a slingshot.) My dad would roll his eyes when my mom would pay some kids $5 for a frog with a broken leg so she could take it to the veterinarian and get it set and splinted. Animals and injuries and healing were part of my growing up.

In our last book I told of how a nuthatch landed on my head, I brushed it off thinking it was a bug or a branch, it flew up to a branch, looked at me, and flew right back and landed on my head again. I took that as a sign and feel an affinity for nuthatches now. Ted Andrews writes of nuthatches that they are one of the few birds who descend down a tree head first. "This reflects the need to learn to bring down the Tree of Life the wisdom and apply it to the world . . . learning to manifest the spiritual within the physical."[21] That is what we are doing in this book.

I have also been quite fond of kingfishers. When I was in New Zealand, our rehabilitation team was called the *Kōtare* Team. This is the Māori word for kingfisher. Kingfishers live throughout the world. I recently saw beautiful kingfishers in Fiji, and I have seen Australian kookaburras, the largest of the family kingfishers. The *kōtare* is also called the "Sacred Kingfisher," as it was a holy bird for the Polynesian peoples who thought that it could calm the ocean waves.[22] I used to see the sacred *kōtare* frequently when I walked along Tamaki Drive in Auckland. Ted Andrews says of the kingfisher that it often "requires that you dive headlong into some activity, but it usually proves to be beneficial."[23] That accurately describes the experience of working with Joseph!

---

20 My father, Thomas Raymond Kopacz, is a study in initiation and transformation. He wanted to be a pilot when he was in high school, but a small-minded guidance counselor told him he could never be a pilot as he wore glasses, so instead he became a carpenter, then a farrier. He built our house. He started taking flying lessons. He got a job with the FAA as a weather briefer, then a job managing an airport at a college. From there he found his first full-time flying job. He worked a number of different flying jobs and eventually worked his way up to being the head pilot for DeKalb Genetics.

21 Ted Andrews, *Animal Speak*, 169.

22 "Sacred Kingfisher," *Wikipedia*.

23 Andrews, 161–62.

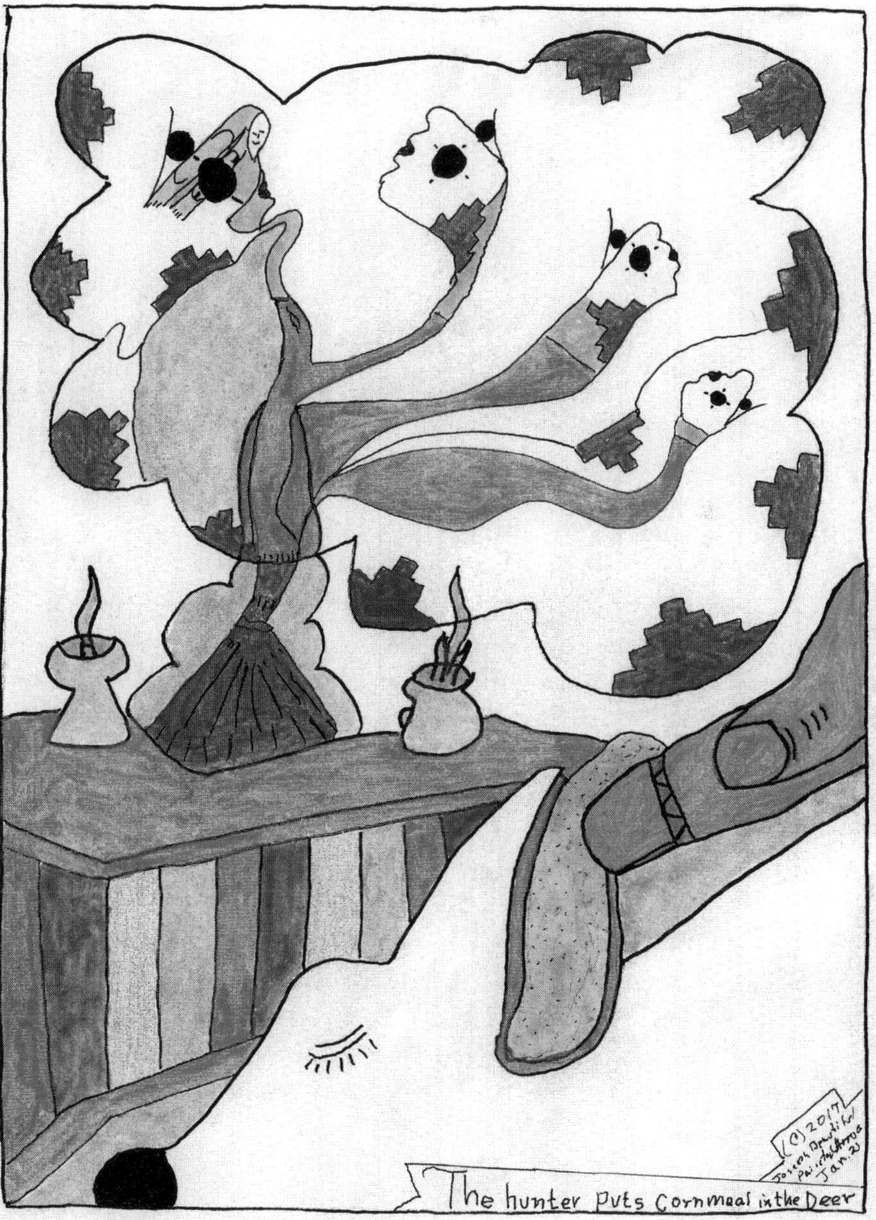

©2019 JOSEPH RAEL (BEAUTIFUL PAINTED ARROW)

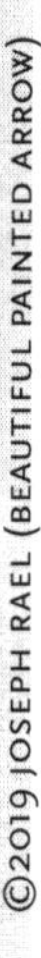

THE HUNTER PUTS CORNMEAL IN THE DEER

A SURPRISING INITIATION

I took a solo backpacking trip, in the late '90s, to walk up Black Elk Peak in South Dakota, the site of Black Elk's formative vision. I had hoped for some kind of spiritual experience, but everything seemed pretty ordinary. The night after I climbed the peak, I got up in what I thought was early morning to go to the bathroom outside the tent. I felt, more than saw, a tremendous pounding of the ground and then saw something large bound away. A deer had bedded down for the night right outside the door of my tent. I could see the outline of where it had flattened down the grass. We both scared each other terribly. It took me a while to figure out what was the pounding of the deer's hooves and the pounding of my heart. I looked up in the sky and it was the middle of the night, but it was brilliantly lit with the moon and the Milky Way. It was definitely an experience where I felt knocked out of this reality. After I no longer felt my heart pounding in my ears, I was a bit disappointed. I had hoped for a more dramatic encounter in this sort of vision quest I was doing. A deer seemed mundane, I would have preferred a wolf or puma. However, as I have worked with Joseph, I have come to appreciate the beauty and unusualness of a deer bedding down right next to me at night, separated by just a thin veil of the nylon tent. Ted Andrews writes that the deer "leads us back to the primal wisdom." "When deer show up in your life it is time to be gentle with yourself and others. A new innocence and freshness is about to be awakened or born. There is going to be a gentle, enticing lure of new adventures."[24] Here is what Joseph says about deer:

"Deer means peh ney. Peh *means straight forward.* Ney *means a space in front of, before creation was made. What that is saying is that if we as a people are going to have peace, we have to go to that space beyond, before creation where Peace was. I did the Deer Dance when I was younger and I think that added to my medicine. That is an important point. The last time we were working a book, my father came in a vision and gave me permission to go forward. Now with this work with the deer medicine, the earlier dances are supporting us to go forward. True Peace is that space before there was anything that could create un-peace.*

"A gathering place for deer is peh mesa, peh mesa.*"* Joseph goes over to a table and brings his hand down flat on it – *peh.* Then he drags it across the surface – *mesa. Peh mesa, peh mesa,* he repeats it several times, looking in my eyes to see if I hear it and understand it. Then he goes to the TV

---

24 Andrews, 263–64.

console – *peh mesa, peh mesa, peh mesa.* Then he goes to the bed spread and does it again – *peh mesa, peh mesa, peh mesa.* Then he says, *"Put that in the book—Joseph Rael made the sound of the deer on the table, then on the console, then on the bed and it was always the same sound and it means 'the power of true perception.'"*

We may not exist, but we are not alone. Joseph teaches us to watch and learn from the animal world around us, as well as to be open to receiving animal and spirit helpers in visionary reality. Animals guide us across thresholds and through liminal spaces. The Great Mystery is that we think we exist but we do not; we think we are alone and separate, but we are not; we are animals surrounded by animals who will teach us the "power of true perception" and will guide us back and forth between ordinary and non-ordinary reality.

MYSTICAL INTERCONNECTIONS

One of my initiations with Joseph has been an enhanced awareness of the mystical interconnections that I have found as I have chased down his leads and researched topics and authors. I have tried to include these different threads and nodes in this work to give you, the reader a sense of these "aha" moments. The Net of Indra is a Hindu concept in which the universe is a vast interconnected web and at the center of each intersecting strand is a gem and this gem reflects all the other gems around it. Reality is thus a great interconnected and reflecting woven web. Joseph often quotes Stephen Hawking, saying "We live in a reflective universe." Physicist David Bohm befriended J. Krishnamurti who met a young Joseph Campbell on a voyage across the Atlantic. I was working with Joseph Campbell's hero's journey when I read Kurt Wilt's book on Joseph Rael (whom I had read more than a decade earlier) and then Kurt introduced me to Joseph—seeing and understanding these interconnections is the initiation. It can all seem like distraction, but focus on the relationships that form when you are on a secret journey, when you are seeking initiation. There is a saying that "the teacher appears when the student is ready." The people and the books that come into your life are pointing to a hidden order of things that exists below the surface details. Ancient wisdom is a culture of relationships, but we often cannot see it because the contemporary world is a culture of information and we only see details without seeing how these details are deeply interconnected.

DARK MATTER DEER MEDICINE

In many traditional settings a teacher might send a student off into the wilderness, into a cave, into the darkness to seek for the unity within the Self. In my work with Joseph, he sends me down a seemingly endless series of rabbit holes, or maybe fox holes:

> *"Put something in the book about Pope Francis, my foster mother had a statue of St. Francis of Assisi and I did a dance there once.*
>
> *"We'll need to put something in the book about ETs, at Picuris they often spoke about the extraterrestrials visiting and some of the people disappeared, and were never seen again, I think maybe they went with the ETs . . .*
>
> *"Here is an article on transposons in DNA, they jump around like we used to jump around doing the Deer Dance—there is something there we should put in the book . . .*
>
> *"I'm reading this book by Lisa Randall called* Dark Matter and the Dinosaurs, *I think you should get a copy of this book and we can put something in our book about dark matter; maybe we should try to talk to her, too . . .*
>
> *"Ponce de León was looking for the fountain of youth in* La Florida, *I think we should have something about that in the book . . .*
>
> *"You should call the University of Wisconsin Library, not the undergraduate, but the graduate library and ask for a copy of the* Forty-Third Annual Report of the Bureau of Ethnology, 1925–1926 *because the Picuris Children's Stories are in there by John P. Harrington and Helen H. Roberts. I think that those Children's Stories are the metaphors of ancient secrets."*

Those are some rough paraphrases of some of the conversations, phone messages, and notes I have received from Joseph. I often feel like I am going in circles in chasing down these various, seemingly unrelated topics. I have learned to have some faith in the process, though, and that as I follow the leads and trails, interconnections emerge. Researching this book has taken me in many directions and has at times been exhilarating fun, an excuse to buy *a lot* of books, and at times been incredibly frustrating as I wonder why in the world I am researching some of these things. With dark matter/dark energy I have chased down lots of references in physics and spirituality. Renée Weber leads me to David Bohm, David Bohm to F. David Peat who wrote a biography on Bohm as well as a book called *Blackfoot Physics*. Bohm and Peat lead me to a DVD called "The Language of Spirituality," which was part of a series of dialogues between physicists and Native American sages—as I watch this I hear a familiar voice and then see a young Beautiful Painted Arrow speaking. Joseph says, "Oh yeah, I met with some of those physicists in Albuquerque some years ago."

Father Bede Griffiths, who came to Shantivanam near the end of Abhishiktananda's life, has written about finding wisdom in the darkness in both the Christian and Hindu traditions. "In the Hindu temple, the inner sanctuary is always dark. . . . When you come to the inner sanctuary you come to the . . . inner center of your own being, and you encounter God in the darkness." He compares the teachings of Dionysius the Areopagite who "speaks of the divine darkness: You must go beyond all imagery, beyond your thoughts, into the divine darkness. That's where you meet God."[25] This seeking wisdom in darkness seems to lead us from the darkness of the cave or the inner temple into the darkness of dark matter and dark energy.

Another thread was when I found the book *The Mystic Heart: Discovering a Universal Spirituality in the World's Religions* by Wayne Teasdale. I come across the term *guhā*, the cave of the heart. This "place" of mystic oneness with God leads me to the life and writings of Abhishiktananda, a Benedictine monk who went to India and spent the rest of his life integrating Christianity and Hinduism. Abhishiktananda's successor at the ashram in India was Father Bede Griffiths who was interviewed by Renée Weber and who also was a mentor to Wayne Teasdale who was one of the members of the Parliament of World Religions in 1993 in Chicago, a few miles from where I was just starting residency. These interconnections could all be dismissed as the mind trying to find connections where there are none, but Joseph would say, "*Ahhhh, that means we are on to something. We are doing good work if these things are coming together like that.*"

THE PATH OF INITIATION

Our seeking takes us to the *guhā*, the cave of the heart, where we are initiated. There in the inner darkness something stirs—*Wah-Mah-Chi*, Breath-Matter-Movement is found there. This is the place of giving and receiving: we are given initiation and we receive initiation. The ordinary heart is always giving and receiving blood. The non-ordinary heart is always giving and receiving *Wah-Mah-Chi*. The heart is the organ of transformation and transformation is initiation into a new way of seeing,

25 Renée Weber, *Dialogues with Scientists and Sages*, 176–77.

into a new way of being. The heart is the medicine bag in which we are carrying the sacred objects of divinity back to ordinary reality.

MEDICINE WHEEL INITIATION

Let us circle back around to the medicine wheel initiation that Joseph taught me. As I was sitting in the center of the medicine wheel I remembered that Joseph said that I should first center, then shift to a perspective of watching myself outside of the medicine wheel. My back started hurting, an old injury. "Too much sitting on the plane ride over here," I thought. Then through visionary perspective I saw a rabbit hopping in from the west, the direction of the physical. (I had seen a little rabbit earlier as we were leaving offerings at the shrines.) The rabbit hopped up and started sniffing at my back. Then he started gnawing at the spot where the pain was. That freaked me out at first and I wondered if this should really be happening. Then I remembered something about incorporation of an animal spirit through eating it and also how many times shamans go through a ritual dismemberment as part of their initiation process, so I let it go and the pain started to abate a little bit. Then a larger animal came in, it seemed like a badger and it grew quite large and powerful. When it set in to gnawing on the spot it quickly ripped off all my flesh and I was looking at myself as a skeleton lying in the sun on the ground.

I started to feel my eyes rotating clockwise, half the rotation in light, half the rotation in darkness. It seemed like watching time speed up and my bones began to decay. They disappeared completely into the dust of the earth. The cycles of light and dark continued, then a sprout appeared, it slowly grew into a large cottonwood tree, gradually a limb would fall off here and there and gradually the tree decayed into dust and disappeared. Another sprout appeared and grew into a different shaped tree, maybe an oak. That tree too, decayed. I had a sense of what Joseph means when he says "we do not exist." Breath-Matter-Movement came and went with the cycling of light and darkness, like pulses of existence like fireworks building, peaking, and dissolving back into source. "I am the Source of All Origination," I heard in my mind. With my consciousness outside of my momentary form there seemed to be no separation between "me" and the universal process of coming into form and dissolving out of form—an experience of non-duality.

THIS BOOK AS INITIATION

> *I thank the Creator for this food and I invite all the Ancient Ones to this meal, the Ancient Ones who have made us who we are today, from our very beginnings in the first man, the namer who named all things. We are the light of the Ancient Ones shining forth into the present.*
>
> JOSEPH'S PRAYER BEFORE EATING

Writing this book is part of my initiation with Joseph. Initiation is a new state of being and a new sense of one's interrelationship and non-duality. Initiation is to realize that each of us is "the light of the Ancient Ones shining forth into the present." Initiation is entering into a living spirituality where there is no separation between mind and body or between spirit and matter. Initiation is not something you do once and are done with; rather it is an understanding that "we do not exist" and yet we are perpetually coming into being and being reborn every moment.

"Work is worship," taught Joseph's Grandfather. The work of this book has been a form of worship for me, a continual process of learning and a ceremony seeking to breathe the living spirit into the words on the page.

I recently took a trip to Australia, New Zealand, and Fiji (with stops in Hawaii and LA) and I brought along a hard copy draft of the book for editing. After I returned from my journey, I was talking with my friend and colleague Henri Roca one morning and he was asking me what land I am oriented to and that recharges me. I had the flash of insight of burying this draft of *Becoming Medicine* in my backyard! I had carried this physical object of the book from Seattle, to Hawaii, to Sydney Australia, Auckland New Zealand, to Fiji, LA, and then back to Seattle. Not only did I physically carry this draft of the book, I also carried sacred "objects" I have learned from Joseph in the medicine bag of my heart and acquired new sacred objects. After making this trip across the Pacific and back, down under and back, it seemed the obvious thing was to plant this book, which I had been carrying in my hands and in my heart, like a seed into the ground and to see what grows from it. That is exactly what I did. I dug a hole in the Northwest corner of the yard and buried the manuscript, and then covered it with *nah-meh-neh* and some rocks, and now I sit and meditate sitting on top of the book planted in the ground. If you can understand what I mean by this, then I have done my work in explaining initiation—if not I guess I have to go dig up the book and try harder!

Joseph says that the seed is *hchole* and that "*the seed is the circle . . . and the circle is the medicine wheel . . . and we are all one seed of the universe.*"

THE COMING OF THE MOON DANCE BY THE TREE SPIRITS: TREE SPIRIT INITIATION (9/10/15)

In the summer we would sometimes do a tree-spirit watching ceremony. We'd go up around the big trees, lie down on sleeping bags, and just watch. Pretty soon, we'd see the lights of the trees, almost like they were Christmas trees, and then we'd see the beings of the trees. They would manifest into some kind of humanoid appearance or something else.[26]

JOSEPH RAEL

I am back at the Magpie Newsstand Café in Durango, having a coffee and writing on my laptop. I just finished meeting with Joseph. We started the day at 4 AM to watch the moonrise and watch for tree spirits. Joseph instructed me to slit my eyes and not to blink. "*It is like a prolonged camera exposure,*" he said. The sky was magnificent with the Milky Way and stars everywhere. We sat in his truck and right away I started to see something.

It is kind of like imagination and letting the mind wander, but it was definitely a formed image and didn't feel like make believe. I saw a pale, glowing green figure, wispy—moving in a dance. I heard in my imagination the chant, "*Hey-Oh-Wey.*" The figure was very supple, swaying and bending as it danced. Gradually this elaborated more and I was surprised to feel the spirit rush toward me and "pull me on to the dance floor," so to speak. Part of the surprise was that I expected the tree spirits to be confined to the tree and not able to move about in the field in front of the trees. I felt this pull of the invitation to dance several times during our time, the pull and desire for me to join in the dancing, which I did through my imagination, not with my physical body. Joseph had said beforehand. "*They are as curious about us as we are about them.*"

The dance elaborated more, or I became gradually more aware of different elements of it. The "*Hey-Oh-Wey,*" chant was for linear movements forming a cross around the tree. These alternated periodically with a circular dance around the tree trunk with a chant of "*Lak-ah, Lak-ah, Lak-ah,*" then back to "*Hey-Oh-Wey, Hey-Oh-Wey, Hey-Oh-Wey.*"

The dance further elaborated as I suddenly became aware of the

26 *House*, 36. Mary Elizabeth Marlow also describes Joseph often teaching his students to see tree spirits. She writes, "Seeing the spirit of the tree is one way of recognizing that all life is an expression of the Divine," (*Walking with Cosmic Dancer Joseph Rael*, 19).

whole field of tree spirits dancing in unison. Sometimes they would go in opposite linear directions in synchrony. It was a beautiful image that made me sigh and relax into my seat. I became aware that the spirits were not just dancing on the surface of the ground, but they were also moving beneath the surface. At some point I felt pulled below the surface, and I got somewhat scared as I peered up to the light of the stars through the second darkness of the earth. I can't be certain of what I saw as I kind of came in and out of it a few times, trying to see the image, but also working with my fear of being underground.

The next elaboration of the dance was a sense of three-dimensionality as a globe formed, encircling the top of the branches down to the tips of the roots. These globes then moved in the alternating backwards/forwards, side-to-side linear movements (with the chant, "*Hey-Oh-Wey*") and the circular movements (with the chant, "*Lak-Ah, Lak-Ah, Lak-Ah*"). Then I had the image from above of the whole line of trees along the river moving, chanting the Coming of the Moon song. Then this moved even further up, viewing the globe with the light circle of the moon sweeping from east to west and all the trees from the northern tree line to the southern tree line all dancing the Coming of the Moon.

I remembered Joseph telling me how earthquakes and lighting balance the energy of the earth and I came to think of this as like how cracking your knuckles or a joint can feel good and relieve tension. I imagined that the trees dancing above and below the ground were balancing the earth and the sky and bringing them into harmony. Oh, this was one of the confusing things underground—sometimes it seemed like the whole tree, from the roots to the branches, was dancing, but it also shifted to a mirror image of the tree in the roots, upside down, dancing on the surface of the sky the same way the above-ground tree was dancing on the surface of the earth—a little disorienting. It reminded me of the scene in Richard Bach's *Illusions* where Richard walks on water and then almost drowns in the liquid earth.

As I squinted, sometimes I would see the stars seeming to move. Occasionally I think it was a plane or a satellite, but other times, when I opened my eyes it was the same star, stationary. Eventually the moon rose, just a sliver, crescent, accompanied by a bright, companion star off to the upper right. I noticed once the moon rose, the chant changed slightly, "*Hey-Oh-Wey-Oh*," with the same "*Lak-Ah, Lak-Ah, Lak-Ah*."

This may all sound quite fantastic, and it was amazing. I would say the difference between a vision and a hallucination is that if I opened my eyes all the way, the scene turned ordinary again (except for some weird pulsating of the background of the sky, kind of like a waving curtain—you can call this an optical illusion or a sensation of the flux of energy with the coming of the moon, like the *spanda*, the Divine Creative Pulsation). I could shift between what Joseph calls *ordinary* and *non-ordinary* reality at will. I was not out of touch with reality in that sense, as much as I was in touch with an additional reality. I was not on any substances, although I was a little tired.

After moonrise, Joseph said, "*Ok, now ask them a question, they are in agreement with what we are doing in the book and ask them now for advice on how to proceed.*" What grew in my imagination was a view of the interaction of the hard work of the roots growing into the ground and the joyousness of the branches, waving in carefree celebration. It seemed to me that the work of the roots was the intentional work with the book, all my years of background reading, the intentional focus of an hour of staring at that edge of the trees and the gradually lighting sky. The roots were the effort. The branches with leaves and flowers, were radiant and carefree in celebration. I had the sense that the harder I worked, the deeper the roots would go and the higher the branches would grow and the more they would flower and fruit. The above was the fruits of our labors and the below was our toil and labor. What this meant to me was to keep focused on the behind the scenes, the below the surface work, rather than on what it was that other people would be seeing. In a sense, this means the finished product is an after-thought or a by-product of *work is worship*. Remember, this book is not in your hands, it is growing in the *nah-meh-neh* in the backyard where I planted it.

CHAPTER 0

NA-YO TI-AY WE-AH (WE DO NOT EXIST)

These are the ancient mysteries. They were set up this way. In the end, the mystery is the infinite void and the mystery of the void is all of us remembering, because, truly speaking, we do not exist.

We exist and we do not exist. We are the infinite void; we are relativity; we are awareness; we are 'the people' which nature called, and 'the people' which means vibration.[1]

JOSEPH RAEL

Ah dah lah pi ah chi.

JOSEPH RAEL

NA-YO TI-AY WE-AH

This is a difficult concept to explain, and yet Joseph is constantly teaching me this. How can you explain something to someone when they do not exist?

I asked Joseph what the Tiwa word for "zero" is. "*Y-we-ah*" he said, "*the flesh does not exist.*" And then he said:

"Ok, hold it right there. We are not going to go to the East or the West, we are not going to go to the North of the South. We are not going to go up or down. Write this down, I'm going to say it to you in Spanish. La vida no mas un sueño es. *In English that means, 'Life is but a dream.' This life is not real. This life is a dream. We have talked ourselves into believing we are our ordinary reality bodies. We use these ordinary bodies to complain, to get in the car, to go around. In this life we are addictable. Use that word, I know I am making things up—we are addictable, we are addicted to this life of ordinary reality. We think we are going from 1 to 10, but we are already at ten* (tehn-ku-teh). *We were at number eight 10,000 years ago, but we are stuck because we are very addictable, we are stuck hanging on to life, we are hung up on the physical. Enticing as life is, it is a dream. Now, 99% of people are going to disagree with this. They are supposed to disagree because they decided*

1 *B&V*, 75, 77.

to go with teamwork. All these generations have been stuck because we are very addicted to the idea of being solid, physical ideas—this leads to the idea of property and property leads to conflict. So now we have property problems between the Indians and the United States.

"The point for me—I'm being told, 'Look you dummy, you are going around in circles, 10,000 years and you are still going around in circles.' Every now and then, I see ancestors looking down from above—I climb and climb and climb all the way up there. They tell me, look, your ancestors got hooked on the physical. That is why they are still here but they are not supposed to be, they were supposed to have moved on. The trees stayed here with us because they love us. Plants stayed and that is where we got our language from. The mermen were planted in the ocean and now they are stuck here with us, too. It is like that man in the Bible *who was stuck inside a whale—that's us! We got addicted to the sunrise and the sunset, to seeing rainbows, then we got stuck in going to school, going to college, learning things so that we could get rich. We got stuck getting rich, traveling all over the place.*

"We better start getting the message, La vida no mas un sueño es. *It is dream, dream, dream! We have invested in our landedness, we get money and we buy land. We get a little money and then we buy property and we are stuck with ownership.*

"This is what the Story Teller was telling us in the Picuris Children's stories. I heard these when I was eight or nine years old. [He speaks for a while in Tiwa]. 'Look up at the stars, they are like little bits of sand. That is where our ancestors are living. We are down here and we are supposed to be up there.' Then they put you in a square sand box and you play with the sand. Look at people's attraction to the ocean. They'll travel across the world to put their feet in the sand and the ocean. They are trying to realize that they are the grains of sand and the grains of sand are the stars and that we do not belong here.

"It's raining right now—finally I'm saying something worthwhile. This is more rain than I have seen in ten years. They're saying, 'Dang, David, you finally got it—you and that crazy Joseph Rael!'

"I was driving this morning and I saw a giant cloud and there was a rainbow up front on the left and then it went over and it was on the right, too. I was driving through it. The last time I saw that was driving back from Madison when I was in graduate school. It was around a place on the border of New Mexico and Texas called Texico. I drove through that rainbow and I thought, 'It's time to call David!'

"There's something going on here that I'm not even going to try to explain."

I totally resonate with this last statement and momentarily wonder if I can just say that in the book: "There's something going on here that I'm not even going to try to explain!" But then Joseph continues and he tells me I do need to explain some things.

"We're supposed to be here, you and I, for some dastardly reason. We need to put something in the book about what all this flooding in the world is about according to the mystic. Schools should be teaching this to kids. We need to understand that in non-ordinary reality we can leave these ordinary bodies behind. We can go out into outer space, to the moon, to other planets.

"We need to start with the premise that everything becomes its opposite. You are a scholar, you can explain this. We started with Pangea, the Indians came across the land bridge, across the straits. You need to orient people to where they come from and then tell them the statistics of what will happen with the flooding and rising oceans on the coasts. You have to look at where there is a lot of land and sooner or later that will turn into its opposite, a lot of water.

"I'm going to send you an art piece. In it I am asking for the people from outer space to come give us some technology. They can do it in our dreams, maybe the dream of a young scientist who will then get that idea to make something."

Joseph says a lot here. I had been thinking about giving this chapter the number zero and I had also been remembering Joseph's phrase from the foreword of Kurt Wilt's *The Visionary*, "*La vida no mas un sueño es.*"[2] He touches on both these themes and that leads him to talk about the ancestors in outer space. "We do not exist. To understand this truth requires a transformation of one's way of understanding the cosmos," Joseph wrote.[3] It is still confusing to me sometimes, although other times I feel it making some sense, "*we do not exist.*"

LA VIDA NO MAS UN SUEÑO ES (LIFE IS BUT A DREAM)

Joseph is not the only one to say that this reality that we think is real is actually a dream. Hinduism and Buddhism speak of *maya*, the "illusion" of reality. In Hinduism, this world is sometimes said to be the dream of Vishnu, who lies asleep, dreaming on the Cosmic Ocean. In this form Vishnu is often called Narayana, "the Supreme God in his infinite

2 *Visionary*, ix.

3 *Sound*, 1.

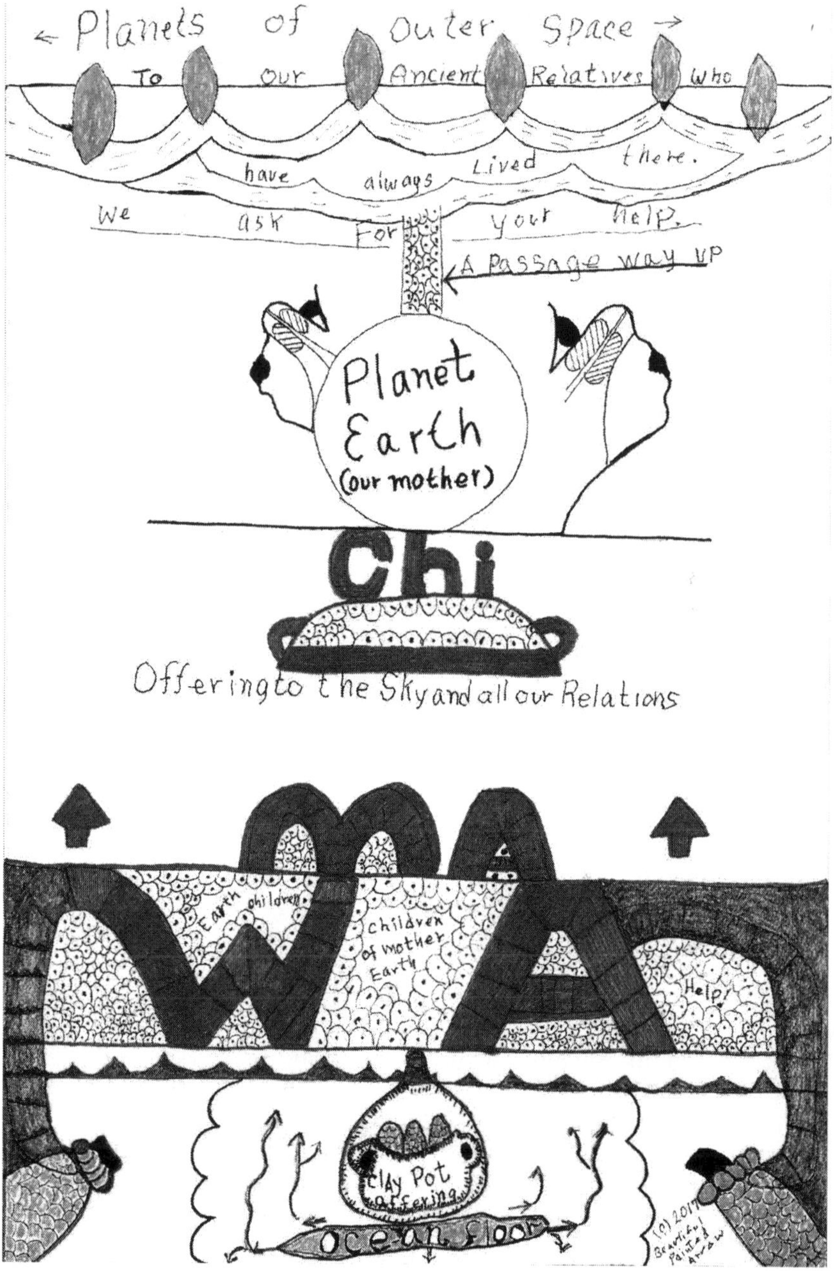

PLANET EARTH (OUR MOTHER)

all pervading form . . . [who] pervades whatever is seen or heard in this universe from inside and outside alike."[4]

In many spiritual traditions, the discussion of the illusion of this reality leads us to the one being who is the dreamer, much like Joseph's Vast Self. Hank Wesselman, in his work with Hawaiian holy man, Hale Makua, was taught that this world is a dream, although the concept was not entirely new to him.

> In my work as an anthropologist, I have heard a singular statement regularly repeated in various forms among indigenous peoples I have lived with across the years—the proclamation that we are all actually dreaming twenty-four hours a day, that the dream world is the real world, and that this physical world we all take so much for granted is a manifestation of the dream, not vice versa.[5]

This reversal of what is the most real transports us from materialism to the realm of spiritual interconnection. Joseph observes that we are *addictable* and stuck in property, ownership, and materialism. This is because we do not realize that "things" do not exist. We are like dreamers clutching at phantasms, while the thing that materialists think is fantasy is *Reality*.

(WE EXIST IN A STATE OF BECOMING)

Maybe it is almost right to say that we do not exist, but we exist in a state of becoming. Joseph has written, "We exist and we do not exist."[6]

We do not exist, could be the bridge to change and creation. *We do not exist* is the same thing as *becoming medicine*. Medicine is healing and creative and we heal and create through letting go of our previous existence so that we can be continually reborn, remade into new existence and this is how we change and this is how we actually do exist, by not clinging to existence.

---

4 "Narayana," *Wisdom Library online*. Further etymology and definition continues: "Another important translation of Narayana is The One who rests on Water. The waters are called narah, [for] the waters are, indeed, produced by Nara [the first Being]; as they were his first residence [ayana], he is called Narayana. In Sanskrit, 'Nara' can also refer to all human beings or living entities (Jivas). Therefore, another meaning of Narayana is Resting place for all living entities. The close association of Narayana with water explains the frequent depiction of Narayana in Hindu art as standing or sitting on an ocean."

5 Wesselman, *The Bowl of Light*, 83.

6 *B&V*, 77.

Sound. Vibration. Flowing outward into manifestation. Returning inward to the void which is the Source of our creation. Joseph teaches that it is more correct to think of ourselves as sound echoing throughout creation than as solid beings struggling to exist and persist. One of the struggles in theology is how to understand our relationship to *Wah-Mah-Chi*/God/Source through our separation and seeming existence as objective beings in the world. Dualism separates us from God and we fall into categories of separation: God/Human, spirit/body, heaven/hell, good/evil, man/woman, us/them. Rather than dualism and separation, Joseph teaches us that we are connected, interconnected, in fact we are the breath of God. Everything we see, feel, think and interact with is the breath of God, is *Breath-Matter-Movement.*

> God's breath is the power, the energy of matter in movement. Because of this on-off-on pulsation, we become matter. We matter because we move. We move because God breathes. On the one hand, we each move in patterns unique to ourselves, but on the other hand, we do not exist at all: we are nothing.
>
> The teachings collected here under the title *Sound* are all based on one central fact: The true basis for Universal Intelligence is sound. Out of sound comes everything. . . .
>
> I suggest that you read this book in the same way you would listen to music. If you can approach this experience with all your doors of perception wide open, perhaps the words and images here might seep into your being through the spaces of your nonbeing, and you will be forever changed.
>
> Enter this book of my teachings as if you were climbing down into a kiva for a sacred ceremony. Do not come to be instructed. Come to be initiated.[7]

"We do not exist" means that the things that we take for granted and think and say about our identity and our reality are not correct. This is the first sense of *we do not exist*—it is a negation of that with which we commonly identify. Many spiritual, mystical traditions have devoted many words and pages to attempt to convey the insight that words and pages cannot capture the true nature of reality. This is similar to what Joseph speaks about with the difference between noun-pronoun language and verb language. Noun-pronoun language is about separation, fragmentation, and objectification.

---

7 *Sound*, 2–3.

It is the process of taking the *breath-matter-movement* of life and turning it into a fixed thing, an object which appears to exist separately from its surroundings. Verb language, on the other hand, captures the movement of perpetual arising. It is process rather than static. It is circular rather than linear. Verb language dances around the medicine wheel and continues to return. The place that it is perpetually returning to is Source. It is the place of all arising. When we return to Source, this is the same thing as tasting healing because we are re-made, re-born, re-newed when we dance back into Source where we are unmade and then remade.

The word *theophany* means revelation of God. The word *epiphany* means a sudden manifestation of the divine. In ordinary reality we think that theophany and epiphany are made-up superstitions, or at best we think they are things that happened to other people, saints and founders of religions, hundreds and thousands of years ago. A mystic, a visionary, a shaman, however, works on becoming more capable of theophany and epiphany. This is the in-breaking of non-ordinary reality into ordinary reality. Mystics, visionaries, and shamans strive to live as much in non-ordinary reality as they can. Joseph says that a vision is the soul drinking light. Mystics, visionaries, and shamans have an insatiable and unquenchable thirst for the divinity of non-ordinary reality.

> I have learned that there is only one actor in the cosmos, and that actor is creating billions and billions of resonating images that continually manifest and return to the One. Sound is the soul of the One who drinks the light that It is creating moment by moment in order to continue existence. This House of Shattering Light—this perceptual reality in which we live and of which we are part—exists only for the soul's continuing.
>
> Now it is time for death's illusion to give way, along with the illusion of material form, before the reality of these vibrations. I believe that if we learn to listen, the vibrations will give forth their meanings, encoded in the crystal soil of our native earth, to fill the close-pressed ear with song.[8]

Here Joseph invokes what he calls "Vast Self," the one actor who is continually creating and absorbing vibrations. He tells me that House, *tuh-neh*, means "shattering," and that it also means "healing." "*Whatever is broken may be healed. Any time you are doing something around the house and something breaks, one of your ancestors is needing healing.*" The *House*

8 *House*, 19–20.

of Shattering Light is this *Being & Vibration* of coming into existence and being drunk back in by Vast Self.

THE NEW SCIENCE OF QUANTUM PHYSICS AND ANCIENT WISDOM

Quantum physics is another tradition that tells us that *we do not exist* in the way we think we exist. Quantum physics tells us that what we think of as solid matter is actually moving energy.

Fritjof Capra trained as a physicist and has studied spirituality after having a visionary experience. His intense visionary, mystical experience brought his intellectual knowledge of physics into a spiritual realm and this visionary insight has shaped his life and work.

> I was sitting by the ocean one late summer afternoon, watching the waves rolling and feeling the rhythm of my breathing, when I suddenly became aware of my whole environment as being engaged in a gigantic cosmic dance. . . . As I sat on that beach my former experiences came to life; I 'saw' cascades of energy coming down from outer space, in which particles were created and destroyed in rhythmic pulses; I 'saw' the atoms of the elements and those of my body participating in this cosmic dance of energy; I felt its rhythm and I 'heard' its sound, at that moment I *knew* that this was the Dance of Shiva, the Lord of Dancers worshipped by the Hindus.[9]

Capra's "new vision of reality" led him into the work of deep ecology and seeking the interconnectedness of all things. He writes that this "sense of oneness with the natural world, which is characteristic of spiritual experience, is fully borne out by the understanding of life in contemporary science." Capra developed the idea of "quantum interconnectedness" which illustrates that everything is part of a "unified whole," although it appears to be separated into different objects.[10] He quotes the Buddhist teacher Nagarjuna who reached the same conclusion as the physicists·that things are all interconnected, "Things derive their being and nature by mutual dependence and are nothing in themselves."[11] This statement of Nagarjuna's perhaps gives some clarity on Joseph Rael's statement that "we don't exist." We do not exist in and of ourselves as separate entities

9 Fritjof Capra, *The Tao of Physics*, 11.

10 Ibid., 9, 309.

11 Ibid., Nagarjuna quoted in Capra, 313.

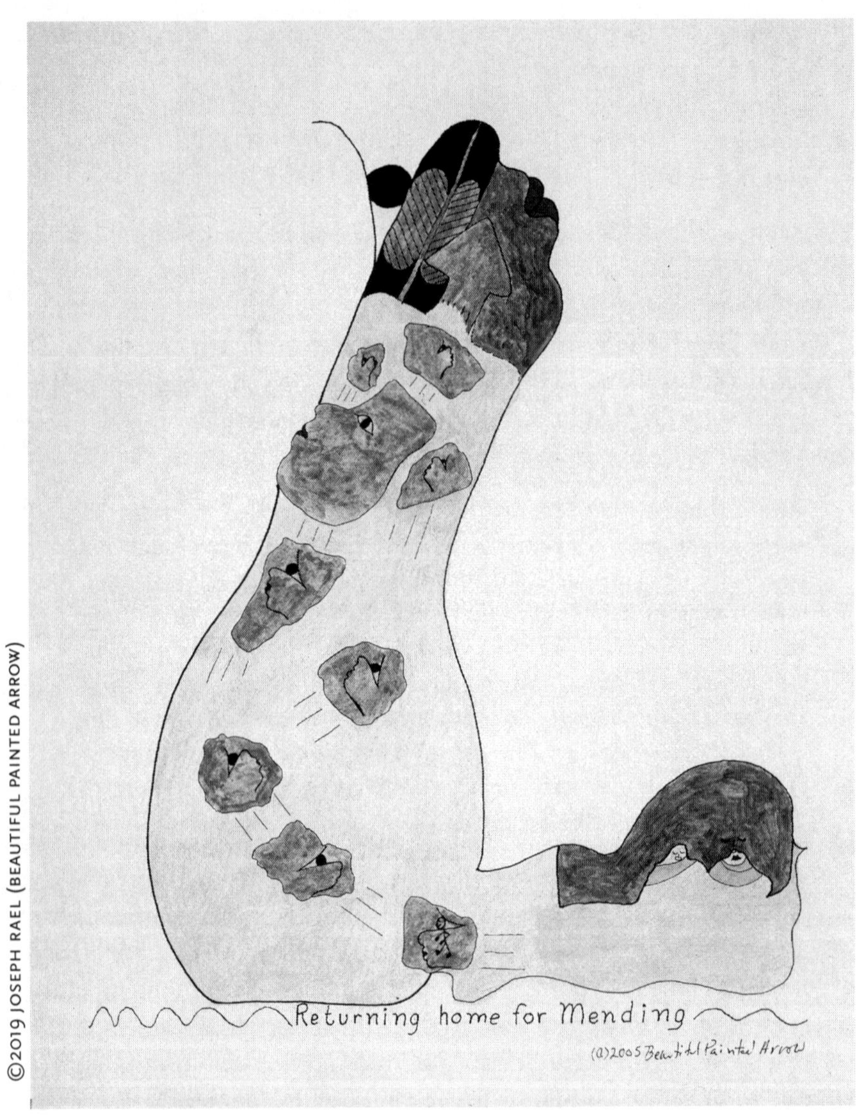

RETURNING HOME FOR MENDING

persisting through time, rather we exist like sunlight dancing on rippling waves in the cosmic ocean.

Contemporary applied science and the materialistic world view depend on the separation of subjects and objects and the scientific method works through a process of objective detachment. However, the quantum physicists of the last century have been discovering that there is no such thing as objectivity at the quantum level—the very act of observation changes the results of the experiment, indicating a deep interconnection and interaction between observation and what is observed. This enters the realm of mysticism which can be thought of as a counterpart to the objective investigation of science. Mysticism is a subjective investigation of reality, as Capra explains.

> Mystical knowledge can never be obtained by detached, objective observation; it always involves full participation with one's whole being. . . . Mystics in deep meditation arrive at a point where the distinction between observer and observed breaks down completely, where subject and object fuse. . . . So we have physicists probing into matter with the help of sophisticated instruments and mystics probing into consciousness with the help of sophisticated techniques of meditation. Both reach nonordinary levels of perception, and at these nonordinary levels the patterns and principles of organization they observe seem to be very similar.[12]

Capra introduces the word "nonordinary" which is a word that Joseph Rael frequently uses to describe visionary reality. He also points to the place of unity and oneness which is the ultimate aim of becoming medicine—of recognizing the unity and oneness underlying non-ordinary reality.

DAVID BOHM AND THE HOLOMOVEMENT

David Bohm is another quantum physicist who was also a mystic.[13] Bohm developed the concept of the "holomovement" a unitary essence of reality which could unfold into the *explicate order* (manifested existence) and enfold back into the underlying *implicate order* (potential existence). This is in keeping with the findings of quantum physics that matter is actually not solid, but rather made up of moving energies. We, in ordinary reality, experience matter as a solid, separate objects, but in non-ordinary reality matter is perpetually moving energy that has briefly taken a form that appears as solid and separate. We can live our lives on the basis of

---

12 Ibid., 331, 339.

13 Bohm was an American-born physicist who left the US in 1949 due to McCarthyism and lived in Brazil and England. He continued his ground-breaking work in quantum physics and also was friends with spiritual teacher, J. Krishnamurti. They engaged in many dialogues over the years which are published as *The Ending of Time: Where Philosophy and Physics Meet*. Like Joseph, Bohm and Krishnamurti challenge our language and underlying views of ourselves as separate objects.

appearance (ordinary reality) or we can strive to base our lives on the basis of movement (non-ordinary reality). The dance back and forth between the explicate and implicate order reminds us of the *spanda*, the divine creative pulsation that flashes into manifest existence only to disappear into un-manifest existence (potential existence).

The Dalai Lama called Bohm "one of my scientific 'gurus."[14] Bohm was friends with Krishnamurti and they had many discussions together and shared many insights. Bohm also wrote a textbook on quantum physics and developed ideas that many more creative and spiritually inclined people have gravitated toward: the holomovement, and the explicate and implicate orders. We spoke of him earlier in regard to verb language. He created a physics that was holistic and shares a lot with Joseph Rael's concept of reality not being a static noun, but rather a pulsing enfolding and unfolding reality. The editor of *The Essential David Bohm*, Lee Nichol, wrote:

> He proposed that what we normally think of as a particle is actually a temporary localized pulse emerging from a larger field, very much as a vortex temporarily forms from the dynamic flow of a stream. In Bohm's words, "the field structure associated with two pulses will merge and flow together in one unbroken whole."[15]

Bohm also spoke of the inherent integration of matter and movement (recalling Joseph's Breath-Matter-Movement). He wrote, "motions are . . . inherent and indispensable to what matter is, so that it would in general not even make sense to discuss matter apart from" motion. As matter is internally and externally in motion, Bohm stated that it could not exist in a static and persistent state and that motion of matter would lead "eventually to destruction or decay, to be replaced by new kinds of things. . . . This process, in which exist infinitely varied types of natural laws, is just the process of *becoming*, first described by Heraclitus several thousand years ago."[16] Matter, in this sense, does not exist as fixed matter, but rather is perpetually ceasing to exist and then giving rise to *new kinds of thing*s in a *process of becoming*.

---

14 In *The Essential David Bohm*, ed. Lee Nichol, x.

15 Bohm, Ibid., 3.

16 Ibid., 27–28, 32.

PHYSICISM & MYSTICISM

> *What is mysticism? The word "mysticism" is based on the word "mystery," implying something hidden. Perhaps the ordinary mode of consciousness which elaborately obscures its mode of functioning from itself and engages in self-deception might more appropriately be called "mysticism." Or we could call it "obscurantism," and say there's an opposite mode that we could term "transparentism."*[17]
>
> DAVID BOHM

Bohm's study of physics took him into mysticism. As so often in the quantum world, reality turns on its head and Bohm suggests that we call the ordinary consciousness *mysticism* or *obscurantism* because it gives us a false sense of separation from underlying reality. "So we say deep down the consciousness of mankind is one," concludes Bohm. This sense of oneness shifts our view of empty space as something that surrounds and separates objects to an active and vibrating matrix within which objects are embedded and connected.

> But if we looked at it as a holomovement with this vast reserve of energy and empty space where matter itself is that small wave on empty space, then we should really say that the space as a whole is the ground of existence and we are in it. So the space doesn't separate us, it unites us. . . . In that sense there are no separate people.

If *there are no separate people*, then, logically, *we do not exist.* This statement that *space doesn't separate us, it unites us* is quite profound. The thing that we think separates us actually connects and unites us with what Joseph calls Vast Self. Joseph's teaching that we are *being & vibration* is echoed by Bohm when he wrote, "I'm saying that what we call real things are actually tiny little ripples."[18]

"I HAVE LOOKED AT REALITY AND SEEN THAT IT IS AN ILLUSION"

Physicist and mystic, F. David Peat was friends with Bohm and continued on in the SEED, Language of Spirituality conferences in New Mexico after Bohm's death. In *Infinite Potential: The Life and Times of David Bohm*, Peat describes both Bohm's science and his mysticism. Peat

---

17 Ibid., 151–52.

18 Ibid., 149–50.

has a deep understanding of both fields and wrote that, "For Bohm, physics was an inner journey grounded in the conviction that his own body was a microcosm of the universe," and that "Bohm sought a holistic physics . . . the holomovement, is the movement of the whole."

Bohm's work with Krishnamurti stimulated his own ideas about physics and the nature of reality. Both Bohm and Krishnamurti saw our ordinary consciousness as creating the illusion of separation, where, in fact, there was connection and unity. As Peat writes:

> In this act of separation, and in the subsequent reification of the thinker and the thought, lie the origins of human problems. Krishnamurti's observation that the 'thinker is the thought' and 'the observer is the observed' struck Bohm as resembling his own—and Niels Bohr's—meditations on the role of the observer in quantum theory.[19]

The difference between many physicists and mystics is that physicists think about and measure reality whereas mystics seek to experience reality and report back to us. Bohm, however, was both a physicist and a mystic as he had the experience as well as the theoretical knowledge. As he said, "Well, let's say I have seen some of the things Krishnamurti talks about. I have looked at reality and seen that it is an illusion."[20]

We will close this section on David Bohm with a description of a vision he had that sounds very much like the Hindu and Buddhist concept of the "Net of Indra" found in the *Avatamsaka Sutra*. The Net of Indra describes a vast net of jewels that stretches out in all directions and each jewel reflects all of the others. The idea of individuality, here, is subsumed as a reflection of all the other "individual" jewels in the net. Although each jewel seems separate, it is connected through the net as well as connected in reflecting all the other jewels. Both William Keepin in his book *Belonging to God* and Fritjof Capra in *The Tao of Physics* describe Indra's Net and its implications for both science and mysticism.[21] Here is Peat summarizing Bohm's vision:

> While he was in Copenhagen, Bohm had an insight into the nature of infinity, an issue he had been thinking about for some years. The vision came to him in the form of a large number of highly spherical

19 F. David Peat, *Infinite Potential: The Life and Times of David Bohm*, 77, 258, 199.

20 Bohm, Ibid., 274.

21 William Keepin, *Belonging to God: Spirituality, Science & a Universal Path of Divine Love*, 175–76. Fritjof Capra, *The Tao of Physics*, 296–98.

> mirrors that reflected each other. The universe was composed of this infinity of reflections, and of reflections of reflections. Every atom was reflecting in this way, and the infinity of these reflections was reflected in each thing; each was an infinite reflection of the whole. This image possesses almost mystical connotations in its vividness, and at the metaphorical level at least, it contains the seeds of the concepts that Bohm was later to call the implicate order.[22]

REALITY

Peter Kingsley has worked with *Reality*, his book by that name is a vast tome that reminds us of the ancient wisdom that Joseph speaks of: *we do not exist.* Kingsley continually returns in his books to remind us of our beginnings, of the secret and lost teachings of the founders of the Western world. He reminds us that we have in our world teachers who have taught us that reality is but a dream, much the same as Joseph teaches us. We have shamans, mystics, and visionaries in our Western blood, but the Western mind continually is covering up and burying the truth of reality. Kingsley reminds us that there are visible and invisible traditions of knowledge and wisdom. The invisible traditions, are found in the *Dark Places of Wisdom* (the name of another of his books), and they "appear and disappear." He tells us that the invisible traditions "manifest in periods and in places where a particular understanding of timelessness is called for; where a certain quality of need, of deep dissatisfaction, means a time for renewal has come." While science and Western philosophy pride themselves on overcoming superstition to unveil rational, objective reality, Kingsley argues that just the reverse is true—our scientists and philosophers have been pulling the wool over eyes so that we seem to have lost touch with the roots of our vision into the vibratory and fluctuating nature of reality.

Kingsley argues that we can view the history of Western thought as a similar kind of forgetting and remembering of reality. From Kingsley's perspective, our glorification of rationality, objectivity, and materialism is a kind of traumatic veiling of what Joseph would call non-ordinary reality. Kingsley whispers to us that "the secret is to be able to see this whole world as an illusion and still function in it as if it is real."

> Purification or *katharmos* was the traditional first stage in the mysteries, followed by *paradosis* or transmission of the mystery teaching itself. Only then, after the transmission had taken place, came the stage of

22 Peat, *Infinite Potential*, 186.

> *epopteia*: of overseeing . . . [which is] a bewildering experience—to lack nothing, to contain everything you will ever need inside yourself . . . [the initiated] holds, inside himself, the germs of a teaching that most people have not even the slightest desire or use for. And he has to do what from any normal human point of view is absurd: to care for things he is unable to see or hear or touch.[23]

Initiation can seem useless from the perspective of ordinary reality, but it opens up a whole new world of invisible realities, and with it there are invisible responsibilities in caring for the ongoing growth. The initiation is into non-duality, into metaphysical Oneness as "you discover that nothing exists apart from you. There is nothing outside you any more: nothing there at all. You are everybody, everywhere." Reality is not so much "reality" as it is a book that we are writing as we go along.

> For everything is your book. Even you are your own book as you write yourself in the depths of your being so you can read it in each episode of the life you seem to live. And every word ever written or spoken is spoken and written by you, for yourself.[24]

THE SEED OF LIFE

For Joseph, the medicine wheel harmonizes the initial moment of creation with the present moment (which is also a creation). Joseph says that "*we don't truly exist*," however he will also say that we exist only for brief moments of time, like flashes of light. I understand this to mean that we only exist when we are being creative and new and original, when we are letting our own light flash out from within our souls (using our hollow emptiness to be the space for God's light flashing through us). Every moment is a new creation and creation always follows the same format—a flash of light and sound exploding into being from within the darkness of the void.

> In the beginning was a flash of light in which everything was known and seen. In that moment was the beginning, the end and everything in between. The original vision came from this being we will call Inspiration, and we were that original vision. We are the original vision of the Being of Drinking Light, the soul.
>
> That flash was a circle with a center made of heart and a periphery made of beyond. . . . We exist and we do not exist. We are the infinite

23 Peter Kingsley, *Reality*, 498, 449, 532.

24 Ibid., 556, 557.

> void; we are relativity; we are awareness; we are the "people" which nature called, and "the people" which means vibration.
>
> The flash of light is the "seed of life". . . . The seed is in the land which gives us the initial clarity to discern right living. The land is materialized vibration which forms other vibrations, as we live on it, work on it, and eat the foods that grow from it. What's going on is that the heart is integrating with innocence, with teachableness, with that state in which there is no ego, when one is simply soaking it all up, like a sponge.[25]

Joseph writes that visionary experiences give insight into the process of creation as well into the medicine wheel which is a circle of creation. "For anyone who has had a visionary experience, it is perhaps easier to understand how we became the original medicine wheel. When I had my first visionary experience, I got a flash of light, similar to the original flash of light that made us all, and then came the vision." A visionary experience is the same process as the creation of the universe or the creation of life. There is thus a unity in life and creation. Existence—of the universe and of the individual—is a continuing lightning bolt bang of sound and vision. Insight strikes, illuminates, energizes, inspires—it is the breath, the inspiration that brings spirit into the physical body—existence is the vital experience of Breath-Matter-Movement all combining. Our minds separate the unity of Breath-Matter-Movement, into breath; matter; movement.

> So you see, the medicine wheel or circle really doesn't exist. It really doesn't exist because we do not exist. This has to be made very clear. We don't exist the way we think we do. We are energy that appears and disappears and appears and disappears. When it is no longer there, it automatically goes into silence. When it reappears again, it is not the same person because in some ways it has changed. And that is the key to evolution.[26]

Joseph's teachings can be esoteric at times. It is difficult for us to understand what he means when he says that "*we do not exist.*" However he also says we do exist when we have a flash of inspiration, when we are struck by a lightning bolt, when we embody the original creation of the universe in the big bang through having a sudden spark of illumination within ourselves, in which we momentarily flash into existence. Some

25 *B&V*, 76–78.

26 Ibid., 78-81.

of the difficulty in understanding this is its simplicity, some of it lies in its complexity. Most of the challenge is that the teaching is asking us to change the way we experience life and ourselves, from a sense of ourselves as separate material objects surrounded by material objects (a form of materialism) to a sense of ourselves as a spiritual process, a sense of ourselves as circle beings of flashing, pulsating, divine creative light.

WE DO NOT EXIST: WE ARE ONE

In many traditions, enlightenment is the state of realizing God in one's self. Spiritual teacher Narayana Guru describes the "ultimate teaching is that there is one Reality alone. As there is but one single Reality, each person is inseparably one with the whole, with the one changeless Reality underlying all that is changeful."[27] Narayana Guru (1856–1928) was a spiritual leader and also advocated for social reform of the caste system and taught a kind of spiritual democracy that the path to God was open to all people, regardless of caste. Narayana Guru's universal prayer, *Daivadaśakam*, expresses his non-dualistic philosophy and his *Garland of Visions* describes ten different paths to enlightenment, teaching that many different paths lead to the one Reality, including, for instance, paths of action (*karma*), knowledge (*jñāna*), love (*bhakti*), union (*yoga*), and understanding the illusory (*māyā*). Each of these paths could be followed singly to approach enlightenment, but Narayana Guru taught his students to pursue each of these paths to their endpoint and to wear them as a garland of beads around one's neck.

> The non-dual ultimate Reality is to be intuitively perceived by the seeker-student as that which gives room for all such varying visions. It, in other words, remains invisible and unstated in this work, like the invisible thread that strings all the beads together. The job of the reader or rather of the seeker-student is seeking out this invisible thread, and stringing together all the visions into a garland to be worn around his own neck. Real *jñānins*, the enlightened ones, on the other hand, are those who are already having this garland around their neck.

Enlightenment transcends duality and this is called non-duality. There is no difference between the knower, the known, and the act of knowing. Enlightenment entails perceiving non-difference between "*dṛk* (the perceiver), *dṛśya* (the perceived) and *darśana* (perception); or simply the

27 Swami Muni Narayana Prasad, *Garland of Visions: The Darśanamālā of Narayana Guru*, v.

knower, the known and knowledge. These factors together in Vedānta are known as *tripuṭi*. . . . It is the seekers own heart (*hṛt*) that is to be attuned to the Reality that transcends the bounds of *tripuṭi*."[28]

Thus, we do not exist, because only the One exists. The perceiver, the perception, and the perceived are all one. The *knower* is the *known* and the act of *knowing*.

ALL IS ŚIVA—ALL IS VAST SELF

> *All of my teachings tie into the reality that there is a Seer seeing everything. We call it God, the higher power, or whatever. It is simply the Vast Self seeing itself creating itself. We humans perceive ourselves and the world around us as solid objects, as flesh and bone, sitting on a padded chair, or on grass-covered earth. But all these things, the flesh, bones, chair, grass and earth, are artifacts of one great collective act of perceiving in which all beings participate. What we perceive as solid, having dimensions and colors and other properties, are really just pulses of energy moving or vibrating, each in its unique pattern, so as to interact with our patterns, to excite our senses and create patterns of perception.*[29] (Joseph Rael)

> *Where all splendors are in the light*
> *And all darknesses in the dark*
> *brilliant light and gloomy darkness!*
> *I praise that transcendent light.*
> . . .
> *Always new, hidden,*
> *Yet old and apparent to all,*
> *The Heart, the Ultimate*
> *Shines alone with the brilliance of the Supreme.*[30]
> (Abhinavagupta)

---

28 Ibid., 7, 261–63.

29 *Sound*, 1.

30 Abhinavagupta, in Muller-Ortega, 204. Abhinavagupta (c 950-1016 CE) lived in the Kashmir region of the Indian sub-continent. He was the author of a number of books on mysticism. Paul Eduardo Muller-Ortega bases much of his book, *The Triadic Heart of Śiva: Kaula Tantricism of Abhinavagupta in the Non-Dual Shaivism of Kashmir*, on Abhinavagupta's work. Muller-Ortega is one of a number of contemporary scholars (who are often practitioners as well) of Kashmiri Shaivism, including Mark Dyczkowski, Daniel Odier, Jaideva Singh, Christopher Wallis, and Lorin Roche.

As Joseph Rael describes Vast Self as *a Seer seeing everything* and creating reality out of itself, so too do many Hindu traditions speak of one ultimate being, Brahman, or Śiva, as the only reality and the foundation of consciousness and matter. This one being is also vibration, as Joseph speaks of *being & vibration* and *Wah-Mah-Chi* (Breath-Matter-Movement), so does Kashmiri Shaivism speaks of *spanda*, the divine creative pulsation and *sat-cit-ananda* (being-consciousness-bliss).

> The Heart of Śiva is not a static or inert absolute, however. In fact, the non-dual Kashmir Shaiva tradition considers it to be in a state of perpetual movement, a state of vibration (*spanda*) in which it is continuously contracting and expanding (*saṃkoca-vikāsa*), opening and closing (*unmeṣa-nimeṣa*), trembling (*ullasitā*), quivering (*sphuritā*), throbbing, waving, and sparkling (*ucchalatā*). The intensity and speed of this movement is such that paradoxically it is simultaneously a perfect dynamic stillness.[31]

From the heart of Śiva emerges the feminine vibration of Śakti, which emanates out, creating all reality and then returning back into the silence of Śiva. Joseph describes the feminine as descending, creative energy. Just as Kashmiri Shaivism describes how creation unfolds through the interplay of masculine Śiva and feminine Śakti, so too does Joseph describe the dance of the feminine and masculine in creation. Compare these quotations, the first from Kashmiri Shaivism and the second from Joseph Rael:

> The silence of the Supreme is shot through with a creative tension, a primordial urge, an impelling force. This force is the śakti, the power of the Ultimate . . . which is responsible for the wave motion within the absolute. Thus, the absolute is continually arising into waves which create the slight and imperceptible movement or vibration that characterizes consciousness, and which allows consciousness to be the foundation and essence of all manifest reality.[32] (Muller-Ortega)
>
> We all want to be initiated into womanhood because it is the feminine that helps us to slip through the crack between the two slices of light, and for a split of a split second, we exist. It's the feminine, not the masculine, that is that power of inspiration. When the inspiration unfolds, then it is masculine. The feminine is the descending light itself, and the masculine is the unfolding of the feminine.[33] (Joseph Rael)

---

31 Muller-Ortega, 82.

32 Ibid., 120.

33 *Ceremonies*, 15.

The creative masculine and feminine energies, emerging out of the void, in play, lead to creation. There is a meditation in Kashmiri Shaivism of concentrating on the subtle space between things rather than on the things themselves, whether these "things" be thoughts, breaths, emotions, or material objects. As Joseph Rael says, "*God is in the spaces, not in the words.*" We find that which we are seeking not by reaching out toward the object, but rather by embracing the fact that through the space around ourselves and the object, we are already one. [The] "omnipresence of the Ultimate . . . may be located between the experience of any two thoughts, objects, or emotions. . . . Thus, when one penetrates into the interval between any two things or ideas, one will not encounter a nothingness, but rather the fullness of totality." It is by piercing through the dualistic illusion of separation that one reaches the non-dual state of non-ordinary reality. Joseph Rael tells us that in the center of the medicine wheel is the heart, which is the source. So too does Kashmiri Shaivism direct us toward the heart, the heart of Śiva. "The play between opening and closing, between expanding and contracting, is the essential characteristic of the Heart. The Heart itself constitutes the highest method for reaching the condition of non-duality which finally unifies the open and the closed, the expanded and contracted." In the darkness of the *guhā*, the cave of the heart, there exists a gleaming light. Once this light is found and activated it "can in no way be held back: it is unconcealable and unbounded. It begins to spread out from the inner reality of the Heart and invades the entire structure of finiteness. When this happens it transforms the inertness of finitude into the vibrancy of life."[34] This is the state that Eliade calls the *sacred* and we are calling *a living spirituality*. There is but one heart, just as there is but one Seer. The initiation is realizing that *we do not exist*, but that we are continually emanating out from and returning back to the One Heart through *spanda* and waves of *being & vibration*. We have within us a hidden treasure.

> [I]t is not that we must travel far beyond the manifested world in order to locate the interior universe of the ocean within the Heart. To speak of distance, of return, of a path, may be useful aids for the spiritual practitioner; in reality, however, all objects, all beings, all possible experiences are continuously and eternally bathed in that ocean . . . Abhinavagupta's images of the ocean and waves derive from the experiential absorption (*samāveśa*) in the Heart.[35]

---

34 Muller-Ortega., 93, 120, 188.

35 Ibid., 148.

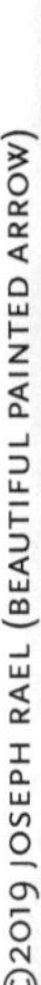

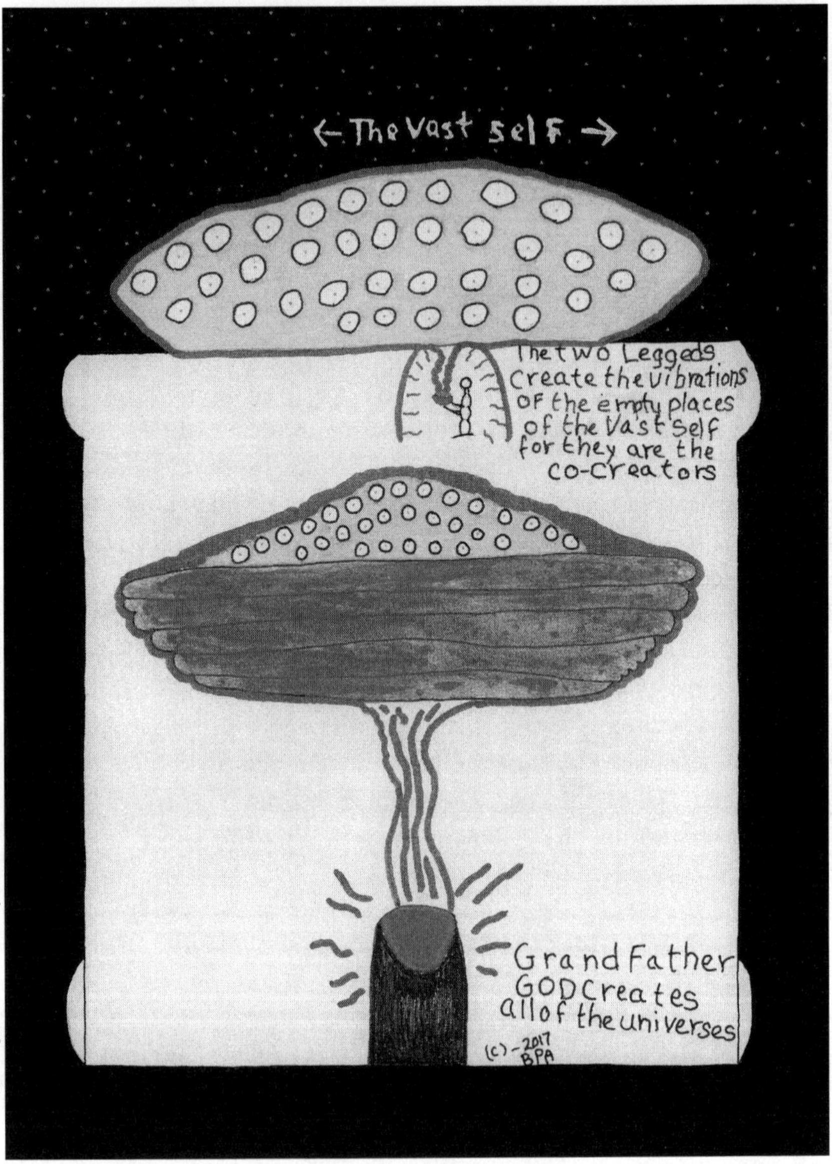

GRANDFATHER GOD CREATES ALL THE UNIVERSES

THE DOCTRINE OF VIBRATION

Mark Dyczkowski describes the *śakticakra* as a spinning circular wheel of energies that underlies reality in much the same way as the medicine wheel is an organizing and orienting structure.

> The arising and subsiding of each wave of cosmic manifestation is marked by a regular sequence. . . . Following one after another in recurrent cycles, each sequence is aptly symbolised by a rotating wheel (śakticakra), the spokes of which are the aspects of divine creative energy of consciousness brought into play as the wheel revolves. Thus these Wheels collectively represent the primal form or 'archetype-field structure' of all experience. . . .
>
> As each Wheel rotates, one power after another becomes active, taking over from the one that went before it and blending into the one that follows. The flow of the energy of consciousness moves round the circle in harmony with the rhythm of its pulsation. . . .
>
> The Doctrine of Vibration teaches that there is an essential identity between the inner world of the subject and the outer world of the object. The universe is equally the outer physical world and the inner world of mind and body. Thus the emanation of these Wheels corresponds to the creation of both of these worlds.[36]

We could easily substitute "medicine wheel" for *śakticakra* (the chakra of *śakti*, or manifestation) and the statements would be congruent. The medicine wheel also has both inner and outer wheels that are in relationship with each other and that create our reality. Both can be considered organizing archetypal structures for reality and experience. The *Doctrine of Vibration* orients us not only to the *śakticakra*, but also to the *spanda*, the creative pulsation that underlies reality, much as Joseph teaches that sound, being, and vibration are the foundations of our reality.

> [The] Doctrine of Vibration stresses . . . the importance of experiencing Spanda, the vibration or pulse of consciousness. . . . Every activity in the universe, as well as every perception, notion, sensation or emotion in the microcosm, ebbs and flows as part of the universal rhythm of the one reality, which is Śiva, the one God Who is the pure conscious agent and perceiver. According to the Doctrine of Vibration, man can realise his true nature to be Śiva by experiencing Spanda, the dynamic, recurrent and creative activity of the absolute.[37]

36 Mark S.G. Dyczkowski, *The Doctrine of Vibration*, 117–18.

37 Ibid., 21.

The Doctrine of Vibration is very similar to Joseph's *Being & Vibration.* We do not exist, Joseph tells us, instead we flicker in and out of existence. We do not exist teaches the Doctrine of Vibration, instead all is the pulsation of the one reality, Śiva. We do not exist says Joseph, instead there is One perceiver, perceiving everything, Vast Self. This is non-duality, since what appears as separate objects is simply brief pulsations, flickers, or waves of the cosmic ocean. The Doctrine of Vibration tells us that in "reality nothing arises, and nothing subsides, only the divine *Spanda-śakti* which though free of succession, appears in different aspects as if arising, and as if subsiding."[38] Not only does creation emanate out from the wheel, but through meditating on the wheel one can cease to exist, to dissolve back into the wheel, as the sage, Abhinavagupta, describes.

> This supreme wheel goes out from the Heart through the spaces of the eyes, and so forth, and ranges over the various objects of the senses . . . one should meditate on the great wheel which revolves and is the overflowing of the true Self. Because of the dissolution of all that could be burned, and because of the destruction of even the remaining latent impressions, the practitioner should meditate on that wheel as becoming calm, then as pacified, then as tranquil quietude itself. By this method of meditation, the entire universe is dissolved in the wheel, in that consciousness.[39]

Initiation is the term that is used for any transformational process that moves one from one state of being into another state of being. One becomes someone different, takes on a new identity and leaves an old identity behind. When Joseph says we do not exist, he is inviting us to become initiated. The initiation is letting go of our old, seemingly solid, separate identity. "What we perceive as solid, having dimensions and colors and other properties, are really just pulses of energy moving or vibrating, each in its unique pattern, so as to interact with our patterns,

38 Jaideva Singh, *Spanda-Kārikās*, 22. Another similarity involves a change in our relationship with suffering. The medicine wheel reorients us, incorporating pain and suffering as potential initiations into higher states of being & vibration. In the *Doctrine of Vibration*, "when in that noble person who attentively pursues the teaching, the *Spanda* principle, whose quintessence is flashing, throbbing consciousness, becomes manifest, then even when experiences of pain, pleasure, object, subject, or their absence occur, they are considered by him as naught, because to him everything appears only as the quintessence of the delight of *Spanda*," (48).

39 Abhinavagupta, in Paul Eduardo Muller-Ortega, *The Triadic Heart of Śiva*, 197.

to excite our senses and create patterns of perception."[40] Our separation is the experience of coming into form, into matter. The Latin word *mater*, the etymological root of "matter," means "mother"—so we are continually being born of *Mater* Earth into matter. Our initiation is when we let go of what seems like our solid identity.

"Die before you die" say the Sufis.[41] "Submit to love without thinking,"[42] says Rumi, meaning let yourself reside in the essential bliss of flashing into and out of existence. Rumi translator, Nevit O. Ergin, describes *annihilation* as medicine. "Without *fanâ* [annihilation], everything in the world exists. . . . *Fanâ* is the medicine for all of this. If a person reaches *fanâ*, they see that everything in the world is just a dream."[43] The Sufi seems to travel in the same circle as Joseph Rael, moving through *we do not exist* (*fanâ*) to *la vida es un sueño es* (life is but a dream). In fact, Joseph has told me on a number of occasions that he once had a Sufi initiation.

A SECRET TREASURE

Lord, said David, since you do not need us,
why did you create these two worlds?
Reality replied: O prisoner of time,
I was a secret treasure of kindness and generosity,
and I wished this treasure to be known,
so I created a mirror . . . [44] (Rumi)

GRADUATION DAY

One day I walked out of work and heard a kind of screeching sound. At first I thought it was a gull, but it did not sound quite like a gull. As I climbed up to the fourth level of the parking deck, I kept hearing it and thought maybe it was the construction going on nearby. When I got to the top I saw one (*weh-mu* – the seed, to slip), two (*weh-seh* – duality, the power to cry) bald eagles circling close together. They were not screeching, more

---

40 *Sound*, 1.

41 Ergin and Johnson, *The Rubais of Rumi*, p. 11.

42 Rumi translated by Coleman Barks, from the poem "More Range," first line "We're friends with one who kills us, who gives us to the ocean waves," *The Soul of Rumi*, 24.

43 Ergin, *Unknown Rumi*, 44.

44 Rumi, "Be Lost in the Call," Kabir Helminski (trans.), *Love is a Stranger: Selected Lyric Poetry of Jelaluddin Rumi*, 64.

of a calling or keening. Then I saw number three (*paah-chu* – movement in all directions) and then looked up and saw another, four (*wiii* – the power to climb, ascend). I had never seen this, four eagles, not just flying over, but circling and circling over the building. When I told this sight to Joseph, he exclaimed:

"*You just graduated with your PhD!* Weh-mu, weh-seh, paah-chu, wiii – *now you are at five,* paah-nu, *now you have to give something – you are going to give your physical body to the Sun Moon Dance. You are going to become the 'give-away' because you have to suffer. You have to suffer mentally, physically, emotionally, spiritually. My foster Father's name was* Where Eagles Perch – *you saw four eagles. You have passed! Now you are ready to go into non-ordinary reality and get rid of all that junk you have accumulated in your physical body.*"

After talking, I look up *paah-nu* in *Ceremonies of the Living Spirit*:

> At that point of inspiration, everything disappears. The eagle disappears.
> I disappear. The self disappears. It's all nothing.
> We're not there. We're everything, but nothing simultaneously.[45]

---

45 *Ceremonies*, 73.

G o d

i s

I n

t h e

S p

a c

e s

N o t

I n

T h e

W o r

d s

PART III

RETURN (GIVING)

The hero, therefore is the man or woman who has been able to battle past his personal and local historical limitations to the generally valid, normally human forms. Such a one's visions, ideas, and inspirations come pristine from the primary springs of human life and thought. Hence they are eloquent, not of the present, disintegrating society and psyche, but of the unquenched source through which society is reborn. The hero has died as a modern man; but as eternal man—perfected, unspecific, universal man—he has been reborn. His second solemn task and deed therefore . . . is to return then to us, transfigured, and teach the lesson he has learned of life renewed.[1]

JOSEPH CAMPBELL

The seed begins to root
It grows downward
And to all the other directions
For it carries the heart
of life, of the clarity of
All the heavens.
It now has a creation of songs and sings
Its beauty. It carries
On it return to oneness of Maa-Hay-Nay
The farmer's hand, the
Sower of Life.[2]

JOSEPH RAEL

The return and reintegration with society, which is indispensable to the continuous circulation of spiritual energy into the world, and which, from the standpoint of the community, is the justification of the long retreat, the hero himself may find the most difficult requirement of all."[3]

JOSEPH CAMPBELL

1 Joseph Campbell, *The Hero with a Thousand Faces*, 14–15.
2 *Inspiration*, 55.
3 Joseph Campbell, *The Hero with a Thousand Faces*, 29.

CHAPTER 12

RETURNING TO THE LAND

I believe Native American spirituality is a gift to us from North America herself. It is the natural spiritual path for those who live on this continent.[1]

LEWIS MEHL-MADRONA

RETURNING & CARRYING

> Before I studied Zen, mountains were just mountains and rivers just rivers. When I first took up the study of Zen, mountains were no longer mountains and rivers no longer rivers. But now that I've really got some understanding of Zen, mountains are once again mountains and rivers are once again rivers.[2]

This Zen saying captures the essence of our return back to where we started, transformed, but in many ways just who we are, present in the moment. The secret of returning is that we never left. That is why in the Zen story we end up at the same place where we began, but in the middle we realize that things are not as we thought they were.

Throughout this book we have been returning to the framework of separation, initiation, and return. In separation we begin seeking. Through initiation we find and receive that which we were seeking. In returning we feel the fullness of fulfillment and we naturally overflow with giving. We return back to the Source, to the place of origin. However, when we are returning we have passed through non-ordinary reality and been initiated into a new world and we are returning with new eyes. To return is to re-turn, that is to begin a cycle of circular movement once again. We return to the starting point, it is our old home, but it is different because now it is our new home. When we return we are changed, we have had new mental,

1 Lewis Mehl-Madrona, *Coyote Medicine: Lessons from Native American Healing*, 288. Mehl-Madrona continues, "Native American people have been preservers of this spiritual path for centuries, but they do not own it. No one can own a spiritual path. The proper response to the current interest in Native American spirituality is to correctly transmit this spiritual path to all who wish to learn from it. This ensures both its preservation, its accuracy, and its authenticity."

2 Quoted in Renée Weber, *Dialogues with Scientists and Sages*, 17.

emotional, physical, and spiritual experiences. We are not only changed, we are transformed because we have been initiated into a new vibration of being and we see our origin with new eyes. We are now spiritualized and every "thing" in our environment is spiritualized. We are now in a place of Unity and Oneness. This changes our relationship with ourselves, with others, and with the Earth.

Joseph says that we are "*built as adventurers, as inventors . . . death is not the end for us, it's really just the beginning of our next adventure . . . we are eternal beings.*" Every moment we are returning, every moment we are re-turning the medicine wheel. Each turn of the medicine wheel goes through the outer directions of east, south, west, and north. Every turn of the medicine wheel goes through the inner directions of mind, emotion, body, and spirit. Every turn of the medicine wheel goes through the vowel sounds of A, E, I, O, and then returns to the center, to U, which is about *carrying*. Joseph told me one day about how he came to put so much emphasis on the vowel sounds of A, E, I, O, U, and how they relate to the directions of the medicine wheel.

"So this came from a vision. The vision came that said, 'The secret is in the A, E, I, O, U.' If people will just learn the concept and for those who don't learn the concept, then they need to go to a sound chamber and just chant the damn thing. Ahh, Ehh, Eee, Oh, Uu. And then you can make a song and sing Aaaaaaa-aaaa-eee-a-a-eee-iiiiiii-oooooo-uuuuu. Now look how I do it. [He chants the vowels for a while, varying the pitch high and low].

"I made a song out of the Ahh, Ehh, Eee, Oh, Uu, Ahh, Ehh, Eee, Oh, Uu, Ahh, Ehh, Eee, Oh, Uu. I'm moving my feet. I'm moving my body. Ahh, Ehh, Eee, Oh, Uu. The North, the South, the East, the West. I am the one, the only one, I am the future and the past. Here and now. I dance, I dance, he dances. Divine presence walks with me, dances with me. Ahh, Ehh, Eee, Oh, Uu.

"Pure music, that's all we are."

I asked Joseph, "When you showed the motion for *Uu*, and you showed the movement for carrying, I noticed you brought it toward your heart. When you lift something with your arms, they don't go out, they go in toward your heart, and that's what I see this next book, *Becoming Medicine* is about that last vowel, about the *Uu*, the essence of the heart at the center of the medicine wheel, which is carrying. Can you say anything more for this next book about *Becoming Medicine* and the center of the medicine wheel and *Uu*?" He replied:

"We are cursed with a body—all we are going to be for as long as we live is carrying. We're going to carry our physical bodies, we are going to carry our thoughts, and we are going to carry our goals and objectives with us. They are in our bodies. And they are waiting for us out there, those goals to be manifested, and that's what the book is about. It's about people understanding that whatever they are seeking for is not out there anymore, it's in here. If you are born, the goals and objectives of what you are going to be are already instilled in here. All that stepping forward does is that it is allowing you to go through one door, closing it, that's one moment, right? Or one year. And then you open the door and close it."

The center of the medicine wheel is the place to which we are always returning and the place from which we are always separating from (however the center contains everything, so we are not really separating). When we return we connect to the heart center, to the principle of carrying. It is here that Joseph says that we are a medicine bag and that we are carrying sacred objects. These objects are the mental, emotional, physical, and spiritual experiences of our lives.

When we separate from the heart center, we leave homeland, family, childhood and then we return—entering into a new relationship, a spiritual relationship. We are continually leaving ordinary reality and entering into non-ordinary reality. In this way, the path of the visionary, the mystic, and the shaman is to be re-spiritualizing ordinary reality, which really means that this is the purpose of all of our lives, to be re-spiritualizing reality because we are all mystics, we are all visionaries, we are all shamans.

We are always separating, we are always initiating, we are always returning. When we separate we are seeking. We have been initiated into the center of the medicine wheel, and although we know we do not exist, we are returning with a new mission and vision. We are returning with a new orientation to the North, South, East, and West of the medicine wheel. We are returning with a new orientation to the Land of our birth.

RETURNING TO THE LAND

> When anything is occurring, in any moment in time, it is occurring not only to the individual, but it is also occurring to that geography—to that physical geography. What is happening to me is also happening to this place, this continent, this Planet Earth, this galaxy. I am giving and I am receiving energy back from the Earth, and so are we all. We are receiving it, each according to what he needs, and translating the energies we are receiving according to what we think is happening right now.[3] (Joseph Rael)

Joseph points out the correspondence between the land and the individual who lives on the land—what happens in one happens in the other, there is no separation. The microcosm and the macrocosm are in relationship with each other. We all share this land with each other, but what do we call this land from which we come, upon which we walk, and to which we return?

We not only live on the land, but we are of the land. That is what the word, "indigenous" means, to be of the land, born from the land.[4] The stuff of our bodies comes from the plants and animals of the land. We are all children of this land, Mother Earth, growing out of, being made of, and returning to her body. Western archaeology tells us that the indigenous peoples of what we now call North America came across a land bridge from Siberia some 15,000 or more years ago. Different tribes have their own names for this land. The name "Turtle Island" is sometimes used as a name for this land prior to European colonizers. Joseph has at least one painting with this name in it. The name "America" comes from the name of Italian sailor Amerigo Vespucci who realized that Columbus had not found the passage to India, but rather lands unknown to the Europeans. Columbus sought to find a passage to India, and when he landed in the what is now called the Bahamas and Hispaniola he called the people "Indians."

When the Indigenous peoples of the Bahama Islands first met Columbus, they offered many gifts to him. Columbus wrote in his log "They would make fine servants. . . . With fifty men we could subjugate them all and make them do whatever we want. . . . I took some of the natives by force

---

3 *Sound*, 177–78.

4 The *Online Etymology Dictionary describes the roots of indigenous*: "born or originating in a particular place," 1640s, from Late Latin *indigenus* "born in a country, native," from Latin *indigena* "sprung from the land, native," as a noun, "a native," literally "in-born," or "born in (a place)."

in order that they might learn and might give me information of whatever there is in these parts."[5] Columbus began taking prisoners and when the Indigenous peoples resisted, two of them were killed. Columbus, like Cain in the Bible killed his own brothers and felt righteous in doing so because of his interpretation of Christianity and his greed for material things.

What do we call this land? Should we simply call it "the Land," or maybe we should call it Mother Earth. The history of the United States of America is one of taking and renaming land, so that now it is confusing to even know what the land is called or what to call the original indigenous inhabitants and what to call ourselves.

It is important to remember how we started off in this place if we do not want to end up back where we started. "On Being" columnist, Omid Safi writes that "America is and has always been a dream wrapped around a nightmare."

> Yes, America is and has always been a dream wrapped around a nightmare, but there is still something noble about this flawed experiment. And we have to love this experiment enough to dream of a better America, and a better humanity.
>
> I still have hope that if enough of us reach out together, and march forward, that light will have victory over darkness, love over hatred, and unity over division . . . hope for a more perfect union.[6]

The Americas were a dream home for her indigenous inhabitants, but this dream became a nightmare as their lands were taken, their children were taken away, their language and religion was outlawed, and they were pushed to the margins of America. Roxanne Dunbar-Ortiz, in *An Indigenous People's History of the United States*, calls the nightmare a "culture of conquest—violence, exploitation, destruction, and dehumanization," and further, "genocide."[7] The Indian wars lasted nearly 400 years and in some ways they are still going on with the occupation of Alcatraz in 1969, the events at Wounded Knee with AIM (the American Indian Movement) in 1973, and even in 2016 with the Water Protectors at Standing Rock.

---

5 Howard Zinn, *A People's History of the United States*, 1-2. In what seems like blasphemy to modern ears, Columbus wrote "Let us in the name of the Holy Trinity go on sending all the slaves that can be sold" (Howard Zinn, *A People's History of the United States*, 4). Zinn describes the Indigenous people that Columbus encountered "Arawaks," while Charles Mann speaks of the Taino.

6 Omid Safi, "We Need Hope That's Gritty and Grounded," *On Being* Blog, 11/17/16.

7 Roxanne Dunbar-Ortiz, *An Indigenous People's History of the United States*, 32. See also Dee Brown's *Bury My Heart at Wounded Knee*.

The nightmare for African people started when they were brought to these shores against their will and sold as slaves. Slavery was legal in all thirteen colonies and in the newly formed United States of American up until the thirteenth amendment in 1865. The struggles for equality and acceptance still continue to this day. We cannot separate what we have done on this land from the land itself, for what we do to the land, we do to ourselves and the people of the Americas as well.

We will get to the dream of the United States of America in another chapter, but we first need to deal with the nightmare. Carl Jung spoke about the archetype of the "shadow" and that when we do not meet, and "own," and integrate our shadow, we project it off on others. Native Americans and African Americans have borne a tremendous burden of the weight of the Europeans shadow, the darkness our ancestors refused to own and projected off on to others. The land, itself, is a place that European Christians projected their shadow. The Puritans saw the forest as evil and demonized religions that sought harmony with nature. Our bodies are also a place of unconsciousness for us because they are made of same earth that we believe we are separate from. Life is a *psychosomatic* experience, meaning a coming together of mind (psyche/soul) and body, yet we have split ourselves off from life.

Indigenous cultures do not have the pronounced split between spirit and matter that we do in the industrialized world. The material is the place where the spiritual manifests. There is such an integration of spirituality into everyday life, the Pueblos do not even have a word for "religion" that is apart from daily life. Joe Sando, a Towa (similar to Tiwa) language speaker from Jemez Pueblo writes the following:

> The Pueblos have no word that translates as "religion." The knowledge of a spiritual life is part of the person twenty-four hours a day, every day of the year. . . . The tradition of religious belief permeates every aspect of the people's life; it determines man's relation with the natural world and with his fellow man. Its basic concern is continuity of a harmonious relationship with the world in which man lives.[8]

Indigenous traditions teach that we are rooted in the land, that we are of the land and that we are the land. *Indigenous* means to be of or from the land, born in and of the land. The land is our Mother Earth and up above

8 Joe Sando, *The Pueblo Indians*, cited in Wilt, *The Visionary*, 38.

is Father Sky. Many indigenous traditions have stories about the creation of the earth occurring from the separation of the primal parents embrace. Usually the male principle is pushed skyward and the feminine principle remains as the Earth. In the Māori creation story, the Earth is the body of a woman who is separated from her lover and this separation creates the space for all creatures to flourish. Our flesh is from the flesh of this mother Earth, the carbon, oxygen, nitrogen and other compounds that comprise our physical bodies are all from the Earth and they return to the Earth. In this way, we are like an eruption from the surface of the Earth that arches through a brief time of being and then is re-absorbed back from whence we came. This view of the Earth as our Mother creates a far different relationship than in technological culture where the Earth is a dead pile of resources for us to use to create more material objects and progress and profit for the ego.

David Abram, a cultural ecologist and philosopher, writes that indigenous healers' power comes from being in the service of the larger natural world, rather than being solely at the disposal of the human world and human society. "The medicine person's primary allegiance," he writes, "is not to the human community, but to the earthly web of relations in which that community is embedded—it is from this that his or her power to alleviate human illness derives."[9] This healing is not just the personal healing of illness, but the healing of the wound of our culture. Abram, as well as many other contemporary writers, seeks to return to a sense of wonder and connection with the natural world that we have lost through the development of our Western rationality, intellect, and objective science. "Becoming earth. Becoming animal. Becoming, in this manner, fully human," his vision is congruent with what we are doing in this book, *Becoming Medicine*. Abram develops the idea that we can only have a sense of self develop in relationship to others whom we are interconnected with. He calls this our "Interbeing with the earth."[10]

9 David Abram, *The Spell of the Sensuous*, 8.

10 David Abram, *Becoming Animal: An Earthly Cosmology*, 3, 38.

THE LAND: NAH-MEH-NEH

Joseph Rael's teachings often relate to the land and specific landmarks of his life. As a child living at Picuris Pueblo, he realized that the people and the land are the same thing, the same vibration, the same being.

> As we plowed and planted the land each spring, we were revitalizing and empowering ourselves. As we tended crops we were revitalizing and empowering our own personal individual strengths. . . . I had the revelation that the original ideas that make up our human bodies were vibrations instilled in matter, instilled in soil and seed and grain.[11]

We are not separate from the land, we are extensions of the land. Ceremonies are about this realization and harmonize the land of our bodies with the land outside us. We think of our lives as our own, however, Joseph tells us that the "land is telling the story," and that we are being told rather than telling. Our lives are not our own. Our lives are the story of the land. Even further, the "story of the land" is "the Vast Self, speaking about what it knows it is."[12]

Joseph still lives in the land of his mother, on the Southern Ute Reservation. He also lived on the land of his father, at Picuris Pueblo. Joseph has traveled the world, yet he lives near where he grew up. The Native American relationship to the land is like that of an adult child to his or her mother—respect, care-taking, stewardship. These aren't just words, the indigenous identity is rooted and grounded in the land, the particular tribal land, in a way that is analogous to how technological society grounds its identity in the ego and material, rather than a particular place. This is often described as the Westerner having a "portable" identity, whereas Indigenous people have an identity that relates to a particular land.

THE INFLUENCE OF THE SOIL ON THE SOUL (PSYCHE)

Carl Jung observed that people who move to a new land absorb through their unconscious the qualities and influence of that particular land. He noticed this primarily in Europeans who colonized the United States. In an essay called "Mind and Earth," he wrote that "we can confidently expect this human group to undergo certain psychic and perhaps physical changes

11 Joseph Rael, "The People and the Land," in Jonathan Greenberg and William Kistler (eds.), *Buying America Back: Economic Choices for the 1990s*, 541.

12 *Ceremonies*, 6–7.

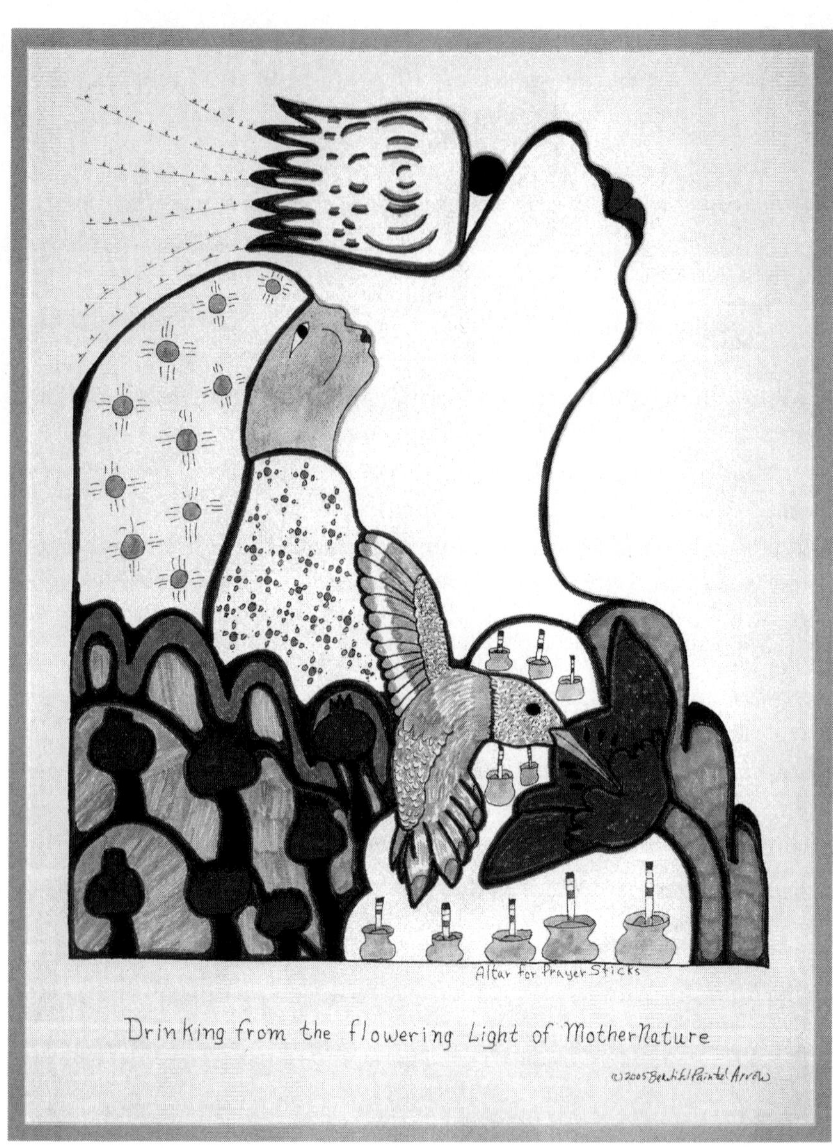

DRINKING FROM THE FLOWERING LIGHT OF MOTHER NATURE

over the course of the next few generation, even without the admixture of foreign blood." He calls this the "mysterious Indianization of the American people."[13] In working with Americans in therapy, he first saw their outward behavior seemed more African than European, but as he got deeper into the unconscious psyche he encountered Native American attitudes toward initiation. He saw this *Indianization* manifested unconsciously in the American love of sports, the single-minded pursuit of work, and also in religious expression. He observed that American's fantasy of the hero was influenced, unconsciously, by the Native American warrior and shaman.

> In everything on which the American has really set his heart we catch a glimpse of the Indian. His extraordinary concentration on a particular goal, his tenacity of purpose, his unflinching endurance of the greatest hardships—in all this the legendary virtues of the Indian find full expression. . . . I have found in my American patients that their hero-figure possesses traits derived from the religion of the Indians. The most important figure in their religion is the shaman, the medicine-man or conjurer of spirits. . . . [American religion] possesses a strength derived from the soil.

As Jung speaks of the influence of the *soil*, he also talks about the *soul*, words that sound similar in English. From his work in psychotherapy with Americans, Jung came to see Americans as Europeans who exhibited African behavior from the influence of slavery (e.g. Jazz music), and had "an Indian soul." He demonstrated the influence of *soil* on *soul* in his work. This reminds us of Joseph's explanation that the Tiwa word for soil is *nah meh neh* and that the word for self is *nah*. Who we are is part of the soil of the Earth. When we move to different land, we absorb the influence of the *soil* into our *soul*. Joseph also points out that when we drink water, our throats make the sound "soul" with each swallow. Drinking the water of a land is bringing in its soul into our soul with every gulp. Anyone born on American soil could be considered "Native American," which is why this is not the best term to refer to the indigenous peoples of North America. Jung pointed out that some Australian aborigines believe that "one cannot conquer foreign soil, because in it there dwell strange ancestor-spirits

13 Jung, *Civilization in Transition* CW 10: 45, 46. Jung's *Symbols of Transformation* draws heavily upon his work with an American woman, Miss Miller's, imaginations of the creative unconscious which included many references to the story of Hiawatha. Jung ran a 5 year seminar, from 1930-1934, called "The Interpretation of Visions," which focused on his psychotherapeutic work with another American woman, Christina Morgan.

who reincarnate themselves in the new-born." He found that there is a "great psychological truth" expressed in this belief and concludes that the "foreign land assimilates its conqueror."[14]

Jung saw a secret counter-force at work where the colonizers took on attributes of the colonized, mediated through the land itself. The flow of influence on empires reveals *reverse cultural diffusion* which flows from the colonized back to the colonizer. In England you can readily find curry shops which diffused back from the former colonies of India and Pakistan. Asian religions surged back into the United States after the Korean and Vietnam wars. The Islamic Sufi poet, Rumi, has been the most popular poet in the United States (after years of occupation and preoccupation with the Middle East).[15] Contact between cultures results in a two-way exchange and influence, regardless of whether one culture politically, economically, or militarily dominates the other. Connection is connection and flows both ways.

Jung pointed out that as the Roman Empire militarily and politically conquered Asia Minor, the religions of the East came back in the form of the Mithraic cult. He showed that religions often borrow from earlier religions. Jung writes that it does seem that the East is sparking "the spiritual change" we are going through in the West. However, he writes that "this East . . . lies within us. It is from the depths of our own psychic life that new spiritual forms will arise."[16]

THE INVISIBLE COUNTER-PLAYER

Joseph Campbell spoke of a similar concept of the "invisible counter-player,"[17] to represent the influence of cultures which exerted a hidden, unseen influence on later cultures. Campbell borrowed this term from ethnologist and archaeologist Leo Frobenius who used it to describe the influence of a culture whose artifacts were less durable and decayed quicker than another cultures. For instance, a culture who worked with wood and cloth would not have as robust of an archaeological presence as one that worked with stone or metal. Campbell applied this concept to the influence of pre-Aryan, Dravidian culture of India (such as Mohenjo-daro) on the invading Aryan, Vedic culture. Campbell traces images of

14 Ibid., 48, 49, 49.

15 Jane Ciabattari, "Why is Rumi the best-selling poet in the US?" *BBC* online, 10/21/14.

16 *MMSS*, 217.

17 Joseph Campbell, *The Masks of God, Volume 2: Oriental Mythology*, 154. Campbell borrowed this term from archaeologist, Leo Frobenius.

the god, Śiva,[18] back to Dravidian and perhaps earlier sources. The Śiva complex is an example of the influence of an invisible counter-player in which elements of pre-Aryan yoga, meditation, association with animals (possible shamanic elements?), and also the goddess (for instance, Kali) integrated with the later over-lay of Vedic, Aryan elements.

> For the calmly ruthless power of the jungle and consequent orientation of its folk . . . has supplied the drone base of whatever song has ever been sung in India of man, his destiny, and his escape from destiny. New civilizations, races, philosophies, and great mythologies have poured into India and have been not only assimilated but greatly developed, enriched, and sophisticated. Yet, in the end (and, in fact even secretly throughout), the enduring power in that land has always been the same old dark goddess of the long red tongue who turns everything into her own everlasting, awesome . . . self.[19]

BLAST AND COUNTERBLAST

Nataraja Guru, in his chapter "Blast and Counterblast," picks up this same theme of the Dravidian influence of the Śiva complex on the later development of various forms of Hinduism.

> [T]he nature of the blast and counterblast, the thesis and antithesis, in the process of the formulation of the Word in its Indian 'home.' We have seen how the Śiva tradition, far from being overcovered during the five thousand years and more from its earliest visible appearance in Mohenjo-Dāro, still survives as the dominant spiritual note in common Indian life to the present day.[20]

Nataraja Guru describes the Aryan invasion as the "blast" and the "counter-blast" as the hidden influence of the strength of Dravidian Śiva tradition that influenced the invaders and the eventual hybrid culture that developed. The counter-blast is similar to Campbell's "invisible counter-player" and our discussion of counter-cultural diffusion. One element that is relevant to our current book is that Nataraja Guru weaves an additional thread into his discussion of the historical influence of one

18 The Sanskrit word, "Śiva," is often Anglicized to "Shiva." We will generally use the original Sanskrit, Śiva, in this book, roughly pronounced in English, "Shiva."

19 Campbell, Ibid., 164.

20 Nataraja Guru, *The Word of the Guru: The Life and Teachings of Nārāyana Guru*, 179. For a more recent discussion of the historical and mythological influence of the ancient Śiva complex on later culture and consciousness, see Sadhguru Jaggi Vasudev and Arundhathi Subramaniam's *Adiyogi: The Source of Yoga* (2017).

culture on another: the influence of *the Word of the Guru*. He writes of his own teacher, Nārāyana Guru and the oral tradition of *Word-wisdom* that stretches back through oral history into ancient times and is interwoven with the land itself. In this way, the Word of the Guru is a counter-blast and invisible counter-player to the distractions of ordinary reality and is constantly reminding us of the hidden reality of non-ordinary reality that is continually vibrating with the silent Word that shapes reality.

> Here therefore we have the essence of the formulation of the Word of wisdom in a typical situation of opposition. . . . Between these bellowing challenges the Word is again formulated. One hears its silent, still voice. In subtle reciprocity, one shrill blast evokes and implies its counter-blast, and in that delicate relationship is the secret of silence, of the Word-wisdom of the *guru*.
>
> The silent Guru of Varkala, sitting on a hill-top at the southern extremity of Mother India, steeped in the silence of non-dual unitive vision, integrated all the contributory views and visions into one whole, brought all within the scope of one contemplative Word-Wisdom, by which human dignity could be held high everywhere and all mankind become free.[21]

These inter-related terms, *counter-blast, the invisible counter-player, counter-cultural diffusion*, and *Word-wisdom*—all tell us that the hidden, the secret, the ignored, and the conquered still exert an influence on our consciousness and culture. This hidden secret is woven into Reality, into our consciousness, our bodies, and the land upon which we walk. Jung saw the land, itself, having a role in this—that the energy of the land influences the people living upon the land. He often wrote of the *anima mundi*, the "world soul." Jung's idea of the anima is that it was the inner, feminine aspect of a man's soul. *Anima*, in Latin, means soul. The *anima mundi* is the soul of the world. As American Indians often refer to the earth as Mother Earth, we can think of the *anima mundi* also as feminine—the nurturing and sustaining aspect of life. In coming into relationship with our own souls we can also go deeper until we come into contact with the *anima mundi*, the world soul. To know the land is to know ourselves.

21 Nataraja Guru, *The Word of the Guru: The Life and Teachings of Nārāyana Guru*, 174, 189.

DAVID'S ANCESTORS & THE LAND[22]

Joseph told me to get my DNA traced through National Genographic and that piqued my interest in the relationship of my ancestors to the lands of North America, Europe, Southwest Asia, and Africa as I followed the threads backward in time.

My father's family all emigrated from Poland in the early 20th Century. My mother's family had a line of recent emigration from Wales in the early 20th Century and then also stretched back to the early English colonies, and further back to Ireland, Wales, England, and Northern Europe. I, David, was born in Naperville, Illinois. The word "Naperville" comes from the "Naper" settlement of 1831 by Joseph Naper. The word, *Illinois*, can be traced through the French interpretation of a Native American root word through Miami-Illinois, Ojibwe and Ottawa dialect, originally meaning "he speaks the regular way."[23] I grew up in rural Yorkville, Illinois until age 4. My parents rented an old farm house on High Point Road, a gravel road.

There are no Indian reservations in Illinois, although it was once home to numerous native peoples. These peoples were pushed off the land through war, treaties, and disease. Their languages linger on in place names like *Oswego*, *Waubonsee*, and *Chicago*. Sometimes it is difficult to find the history of native peoples and the land they lived on in the United States. Our public and written histories are largely told from the perspective of the European colonizers. We are told the names of the colonizers who first arrived and they are glorified, but we are not often told the names of the people who lived here prior to being dispossessed. Just as we have a responsibility to know ourselves, we have a responsibility to know the deeper history of the land we are living upon. A place to start with this is the *Native Land* website and app. According to *Native Land*, Oswego, Illinois was home to the Miami, Potawatomi, Peoria, and Očeti Šakówiŋ (Sioux).[24] The Potawatomi, Ottawa, and Ojibwe are said to have once been one tribe that came into Wisconsin and Illinois from Michigan. The three tribes formed a federation called the "Three Fires."[25]

22 My sister, Karen Kopacz, is writing a book called *If Land, Then Peace* that also takes a look at the lands that we live upon. She combines drawing, lived experience, and environmental research, focusing on different sites across the Midwest.

23 "Illinois," *Wikipedia*.

24 Native Land website, https://native-land.ca/, accessed 11/26/18. *Wikipedia* also lists Ottawa and Chippewa for this region.

25 Wayne Temple, *Indian Villages of the Illinois Country*, 126.

The Potawatomi were the keepers of the council fire and thus were given their name, which means "Keepers of the Fire."[26] Even when we try to learn the native history of the land in the United States it is often distorted through the intervention of the colonial perspective and influence. For instance, the Potawatomi were more closely allied with the French in the wars against the encroaching English. The colonial powers would often favor one people over another and this led to conflicts, war, and changed the relationship of peoples to the land.[27]

In New Zealand, Māori introductions include three points of orientation: the mountain closest to one's childhood home, the closest river, and the *waka* (ocean-going canoe) that brought your ancestors to New Zealand. I would always say that Air New Zealand was my *waka* that brought me to New Zealand. I consider High Point Hill, where we lived in rural Yorkville, my orienting mountain. It is the highest point in Kendall County at around 800 feet elevation. In the spring, after the farmers plowed, my parents found arrowheads in the fields, reminding us of the lands connection to Native Americans. My dad built a house in Oswego and we moved there when I was four years old and my sister was born that same year of 1971. Our house was still in the country, but a little closer to town and it was near a branch of the Waubonsie Creek and I consider that my river.[28] As a child I would walk down to the creek and fish, or wander. It was my own little wild place. There was an Osage orange tree a little north of the creek and that was another favorite hang-out, particularly when the large, green softball size fruit would fall.

I like to imagine the land before European colonizers arrived. It is difficult to relate to generic people, so I imagine the lives of specific people, a native man and a native woman. *Waish-Kee-Shah* was a Potawatomi woman who married an American settler, David Laughton and they had a son named Joseph. There is a historical record of a land deed in her

26 R. David Edmunds, *The Potawatomis: Keepers of the Fire*, 3–4.

27 I have gathered this little bit of information from books and the internet. I have made an initial attempt at communication with the Potawatomi Nation. My understanding is that the Prairie Band Potawatomi Indian Reservation is where the peoples who lived on the land before me where forcibly relocated to. However, I have not yet been able to hear the history of the people from their own mouths.

28 "Oswego" is said to derive from Mohawk language meaning "outpouring." There is an Oswego, New York, as well as in Kansas. Waubonsie was a Potawatomi chief in the 1700s whose name means "Break of Day" *(waaban-izhi)* or "He Causes Paleness" *(waabaanizii)*.

name. When I was a kid, we would drive out to Waa Kee Sha Park.[29] I only recently learned this park is named after this woman. I picture her standing on this land that is now a park, stopping whatever work she was doing and listening to a distant bird.[30]

There is more written information about *Wabanzi (Waubonsee, Wabanzi)*, a Potawatomi man—a warrior, diplomat, and a man whose name is still spoken: Waubonsie Creek, Waubonsie Valley High School, Waubonsee Community College. Wabanzi fought with the British against the Americans in Tecumseh's War, the War of 1812, and the Battle of Tippecanoe. Later, he supported the Americans in the attack on Fort Dearborn and in the Black Hawk War. He visited Washington D.C. twice and signed the treaty removing the Potawatomi from Illinois and Indiana. There are at least two paintings of Wabanzi that can be found on-line. I picture him standing at the mouth (*oswego*: "outpouring") of the Waubonsie Creek where it meets the Fox River. Wabanzi was given a house, in the forced relocation of the Potawatomi, near present day Tabor, Iowa, (where there is a Waubonsie Avenue), not too far from Omaha, Nebraska.

What does it mean when a person's name continues to be spoken after his or her death? On the one hand, there is cultural appropriation—the hollow honoring of one native person after the removal of an indigenous nation. On the other hand, Joseph might say that there is a meaning and a power in those words and letters that keeps alive an energy of the land. We remember names and say them because the land wants us to remember something.

There was a man who went by the nickname, "The Fox." He was an environmental activist whose righteous anger from seeing a family of ducks dead from industrial pollution on the Fox River led him to take action and raise awareness about the effects of industrial pollution.[31] We

29 Roger Matile, *Oswego Township: Images of America*, 9. There is a forgotten history that our parks were once Indian reservations, for instance see Robert Keller and Michael Turk's *American Indians & National Parks*.

30 I realize that my imaging of a lone Indigenous person could be a form of the colonial trope of the "vanishing race," in which Indigenous people are idealized in their passing away. That is not my intention, but rather to raise awareness of the history of the land and the names we still use. Would statues of Waish-Kee-Shah and Waubonsee with information about who they were, their people's life on the land, and where their descendants now live honor them or appropriate them?

31 Ray Fox wrote a book about his work called, *Raising Kane: The Fox Chronicles*. There is also a recent documentary on him called *The Legend of the Fox: World Famous Eco-Hero* (2018).

heard about him when we were kids—in fact, we wrongly suspected one of our high school teachers to be The Fox, because he talked about him all the time. What spirit possessed him to speak up for the environment, particularly the waters of the Fox River and her tributaries, like Waubonsie Creek? The Fox was featured in National Geographic and Mike Royko, a *Chicago Tribune* columnist used to write about him. I have not been able to figure out if the Fox River is named after the animal the fox, or after the Native American peoples, the *Meskwaki*, called the Fox, in English. There are two Fox Rivers, one in Illinois and one in Wisconsin, both in the one-time territories of the Fox (Meskwaki).

I grew up surrounded by farmland that grew soybeans and corn. We would eat young soybeans or young field corn as we wandered through the fields. We would run through the corn fields at night when it was hot and humid and the sharp leaves would make small "paper cuts" on bare arms. When the corn was high we would disappear into the ocean of green. The Midwest *was* once an ocean, the Western Interior Seaway (or as Tim Flannery calls it, the Bearpaw Sea). There is a small, extinct marine creature called *Tentaculites oswegoensis*, found fossilized around Oswego and the Waubonsie Creek. This little sea creature became extinct around 350 million years ago at the end of the Devonian period.[32] Fossils of shells were plentiful in the limestone in the area. The rich Midwestern soil was once ocean floor and it also benefited from the glaciers that pushed down topsoil from the north. These glaciers began retreating around 18,000 years ago.[33]

32 "Tentaculites oswegoensis," *Wikipedia*.

33 A fascinating history of North America is *The Eternal Frontier*, by geological ecologist Tim Flannery. Henri Roca recommended this book a couple times to me as I spoke with him about *Becoming Medicine*. Flannery examines the geological structure of the United States and North America and finds interesting, unique features, such as it being the only continent to have two parallel mountain ranges running North to South. This "climatic trumpet" serves to amplify climatic changes in the world, making them more extreme. Flannery hypothesizes that this structure of the land influences the evolution of organisms living on the land and tends to create extremes of diversity through periods of "ecological release" with rapid expansion, followed by extremes of diversity when the limits of expansion are reached. He also sees the effects of the vast frontiers in North America shaping its organisms and peoples. He sees this happening first with humans during the rapid expansion of the Clovis culture around 13,000 years ago which rapidly spread across North America. There followed the extinction of the mega-fauna of mastodons and the like, and then a splintering of Clovis culture into the myriad of Native American cultures. Flannery sees the recent history of the United States expansion across the frontier as possibly paralleling ancient history. "The very essence of the frontier experience lies in the extent of its resources, and when the resources are boundless, why conserve them efficiently? The principal goal is to exploit them as quickly

The land is our connection to ancientness and if we want to know who we are, we must learn not just psychology, but history and even ancient history of our ancestors and of the land.

Carl Jung taught us that there are centers of consciousness within us that do not derive from the personal memories of the ego, but reach back into ancient history. Our bodies carry DNA that reaches back to the first human beings in Africa. The foods that we eat have histories that stretch back thousands of years. I ate from the fields of corn and soybeans and breathed in the oxygen the plants produced. Corn is native to North America, however, soybeans are originally from Southeast Asia and were domesticated by the Chinese around 6000 – 7000 BCE. *Maize* (Corn) was domesticated in the Americas possibly as early as 9000 BCE.[34] It is interesting that I (whose genetic heritage is of the "West") lived on the land of the Potowatomi, Ottawa, and Ojibwe, and was surrounded by an alternating intermingling of plant peoples from the East and the indigenous (albeit highly modified) North American maize. In some ways the Americas can be seen as a third place between East and West. Columbus initially could not comprehend that there was something other than "East" and "West" when he stumbled upon a third place.

After 17 years in Yorkville and Oswego, Illinois, I moved downstate to Champaign-Urbana for undergraduate, then up to Chicago for eight years of medical and psychiatric education, out to Omaha, Nebraska for two years, then back to Champaign for 11 years. Most of my life was spent living on the rich humus of the Midwest. Maybe this influenced my creativity, the years of putting down deep roots and drawing nourishment from *nah-meh-neh* that still resonated with the ancient ocean waves of the Bearpaw Sea. In 2010 we picked up and moved to New Zealand for three and a half years. I had never been there, but knew I always wanted to go there. We lived on the sea, on *Tīkapa Moana* (the Hauraki Gulf), looking out at the relatively young volcano, *Rangitoto*. Every day I would look out at the sky, the ocean, and the volcano.

I was familiar with Jung's ideas of how the land influences the unconscious of the people living on it, as well as with American Indian

---

as possible, then move on. It is this frontier attitude to resource utilisation that lies at the heart of much capitalism, and which presents a major challenge to conservationists today. In this sense, the legacy of the American frontier is still very much with us," (292).

34 The word, "maize," comes from the Taíno language, *mahiz*. Like potatoes, peppers (capsicum) and squash, maize was exported from the Americas and has become a staple food source world-wide. "Maize," *Wikipedia*.

concepts of the land as our Mother when I moved to New Zealand. The indigenous Māori of New Zealand also had a similar concept which can be seen in the root of the word *whenua*,[35] which means "placenta" as well as "the land." The land is that which sustains the people, just as the placenta is that which sustains the fetus. I knew of these concepts when I first walked upon New Zealand soil, but I did not remember them as I struggled my first year there, trying to "fit in." At times I felt like the land was indifferent to me, that I could not establish a root connection or sense of grounding during that first year. I also had several minor to moderate knee and hip injuries or pains that made it difficult for me to walk at times. Sometimes I even felt that the spirit of the land (the spirit of the Māori people) was openly hostile toward me. I would feel this at night sometimes when I awoke and would hear arguments outside our flat in the park across the street. I had this sense of fear and not fitting in that was greater than I had ever experienced before. I was yet another colonizer whose family history reached back to Europe. Blood was spilled on the land of New Zealand, Māori blood, European blood. Looking back it makes sense to me that I had to go through a period of physical and emotional adjustment to living on this land.

We lived in Mission Bay in Auckland. Mission Bay is named for the Melanesian Mission School that was set up there to teach Melanesian boys Christianity and Western education. This land was the *whenua* of *Ngāti Whātua iwi* (tribe) at the time of English colonization. Up the hill from where we lived was *Kohimarama* (Bastion Point) which was a large open space of a public park and a *marae* (a Māori communal/sacred building and meeting place). This same place was taken over by the New Zealand government in 1885 and made into a military fort. There are still concrete bunkers on the top of the hill. In 1977 there was a New Zealand government plan to build a housing development on this site. It was occupied for 2 years by the Orakei Māori Action Committee and a new *marae* was built and they began growing crops again on the land. In 1980, the land was returned to the *Ngāti Whātua iwi*, part of which is a public park.[36]

35 Richard Katz writes of the Fijian word, *"vanua"* which seems to be related to the Māori word *"whenua."* "Vanua is one of the most important words in the Fijian language, describing the heart of Fijian culture. Vanua is an experience; it means the 'land' but more concretely 'the land and the people who live on it' or 'our place, our culture and its traditions," (Katz, *Indigenous Healing Psychology*, 344).

36 "Bastion Point," *Wikipedia*.

This land where I lived has a complicated history and it is no wonder that I had a complicated time my first year coming to terms living on it. The adjustment was difficult at first as I struggled to put down roots in the rocky soil and come into a relationship with the land. There is much of great value buried in this land. This was my *whenua* in New Zealand, the placenta that at first seemed to reject my presence. Eventually, I came to feel accepted by the land and by the people of New Zealand and I felt nurtured by the *whenua*. I came to thrive there and there is a part of me that relished the sense of belonging and also being an outsider at the same time. Maybe I needed some distance from where I grew up, or maybe I needed to be closer to an active and living ocean after years of living where the echoes of the waves were ancient. Or, maybe I needed the volcanic and tectonic activity and the powerful energy moving beneath the surface of the Earth. Something happened to me in New Zealand and my writing shifted and expanded and I wrote my first book there.

When I left New Zealand, one of the gifts I was given was a colored pencil artwork which depicted me sitting in full lotus position, surrounded by a glowing light while a vast blue face was above me, next to me was a woman with arms raised and Maui, the cultural Māori hero was holding the sun. There was a written text on the back of this artwork.

> Dr. Dave's moment of Satori at Takapuna Beach in the middle of the night. Ranginui the sky father is present giving you his blessings of a safe trip home. Papatuanuku the Earth goddess is praying to Ranginui hoping you will visit Aotearoa's shores some time again in your future. Maui has caught the sun slowing down its course across the sky so there is enough daylight for life to be reborn again.

Then we moved to Seattle in the Northwest of the United States, where I have been now for five years. Seattle is named after Chief Seattle (*Si'ahl*) of the Duwamish and Suquamish peoples who lived on this land prior to European and American colonization. I visited this land often in my early adulthood, visiting family and friends, and sleeping on the mountains, in the forests, and on the shores of the ocean. I have also felt this sense of trying to come into connection and harmony with the land. In some ways I feel more "alien" here than I did when I left New Zealand. It is also a place that I have long felt was a "home away from home" as I had travelled out many times and camped and lived on the land. Sometimes I think that I am supposed to try to connect to all the lands of the Earth,

to be a Planetary Citizen, a Global Citizen, a Cosmic Citizen. This land has been very good for me professionally and creatively. The soil here is quite different than the Midwest; it is very rocky, but the dirt is blacker than the New Zealand soil where we lived. We are not as close to the ocean, but I can still feel it in the air some days and other days I feel the cold, mountain air coming down. Things grow well here with all the rain and the temperate climate. My work here has taken root, but my work is also in what seems like the opposite climate, the dry, high desert of the Southwest where I frequently visit Joseph.

I do not remember as much of a conscious and unconscious struggle when I moved to Omaha, Nebraska, although I do remember the feeling of it being familiar and also different, "Western." I remember learning that Omaha was a meeting point of three different ecosystems and that made sense to me and I relaxed in some way. How much are we to return to our past and how much are we to move forward into the future? Where is my home: Seattle, Auckland, Champaign-Urbana, Omaha, Chicago, Oswego, Yorkville? I remember feeling in New Zealand a tension between trying to fit in and to maintain my past connections. This was obvious in maintaining relationships, but it was also playing out on a larger as well as more internal field. Some of my alienation in Seattle, even as I am flourishing professionally, creatively, spiritually, comes from my sense of separation as much as from my sense of belonging. Joseph Rael describes himself as a world citizen and sometimes I think that means that there is a tension between a focused sense of place-identity (when expressed negatively this becomes fundamentalism and parochialism) and an expansive sense of world-identity.

People in the United States have a very different relationship with the land. Tim Flannery writes that the United States was born out of "two remarkable movements—a revolution and an act of union."[37] He sees this tension playing out in our history and he links the adaptation of human beings and other organisms to the realities of the land upon which they live. He sees the frontier mentality as "ruthless exploitation, greed and senseless environmental destruction," but he also sees "one of the most striking aspects of the North American people is their ability to reinvent themselves."[38] Flannery sees a glimmer of hope that living harmoniously with the land may prove stronger than the frontier mentality of exploitation. "If the frontier dreaming of North America has to be destroyed so its environment and people can move into the future, then I'm sure it will be done. . . . After all, the frontier is a state of mind as much as anything, and even now the minds of its citizens are changing rapidly." North Americans continue to expand the frontier, exploring space and moving into the vast open space that we have come to call the internet. However, we can no longer afford to view the land we live on as an eternal frontier and we must learn to live in harmony and preservation of the land because we ourselves are the land.

JOSEPH'S ANCESTORS AND THE LAND

Joseph comments throughout the book on different places and experiences, so we will just give a brief discussion here. Joseph's mother was Southern Ute and he also says she had French blood. His father was from Picuris Pueblo. Joseph was born on the Southern Ute reservation[39] and lived there until his mother died when he was about six years old and then moved 200 miles away to live with his father's people at Picuris.

37 Tim Flannery, *The Eternal Frontier*, 281.

38 Ibid., 337, 353–54

39 The Ute People were divided into the Southern Ute Reservation, the Ute Mountain and Uintah-Ouray Reservations. Dee Brown's *Bury My Heart at Wounded Knee* has a chapter entitled, "The Utes Must Go!" that recounts the animosity miners and settlers had toward the Utes as they pushed into their ancestral lands and relocated them.

Joseph attended the Santa Fe Indian School as a teen and studied art with José Rey Toledo of Jemez Pueblo.

Joseph attended undergraduate at University of New Mexico in Albuquerque and went to graduate school at University of Wisconsin in Madison. He returned to the Southwest and worked for tribal organizations, the All Indian Pueblo Council, and HUD. He also got certified in hypnosis and worked as a substance abuse counselor with the Indian Health Service. His work took him across New Mexico and Arizona. Joseph grew up on the land of Northern New Mexico and Southern Colorado and he lives there still.

For a time, though, Joseph lived in New York City and from there traveled the world, taking his vision of the Sound Peace Chambers to the United Kingdom, Europe, Australia, New Zealand, Canada and South America. He has traveled back and forth across the Atlantic and Pacific Oceans. Joseph has told me on several occasions that his sense of not fully belonging to one people fully led him to become a Global Citizen.

LAND IS THE LOVING-SELF PLACE

Joseph wrote to me, "*We who live on Planet Earth are her children, we are the people of the Land & Sky, the Sky Our Father.*" In a chapter called, "People of the Land," Joseph writes about the interconnection of the people with the land and sky, and also how the very Tiwa language comes from the sound vibrations of the land. He calls *home* "the loving-self place."

> I saw the connection that all the natural sounds, the vibrations of nature that were in the spoken English or spoken Tiwa languages also vibrated in the land and the sky. . . .
>
> The land on which we live is the means by which we are making ourselves anew. At Picuris our home was the "loving-self place" and homegrown food from our vegetable gardens, fruit trees, wildberries and root were all composed of the energies of this loving-self place.

Joseph describes the resonance between land and language and that the land is the place where we love ourselves. To nurture the land is to nurture ourselves. He continues in describing how when we lose this connection, we fall into black and white thinking of division and polarization. He then tells us of his return to Picuris after being away for years.

> After I had been gone from Picuris for 36 years . . . on my return, at the precise moment I entered the fence line walking toward our

> ranch house, I sensed an energy similar in vibration to my own physical energy. The knowingness that I had just received was that the land and I were the same . . . I had rediscovered myself![40]

Indigenous traditions find our place of belonging in the active relationship with Mother Earth and specific, ancestral land. Many mystical spiritual traditions place our true home as elsewhere from the Earth—Christian views of exile from the Garden of Eden, the journey back to Heaven, and Jesus' statement "I am not of the world;"[41] the Sufi recognition that we are not from here and will return elsewhere; and the views of many Hindu and Buddhist traditions that the physical world, our bodies, and even our egos are *maya* (illusion)—all these teachings point our spiritual goal as somewhere other than our bodies and the physical Earth. So, I asked Joseph what it means that so many people in the US do not have this relationship to the land. Joseph said, "*Well, I think that these are the generations of humans that are getting ready to go up into space, you know, to go up with the ETs.*" Joseph says that this is consistent with the teachings of the Native peoples of the Southwest—either we came from elsewhere, or some of us left here and will come back later. He cites drawings of spaceships and teachings of sky beings who came to Earth in machines, as well as his own visions.

Our bodies are made of the land. The land is the body of Mother Earth. Mother Earth is made up of the elements created from the deaths of generations of stars. We are of the land, we are of the stars. Indigenousness is our relationship to "a particular place," to be "sprung from the land." We are the indigenous people of Mother Earth, we are the indigenous people of the stars. When I have asked Joseph why he thinks Europeans and so many other people now are spreading across the globe, away from the particular place and land that they were born in, he speaks of the need for us all to be world citizens. The goal then would be to spring from the Earth, to belong to the entire planet. Our connection to the Earth and to particular places is through the material of our bodies and our bodies are made of the Earth. More and more people are eating food that is sourced from the entire Earth, not just their local land. While there are costs to this, there is also the hidden teaching that we eat of the land of the Earth: North America, South America, Asia, Australia, New Zealand, India,

40 Joseph Rael, "The People and the Land," in Jonathan Greenberg and William Kistler (eds.), *Buying America Back*, 541, 541-544.

41 John 17:16, *The Holy Bible: Revised Standard Edition, Second Catholic Edition*.

Africa, Europe. If we eat this food with the awareness of thanksgiving and gratitude toward our Mother Earth, our spaceship Earth, we can grow in a sense of being part of, connected to, and relationship with the whole Earth.

THE ORDER OF THE SACRED EARTH

Coming out of Creation Spirituality, Matthew Fox, Skylar Wilson, and Jennifer Berit Listung have recently called for the formation of a post-religious, post-denominational Order of the Sacred Earth. The vow to join this Order is very simple, "I promise to be the best lover and defender of the Earth that I can be." Fox calls for us to become "the best lovers (mystics) and defenders (warriors)" as part of this "*Spiritual Order*."[42]

It is movements like this, which bring people together rather than separating them, and that brings us back into a spiritual and harmonious relationship with the land that we most need right now. We can take vows such as these, *I promise to be the best lover and defender of the Earth that I can be.* Returning to the Land is, at the end of the day, returning to ourselves. Land is the loving-self place, the place that we are found after being lost and the place that we find love and give love. When we recognize the land in ourselves and ourselves in the land, we find out who we are and that we are all one.

---

42 Matthew Fox, Skylar Wilson, and Jennifer Berit Listug, *Order of the Sacred Earth: An Intergenerational Vision of Love and Action*, xvii, 4.

CHAPTER 13

WE ARE ALL PANGEANS — WE ARE ALL RELATED

"Was there life back then? Whether we like it or not, we all come from there, we are all one."

JOSEPH RAEL

At its dawn all the world's continents were joined into one vast landmass known as Pangea, which was inhabited by many kinds of animals and plants. Pangea was destined to divide into two supercontinents, known as Laurasia and Gondwana, and by the end of the era these landmasses had begun to fragment, giving rise to the contemporary continents. . . . Most of the existing continents were formed by fragmentation: Australia, Antarctica, South America and Africa all came into existence as a result of the break-up of the supercontinent Gondwana. North America, however, was created differently—it resulted from a victory of the forces of union.[1]

TIM FLANNERY

INDIGENOUS

We often hear cultures divided up into "Western" and "Eastern" or "Western" and "Native American." All these terms are open to critique as being imprecise or vague. Many indigenous people of the United States have pointed out that there is no such thing as a unified concept as "Native American," rather there are numerous tribes (573 federally recognized) and that it is more correct to refer to a specific tribal affiliation rather than to use the broader term "Native American" culture.

When I was living in New Zealand, I first heard a critique of the term "Western" at "World Dreaming," the 6th World Congress for Psychotherapy conference in Sydney, Australia in 2011. The speaker put forward the concept of "Southern Philosophies" saying that he did not feel that the term "Western" was meaningful to those living in the Southern Hemisphere. I had never really thought about it before, but it made sense.

1 Tim Flannery, *The Eternal Frontier*, 9–10.

We use the term Western, which is a compass direction, yet what we really seem to be referring to is an approximation which includes many people of different cultures and languages who are in Europe or whose ancestors came from Europe and colonized the Americas, New Zealand, Australia as well as other places. In some ways "Western" could be taken to mean "white skinned" or "Caucasian," or "European." Yet it is a fuzzy concept. Are my Polish ancestors from Eastern Europe Westerners? If I am genetically 19% Southwest Asian (according to National Genographic project) am I still a Westerner? On one hand the concept is useful, but on the other hand it is not. The term came into use as a way of dividing and contrasting people, and yet the work we are doing in this book is trying to find a path to unite people.

Sometimes we forget where we came from. We all come from Africa some 200,000 years ago. International trade has existed since Homo sapiens first walked out of Africa. Trade occurred throughout the Americas prior to the arrival of Europeans.[2] In his book on the silk roads, Peter Frankopan writes, "We think of globalisation as a uniquely modern phenomenon; yet 2,000 years ago too, it was a fact of life, one that presented opportunities, created problems, and prompted technological advance." Frankopan describes how it was the place where east and west met, the bridge between them, that was the place of growth, "as they traded and exchanged ideas, they learnt and borrowed from each other, stimulating further advances in philosophy, the sciences, language and religion."[3]

Historian of ancient philosophy, spirituality, and culture, Peter Kingsley, writes, "Where the paths of cultural contact exist there's a standing invitation for the seeker." He describes how not only were there ancient networks of trade, but also networks of trade in ideas, teachings, and initiations. He describes the shamanic travels and teachings of those who were called in ancient Greek, *Iatromantis*—prophetic healers.

---

2 "By 1000 A.D., trade relationships had covered the continent for more than a thousand years: mother-of-pearl from the Gulf of Mexico has been found in Manitoba, and Lake Superior copper in Louisiana," Charles Mann, *1491: New Revelations of the Americas Before Columbus*, 29. Mann describes the Americas as a "thriving, stunningly diverse place," with a "tumult of languages, trade, and culture," much of this world "vanished after Columbus, swept away by disease and subjugation." "So thorough was the erasure that within a few generations," Mann writes, "neither conqueror nor conquered knew that this world had existed. Now, though, it is returning to view. It is incumbent upon us to take a look," (31).

3 Peter Frankopan, *The Silk Roads: A New History of the World*, 13, xvii.

> We now think of East and West. But then there were no real lines to be drawn. The oneness experienced by the Iatromantis on another level of awareness left its mark in the physical world. Even to talk about influence is to limit the reality of what was one vast network of nomads, of travelers, of individuals who lived in time and space but also were in touch with something else.[4]

Joseph tells me that he thinks that the reason that Europeans came to the Americas is because they needed something that was missing in their culture. Joseph called me up and said he had a vision that we need to understand something in terms of cycles of time including events in Europe and the Americas. He encourages me to look at 400 year cycles going backward and forward from the 1400s. In 1492 Columbus set sail for what he thought was India, instead he found the Americas and mistakenly called the indigenous people "Indians." Jumping 400 years ahead we are in the late 1800s and Joseph highlights President U. S. Grant's formation of the reservations. "*Something happened 400 years before Columbus came that set things in motion for his voyage*," Joseph tells me. This gets me looking deeper and deeper into the past.

It does seem true that we "Westerners" have lost something. All colonists have lost a connection with their homelands. Science, technology, capitalism, consumerism have objectified and commodified everything, including ourselves. Many descendants of European colonists either idealize or devalue indigenous peoples. Many tribal people feel they need to protect their traditions and remain separate from the former European colonists, however, some indigenous people feel that they have something to teach the larger culture of the United States. Those of us of the former European colonies who now call ourselves Americans, Kiwis, Australians, Canadians, or South Africans, often look to the indigenous peoples who seem to have a living spirituality and are able to live in harmony and integration with the land. There are both positive and negative aspects to this. It can lead to what is sometimes called "playing Indian" where someone picks and chooses aspects of an indigenous culture. This can lead to appropriation of traditional practices and concepts. I am cautious about this in my work with Joseph.

---

4 Peter Kingsley, *In the Dark Places of Wisdom*, 17, 114.

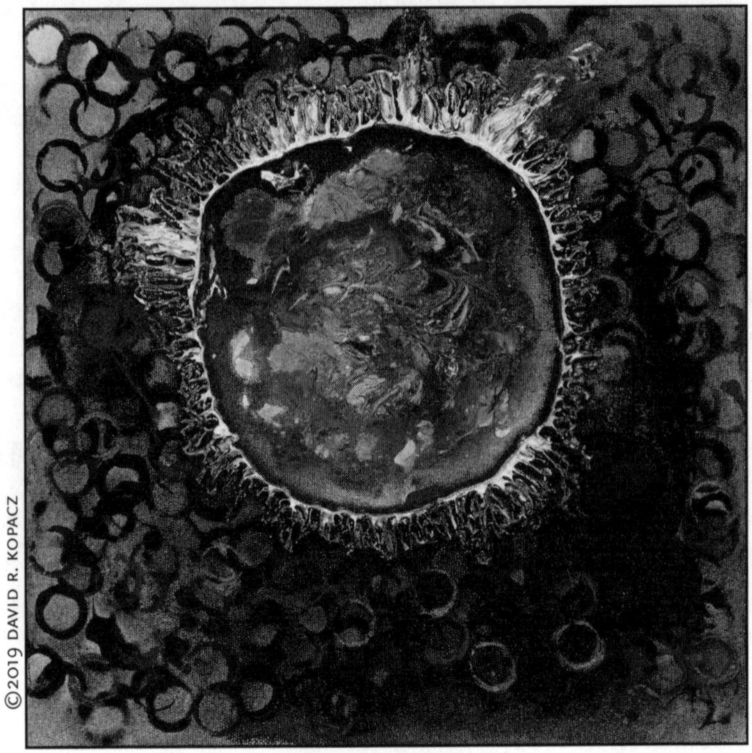

OUT OF ONE, MANY

THE INDIGENOUS ONE

Fred Gustafson was a Jungian therapist who worked closely with several Native American tribes. He says that we need to reconnect to the archetype of the "Indigenous One." An archetype is a conceptual structure, an organizing framework, which shapes our experiences of ourselves and the world. Gustafson feels that we can learn from Native American peoples, but that what we are learning is to connect to our own inner sense of indigenousness. Gustafson points out that the etymology of the word, "indigenous," "means 'to be born from within' (Gk. *genes*=one born, *indu*=within)," and further that if we lose a sense of our own indigenousness we "lose any sense of our earth as a womb and home that brought us into being."

Gustafson describes Jung's view that an "Indianization process . . . happened to all non-Indian immigrants in a mostly unconscious way but which came to distinguish them from their homes of origin. It is as though the soul of the American soil and its first peoples rises up and influences and even wants to adopt the outsider. In our own land it has been seen as the conqueror taking on the attributes of the conquered."

Gustafson cautions us that if we do not see ourselves as keepers of the land now and only think that indigenous people are the only keepers of the land, then we are neglecting an important, but forgotten deep aspect of our beings and neglecting our responsibility to the land.

> What we must now realize, however, is that we of the technologized world are indigenous peoples somewhere deep within ourselves and, at one time, we had a living indigenous past with a sense of intimately belonging to the earth. Indigenous really refers to an attitude and a way of life that respects the unity and relationship of all things on the earth.[5]

We can look at the things that divide us or we can focus on the things that unite us. I write this the week of the violence in Charlottesville, Virginia between those who seek to divide and separate and those who imagine the unity of humanity. What is going on in our hearts?

Gustafson's concept of the archetype of the "Indigenous One" postulates that we each have within us a constellation of the past, a nexus of ancient wisdom and relatedness to the Earth and all her beings. All peoples arose from cultures that were in harmony with the Earth. For instance, I can trace back to Irish and Welsh Celtic peoples who valued the natural world as a source of spirituality and I can trace back to the pre-Christian Slavic peoples of Poland and Eastern Europe who were "pagan" people who lived in harmony with the land.[6] My parents, early in their marriage "went back to the land," although neither of them grew up in the country, they went away from the cities and surrounded themselves with animals and that is the world I grew up in. Even though we have largely lost our cultural connections with the land and have lost our cultural sense of indigenousness, Gustafson says that we can always look within us to find this ancient source of connection wisdom: the *Indigenous One*. Buried within us, in our genes, our bodies, and our psyches, is the archetypal template of *being of the land*. Gustafson tells us that it is possible to connect to this inner *Indigenous One*, and through this inner connection come into union and harmony with the land in which we live.

5 Fred Gustafson, *Dancing Between Two Worlds*, 40, 75, 79.

6 Interestingly, the word "slave" derives from the word "Slav," due to the frequent enslavement of Slavs. See the etymology of "slave," and also Frankopan's chapter, "The Slave Road," in *The Silk Road*.

> I refer to the "Indigenous One" as a reference point for the antiquity of the human soul. We came from somewhere. . . . Our own inner Indigenous Ancestor has been pushed aside and all but forgotten. If the entire book can be put into one thought it is this: not only have we lost a connection to our own indigenous root, but alongside this there exists a profound sadness and longing for its return.[7]

GETTING TO THE ROOTS OF DNA

> *When you look in the mirror you see not just your face but a museum. Although your face, in one sense, is your own, it is composed of a collage of features you have inherited from your parents, grandparents, great grandparents and so on. . . . We carry the past around with us all the time, and not just in our bodies. It lives also in our customs, including the way we speak. The past is a set of invisible lenses we wear constantly, and through these we perceive the world and the world perceives us.*[8]
>
> DAVID W. ANTHONY

When Joseph and I were working on *Walking the Medicine Wheel*, he advised me to get my DNA traced back to its roots. He said that veterans should do this too, because then they would realize that everyone is their brother and sister. I used two different DNA searches, Ancestry and National Genographic. Ancestry gives a more recent DNA regional review and I came up: 40% Eastern European, 31% Western European, and 20% Irish/Scottish/Welsh. National Genographic goes back deeper in time, even tracing back to our common roots in Africa. Going back to 500-10,000 years ago, my results were: 43% Northern Europe, 36% Mediterranean, and 19% Southwest Asian.

My paternal great grandparents both came from Poland. Poland was not Christianized until 966 CE and prior to that had a Slavic spirituality with nature spirits and a pantheon of gods and goddesses. The Poles readily adopted a cult of the Virgin Mary and some speculate that the Black Madonna of Częstochowa represents pre-Christian nature goddess worship.[9]

---

7 Gustafson, 6–7.

8 David W. Anthony, *The Horse, The Wheel and Language: How Bronze-Age Riders from the Eurasian Steppes Shaped the Modern World*, 3.

9 Fred Gustafson in *The Black Madonna* discusses various theories behind the dark-skinned Madonnas found in various sites throughout the world.

On my mother's side, I have roots back to Wales through my maternal Great Grandfather Iorworth Roberts, and a mix of Irish, English, and European ancestors that trace through the early days of colonization of the United States. Five of my eight great grandparents immigrated to the United States in the 20th Century. Tracing the Irish/Welsh/Scottish and English history, there are deep Celtic roots and later Anglo Saxon influences. The Romans arrived in Britain starting in 43 CE, but never conquered Ireland. Christians first arrived in Ireland around 400 CE. Prior to that it was Celtic. History is often written by the victors, and the Romans described the Celts as barbarians. The Latin and Greek roots of the word "barbarian" originally meant something more akin to "foreigner" than "uncivilized."[10] However Graham Robb has uncovered a vast network of ancient roads and networks across Celtic Europe prior to the Roman invasion. He describes a complex and developed culture in which the sages and scholars called "druids" studied history, geography, moral philosophy, religion, and theology for 20 years of education.[11]

Looking at the last thousand years of humanity, I could be considered to have Roman Catholic and Protestant roots. However, if we go back deeper in time, I am Celtic and Slavic and both of those cultural groups have shamanic historical elements. Further back, I am Southwest Asian and African, and also 1.8% of my DNA is Neanderthal (*Homo neanderthalensis*) and 0.2% Denisovan (*Homo denisova*).

The word "shaman" has roots in Asia, but also connects to many different languages, as the etymology shows.

> Shaman (n)
> 1690s, "priest of the Ural-Altaic peoples," probably via German *Schamane*, from Russian *shaman*, from Tungus *saman*, which is perhaps from Chinese *sha men* "Buddhist monk," from Prakrit *samaya-*, from Sanskrit *sramana-s* "Buddhist ascetic" [OED].[12]

---

10 "Barbarian," *Online Etymology Dictionary*.

11 Robb, *The Ancient Paths: Discovering the Lost Map of Celtic Europe*, 109-116. Robb describes the etymology of the word "druid" as a riddle that is difficult to decipher. "The word 'Druid' was a cleverly tangled knot of meanings and unravelling it would have required a long lecture on historical semantics. The *'uid'* belongs to the same family as the Sanskrit *'veda'* ('knowledge') and the Latin *'videre'* ('to see'). The *'dru'* could mean either 'very great' or 'oak'. Welsh and Breton forms derived from *'do-are-wid'* contain the word 'are', meaning 'eastward', 'in front of' or 'into the future'. Other words that were etymologically unrelated may have woven their connections into the puzzle: *'druta'* ('swift'), *'drutos'* ('strong' or 'solid'), *'uidua'* ('tree' or 'wood')." (Robb, 115).

12 "Shaman," *Online Etymology Dictionary*.

I have always been interested in the roots of words and in the past few years came across the Proto-Indo-European language as a common shared linguistic and cultural heritage of many of the peoples of the Earth, spoken perhaps 5,000 years ago.[13] This language is not in a pure written form, but linguists put together the clues to its existence by the common roots of languages that grew out of Proto-Indo-European, which make it the largest human language group, including: Celtic, Italic, Germanic, Baltic, Slavic, Albanian, Greek, Anatolian, Armenian, Indo-Aryan, Iranian, and Tocharian.[14] I looked for any possible additional roots of the word "shaman" in Proto-Indo European (PIE) and found a couple of possibilities. In PIE the word *shómen-* means "song." Singing and chanting is a common part of being a shaman. The Sanskrit (from Indo-Aryan) word that derives from *shómen-* is *sāman*,[15] which also means "to breathe, live"[16] and this is also quite connected into the work of the shaman as a healer and the word for "breath" in many languages has connections to spirit (inspiration) and to healing.

Hank Wesselman, PhD, a paleoanthropologist and shamanic teacher, writes that we all have roots in shamanic worldviews if we go back far enough—during the late Stone Age period 26,000 to 12,000 BCE, he writes, "the dominant spiritual practice was shamanism—nature-focused spirituality."[17]

Scientists say that the human species, *Homo sapiens*, originated in Africa around 200,000 years ago and then spread throughout the rest of the world. My "Deep Ancestry" through National Genographic traces back 1,000–100,000 years ago to my (and all of our) ancient homeland of Africa. My oldest maternal line is L3 which traces to East Africa around 67,000 years ago. The L3 line is a descendent of "Mitochondrial Eve," the common human mother of all living humans, who lived about 180,000 years ago. My oldest paternal line is P305, and goes back about 100,000 years ago to Africa. Further back is "Y Chromosome Adam" the common human father of all living humans who lived somewhere between 150,000 and 300,000 years ago.[18] National Genographic also traces the migration

13 Anthony, *The Horse, The Wheel and Language*, 42.

14 J.P. Mallory and D.Q. Adams, *The Oxford Introduction to Proto-Indo-European and the Proto-Indo-European World*, 12.

15 Ibid., 356.

16 *Sanskrit Dictionary*.

17 Hank Wesselman, *The Re-Enchantment*, 124.

18 Source information is from the National Genographic analysis of my DNA and includes general history as well as history specific to my own DNA.

patterns that are specific to a person's DNA so you can see the various routes out of Africa that your ancestors traveled.

Joseph gave me his National Genographic results and said they were important to have in the book. Like many Native Americans, his DNA has been intermingled with the colonizing Europeans, he knows that he has Spanish blood and that is where the name Rael comes from. Joseph's National Genographic results for the range of 500–10,000 years ago are: 46% Native American, 19% Mediterranean, 17% Northern European, 9% Southwest Asian, 6% Northeast Asian, and 2% Southeast Asian. His oldest maternal line is the same as mine, L3, tracing back to 67,000 years ago in East Africa (so we are brothers through our mothers' lines!). Joseph's oldest paternal line is M42 that traces to Africa around 75,000 years ago. I have this line also, but I also have an even older line P305—so I guess this makes Joseph my younger second cousin on my father's side!

PANGEA

I am sitting at Union Station in Denver.[19] It is a beautifully restored train station. I am sitting at a table that could be in a library, reading lamps, power outlets in the table. It is in a vast open space of the lobby of the old station. An eclectic mixture of furnishings are here, including old benches. I am here in Denver to present at a conference a presentation, "Becoming a Whole Person to Treat a Whole Person." Earlier in the week I was in Durango with Joseph talking about Pangea. He said, "*Scientists tell us that once all the land of the earth was in one place. It was a smaller place than it is now, because the earth is always making more land. Everyone had to live in one place and they had to get along. The scientists know that it was all one land once, because you can fit the pieces of the coastline together. You can fit Europe with North America. But then there started to be splits, and the continents drifted apart into separation. We had more space and were separated, so we didn't have to get along anymore.*"

While going through my notes, here at Union Station, I am listening to Miles Davis' *Pangea.* This recording was the evening set and the earlier set was recorded and released with the name *Agharta. Pangea* has just two tracks, "Gondwana," and "Zimbabwe." Pangea broke in two, into Laurasia (in the north) and Gondwana (in the South, which eventually separated into Africa, which would include Zimbabwe) and the southern continents.

19 The journal and diary entries that I have in this book are not in chronological order.

Pangea was a single land-mass continent that existed on earth from 300 to 175 million years ago. The word "Pangea" is "derived from Ancient Greek *pan* (πᾶν, "all, entire, whole") and *Gaia* (Γαῖα, "Mother Earth, land")."[20] The continent Pangea was surrounded by a single ocean, Panthalassa. It eventually broke into the continents of Laurasia and Gondwana. The one ocean, Panthalassa, split into the Pacific and the Tethys oceans. Thethys was a Greek goddess, the sister and wife of the god Oceanus. Tethys is said to have given birth to all the fresh water rivers, whereas Oceanus was associated with salt waters. Joseph Rael has had a number of visions involving Oceanus and the oceans and often works with issues around water.

Miles Davis' album, *Pangea* sounds tired and muddy to me. In 1975 Miles Davis was at the end of a period of intense innovation, creativity, as well as physical pain and addiction. Davis was reportedly "depressed, exhausted and suffering ever mounting health problems, retreated from the music scene."[21] He released nothing for 6 years after these live performance albums. Musician Bill Laswell[22] reconstructed and remixed some of Miles Davis' fusion era albums from 1969-1974 and he called the album *Panthalassa: The Music of Miles Davis 1969–1974, Reconstruction and Mix Translation by Bill Laswell.* Most of *Panthalassa* was taken from Davis' albums *In a Silent Way* (1969), *On the Corner* (1972), and *Get Up with It* (1974). Laswell's music often combines multiple different genres and perspectives: jazz, world music, dub, rock, ambient and complex bass lines and strong percussion.

I spoke with Bill Laswell by phone and asked him about Miles Davis, John and Alice Coltrane, and about some of the topics in this book. Bill spoke about working with the original multi-track recordings of Davis' *In a Silent Way.* He found that the original studio tracks had a musical theme that was edited out of the final recording. In a way, a kind of secret influence that was removed, "What you hear them playing on the original is them playing around the theme that you never hear, which is interesting," Bill said. The finished recording combines the hiding of the main theme with improvisation around it. Laswell continues, "*In a Silent Way* . . . came out completely random and spontaneous, unexpected,

20 "Pangea," *Wikipedia*.

21 "Pangea (album),"*Wikipedia*.

22 Bill Laswell was born in Salem, Illinois, not too terribly far from Alton, Illinois where Miles Davis was born.

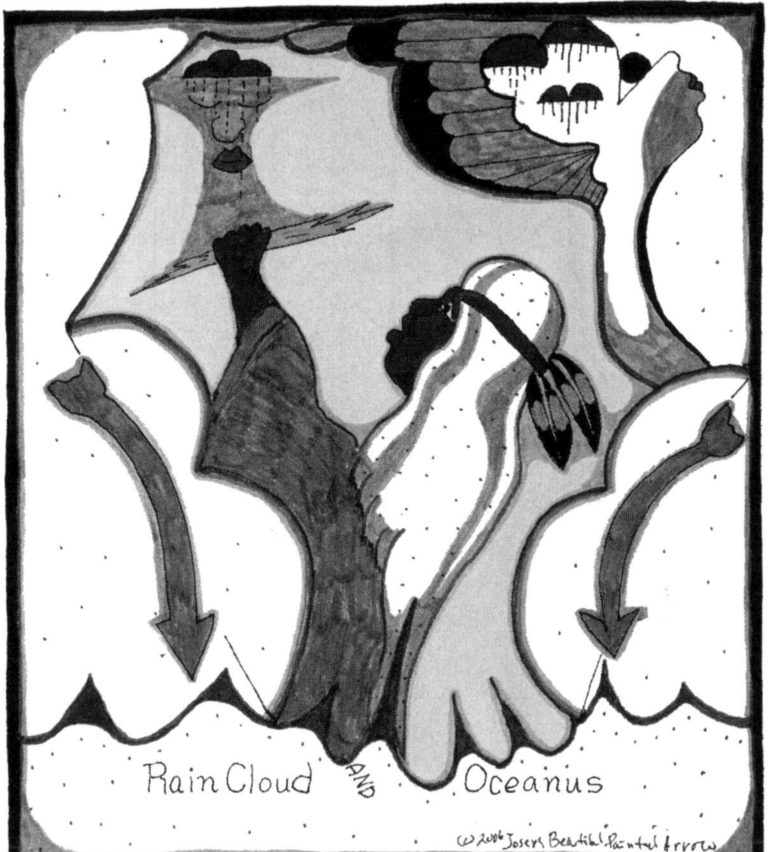

RAIN CLOUD AND OCEANUS

not planned, certainly not anticipated and they came from that which means maybe they are coming on their own. They had their own kind of transmission." This view of musical creation has strong elements of what we have talked about regarding initiation and the secret journey.

In describing his own musical work, Laswell said, "it's that kind of commitment or sacrifice to getting into something and letting go of everything to get to a place you haven't been or no one's been and then you don't know if that was real or not, but I'm glad that I was pulled in that direction."

I asked Bill about the element of spirituality in his music and he talked about his gradual steps into West African, Indian, and Central American music.

> The word "spirituality" gets thrown around a lot these days. To me, it is sort of more about getting kind of lost in the moment and something else takes over. It's not just a routine or a kind of theory. Musicians just sit down and play music, but there's always something to me that's kind of out there like you get lost and into something, and you sacrifice everything in hopes that you will come out the other end safely. That's why I deal today with a lot of improvisation, because I believe that's, whether we know it or not, we're playing somebody's future music and it's not based on a routine or a style or genre. It has more to do with communication, but then again a kind of secret, a special way, it's like a non-verbal dialogue that just drifts in and out of sight.

Pangea teaches us about an underlying unity separating off into pieces as well as Miles Davis' health and career fragmenting and falling apart and going underground for 6 years. We have Bill Laswell reconstructing Panthalassa, the ocean around Pangea. We have Oceanus and Tethys, giving birth to the rivers and the 3,000 sea nymphs who were the spirits of bodies of waters and even clouds. Pangea leads us to Oceanus, whom Joseph describes visiting in visionary journeys, which led to him holding purification ceremonies for the ocean on the 7th of every month in the Sound Chambers. It makes sense that in order to bring peace to the land, Joseph would journey to the oceans. In holding the awareness of our original unity in land and water, Joseph can better hold focus on the peace that comes from Unity. Joseph says, "*We are the reflection of the reflection*." He says that Stephen Hawking said something similar, that "We live in a reflective universe."

In the non-ordinary universe of the visionary, everything is reflective and everything is interconnected. Originally all was One, but in the evolution of our consciousness we have moved to a point of extreme separation and we have lost sight of the fact that with each separation, there is a pairing which reflects the wholeness. Man and woman, sun and moon, light and dark—we see these as opposites, but they are reflections of each other, sounding the truth of a reflective universe.

Biologists are starting to speak of a "New Pangea" which comes from the increase in travel and globalization and the intermingling of species that had long been kept separate. Different species develop to adapt to different conditions—this is what Darwin spoke of in evolution. These changes occurred over long spans of years. Now, though, we have species being introduced, purposefully and accidentally all the time, bringing together what was once apart.

Scientists believe that all land started in the mega-continent of Pangea and that this has slowly split apart. The separation of habitats led to the creation and evolution of a tremendous diversity of species and human cultures. Currently we are in a phase of globalization, in which separation is shifting into integration. Scientists predict that continental drift will continue and eventually we will be back into most land being unified mostly in one vast continent, "Pangea Ultima"—250 million years from now. With Pangea Ultima, the land that was separated will be brought back together through a vast reconnection, and what was separated will once again be whole.

It is often said that "we are all Africans" because scientific evidence shows that *Homo sapiens* originated in Africa and spread outward throughout the rest of the inhabitable globe. There are two circular forces. One is centrifugal which encourages movement outward from the center. The other is centripetal which pulls what is outward toward the center. We see both movements with the drift of the continents, first beginning as Pangea, then separating into the continents we know now, and then moving back toward union again in Pangea Ultima. Hindus see the whole of the universe as arising and dissolving back into Union through breath. "Breathing is a manifestation of the Cosmic Rhythm to which the whole universe moves and according to which it appears and disappears."[23]

Whereas the continents move very, very slowly, we *Homo sapiens* are picking up speed. After moving out of Africa some 70,000 years ago, we have colonized the known earth and lived for thousands of years in separation from each other. While it is true that there were a great many trade connections between the different cultures on different continents, it was not until Cristóbal Colón (known to us as Christopher Columbus, born in Italy as Cristoforo Colombo) sailed across the Atlantic Ocean that human beings began to complete a circle that anticipated the slow centripetal, geological movement toward Pangea Ultima. In fact, historian Alfred W. Crosby said that Colón's accomplishment was "to reknit the seams of Pangea."[24] It is of interest to note that the Spanish name, Cristóbal Colón, has within it the root of the word *colon*-ize. The etymology of

23 Sir John Woodroffe, *Śakti and Śakta*, 204.

24 In Charles C. Mann, *1493: Uncovering the New World Columbus Created*, 7.

colonize comes from the Latin *colonus* "tiller of the soil, farmer."[25] The word "colony" predates Cristóbal Colón, but Joseph would say "pay attention" to such coincidences.

The Spanish search for gold and silver and trade routes to India re-connected the peoples of the earth in a way that had not been for tens of thousands of years. Of course there is a long history of trade along the silk roads and people, goods, and ideas flowed back and forth between Europe, the Middle East, India, and China. Further back, maybe 4000-6000 years ago there was a common language, Proto-Indo-European. This search for deeper and deeper proto-languages has something of the spiritual quest about it—seeking the lost, hidden roots of languages that are buried beneath the aeons.

Joseph has written about this linguistic research into Proto-Indo-European language. Reading about it piqued Joseph's interest, leading him to search back even further into the depths of time for the "Mother Tongue," the first language spoken by human beings. For Joseph, the Tiwa language was not created by humans, but rather it is "a language that was constructed according to the different vibratory levels of mother nature."[26]

We can ask what drove Columbus' and the European conquest of the Americas. The simple answers are greed, gold, land, and evangelization. We can wonder if there was also some unconscious drive toward unity and re-unification. Columbus landed on the Caribbean island of Hispaniola (home to the Taino and Arawak people), but his journey was a stepping stone toward what became a vast Spanish network running gold and silver from the Americas to Europe, and from the Americas to China (via the Spanish colony of the Philippines).[27] Columbus' voyage led to what has been called the "Columbian Exchange" which moved peoples, diseases, precious metals, animals and plants across the oceans, re-linking the continents. "The Columbian Exchange had such far-reaching effects that some biologists now say that Colón's voyages mark the beginning of a new biological era: the Homogenocene."[28] The term "homogenocene" picks

25 "Colonize," *Online Etymology Dictionary*.

26 *B&V*, 61. Joseph describes an even earlier vision of the Mother Tongue he had as a child, sleeping back to back with his Grandfather and feeling a transmission of knowledge. "Due to that moment I would want to investigate the sounds of the different languages and would search for the Mother tongue. Out of that moment would come the longing and wanting that created the impetus to write this book based on sound vibration language." (45–46).

27 Mann, *1493*, 23–32.

28 Ibid., 23.

up a dual meaning, with *homo-* meaning homogenizing on the one hand, but also a historical epoch instigated by *Homo sapiens*.

IN A SILENT WAY

When saxophonist John Coltrane left Miles Davis' "first great quintet" in 1957, it has been said that this created the rift between two trends in modern jazz, one evolutionary branch with Coltrane led to free-jazz with ever more dissonant and arrhythmicism. The other evolutionary branch led to fusion jazz which blended in other influences.[29] After the ending of Davis' "second great quintet" in 1968, a new way opened up in Davis' music, leading to his electric, or fusion period. Davis is often credited with ushering in a number of paradigm shifts in jazz over his career. *In a Silent Way* was recorded on one session date, February 18, 1969, and released July 30, 1969.

I first heard *In a Silent Way* through Bill Laswell's *Panthalassa*, as mentioned above. I had long been a fan of Miles Davis, but had somehow skipped over this phase of Davis' work. When I was in New Zealand I was working on my first book, *Re-humanizing Medicine*, and I was looking for long, instrumental music tracks that were good for long sessions of writing and editing. I came upon *In a Silent Way* and I was immediately taken with it. Three years later, this album came to serve as a bridge for me back to the United States when I moved to Seattle in 2013.

Leaving New Zealand stirred up complex feelings for me. I had taken on the Clinical Director role at Buchanan Rehabilitation Centre, but we had already stayed in New Zealand for 3 years and my wife Mary Pat was desperately wanting to return back to the United States. I felt guilty having taken on the role and then leaving. I also was at a pinnacle of my career in a leadership role and I loved my work and Buchanan. My move back to the US was complicated by the 2013 lack of a congressional budget late that year and also the excruciatingly slow human resources process with the VA. I gave 90-day notice in New Zealand when I received my job offer from Puget Sound VA, however 90 days came and went and I still did not have a signed contract. Our belongings were packed up and shipped out. I moved out of the apartment and into a series of hotels and friend's homes. I extended my work in New Zealand two weeks—still no contract. I extended two more weeks—still no contract. I had no job, was

29 Paul Tingen, *Miles Beyond: The Electric Explorations of Miles Davis, 1967–1991*, 31.

in the middle of an international move, Mary Pat did not have a job as she had been working to get details arranged on the Seattle side. My dad was going in for back surgery before Thanksgiving and I felt I just had to jump. I figured if I arrived in Seattle and still did not have a job after visiting my parents in Illinois, I would just scramble and get the first job I could find.

The transition from New Zealand to Seattle was a difficult one for me. The job did eventually come through for the end of December. It took months to feel settled at work, and longer to feel settled in the United States again. My transition gave me a small glimpse of what it must be like for veterans returning back to US civilian culture after having been deployed to other countries. I often felt completely lost and irrelevant back in the United States. We had thought we were "moving back" to the US, however we had never lived in Seattle. It ended up feeling like we had moved to a third place that was not "home" and was also not New Zealand.

The place that I found solace and a sense of home was in listening to Miles Davis' *In a Silent Way*. I listened to it over and over again as I drove back and forth to work. I found something peaceful in its sparseness as well as its fullness. The second track, "In a Silent Way/It's About That Time," in particular, I found otherworldly. I always imagined being deep in the ocean, or far out in space as the haunting and tentative notes of John McLaughlin's guitar sound out into a void of silence and various electronic noises and spaces.[30] Then Miles' trumpet comes in picking up the guitar theme. I can feel a wind through my hair, or even through my soul and I have an acute feeling of being made up of "matter" that is blowing like wind chimes in a wind, while also feeling like I am "movement" through empty space—it is like the feeling of being and not being at the same time.[31]

In a Silent Way became the cave that I returned to again and again, while it felt like I was dying and only felt alive in listening to it, eventually that cave became a place of re-birth. I have never tired of listening, it seemed I could go ever deeper and deeper into it. I only felt at home in the vibrations and stillness of *In a Silent Way*.

Murray Bodo wrote about St. Francis' solace he found in a cave as

30 Paul Tingen tells the story of how McLaughlin thought he was actually auditioning for the band, but Miles was recording it and used it as the master take, (Tingen, *Miles Beyond*, 58).

31 I wrote about "In a Silent Way" on my blog, *Being Fully Human*, in an entry entitled "Coniunctionis.21: In a Silent Way," June 2, 2014.

he was recovering from being imprisoned, convalescing from illness and then recovering from the shame of having set off on a crusade as a knight only to return the next day because the voice of God told him to return back to his home. Just as Francis only felt at home in the cave, I only felt at home in the vibrations and stillness of *In a Silent Way*. "Every day it became harder and harder to leave his cave and meet the harsh light of all the staring world. The farther into the cave he retreated, the more comfortably insulated he felt," writes Bodo.[32]

Music has long been a cave for me, I could retreat into it, seek wisdom, find solace, venture into the dark places of wisdom. To give one's self to the throb and beat of the music, to get lost in the soundscape and then to find one's self there is like a shamanic journey. When I was in high school and college I listened to a lot of New Order and Joy Division. I marveled at how entering into the darkness of some of that music could lead to a sense of spaciousness and release. "This is the hour when the mysteries emerge, A strangeness so hard to reflect," sang Ian Curtis on "Komakino." In the early 2000s I wrote a column called Coniunctionis that explored the topic of "Trauma, Transformation, and Punk Rock." One particular installment of the column I called "What Did You See There? Ian Curtis and the Visionary Quest of the Shaman (Trauma, Transformation and Punk Rock Part IX)."[33] I realized that listening to Joy Division was like a dangerous shamanic journey into the darkness as Ian Curtis sang "I've been waiting for a guide to come and take me by the hand,"[34] and "I never realised the lengths I'd have to go, All the darkest corners of a sense I didn't know."[35] Music can be a cave, it can be a secret journey, it can take you to a place you didn't know. Music can take us deeper into ourselves as we get lost in it.

THE ONE BEING

Joseph Rael is saying that when we are fully in our physical being we are also in the body of the Earth and of the Vast Self. It is being one with Oneness. Just as there was one Pangea that split into many different continents and lands, so too, there is one Vast Self, that is a primal unity

32 Murray Bodo, *Francis: The Journey and the Dream*, 9.

33 These columns can be found on my website, DavidKopacz.com, under "Creativity," "Coniunctionis."

34 Joy Division, "Disorder," from *Unknown Pleasures*. Lyrics available Deborah Curtis, *Touching from a Distance: Ian Curtis and Joy Division*.

35 Joy Division, "Twenty-four Hours," from *Closer*.

manifested into diversity. "All these ideas tie into the reality that there is a Seer seeing everything. We call it God, the higher power, or whatever. It is simply the Vast Self seeing itself creating itself."[36]

After his vision of the sound peace chamber, Joseph "had this inner determination that I needed to do things that would help bring about a more spiritualized reality."[37] Healing, then, is not something to be done in isolation—for it is isolation that is actually the disease. Rather, healing is what occurs through bringing the person and the land back into a harmonious relationship. Separation of the body from spirit and the body from nature is what leads to illness and dis-ease. *Becoming medicine* is reconnection and this heals both the separated body and the separated land.

The other day I did the center of the medicine wheel ceremony Joseph taught me. After working out in the gym I have taken to doing this ceremony in the heat of the sauna (the closest thing to a sweat lodge in my daily environment). When I did this ceremony recently, suddenly the breath was knocked out of me as a thousand black crows flew into my back, coming from the west. I try not to analyze what is happening in the moment, but just to let it happen and after the first bit of resistance, I allowed and accepted this influx of a thousand black birds into my being. I then had the awareness, *they are coming to give me physical support in my work during these difficult times*. This felt very supportive to have this energy and movement from the physical direction of the west enter into me.

The scientific history of Pangea tells that the land on Earth was once one continent and all the seas were one vast ocean, Panthalassa. Human beings evolved in Africa and ventured off across all the lands and seas of the globe. Taking it further back, all matter denser than hydrogen and helium originated in the explosive deaths of the first stars and the first stars originated in the Singularity—the Big Bang. Joseph says that although we seem to be many diverse beings, really we are all One—the Vast Self watching the pulse of creation unfold out of itself.

---

36 *Sound*, 96.

37 *House*, 130.

RETURNING TO PEACE

Go far into the Void, and there rest in quietness.
All things arise, and bloom in their time, and then they return to their root.
Their returning is peace.
Peace is surrender to the Supreme Will; and he who surrenders
becomes part of Eternity.
To know Eternity is Light; and not to know it is darkness.
He who knows Eternity has all things in his heart: he is universal; he is greatness; he is in heaven; he is in TAO.
Tao may pass away, but his spirit lives on for ever.

TAO TE CHING[38]

To be returning to peace is to be returning to the heart, and the heart is the place of transformation, it is the place where we can separate from ordinary reality, become initiated in non-ordinary reality, and then return to ordinary reality carrying peace in the medicine bag of our hearts. By returning to a living spirituality we bring *Wah-Mah-Chi* into every moment, bringing Breath-Matter-Movement into reality. This changes our relationship with ourselves, with each other, and with the Earth. In non-ordinary reality everything is not just interconnected—All is One. As Joseph Rael tells us:

"I am you and you are me. There's only one being here, and even though you have a different body, I have a different body, and a different moment, but we are in this together, you know, and people don't understand that."

38 *Tao Te Ching XVI*, rendered by Juan Mascaró, in *Lamps of Fire: The Spirit of Religions*, 217.

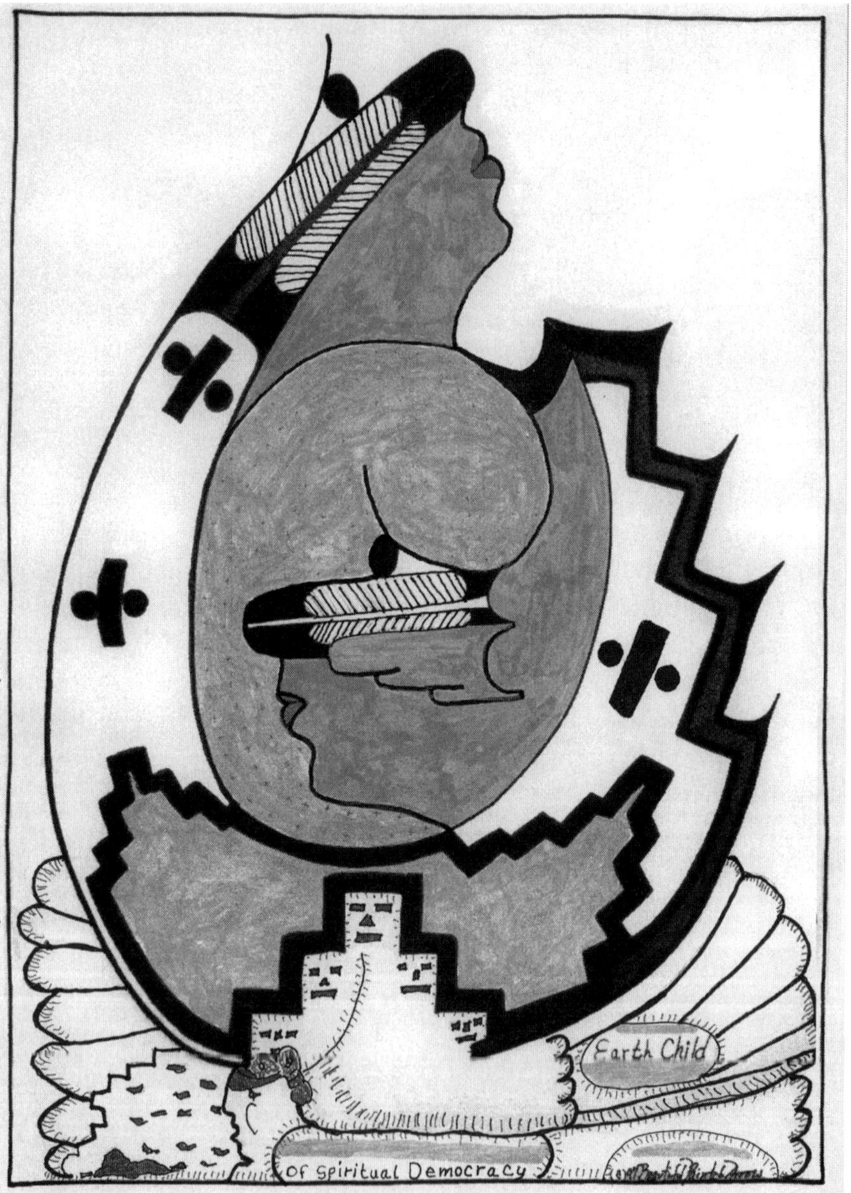

EARTH CHILD OF SPIRITUAL DEMOCRACY

CHAPTER 14

SPIRITUAL DEMOCRACY

Spiritual Democracy is a living connection, allowing the flow of spirituality through our lives, embracing the divinity in all creatures and the divinity of the Earth. Spiritual democracy is the way we treat others when we learn to see the divine in all things and that we, too, are part of divinity. It is a sacred way of being.

Periodically, we forget that we are divine as we live in this world of matter and go through its trials and travails. We, as individuals, as well as we as people, need periodic renewal at the font of spiritual democracy. To seek renewal is to be a Seeker, yet so many "religious" people are becoming fundamentalists.

Father Gerald Arbuckle has written a recent and very topical book about fundamentalism. He sees fundamentalists as "boundary-setters . . . marking themselves off from others." This heightened distinction between self and others sets the scene for potential discrimination and violence. Arbuckle describes a current "global epidemic of fundamentalism both religious and plural" that is a "form of organized institutional or civic religious anger in reaction to secularization, political changes, and globalization; it often intimidates or coerces people to achieve its ends." A strong aspect of fundamentalism, then, is a resistance to change and a desire to keep things as they are. I understand Joseph Rael's teaching that "we do not exist" to mean that we only exist when we are changing, growing, and evolving. When we are striving to persist, we become fundamentalists trying to stop the flow of change, which is the flow of spirit. Arbuckle writes that we all as individuals and all cultures and countries have the propensity for fundamentalism. Bringing the lens of an anthropologist and theologian, he traces out the global epidemic of fundamentalism, including its manifestation in the United States as "Trumpism," which he sees as built on "fostering fear, hatred, and violence."[1]

Spiritual Democracy is the opposite of fundamentalism—it is about opening our hearts to others and seeking to act in such a way that it encourages others to open their hearts. Fundamentalism is idolatry—the

1 Gerald Arbuckle, *Fundamentalism At Home and Abroad: Analysis and Pastoral Responses*, 9, 28, 81.

worship of a fixed thing. Spiritual Democracy is about allowing ourselves to be shaped and continually reshaped by *Wah-Mah-Chi*, by Breath-Matter-Movement.

JOSEPH RAEL ON THE SOUL AND RELIGIOUS FREEDOM

Joseph called me on the winter solstice and left a voice mail while I was at work.

"Hi Dave, how is your day going today? I know it is going well because it is going well for me.

"I was looking at your writings and there is the quote 'The Founding Faith, then, was not Christianity, and it was not secularism. It was religious liberty—a revolutionary formula for promoting faith by leaving it alone.[2]

"Religious liberty happens to every single human baby child when the human being swallows and drinks the milk from its mother's breast at feeding time. Thus the American soul is in the making stage.

"What I am saying is we have to start at the foundation of what makes a human being to grow up in that religious liberty. That is the only way it is going to work if we are really going to follow the real way that we become individuals. If we don't start at the beginning. . . .

"Where I learned this was from a nun who was teaching religion on the islands. She came and visited me and spoke with me in Pennsylvania. She said, 'Why did the Indians accept Christianity so easily?'

"I said, 'Just listen when you drink water, like take that bottle of water over there and drink and listen to the sound it makes as you swallow. You will hear the sound soul with every swallow.'

"Her eyes got real big and she said, 'So you already knew about the soul and the teaching of Christianity?'

"So I am telling you now as I am reading your paper that the idea of religious freedom was already being educated through the sound, and the being and vibration of every single swallow of swallowing-ness every time the baby was drinking its mother's milk. This is my contribution to the idea of spiritual democracy and religious freedom."

---

2 Waldman, *Founding Faith*, xvi.

SPIRITUAL DEMOCRACY AS HEART MEDICINE

Steven Herrmann has written a book on *Spiritual Democracy*, which is where I came across this term. Herrmann, in turn, found the term in the work of Walt Whitman (1819–1892), the American ecstatic poet. The way Herrmann describes Spiritual Democracy reminds me of the path of the hero's journey that begins in separation and ends in re-union. We, as a country, went through such a journey in the Civil War. We separated from our brothers and sisters and saw them as enemies and then went through the Reconstruction of re-uniting the country. As a country, these old fault lines are active again in present day, sending earthquakes and aftershocks across our land and through our people, threatening to divide us once again from each other. "We as individuals and as humanity suffer from a lack of connection to other people . . . to the point where our very survival as a species is in question," Herrmann writes. The symptoms of this lack of connection are poverty, war, inequality and environmental degradation. The cure is Spiritual Democracy.

> Adopting the big idea of Spiritual Democracy, the realization of oneness of humanity with the universe and all its forces, can help people feel joy, peace, and interconnectedness on an individual basis. It can also inspire us to undertake sacred activism, the channeling of such forces into callings that are compassionate, just, and of equitable heart and conscience, and give us some tools to start solving some of these grave global problems, while uniting people on the planet.[3]

We grow through recognizing our oneness. *Becoming Medicine* means taking the hero's journey from separation to union. This is what Herrmann says Spiritual Democracy consists of, "the realization of oneness of humanity with the universe." When we see ourselves in relation and as part of other people and the earth, we act in a different way than when we see ourselves as separate, isolated beings.

The entire spiritual journey is simply a continual struggle to return to our hearts. The heart, like the medicine wheel, holds four sacred chambers, and yet it is one greater whole that gives us our lifeblood and rejuvenates the "wretched, tired and poor" blood of our veins and transforms it into the vibrant vitality of our arteries. Every beat of our heart says *E plurbus unum*—out of many, one. This is heart medicine that is the goal of *becoming*

---

3 Steven Herrmann, *Spiritual Democracy: The Wisdom of Early American Visionaries for the Journey Forward*, xiii.

medicine. Herrmann speaks of the medicine of Spiritual Democracy:

> Whitman's role as a poet in helping to spread Spiritual Democracy as a universal medicine might help us alleviate at least some of our suffering during a time of political, economic, and religious upheaval. His vision of religious equality for women and men is a living "seed" of "becoming" in the general populace that we would be wise to cultivate into a new myth for our times. . . . If Spiritual Democracy as Whitman envisioned is truly to "become the world," then the peace at the center of such a vision must radiate outward to speed up the process of bringing it about through sacred actions, day by day, minute by minute, by each of us and all of us. For ultimately, everything we do in time is patterned by peace, friendship, and brotherhood in Whitman's vision, and it can be realized by anyone in the perpetual now.[4]

There are multiple correspondences between how Herrmann describes spiritual democracy with our work in this book. Spiritual democracy and becoming medicine are similar *seeds of becoming* for growing peace and these are found through a shamanic journey.

THE INNER JOURNEY OF THE DEMOCRATIC SHAMAN

Herrmann writes about Whitman as a shaman and a prophet who goes through his own spiritual journey, returns, and then speaks and sings to share with others his visions. Herrmann describes Whitman's view that the spiritual is not necessarily found in religions or dogmas, but rather is found in an "overarching 'consciousness,' a spiritual conscience that is unitary, latent in every person."[5]

The search for this inner light is the journey of the shaman, the mystic, and visionary. The shaman is the vehicle that connects the different worlds of ordinary and non-ordinary reality, the known and the unknown, matter and spirit. Herrmann writes that his central premise of his book, *Walt Whitman: Shamanism, Spiritual Democracy, and the World Soul,* "is that we can only know what shamanism is through direct living experience and it is the shamanic archetype that gives Whitman his medicine-power to mediate between the two worlds of existence, the known and the unknown, the seen and the unseen."[6]

4 Herrmann, 20.

5 Herrmann, xvii.

6 Herrmann, *Walt Whitman: Shamanism, Spiritual Democracy, and the World Soul,* xxi.

The shaman's ability to move backward and forward in time also allows him or her to return all the way back to Source, back to the Garden of Paradise, the beginning of time—and then to connect the present with the beginning of creation, which leads to a re-birth by connecting a current of life energy, leading to a re-birth and re-discovery of who we are and what our mission is here. Mircea Eliade wrote that the shaman "abolishes the present human condition and, for a time being, recovers the situation as it was in the beginning. Friendship with animals, knowledge of their language, transformation into an animal are so many signs that the shaman has re-established the 'paradisal' situation lost at the dawn of time."[7]

Herrmann's view of Whitman as a prophet of democracy and a shaman of bodily and spiritual ecstasy draws on Whitman's use of incantatory rhythms in his poems leading to altered states of consciousness in which the ecstatic bliss of Oneness is experienced. His words are sound-medicine. Herrmann writes about the American Indian influence on Whitman's work and references several books on Whitman that pick up this theme.[8] In moving deeply into one's self, one finds a relationship to the land and to all who live upon it. Herrmann sees outer "sacred activism"[9] as beginning with the inner journey of finding the star within us that, like walking the medicine wheel, can orient and guide us on our inner and outer journeys. Following the inner journey to the Source of Oneness comes the outer journey of sacred activism.

> Each of us, it seems, is guided by such a star and it varies in its fixed orbits, in different fields of sacred action, in every person's life. A central existential task is to discover what that star is and to make its light, the inner fire of human love, burn brightly against the darkness, as a calling to live by. . . . Sacred activism is a spiritual practice for bringing about planetary changes through a receptivity to, and response to, experiences of a mysterious energy, force, or power, which move through the human body, psyche, and entire cosmos in an effort to bring about alterations of consciousness, cultural transformation, and ultimately: world peace.[10]

---

7 Mircea Eliade, *Shamanism: Archaic Techniques of Ecstasy*, 99.

8 Notably George Hutchinson's *The Ecstatic Whitman: Literary Shamanism & the Crisis of Union*, James Nolan's *Poet-Chief: The Native American Poetics of Walt Whitman and Pablo Neruda*, and Ed Folsom's *Walt Whitman's Native Representations*, Herrmann, 51.

9 He credits Andrew Harvey for originating this term.

10 Herrmann, *Spiritual Democracy*, xvii–xviii.

After the American Civil War ended there was a time of coming together after violent separation. It was a time of coming full circle back to the founding ideas of American democracy. Whitman served as a nurse on the front for the Union. He was not a fighter in the physical world, more of a lover and a poet. He saw up-close the wounds of war and he then sought to heal them through his vision of a world at peace. He realized this peace had to be found within people—unifying body and spirit, as well as in the outer world—unifying all humans and all of creation in brotherhood and sisterhood.

THE AMERICAN SOUL

Jacob Needleman wrote *The American Soul: Rediscovering the Wisdom of the Founders* (2003). As a philosopher, he speaks of the "idea of America" and the "inner meaning of democracy." He feels that there is an urgent need to rediscover the power of the realm of ideas and particularly the idea of US America[11] and the idea of democracy because he sees a nation that is losing touch with its philosophical and spiritual roots through an over-emphasis on individualism and materialism. He writes that the root of materialism "is a poverty of ideas about the inner and outer world. . . . Materialism is a disease of the mind starved for ideas . . . the neurosis of materialism leads us into despair."[12] Similar to the idea of *Becoming Medicine*, Needleman, sees the interconnection of the individual search for spirit and meaning with the outer activism of being good to our brothers and sisters of the world. Needleman writes, "Although our inner nature is cosmic, our finite life is on earth; our duties are to both the immortal presence within and, while on earth, to our temporary role in the social order. Our task is simultaneous inner freedom and full outer engagement."

The path of *becoming medicine* is this simultaneous cultivation of inner depth and outer engagement. Medicine must be prepared in a loving and sacred manner, but then it must be given wherever there is pain and suffering. Needleman sees materialism and excess individualism as a social disease and he sees the inward search for inner democracy as leading to the treatment of social ills through outer democracy. "To a significant extent, democracy in its specifically American form was created to allow men and

---

11 As we get into this section, several authors speak of "America" as a term referring to people of the United States of America. This term is imprecise it could also refer to all the inhabitants of North and South America. We will use the terms "US America" or "US American," when possible.

12 Needleman, 6–7.

women to seek their own higher principle within themselves."[13]

Needleman speaks of the "promise" and the "crime of America." The *promise* is the *idea of the United States of America*, a second, inner, spiritual history "that flows from the efforts of more inwardly developed men and women to introduce truth and wisdom into the life of humanity."[14] This "second democracy," Needleman describes as "the democracy that actually tries to live inwardly according to the ideals of self-determination, liberty of thought and conscience, respect for the selfhood of one's neighbor."[15] Needleman distinguishes "individualism" from "authentic individuality." This is different than someone being a selfish person and simply gratifying their material desires. US American independence and individuality requires an outer form of democracy that protects the right of individuals to pursue the inner search. The inner search, in turn, provides the idealism to maintain the outer democracy. Inner democracy without outer democracy is isolated spiritual materialism—building up spiritual experiences without social engagement, a criticism often made of new age pursuits. Outer democracy without the development of inner democracy leads to the freedom to exploit others for one's own gratification—this is what Needleman refers to as the "crime of America." He examines this through our history in relation to slavery and the oppression and genocide of the American Indians.[16] Needleman balances the call for inner connection to the "American soul" with bearing witness to the times when we have failed to live up to our ideals and have created political structures of oppression that deny freedom to others.

Our ancestors committed crimes in founding the United States of America. We have great ideals, but a tainted record of implementing these ideals. Joseph Rael tells us that we are doing things now for those who came before us. Healing is not just of this moment in time, but stretches backwards and forwards in time. Once blood is spilled it requires some kind of ceremony to bring life back into balance. We have not sufficiently done that in the United States. The genocide we perpetrated against Native Americans and the enslavement of Africans are pushed down

---

13 Ibid., 9.

14 Ibid., 15.

15 Ibid., 18.

16 Further reading on the American Genocide can be found in Dee Brown's *Bury My Heart at Wounded Knee*, Roxanne Dunbar-Ortiz's *An Indigenous Peoples' History of the United States*, and in Charles Mann's *1491* and *1493*.

into our collective cultural shadow. Psychology tells us that if we do not face our darkness we will act it out, the same is true for us as a people as it is for each of us as a person. Joseph Rael has seen, in his lifetime, his people being second-class citizens, not being able to vote, not being able to practice their religion, and he himself went to boarding school. US American democracy is still an idea that has not been fully realized, yet that does not mean we should stop trying. Our motto is *E plurbus unum*, "out of many, one." We accept great diversity and our founders envisioned a unification of people coming together through the best of human ideals, yet there are contemporary forces seeking homogenization through exclusion of the "other," who in reality is actually our brother and sister, and in a very real way is even our very self. Unification through the inner recognition of our unity despite outer differences is the *idea* of US American democracy, unification through force and exclusion of "otherness" is totalitarian fascism.

> But the question that now needs to be asked concerns the interior, human meaning of this fundamental goal of democracy and the inner as well as the outer conditions that are necessary for its realization. Can there be any real and enduring relationship between disparate peoples and nations unless there also takes place within the soul of the individual human being a similar movement of relationship between the disparate parts of oneself? Can there be an American nation unless there also exists within oneself a unified *American soul*?[17]

Needleman states the purpose of his book, "is to call for the return of the inner meaning of America to our hearts and minds." He sees democracy as a kind of medicine that can heal the individual as well as the collective through its realization and application. He writes that "when it is forgotten that the world is what it is because human beings are what they are, and that nothing essential in human life can be changed for the better without first attending to the inner disharmony, then, inevitably, there arises the dominance of 'politics,' leading to violence and war in all its many forms."[18] Outer war is thus a consequence of inner war. Inner war can only be healed by searching out the inner medicine. One then becomes medicine and must apply oneself to the outer war in order to bring about outer peace.

---

17 Needleman, 25–26.

18 Ibid., 27.

Needleman discusses a Founding Father not often recognized in schoolbook history—Hiawatha, and the founding of the Great Law of Peace that brought together the five Northeastern tribes of the Haudenosaunee (Iroquois) Confederacy.[19]

BRINGING THE NEW MIND OF THE GREAT PEACE

The creation story begins with twin brothers, whose Anglicized names are "He Grasps the Sky With Both Hands" and "He Who is Crystal Ice." When He Grasps the Sky With Both Hands is born, he looks around creation and says "I know from where I come, and that is the sky . . . I will not forget that. I will continue to grasp with both hands the place from where I come." When He Who is Crystal Ice is born, however, he says "I am not thinking about the place from where I came. . . . It is sufficient that my mind is satisfied with having arrived at this place. . . . This place will become exceedingly delightful and amusing to the mind." Needleman comments that "Few legends of the world's traditions make it so clear that the real root of all that we call evil is primal forgetfulness of our Selves."

He Grasps the Sky With Both Hands creates humans and puts a portion of himself in them, giving them his own mind, his own blood, his own power, and his own breath. Before withdrawing from the earth, He Grasps the Sky spoke to the human beings and gave them their original instructions.

> Do not ever forget this, that in the days and nights to come a grave thing will come to pass if ever you forget peace. You will not continue

---

19 Needleman lists his source as an unpublished manuscript by Maril Rianna Blanchard as well as J.N.B. Hewitt's *Iroqouian Cosmology*, second part. His sources for the story of the founding of the Iroquoian Confederacy are Paul Wallace's *White Roots of Peace* and personal communication with Chief Oren Lyons. See endnote 94, p. 368 in Needleman.

Needleman states that he has greatly condensed this story (which runs 26 pages) in his book. We have further condensed this story. Our apologies to any who feel this is not our story to tell, however it is so relevant to the topic of the book and it is in the public domain and may have influenced the foundational ideas of US American democracy. It is a beautiful story and we hope we have offered it with proper reverence and acknowledgement. We also hope to correct the recent use of "Hiawatha" as a racial slur, as it is a name that holds great beauty and meaning for spiritual democracy.

The Hiawatha that Needleman tells of is different than the one that Longfellow wrote about. Longfellow's poem also later influenced Jung's understanding of the indigenous people of what is now the United States. See "Hiawatha," *Wikipedia* for more discussion on this confusion. There is also a recent publication by Kayanesenh Paul Williams for further reference, *Kayanerenkó:wa: The Great Law of Peace* (2018).

> to live if you forget peace. . . . The time will come to pass when there will be great divisions between the minds of human beings, and there will be nothing but contentions, and the people will forget happiness, peace, and me. . . . Then I will come again.[20]

The time came to pass that the human beings forgot peace. War, discord, separation, strife, suspiciousness, materialism took root. True to his prophesy, He Grasps the Sky With Both Hands intervenes by sending his emissary, Great Peacemaker. Needleman writes that "we are thus given to understand peace not as something passive, not as a mere absence of conflict, but as a force that can harmonize the actions and impulses of human life in all their multiplicity and opposition to each other. Peace—a unifying energy that paradoxically also allows each element to flourish in its individuality." The force of peace is also known as "the new mind" which Great Peacemaker brings to all peoples. This new mind "shows them the real essence of their ideals of what it means to be human beings and to care for each other. This is peace as the field of life in all its vibrancy, peace as the call to serve what is far greater than oneself."[21] However there is one who resists the new mind of peace, Atotarho, a wizard and chief of the Onondagas.

Great Peacemaker travels, meeting all the tribes and invites them to take into their hearts the new mind of peace. However, Atotarho resists and does not join. Before Great Peacemaker can face this last resistance, he seeks out the tent of a certain woman who lives along the "warrior's path" that travels east to west. Needleman states that it "is through the mediation of a woman that the mission of peace takes form in the world, and in fact it is women's power of judgment that will ultimately determine the leadership of the Iroquois Confederacy." When Great Peacemaker meets this woman, she asks who he is. Great Peacemaker replies, "I carry the mind of the Life of God . . . and my message will bring an end to the wars between east and west." He then gives the vision of the Longhouse, where "All shall live as one house-hold under one chief mother." Then he tells the woman, "Thinking shall replace killing." The woman sees the goodness of his message and says, "I take hold of it. I embrace it."

Great Peacemaker then says that women will be in charge of the Longhouse and that they will choose the chiefs because "you, my Mother,

---

20 Ibid., 204, 210–11.

21 Ibid., 214–15.

were the first to truly grasp and accept the message of the peace that is power." He then gives her a new name, *Jigonhsasee*, which means New Face, and he tells her, "Out of the womb of the New Mind the nations will be born anew."[22] She asks where he will go next, and Great Peacemaker says he will head east, toward the sunrise. Shocked, she warns him that there is a great danger that way, there is a house of a man who eats humans. Great Peacemaker takes his leave and New Face spreads the word to all the warriors that she feeds as they travel the warrior's path in front of her house.

Great Peacemaker comes to the home of He Who Eats Humans, who turns out to be none other than Hiawatha, who lives in a state of human degradation, eating his fellow human beings. Great Peacemaker climbs on the roof and looks down into Hiawatha's home, seeing the fire pit and the kettle where he cooks the humans. Hiawatha returns home carrying a human body and puts the kettle on the fire.

> Just at that moment, the man in the house bends over the kettle and sees not only the body of the human being he has killed and is about to eat, but also a face looking up at him. He is amazed. It is the Great Peacemaker's face, reflected in the water, that is looking up at him, but the man thinks it is his own face! And there was in this face such wisdom and strength as he had never seen before nor ever dreamed that he possessed. . . .
>
> "This is a wondrous thing," he says to himself. "Such a thing has never happened before as long as I have lived in this house. I did not know I was like that. It was a great man who looked at me out of the kettle."
>
> He goes over to the kettle to look again, and there again is the face of a great man looking up at him.
>
> "It is true," he says. "It is my own face in which I see wisdom and righteousness and strength. It is not the face of a man who eats humans." And he takes the kettle out of the house and empties it by the roots of an upturned tree.
>
> "No more will I do this thing that I have done for so long. No longer will I kill humans and eat their flesh."
>
> The man falls silent and then speaks again to himself. His voice is breaking with remorse.
>
> "But that is not enough. The mind inside is more difficult to change. I cannot escape the suffering I have caused. I cannot bring back the

22 Ibid., 218, 221.

dead. I cannot erase the cries of the women and children."

This beautiful passage reminds us of Joseph Rael's teaching that there is a place of held-back goodness within all our hearts. No matter how far astray we go, no matter how lost in darkness we become, there is the possibility of having mirrored to us our own goodness. Hiawatha seeing the reflection of Great Peacemaker superimposed over his own face comes to recognize his own inner goodness. Needleman comments on this further:

> Here we feel the scale of this legend and of the source from which it has come. For here the legend speaks of a human crime for which no ordinary action can atone. Here the story may well be heard as speaking to our own remorse as we see in a clear light what has been done to an entire people. And here the tale echoes the constitutive legend of our own culture—the crime for which no ordinary action can atone, a level of self-remorse which demands of man an action of an entirely new quality. And for this action the man needs now to turn to the greatness he has seen in himself.[23]

Great Peacemaker comes down from the roof and consoles Hiawatha who is crying out of remorse for the greatness he has seen reflected within him and the terrible nature of his deeds. Great Peacemaker says,

> The New Mind has come to you . . . and you are miserable because the New Mind does not live at ease with old memories . . . Now you will work with me to bring justice and peace to those places where you have done injury to man. We will work together to bring to the earth the new idea of the peace that is power. Such is the work given to man by the Creator of Life.[24]

Great Peacemaker gives to Hiawatha the *Kayanerenhkowa*, the Great Law of Peace. Hiawatha says, "I take hold, I grasp it. . . . Now what work is there for us to do?" Great Peacemaker tells Hiawatha that he must take this New Mind to the evil wizard, Atotarho. Great Peacemaker describes Atotarho as a man of great power who kills and eats men who approach him. He has a twisted body and his mind is twisted and his hair is a mass of snakes. However, he is one of Hiawatha's people and the Great Peace cannot manifest without Atotarho. Hiawatha is also a man who has eaten other humans and he can relate to the twisted mind of Atotarho, however

23 Ibid., 223–24.

24 Ibid., 224.

now he has a New Mind, a mind of peace that he can bring to him. Great Peacemaker says that although Hiawatha must go and speak to Atotarho, "He will not listen to you. He will drive you away. But you will go to him again and again and at last you will prevail—*if you do not give up*." Again, Great Peacemaker whispers, "*Do not give up*." He then gives Hiawatha his name, "You will be called Hiawatha, He Who Combs for you will comb the snakes out of Atotarho's hair."[25]

Hiawatha goes to Atotarho, and sure enough, he is rejected and Atotarho shrieks his name, "Hiawatha-a-a-a-a!" He is overcome by a sense of foreboding. His three daughters fall ill and die. Hiawatha loses heart and says, "Because of this thing that has befallen me . . . I can no longer do the work of the Good Mind." The people seek to comfort him in his despair, but suddenly a strange great bird falls from the sky, startling the people. The crowd panics and running accidentally tramples Hiawatha's wife to death. Hiawatha further despairs, he shuns human beings, he wanders the forest alone. He walks without direction, searching for "someone with a grief as deep as his own." He has forgotten Great Peacemaker's words, "*Do not give up*." Needleman writes that Hiawatha's mind becomes almost as dark as Atotarho's and that "man must experience *himself* as the force that resists the good." This is the dark night of the soul.

On the twenty-third day of his wandering, Great Peacemaker comes to Hiawatha and says, "I wipe away the tears from your face . . . using the white fawn-skin of pity. . . . I make daylight for you. . . . I beautify the sky. Now you will think with a quiet mind when your eyes rest on the sky, which the Maker of All Things intended should be a source of happiness to man." Hiawatha looks above himself into the beauty of the sky and his mind clears of grief. Great Peacemaker addresses him and says, "Now . . . Reason has returned; your judgment is firm again. You are ready to carry the New Mind to others. Let us work together now and make the laws of the Great Peace."[26]

Together Great Peacemaker and Hiawatha go to face Atotarho. They withstand the blast of his screams and bring the New Mind to him. Needleman describes what happens as one who has forgotten their own inner goodness finds this goodness again within him- or herself.

> But he has not understood where power and energy come from; and

---

25 Ibid., 225.

26 Ibid., 230.

> without this knowledge and experience all the force within him is turned outward toward violence and inward to doubt and despair . . . if it is not turned toward the striving to obey the Master of Life and to overcome one's own weaknesses, it will be turned toward violence; if this energy is not turned toward helping one's neighbor, it will be turned toward killing one's neighbor. Atotarho is power without understanding; he is the desire to live without knowing the Good. And nothing can overcome this force of violence except the direct experience of the Good within oneself, an experience that turns all the energies of man around so that they serve what they are created to serve.[27]

Great Peacemaker explains the Great Law of Peace to Atotarho, but Atotarho says "Who will bring this about? There is no one." Great Peacemaker says that Atotarho, himself, will bring about the Great Peace. "It is you yourself who will bring it about, *if you desire it*. You shall be the head chief of the Five Nations." But to this Atotarho just shrieks, "It is not yet!" Hiawatha approaches Atotarho and combs the snakes out of his hair and his mind is made straight, he now has the New Mind. He becomes the strong and good head chief of the Five Nations.

Needleman comments that "it was necessary to go into the broken heart of human evil and comb the snakes out of man's mind and soul that brought upon him despair and out of despair a thick coat of anger and bloodshed."[28] Applying this story to ourselves, as contemporary Americans, Needleman asks us how we can atone for the crime of what we, as a country, have done to the American Indian peoples of this land.

> If we glimpse even a little that America killed something that was divinely ordained, not only for the Indians themselves but for all of humanity and for all the earth . . . only then may we perhaps approach a true response and a true direction of recompense, not only to the Indian spirit, but to what we ourselves may recognize as the Good—why not call it God? Can we now do for man and for the earth what the culture of the Indian was designed to do? Can we help bring to the world and to ourselves the energy of the Great Peace? Although America betrayed all its ideals by slaughtering the Indian, can it—or any of us—accept that there is no recompense for this crime except to continue the work that formed the essence of the Indians' culture,

27 Ibid., 232.

28 Ibid., 235.

> the same work that we find as well at the heart of our own ideals . . . ? We are obliged, by the laws of conscience, to bring to the earth what the Indians brought. Without that, all other compensation and atonement will be perilously incomplete.[29]

Needleman tells us that we must make atonement for the sins of our forefathers. Atonement recognizes the crime of America and that wrong has been done and it seeks to make it right. Joseph Campbell speaks of a phase of the hero's journey called at-one-ment. In order to return on the hero's journey, we must let go of our fragmentation and return to oneness. Needleman tells us we must continue the work of the Haudenosaunee (Iroquois) Confederacy and carry on in our hearts the work of the *Kayanerenhkowa*, the Great Law of Peace. Joseph Rael tells us that work is worship and so we must make *Kayanerenhkowa* our work, we must make peace our worship so that we can make the peace for our ancestors, make the peace for ourselves, and make the peace for Mother Earth who is stained with the blood of her sons and daughters.

Needleman encourages us to go into the broken heart in order to learn. We will next turn to Parker Palmer who speaks to us of the different ways that the heart can break and how we can develop a "politics of broken-heartedness" that grows compassion and connection rather than separation and wounding.

HEALING THE HEART OF DEMOCRACY

Parker Palmer is a Quaker, an educator and change agent. His organization Courage & Renewal seeks to address burnout in teaching, business, and health care through helping people lead an "undivided life." I traveled up from New Zealand to Minnesota in 2013 to participate in the "Integrity in Health Care: The Courage to Lead in a Changing Landscape" program. I have continued to write guest blogs periodically for the organization and I feel a real resonance with their work and message. Courage & Renewal has chosen both *Re-humanizing Medicine* and *Walking the Medicine Wheel* as selections for their annual Favorite Courageous Books.

Palmer sees the United States' crisis of democracy as a kind of heart trouble. Throughout the book, Palmer focuses on President Lincoln, who sought to preserve our Union during the Civil War, and who struggled with depression throughout his life. Parker Palmer has written about his own

29 Ibid., 236.

PEACE MAKERS OF THE RAINBOW LIGHT

struggles with depression, including while writing of *Healing the Heart of Democracy*. Depression, despair, hopelessness, rage, anger, and verbal violence are common emotions in politics these days. Now, maybe more than ever, we need to attend to the suffering heart of democracy. From the beginning, English colonists were striving for their own freedom even while oppressing others, particularly the native inhabitants of this land and the African slaves that they brought here to work the land. This fact, and the larger struggle of the Civil War, warn us that there is something divided within us as individuals and as a people that we are struggling to come to terms with and unite.

Palmer cautions that the failure of democracy can only occur if our hearts are separated and divided internally and between ourselves as a common people.

> If American democracy fails, the ultimate cause will not be a foreign invasion or the power of big money or the greed and dishonesty of some elected officials or a military coup or the internal communist/socialist/fascist takeover that keeps some Americans awake at night. It will happen because we—you and I—became fearful of each other, of our differences and of the future, that we unraveled the civic community on which democracy depends, losing our power to resist all that threatens it and call it back to its highest form.

One of the key concepts in Palmer's book is the idea of holding tension when conflict arises rather than trying to immediately disperse it. He writes, "*It is in the common good to hold our political differences and the conflicts they create in a way that does not unravel the civic community on which democracy depends.*"[30] The unity of democracy comes out of the clamor of our diversity. *E plurbus unum* is our national motto, *out of many, one*. However, this one is not a totalitarian or fascist imposition of imposed identity, rather our unitary identity is made up of many identities—just as the stars in the sky are all part of a larger whole, and yet each one burns brightly on its own. The beauty of the sky is in its variation, not in its uniformity.

Palmer tells us that we can transform our suffering for the purpose of personal, national, and global transformation. He speaks of the two ways the heart can break: it can shatter, wounding self and others with its shards; or it can break open, opening to the potential wisdom of suffering. Palmer describes the work of writing his book, "I began this book in a season of heartbreak—personal and political heartbreak—that soon descended into a dark night of the soul. It took months to find my way back to the light and six years to complete this book." Thus begins Palmer's book, published in 2011, situating personal heartbreak within political heartbreak. What he struggles to find is how we can find a "politics of the brokenhearted" rather than a "politics of rage" or a politics of apathy. He asks us a series of questions.

30 Palmer, *Healing the Heart of Democracy*, 9, xxvii

> How did we forget that our differences are among our most valuable assets? . . . When will we learn that violence in the long run creates at least as many problems as it solves? Why do we not value life, every life, no matter whose or where? Or understand that the measure of national greatness is not only how successful the strong can be but how well we support the weak?

In seeking to address his personal and political heartbreak, Palmer tells us "In my experience, the best therapy for personal problems comes from reaching out as well as looking within."[31] This fits with our theme in this book of the interconnection and unity of inner and outer work. The heart is the place where the inner and outer meet. Quite literally this is true as the heart and lungs work together, bringing our depleted blood into contact with the oxygen of the outside world and pumping this rejuvenated blood throughout our bodies. This is a two-way exchange as we breathe out carbon dioxide and breathe in more oxygen. This connects us to the outside world with every breath and every breath connects us with all of the green and growing things of the earth as they breathe in our carbon dioxide and breathe out oxygen.

Palmer seeks to reclaim the original meaning of *heart*. His definition fits nicely with Joseph's teaching that the heart is the center of the medicine wheel, the place of integrating the outer directions of north, south, east and west with the inner directions of spirit, emotions, mind, and body.

> Heart comes from the Latin *cor* and points not merely to our emotions but to the core of the self, that center place where all our ways of knowing converge—intellectual, emotional, sensory, intuitive, imaginative, experiential, relational, and bodily, among others. The heart is where we integrate what we know in our minds with what we know in our bones, the place where knowledge can become more fully human.

Without healthy spiritual hearts, we cannot have spiritual democracy and Palmer is seeking to help us create *a politics worthy of the human spirit*. Just as the heart is continually pumping and helping us transform what is used up into what is new and vital, we must, as individuals, as a nation, and as a global people, be continually renewing and revitalizing ourselves and our democracy. To do this we must continually come out of our heads and down to our hearts.

---

31 Ibid., 1, 2, 4.

> For those of us who want to see democracy survive and thrive—and we are legion—the heart is where *everything* begins: that grounded place in each of us where we can overcome fear, rediscover that we are members of one another, and embrace the conflicts that threaten democracy as openings to new life and for our nation.[32]

I have wondered how this could practically be implemented, what would happen if every politician were to ask him- or herself before speaking or legislating—"Am I starting with my heart? Will my actions make the world a more loving place?" It seems we would live in a much different country if these were the motivations in the hearts of all of us as citizens and public servants—for we are all, in a democracy, public servants, seeking the greater common good.

Coming from the Quaker tradition, Palmer uses a process called the "clearness committee," which he says is based on "the belief that every person has an 'inner teacher'—a soul-deep source of whatever truth the person needs to hear and the best possible source of counsel in challenging times." It is through seeking this inner source of wisdom that a person should make big decisions and the clearness committee functions to support a person to turn his or her attention inward to this source. It is like saying that in the cave of the heart there dwells one's own inner teacher, one's own inner guru, who can give the best advice for you during the times that try the soul. Palmer sees that our outer ability to engage in democracy is made possible through our inner practice of self-connection, which is also divine connection. "If we are to be citizens of a democracy, we must spend time in conceptual spaces defined by personal experience, not by the mass media, spaces where we can get the news that comes from within."[33]

Palmer quotes Rilke about doing the "heart-work."[34] This concept of *heart-work* is a useful one for our book, as that is the kind of work that takes one to the center of the medicine wheel and it is the kind of work that is done in the center of the medicine wheel, and it is the kind of work that reconnects once from one's deepest center to the world and universe. Palmer writes that to "reclaim our democracy, we need to do

32 Ibid., 6, 10.

33 Ibid., 146, 154.

34 Rilke, "Turning Point," cited in Palmer, 175. We previously discussed this concept of "heart-work" and some of Palmer's ways the heart can break in *Walking the Medicine Wheel*, 139–40, 156–58.

the challenging heart-work of examining our myths, seeing how far they are from the reality of our national life, then reclaiming their embedded visions and doing the hard work necessary to bring reality closer to them."[35] Thus we must go into the visionary space of the heart in order to reconnect with the source of democracy, what Joseph Rael would call "the principle ideas" of democracy—that place where we feed our souls on the Mother Earth's milk of spiritual democracy. We must seek deeply the truth of each of our hearts. What our hearts tell us is that the heart is never alone, it is always reaching deeply inward toward the divine which is simultaneously stretching outward to embrace all of reality as One.

JOSEPH'S TEACHINGS ON SPIRITUAL DEMOCRACY & ESOTERIC KNOWLEDGE

Joseph recently sent me a couple of drawings. The first is a pueblo structure. There is a ladder leading up to another pueblo structure and then another ladder leading up to a very large pueblo structure, composed of many layers and tiers of rooms and it is surrounded in a cloud in the sky. I could see that there was some writing below the ordinary and non-ordinary pueblos, but it had been erased.

The other drawing is the floor plan of Joseph's home as a child in Picuris and shows the bed where he slept. One interesting thing about the drawing is that the Holy Room is as large as the bedroom, common room, and kitchen combined. Joseph wrote some things on this drawing. "Not to scale house where BPA [Beautiful Painted Arrow] lived and dreamed at night." "How the principle Ideas visited my dreamtime from the Holy Rooms so we could travel to the upper village located in the Heavens."

On the back of this drawing is another that shows a rectangle of "BPA's house," and then layers of rectangles above as the "upper village." There is an arrow from the upper village to more text. "Each of the squares is a universe and there are billions. The Spirit Helpers belong to all humans as our teachers."

Joseph called one day and I asked him about the text that had been erased on the drawing he sent. Here is what he said:

"Tiwa knowledge is held in the above, not in the ordinary Tiwa, but in the Tiwa in the sky.

"The esoteric knowledge is held in the city above the city. We talk about

35 Palmer, 183.

the Sky City, which exists above the ordinary city. Up there all of the esoteric knowledge dwells, because when I talk about non-ordinary reality or the esoteric, I am speaking about eternity. What is in eternity is there for all time.

"I had a student asking me about what is meant by 'esoteric knowledge,' he said he didn't understand what 'esoteric' meant. I told him that when you are going to dig post-holes for a fence, you should get a cup of water. Take the cup or water outside to make an offering to the rising sun. Offer water in the four directions. Then go inside and eat your breakfast and then go do your work. Remember that I teach that work is worship, so when you are doing your work you are worshipping and you are bringing the esoteric knowledge down from the sky and into ordinary reality. As you dig the hole you are there with the hole and you dig down 12 inches, 13 inches, maybe 15 inches. Then you put the cedar pole in the ground. Then you put an inch of earth around the pole and you tamp it down as hard as you can. Then you put another inch of earth around the pole and you tamp it down. Then you gradually put in more earth, but you don't have to tamp it down as much. That pole will stay in place more than if you put it in concrete. That way you are bringing together the spiritual, the emotional, the mental, and the physical. You are bringing together Wah-Mah-Chi, *Breath, Matter, Movement.*

"The esoteric knowledge is in the sky and what we do is we bring it down into ordinary reality. It is not human beings who are doing the work, it is the esoteric knowledge. Human beings just need to learn how to connect to that esoteric knowledge. So what you do is in meditation you learn to go to the city in non-ordinary reality, the Sky City. You can go there and look for someone who is teaching there and you can learn what you need to learn and then you bring it back down to the earth. Up there you can come into contact with all the various spirit helpers.

"You sit in meditation and eventually you find yourself in the upper realm. I would sit and meditate and I would look around for the ladder that leads up to the esoteric knowledge. The way that you develop the ability to go up to the esoteric knowledge is by living a life of piety. You live in piety and pretty soon the spirit helpers get used to seeing you and they think you are all right and they start to help you.

"In the old times priests would go into caves when they were seeking esoteric knowledge and contact with God. In Greek times, from what I have read, the Greeks used to go into caves for their esoteric knowledge. The trouble began when they brought their ceremonies out into the light of day and then they did not work as well. In the light that illuminates ordinary reality, there are a lot of

distractions. I don't mean like the Christians do that there are demons that are trying to lead you to evil. I mean that there are many different things to look at and these can be distractions from the esoteric knowledge. When you go into darkness, you can see into the dark matter and this connects up to the esoteric.

"You are in Seattle, right? And that is named after Chief Seattle. So what you can do is go into meditation and look for a ladder that leads up, 10 miles up, and you can go there and you can talk with Chief Seattle about what his esoteric teachings are. They are always there for those who know how to access them.

"When you are seeking esoteric knowledge, you shouldn't ask questions. Remember how I have told you that when you ask a question you are setting up the human template to miss? It is like an arrow. If you are going to hit something you imagine yourself hitting it, you don't ask, 'how am I going to hit it,' or 'why does that deer move so quickly and quietly?' If you do that you are setting yourself up to miss. The esoteric knowledge is a lot like a deer, quiet, fast, elusive. To find it you have to imagine yourself finding it. If you say 'Why, why can't I find it?' you will never find it. When you question you separate yourself from it, but it is already there for you to find in an instant and you are there.'

One of the last things Joseph said to me was, "*See, there are always synchronicities, you just have to look for them.*" Earlier he had said, "*You can go into meditation and find esoteric knowledge and then when you see something on a billboard in California, or Denver, or Seattle, you can look at it and understand it and say, 'God is talking to me through this billboard.'*" Oftentimes when I am working intensively on something, Joseph will call me and I want to ask him linear questions about the topic. Sometimes he is teaching something that is obviously about the topic. Other times, no matter how many times I ask him he goes off on (seeming) tangents that keep looping and circling around the topic without (from my perspective) seeming to hit it.

I asked Joseph about his ideas on "spiritual democracy" and "America," but instead he spoke about esoteric knowledge. Extrapolating from his teachings we could say that Spiritual Democracy exists in an upper level in the Heavens. There is an ordinary United States of America and there is a non-ordinary, esoteric United States of America. The esoteric wisdom of the Founders of this land (including both the European and the American Indian Founders) is still accessible for those who know how to reach it. We can allow ourselves to be taught by becoming seekers. If we simply ask a lot of questions, however, we will not find the answers, but only more distractions. Spiritual Democracy can be found by movements upward as well as downward. Going into the darkness, one can more easily connect with the "dark matter" of the esoteric without the distractions that light up in ordinary reality. The way up to the esoteric is by first quieting and going inward into the darkness of meditation and from there one can travel upward. If we were to come into contact with the principle idea of the United States of America, we would do this through each of our own hearts and from there connect to the USA that exists above the ordinary USA we live in most of the time. There is the ideal and there is the ordinary. We renew Spiritual Democracy through a continual process of re-connecting to the Upper United States of American (UUSA) which exists in eternity, in the ideal realm above us. We bring this esoteric knowledge down from Father Sky to become embodied in Mother Earth.

Joseph often speaks of spirit helpers who we come in contact with and who guide and instruct us in our seeking. Maybe this is why the names Washington, Hamilton, Lincoln, Black Elk, Hiawatha, and Chief Seattle continue to inspire us. To be inspired means that one is breathed into. If we only think of ourselves in isolation, we are breathing recycled air that gets stale. If we re-remember and re-connect to the principle idea of Upper United States of American, we are allowing ourselves to be a vehicle for the spirit helpers of UUSA. We can be inspired by the Indigneous and colonizing Founders of the United States of America and we can be seekers and distributors of divine wisdom.[36] Just as individuals, nations too, require continual re-orientation toward the divine and continual infusions of divine wisdom. This is what Joseph means when he says "we do not exist." We do not exist as concrete, separate, individuals. We only exist when we come into relation with the Source of being who is continually recreating us. Seeking to stay the same is death and fundamentalism. Allowing ourselves to be continually inspired and recreated is life, liberty, and the pursuit of happiness.

The abbreviation for the United States is *US*. This is also telling us that when we are speaking of the United States, we are speaking of US. Esoteric knowledge teaches us to pay special attention to synchronicities like this. When we speak of the United States, we continually hear the whispered reminder—*US*. The United States of America is abbreviated

36 By "Founders" we mean our Native brothers and sisters as much as the Europeans and their descendants. Any name that is remembered and revered is an ancestor and Founder of the land.

the US of A. This reminds us that the idea of the USA is beyond the little *us* of citizens of just this one country, and that we are speaking of the big *US* of the Americas—and even more the *US* of the world.

WORKING FOR PEACE AFTER WAR

Following World War I, the people of many nations of the world got together to create the League of Nations in 1920. This was brokered by a number of people, including Lord Bryce from the UK, US president Woodrow Wilson, and South African, Jan Smuts.[37] The League of Nations lasted from 1920 to 1945 when it was replaced by the newly formed organization, the United Nations. The UN is an organization dedicated to promoting world peace and human rights. While it has become trendy amongst the populist right wing in the United States to demonize the UN and seek to limit its powers or even to speak of withdrawing from it, we need an organization dedicated to promoting peace in this world. How will we ever be able to come together as one people of the Earth if we do not have organizations that are forums for every nation to have a voice? The idea of the UN is to create a council of world leaders who will hold the identity of global citizenship above the narrow identity of tribes and nations. This is one of the foremost organizations working for peace on the planet. The UN brings together soldiers and diplomats from all over the world. The soldiers serving as "Peacekeepers" wear blue helmets, no matter what country they come from.

---

37 South African Jan Smuts has an interesting history. Smuts was a Field Marshall, a member of the British War Cabinet, a Prime Minister of South Africa and is the only person to have signed the peace treaties ending both World War I and World War II. However, Smuts was a proponent of apartheid (separation of whites and blacks in South Africa) and was the opponent of Gandhi in his work for civil rights for the Indian population living in South Africa. I choose the word "opponent" rather than enemy, since, even though they were on opposite sides of an argument, Gandhi still gave Smuts a pair of sandals as a gift, made with his own hands. This tells us something of Gandhi, who took the time to hand-make sandals for his opponent who favored segregation. Not only that, Gandhi made the sandals whilst he was imprisoned. Smuts returned these sandals to Gandhi in 1939, on Gandhi's 70th birthday with the following note, "I have worn these sandals for many a summer, even though I may feel that I am not worthy to stand in the shoes of so great a man," (Mahatma Gandhi, *The Essential Gandhi: An Anthology of His Writings on His Life, Work, and Ideas,* ed. Louis Fischer, 98). We can speculate what effect having Gandhi as an opponent may have had on Smuts. Even though Smuts was a proponent of racial segregation and opposed rights for non-whites in the early 1900s, he later did much to promote peace. He was also a philosopher and in his 1926 book *Holism and Evolution* coined the word, "holism" the concept of unifying separate parts into a greater whole (which is greater than the sum of its parts).

Joseph received a letter from the United Nations in regard to his work with the Sound Peace Chambers and ceremonies to promote world peace.

UN LETTER, KATHERINE SPRINGER, 20 FEB, 1989

1. It is with great pleasure that I acknowledge the contributions of Mr. Joseph Rael to activities furthering world peace. This is a primary objective for the United Nations, for whom I work, and the U.N. Peacekeeping Forces have recently received the Nobel Peace Prize for efforts in this area. Mr. Rael is known in a number of countries around the world to be dedicated to the cause of world peace and to undertake activities which further its achievement.

2. Among Mr. Rael's numerous activities is organizing group prayer, particularly in connection with Peace Chambers. Such groups chant for world peace, accompanied by rattles, drums, and eagle feathers which are essential to the inspiring performance in many traditional and non-industrialized societies. It is hoped that Mr. Rael will continue to expand his activities to other countries in our common pursuit of peace on this planet.

KATHERINE SPRINGER
Technical Advisor
20 Feb, 1989

The United Nations Declaration on a Culture of Peace states that, "since wars begin in the minds of men, it is in the minds of men that the defences of peace must be constructed."[38] Needleman tells us that we need a New Mind to bring the *Kayanerenhkowa* (Law of Peace) into our minds and hearts. Joseph tells us that war stems from a state of mind (and of heart) in which we falsely strive to persist in our separated, individual identities. Through atonement for the crimes of America, we can bring *at-one-ment* which brings a change of consciousness and identity. Then we can all share, Native Americans, European Americans, African Americans, and all peoples of the Earth, that peace and abundance of the Horn of Plenty.

The original Founders of Spiritual Democracy are Father Sky and Mother Earth and they have given us this teaching of peace. It is up to us to listen to this teaching. We can renew Spiritual Democracy by listening to the depths of our hearts, by listening deeply to the land, and by listening with all our being to the sky.

38 The United Nations Education, Scientific, and Cultural Organization constitution, signed 1945.

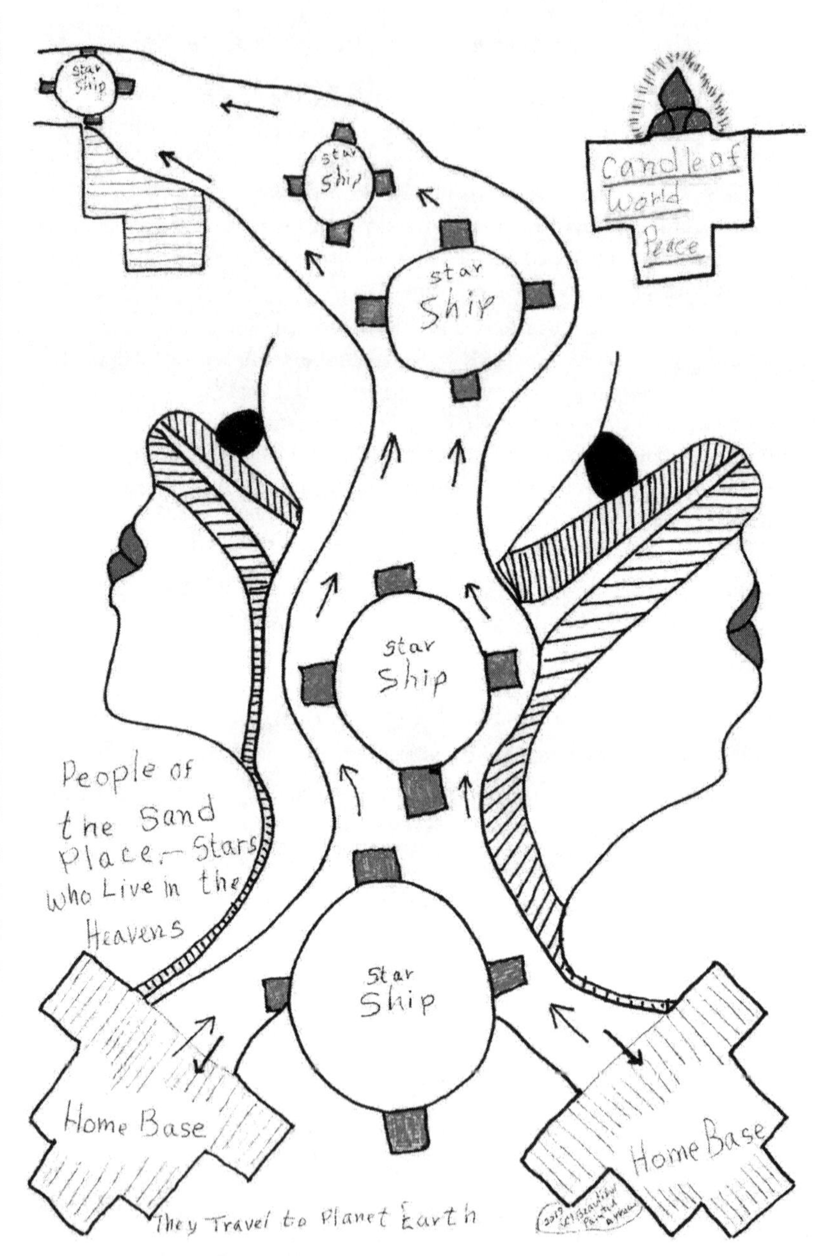

CANDLE OF WORLD #2 – PEOPLE OF THE SAND PLACE – STARS WHO LIVE IN THE HEAVENS - THEY TRAVEL TO PLANET EARTH

CHAPTER 15

REFOUNDING

By refounding I mean the process of returning to the founding experience of an organization or group in order to rediscover and re-own the vision and driving energy of the pioneers. . . . To refound formation is to re-enter the sacred time of the founding of religious life itself. . . . There having re-identified with Christ and his prophetic mission to the world, we then struggle collaboratively to build radically new formation structures and processes in harmony with Christ's mission to the Church and world. . . . This model of symbolic death and rebirth, which is made up of three stages – separation, transition/liminality and reaggregation – also has a powerful scriptural foundation.[1]

GERALD ARBUCKLE

[I]nitiation lies at the core of any genuine human life. And this is true for two reasons: the first is that any genuine human life implies profound crises, ordeals, suffering, loss and reconquest of self, "death and resurrection"; the second is that whatever degree of fulfillment life may have brought us, at a certain moment everyone sees life as a failure. . . . The hope and dream of these moments of crisis are to obtain a definitive and total renovation, a renewal capable of transmuting life. Such a renewal is the result of every genuine religious conversion.[2]

MIRCEA ELIADE

But no religion is completely "new," no religious message completely abolishes the past. Rather, there is a recasting, a renewal, a revalorization, an integration of the elements—the most essential elements!—of an immemorial religious tradition.[3]

MIRCEA ELIADE

1 Gerald Arbuckle, *From Chaos to Mission: Refounding Religious Life Formation*, 3–5.

2 Mircea Eliade, *Rites and Symbols of Initiation*, 203–04.

3 Mircea Eliade, *Shamanism*, 12.

REFOUNDING

I recently traveled to Sydney, Australia for the Australasian Doctors Health Conference. Whilst I was there, I finally met Gerald Arbuckle, who I had been corresponding with for several years. We spoke at length about the world political situation, fundamentalism, initiation, and the concept of "refounding." Gerry sees a need for continual refounding in institutions because as institutions function they lose their original vision and mission and become overly focused on the perpetuation of the institution. I think of this as being similar to what Joseph Rael says about ourselves as individuals—that when we seek to persist as fixed entities, we cease to exist. To exist means we are perpetually dying to the old and being reborn in the new. In other words, we are continually undergoing a process of initiation. We can think of refounding as a somewhat analogous process to the continual process of initiation. Whereas initiation is an individual process, refounding is a communal process which is often sparked by an individual, a "refounding person."

> A refounding person is one who, in imitation of the shock that the original founding person experienced on perceiving the gap between their deeply held values and the world of their time, acutely sees a . . . chasm between these values and their contemporary reality, and moves, through quantum-leap creative strategies, to bridge the gulf, and at the same time restlessly summons others to undergo a similar conversion to share in the vision and to venture collaboratively into the unknown in order to implement these strategies.[4]

Gerry sees the power or ability of the refounding person to transform the institution as coming through a "liminal initiate experience." This connects the individual back to the sacred time, or power of the original founder of the institution. We can think of this as building *mana* or *medicine*.

> The initiation liminal experience of the refounding person is the transformative process of returning to the founding myth of an institution. He/she relives the founding experience in which the original founder was so shocked at the gap between their desired values and the realities of their world. The refounding person is alerted to

4 The quotes in this section are taken from an email exchange that Gerald Arbuckle and I had in October, 2018. Also see Gerald A. Arbuckle, *Out of Chaos: Refounding Religious Congregations* (New York: Paulist Press, 1988), 89.

> the contemporary gap between values and the world around them. They are contemplatives who act; they move to bridge the gap, not by tackling the symptoms of the gap but by struggling to remove the *causes* of the gap. This is what is meant by the expression "quantum-leap creative strategies."

As a *contemplative who acts*, the refounding person's work becomes a call for the community to go through a similar initiation process. This recalls Jung's view that in psychotherapy the therapist first goes through the painful process of growth and change and then leads the client through it. In the case of a refounding person, it is the relationship between a spiritual leader and a community rather than between two individuals.

> Refounding persons are not loners in molding new identities for institutions amid changing contexts. They recognize their limitations and the need for collaborators to sharpen their understanding of their creative vision, to plan and ensure its implementation. Refounding persons commonly begin with a vague intuition of what should be done. By involving others in the planning and implementation of a project the refounding persons are slowly able to refine their insights and strategies. But collaborators cannot act *unless* they themselves experience the pain of the contemporary gap between values and realities, in imitation of the original founding pain.

Refounding is a dance between the individual and the collective. It is akin to the hero's journey in which an individual goes through their own deep, personal process, and then serves as a guide for others to go through their own initiation processes.

> Refounding is a collective event in society, BUT it can never happen without refounding persons to lead it. A collectivity by itself cannot act alone. The cultural status quo seduces people away from their liminal experience. The call to constantly avoid the seduction demands the presence of refounding people who seek to live *permanently* their original transformative liminal experience of shock and response. A collectivity left to itself loses energy, becomes seduced by desires for order and predictability. Order and predictability, that is culture, destroys ongoing transformative liminal experience. St Francis of Assisi is such a liminal person – always remaining an initiate, challenging the ever-present status quo. He demanded this of his followers also. Eventually, however, his followers forgot this. When this happened the Franciscan refounding process ceased.

Gerry writes that refounding people "seek to live permanently" in their "original transformative liminal experience." This is similar to the work of a shaman, a visionary, or a mystic, who seeks to dwell permanently in *Wah-Mah-Chi*, in God. The refounding person who can do this lives in a state in which every moment is a theophany and every moment is an epiphany and they are able to serve a function for the community by reminding them of the call to Spirit.

Today many people feel that our institutions are in crisis and are not reflecting the values of the founders. We are in desperate need of renewal and refounding. Re-working the foundation is dangerous work and there can be an impulse toward making structures rigid, narrow, and brittle, which Gerry Arbuckle warns is the motivation behind fundamentalism. Fundamentalism closes off and tries to preserve an imagined past, whereas refounding opens up and creates space for living spirituality to be infused in the structure, so that the structures are living Breath-Matter-Movement, rather than being static and deadened.

REFOUNDING MOTHERS OF DEMOCRACY

As I was doing the background reading for this chapter, I kept seeing the term "Founding Fathers" and no one mentioned the Founding Mothers of Democracy. In a patriarchal society, women and minorities are often left out of the historical narrative of war-fighters and kings. We will look at the contribution of the feminine in terms of giving birth to creativity, hope, human rights, and democracy.

Joseph Rael's culture is matriarchal and believes mothers are the source of the baby's first contact with soul. He told me that Spiritual Democracy has to do with babies drinking their mother's milk, because swallowing makes the sound, "soul." Every time a baby drinks from the mother, there is the sound of soul being brought into this world and that leads to a spiritual democracy.

Some of the founding mothers in the history of US democracy are Betsy Ross, Abigail Adams, and Martha Washington. Periodically, re-founding is needed and many women have been part of refounding movements, such as Harriet Tubman and the Underground Railroad, and civil rights activists like Rosa Parks. There are contemporary refounding mothers of democracy, such as: Rachel Carson, author of *Silent Spring*, whom we can consider the mother of the modern environmental movement in the

United States; Vandana Shiva with her concept of "Earth Democracy"[5] and her work on creating living economies, living democracies, and living cultures; or Marianne Williamson, author of *Healing the Soul of America: Reclaiming Our Voices as Spiritual Citizens*. Given considerations of space, we will focus on two contemporary refounding mothers of democracy who have influenced me, Anoushka Shankar and Rebecca Solnit. We will also write about the original founder of spiritual democracy and earth democracy, Mother Earth.

RETURNING HOME: ANOUSHKA SHANKAR

I have repeatedly listened to Anoushka Shankar's 2015 album, *Home*, as I have worked on this book.[6] The idea of home has been foundational for me the past few years—while I was living "away from home" in New Zealand, when I returned "home" to the United States and worked to feel at home in Seattle in the Northwest, far from the Midwest where I spent most of my life, and lastly as I have worked daily with veterans who have returned "home" from war, but who do not feel at home in their own country, in their own communities, in their own families, or even in their own skin. Home is such a central concept for us as human beings, and yet the spiritual seeker is one who wanders far from home, and if lucky finds a sense of home deep within the cave of his or her own heart.

I was lucky enough to see Anoushka Shankar and Ravi Shankar perform in Champaign-Urbana, Illinois at Krannert Center for the Performing Arts, which must have been around 2000. The thing I noticed was that Ravi barely moved his body as his fingers went up and down the sitar. Anoushka, on the other hand, looked a little bit like a rocker as she played. I wondered if that was due to a difference in experience or belonging to different generations.

Anoushka Shankar is the daughter of Sukanya Shankar and world famous Indian musician, Ravi Shankar (who was 61 when she was born).

---

5 "Earth Democracy," according to Vandana Shiva, "connects people in circles of care, cooperation, and compassion instead of dividing them through competition and conflict, fear and hatred. . . . Earth democracy globalizes compassion, justice, and sustainability," (Shiva, *Earth Democracy*, 10). The concept of Earth Democracy shares elements with Whitman's and Herrmann's "Spiritual Democracy" and adds an engaged activism.

6 I find it useful to have a couple of foundational pieces of music to listen to as I write a book. Shankar's *Home* and Miles Davis' *In a Silent Way* have been the anchors for this book, along with John and Alice Coltrane, Ben Lee's *Ayahuasca: Welcome to the Work*, and Bill Laswell.

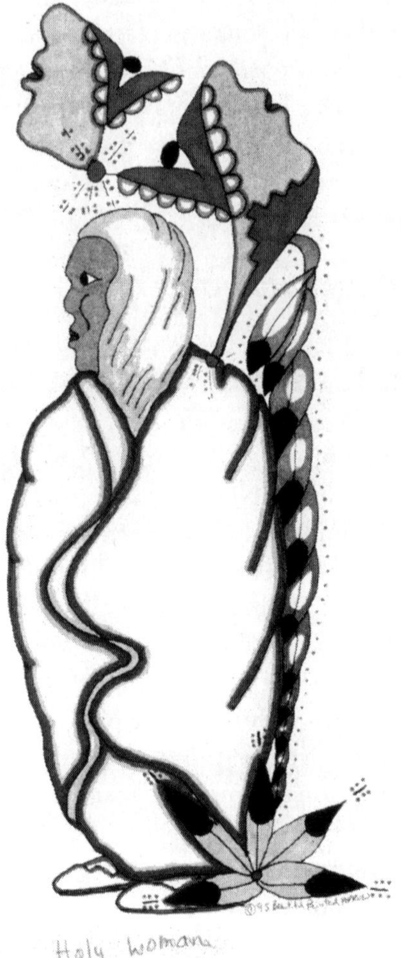

HOLY WOMAN

She was born in London in 1981 and her early childhood was in London and Delhi. As a teenager she moved to Encinitas, California, and graduated with honors from San Dieguito High School Academy in 1999. She was the Homecoming Queen of this American high school. She followed in the footsteps of her father, who became her musical guru, and she became an accomplished sitar player and performer. She assisted her father in putting together the amazing 1997 album, *Chants of India*, which was produced by former Beatle, George Harrison. In 2002 Anoushka Shankar performed live at "The Concert for George," a musical tribute to George Harrison's life and music. One of the songs she performed was "The Inner Light."[7]

Her website describes her albums, the creative process, and the meanings and influences behind her work. Her album, *Home*, was an homage to her father.

> Home features two ragas, one of which is a creation of Ravi Shankar's, and with them Anoushka shares an intimate, heartfelt live performance in the traditional style. Indian classical music is not written down, but has been improvised and passed down through an oral tradition for centuries; Home is a paradigm of this genre, exemplifying the unique dichotomy between the ancient structure and in-the-moment improvisations.[8]

Anoushka Shankar's life and music have been a blending of ancient traditions and the modern (similar to the work that Joseph and I are doing with this book, bringing together ancient wisdom into the modern day) She has brought in Western as well as classical Indian elements to her music, collaborating with Karsh Kale, Thievery Corporation, Jazz pianist Herbie Hancock, as well as with her half-sister, Norah Jones. Her most recent album, the influential *Land of Gold*,[9] has been remixed by Karsh Kale, Shiva Soundsystem, and even Scottish rockers Mogwai. Increasingly, Anoushka Shankar has also become a champion of women's rights and human rights.

> Separate from my desire to have an established core sound at the musical heart of this album, thematically, I wanted to integrate the authority of the female voice, and the drive for women to establish personal autonomy and dignity in situations where the female perspective is often, sometimes forcibly, subdued. I have been lucky to collaborate with some incredible female guest artists who helped me to bring this across.[10]

---

7 Details of Anoushka Shankar's life and recording history from an interview with Kavita Chhibber (3/18/05), "Anoushka Shankar Biography" by Eve M. B. Hermann on MusicianGuide.com and also see her Anoushka Shankar.com webpage, "biography." We have earlier discussed the origins of that song from the correspondence of Juan Mascaró and George Harrison around the genesis of "Inner Light."

8 AnoushkaShankar.com, "Albums," "Home."

9 When I am writing and listening to *Home* it flows into listening to this album, *Land of Gold,* so I often listen to these two albums back to back.

10 Writing about her album, *Land of Gold* from her webpage.

Anoushka Shankar is an exceptional musician who has been nominated for six Grammy Awards, but beyond her music she has taken on a greater role as an activist and spokesperson for humanity. She and her father were spokespeople for People for the Ethical Treatment of Animals (PETA), and she is also the spokesperson for the United Nations World Food Programme in India.[11] She spoke out about the 2012 horrific gang-rape of Jyoti Singh Pandey in Delhi. Anoushka Shankar released a song titled "In Jyoti's Name" on her 2013 album "Traces of You," and joined the online campaign One Billion Rising on Change.org, which demanded an end to crime against women. She described her song

> "In Jyoti's Name" [is] probably the angriest piece of music I'd ever written, and we played it around the world, and we kept talking about it, and sharing it, and dedicating it to her. So there's a way in which you could tie it to the dialogue, simply by playing that piece of music. I do feel like in a quasi-spiritual sense, you're offering something up. . . . Pain is a great music tool.[12]

In support of Jyoti and women everywhere, "she released a video in which she demanded an end to crime against women, and revealed she had been sexually abused for many years as a child."[13] This public revelation of her own childhood abuse presaged the #metoo movement. Speaking up for the human rights of women and girls is the ultimate refounding as we are all born of mothers and yet our contemporary world is often a hostile place for those who are our mothers.[14]

Shankar's 2016 album *Land of Gold* takes on many personal and world issues as its genesis. She describes the process and journey of this album on her website.

---

11 "Anoushka Shankar," *Wikipedia*.

12 Fabi Reyna, "Sitarist Anoushka Shankar on Corroborating Activism and Fusing Musical Worlds," *She Shreds* magazine, 6/27/17.

13 AnoushkaShankar.com, "biography."

14 Since Jyoti, other rapes and murders of girls on the Indian sub-continent have captured the attention of the world. Zainab from Pakistan and Asifa from India are two tragic cases. The abuse of women and girls is a crime against Mother Earth and the Divine Feminine. As Llewellyn Vaughn-Lee writes, rape is not just something that happens to women, it is a denial and desecration of the divine feminine, which is, ultimately, self-abuse. He writes: "When we deny the divine mystery of the feminine we also deny something fundamental to life. We separate life from its sacred core, from the matrix that nourishes all of creation. We cut the world off from the source that alone can heal, nourish, and transform it," (Vaughn-Lee, *The Return of the Feminine and the World Soul*, 3-4).

> Everyone is, in some way or another, searching for their own "Land of Gold": a journey to a place of security, connectedness and tranquillity, which they can call home. This journey also represents the interior quest that we all take to find a sense of inner peace, truth and acceptance – a universal desire that unites humanity.
>
> The seeds of *Land of Gold* originated in the context of the humanitarian plight of refugees. It coincided with the time when I had recently given birth to my second child. I was deeply troubled by the intense contrast between my ability to provide for my baby, and others who desperately wanted to provide the same security for their children but were unable to do so. . . .
>
> As I watched this nightmarish trauma unfold, graphically crystallized by the heart-wrenching images of the lifeless body of Syrian infant Aylan Kurdi washed-up on a Turkish beach – an event that shaped the album's title song, "Land of Gold" – I felt overwhelmed with a sense of powerlessness to alleviate the suffering and injustice taking place as the world looked on. However, like many others, I was painfully aware that, while I was physically remote from their harrowing experience, it was impossible for me to deny my emotional connection, as a human being.
>
> Land of Gold is the culmination of my journey to the interior, channelling my distress at the situation in a constructive way, exploring the stories of the voiceless and dispossessed. I believe that art can make a difference – it connects us to our hearts, bringing us back to what really matters. Music has the power to speak to the soul.[15]

The *land of gold* was what the Spanish were searching for when they conquered and exploited the peoples of America and it is also similar to the idea of the fountain of youth or the garden of paradise. Anoushka Shankar's idea of the *land of gold* is similar to the idea of *home*, the search to find where we belong, where we are safe, and where we are accepted. She describes this as an inner journey, an "interior quest," that we all must make and, yet, somehow, this most personal of quests connects us to our universal humanity. Bringing this back to the theme of our book, we could say that everyone has a land of gold within them, deep within the cave of each person's heart (Joseph sometimes speaks of the "held-back place of goodness within each of our hearts"). We must search for this gold and bring it to the surface of our lives, bring it out from the depths into the light of day and that, in that way, we can be creating the land of

15 AnoushkaShankar.com, "music."

gold in our communities and world. Our hearts connect us to the sacred in ourselves and the sacred in others. It is the heart that leads to the *land of gold.*

> Find the kind heart, rest your feet and soul
> May your kind heart find the land of gold.[16]

Anoushka Shankar is a true world citizen who brings worlds together, integrates the ancient and the modern in her music, and uses her interconnection to promote peace and human rights for women, immigrants, and all human beings. She goes into her heart and transforms her own pain to speak out for others who are in pain. Bringing together what has been separated and reconnecting to ancient wisdom are functions of the *Refounding Mothers of Democracy.* While it could be said that many musicians and artists work to make a difference in the world, Anoushka Shankar re-spiritualizes modern music by bringing the ancient spiritual music of Indian into the present day and integrating it with contemporary music and modern problems. The problem of peace is both ancient and modern, and artists and visionaries have been working to manifest the vibration of peace in the world just as long as others have been bringing the disharmonious vibrations of war, discord, pain, and oppression. For me, listening to Anoushka Shankar is an experience of refounding ancient spiritual wisdom in the present day.

REBECCA SOLNIT: RE-BECOMING AMERICAN

Another *Refounding Mother of Democracy* for me is Rebecca Solnit, an American from the United States whom I first read whilst I was living abroad. I spent three and a half years in New Zealand and there was a part of me that did not want to come back after my journey down under. Perhaps to truly become American, I had to leave and return and it has been work, at times, re-becoming an American.

In 2010 I had just moved to New Zealand and was consciously working hard to acculturate. In becoming a Kiwi (I have a permanent New Zealand resident stamp in my passport), I found myself often thinking about what it meant to be an American. One day I was browsing at Unity Books in Auckland and I came across Rebecca Solnit's book, *A Field Guide to Getting*

16 Anoushka Shankar, "Land of Gold," sung by Alev Lenz, from the album, *Land of Gold.*

Lost. I love the way that Solnit interweaves the personal, the historical, the political, and the transformative. In this book she traces out all the ways that a person can become lost: from being lost in the outer world, or lost in the inner world, lost in drugs, sex, and rock and roll, or lost in suicide. Like Dante's journey, finding himself lost in the woods at mid-life, so too I was lost from America, trying to find the path in New Zealand.

Living abroad also gave me a new perspective on "Americans" and I came to be able to speak of "Americans" and to think of myself as a New Zealander, a Kiwi, as well as being from the United States. Rebecca Solnit reminded me of some of the best things about being an American from the United States, whether it was punk rock, the beauty of the North American landscape, the writing of Henry David Thoreau, or of being a people who sometimes embody the optimism of hope. Solnit saw the value of getting lost, of learning in the darkness, while all along protecting that sometimes vulnerable and yet always strong flame of "hope in the dark." Her book, *Hope in the Dark: Untold Histories, Wild Possibilities* is a manifesto for how to remain optimistic *and* realistic. Her call to social activism draws its strength not out of the hope for success, but out of a strong inner connection with what is the right and good thing to do. She writes, "To hope is to gamble. It's to bet on the future, on your desires, on the possibility that an open heart and uncertainty are better than gloom and safety."[17] We all have to place a bet, but we have no reassurance of how it will turn out. Solnit writes that the "future is dark, with a darkness as much of the womb as of the grave."[18] She reminds us that darkness can symbolize both death and rebirth. We all have no choice but to go through the pains, but we do have the choice as to whether we interpret those pains as the pain of dying or the pain of giving birth continually to something new—or as Solnit often seems to argue, both together.

Hope in the Dark is about learning to sustain one's self as a citizen-activist. Solnit writes, "I use the term activist to mean a particular kind of engagement—and a specific politic: one that seeks to democratize the world, to share power, to protect difference and complexity, human and otherwise." She describes citizenship as a kind of heroism that builds "a sense of connection and commitment to the community" even in the face of tragedy. Solnit sees the goal of activism not as seeking an end, but as a continual state of active engagement in the world.

17 Solnit, *Hope in the Dark*, 4.

18 Ibid., 6.

> The question, then, is not so much how to create a world as how to keep alive that moment of creation, how to realize that Coyote world in which creation never ends and people participate in the power of being creators, a world whose hopefulness lies in its unfinishedness, its openness to improvisation and participation.[19]

Rebecca Solnit argues that human beings are at heart good in her book, *A Paradise Built in Hell: The Extraordinary Communities that Arise in Disaster*. This is much like Joseph Rael's teaching that there is a "held-back place of goodness" in everyone's heart and that this potential goodness is always accessible with effort. Disaster can serve as a kind of traumatic shake-up that frees up this human goodness as it breaks down barriers and separation between people. She describes that a kind of paradise of humanity can arise in the worst of times. "The possibility of paradise hovers on the cusp of coming into being, so much so that it takes powerful forces to keep such a paradise at bay. If paradise now arises in hell, it's because in the suspension of the usual order and the failure of most systems, we are free to live and act another way."[20] This idea that powerful forces hold back paradise in daily life is reminiscent of the idea of initiation—a separation, sometimes traumatic, from the mundane and profane life. Victor Turner's concept of *communitas* describes how this state of diminished social boundaries is generally inhibited under the structure of society. It is only during times of break-down (whether traumatic or ceremonial) that the sense of separation between peoples can be transcended to experience a state of connective unity.

Solnit traces the way that communities arise during war and disaster, such as in the blitz during World War II, between soldiers at war, and in New Orleans after Hurricane Katrina. There is something about disaster that stirs our goodness that we otherwise are too busy to access and leads to "abandoning the illusion of one's sense of separateness."

Without glorifying disaster, Solnit sees that there is something golden that disaster can awaken in us—our slumbering humanity and love of others as ourselves, which is reminiscent of what Victor Turner calls *communitas*.

> The joy in disaster comes . . . from that purposefulness, the immersion in service and survival, and from an affection that is not private and personal but civic: the love of strangers for each other, of a citizen for

19 Ibid., 18, 52, 108.

20 Solnit, *A Paradise Built in Hell*, 7.

> his or her city, of belonging to a greater whole, of doing work that matters.
>
> These loves remain largely dormant and unacknowledged in contemporary postindustrial society: this is the way in which everyday life is a disaster. For acted upon, given a role, this is a love that builds society, resilience, community, purpose, and meaning.[21]

Upon returning to the United States, I saw Rebecca Solnit speak in Seattle, June of 2014. I was excited to see this living heroine speak in-person. I brought my copy of *A Field Guide to Getting Lost* that I had brought back from New Zealand and Rebecca Solnit signed it. This book served as a bridge between New Zealand and the United States for me.

In Solnit's book, *The Mother of All Questions* (2017), she gives an argument for a creative and productive life that does not include children. As my wife and I also chose not to have children, I was interested in this essay. In "The Mother of All Questions," she writes, "I have done what I set out to do in my life. . . . I set out to write books, to be surrounded by generous, brilliant people, and to have great adventures." She writes that biological parenting is only one of many ways to love and that "there are so many things to love besides one's own offspring, so many things that need love, so much other work love has to do in the world."[22] I often think of my books as children and my professional work as a psychiatrist and healer involves a lot of nurturing. The gift of initiation is fulfilling and enlightening, one automatically starts to be a gift to others. Reciprocity of giving and receiving is the basis of the spiritual realm and the natural realm.

Solnit continues to provide a much needed voice crying out in the wilderness that re-orients us to what is most important for life on this world. Her latest collection of essays, *Call Them by Their True Names*, diagnoses the current social ills of our time as stemming from the disease of isolation. This isolation and separation is so profound that meaning is being separated from facts, resulting in a *deregulation of meaning*. She warns us that the ideology of isolation "becomes nihilism, trying to kill the planet and most living things on it with a confidence born of total disconnection." As Joseph and I pointed out in *Walking the Medicine Wheel* and in this book, war comes from separation and isolation and peace comes from recognizing our brotherhood and sisterhood with

---

21 Ibid., 118, 306.

22 Solnit, *The Mother of All Questions*, 8, 9.

human beings and the natural world. Solnit points out how this ideology of isolation and separationism infects not just our relationships with other human beings and the world, but becomes a linguistic crisis.

> What keeps the ideology of isolation going is going to extremes. If you begin by denying social and ecological systems, then you end by denying the reality of facts, which are, after all, part of a network of systematic relationships among language, physical reality, and the record, regulated by the rules of evidence, truth, grammar, word meaning and so forth. You deny the relationship between cause and effect, evidence and conclusion; or rather, you imagine both as products of the free market that one can produce and consume according to one's preferences. You deregulate meaning.[23]

I am grateful for Rebecca Solnit's tenacious democracy, environmentalism, and how she openly shares her personal life and interweaves it with the political. She influences me as a writer and her work is a crucial part of my re-birth in re-becoming an American from the United States.. Her kind of love for the land and for others is what makes her a *Refounding Mother of Democracy.*

MOTHER EARTH—THE ORIGINAL MOTHER OF SPIRITUAL DEMOCRACY

Mother Earth is not only our home, we are made out of her substance, her body—we come from her and we return to her. We are all children of Mother Earth. The Indigenous American traditions teaches us *relationship* rather than *ownership* and we are encouraged to think of the Earth as our Mother. Here is what Joseph writes:

> I believe that it is now time for the elders all over the world to talk to their people and instruct them. As elders we have more responsibility . . . a responsibility to talk about the sacredness of the Earth, and the sacredness of the people on the Earth. One of our journeys is to help the people as they walk on Mother Earth. Mother Earth is our land and she belongs to us because we are her children. She belongs to us and we belong to her. So we can take care of her the way she has been taking care of us.[24]

---

23 Rebecca Solnit, *Call Them by Their True Names*, 50. She writes that "one of the crises of this moment is linguistic," (4).

24 *Sound*, 256.

Pope Francis echoes this language of "mother earth" in his encyclical *Laudato Si': On Care for Our Common Home.* Pope Francis encourages us to engage in the mysterious relationship we have with the earth our mother.

> Rather than a problem to be solved, the world is a joyful mystery to be contemplated with gladness and praise. . . . Everything is related, and we human beings are united as brothers and sisters on a wonderful pilgrimage, woven together by the love of God has for each of his creatures and which also unites us in fond affection with brother sun, sister moon, brother river, and mother earth.[25]

We arise from Mother Earth and after we die our bodies return to Her. Joseph will often speak of Father Sky and Mother Earth, but in contemporary society we have lost connection to Mother Earth and this is a symptom of disconnection from the Divine Feminine. This has led to the despiritualization of nature, of Mother Earth, and of our own bodies. We are orphans who do not realize we are walking on our own Mother and that we are physically created out of our "lost" parent. Theologians speak of God as "Him," but God is also a "Her." Without Mother Earth we have no life in the same way that without our biological mother we would not have been born. Without a relationship to the Feminine we are one-sided. Mother Earth is always giving birth to us and Meister Eckhart wrote that we are also giving birth. "We are all meant to be mothers of God. For God is always needing to be born."[26] Creation is impossible without birth and new creation is impossible without re-birth. This is why we speak of Mother Earth as a *Refounding Mother of Democracy*: *Refounding* because her work is never finished; *Democracy* because She is always and continually giving birth to all of her children equally.

Sufi teacher Llewellyn Vaughn-Lee writes that our current global crises stem from our loss of connection to the Sacred Feminine. "Without the feminine nothing new can be born, nothing new can come into existence—we will be caught in the materialistic images of life that are polluting our planet and desecrating our souls." In the realm of the soul we are all interconnected—what we do to the soul of Mother Earth we do to our own souls as well. Vaughn-Lee tells us: "The world is a living spiritual being. This was understood by the ancient philosophers and the

25 Pope Francis, in Vaughn-Lee, *Spiritual Ecology: The Cry of the Earth*, ii–iii.

26 Meister Eckhart in Matthew Fox, *Original Blessing*, 222.

alchemists who referred to the spiritual essence of the world as the *anima mundi*, the 'Soul of the World.'" The *anima mundi* is the soul of Mother Earth, the essence of the creative life force animating all of our bodies and all of nature. Not only is Vaughn-Lee telling us that we are related and interconnected with the soul of Mother Earth, but we *are* actually *her!* "In the depth of ourself we discover this essential oneness. This is the same awareness as the yogi's realization that one's true nature and unchanging self (*atman*) is the Universal Self (*Atman*). What is within us is within everything."[27] The connection with Mother Earth, who is our very self and soul, brings us not just into the connection with physical matter (remember the Latin word for "mother" is *mater*) but brings us deep into the realm of mystical oneness. As Vaughn-Lee speaks of soul to Soul and *atman* to *Atman*, Joseph tells us that we are all part of Vast Self. If we look at Mother Earth's initials, we find "ME." This tells us that we are the same person.

RECOGNIZING THE EARTH AS A PERSON

If we were to see ourselves in relationship with Mother Earth, rather than having dominion over Her, or seeing Her as nothing but material resources to burn through, we would have feelings for Her as a person.

On March 16th, 2017, the Whanganui River in New Zealand was granted the status of personhood as part of the *Te Awa Tupua* (Whanganui River Claims Settlement) Bill. This third largest river in New Zealand has now been officially recognized as an ancestor of the Māori Whanganui *Iwi* (tribe). Gerrard Albert, lead negotiator for the *iwi* said that

> [W]e consider the river an ancestor and always have. . . . We have fought to find an approximation in law so that all others can understand that from our perspective treating the river as a living entity is the correct way to approach it, as an indivisible whole, instead of the traditional model for the last 100 years of treating it from a perspective of ownership and management.[28]

Influenced by the New Zealand decision to grant the Whanganui River personhood status, India followed this precedent granting the Ganges River "the rights of a human being." The Ganges is considered holy by the

---

27 Llewellyn Vaughn-Lee, *The Return of the Feminine and the World Soul*, 49, 99, 111.

28 Eleanor Ainge Roy, "New Zealand river granted same legal rights as human," *The Guardian Weekly*, 24–30 March, 2017.

MOTHER EARTH DREAMING ALL THE TWO LEGGEDS INTO BEAUTY

more than one billion Hindus.[29]

Recognizing rivers as human beings makes implicit sense from an indigenous or spiritual earth perspective. We come from the earth and return to the earth. The earth is truly our mother, Mother Earth. Who would not treat their mother as a person?

Joseph called me one day and left a message that speaks to the view of the earth as holding spiritual significance and for treating rivers and oceans as ancestors:

---

29 Simon Waters, "India makes Ganges a person; praises Whanganui River laws," *New Zealand World Herald* online, Mar 24, 2017.

"When someone dies in the village, the people will wash the body in the river and bury the body in the cemetery. You might think that the dead person lies in the cemetery, but that is not the way to see it. When the person's body is washed in the river, his or her spirit flows into the river, the body is buried, but the spirit continues on in the river. The river flows to the ocean and the person's spirit is in the river and the ocean. Then the sun heats the ocean and the water from the ocean goes into the sky, so does the person's spirit which is now in the sky. The clouds come back over the village eventually and the rain falls on the crops, so too falls the ancestor's spirit. Then when we eat the crops, we are eating the spirit of our ancestors."

This view of the interconnectedness of spirit draws together what seems to be separated and disconnected. The land is truly our mother, Mother Earth, and the sky is truly our father, Father Sky. If we viewed all rivers, lakes, and oceans as containing our ancestor's spirits and as being persons in their own right, we would have a far different relationship with the land and pollution would be unthinkable as it would be equivalent to assaulting or declaring war on the river people who are our very ancestors and who are our very selves.

MITOCHONDRIAL EVE

We mentioned Mitochondrial Eve in *Walking the Medicine Wheel.* It is worth mentioning again that science is telling us that we are all brothers and sisters and come from the same mother. Quite literally, we are all brothers and sisters. Think about that. This is not just a feel good statement of affiliation but a true bond between all living human beings on this planet. Here is what Dr. Siddhartha Mukherjee writes in his book, *The Gene.*

> For modern humans . . . each of us can trace our mitochondrial lineage to a single human female who existed in Africa about two hundred thousand years ago. She is the common mother of our species. We do not know what she looked like, although her closet modern day relatives are women from the San tribe from Botswana or Namibia.
>
> I find the idea of such a founding mother endlessly mesmerizing. In human genetics, she is known by a beautiful name—Mitochondrial Eve.[30]

The initials of Mitochondrial Eve and Mother Earth are the same: ME, which also has something to do with you and me, and each and every

30 Siddhartha Mukherjee, *The Gene*, 338.

one of us. We are all ME, we each identify with that when someone asks "Who is there?" and we point to our chests and say "ME." Every time you say "ME" you are echoing the vibration of Mitochondrial Eve and the vibration of Mother Earth. We are all *ME*, as a diversity and also as a Unity.

We have within, all of us, the ancient mitochondrial DNA of *ME* (Mitochondrial Eve). We are made of *ME* (Mother Earth), she is our foundation, and yet we lose our sense of connectedness to Her and to all of her children, our brothers and sisters. When we lose our foundation, we must go through a refounding process. Mother Earth is continually teaching refounding to us as we cycle through the seasons each year—seasons of awakening, seasons of growth, seasons of harvesting abundance, and seasons of decline and dormancy. Each spring the Earth goes through refounding.

To realize our indigenousness, our being of the land, we must harmonize the matter of our bodies with the *mater* of Mother Earth. Our bodies never forget who our Mother is, and yet we do. We treat Her with disrespect when we despoil the environment, when we take from Her without giving back, or when we mistreat our brothers and sisters of the Earth. Mother Earth is always reminding us externally and Mitochondrial Eve is reminding us internally that we are all ME. There is non-difference between us and we are all related.

COMMUNITAS

Gerald Arbuckle tells us that refounding occurs when an individual makes the journey back to the source of an institution's founding vision and then returns, transformed, to the institution and serves as an inspiration to the community. Anthropologist Victor Turner wrote about *communitas*, a state representing genuine and authentic human-human relationship rather than the often societal role-mediated relationships and transactional relationships that people have throughout their days. Turner discusses the work of theologian Martin Buber who also wrote about *communitas*. It fits his sense of the "I-Thou" relationship, rather than the "I-It" relationship. When this occurs in groups, Buber called it the "essential *We*."

Perhaps we can think of *communitas* as a kind of communal initiation—there is a crisis in orientation, the usual structure breaks down, and there is the opportunity for initiation and transformation. Turner compares two historical examples of *communitas*: the Franciscan order that St. Francis established in the 13th Century and Caitanya and the Sahajīyās of 15th–16th

Century India. Francis' vow of poverty placed him and his followers into a state of "permanent liminality." After his death this led to a crisis between those who wished to follow his spirit of poverty and as the institution grew, those who wished to relax the rules a bit. Caitanya was considered an avatar of Krishna and he started a social movement of revitalization of bhakti yoga that ritually broke down the usual social norms in which individuals identified with Rādhā and her divine lover Krishna in highly ceremonial ritual intercourse in a way that was "essentially religious in nature, treating the act of sex as a kind of sacrament." Turner draws parallels between Francis' love of Lady Poverty and the Sahajīyās enactment "using various cultural and biological means to attain a structureless state of pure social communitas . . . [in which] each devotee would be an incarnation simultaneously of Krishna and Rādhā, a complete human being."[31]

Communitas can be thought of as a liminal state for a group in which love, devotion, and communal bonding occurs. Culture and society generally do everything they can to prevent states like *communitas* as it is a breakdown of the structure of expected social norms. *Communitas* is the energy of refounding where people feel a sense of communal oneness with each other that transcends the separation and differences that so often divide us from our brothers and sisters.

CULTURAL REVITALIZATION

Alice Beck Kehoe writes about the cultural revitalization movements that occurred as Native American tribes were under stress and assault from the influx of European-Americans heading West. The idea of revitalization and millenarian movements is a similar process to what Gerald Arbuckle describes as *refounding* and what Victor Turner describes as *communitas.* Black Elk's organizing vision of spiritual rebirth for his people is an example of revitalization and refounding.

> Today I send a voice for a people in despair. . . . To the center of the world you have taken me and showed the goodness and the beauty and the strangeness of the greening earth, the only mother. . . . At the center of the sacred hoop you have said that I should make the tree bloom. . . . It may be that some little root of the sacred tree still lives. Nourish it then, that it may leaf and bloom and fill with singing birds. Hear me, not for myself, but for my people; I am old. Hear me that

31 Turner, 137–63.

> they may once more go back into the sacred hoop and find the good red road, the shielding tree![32]

Black Elk's voice went out, not only to the Great Spirit, but also to generations of American youth, seeing the despair and devitalization in their own culture in the 1960s and 1970s and into the present day. I know, for myself, Black Elk's visions were a source of hope that we can get back to the root of a living spirituality. This is what I have learned from Joseph Rael, also—ancient wisdom is something that is always present if only we seek it. That is why I climbed Black Elk peak and sought a revitalizing or refounding experience. We, as individuals, find ourselves in these places in our lives where nothing makes sense and the way we have been is not working any longer. Cultures need periodic revitalization and refounding if they are to remain healthy and vital, particularly those cultures which are under stress as Native American tribes of the late 1800s were, or even as our US American culture is now—divided, distrustful, fragmented, gridlocked. Arbuckle cautions us, though, to avoid the trap of fundamentalism, which is not a refounding movement that revitalizes, but rather a narrowing and hardening of attitudes that further separates and fragments. Beck Kehoe writes "Without change, adaptation, reformulation, revitalization, transformation (call it what you will), a society—Indian, European, *any* society—cannot continue."[33] This is the place that we are struggling within the United States: how can we find a place of *communitas* that includes everyone instead of fragmenting into *us* vs. *them*?

WOVOKA'S VISION OF THE GHOST DANCE

Alice Beck Kehoe's main focus in her book is Wovoka (Jack Wilson, 1865–1932), a Paiute man who had visions of a way to revitalize the struggling Native American communities through a dance that would bring back the ancestors and the buffalo. This came to be called the Ghost Dance because it would bring back the ancestors. Wovoka actively sought to spread his message to other tribes where the Ghost Dance ceremony was rapidly taken up. Uneasiness about the "restless natives" was one of the factors that led the American military atrocities of Wounded Knee

---

32 Black Elk, quoted in Alice Beck Kehoe, *The Ghost Dance: Ethnohistory and Revitalization*, 53.

33 Kehoe, 144.

in 1890, even though Wovoka preached peace, pacifism, clean living, and honesty. James Mooney, an ethnographer, was commissioned by the United States government to investigate the Ghost Dance, concluded that the "doctrines of the Hindu avatar, the Hebrew Messiah, the Christian Millennium, and the Hesûnanin of the Indian Ghost Dance are essentially the same, and have their common origin in a hope and longing common to all humanity."[34]

We can view the visions of Beautiful Painted Arrow (Joseph Rael) as similar *refounding visions* that have "their common origin in a hope and longing common to all humanity." Since his visions in the 1980s, Joseph has been working for world peace and unity through the creation of Sound Chambers and the dances he has led from his visions. Even in his statement "we do not exist," we can see that he is always challenging us to be perpetually in a state of *refounding* as we let go of static forms, return to source, and are reborn into a new *being & vibration*. Joseph reminds us that we are a "hollow bone" for *Wah-Mah-Chi*, Breath-Matter-Movement, God to pass through and do the work and worship of peace in the world. Joseph teaches us that ancient wisdom is always accessible when we are in the state of becoming visionaries. Then we learn that we are all children of Mother Earth and that we are all brothers and sisters: people, animals, rocks, stones, plants, trees, air, water, and the soil of the Earth. Joseph also is open to new learning through science and does not see science and spirituality as opposed, but as reaching for the same truth in different ways.

COMING FULL CIRCLE

When I was 21 years old, just after graduating from college, I took a 50-hour Greyhound bus trip from Chicago to Seattle. I was starting medical school in the fall and I felt that I needed to do some kind of adventure, and maybe even a vision quest of sorts. So in July of 1989 I set off across the US by Greyhound bus, a new backpack, some borrowed equipment, and probably too many books. My literary companions on the trip were Henry David Thoreau, Alan Watts, Chuang Tzu, D.T. Suzuki, Richard Bach, and Donald Shimoda, but otherwise, I spent two weeks alone in the Olympics, meeting only an occasional hiker. I did spend one night where another camper shared the alpine camp site. He turned out to be a high

---

34 James Mooney, cited in Kehoe, 154.

school teacher from the town I was born in, Naperville, Illinois. We talked a while over dinner. The thing I remember most that he taught me was that there had been a study of astronauts and they tended to come from small towns. The idea was that you needed to be able to dream, think big, and to see beyond the narrow confines in which you grew up—in order to be able to imagine other worlds.

I remember meeting a number of people on the bus trip back and forth. I remember one man, who seemed old, but was maybe younger than I am now, who said that the best two investments are education and travel—because both broaden your horizons.

The trip was transformative to me in many ways. Sometimes you don't realize what you have learned until time has passed. Looking back now, this trip was a rite of passage for me—I felt like I became a man, relying on myself out in the world. In fact it earned me the nickname "Mountain Man Doctor Dave." I had to come up against myself and the chatter of my mind as I spent so much time alone in the woods. Eventually there was a calm place that I reached and even more importantly, I know that there is a calm place of peace at the center of my being that I can always access. It probably helped that I had along so many books on spirituality, meditation, and nature mysticism. I had to face my fear and face the limits of my control. I remember one night, lying in my tent, freaking myself out, running thought experiments of a deranged killer living in the vast woods who killed people in their tents at night. I came to the decision that if that happened, I would respond, but that I couldn't live my life in fear of something that "might" happen. I learned that the world was more beautiful and vast, and filled with more interesting people than I had imagined. I met people from England, Poland, and Pakistan, as well as from all across the US on the trip.

Early on in the trip I was supposed to go to Sol Duc Falls and meet my friend Glenn one afternoon and we would camp that weekend. It seemed likely, but not certain. I waited at the falls for a few hours with nothing to do but wait and stare at the water perpetually cascading down. As I watched I would catch glimpses of single droplets of water separate out as they fell and then rejoin at the bottom of the falls. How many droplets forming and unforming? I imagined that is how we are as individuals, momentarily separating out of the cosmic ocean and then rejoining after what seems like almost an instant. I wondered about the "lives" of the water droplets, how they came to be separate and understood their state of separation, what their brief lives might be like, how much like a terrible thing "death" must seem as they neared collision with the water—only to be absorbed back into a greater unity.

As I write this, I am again on the Pacific Coast of the Olympic Peninsula of Washington state. Once again I am surrounded by this vastness of the Pacific Ocean, the "ocean of peace" that reaches out and connects to other places I have just recently been this past year: Hawaii, Fiji, New Zealand, Australia. At one point, I realized that if you step in the ocean, you are connected to all the ocean water of the Earth and also connected to all the coastlines throughout the world. We create arbitrary boundaries between things and nowhere is this more apparent than with oceans and seas. I once stood at the Northernmost tip of New Zealand, Cape Reinga, and I could see the confluence of the Tasman and the Pacific—there was a distinct line that could be seen extending out from the Cape, but the water was the same water, maybe there was a different energy to it, or different temperature, but the water that washes over my feet in Washington state is connected to the water of Fiji, where I just spent a week, and to the water of New Zealand, where I lived on the water. It also connects to the coastline of Antarctica, to the ice of the Arctic, to the shores of Iceland and the United Kingdom, where I will be in a few months. It is easier to see our Oneness and interconnection with water than it is with land, although all you have to do is look underneath the oceans and you see that the Earth is all one vast land mass that only appears to be "divided" up into continents—we are still living in the land of Pangea surrounded by the One Ocean, Panthalassa.

I took our dog, Corbin, on a walk in the woods where we are staying. It was raining gently, not enough to get really wet, but enough that you felt it and it breathed it in. I was breathing in Panthalassa, this water that we breathe in and the 70% of us that is water is Panthalassa. We walked down the trail and came to a stand of trees. Since working with Joseph I feel like I can sense that certain trees in the forest have something about them, more *gravitas*. They seem like sentinels and that is why I call them, Sentinel Trees. They seem more sentient than other trees; they have personalities, often have some kind of deformity or characteristic that makes them stand out. This clump of three trees was growing out of a nurse tree. A nurse tree is an old tree that falls and as it starts to decay seeds sprout in it and new trees grow out of it as its body becomes nutrients for the next generation of life. This can create a large mound with tree roots snaking about. The body of the nurse tree gives itself to new life; spaces open up when the older tree decays. There was a hole under the roots that looked obviously like some good-sized animal had its burrow there. I put a hand on one of the trees growing out of the nurse tree and communed with it for a while, looking down at the hole and marveling in my imagination about how these nurse trees create a different habitat for not only the trees that grow out of them, but for the animals as well.

I thought about how shamans are liminal beings, they are comfortable moving between worlds. I realized that trees are liminal beings, their trunk and branches reach up into the air and their roots reach down into the depths of the Earth. Maybe this is why these tree root caves are so important, trees remind us of the darkness within the Earth and the darkness within ourselves. At the same time they connect us to the heavens, reaching ever upward while reaching ever downward. "The World Tree," I thought to myself. That axis point where worlds meet.

We walked on for a while, Corbin grew quiet and interested and did not seem to mind standing in the rain while I communed with trees. We walked on and came to a giant tree on its side, its trunk on its side was taller than I am. There was a space where the tree had broken in two and it provided a narrow path that Corbin and I could fit through. As we slipped through this space, there was an opening in the old hollow tree that stretched back into the darkness of the interior—a perfect cougar den was my first thought! We slipped through quietly and I imagined we stepped into a different world—we were now in non-ordinary reality. I took my hood off so I could experience it better, even though I was getting more wet.

We explored a while and I thought we would have to cross back into ordinary reality. That saddened me, so we walked some more, we started to circle around the tree to come back to the opening, but from the ordinary reality side again. We passed through the opening again, I relaxed my breathing and the focus of my vision. We found an "obvious" trail, which was not the main trail. There were many "obvious" trails as we walked and I thought how easy it would be to get lost in this dense woods. Then I opened my hearing and could hear the roaring of the ocean surf and realized that we would have our bearings from that, so I relaxed gradually and didn't worry as much about finding visual cues for the trail.

We came to another very prominent tree, very tall with many, many small moss covered branches sticking out of the trunk. The tree looked like it had slithered along the ground for a while because the trunk ran parallel to the ground a ways and then turned upwards—another Sentinel Tree. It provided a good landmark that was visible from any direction. We looped back around to ordinary reality to make another pass through the tree into non-ordinary reality. I looked a little deeper into the cavernous hollow, sensing my fear and also being respectful if there was someone in there, just a quick look, then we went through again. This time we followed a "trail" to the right. "The truth is a pathless land," wrote Krishnamurti, but here we were finding trails every way we looked. Also, going downhill there were "obvious" trails, but then going back up other "trails" became obvious. I had been reading Fred Alan Wolf's book *The Eagles Quest*, earlier that morning. Wolf quotes quantum physicist, Werner Heisenberg about quantum physics, "The path comes into existence only when you see it."[35] That is what was happening, as Corbin and I spent more time circling around, imagining ourselves deeper into non-ordinary reality, we were able to see paths were none existed before. It was like what Joseph Campbell writes about the hero's journey, that doors will open for you where there were no doors.

Wolf had also written something that reminded me about watching droplets of water individuate and then rejoin unity at Sol Duc Falls. He wrote that the ego's body and even consciousness is a trap because it "keeps seeing only itself apart from the rest of the field or ocean of consciousness. Yet it is a drop of the ocean that, because of the working surface tension forces, tends to hold itself as a drop, separated from other drops, separated from the ocean of consciousness."[36]

As we walked around the large tree trunk, there was another hole in the hollow tree, big enough for a puma—a perfect puma den, open on both ends like a hollow tube or a hollow bone! I remembered Joseph calling the cats when he was a boy, "Here *mossa, mossa, mossa*!" He said he thinks this is why he has a special bond with cougars and why they left him a deer carcass recently. Joseph also said it prepared him to be a visionary because when you say "*mossa, mossa, mossa*," it sounds like "Moses, Moses, Moses," and so he was preparing this visionary energy in himself. I said "*mossa, mossa, mossa*" a few times and Corbin looked at me quizzically and we walked on.

35 Wolf, *The Eagles Quest*, 145.

36 Ibid., 260.

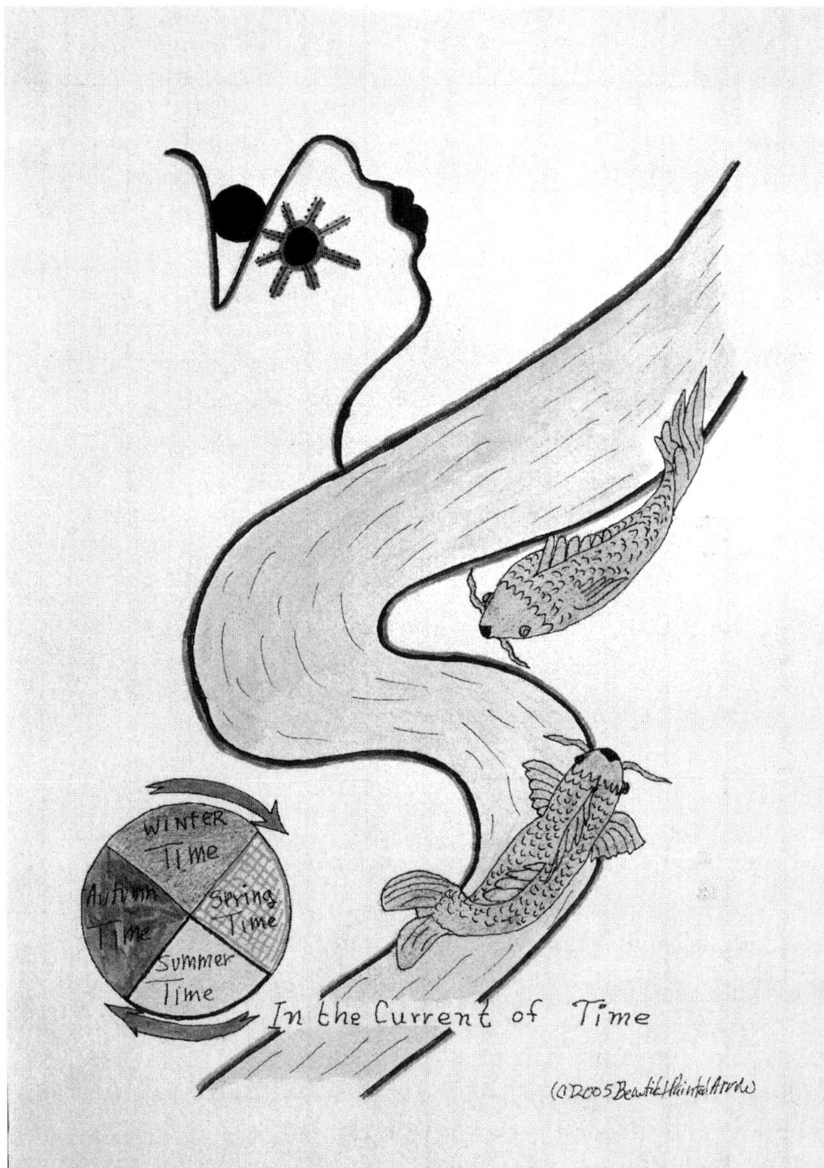

IN THE CURRENTS OF TIME

CHAPTER 16

A LIVING SPIRITUALITY

Each of us is a ceremony, a vibration of the All-That-Is. We ourselves are the Vast Self, that One Actor in the universe, who creates continually in all moments. We are the Vast Self playing in creation as creatures, as individuals.

In the experiences of my life, through loss and transformation, ceremony and story, I learned how to emerge continually from the individual self that is Joseph Earl Head Rael into the Vast Self again. In the kiva, in the sweat lodge, in the sun dances and long dances. I have learned to die to myself in order to know the Self, dying from this House of Shattering Light into states of ecstasy, and then returning again, that the Vast Self might drink continually of the light that It is creating.

To know ourselves as the Vast Self playing is to be both human and divine. It is for this we all are born, to be mystics, fully alive and dancing.[1]

JOSEPH RAEL

The purpose of the visionary, mystic, and shamanic initiations we have been studying in this book is to come to a place of *a living spirituality*. Joseph was brought up in a culture in which spirituality was inseparable from everyday life: walking, plowing, drinking, hunting, eating, dreaming, working—all of these are done with spiritual awareness in the indigenous world where Joseph was raised. For many of us in the modern, industrialized, and digitalized world, we have lost a sense of living spirituality. Maybe we had it as children when a blade of grass or a butterfly could captivate us and move us into a state of awe, but as adults the spiritual is largely lacking, even from our religious institutions. We have separated off the "spiritual" to an hour on Sunday morning if that.

I put "spiritual" in quotes because there is a lack of spirituality in many contemporary houses of worship. *A living spirituality*: hearing God's voice, talking with God, having spiritual dreams and visions, and spiritual initiations have all been placed in the past, inaccessible to us,

---

1 *House*, 199–200.

except vicariously through worshipping someone else who was privileged to have these spiritual experiences. Religion has become something like a spectator sport, we only get to watch our favorite team play and we never have a chance to get on the field ourselves. Without a living spirituality, religion becomes like a social club or a competitive identity like putting on your favorite team's jersey for the game and wanting the other team to get beaten to a pulp and defeated.

A living spirituality is different than the way the majority of religion is practiced today. One needs to develop a counter-curriculum to the way many religions teach as a way to get one's spiritual needs met in a vital spiritual way. I wrote, earlier, about how the Catholic Church lost credibility when they tried to teach me that animals do not have souls. This did not fit with my lived experience and that belief creates a separation between man and nature. D.T. Suzuki captured the essence of this duality in a comment he made at an Eranos conference in 1953, "Nature against Man, Man against Nature; God against Man, Man against God; God against Nature, Nature against God; very funny religion!"[2]

Initiation into a living spirituality comes through seeking, receiving, and then giving. It is a gift that one receives and then one becomes a gift to others. The essence of a living spirituality is moving from states of separation into greater and greater states of interconnection, until, finally, this interconnection is so complete that there is Oneness, non-duality. At this point, one does not need to be bullied or intimidated by religion to "be good" and to "do the right thing," because Unity is goodness which comes out of the awareness of our sameness with the land, with animals, with people, with life, and with *Wah-Mah-Chi*, with God.

A living spirituality is an internal and deeply personal process that one finds through initiation in which one develops a deeper and deeper connection with Heart. At first this is a connection with one's own personal heart, and then into the *guhā*, into the cave of the heart. There one finds the center of the medicine wheel, *the center of the center*, and one becomes One.

We are born into a living spirituality, this is what Matthew Fox calls *the original blessing*. However, we are separated from this and lose this often through the process of becoming an adult, with adult responsibilities in the ordinary world of material existence. Because we do not exist, we need to continue to be re-born into a living spirituality. Being re-born happens

2 Stephen and Robin Larsen, *A Fire in the Mind: The Life of Joseph Campbell*, 361.

through initiation—through separation, initiation, return; through seeking, finding, and giving.

My path has taken me through different fields of study, different fields of nature, and to different guides and teachers. Even looking back to when I turned to my path of knowledge, *jñana*, in learning to read Carl Jung, I see that my path was already marked out for me and yet it has still been many long years in walking. Jung's *Modern Man in Search of a Soul* ends with the following:

> The living spirit grows and even outgrows its earlier forms of expression; it freely chooses the men in whom it lives and who proclaim it. This living spirit is eternally renewed and pursues a goal in manifold and inconceivable ways throughout the history of mankind. Measured against it, the names and forms which men have given it mean little enough; they are only the changing leaves and blossoms on the stem of the eternal tree.[3]

SPIRITUAL ECOLOGY

The word ecology comes from the Greek word *oikos*, which means "household," thus ecology is the study of the "Earth Household." In other words, in turning to ecology, we are once again discussing our home, just as the spiritual body and the spiritual earth are also our homes. Capra and Luisi remind us that ecology is a holistic, rather than a reductionistic science. "The basic tension [in science] is between the parts and the whole. The emphasis on the parts has been called mechanistic, reductionist, or atomistic; the emphasis on the whole, holistic, organismic, or ecological." The kind of ecology that is holistic is called "deep ecology" and Capra and Luisi see that "deep ecological awareness is spiritual awareness."[4]

> Only if we perceive the world differently will be able to act differently. So we need a change of perception, a shift of paradigms in our thinking and in our values. We need a shift from fragmentation to wholeness, from a mechanistic view of the world to an ecological view, from domination to partnership, from quantity to quality, from expansion to conservation, from efficiency to sustainability.[5]

---

3 *MMSS*, 243.

4 Fritjof Capra and Pier Luigi Luisi, *The Systems View of Life*, 341, 4, 13.

5 Capra cited in Gail Bernice Holland's *A Call for Connection: Solutions for Creating a Whole New Culture.*, 114.

The idea of Spiritual Ecology asks us to shift our paradigm and move toward a sense of interconnectedness with all of our relations—plants, animals, fish, birds, people, stones, trees, and Mother Earth, herself.

Sufi teacher and scholar Llewellyn Vaughn-Lee has put together an edited volume called *Spiritual Ecology: The Cry of the Earth*. Vaughn-Lee offers us a possible definition of spiritual ecology, showing that caring for the world and caring for our soul is one and the same spiritual work. He echoes Pope Francis in saying,

> The world is not a problem to be solved; it is a living being to which we belong. The world is part of our own self and we are a part of its suffering wholeness. . . . Only from the place of sacred wholeness and reverence can we begin the work of healing, of bringing the world back into balance. . . . Each in our own way, we need to return to our ancient heritage as guardians of the Earth, so that we may once again be present here, holding the Earth with our hearts and souls as well as with our minds and hands.[6]

INTERSPIRITUALITY

Spirituality . . . is an essential resource in the transformation of consciousness on our planet, and it will be enormously beneficial in our attempts to build a new universal society. Spirituality, intermysticism, and interspirituality can clear a path for a return of the sacred in the wider culture. This return is necessary if we are to create an alternative to what now exists. I believe there is a real possibility for a genuine renaissance of the sacred, and with its dawning comes the hope of a universal civilization with a compassionate, loving heart. If that compassionate, loving heart is cultivated in a large number of people, then the universal age will be born. It all depends on . . . intermysticism that is open to all.[7]

WAYNE TEASDALE

This quote from Father Wayne Teasdale comes from a book that I found at Powell's Books in Portland, Oregon. That bookstore plays an important role in this story because it was at Powell's that I found Kurt Wilt's book on Joseph Rael, *The Visionary*, which led me to Joseph. I came across Wayne Teasdale's book *The Mystic Heart: Discovering a Universal Spirituality in*

6 Vaughn-Lee, *Spiritual Ecology.*, v-vii.

7 Teasdale, *The Mystic Heart*, 249.

the World's Religions. It was through this book that I realized that the 1993 Parliament of World Religions was happening three miles from where I was just starting my education in psychiatry. I had mused earlier that perhaps when I lost my soul it went over to study at the Parliament!

A common theme in my life since medical school is recovering soul, spirit, and humanity—*re-humanizing* medicine as well as ourselves when we lose our humanity. In our current book, Joseph and I are looking at *re-spiritualizing medicine* and to revitalize ourselves and society. This is the path of *becoming medicine* and the path of re-discovering our common unity, the unity within our hearts and souls as well as the unity within all of us as a common people who have a foundation in unity even though we have been walking the road of separation for so long.

Many people in the modern era do not have a single, "home" religion that they identify with. There is a growing movement of people who consider themselves "spiritual" but not religious, for many people have difficulty believing a single religion has the whole truth. Many people of today see each religion as having a slice of the truth. Like the parable of the blind men trying to describe an elephant, we each come to our limited version of *Wah-Mah-Chi*. By developing more complex identities and affiliations we become more and more interconnected. Since we are made of Breath-Matter-Movement, it is possible for us to allow a living spirituality to be born in us.

A risk of blending religions is a superficial collecting of trivia. However, many people pick and choose superficial aspects of "their" religion, resulting in being "religious but not spiritual." From a cultural perspective, religions grow from the visionary, mystical, and shamanic spiritual experiences of a founder or founders. The spiritual founder then seeks to share with others his or her spiritual experience and insight. The students become followers and gradually a religion is born. However, Buddha was not a "Buddhist" and Christ was not a "Christian." The religion that is built up around the founder often loses the living spiritual message that was the life of the founder. For instance, Jesus in the Bible appears to be a pacifist and socialist and yet the majority of Christian societies are by no means pacifistic or socialistic. In many ways, free market capitalism seems incompatible with a living Christianity. All religions pick and choose elements of the original teachings and add new teachings. This often leads to a rigid dogma and doctrine that seeks to persist—to perpetuate itself. This leads to separation from the living spirit, separation between "true believers" and "others" and even between members of the same religion resulting in schisms. The foundation of religious violence is a lack of living spirituality. There is no such thing as spiritual violence, only *religious* violence.

Indigenous cultures have spiritual practices that are connected to a specific people and land. Indigenous peoples, particularly who have experienced the ravages of colonialism, consider their religion and spiritual practices to belong only to them. With the renewed interest of Westerners in shamanism and Indigenous ways, indigenous people often feel that the dominant culture is appropriating its religious and cultural traditions. It is important to keep in mind what Fred Gustafson teaches about the archetype of the "Indigenous One" we each have within us—what Westerners can learn from Indigenous traditions is how to connect to our own *indigenousness* of being of the land. A living spirituality must honor that some peoples wish to keep their ways secret and for their own peoples. Other teachers coming out of the indigenous tradition, such as Joseph and Lewis Mehl-Madrona, tell us that there is wisdom that all people need and can use that comes out of indigenous ways of being. The place of living spirituality is always to be found within one's own heart, although we can find guides in the traditions of many different peoples who can all re-direct us to our own heart.

The history of World Religions is a history of interconnection and interaction. Jesus was a Jewish Rabbi who spoke Aramaic. The *Bible* was later translated into Greek, then Latin, and eventually into English and other languages. Mohammad was an Arabic speaker and Islam spread from the Middle East through Africa, Central Asia, and into the East. The land of India supports many living spiritualities. Waves of invasion and migration brought the Aryan Vedas and Islam to the land of India. Hinduism reaches back into the indigenous past and absorbed many different traditions. India is the birthplace of Hinduism, Jainism, Sikhism, and also Buddhism. Buddhism spread from India, northwards, to Tibet and China, blending with the shamanic Bon tradition of indigenous Tibet and with Taoism in China to form Zen Buddhism, which then spread to Korea and Japan and even now to North America (home to every major religion). Amongst the indigenous peoples of North America, the Ghost Dance religion from the visions of Wovoka, spread across many different tribes.

Religions seem to seek expansion. It is as if the divinely revealed principle ideas spread like wildfire through the consciousness of peoples across the globe. We can look at religious ideas as being freely adopted as people "convert" from one religion to another. We can also look at some religions as being imposed or forced upon others. This occurs when religion is bound up with colonialism the way it has been with Christianity across the globe. Sometimes there is a mixture over years of a religion forcefully entering a land and then being adopted through force, through cultural utility (opening up more cultural or economic opportunities), or through a sense of philosophical embrace of its principles.

For American Indians, Christianity was largely forced upon them and their old ways, language, and religion were suppressed and even outlawed. It is no wonder, then, that some American Indian peoples would feel very uneasy about the dominant European culture now adopting or "appropriating" their religious and spiritual practices, particularly when done in an insensitive and superficial way. Yet there is something the dominant culture of the United States needs to learn from American Indian cultures. What we can learn is to listen to the heartbeat of Mother Earth who teaches us living spirituality. As I realized when Joseph did the tree spirit ceremony, it is not that the trees sing like Native Americans, rather, Native Americans sing the way they do because they learned it from the Earth and from the trees. This is why Black Elk says that the birds' religion is the same as his peoples' religion. If the Earth taught Native Americans their religion, then Native Americans can teach us (if we are willing to truly listen) the religion of the Earth. If we practice Earth Religion, we will end up practicing similar religions because we are learning from the same source. Our religion will end up having similarities with Black Elk's religion and the religions of the birds and the trees.

Thomas Jefferson thought all Americans would become Unitarian Universalists in the new United States. It makes sense that in uniting a people, he would think that religions could also be united. In 1822, Jefferson wrote, "I trust that there is not a young man now living in the United States who will not die a Unitarian." Further, Jefferson once speculated on the kind of religion he would create if he were able to found a new religion. He wrote that he would call the followers of such a religion "Apriarians, and after the example of the bee, advise them to extract the honey of every sect." [8]

---

8 Jefferson, cited in Steven Waldman, *Founding Faith*. 185–86.

BELONGING TO GOD

William Keepin, in his book *Belonging to God*, gives a brief history of some of these terms we have been discussing. Keepin cites Brother Wayne Teasdale as coining the term, "interspirituality." Keepin speaks of "multiple religious belonging" as "bridging two or more religions."[9] One of the ways that we can become global citizens is through bringing into our own hearts the seeds of divinity from the spiritualities of all the peoples of the Earth. *Multiple religious belonging* is not putting on different costumes, but expanding the room in your heart for different understandings to take root. This is what happened to Henri Le Saux when he planted the seeds of Hinduism alongside the seeds of Christianity and he was transformed into Abhishiktananda. Belonging to world religion means allowing Jesus, Buddha, Mohammad, Raven, Coyote, Fox, Badger, Nuthatch, Ganesha, Śiva, Krishna, Moses, Rumi, Kabir, Eckhart, Mary, Mira Bai, Kali, Durga, Śakti, Black Elk, Wovoka, Saint Francis, Saint Clare, Hildegard of Bingen, and Theresa of Ávila to be born in your heart. If a particular holy person or deity speaks to you, enter into a living dialogue and allow yourself to be a hollow bone through which the various manifestations of *Wah-Mah-Chi*, Breath-Matter-Movement speaks.

All religions and all spiritual practices are paths to God. Keepin writes, "God includes and transcends all religions. Every major religion offers a unique pathway to the infinite and eternal Supreme Reality that dwells within and beyond all beings."[10] The idea of a universal, integrative religion is found in the words of many holy people. Black Elk said, "Birds make their nests in circles, for theirs is the same religion as ours."[11] In the introduction to his book *Belonging to God*, William Keepin quotes Gandhi and Rumi who seem to make contradictory universal statements: "I am a Muslim, a Hindu, a Christian, and a Jew—and so are all of you!" (Gandhi) and "I am neither Christian, nor Jew, nor Zoroastrian, no Muslim. . . . I know none other except God" (Rumi). Discussing these two seemingly opposing quotes by Gandhi and Rumi, Keepin writes the following:

> Gandhi belongs to every religion. Rumi belongs to no religion. So it is with all those who belong to God. . . . The spiritual path of divine

---

9 This calls to mind Michael H. Cohen's concept of medical pluralism, multiple religious belonging is like religious pluralism or religious democracy.

10 Keepin, xvii.

11 John Niehardt, *Black Elk Speaks*, 155.

> love is found in one form or another within all major religious and spiritual traditions, and exists beyond them as well. It is the hidden path to the heart to God, entered through an invisible doorway deep within the heart.
>
> Like Rumi and Gandhi, those who tread the path of divine love belong to all religions—and in a sense they belong to no religion, because they have given themselves utterly and exclusively to the Infinite Supreme Reality, which is often called "God." Hence, they *belong* to this Supreme Reality, aka God, and to nothing else. The path of divine love is thus a kind of universal religion that leads to a mystical mergence into the very essence of God (or Brahman, Allah, Yahweh, Nirvana, Tao; there are many names for the Supreme Reality).[12]

Both Rumi and Gandhi are correct, although they could seem to contradict each other. Rumi belongs to no single religion but God, because no single religion is capable of containing all of God. Gandhi belongs to all religions to get closer to the God behind religion. Religions, as practiced, often separate and divide, but the living spirituality behind religions unites. Religions are tools to approach the divine that human beings have codified into rules and regulations. Sometimes religion is like putting a tool upon a shelf and worshipping it. A living spirituality views tools as a supports to use to pursue the secret journey of seeking. Belonging to God means that we can use any of the tools at our disposal in order to become hollow bones for a living spirituality.

When we enter into a living spirituality, we no longer belong to ourselves, we belong to *Wah-Mah-Chi*, Breath-Matter-Movement. The more we make ourselves *capable of God*, the more we identify with the unity within the religions and spiritual practices. When we embark on the spiritual path of divine love, we enter the invisible doorway deep within the heart (the cave of the heart) and we find that the doorway within our heart is the path that leads to the heart of God. When we attain mystical realization, we understand that there is only one heart in all of creation and that the heart of God is the same heart that beats in our chest and that we are all together in the heartbeat of creation.

---

12 Keepin, *Belonging to God*, xiii–xiv.

DEMOCRATIC SPIRITUALITY

Bringing together all spiritual and mystical traditions into the cave of the heart gives off a multi-colored light like a rainbow. We wrote, earlier, of *spiritual democracy*, here we look at the idea of a *democratic spirituality* that brings together the colors of the rainbow into a larger and more vibrantly beautiful whole. Wayne Teasdale calls for a universal order of *sannyasa*, "an interspiritual order of monastics and contemplatives open to all people . . . that welcomes as members individuals from all the world's religions and even from no tradition at all." He says that a *sannyasi* is a renunciate and that the term "refers to an extremely ancient state probably considerably older than Hinduism itself."

> Sannyasis transcend religion because they seek integration with the absolute, which is infinitely beyond our spiritual institutions and all our conceptual and theological formulations. Sannyasa is a call to the mystical life. What mysticism seeks cannot be encompassed by any religion, even though sannyasa remains part of Hinduism. . . .
>
> A universal or intermystical order of sannyasa, of contemplatives or mystics, would act as a meeting point for all traditions. It would also democratize the spiritual life as a state in which people could help one another, sharing their insights and spiritual resources. . . . It is these resources that we desperately need as we build the civilization with a heart, a universal society capable of embracing all that is, putting it to service in the transformation of the world.[13]

This idea of a democratic spirituality, open to all equally, pulls together many of the threads we have been exploring in spiritual democracy and spiritual ecology. While there are several organizations that have sought to bring religions together in an interreligious or interfaith dialogue, these organizations often have sought to maintain the boundaries of belief between religions. Rather than seeking to integrate spirituality, they have sought to create something akin to a United Nations of Religions. The analogy with the UN is that the boundaries or borders of different states remain firm, but a dialogue across boundaries is opened.

Many modern seekers, including myself, do not come solely from the framework of one religious tradition. The essence of mysticism is a dissolving of boundaries and a sense of interconnection and even a sense of mystical union. Teasdale thus speaks of *intermysticism*, a path of mysticism

13 Teasdale, 248–50.

that includes many different traditions in the search. In a rainbow, each color is unique and beautiful, but it is part of a larger whole, something that is beyond the imagination of a single color. Red is a beautiful color, but can the color red even imagine the color blue? Neither red nor blue are better than the other, both are beautiful, we have red sunsets and the blue sky of day under ordinary conditions. Rainbows appear under non-ordinary conditions; only from time to time are we reminded of the larger Unity within diversity. Just as the motto of the United States is *E plurbus unum*, "out of many, one," so too the rainbow reminds us of the diversity hidden in light. Peace comes when diversity and unity are in harmony. "May the mystics lead the way to this rebirth of the human community that will harmonize itself with the cosmos and finally make peace with all beings," Teasdale writes.[14]

BECOMING WORLD RELIGION

I have been thinking about what term to use to describe a religion of unity. One of the central themes of this book is mystical Unity, which itself, can be described with different terms such as Oneness, or non-dualism. One day I thought of the simple and obvious term "world religion" and maybe this can be useful for some time.[15] After all, we will not find one term to describe the indescribable or a word to capture the Unity of God. Joseph might say that we could capture it in a sound, but not in a linear concept. In Tiwa, God is *Wah-Mah-Chi*, breath, matter, movement. Hinduism might suggest a similar triad of words, *Sat-Cit-Ananda*, Being, Consciousness, Bliss. Hinduism also has the sound *om*, which is sometimes written *aum*. *Aum* is composed of three letters, three sounds, and then echoes off into silence. In speaking of the name, *Allah*, the sounds have meanings that add extra dimensions of meaning, similar to the way that for Joseph sounds are meaningful spiritually, above and beyond the intellectual meaning of letters and words.

> The name Allah is also a sound, and as a sound its real meaning is to directly evoke and point toward the unpronounceable essence behind all the Names. The sound that you make when you say Allah represents the greatest Name, or the 100th Name, which itself has no

14 Teasdale, 250.

15 Hank Wesselman speaks of a similar term, "New World Religion," "which is coming into being [and] will unify all faiths as humanity shifts away from wars between religions to create unity between them," (*The Bowl of Light*, 94).

> sound. . . . There are two syllables: "Al" + "lah." *Al* is affirmation. . . . *La* is negation. . . . The breathy sound of the final "h" of Allah is the beginning of the sacred syllable *hu. Hu* transcends both the positive and negative elements: the *al* and the *la*. . . . The opposites included in the Name Allah produce a certain effect on the mind, leading to the still point, which is the *hu. Hu* is called the secret of the secret . . . because it is included unpronounced in an abbreviated form within the name Allah. The letter 'h" is the first letter of the word *hu* and is called the secret of the secret of the secret.
>
> Sufis call this "H" sound the breath of infinite compassion, with which God created the universe. God's love is the secret of *hu*. A sacred tradition (*hadith qudsi*) of the Prophet Muhammed, one where he speaks in the voice of Allah, says, "I longed to be known myself so I created the heavens and earth with the breath of infinite compassion."[16]

I wonder if the secret of the secret of the secret of the secret might be, "u" the second part of *hu*. I like this idea because it means that this secret is hidden in *u* (*you*). *U* is also the sound of the center of the medicine wheel, according to Joseph, the hidden still point from which the wheel of creation emanates and to which it returns.

In the word *aum* we have three parts that make up a unity. The number 3 is of great significance in many religions. In Christianity there is the trinity. In Hinduism there is Brahma, Vishnu, and Shiva as well as *sat-cit-ananda*, which is being, consciousness, and bliss. In Tiwa, God is *Wah-Mah-Chi*. Manulani Aluli Meyer describes a number of spiritual triads from various world traditions in her paper "Holographic Epistemology: Native Common Sense."

> In ancient systems around the world there are inevitably three main ways in which to view and experience knowledge: (1) via the objective, physical, outside world, the world of science and measurement, density and force; (2) via the inside subjective world . . . ; and finally (3) via the quantum world . . . a spiritual dimension un-linked to religious dogma, described in ethereal, mystic, and yet experiential terms: ie: *All my relations;* or in Science: the *Implicate Order*. Simply put: *body, mind, spirit*; or in Maori: *tinana, hinengaro, wairua*. Hawaiians refer to this epistemologic trilogy as: *manaoio, manaolana*, and *aloha;* Fijians see it as *vuku, kilaka* and *yalomatua*.

16 Wali Ali Meyer, Bilal Hyde, Faisal Muqaddam, and Shabda Kahn. *Physicians of the Heart: A Sufi View of the Ninety-nine Names of Allah*, 2–3.

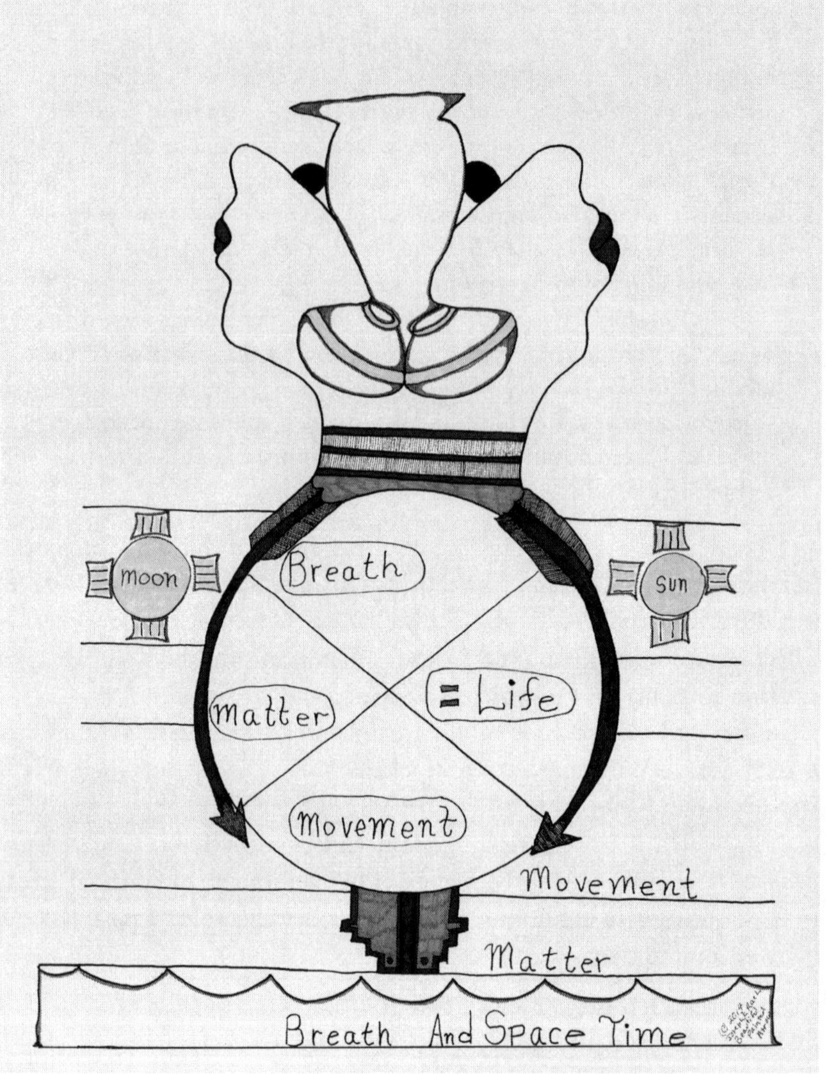

BREATH AND SPACE TIME

Meyer describes these three different dimensions as having a holographic relationship—happening simultaneously and holistically rather than linearly. She calls this a "triangulation of meaning" and also describes the importance of relationships as verbs, not nouns (similar to how Joseph Rael speaks of Tiwa as a verb language rather than the noun language of English). She concludes, "*Everything is alive and we are all relatives.*"[17]

17 Manulani Aluli Meyer, "Holographic Epistemology: Native Common Sense," 94, 100.

RELIGION: TO GO THROUGH AGAIN

> religion (n.)
> According to Cicero derived from *relegere* "go through again" (in reading or in thought), from *re-* "again" . . . + l*egere* "read." . . . However, popular etymology among the later ancients . . . and the interpretation of many modern writers connects it with *religare* "to bind fast" . . . via notion of "place an obligation on," or "bond between humans and gods."[18]

The etymology of the word religion shows several threads. The often cited *religare* "to bind fast," seems more like our distorted version of religion which binds us up and is a place of obligation, rather than of celebration. Cicero's etymology of "go through again" which links to "again" and to "read" is closer to Joseph's concept of the medicine wheel which we continue to cycle through again and again. While many fundamentalists like to teach that their religion is the "one true religion," the history of religion shows that our spiritual life as human beings is more like a series of interconnected circles overlapping with one another. Christianity borrowed holidays and symbols from earlier religions and often built churches over sites that were holy to the Celts and Europeans.[19] For the first few hundred years after the Buddha's death, no statues were made of him, perhaps it was contact with Christian statues in India that led to the adoption of what is now a universal Buddhist symbol. What would it be like if we saw religion not as competing ideologies but as a vast and complex tapestry in which we are all interwoven? Rather than bound in obligation and finality, we could see in each other and each religion *a going through again.*

We often think of history in terms of "clashes" between religions. However, Peter Frankopan in *The Silk Roads*, argues for the ways that religions borrowed and grew from contact with each other.

> It was not only goods that flowed along the arteries that linked the Pacific, Central Asia, India, the Persian Gulf and the Mediterranean in antiquity; so did ideas. And among the most powerful ideas were those that concerned the divine. . . . It made for a rich melting pot where ideas were borrowed, refined and repackaged.

---

18 "Religion," Online Etymology Dictionary

19 For example, I recently visited St. Non's Chapel near St. David's, Wales. The ruins of the original chapel are within an older circle of Celtic standing stones.

> As religions came into contact with each other, they inevitably borrowed from each other . . . the halo became a common visual symbol across Hindu, Buddhist, Zoroastrian and Christian art, as a link between the earthly and the divine . . . even poses—like the Buddhist vitarka mudra, formed from the right thumb and index finger of one hand touching, often with the other fingers outstretched—were adopted to illustrate connections with the divine, favoured particularly by Christian artists.[20]

Becoming World Religion would mean that we would go through again the circles of our spiritual growth and development. True World Religion would recognize, at an institutional level, what Joseph is always saying about individuals, "we don't exist!" The way World Religion could exist is by it not existing as a fixed, fundamentalist view imposed on others. The way World Religion could exist is if it recognized that it is always interconnected with all religions and spiritualities, that it is continually being re-created and re-read from *a living spirituality*.

A NONE'S JOURNEY

Corinna Nicolaou shares her journey of seeking in her book *A None's Journey: Searching for Meaning Inside Christianity, Judaism, Buddhism & Islam*. The word "none" is a play on words as it sounds like "nun," but it is a growing category of people without a religious affiliation. "Nones" she says, are the fastest growing self-reported religious affiliation. This is the group of people who do not identify with a particular religious affiliation. However, this does not mean that they are not spiritual or do not pray or even believe in God. She says that Nones are different than Atheists, by ticking the box of "none" for religious affiliation, they are more rejecting organized religion than spirituality or God. She cites research that 30% of people under the age 30 report no religious affiliation. She quotes Putnam and Campbell's book *American Grace: How Religion Divides and Unites Us*, that Nones distance themselves from religion because "they think of religious people as hypocritical, judgmental, or insincere."[21]

In *A None's Story*, Nicolaou writes that she started her quest through "a desperate search for the bits and pieces that might make my pot whole."

---

20 Frankopan, *The Silk Roads*, 28, 57.

21 Corinna Nicolaou, *A None's Story: Search for Meaning Inside Christianity, Judaism, Buddhism & Islam*, 030. I previously published a summary of Nicolaou's book on my blog *Being Fully Human*, "Search for Meaning Book Festival."

With a sense of humor and the spirit of a true seeker, she embarked on a four-year journey of church, temple, and mosque attendance, seeking to learn from the inside what each of these religions has to offer and to teach. She spent four years exploring Christianity, Judaism, Islam, and Buddhism. I saw her speak at Seattle University's annual Search for Meaning Book Festival in 2017, where she said that "Religions provide a space to ask the questions about living and dying." In her book she concludes:

> No matter what religious road I was on, it seemed to lead back to the idea that we come from, and eventually return to, a common source. We are parts of a whole. We can be different and still make up a healthy totality. I had long ago given up trying to make sense of how I might define 'God.' I figured God was too complex a concept and could be imagined a number of ways. I was driving in my car one afternoon not even thinking about any of this stuff when these words popped into my head: God is that which unites us all. . . . I suppose that's the best definition I'll ever have of God.[22]

A person in the audience at the talk asked her about the loneliness of not belonging to a particular religious community. Her response sparked a question of my own that I wrote in my notebook, "What to do when no one religion feels like home, but all do?" In her book she writes about this.

"To commit to none, but to call on all: what would that look like on day-to-day practical terms? With no official place of worship to call home, my spiritual practices will be mostly self-guided." She jokes about making the rounds of religious places of worship again, "A-to-Z," and that she could "draw the boundaries of my spiritual identity ever larger."[23]

I contacted Corinna Nicolaou and we had a chat on the phone about her work and experiences of going to different religious services. I asked her about how she describes religion sometimes being used as a way to separate and divide people.

> I think it's such human nature — how we're built. Religion is, to me, a tool to get us out of our natural instincts. Our natural instincts are to break off into groups and to define ourselves as opposed to the other. You know, if we have an "other," then we have a more definite boundary and it is easier to define ourselves. Religion is the encouragement to not think like that, which I think, we feel safer when we are thinking like that somehow. It's scary to let our boundaries and our definitions

22 Ibid., 005, 266.

23 Ibid., 283, 285.

> loosen and to be wider and more encompassing. That's scary, because then who are we? And then maybe we will disappear or I don't know, but that's the anxiety thing that will take over. Boundaries help us be less anxious or we think they are doing that for us when they really just get us stuck in that thinking instead of going beyond it; but it is scary to not have an us-versus-them, to move from that and so I get it that people will use anything to create those definitions between them and other people, even using religion for that purpose. And that is kind of the greatest irony, right? The cure is, I think, the teachings upon which religions were based and they are the opposite of our natural inclination.[24]

Nicolaou describes how we try to define ourselves through making people more "other," which lessens our own anxiety of the unknown. This kind of dehumanization, however, makes us all less human. Using religions to create boundaries to lessen our anxieties is reminiscent of what Joseph Rael speaks of when he says that "we do not exist" as separate, isolated individuals. Rather than trying to create static boundaries and *persist*, we should relax into the sense of interconnectedness that is our deeper truth. Rather than struggling to *exist* and define ourselves through boundaries, Joseph would encourage us to "disappear," and let go of our attempts at building boundaries. As all mystical traditions teach: we find who we are by going inward into our hearts and finding unity. The idea of "building walls" is not part of the language of any living spirituality.

CREATION SPIRITUALITY

Creation spirituality is *a living spirituality.* It views creation not as an ancient act of history, but as an ongoing revelation of God through our actions and by receiving epiphanies. This reconnects us with the ancient mysteries and truths of our indigenous roots in which everyone "expected the divine to burst out at any place at anytime." Creation spirituality views life and creation as an *original blessing* and brings together Eastern, Western, and indigenous traditions. This term was popularized by Matthew Fox, the Catholic priest excommunicated from the church by Cardinal Ratzinger (the future Pope Benedict). Fox traces elements of creation spirituality through all religions, but he has a particular focus on indigenous religions, whose origins pre-date other religions. "I see the recovery of the ancient

24 Transcript edited by Corinna Nicolaou from our phone conversation.

tradition of creation spirituality as a gift for our times," he writes.

Matthew Fox states that creation spirituality, "helps heal the division between history and mystery, prophecy and mysticism, social change and personal growth, humanity and creation." Thus the goal of creation spirituality is similar to the goal of this book, to heal the divisions and separations that exist within individuals, between individuals and others, and between humans and the earth. The benefits of journeying on this path and accepting the gifts of God are that, "this process of re-visioning equips us with powerful tools for understanding our journey today, for exciting the imagination, without which that journey cannot happen, and for replacing us in the joyful company of a veritable community of saints."[25]

What got Matthew Fox in trouble with the Catholic authorities was his inclusiveness, his bringing together of all religions as democratic equals, and his emphasis on divine blessing rather than original sin and punishment. "Creation, then, at its core, is about relation," Fox writes. He sees Creation Spirituality as an antidote to our materially "overdeveloped" and spiritually "underdeveloped" culture. Creation Spirituality "encourages a great mystical awakening in our time."[26] It brings us into relation, not only with each other, but with all of creation and the mystery of being. This initiation brings us into relationship with creation, which according to Joseph Campbell serves "to awaken in the individual a sense of awe, wonder, and participation in the inscrutable mystery of being."[27]

A LIVING SPIRITUALITY

Breath-Matter-Movement is a current of living spirituality that is flowing through all of creation, thus creation spirituality is consistent with Joseph's teaching. A living spirituality is an understanding that every moment is a new initiation, a new inspiration, and with each expiration there is the realization that we do not exist, and yet the world is being perpetually re-created with divine abundance.

In 2006, Joseph Rael had a vision of the Horn of Plenty. He was doing a dance in Australia and a giant Horn of Plenty appeared above the dance arbor. The abundance of the horn began to fall on the dance ground and the horn changed into the spiral pattern of the galaxy. He saw spirals of seeds spilling out, all different colors of seeds.

25 Fox, *Creation Spirituality*, 32, 33, 14.

26 Ibid., 30.

27 Joseph Campbell, cited in Fox, 30–31.

> The spiral is the energy or action of germination. We call this *huh-leh-neh. Huh* means seed that now is being spread all over. I saw the Horn of Plenty spilling seeds into *huh-leh,* which means they are going to germinate. They are going to germinate on Planet Earth as well as in this galaxy. . . .
>
> The Horn of Plenty to me is like a medicine bag. The medicine bag is where the medicine man puts all his powers. Now it is open and it is spilling out its fruits into the galaxy. . . .
>
> The Horn of Plenty is here now and it is here to stay. We can begin to recognize ourselves as the true peacemakers because we are alive and we are living in this time as the peoples of the global societies.[28]

For Joseph, the Horn of Plenty vision represented the goodness of the cosmos of creation coming to us and one of the most important gifts is the fruit of peace. It is the cosmic medicine bag that is spilling out its powers of goodness for all those who are working for peace. It is a tremendous source of support and nourishment and it is through opening to a living spirituality that we create the space for this divine abundance to flow through us.

28 *Sound*, 35–37.

CHAPTER 17

RETURNING TO THE GARDEN OF PARADISE

It is the Holy Spirit, the divine itself, that is accomplishing a process of healing in us. This is what Thomas Keating calls the Divine Therapy. *The human condition, as we have seen, is basically one of illness. We feel isolated or separated from God. The mystical life is a way in which God can gradually heal our illness by slowly restoring us to a unitive relationship with him. We are ill precisely because we mistakenly think we are separate from God. This Divine Therapy also includes our contribution of practicing the virtues, and communicating love, compassion, kindness, and mercy in all our relationships.*[1]

WAYNE TEASDALE

We are separated from the Garden by a paper thin space. It is a parallel reality. You are there without going there. We don't have to walk there or even have to travel there. You travel with thought, not with physical energy and it pulls you there rather than you having to put effort on your part to get there.

JOSEPH RAEL

After having developed the ability to consistently maintain paradisal consciousness, the hero returns to the mundane world with a healing balm. Having found Heaven, he must share it—which means sharing himself, his state of being. For the individual, the return is the culmination of the journey, but the quest is not complete until the world has been restored.[2]

RICHARD HEINBERG

1 Wayne Teasdale, *The Mystic Heart*, 134.

2 Heinberg, *Memories and Visions of Paradise*, 252.

SEEKING RENEWAL IN THE NEW WORLD

The impulse to seek renewal is an intrinsic aspect of being human. Seeking renewal is the hero's journey and the initiation of mystic, visionary, and shaman. Many indigenous tribes have stories about floods, destruction, and multiple worlds. The Hopi people in Southwestern United States believe that there are a series of worlds.[3] Joseph Rael also teaches that there have been four previous worlds and that we are entering a new world, the fifth world. In the Christian tradition there is the story of the deluge, the flood which destroyed all of the world except for the people and beings on Noah's ark. Noah sends out birds from the ark and eventually a dove returns holding an olive branch, which shows that there is a new world and once again there is land to live upon. Carl Jung believed that deep waters, such as the flood, represent the unconscious, "water is a favourite symbol for the unconscious."[4] Thus the flood would be the periodic flooding of the unconscious into conscious life.

Joseph told me that we should put something about Ponce de León and the Fountain of Youth in the book. He tells me, "*Things are not random, they don't happen for no reason, but are planned out. We live in cycles of time, 4 years, 100 years, 400 years, 500 years. We are living in the time frames that the Planet Earth is using to complete a circle.*" Ponce De León set off to La Florida in the year 1513. Five hundred some years later, Joseph Rael tells of his visionary journey to Florida to visit and assist his friend Kurt Wilt who was in a coma and was lost and wandering in non-ordinary reality.

"After the surgical operation and the removal of Kurt's brain tumor, which was as big as a golf ball, Kurt said that he was getting answers to all of the religious questions that he had pondered in his years of teaching at St. Leo's College. Ponce died of an arrow, and my name is Beautiful Painted Arrow, and I went to get him [Kurt] and put him back in his body.

"In this era here we are going to travel to the stars up there like Beautiful Painted Arrow travelled from the Four Corners, from the Ute Reservation. Kurt Wilt was lying in bed and he went to Florida in less than a second and went there and helped one of his friends when he was lying in his death bed and his soul was lost, and he found him before he crossed the river of forgetfulness and brought him back to his body so he could die a peaceful death. Beautiful Painted Arrow went to look for him and help put him back in his body and

---

3 See *The Book of the Hopi* by Frank Waters.

4 Jung, *The Archetypes of the Collective Unconscious, CW* 9, I, 322.

all that happened in less than a second. So we are going to be able to travel billions and billions of miles. Because above the house of Beautiful Painted Arrow's sound chamber there is a ship waiting, but we can't see it because it is invisible and Beautiful Painted Arrow told you that you could sleep in that bedroom which is where the ship is. When we as humanity can reach 95% of us understanding this, then the ship will become visible. Beautiful Painted Arrow is just a "hollow bone." I allow things to be done through me rather than doing things myself and I was able to help a professor at St. Leo's College. When the whole of planet earth gets to that 80% level of understanding, we will come to the Ute Reservation and get into this ship, this tube and travel and go to far distant universes. Beautiful Painted Arrow has shown this by being in two places at once and quantum physics shows this to be true.

"Is Beautiful Painted Arrow a miracle worker? No, he is just a regular guy who eats chile and beans and whose wife tells him to eat healthy. He can't even speak proper English, but he likes to talk—talk, talk, talk.

"Because he belongs to two tribes, Southern Ute, Ignacio, near Four Corners, and he also belongs to the Picuris in North Central New Mexico, every once in a while he gets confused of the being & vibration that are spoken between those two tribal languages—Ute-Aztecan language for the Ute and the Tiwa of the Picuris. The two languages tend to collide in his mind and he says one thing and it comes out more like a statement coming out of the philosophy of a very high sounding mystical language spoken in the ancient histories of the then worlds that were carrying the mystical teachings of the ancient ones of the old world, such as Africa, all those worlds, not necessarily just Europe but all the others. There is a program National Geographic is doing with DNA. This shows us through science that 'I am my brother's keeper.' I am a little bit Japanese and a little Chinese and then you can see the other vibrations that I am."

As I follow Joseph's visionary flight, I see connections, bridges forming between these seemingly unrelated paths. That is my job: seeking to find bridges and connections that translate his teachings of the web of interconnectedness into the English language. But as I started chasing around Joseph's suggestion that we look into Ponce de León and the fountain of youth, I did not know where to begin. I did what I usually do—look for books and do internet research. It turns out that scholars and historians think it is a myth that Ponce de León was actually looking for the fountain of youth. At first I was disappointed, but then tried to look at it as Joseph would. If pretty much everyone you ask (except apparently professional historians) "Why did Ponce de León go to Florida in 1513?"

they would say "because he was looking for the fountain of youth." *Florida* means "full of flowers" in Spanish, so we know that the Garden is relevant here. There is something that captures the imagination of this Spanish conquistador setting off into the swamps of Florida in search of a fabled fountain that keeps one forever young. There is a *need* for this myth in the human psyche, we could say. Joseph Campbell said, "Myths are clues to the spiritual potentialities of the human life."[5] I read about Ponce de León and learned he did die after being shot with an arrow, possibly a poisoned arrow. I went in circles for a while and the story did not seem to lead anywhere until as I read about the Spanish conquest of Florida, I remembered the story of Álvar Núñez Cabeza de Vaca whom Rebecca Solnit wrote about in her book *A Field Guide to Getting Lost*. Cabeza de Vaca was one of four survivors of the 1527 Narváez expedition of five ships to La Florida. He and the other survivors spent eight years living through hurricanes and encounters. They were greeted as visitors as well as enslaved by different tribes. They were captured and escaped. They were thought to be healers and gathered followers and devotees as they sailed, rowed, and walked starting from modern day Dominican Republic to Florida, across the southern states, and across modern day southern US and Mexico all the way to the Gulf of California and then south to Mexico City. At first Cabeza de Vaca rejected the role of healer that was projected upon him, but after some initial success, he embraced this role and lived as the indigenous people of the areas lived. Solnit quotes Cabeza de Vaca's statement "we became physicians, of whom I was the boldest and most venturous in trying to cure anything." After wandering for nine years Cabeza de Vaca and his group of indigenous wanderers came to a place called the Village of Hearts and learned of Spanish conquistadors in the region. They came upon the conquistadors who did not recognize Cabeza de Vaca as Spanish and they had to flee. The indigenous people accompanying him could not believe that he was of the same people "because we came from the sunrise; they from the sunset; we healed the sick, they killed the sound; we came naked and barefoot, they clothed, horsed, and lanced; we coveted nothing but gave whatever we were given, while they robbed whomever they found and bestowed nothing on anyone." Solnit says of Cabeza de Vaca:

> He was among the first, and the first to come back and tell the tale, of Europeans lost in the Americas, and like many of them he ceased

5 Campbell and Moyers, *The Power of Myth*, 5.

> to be lost by not returning but by turning into something else. . . . [T]hese strays and captives felt that they were far from home, distant from their desires, and then at some point, in a stunning reversal, they came to be at home and what they longed for became remote, alien, unwanted. . . . Somehow for these castaways the far became near and the near far. They did not reject the unfamiliar but embraced it, in the course of which it became familiar. By the end of his decade of wandering, Cabeza de Vaca was no longer in harmony with his own culture, but he had kept it as a destination, a goal, that kept him purposeful and moving, even though arrival was another trauma.[6]

Cabeza de Vaca's travels followed the hero's journey with ups and downs, adapting to another world and culture and becoming part of that culture, and then returning to his own culture. His is a story of continual initiation. He was given a hero's welcome upon his return, but later was arrested for poor administration of Buenos Aires when he was in command of that Spanish outpost. He was said to have had an unusually sympathetic view of indigenous peoples that may have put him at odds with other Spanish colonials. He was arrested in Buenos Aires and deported back to Spain, however he was not tried and eventually died in Seville.

In contrast to the majority of colonial narratives of conquering, plundering, and Christianizing the natives, Cabeza de Vaca's journey put him in the role of an anthropologist and a seeker of initiation as he adapted to and learned about various indigenous cultures. The Spanish title of his book about his experiences was *La relacion y comentarios del gouernador Alvar Nuñez Cabeza de Vaca*. The word *relacion* brings to mind the concept of relations and affiliations. Rather than colonial oppression and exploitation, he developed an attitude of *relacion* with the land and peoples of what came to be called North America.[7] Cabeza de Vaca found a place of renewal in the Land. He found a home in the Garden.

In all cultures there are times of refounding crises that bring about large cultural shifts in which people and society are in turmoil and chaos and a movement arises focused on spiritual, cultural and personal renewal. The Spanish invasion of the Americas brought about significant disruption in the Native American peoples they encountered. We have spoken about

---

6 Rebecca Solnit, *A Field Guide to Getting Lost*, 69, 70, 71–72.

7 Sources for the life story of Cabeza de Vaca are found in Rebecca Solnit's *A Field Guide to Getting Lost*, 65–72; Andrés Resénez's *A Land So Strange: The Epic Journey of Cabeza de Vaca*; and *Cabeza de Vaca's Adventures in the Unknown Interior of America*, transl. and ed. by Cyclone Covey.

Wovoka's visions that led to the creation of the Ghost Dance, a millenarian movement of revitalization and renewal.

THE FIRST AMERICAN REVOLUTION

Another renewal movement that occurred amongst the Native American peoples was the Pueblo Revolt of 1680, in which the Pueblo tribes banded together and pushed out the Spaniards from modern-day New Mexico for 12 years. It has also been called "The First American Revolution," taking place almost 100 years before the American Revolution further east.[8]

Joseph often tells me stories about the 1680 revolt and how he was involved in the ceremonial races that commemorated the 300 year anniversary of the revolt in 1980. Joseph says that the success of the revolt and the temporary expulsion of the Spanish from the Pueblo region is part of how the Pueblo peoples were able to keep as much of their culture as they did. Alfonso Ortiz, from San Juan Pueblo, writes that the "Pueblo Revolt of 1680 . . . represents the story of the Pueblo peoples' restoration of their commitment to their beginnings. It is, therefore, to be understood first and foremost as a religious restoration."

> They knew that they must restore fully to life the vision expressed in the ancient prayers: "As it has been left among us from the time of the earth's dawn, when all was young and green." This vision of the beginning, a fresh, ever-renewable and vigorous beginning, had fully to be restored and reaffirmed or the vitality that it had always given them as free peoples would eventually be sapped by the Spaniards.[9]

The 1680 revolt was thus a *refounding* movement for the Pueblo peoples and it restored the vibrancy of living spirituality of the Garden in

---

8 Joe S. Sando, "The Pueblo Revolt," in *Po'Pay: Leader of the First American Revolution,* 50. The European colonizers often viewed Native Americans as less than human, there was a major debate in Europe and the Americas whether or not Native Americans had souls. Once it was decided that they did, there then began a "crusade" to bring about conversions, often forced through the destruction of the native religion, (See Sando, 9-21). Even in Joseph's time, he grew up with the name Earl until age 12 when he was renamed by the priests as Joseph. The Pueblo peoples suffered greatly under the Spanish, with forced conversions to Christianity, the destruction of their sacred objects used in their religion, and the suppression of their religion—still they were granted citizenship in 1820, and then lost citizenship in 1855 under United States rule after the Spanish territory became part of the United States. The right to vote was not re-established for Pueblo peoples until 1948.

9 Alfonso Ortiz, "The Pueblo Restoration of 1680," in *Po'Pay: Leader of the First American Revolution,* 4.

the desert. The symbolism of the Garden of Paradise is a place of continual renewal and refounding.

RETURNING TO GARDEN OF PARADISE

Joseph Rael says, *"If you pray long enough, sooner or later you are going to meet God."* One day, Joseph called me to discuss a small group of tribal people connected to the land.

"This connection is such that the people are the land. These people through their connection went back and forth between the ordinary and the non-ordinary realms, they didn't know that they were doing so, but they did know, too. They became the land itself and this land is not just dead matter, but is alive and buzzing with spirit infused and inspired into it. On the land grows grass, when you touch grass it makes the sound, tschlay, *which means 'the ancients.' Thus when we walk on the grass, we are connecting to the ancients and this occurs through the land at the boundary between the land and the sky. People think they want green lawns, but what they are really striving for is connection to the ancients.*

"When the Spanish came, looking for gold, the people left. They shifted over dimensional vibrations. In some ways the ancients are still here, living in another dimension which is also this dimension. Another way of saying this is that the ancients left with the ETs (the kachinas in their spaceships). Some stayed, sure and became the Pueblo peoples, but many left. These people, through their deep connection to the Earth connected to something beyond the Earth (as the seeds of what became the Earth are actually from a place beyond, above the Earth).

"Our job in this book is to help people develop the ability to cross-over before we die—to shift dimensions with our awareness."

Joseph is saying through oneness with the Earth we will open a portal to what lies beyond, to that place where the Earth came from, a doorway into the Garden. When we connect to the Earth in this way, we are in the Garden of Paradise. This is what Joseph Campbell has said, that we are already in the Garden of Eden.

> "The kingdom of the Father is spread upon the earth, and men do not see it" . . . this is Eden. When you see the kingdom spread upon the earth, the old way of living in the world is annihilated. That is the end of the world. The end of the world is not an event to come, it is an event of psychological transformation, of visionary

RAINBOW BIRD AND BLUE STAR WOMAN

> transformation. You see not the world of solid things but a world of radiance.[10]

In one sense we are always separating from the previous moment and being born again in a new moment. This is what Joseph Rael points to when he says "we do not exist." *Na-yo ti-ay we-ah*, "I don't exist." The corollary of not existing is that we are continually being reborn in a new moment. In one sense we feel we have separated from something and we are seeking to return to it. It is true, we have separated from ourselves and from the previous moment, but we have also returned into a new moment in every instance. In this sense, when we allow ourselves to continually die we are continually being reborn. If we can be in that state of being, we are already in the Fountain of Youth of continual renewal and we are already in the Garden of Paradise and Peace. We are in this place when we are living in the center of the medicine wheel.

> He who bathes in that spring will be preserved forever of all taint. If someone discovered the meaning of the mystic Truth, it means he has attained to the spring. When he emerges, he has gained the aptitude that makes him resemble that balm, a drop of which distilled in the palm of the hand, if you hold it up to the sun, passes through the back of the hand.[11]

Joseph tells me that we are barely separated from the Garden and that we can learn to return there.

"We are separated from the Garden by a paper-thin space. It is a parallel reality. You are there without going there. We don't have to walk there or even have to travel there. You travel with thought, not with physical energy and it pulls you there rather than you having to put effort on your part to get there.

---

10 Campbell and Moyers, 285.

11 Corbin, from Suhrawardī's spiritual autobiography, in *Alone with the Alone,* 59-60. Corbin describes Suhrawardī's initiation with the Purple Archangel, "the mystic is initiated into the secret which enables him to ascend Mount Qāf, that is, the cosmic mountain, and to attain the Spring of Life." The Purple Archangel consoles Suhrawardī, who is frightened by the enormity of the task before him, by saying "Put on the sandals of *Khiḍir.*" Corbin describes this as coming into a relationship and assimilation of this saintly hero, Khiḍir. Corbin continues, "This suggests what it means to be a disciple of Khiḍir. . . . Khiḍir is the master of all those who are masterless, because he shows all those whose master he is how to be what he himself is: he who has attained the Spring of Life, the Eternal Youth . . . he who has attained the . . . mystic, esoteric truth . . . which frees us from the literal religion." Picking up this spiritual autobiography of the 12th Century Persian mystic, Suhrawardī, brings us back into secret journey of seeking the fountain of youth, however what is attained is not so much the fountain as an identification with divinity.

"When I was helping people in the hospital, I would light a match, between the time that the match lit to when it went out they could use that light as a channel to move to the other side. From the time you light the match to the time that the flame comes up. The word for light is fii-aah. *That is what the light says when you light it.*

"Fii – *means root, where is our root, garden of paradise and we are returning, right? So when you light a match or a candle at church you articulate rootness. At the bottom of the flame is the root and the light is what takes you to where you are going. So how can you go anywhere if you are already there? When you light the match the root of the flame takes you into the garden of paradise. So you are already rooted in it when you are here, but you believe you are separated from eternity, but you are not. Consequently we are always home even when we are trying to get there.*

"Aah – *means to wash. The root of our cleansing is the love of God or the love of Divine Presence."*

In the Christian tradition the story of the Garden of Eden is about loss and sinfulness and the "fall." Matthew Fox argues that this is a human distortion and that creation is a gift, not punishment and loss. This is what Fox's concept of Creation Spirituality is all about—creation is a gift.

Another way of reading this story is as a story of initiation. We find ourselves distant from the Divine (*separation*) and we go into a place of challenge and suffering (*initiation*) and then we seek to *return* back again to the Garden. Separation from the Divine occurs in the very act of creation, which is a gift of life, but also sets up Longing for the Divine, and can lead to a quest for Divine Union.

For Joseph Rael, creation starts with one, *weh-mu*, and continues up to ten, *tehn-ku-teh*. Creation is not something that is finished, it requires work, growth, and transformation. The *fall* is built into creation as a step along the journey. At the number one, "*Weh-mu* is to slip and see." This first slip is where we have "slipped into perception." There is another fall built into creation at the number eight, *wheh-leh*, "we have to fall. . . . We were taught not to fall, to avoid falling. Now, at the point of *wheh-leh*, we must embrace the fall."[12]

Creation is a force that arises within the seed of the Unity of *weh-mu*, which increases complexity by separating out from the Unity. We can say that there is this inherent force within Unity, creation through separation and proliferation—a centrifugal force outwards. And yet there is also a

12 *Inspiration*, 50, 96–97.

counter-balancing force, a return force or counter-force, back from the separation of complexity and dualities to seek the original Unity. The return force is the divine longing for re-union, crying for a vision, for an end to separation.

Henry Corbin, writes frequently of the *'alam al-mithal*, in esoteric Islam. This is a third realm, not matter, not spirit, but where *matter is spiritualized and spirit is materialized*. It is a place where we are connected with what Joseph would say is *Wah-Mah-Chi*, God. Corbin sees the philosophical and spiritual catastrophe of the modern age as the loss of the angelic realm of the *'alam al-mithal*, which is the intermediary realm between God and humans. We can look at the Garden in this same way, not a physical place, but a place of the intermingling of spirit and matter, of God and human. In this perspective, the Garden of Paradise is able to be realized or "entered" by the human being who has made one's self *capable of God* (as Corbin describes it). To be *capable of God* is to have opened up one's heart and recognized that one is not simply a material thing, but also a spiritual being. In recognizing this hybrid nature of spirit and matter, not one, not the other, but both in relation, the Garden of Paradise is entered. Under proper circumstances and with proper preparation—or sometimes by accident, trauma, or divine grace—we can re-enter this Garden, which if it is a place at all, is located within the center of our hearts. Through meditation, prayer, and ceremony, we can re-enter the Garden and we can once again be in relationship with *Wah-Mah-Chi*.

The Garden is the place of visionary experience. In ordinary reality, Ponce de León's search for the Fountain of Youth is a myth, an impossibility. However the Fountain of Youth and the Garden exist in non-ordinary reality. What is accomplished through our re-entry, our re-discovery of the Garden is a state of bliss—what the Hindus call *ananda*—a persistent state of bliss and joy regardless of the accidents of the Roman world of matter. This intermediate, angelic realm supplies us with ever-lasting and unrelenting spiritual resources and rejuvenates matter. We give birth to the Garden within our hearts and the Garden gives birth to us continuously. Henry Corbin cites, "The paradise of the faithful believer is his own body." Thus, the heaven that we are looking for is actually *us*—our very selves. "That is why the Paradise of each of us is in the Heaven of his being. . . . There is a degree of Paradise that corresponds to the respective capacity and conduct of each" person.[13] This is why Joseph Campbell says "follow

13 Corbin, *Spiritual Body, Celestial Earth*, 224, 233. See also *Alone with the Alone*, 132–33.

your bliss." "If you follow your bliss, you put yourself on a kind of track that has been there all the while, waiting for you, and the life that you ought to be living is the one you are living."[14] Your bliss leads you into the Inner Garden.

The return to the Garden is an inner journey. The inner Self that must be aligned in order to re-enter the Garden, in this sense it is a state of the mind and imagination—not imagination as in fantasy, but imagination as in allowing the creative powers of *Wah-Mah-Chi* to flow through one's self in order to re-open the gate to the Garden, which has been here all along. As Joseph Rael says, *we travel to the Garden in thought*. Joseph Campbell writes of how our thoughts and emotions can also keep us out of the Garden.

> We're kept out of the Garden by our own fear and desire in relation to what we think to be the goods of our life . . . but then you also have moments of ecstasy. The difference between everyday living and living in those moments of ecstasy is the difference between being outside and inside the Garden. You go past fear and desire, past the pair of opposites.[15]

In discussing this passage from Joseph Campbell, Richard Heinberg writes that, "Paradise—the immaculate conception of mind and emotion that is the objective of every spiritual technique—is immediately available to every human being."[16] This is what we are saying in this book, that the Garden of Paradise is attainable at any moment when we let go of our egos, let go of our attempts at persistence and allow ourselves to exist as pulsations of the *spanda*, divine creative pulsation, in other words, as manifestations of Vast Self. In Vast Self, there is no separation, there is non-difference, non-duality.

---

14 "Now, I came to this idea of bliss because in Sanskrit, which is the great spiritual language of the world, there are three terms that represent the brink, the jumping-off place to the ocean of transcendence: *Sat-Chit-Ananda*. The word '*Sat*' means being. '*Chit*' means consciousness. '*Ananda*' means bliss or rapture. I thought, 'I don't know whether my consciousness is proper consciousness or not; I don't know whether what I know of my being is my proper being or not; but I do know where my rapture is. So let me hang on to rapture, and that will bring me both my consciousness and my being.' I think it worked. . . . If you follow your bliss, you put yourself on a kind of track that has been there all the while, waiting for you, and the life that you ought to be living is the one you are living. Wherever you are—if you are following your bliss, you are enjoying that refreshment, that life within you, all the time," (Campbell and Moyers, *The Power of Myth*, 149–50).

15 Joseph Campbell & Bill Moyers, 134.

16 Heinberg, *Memories and Visions of Paradise*, 200.

NON-DUALITY

The concept of non-duality brings together diversity into unity. From a non-dual perspective we are the thing that we are seeking. In seeking to return to the garden of paradise, we are seeking to return to our Self. The trident of Śiva "symbolizes humankind as the divinity, the temple, and the worshipper—all united in the main branch of the trident." This is the three-in-the-one, the place where the knower, the known, and knowledge are all experienced as One. The place of non-duality is the heart, it is the place where inner and outer merge. As Daniel Odier writes, the "heart realizes that there is no distance between the divine and the profane. Divine is he who perceives the world, for he perceives only the reflection of the divine within him. The tantrika is Shiva/Shakti. No duality. No separation. . . . We are simultaneously the divine, the temple, and the worshipper."[17] The secret journey is a return to a place that we have never left. Not only have we never left the garden of paradise, it is our very nature, we are the Garden. We end the journey where we began.

> This verse describes the end of the journey. A spark of the Divine flame descends into matter and forgets its divine origin. Like an exile it wanders into distant lands and in different forms. . . . A time comes when he is filled with nostalgia, and now begins his journey homeward. He has not far to go. He has only to throw off the mask of the pseudo-I and enter his essential, real I, which is the *Spanda*, the heart-beat of Śiva. He now becomes what he always was. The universe is no longer a foreign land. The I and the This, the Subject and the object become one. That is an experience for which there is no word in the human language.[18]

The realization of non-duality brings the seeker together with what is sought—there is no separation. We are already in the Garden of Paradise. The *universe is no longer a foreign land.* Instead we realize at every moment we are home and our original home is the Garden. In the darkness of the cave of the heart is the Garden of Eternal De-Light.

---

17 Daniel Odier, *Yoga Spandakarika*, ix, 42.

18 Jaideva Singh, *Spanda-Kārikās*, 171.

VISION OF THE NEW WORLD

Joseph describes a 2014 vision of the new world which brings us into the oneness of Vast Self. The New World is the Fifth World. In Tiwa "five" is *pah-nu.*

> *Pah-Nu* cannot happen before you sing at the door. When you sing *Pah-Nu* at the entrance you bring the future and the past into the eternal now. The doorway opens when you sing to it from that being in vibration. You can now step over and cross into the new world. . . .
>
> As soon as you sing to non-ordinary reality you have already entered into it. It moves beyond you and into a new circle of light.
>
> The shamans say, "Where are we now?" and they'll just smile because they know already that the new world is us even though in the ordinary reality we look the same. But we are not the same. We're in new bodies and have new spirits. . . . It is the dialogue between ordinary time and non-ordinary time.
>
> What is time? Time is the seed. They call it *Da-neh* (seed). We're constantly the seed of a plant that is planted in this circle of light that is called the medicine wheel. . . . This reseeding is happening continually so that we are in constant states of renewal.
>
> . . . The one thing that I know for sure is that we are eternal beings. We're not going anywhere and yet we've been somewhere and everywhere.
>
> . . . In the fifth world, the New World, we have *Pah-Nu. Pah-Nu* means the infinite self and the vast self. It is time to awaken into the light that fuses our personal self into the vast self.[19]

Joseph is speaking pure initiation. Singing *Pah-Nu* opens the door and we step over the threshold, but the shamans only smile because they realize that we were already on the other side of the door. We are continually the planter of the seed and the seed that is being planted at the heart center of the medicine wheel in the *nah-meh-neh* (the soil) and into the *nah* (the self). In the heart we are seeking to fuse the "personal self into the vast self," connecting the microcosm and the macrocosm. Joseph says that we must enter into ceremony with more than our minds, but with our bodies and our voices, with our full being & vibration. Once, Joseph invoked the five vibrations, the five fingers of the Hand of God which appeared as five mystics who gave him a mission to capture the War Gods and transform them into Peace Gods.

---

19 *B&V:NW,* 117–20.

> *Teh-ney-ho-tah-ahh* are the five vibrations. When you say these words wait a moment to enter deep silence and open to the Vast Self. *Teh-ney-ho-tah-ahh.* When I sing this the five mystics appear. They are cloaked in black light, and form a hand—the hand of God.

In his vision, after invoking the five mystics who are the Hand of God, Joseph tells us that he went into a visionary state and helped the War Gods get back home, "I thanked them for their service to humankind and showed them the way home as I was asked to do." Now, the War Gods have returned to the New World, but they have come full circle and now they are no longer gods of war, but Peace Gods. The same is true of us, for we "live in a state of transformation. We are constantly transforming." Because we don't exist, we are continually appearing and disappearing. "As soon as we disappear it's like we fall down into another vastness, and that vastness is a place like from where we came the first time—the garden of paradise."[20]

Here Joseph is telling us that the return into vastness, our disappearing, is actually a returning to our Source, to the garden of paradise. To live in the New World is to be continually in ceremony. That does not mean that we have to be always doing something extraordinary, it just means that we have to bring non-ordinary consciousness to ordinary activities. Even drinking a glass of water can be a ceremony. Ordinary water in an ordinary glass can become the fountain of youth.

> The sound of the water as you swallow is "*soul.*" You can hear it as "*Sol*"—a name for the sun. It is also "sole" meaning "placement," with your feet on the ground, and at the same time "sole" means oneness, that you are the One—the Vast Self.

Drinking an ordinary glass of water from a place of the non-ordinary takes us from the separation from God, the journey of the soul from the Sun, down to the feet and the ground, where we undergo initiation and realize that we have already returned to Oneness, that we "are the One—the Vast Self."

> Now we find ourselves here in this new world. We are always, and we will always be beginning new journeys. We will always be there for the ending of journeys. Then we will start all over again because we are forever beings of eternity. We came out of eternity into the sunlight, and into the light beings of the vibration of divineness.[21]

20 Ibid., 121, 128.

21 Ibid., 130, 141.

CHAPTER 18

SECRET JOURNEY TO THE SECRET GARDEN

The word paradise itself comes from the Avestan (Old Iranian) word Pairi-daeza, *meaning a walled or enclosed garden.*[1]

RICHARD HEINBERG

Tibetans and Navajos know the mandala journey to be one and the same with their own paths through life. For them, there is no separation of self and cosmos; we are all divine, only we have not yet fully realized our innate divinity. It is through their respective spiritual scientific processes, in which the sand mandala is the altar, that Navajos and Tibetans are able to realize their seamless unity with the state of Beauty and the Void. Through such rites of transformation, one is reborn/restored/transformed into one's own ideal state, the best version of oneself. These form the focus of the fourth principle of the circle of the spirit: becoming.[2]

PETER GOLD

One night I wake up and cannot sleep. I feel like God is squeezing the juice out of me. I get the image of a string of organic matter and God is scraping and squeezing me—what is *Wah-Mah-Chi* making of me? It looks like a bowstring. If I am becoming a bowstring, then I know that Joseph is the arrow—a Beautiful Painted Arrow. But it would make more sense that he is launching me into non-ordinary reality, maybe I am becoming an arrow like him. Joseph said that in Tiwa my name would mean He Who is Beautiful Who Exists. But then he tells me "we do not exist." How can I exist and not exist? I guess it is a secret, a hidden treasure. The arrow exists to be shot somewhere, into the future or into the past. The existence of the arrow is not important, it is more what you do with it, where you shoot it. In noun language we would look at the object, the thing, at the arrow. In non-ordinary reality we would look at the trajectory of the arrow. In ordinary reality Ponce de León did not find the Fountain

1 Heinberg, 43.

2 Peter Gold, *Navajo & Tibetan Sacred Wisdom: The Circle of the Spirit*, 180.

of Youth. In non-ordinary reality we have a chance to follow the flight of the arrow from ordinary reality into the secret garden of non-ordinary reality where we can find the hidden treasure of *Wah-Mah-Chi* which is longing to be known since splitting off from one (*weh-mu*) to two (*weh-seh*, longing and crying for a vision of unity).

In the foreword of *Being & Vibration: Entering the Fifth World*, Francis Rico recounts a story that Joseph had told him about hunters who carried a special arrow in their quivers that they would only use in dire situations if they had lost their way. This arrow, when shot, would find the home village and create a beautiful rainbow path/bridge that could lead the hunter home.

Are we all ready to go home now? Really *Home*? If I am the bowstring and Joseph is the arrow, then the curve of the Earth must be the bow. We are here. We are lost—we are lost because we think that we exist here but do not. We think that we are separate, isolated beings, but we are not—we are Divine Unity.

I get up to meditate. I place myself in the medicine wheel. It extends north 200 miles, up into Canada. It extends south 200 miles, down past Portland, Oregon. It extends 200 miles east, across the Cascade range and out toward Spokane, Washington. It extends west 200 miles, across the Olympic peninsula and out into the Ocean of Peace—the Pacific Ocean. I see the bowstring planted in the ground like a tree and extending upward to the Sky of Heavens and downward into the Earth—one end anchored in Father Sky and the other anchored in Mother Earth. The wooden bow is thus the World Tree, the Cosmic Tree, roots in Mother Earth and branches in Father Sky.[3] Joseph tells us that "tree" in Tiwa "*tslah-ah-nay*, which means greatness."[4] I am the bowstring connecting the mother and the father, or maybe I am the tree. I submit to God saying, "Help me *Wah-Mah-Chi*, I am so lost." And Breath-Matter-Movement draws back the bow, creating even more tension within me as I stretch and feel like I will hit the breaking point. God releases the tension building in me—the arrow, the Beautiful Painted Arrow, releases and shoots forth,

3 "If you were to draw a tree and draw where the tree roots go into the ground, the part of the tree above ground would be the area of audible sounds and the root of the tree would be the area of the silent vibrations. In order to manifest itself, the silent vibration needs to come above the ground, and then it becomes audible sound. This tree is the cosmic brain. The ground, or the surface of the earth, is where we enter into the inner cosmic self." *B&V*, 59–60.

4 *Sound*, 88.

trailing a rainbow, a double rainbow (because that is another meaning of Beautiful Painted Arrow—a double rainbow). Double means it leads us away. Double means it leads us back Home. The rainbow strikes its mark as it circles back and dives deep into my heart. Our hearts are the home of God that we are seeking and this heart connects us to all creation through the Heart of God.

In ordinary reality, we see the rainbow. The rainbow in non-ordinary reality is an eye, but Beautiful Painted Arrow means "double rainbow," so in non-ordinary reality we have two eyes. There is our eye looking out and God's eye looking inward. We can use our eye to look in either direction, outward into the beauty of creation or inward into the inner darkness that leads to the inner light of God's eye beholding all in unity. The double rainbow reminds us that we are not one eye looking outward, but we are One with God who is looking inwards. The eye works by having a beautiful colored iris—like a flower Garden blooming with the colors of *Wah-Mah-Chi*. The eye works by having a dark center—the pupil. If God is the Teacher, who is the pupil? We, of course, are the pupil—we are the darkness, the black hole, that makes it possible to see the colored rays of light of the rainbow of *Wah-Mah-Chi*. When we look outward we see ordinary reality, when we look inward we see non-ordinary reality—when we combine inner and outer vision, we become a double eye, one eye is us, seeking God, the other eye is God seeking us.

There is a hadith qudsi[5] in Islamic tradition that tells of the Prophet

---

5 I asked my friend and colleague Aysha about where to find the original source quote of the hidden treasure saying. I asked her this because she seemed like a person who might know this. Instead she gave me book references I had to look up. I read the books, thinking they would have the answer, but the quote was not in the books. She told me that the saying is a *hadith qudsi*. Then I went round and round and got lost in trying to figure out what a *hadith qudsi* is. I forgot the original question about the hidden treasure. I still am not exactly sure what a *hadith qudsi* is, but I decided to go back to the original question of the hidden treasure saying (which is a *hadith qudsi)*. In my reading, I have come across multiple variations of the "hidden treasure" *hadith*. I have decided to quote several sources throughout the book.

> I was a hidden treasure and I longed to be known,
> so I created both worlds, the visible and the invisible,
> in order that My hidden treasure
> of generosity and lovingkindness would be known.
>
> — *Hadīth Qudsī*

(Kabir Helminski, *The Knowing Heart: A Sufi Path of Transformation,* 41).

At first I was getting frustrated and focused on trying to find the original quote, but now I like the idea that the origins of the quote are hidden in the veil of creation and that the seeking is more important than the finding. Maybe the reason I cannot find the

David's question to God about the purpose of creation. William Chittick quotes the passage at length.

> David the prophet said in his whispered prayer, "O God, O endless Majesty described by the attribute of perfection and qualified by the description of unneediness! You have no need for anything and You subsist in Your own description. You require nobody and You take help and aid from no one. Why did you create these creatures? What wisdom is there in existence?"
>
> The answer came, "I was a hidden treasure, and I loved to be recognized": I was a concealed treasure and no one knew or recognized Me. I wanted to be known and recognized.
>
> "I love to be recognized" is an allusion to the fact that recognition is built on love. Wherever there is lover, there is recognition, and wherever there is no love, there is no recognition. The great ones of the religion and the Tariqah have said, "No one recognizes Him save those to whom He has made Himself recognized, no one voices His unity save those to whom He has shown His unity, and no one describes Him save those to whose secret cores He has disclosed Himself."[6]

Creation is created out of the desire for Unity to be known, to be recognized by the many. Creation is created out of a super-abundance of love and is an act of giving, such as comes at the end of an initiation process when the seeker is fulfilled and overflows, giving back what has been given. This hidden treasure is manifest in creation, but it is also a secret, hidden in the center of our own hearts, deep in the cave of our hearts. This is our secret journey, *secret* because we keep forgetting it, *secret* because that is what all the visionaries, mystics, and shamans say it is, *secret* because in reality it is not so much a journey from a place of lostness to a place of home as it is becoming capable of double vision—of seeing that we can never be lost because we are, as always, already *Home*. When we make this secret journey we are seeking to have unity shown to us, and in unity we are then becoming that which we are seeking, we are becoming holy beings. Out of our illness of separation, we are healed through *Becoming Medicine of Wah-Mah-Chi.*

---

original source quote is that "In the Sufi tradition these words are attributed to the Creator, the Source of our being." (Helminski, 41). Maybe I should be asking the Creator, rather than looking for the source of these words in the written books of human beings.

6 William Chittick, quoting Maybūdī's Kashf al-asrār, in *Divine Love: Islamic Literature and the Path to God,* 18–19.

THE SECRET GARDEN

Joseph often returns to the Picuris Children's Stories that he heard as a boy and he looks there for secret wisdom, the sacred teachings that the elders gave to the children, woven into stories, and told during the long, dark months of winter. It seems fitting that we will end this secret journey of the visionary, the mystic, and the shaman with a children's story. We started with a *secret journey*, so we will end in a *secret garden*.

Frances Eliza Hodgson Burnett wrote *The Secret Garden* in 1911. It was inspired by her own experience of following a robin to a doorway leading to a secret garden.[7] The book begins with ten year old Mary Lennox's family dying of a cholera outbreak in India. Mary was sent to England to live with her strange, reclusive uncle, who had no wish to see her, and lives in an old house with many rooms that were off limits to her.

Mary is befriended by a kindly servant, Martha, who brings her breakfast. Martha tells her of her own brother, Dickon, who roams the wild moors, befriending animals and living in harmony with nature. Something stirs in Mary's imagination and she begins to imagine that she might like to meet Dickon. She is also befriended by a grumpy old gardener, Ben Weatherstaff. She learns to listen and talk with a little robin in the gardens as she follows Ben the gardener around, pestering him with questions. Mary was quite sickly and yellow when she arrived and in her walks around the grounds she begins to get a little health and life back, because this is a story of the healing power of nature and the power of ceremony.

Mary kept hearing cries in the night and eventually when she went to investigate she found a strange, pitiful, and very spoiled and angry little creature—her cousin, Colin, also ten years old who was emotionally

7 Burnett was born in Cheetham, Manchester, England in 1849. Her father died when she was quite young and the family left England and moved near Knoxville, Tennessee. She began to earn extra money for the family publishing stories when she was about 19 years old. She married Swan Burnett, a physician, and they lived in Paris for two years, where her sons were born. She returned to England, making the trans-Atlantic sailing with her children. Her oldest son died in 1890 of tuberculosis. She lived at Great Maytham Hall in Kent from 1898 to 1907. There she found an old abandoned, walled garden. "Aided by a robin, Burnett discovered the door hidden amongst the ivy, and began the restoration of the garden, which she planted with hundreds of roses. She set up a table and chair in the gazebo, and dressed always in a white dress and large hat, she wrote a number of books in the peace and tranquillity of her scented secret garden." One of the books inspired by Great Maytham Hall garden was *The Secret Garden*." "Great Maytham Hall," *Wikipedia*. Other biographical information from "Frances Hodgson Burnett," *Wikipedia*.

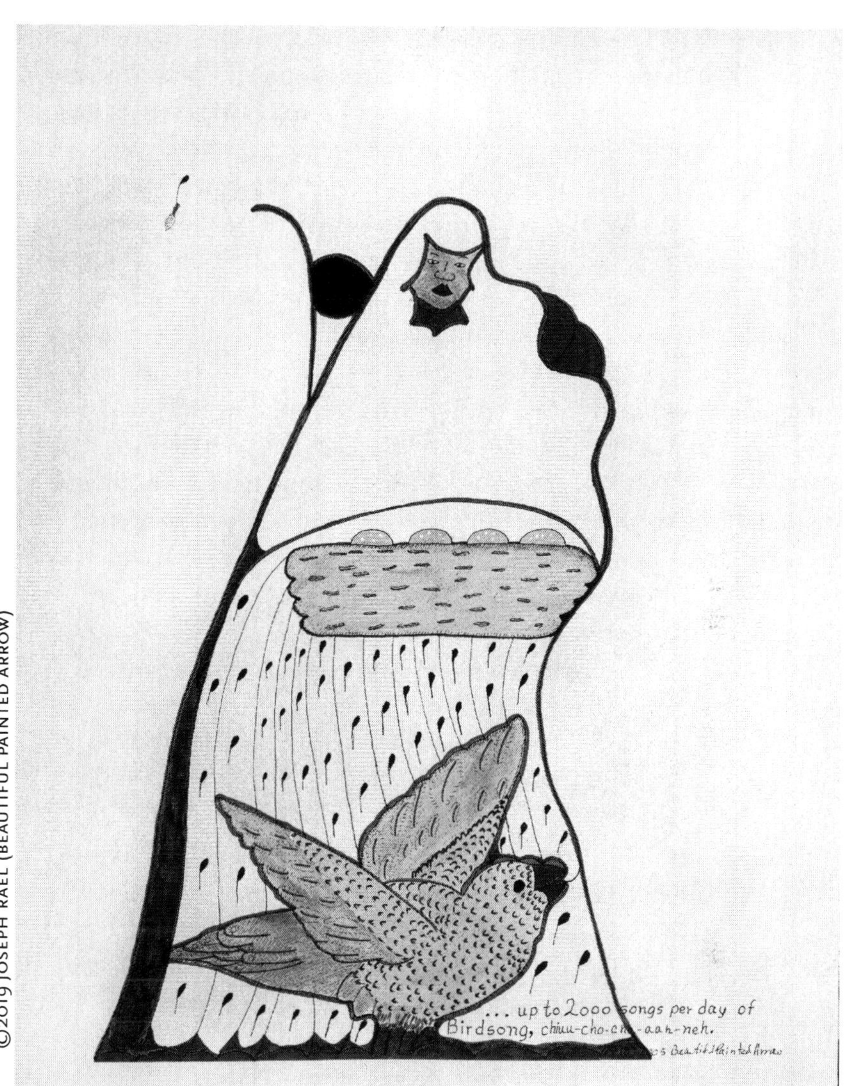

UP TO 2000 SONGS PER DAY OF BIRD SONG CHIUU-CHO-CHA-AAH-NEH

abandoned after his mother died. Colin had never been out of the house in his life and only knew of the outside world through books. The tragic loss of his mother and then the emotional abandonment of his father led everyone to believe that the poor child would not live a long life. Mary, who was also quite spoiled and treated others terribly, slowly befriends Colin and she tells him about the secret garden she has found and also about the boy, Dickon, she has befriended who is an "animal charmer" and wanders about with a pet crow, fox, two squirrels and a newly rescued orphaned lamb. Something in Colin's imagination stirs and he wants to meet this wondrous boy and his creatures and to see the secret garden.

Mary hears of a beautiful woman, the wife of her uncle, who loved flowers, would talk to them and kiss them and who had a special walled garden that she and Ben Weatherstaff planted and tended. She died in a mysterious tragic accident ten years ago and Mary's uncle went mad with grief and shunned the world, going into his own inner wilderness. He locked the garden and buried the key and no one was allowed into it. Mary is enthralled by the idea of this secret garden and begins searching for it. She thinks she has located the outer, surrounding walls, but cannot find a door and circles and circles it. Eventually, her friend the robin helps her out. He gets her attention as he is scratching up some earth and he digs up a key. Mary begins carrying the key with her, but still cannot find the old, locked door. The robin eventually leads her to the locked door which has been covered with ivy vines. She tells Colin about the Secret Garden and they retreat there often.

The story then becomes how Mary and Colin are healed through the growing and living power of the Earth, its creatures, and its plants. There is a blending of Hindu and Muslim spirituality from India (through the young eyes of Mary), shamanism, Celtic spirituality, the healing beauty of nature, and a sprinkling of Christianity.[8]

As Mary and Colin come to life through the healing action of being in contact with the land, Colin seeks to understand what it is that is doing the healing. He comes to the word "Magic" which is the force that pushes and pulls and brings about life and transformation. In this book, Joseph and I speak of *becoming medicine*—in fact we can consider what Colin calls "Magic" and what we call *medicine* to be one and the same thing. Colin decides to embark on a scientific experiment. His experiment is that he will imagine that he is Magic, that the world is Magic, that everything is Magic. He determines to live everyday as *Becoming Magic*, which, of course, we would say is *Becoming Medicine*.

When Dickon and Mary wheel Colin in his wheelchair into the secret garden for the first time, he is in awe. As the sunlight illuminated him, he

8 Some may see colonial, racist, and classist elements in the book, which represent the time in England. While these elements are objectionable, they are historical, and the central theme of healing through connection with nature counter-balances them, which is ahistorical.

cried "I shall get well! I shall get well!" Mary begins calling him the Rajah, as he reminds her of a young Indian rajah she saw in India. Colin gradually transforms from a harsh and selfish bully into a more enlightened force. He wins over old, grumpy Ben Weatherstaff when the children begin speaking in "broad" Yorkshire accents (the language of the land) instead of the more cultured accent of the gentry. Ben assists young Colin in planting a rose as the sun sets on his first day out in the world. He tells Colin to "Set it in the earth thsel' same as th' king does when he goes to a new place." Colin goes into the garden every day, he works with his hands in the earth, he listens to Dickon tell him of all the animal and plant "ways" on the moor. Colin comes into his *medicine* through his experiments with the life magic of growing things. Through coming into harmony with the growing ways of the various creatures and plants of the earth, he begins to feel the stirrings of some unknown force within himself. One day he says:

> "Of course there must be lots of Magic in the world," he said wisely one day, "but people don't know what it is like or how to make it. Perhaps the beginning is just to say things are going to happen until you make them happen. I am going to try an experiment . . . about Magic. Magic is a great thing and scarcely any one knows anything about it except a few people in old books—and Mary a little, because she was born in India where there are fakirs. I believe Dickon knows some Magic, but perhaps he doesn't know it. He charms animals and people. I would never have let him come to see me if he had not been an animal charmer—which is a boy charmer, too, because a boy is an animal.

Colin is pointing out that many of the same *places* to find *magic* are the same as what we talk about in finding and *becoming medicine*: old books, those who go to other cultures and absorb knowledge, and those who live in close contact with animals and nature. Magic is the medicine that creates life, creates a living spirituality.

> "When Mary found this garden it looked quite dead," the orator proceeded. "Then something began pushing things up out of the soil and making things out of nothing. One day things weren't there and another they were. I had never watched things before and it made me feel very curious. . . . I keep saying to myself, 'What is it? What is it?' It's something. It can't be nothing! I don't know its name so I call it Magic. I have never seen the sun rise but Mary and Dickon have

> and from what they tell me I am sure that it is Magic too. Something pushes it up and draws it. Sometimes since I have been in the garden I've looked up through the trees at the sky and I have had a strange feeling of being happy as if something were pushing and drawing in my chest and making me breathe fast. Magic is always pushing and drawing and making things out of nothing. Everything is made out of Magic, leaves and trees, flowers and birds, badgers and foxes and squirrels and people. So it must be all around us. In this garden—in all the places. The Magic in this garden has made me stand up and know I am going to live and to be a man. I am going to make a scientific experiment of trying to get some and put it in myself and make it push and draw me and make me strong. I don't know how to do it but I think that if you keep thinking about it and calling it perhaps it will come. . . . Every morning and every evening and as often in the daytime as I can remember I am going to say, 'Magic is in me! Magic is making me well!'"[9]

This speech comes from a deep place as Colin finds his *medicine* within himself through a deep study of the power within the world of nature and in the being of the Earth. This is because he has entered into non-ordinary reality and he is speaking as a visionary having a vision. The vision is a truth that is revealed through the hollow bone of Colin as he has learned to stop being self-centered and to let life flow through him rather than try to impose his tantrums on life. It is impossible to put into words and explain, and yet in speaking about the difficulty of saying what magic is, he begins to embody it. The speech, itself, is power, it is the movement of Śakti creating in the world; it is the *Hidden Treasure* manifesting, the power of *Wah-Mah-Chi*, of Breath-Matter-Movement; it is the power of Magic revealing itself in life and growth and strength; it is the process of *becoming medicine*—becoming that which grows and heals in the world. His very words are *medicine*.

After speaking this prophetic revelation about the nature of Magic. Colin then engages his listeners again. Checking to see if they are with him, if they are feeling the Magic/medicine. Then, in his visionary state, he sees a ceremony and he invites them to join in this ceremony with him. He asks the little shaman, the animal charmer, Dickon if he thinks the experiment will work.

---

9 Frances Hodgson Burnett, *The Secret Garden*, 140–42.

> "Aye," he answered, "that I do. It'll work the same as th' seeds do when th' sun shines on 'em. It'll work for sure. Shall us begin now?"
>
> Colin was delighted and so was Mary. Fired by recollections of fakirs and devotees in illustrations Colin suggested that they should all sit cross-legged under the tree which made a canopy.
>
> "It will be like sitting in a sort of temple," said Colin. . . .
>
> "I must think only of Magic." It all seemed most majestic and mysterious when they sat down in their circle. . . . Dickon held his rabbit in his arm, and perhaps he made some charmer's signal no one heard, for when he sat down, cross-legged like the rest, the crow, the fox, the squirrels and the lamb slowly drew near and made part of the circle, settling into a place of rest as if of their own desire.
>
> "The creatures have come," said Colin gravely. "They want to help us."
>
> Colin really looked quite beautiful, Mary thought. He held his head up high as if he felt like a sort of priest and his strange eyes had a wonderful look in them. The light shone on him through the tree canopy.
>
> "Now shall we begin," he said. "Shall we sway backward and forward, Mary, as if we were dervishes?"
>
> . . .
>
> "Then I will chant," he said. And he began, looking like a strange boy spirit. "The sun is shining—the sun is shining. That is the Magic. The flowers are growing—the roots are stirring. That is the Magic. Being alive is the Magic—being strong is the Magic. The Magic is in me—the Magic is in me. It is in me—it is in me. It's in every one of us. . . . Magic! Magic! Come and help!"[10]

Colin then insists on walking around the garden in a circle. A procession forms with Mary and Dickon supporting him often, then Ben Weatherstaff, followed by the string of animals. Then the ceremony is completed.

In this children's book we follow two orphaned cousins, a little girl and a little boy, who are both ten years old and have no guidance or initiation into young adulthood. They find each other and they discover the magic/medicine of the Earth through their young guide, the shaman Dickon, who is an animal charmer and explains to them the ways and languages of the birds and plants and animals. The magic/medicine they find at first is outside themselves, and then as on a true visionary, mystical, shamanic journey, they find this magic/medicine within themselves and they come

10 Ibid., 140–44.

to manifest in the rejuvenation and healing of the secret garden and then within themselves. They achieve Oneness and a true integrative spirituality, integrating in their hearts and this ceremony the wisdom of Hindu saints chanting mantras, Islamic fakirs and dervishes, the Christianity of St. Francis, and the ancient ways of shamanism. They hear the Medicine that the Earth is continually speaking to us and teaching us if only we will listen. If, like Mary, Colin, Dickon, and Ben Weatherstaff, we make the secret journey, seeking that which is hidden, we will find the darkness of the cave of the heart—that dark, still place within each of us—and there we will find that each of us has a secret garden and that we were never exiled and expelled from the Garden. Although we all have our winters, the seeds of the garden are always waiting for us to find again so that the spring of life within us may begin to stir—then we are *becoming medicine.*

CALL FROM JOSEPH (7/17/17)

"Hi Dad, ha-ha, I called you 'Dad' maybe that is actually so, maybe you were my dad in a past lifetime or something.

"What I wanted to say is that there is always a little tiny light—when the light comes from up above and into the top of my head or into the side it always has about ¾ of white light and there is a tinge, maybe an 1/8th of an inch that is black. You know you always have to keep the dark and the light balanced out. And in my case when it comes in, it means that the white light predominates which is the goodness and that kind of stuff, and the dark would be badness.

"The other thing is that the caterpillar is a wood grub. It is white and that is what happens when I am going to be sent somewhere on a mission. The light comes from the up above, it hits me on the head, goes through my body, but my body turns into a caterpillar. Before that happens, before the light comes from the up above, which I call it heaven, the light comes down and it always puts down really white, barely a tinge of it is dark energy, ok? It comes from the heavens, hits, pops me on the head—and now here is what is interesting, I am never in my body when this phenomenon happens, I am standing outside of my body looking at this phenomena as it is occurring, light coming from up above, hitting my head, and then it going through this grub. [This] happened with Kurt Wilt, at that moment, as soon as the part of the light reaches there—instantaneously I'm in Florida! After I do my deed, instantaneously I am back here in my body. Why do we use the caterpillar? Because it is called pu-pi, pu-pi, pu- *means 'to get it done,' to get through with it,' 'finish it,' 'make it*

happen.' Let's use 'make it happen,' is the pu-. *And then the* pi- *means 'the heart.' That would be a good ending connection to the thing you did with the heart meditation. I just thought I would give you a closing there. It might be quite appropriate."*

And so we are at the end of our returning. We have gone through separating, initiating, and now returning. We have gone through seeking, finding/receiving, and now we are in a state of giving. Joseph points out a metaphor that is rich with meaning—the blending of white and dark light that comes down and initiates him into a new larval stage, he separates from his body, he becomes a small caterpillar that holds healing transformation within it, but it must crawl and go on a mission. As he goes through the mission of *Wah-Mah-Chi*, of Breath Matter Movement, he unfolds into a beautiful butterfly as healing unfolds—bringing the non-ordinary into the ordinary. Then he returns, back in his body; having completed his mission he has returned home.

We have drawn out this process of separating, initiating, and returning through the length of this long book, however you should not think that every initiation is such a long process. True, the biggest work of vision quests of shamans and mystics often do take long years of preparation and work (as worship). However, initiation can happen in the blink of an eye—one moment you are a human being going about your day, the next minute you are struck by divine inspiration and illumination and you are turned into a caterpillar that must then go on a mission to become a butterfly. You do not do it because you want to be a butterfly for yourself, but because someone is in need of healing and you are the one who has been chosen to do the healing work. We do not become medicine for ourselves, although we can be healed in the process, we are *medicine* for others and for the Earth.

Joseph says that "we do not exist." When we accept this fact that we are momentary flickers of light, *spanda*, coming into being and going out of being, then we are *becoming medicine*. Every moment becomes an epiphany, a theophany—every moment we have made ourselves more capable of God, of *Wah-Mah-Chi*, every moment we are opening to the revelation and manifestation of the divine in the present moment. As Joseph says, the line separating ordinary from non-ordinary reality is razor thin, like the razor's edge that the *Upanishads* speak of. Perhaps, even at this moment, you have crossed that line and are *becoming medicine*.

ENTERING THE HEART CEREMONY

Find a quiet place where you will be able to sit for a while, either inside or outside. Find the center of the space where you will be sitting. Orient yourself to the North and take one step in that direction, honoring the place of innocence. Turn around, facing South, and step back into the Center of your medicine wheel, honoring the place of carrying. Take a step to the South, honoring the place of placement. Turn around, facing North and step back into the Center, again honoring the place of carrying. Turn to the East, and take one step forward, honoring the place of purity. Turn around, facing West, and step back into Center, honoring the place of carrying. Take one step to the West, honoring the place of awareness. Turn around and step back into Center, once again honoring the heart of carrying.

Now you will walk the medicine wheel. Face the East and take one step forward, intone the sound of the letter *A_aaahhhhhhhh*, drawing out the sound as long as you can as you step around the perimeter of the circle to the South and then intone the sound of the letter *E_eeehhhhhhhh*. Follow the wheel around to the West and intone the letter *I_eeeeeeee*. Follow the wheel to the North and intone the sound of *O_oooooooo*. Now step to the Center and intone the sound of the letter *U_uuuuuuuu*.[11]

Now you can sit comfortably in the center of the medicine wheel, this is the place of carrying and it is the heart of the medicine wheel. As Joseph reminds us, the microcosm is the macrocosm, thus this is the heart of the medicine wheel, it is your heart, it is the heart of the Earth, it is the heart of the Universe, and it is even the Heart of God—*Wah Mah Chi*—if you can walk deep enough into the heart.

We will now be going through a series of doorways. First we will enter your personal heart and trace the flow of blood through the medicine wheel of the heart. Venous blood, after giving its oxygen to the body, returns to the heart from the Northwest, the place of connecting spirit and body, entering into the right atrium. Next follow the flow of blood into your right ventricle in the Southwest, the place of the connecting body and emotion. From here the blood is pumped to the North, the place of Spirit and Innocence. Here the blood enters into the lungs and

11 Recall, as discussed in Joseph's books, that the sounds that Joseph uses when intoning the letters of the alphabet are not the typical English pronunciations, but follow the sounds of those letters in Tiwa and Spanish.

is transformed as the inner venous blood connects with the outer oxygen-rich environment coming into the lungs. The venous blood now turns from dark to bright red arterial blood as it carries more oxygen as the physical matter of the body creates a container in which the movement of the blood connects with the movement of the breath—thus we have Breath, Matter, Movement, thus we have *Wah-Mah-Chi* entering at this point. Next, follow the blood as it comes back into the heart from the Northeast, the place of connecting spirit and the mind, as it enters into the doorway of the left atrium. From here the blood travels to the Southeast, the place of connecting mind and emotion in the left ventricle. From here the arterial blood travels North, to the spirit again, and then travels throughout the body, revitalizing it and carrying the breath into matter through the movement of the blood.

The atria and ventricles of the heart are empty chambers that can fill with blood and then empty, a continual process of accepting what life has to give, allowing transformation, and then giving goodness away to the rest of the body. These empty chambers might remind you of the word that Abhishiktananda used—*guhā*: the cave of the heart. Now that you have circulated through your own personal heart, the time has come to enter into the center of your heart, for it is here that you will find the doorway into the deepest chambers of the cave of the heart, which we can also call the secret garden. Move into the center of the heart, this is the still point at the center of all the circulating movement of the burning fire of the blood. In this still center-point, look around for a doorway. It is dark here in the center of the heart, despite the burning of the blood, you can look with your eyes, but you need to see with your inner, non-ordinary vision. You must feel into it with your non-ordinary senses. Locate the doorway—it might be on the wall, or the ceiling, but it could possibly be on the floor as it leads deeper into the heart. Open the door of your heart and step through the threshold into this next larger space of your heart, feeling the opening of stillness and space within your center. You are now in the heart of humanity. Feel your way into this heart of humanity where your heart and the heart of humanity are one.

Once you have acclimated to the heart of humanity, begin looking for the next doorway that opens into an even deeper stillness of heart. Using your non-ordinary senses, locate the door, open it, and step through, entering into the heart of life. Open up into the heart of life where the heart of every living thing is one. Even things that don't have an obvious heart

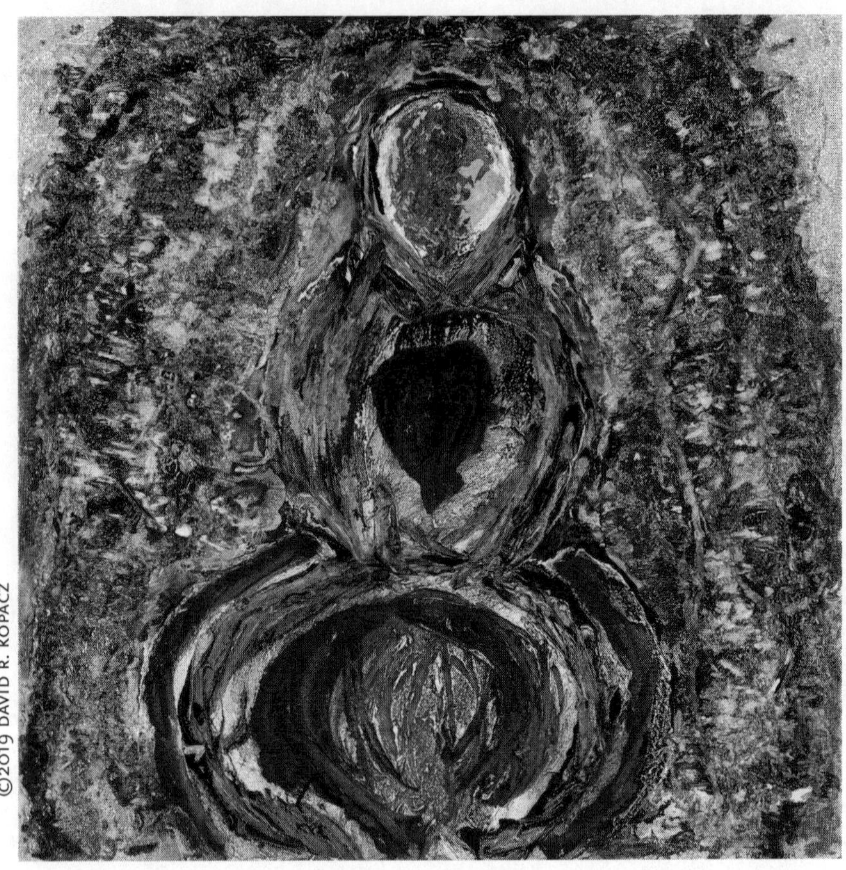

HEART RADIATION

like plants have their center here. Open up into this greater spaciousness, feeling more space open up within your heart and feeling a vastness that you are entering. Take some time getting comfortable in the heart of life.

Start to look around for the next doorway, looking all around with your non-ordinary vision. Find the door, open it, and step through into the heart of creation—this is the heart of every physical thing, all biological beings and rocks, water, soil, and even space. Feel this space open up within the center of your heart as you step forward into this vast space. Spend some time enjoying being one with creation.

There is still another doorway as you begin looking around again with your non-ordinary vision. In this realm, you get used to letting go of your identity—moving from the personal, to humanity, to life, to creation. Find the door, open it, and step through, entering into the Heart of God, the Heart of *Wah-Mah-Chi*—the Heart of the Creator. Here you are One with everything, resting peacefully in the light of the Heart of the Creator. You have taken four steps through four caves of the heart. You have been practicing heart medicine as you have been circling deeper into the heart medicine wheel.

Now it is time to go into the heart of the heart medicine wheel, taking a step into the center of the heart of the heart medicine wheel. By now you should be used to using your non-ordinary vision to find the door, open it, and walk through, as you do so. You now are entering into what Joseph calls Vast Self. This is the place of non-duality. There is not even oneness, because it is before the counting even began. Feel the peace of Vast Self, the place before Creation, the place that watches Creation being created out of itself and yet remaining the same. Be still, be still . . . still . . .

LIST OF SOUND CHAMBERS

Also see http://www.peacechamber.co.uk/

Name	Location
Sweet Beautiful Waters	Arizona, USA
Red Eagle Mountain Spirit (disassembled)	New Mexico, USA
Where God Walks & Talks	Colorado, USA
Unnamed	New York, USA
House of Mica	New York, USA
Unnamed	New Mexico, USA
Unnamed	Michigan, USA
Earth Harmony	Michigan, USA
The Eagle's Nest	Missouri, USA
Thundersong	Colorado, USA
No Name	Colorado, USA
Bud Weaver (disassembled, tree now replaces)	Florida, USA
Earth Song	Michigan, USA
Spirit Earth Path	New Mexico, USA
Circle of Light Chamber	New Mexico, USA
Earth, Spirit of Singing Eyes	New York, USA
Watersong	North Carolina, USA
Soul Fire Sanctuary (originally Earth's Ancestral Voices)	North Carolina, USA
Eaglewatch Peace Chamber	Oklahoma, USA
Happy Heart	Oklahoma, USA
Birdsong	Pennsylvania, USA
Unnamed	Tennessee, USA
Center for Peace	Tennessee, USA
Grandmother's Place	Tennessee, USA
Grandmother Spider Chamber	Texas, USA
Wolf Lodge Chamber	Texas, USA
Song of the Redtail Hawk	Texas, USA
Virginia Beach Chamber	Virginia, USA
Rainbow's End Chamber	California, USA
Blessing of Land for Peace Chamber	Ontario, Canada
Sacred Arrow Peace Sound Chamber	Ontario, Canada
Oca da Paz	Sao Paulo, Brazil
Sacha Runa Peace Chamber	La Paz, Bolivia

Song of the New Dawn	England
Unnamed (disassembled)	England
Sligo Peace Chamber	Éire (Ireland)
Cave of Clay	Scotland
Sound Water Chamber	Scotland
Little Raindrop	Scotland
Skye Chamber	Isle of Skye, Scotland
The Light House	Scotland
Let the Beauty We See Be the Beauty We Are	Scotland
Waterstein Chamber	Isle of Skye, Scotland
Gorslwyd Sound Peace Chamber	Wales
Song of the Cleansing Time	Wales
Heart of the Land	Wales
House of Singing Light	Denmark
To Protect the People Peace Chamber	Denmark
God Wanders as Light	Germany
Beautiful Flower	Germany
Guardians of the Light of the Heavens	Germany
Half of God is Singing; Half Is Listening	Germany
Light from the Heavens	Germany
Little Flames of Life	Germany
One Who Is Speaking	Austria
Unnamed	Austria
Vienna Peace Chamber	Austria
Titra Peace Chamber	Croatia
Fredhus Elisa	Norway
House of Ancient Voices	Norway
Kiama Dojo	Victoria, Australia
Casurina Peace Chamber	Victoria, Australia
Red Eagle	Victoria, Australia
Wind Walker	South Africa
Marimba House	South Africa

ONE SUN AND FOUR MOONS

REFERENCES

Abercrombie, Sharon. "A light in the darkness of the botched pope-animal story." National Catholic Reporter, online, December 16, 2014, http://ncronline.org/blogs/eco-catholic/light-darkness-botched-pope-animal-story, accessed 4/7/18.

Abram, David. *The Spell of the Sensuous*. New York: Vintage, 1997.

—. *Becoming Animal: An Earthly Cosmology*. New York: Vintage, 2011.

Alexander, Stephon. *The Jazz of Physics: The Secret Link Between Music and the Structure of the Universe*. New York: Basic Books, 2016.

Andrews, Ted. *Animal Speak: The Spiritual and Magical Powers of Creatures Great & Small*. Woodbury: Llewellyn Publications, 2015.

Anthony, David. *The Horse, The Wheel, and Language: How Bronze-age Riders from the Eurasian Steppes Shaped the World*. Princeton: Princeton University Press, 2007.

Arbuckle, Gerald. *Fundamentalism at Home and Abroad: Analysis and Pastoral Responses*. Collegeville: Liturgical Press, 2017.

—. *The Francis Factor and the People of God*. Maryknoll: Orbis Books, 2015.

—. *From Chaos to Mission: Refounding Religious Life Formation*. Homebush: St Paul's Publications, 1996.

—. *Out of Chaos: Refounding Religious Congregations*. New York: Paulist Press, 1988.

Atlas Obscura, "The Stone Circles at Odry," https://www.atlasobscura.com/places/the-stone-circles-at-odry, accessed 3/17/18.

Bach, Richard. *Illusions: Adventures of a Reluctant Messiah*. New York: Dell/Eleanor Friede, 1977.

Badger, The. https://issuu.com/antonellavicini/docs/the_badger_october_2017.

Bangley, Bernard (ed.). *Radiance: A Spiritual Memoir of Evelyn Underhill*. Brewster: Paraclete Press, 2015.

Baqli, Ruzbihan. *The Unveiling of Secrets: Diary of a Sufi Master*. Carl W. Ernst (trans.). Chapel Hill: Parvardigar Press, 1997.

Barton, David G. "C.G. Jung and the indigenous psyche: two encounters." *International Journal of Jungian Studies*, Vol. 8(2): 75-84, 2016.

Berkman, Franya. *Monument Eternal: The Music of Alice Coltrane*. Middleton: Wesleyan University Press, 2010.

Bharucha, Ruzbeh N. *The Fakir*. New Delhi: Full Circle Publishing, 2010.

—. *The Fakir: Thoughts and Prayers*. New Delhi: Full Circle Publishing, 2011.

Bible, The Holy. Revised Standard Version, Second Catholic Edition. San Francisco: Ignatius Press, 2006.

Blake, William. *The Portable Blake*. Alfred Kazin (ed.). New York: Viking Press, 1960.

Bohm, David. Nichol, Lee (ed.). *The Essential David Bohm*. New York: Routledge, 2003.

Bodo, Murray. *Francis: The Journey and the Dream*. Cincinnati: Franciscan Media, 2011.

du Boulay, Shirley. *The Cave of the Heart: The Life of Swami Abhishiktananda*. Maryknoll: Orbis Books, 2005.

Burnett, Frances Hodgson. *The Secret Garden*. Snowball Classics Publishing, 2014.

Cajete, Gregory. *Native Science: Natural Laws of Interdependence*. Santa Fe: Clear Light Publishers, 2000.

Campbell, Joseph. *The Hero with a Thousand Faces, Third Edition*. Novato: New World Library, 2008.

—. *Myths of Light: Eastern Metaphors of the Eternal*. Novato: New World Library, 2003.

—. *The Masks of God: Primitive Mythology*. New York: Penguin Compass, 1987.

—. *The Masks of God: Oriental Mythology*. New York: Penguin Compass, 1991.

Campbell, Joseph with Bill Moyers. *The Power of Myth*. New York: Anchor Books, 1991.

Capra, Fritjof. *The Tao of Physics: An Exploration of the Parallels between Modern Physics and Eastern Mysticism, 35th Anniversary (Fifth) Edition*. Boston: Shambhala Publications, 2010.

Capra, Fritjof and Pier Luigi Luisi. *The Systems View of Life: A Unifying Vision*. Cambridge: Cambridge University Press, 2014.

Chapman, Fred. "The Bighorn Medicine Wheel: 1988-1999," *Cultural Resource Management*, Vol. 3, 1999, 5-10. A pdf of this report at http://sacredland.org/wp-content/uploads/2017/07/Bighorn_Medicine_Wheel.pdf, accessed 4/7/18.

Cheetham, Thomas. *All the World an Icon: Henry Corbin and the Angelic Function of Beings*. Berkeley: North Atlantic Books, 2012.

—. *Green Man, Earth Angel: The Prophetic Tradition and the Battle for the Soul of the World*. Albany: State University of New York Press, 2005.

Chhibber, Kavita. "Anoushka Shankar," March, 18, 2005. http://www.kavitachhibber.com/2005/03/18/anoushka-shankar/, accessed 12/16/18.

Chuang Tzu: Basic Writings. Burton Watson (trans). New York: Columbia University Press, 1964.

Chittick, William. *Divine Love: Islamic Literature and the Path to God*. New Haven: Yale University Press, 2013.

Ciabattari, Jane. "Why is Rumi the best-selling poet in the US?" BBC online, 10/21/14, http://www.bbc.com/culture/story/20140414-americas-best-selling-poet , accessed 11/6/17.

Clash, The. "The Sound of Sinners," from the album *Sandinista!* CBS/Epic, 1980.

Cloud Cult. "Living in Awe," from the album *The Seeker*. Rebel Group, 2016.

—. "Unexplainable Stories," from the album *Light Chasers*. Rebel Group, 2010.

Cohen, J.M. and J-F. Phipps. *The Common Experience*. Los Angeles: J. P. Tarcher, 1979.

Cohen, Michael H. *Healing at the Borderland of Medicine and Religion*. Chapel Hill: University of North Carolina Press, 2006.

Corbin, Henry. *Swedenborg and Esoteric Islam*. West Chester: Swedenborg Foundation, 1999.

—. *The Voyage and the Messenger: Iran and Philosophy*. Berkeley: North Atlantic Books, 1998.

—. *Alone with the Alone: Creative Imagination in the Sūfism of Ibn 'Arabī*. Princeton: Princeton University Press, 1997.

—. *Spiritual Body and Celestial Earth: From Mazdean Iran to Shī'ite Iran*. Princeton: Princeton University Press, 1979.

Cousineau, Phil, (ed.). *The Hero's Journey: Joseph Campbell on His Life and Work*. Novato: New World Library, 1990.

Curtis, Deborah. *Touching from a Distance: Ian Curtis and Joy Division*. Faber & Faber, 1995.

Davies, John. *A History of Wales*. New York: Penguin, 2007.

Dellaflora, Anthony. *The Language of Spirituality*. Taos Communications Empire, 2005.

Deloria, Vine Jr. C.G. *Jung and the Sioux Traditions: Dreams, Visions, Nature, and the Primitive*. New Orleans: Spring Journal Books, 2009.

Dick, Philip K. *The Exegesis of Philip K. Dick*. Pamela Jackson and Jonathan Lethem (eds.). New York: Houghton Mifflin Harcourt, 2011.

Draper, Robert, photos by Dave Yoder. *Pope Francis and the New Vatican*. Washington DC: National Geographic, 2015.

Duran, Eduardo. *Healing the Soul Wound: Counseling with American Indians and Other Native Peoples*. New York: Teachers College Press, 2006.

—. "Medicine Wheel, Mandala, and Jung." *Spring: A Journal of Archetype and Culture*, "Native American Cultures and the Western Psyche: A Bridge Between." New Orleans: Spring Journal, 2012.

Duran, Eduardo and Bonnie Duran. *Native American Postcolonial Psychology*. Albany: State Universities of New York Press, 1995.

Duran, Phillip H. *The Condor and the Eagle: Uniting Heart and Mind in Search of a New Science Worldview*. Rio Rancho: Eagle House Publications, 2013.

—. "On the Cosmic Order of Modern Physics and the Conceptual World of the American Indian," pre-publication, 2005, 1-2. This was published in *World Futures: The Journal of New Paradigm Research* Volume 63, 2007 - Issue 1.

Dyczkowski, Mark S.G. *The Doctrine of Vibration: An Analysis of the Doctrines and Practices of Kashmir Shaivism*. Albany: State University of New York Press, 1987.

Edmunds, R. David. *The Potawatomis: Keepers of the Fire*. Norman: University of Oklahoma Press, 1978.

Eisenstein, Charles. *The Ascent of Humanity: Civilization and the Human Sense of Self.* Berkeley: Evolver Editions, 2007, 2013.

—. *The More Beautiful World Our Hearts Know is Possible*. Berkeley: North Atlantic Books, 2013.

Eliade, Mircea. *Rites and Symbols of Initiation: The Mysteries of Birth and Rebirth*. Putnam: Spring Publications, 1994. Originally published as *Birth and Rebirth: The Religious Meanings of Initiation in Human Culture*. New York: Harper & Brothers Publishers, 1958.

—. *The Sacred and the Profane: The Nature of Religion*. New York: A Harvest Book, 1987.

—. *Shamanism: Archaic Techniques of Ecstasy*. Princeton: Princeton University Press, 1964.

Ellenberger, Henri. *The Discovery of the Unconscious: The History and Evolution of Dynamic Psychiatry*. New York: Basic Books, 1970.

Ergin, Nevit O. *Unknown Rumi: Selected Rubais of Mevlana Jalaluddin Rumi and Commentary*. Los Angeles: Powerhouse Publishing, 2015.

Ergin, Nevit O. and Will Johnson. *The Rubais of Rumi: Insane with Love*. Rochester: Inner Traditions, 2007.

Flannery, Tim. *The Eternal Frontier: An Ecological History of North America and Its Peoples*. New York: Grove Press, 2001.

Fleischman, Paul R. *Cultivating Inner Peace*. Seattle: Pariyatti Press, 2011.

Foster, Charles. *Being a Beast: Adventures Across the Species Divide*. New York: Picador, 2016.

Fox, Matthew. *Confessions: The Making of a Postdenominational Priest*. Berkeley: North Atlantic Books, 2015.

—. *Meister Eckhart: A Mystic Warrior for Our Times*. Novato: New World Library, 2014.

—. *Hildegard of Bingen: A Saint for Our Times*. Vancouver: Namaste, 2014.

—. *Illuminations of Hildegard of Bingen*. Rochester: Bear & Company, 2002.

—. *Original Blessing*. New York: Jeremy P. Tarcher/Putnam, 2000.

—. *Creation Spirituality: Liberating Gifts for the Peoples of the Earth*. New York: Harper One, 1991.

—. *Meditations with Meister Eckhart*. Rochester: Bear & Company, 1983.

Fox, Matthew, Skylar Wilson, and Jennifer Berit Listug. *Order of the Sacred Earth: An Intergenerational Vision of Love and Action*. Rhinebeck: Monkfish Book Publishing Company, 2018.

Frankopan, Peter. *The Silk Roads: A New History of the World*. New York: Vintage Books, 2017.

Gandhi, Mohandas K. *An Autobiography: My Experiments with Truth*. Boston: Beacon Press, 1967.

Gandhi, Mohandas K. *The Essential Gandhi: An Anthology of His Writings on His Life, Work, and Ideas, Second Edition*. Louis Fischer (ed.). New York: Vintage Spiritual Classics, 2002.

Gold, Peter. *Navajo & Tibetan Sacred Wisdom: The Circle of the Spirit*. Rochester: Inner Traditions, 1994.

Grey, Alex. *Chapel of Sacred Mirrors*. http://www.alexgrey.com/art/paintings/soul/journy-of-the-wounded-healer/, accessed 7/21/17.

Guénon, René. *Symbols of Sacred Science*. Hillsdale: Sophia Perennis, 2004.

Gustafson, Fred. *Dancing Between Two Worlds: Jung and the Native American Soul*. New York: The Paulist Press, 1997.

Hammerschlag, Carl A. *The Theft of the Spirit*. New York: Fireside, 1994.

Harrison, George. *I, Me, Mine, The Extended Edition*. Guildford: Genesis Publications, 2017.

Hastings, Selina. *The Secret Lives of Somerset Maugham*. New York: Random House, 2009.

Hayes, Ernestine. "*The Tao of Raven: An Alaska Native Memoir*." Seattle Search for Meaning Festival, 2/24/18. The author shared the transcript of her talk. I summarize and quote based on this transcript and also hand written notes I took during the talk.

Heaven, Ross. *The Way of the Lover: Sufism, Shamanism and the Spiritual Art of Love*. Washington DC: Moon Books, 2017.

Heinberg, Richard. *Memories and Visions of Paradise: Exploring the Universal Myth of a Lost Golden Age*. New York: Tarcher, 1990.

Helminski, Kabir. *The Knowing Heart: A Sufi Path of Transformation*. Boston: Shambhala, 1999.

Herrmann, Steven. *Walt Whitman: Shamanism, Spiritual Democracy, and the World Soul*. Durham: Eloquent Books, 2010.

—. *Spiritual Democracy: The Wisdom of Early American Visionaries for the Journey Forward*. Berkeley: North Atlantic Books, 2014.

Hermann, Eve M. B. "Anoushka Shankar Biography." MusicianGuide.com. http://www.musicianguide.com/biographies/1608003982/Anoushka-Shankar.html, accessed 12/16/18.

Hindupedia. "Sanskrit, The Aksharas (letters)." http://www.hindupedia.com/en/Sanskrit, accessed 11/9/17.

Holland, Gail Bernice. *A Call for Connection: Solutions for Creating a Whole New Culture*. Novato: New World Library, 1998.

Hurley, Luke. "The Sound," *The Best of Luke Hurley, 1981-2006*. Monkey Records, 2013.

Hyde, Lewis. *Trickster Makes this World: Mischief, Myth, and Art*. New York: Farrar, Straus and Giroux, 2010.

Ingerman, Sandra and Hank Wesselman. *Awakening to the Spirit World: The Shamanic Path of Direct Revelation*. Boulder: Sounds True, 2010.

Jung, Carl G. *The Red Book: Liber Novus*. Sonu Shamdasani (ed.). New York: Norton & Company, 2009.

Jung, Carl G. *The Psychology of Kundalini Yoga: Notes of the Seminar Given in 1932*. Princeton: Princeton University Press, 1996.

—. *The Development of the Personality, CW 17*. Princeton: Princeton University Press, 1991.

—. *The Archetypes of the Collective Unconscious, CW 9*, Part I. Princeton: Princeton University Press, 1990.

—. *Psychology and Religion: West and East, CW 11*. Princeton: Princeton University Press, 1989.

—. *The Symbolic Life, CW 18*. Princeton: Princeton University Press, 1989.

—. *C. G. Jung Speaking: Interviews and Encounters*. Princeton: Princeton University Press, 1977.

—. *Civilization in Transition, CW 10, Second Edition*. Princeton: Princeton University Press, 1970.

—. *Mysterium Coniunctionis, CW 14, Second Edition*. Princeton: Princeton University Press, 1970.

—. *Memories, Dreams, Reflections*. New York: Vintage Books, 1989.

—. *Modern Man in Search of a Soul*. New York: Harvest Books, 1955.

Katz, Richard. *Indigenous Healing Psychology: Honoring the Wisdom of the First Peoples*. Rochester: Healing Arts Press, 2017.

—. *The Straight Path: A Story of Healing and Transformation in Fiji*. New York: Merloyd Lawrence Book, Addison-Wesley Publishing, 1993.

—. "Education as Transformation: Becoming a Healer Among the !Kung and the Fijians." *Harvard Educational Review*, Vol. 51, No. 1, February 1981.

Kalweit, Holger. *Shamans, Healers, and Medicine Men*. Boston: Shambhala, 1992.

Keeney, Bradford. *Shaking Medicine: The Healing Power of Ecstatic Movement*. Rochester: Destiny Books, 2007.

Keepin, William. *Belonging to God: Spirituality, Science & a Universal Path of Divine Love*. Woodstock: Skylight Paths Publishing, 2016.

Kehoe, Alice Beck. *The Ghost Dance: Ethnohistory and Revitalization*. Long Grove: Waveland Press, 2006.

Kingsley, Peter. *Catafalque: Carl Jung and the End of Humanity*. London: Catafalque Press, 2018.

—. *A Story Waiting to Pierce You: Mongolia, Tibet and the Destiny of the Western World*, Third Printing. Point Reyes: The Golden Sufi Center, 2014, originally 2010.

—. *Reality*. Point Reyes: The Golden Sufi Center, 2003.

—. *In the Dark Places of Wisdom*. Point Reyes: The Golden Sufi Center, 1999.

Kopacz, David R. *Re-humanizing Medicine: A Holistic Framework for Transforming Your Self, Your Practice, and the Culture of Medicine*. Washington DC: Ayni Books, 2014.

—. *Being Fully Human: Living an Integrated Life* blog. https://beingfullyhuman.com/.

Kopacz, David R and Joseph Rael (Beautiful Painted Arrow). *Walking the Medicine Wheel: Healing Trauma & PTSD*. Pointer Oak/Tri S Foundation, distributed by Millichap Books, 2016.

Kornblatt, Judith Deutsch. *Divine Sophia: The Wisdom Writings of Vladimir Solovyov*. Ithaca: Cornell University Press, 2009.

Krishnamurti, Jiddu. *Krishnamurti's Notebook*. Ojai: Krishnamurti Productions of America, 2003.

—. *Total Freedom: The Essential Krishnamurti*. San Francisco: Harper Collins, 1996.

Krishnamurti, J. and David Bohm. *The Ending of Time: Where Philosophy and Physics Meet*. New York: HarperOne, 2014.

Lachman, Gary. *The Secret Teachers of the Western World*. New York: Jeremy P. Tarcher, 2015.

—. *Jung the Mystic: The Esoteric Dimensions of Carl Jung's Life and Teachings*. New York: Jeremy P. Tarcher, 2010.

Ladinsky, Daniel. *Love Poems from God: Twelve Sacred Voices from the East and West*. New York: Penguin, 2002.

Larsen, Stephen and Robin. *A Fire in the Mind: The Life of Joseph Campbell*. New York: Doubleday, 1991.

Lavezzoli, Peter. *The Dawn of Indian Music in the West*. New York: Continuum, 2007.

Lee, Ben. *Ayahuasca: Welcome to the Work*, Album Trailer. https://www.youtube.com/watch?v=YFk9CrbzpQc, accessed 11/19/17.

—. Website. https://www.ben-lee.com/, accessed 11/19/17.

—. "In the Silence." *Ayahuasca: Welcome to the Work*. Ten Fingers Records, 2013.

Lewis-Williams, David. *The Mind in the Cave*. London: Thames & Hudson Ltd, 2002.

Mack, John E. *Passport to the Cosmos: Human Transformation and Alien Encounters*. Guildford: White Crow Books, Commemorative Edition, 2008.

Mallory, J.P. and D.Q. Adams. *The Oxford Introduction to Proto-Indo-European and the Proto-Indo-European World*. Oxford: Oxford University Press, 2006.

Mann, Charles C. *1491: New Revelations of the Americas Before Columbus*. New York: Vintage, 2011.

—. *1493: Uncovering the New World Columbus Created*. New York: Vintage Books, 2011.

Māori Dictionary. "Manaaki." https:maoridictionary.co.nz, accessed 4/30/18.

Marlow, Mary Elizabeth. *Walking with Cosmic Dancer Joseph Rael*. Pointer Oak/Tri S Foundation, distributed by Millichap Books, 2018.

Mascaró, Juan. *The Creation of Faith*. Calgary: Bayeux Arts, 1999.

—. (trans.). *The Upanishads*. New York: Penguin Books, 1965.

—. *Lamps of Fire: The Spirit of Religions*. London: Eyre Methuen, 1961.

Matile, Roger. *Oswego Township: Images of America*. Chicago: Arcadia, 2008.

Maugham, Somerset. *The Razor's Edge*. New York: Penguin Books, 1988.

Mehl-Madrona, Lewis. *Healing the Mind through the Power of Story: The Promise of Narrative Psychiatry*. Rochester: Bear & Company, 2010.

—. *Narrative Medicine: The Use of History and Story in the Healing Process*. Rochester: Bear & Company, 2007.

—. *Coyote Medicine: Lessons from Native American Healing*. New York: Fireside, 1998.

Mehl-Madrona, Lewis and Barbara Mainguy. *Remapping Your Mind: The Neuroscience of Self-Transformation through Story*. Rochester: Bear & Company, 2015.

Meyer, Manulani Aluli. "Holographic Epistemology: Native Common Sense," *China Media Research*, 9(2), 2013.

Meyer, Wali Ali, Bilal Hyde, Faisal Muqaddam, and Shabda Kahn. *Physicians of the Heart: A Sufi View of the Ninety-nine Names of Allah*. San Francisco: Sufi Ruhaniat International, 2011.

Mezirow, Jack. "Transformational Learning Theory," in Jack Mezirow, Edward Taylor, and Associates (eds.), *Transformative Learning in Practice*. San Francisco: Jossey-Bass, 2009.

Miller, Richard. *Yoga Nidra*. Boulder: Sounds True, 2010.

—. "Welcoming All That Is: Nonduality, Yoga Nidra, and the Play of Opposites in Psychotherapy." In John J. Pedergast, Peter Fenner, and Sheila Krystal (eds.) *The*

Sacred Wisdom: Nondual Wisdom and Psychotherapy. St. Paul: Paragon House, 2003.

Muller-Ortega, Paul Eduardo. *The Triadic Heart of Śiva: Kaula Tantricism of Abhinavagupta in the Non-Dual Shaivism of Kashmir.* Albany: State University of New York Press, 1989.

Mukherjee, Siddhartha. *The Gene: An Intimate History*. New York: Scribner, 2016.

NASA Science online: Astrophysics page. "Dark Energy, Dark Matter." http://science.nasa.gov/astrophysics/focus-areas/what-is-dark-energy/, accessed 10/12/15.

Nataraja Guru. *The Word of the Guru: The Life and Teachings of Nārāyana Guru*. New Delhi: D.K. Printworld, 2003.

Natarajan, Priyamvada. *Mapping the Heavens: The Radical Scientific Ideas that Reveal the Cosmos*. New Haven: Yale University Press, 2016.

Needleman, Jacob. *The American Soul: Rediscovering the Wisdom of the Founders*. New York: Jeremy P. Tarcher/Putnam, 2003.

Nicolaou, Corinna. *A None's Story: Searching for Meaning Inside Christianity, Judaism, Buddhism, and Islam*. New York: Columbia University Press, 2016.

Niehardt, John G. *Black Elk Speaks: The Premiere Edition*. Albany: State University of New York Press, 2008.

Oakes, Maud and Joseph Campbell. *Where the Two Came to Their Father: A Navaho War Ceremonial Given by Jeff King, Third Edition*. Princeton: Princeton University Press, 1991.

Odier, Daniel. *The Doors of Joy: 19 Meditations for Authentic Living*. Oxford: Watkins Publishing, 2014.

—. *Yoga Spandakarikas: The Sacred Texts at the Origins of Tantra*. Rochester: Inner Traditions, 2004.

—. *Desire: The Tantric Path to Awakening*. Rochester: Inner Traditions, 2001.

O'Neill, Molly. "At Supper with – Matthew Fox; Roman Catholic Rebel Becomes A Cause Celebre," *New York Times*, March 17, 1993. http://www.nytimes.com/1993/03/17/garden/at-supper-with-matthew-fox-roman-catholic-rebel-becomes-a-cause-celebre.html?scp=1&sq=&st=nyt, accessed 1/21/17.

Online Etymology Dictionary. "Barbarian." http://www.etymonline.com/index.php?term=barbarian, accessed 11/10/17.

—. "Cadaver." http://www.etymonline.com/index.php?term=cadaver, accessed 7/21/17.

—. "Colonize." https://www.etymonline.com/word/colonize, accessed 12/15/17.

—. "Indigenous." https://www.etymonline.com/word/indigenous, accessed, 11/10/17.

—. "Mythopoesis." https://www.etymonline.com/word/mythopoeic, accessed 11/10/17.

—. "Ocean." http://www.etymonline.com/index.php?term=ocean, accessed 9/30/16.

—. "Shaman." http://www.etymonline.com/index.php?term=shaman, accessed 8/5/17.

—. "Vocation." http://www.etymonline.com/index.php?term=vocation, accessed 11/18/16.

Palmer, Parker. *Healing the Heart of Democracy: The Courage to Create a Politics Worthy of the Human Spirit*. San Francisco: Jossey-Bass, 2011.

Panek, Richard. *The 4% Universe: Dark Matter, Dark Energy, and the Race to Discover the Rest of Reality*. Boston: Houghton Mifflin Harcourt, 2011.

Peat, F. David. *Infinite Potential: The Life and Times of David Bohm*. New York: Basic Books, 1997.

Peck, M. Scott. *The Road Less Traveled*. London: Arrow Books 2006, originally 1978.

Penprase, Bryan. *The Power of Stars: How Celestial Observations Have Shaped Civilization*. New York: Springer, 2011.

Police, The. "Secret Journey," from the album *Ghost in the Machine*. A&M, 1981. Lyrics, http://www.sting.com/discography/lyrics/lyric/song/221, accessed 7/23/16.

Polling, Jim. "We Are Story," obituary for Richard Wagamese, *The Minden Times Ontario* online, http://www.mindentimes.ca/we-are-story, accessed 6/22/18.

Prasad, Swami Muni Narayana. *Garland of Visions (Darśanamālā of Narayana Guru)*. New Delhi: D.K. Printworld, 2007.

Rael, Joseph (Beautiful Painted Arrow). *Ceremonies of the Living Spirit*. Pointer Oak/Tri S Foundation, distributed by Millichap Books, 2016 edition.

—. *Being & Vibration: Entering the New World*. Pointer Oak/Tri S Foundation, distributed by Millichap Books, 2015.

—. *House of Shattering Light: life as an American Indian Mystic*. San Francisco & Tulsa: Tri S Foundation and Council Oaks Books, 2011.

—. *Sound: Native Teachings + Visionary Art*. Council Oak Books, 2009.

—. *Inspirations of the Living Spirit*. Tulsa: Council Oak Books, 1996.

—. *Beautiful Painted Arrow: Stories & Teachings from the Native American Tradition*. Rockport: Element, 1992.

—. "The People and the Land." In Jonathan Greenberg, and William Kistler (eds.). *Buying America Back*. Tulsa: Council Oak Books, 1992.

Rael, Joseph (Beautiful Painted Arrow) with Mary Elizabeth Marlow. *Being & Vibration*. Tulsa: Council Oak Books, 1993.

Raff, Jeffrey. *The Practice of Ally Work: Meeting and Partnering with Your Spirit Guide in the Imaginal World*. Berwick: Nicolas-Hays, 2006.

—. *The Wedding of Sophia: The Divine Feminine in Psychoidal Alchemy*. Berwick: Nicolas-Hays, 2003.

—. *Jung and the Alchemical Imagination*. Berwick: Nicolas-Hays, 2000.

Ramana Maharshi. *The Spiritual Teachings of Ramana Maharshi*. Boulder: Shambhala, 1972.

Randall, Lisa. *Dark Matter and the Dinosaurs: The Astounding Interconnectedness of the Universe*. New York: Harper Collins, 2015.

Reyna, Fabi. "Sitarist Anoushka Shankar on Corroborating Activism and Fusing Musical Worlds." *She Shreds* magazine, 6/27/17, http://sheshredsmag.com/anoushka-shankar-12/, accessed 2/25/18.

Robb, Graham. *The Ancient Paths: Discovering the Lost Map of Celtic Europe*. London: Picador, 2014.

Roy, Eleanor Ainge. "New Zealand river granted same legal rights as human." *The Guardian Weekly*, 24-30 March, 2017.

Rumi, Jelaluddin. Coleman Barks (trans.). *The Essential Rumi*. New York: Harper One, 2004.

—. Coleman Barks (trans.). *The Soul of Rumi*. New York: Harper One, 2002.

—. Kabir Helminski (trans). *Love is a Stranger: Selected Lyric Poetry of Jelaluddin Rumi*. Boulder: Shambhala Publications, 1993.

Sadowski, Robert. "Stone Rings of Northern Poland." In D.C. Heggie (ed.), *Archaeoastronomy in the Old World*. New York: Cambridge University Press, 1982.

Safi, Omid. "We Need Hope That's Gritty and Grounded." *On Being* Blog, http://www.onbeing.org/blog/omid-safi-we-need-hope-thats-gritty-and-grounded/9050, accessed 11/17/16.

Sandner, Donald. *Navaho Symbols of Healing: A Jungian Exploration of Ritual, Image, & Medicine*. Rochester: Healing Arts Press, 1979, 1991.

Sandner, Donald and Steven Wong, (eds.). *The Sacred Heritage: The Influence of Shamanism on Analytical Psychology*. New York: Routledge, 1997.

Sando, Joe S. and Herman Agoyo, (eds.). *Po'Pay: Leader of the First American Revolution*. Santa Fe: Clear Light Publishing, 2005.

Sanskrit Dictionary. "Guhā." http://sanskritdictionary.com/guh%C4%81/73318/1, accessed 11/9/17.

—. "Sāman." http://sanskritdictionary.com/?q=saman, accessed 3/31/18.

Schumacher, Michael. *Dharma Lion: A Biography of Allen Ginsberg*. Minneapolis: University of Minnesota Press, 2016.

Schweitzer, Jeff. "Soul Search: Why Pope Francis Is Barking Up the Wrong Tree." *The Huffington Post*, 12/17/14, http://www.huffingtonpost.com/jeff-schweitzer/soul-search-why-pope-fran_b_6344530.html, accessed 4/7/18.

Shankar, Anoushka. *The Land of Gold*. Deutsche Grammophon, 2016.

—. AnoushkaShankar.com webpage http://www.anoushkashankar.com.

Shibayama, Zenkei. *The Gateless Barrier: Zen Comments on the Mumonkan*. Boston: Shambhala, 2000.

Shiva, Vandana. *Earth Democracy: Justice, Sustainability, and Peace*. Berkeley: North Atlantic Books, 2005, 2015.

Singh, Jaideva. *Spanda-Kārikās: The Divine Creative Pulsation*. Delhi: Motilal Banarsidass Publishers, 2014.

Smoley, Richard. "Original Instructions: An Interview with Peter Kingsley." *Quest*, Summer 2011.

Soelle, Dorothy. *The Silent Cry: Mysticism and Resistance*. Minneapolis: Fortress Press, 2001.

Solnit, Rebecca. *Call Them by Their True Names*. Chicago: Haymarket Books, 2018.

—. *The Mother of All Questions*. Chicago: Haymarket Books, 2017.

—. *The Faraway Nearby*. New York: Viking, 2013.

—. *A Paradise Built in Hell: The Extraordinary Communities that Arise in Disaster*. New York: Penguin Books, 2009.

—. *Hope in the Dark: Untold Histories, Wild Possibilities*. New York: Nation Books, 2006.

—. *A Field Guide to Getting Lost*. New York: Penguin Books, 2005.

Somé, Malidoma Patrice. *Of Water and the Spirit: Ritual, Magic, and Initiation in the Life of an African Shaman*. New York: Penguin, 1994.

Subramaniam, Arundhathi (ed.). *Eating God: A Book of Bhakti Poetry*. Haryana: Penguin Ananda, 2014.

—. (ed.). *Pilgrim's India: An Anthology*. Haryana: Penguin Ananda, 2011.

Suhrawardi. *The Shape of Light: Hayakal al-Nur*, Interpreted by Shaykh Tosun Bayrak al-Jerrahi al-Halveti. Louisville: Fons Vitae, 2006.

Sutcliffe, Ron. *Moon Tracks: Lunar Horizon Patterns*. Pagosa Springs: Moon*spiral* Press, 2006.

Taylor, Barbara Brown. "Redeeming Darkness: A Spirituality for the Night Times." Seattle University Search for Meaning Festival, 2/24/18. The quotes are from my handwritten notes of the talk.

Teasdale, Wayne. *Bede Griffiths: An Introduction to His Spiritual Thought*. Woodstock: Skylight Paths Publishing, 2003.

—. *The Mystic Heart: Discovering a Universal Spirituality in the World's Religions*. Novato: New World Library, 1999.

Temple, Wayne. *Indian Villages of the Illinois Country*. Springfield: Illinois State Museum Scientific Papers, Volume II, Part 2, 1966.

Tick, Ed. *The Practice of Dream Healing: Bringing Ancient Greek Mysteries into Modern Medicine*. Wheaton: Quest Books, 2001.

Tingen, Paul. *Miles Beyond: The Electrical Explorations of Miles Davis, 1967-1991*. New York: Billboard Books, 2001.

Tolkien, J.R.R. *The Lord of the Rings, Collector's Edition*. Boston: Houghton Mifflin, 1994.

Turner, Victor. *The Ritual Process: Structure and Anti-Structure*. Piscataway: Transaction Publishers, 2008.

Underhill, Evelyn. *Mysticism: A Study in the Nature and Development of Spiritual Consciousness*. Mineola: Dover Publications, 2002, reprint of twelfth edition 1930.

The United Nations Education, Scientific, and Cultural Organization constitution, signed 1945, http://www.unesco.org/new/en/unesco/about-us/who-we-are/history/constitution/.

Vaughn-Lee, Llewellyn, (ed.). *Spiritual Ecology: The Cry of the Earth*. Point Reyes: The Golden Sufi Center, Second Edition 2016.

—. *The Return of the Feminine and the World Soul*. Point Reyes: The Golden Sufi Center, Third Printing 2013, originally published 2009.

Vedantic Center, The, website. http://thevedanticcenter.org/aboutTVC.html, accessed 3/24/17.

Waldman, Steven. *Founding Faith: How Our Founding Fathers Forged a Radical New Approach to Religious Liberty*. New York: Random House, 2008.

Waite, Dennis. *Sanskrit for Seekers*. Washington DC: Mantra Books, 2014.

Waters, Simon. "India makes Ganges a person; praises Whanganui River laws." *New Zealand World Herald* online, Mar 24, 2017, http://www.nzherald.co.nz/nz/news/article.cfm?c_id=1&objectid=11823920, accessed 12/21/18.

Weber, Renée. *Dialogues with Scientists and Sages: The Search for Unity*. New York: Arcana, 1986.

Weine, Stevan. "Allen Ginsberg's Kind of Psychiatrist," *American Journal of Psychiatry*, Volume 171, Issue 1, January 2014, pp. 23-24, https://ajp.psychiatryonline.org/doi/full/10.1176/appi.ajp.2013.13081084, accessed 2/9/18.

Wesselman, Hank. *The Re-Enchantment: A Shamanic Path to a Life of Wonder*. Boulder: Sounds True, 2016.

—. *The Bowl of Light: Ancestral Wisdom from a Hawaiian Shaman*. Boulder: Sounds True, 2011.

Wikipedia. "Abhishiktananda." https://en.wikipedia.org/wiki/Abhishiktananda, accessed 4/7/18.

—. "Anoushka Shankar." https://en.wikipedia.org/wiki/Anoushka_Shankar, accessed 12/30/16.

—. "Bastion Point." https://en.wikipedia.org/wiki/Bastion_Point, accessed 12/16/16.

—. "Frances Hodgson Burnett." https://en.wikipedia.org/wiki/Frances_Hodgson_Burnett, accessed 4/7/17.

—. "Great Maytham Hall." https://en.wikipedia.org/wiki/Great_Maytham_Hall, accessed 4/7/17.

—. "Hiawatha." https://en.wikipedia.org/wiki/Hiawatha, accessed 12/17.18.

—. "Illinois." https://en.wikipedia.org/wiki/Illinois#Etymology, accessed 9/18/15.

—. "Jiddu Krishnamurti." https://en.wikipedia.org/wiki/Jiddu_Krishnamurti, accessed 1/21/17.

—. "Limen." https://en.wikipedia.org/wiki/Limen_(disambiguation) , accessed 4/7/18.

—. "Maize." https://en.wikipedia.org/wiki/Maize, accessed 12/15/17.

—. "Pangea." https://en.wikipedia.org/wiki/Pangaea, accessed 10/1/16.

—. "Pangea (album)." https://en.wikipedia.org/wiki/Pangaea_(album), accessed 9/12/15.

—. "Sacred Kingfisher." https://en.wikipedia.org/wiki/Sacred_kingfisher, accessed 11/8/17.

—. "Tentaculites oswegoensis." https://en.wikipedia.org/wiki/Tentaculites_oswegoensis, accessed 12/15/17.

—. "We Are All Made of Stars," Moby album *18*. http://en.wikipedia.org/wiki/We_Are_All_Made_of_Stars, accessed 4/7/18.

Wilt, Kurt. *The Visionary: entering the mystic universe of Joseph Rael Beautiful Painted Arrow*. San Francisco & Tulsa: Tri S Foundation & Council Oak Books, 2011.

Wisdom Library online. “Narayana.” https://www.wisdomlib.org/definition/narayana, accessed 4/20/18

Wolf, Fred Alan. *The Eagle's Quest: A Physicist Finds Scientific Truth at the Heart of the Shamanic World*. New York: Touchstone, 1992.

Woodroffe, Sir John. *Śakti and Śākta*. Madras: Ganesh & Company, reprint 2016, third edition originally published 1927.

Zinn, Howard. *A People's History of the United States*. New York: HarperCollins, 2015, originally 1980.

INDEX

ABOUT THE AUTHORS

DAVID R. KOPACZ, MD works as a psychiatrist at Seattle VA in primary care mental health integration. In his clinical work, he has been developing a holistic health class and a hero's journey class, using mythology, narrative, culture, poetry, and art to help Veterans return home after military service. David is an education champion with the national VA Office of Patient Centered Care & Cultural Transformation, where he teaches Whole Health to VA staff across the USA. He is board certified in psychiatry and holistic & integrative medicine and is an assistant professor at the University of Washington. He has worked in many different practice settings, including holistic private practice, community mental health, and as clinical director of Buchanan Rehabilitation Centre in Auckland, New Zealand. David is the author of *Re-humanizing Medicine: A Holistic Framework for Transforming Your Self, Your Practice, and the Culture of Medicine* and *Walking the Medicine Wheel: Healing Trauma & PTSD* (with Joseph Rael).

JOSEPH RAEL, whose Tiwa name is *Tsluu-teh-koh-ay* (Beautiful Painted Arrow), is a visionary healer and artist. He brings together in his person Southern Ute (through his mother) and Picuris Pueblo (through his father) traditions and is a citizen of the Southern Ute tribe and the United States of America. He is the author of many books, including *Sound: Native Teachings & Visionary Art, Being & Vibration: Entering the New World, Ceremonies of the Living Spirit,* and *Walking the Medicine Wheel: Healing Trauma & PTSD* (with David Kopacz). He is a graduate of the University of New Mexico and holds a master's degree in Political Science from the University of Wisconsin. He has worked for Housing and Urban Development, the All Indian Pueblo Council, and the Indian Health Service, using Native American traditions and holistic health care to help those suffering from addiction. In 1983 he had a formative vision of Sound Peace Chambers and has overseen the construction of over 65 chambers on four continents, which led to him being recognized by the United Nations for his work for world peace.